A·N·N·U·A·L E·D·I·T·I·O·N·S

PERSONAL GROWTH AND BEHAVIOR 00/01

Twentieth Edition

EDITOR

Karen G. Duffy
SUNY College, Geneseo

Karen G. Duffy holds a doctorate in psychology from Michigan State University and is currently a professor of psychology at SUNY at Geneseo. She sits on the executive board of the New York State Employees Assistance Program and is a certified community and family mediator. She is a member of the American Psychological Society and the Eastern Psychological Association.

D0165913

Dushkin/McGraw-Hill
Sluice Dock, Guilford, Connecticut 06437

Visit us on the Internet
http://www.dushkin.com/annualeditions/

Credits

1. Becoming a Person: Seeking Self-Identity
Unit photo—© 1999 by Cleo Freelance Photography, Inc.
2. Determinants of Behavior: Motivation, Environment, and Physiology
Unit photo—Courtesy of the World Health Organization.
3. Problems Influencing Personal Growth
Unit photo—© 1999 by Cleo Freelance Photography, Inc.
4. Relating to Others
Unit photo—© 1999 by Cleo Freelance Photography, Inc.
5. Dynamics of Personal Adjustment: The Individual and Society
Unit photo—© 1999 by Cleo Freelance Photography, Inc.
6. Enhancing Human Adjustment: Learning to Cope Effectively
Unit photo—© 1999 by Cleo Freelance Photography, Inc.

Copyright

Cataloging in Publication Data
Main entry under title: Annual Editions: Personal Growth and Behavior. 2000/2001.
    1. Personality—Periodicals. 2. Adjustment (Psychology)—Periodicals.
I. Duffy, Karen G., *comp.* II. Title: Personal growth and behavior.
ISBN 0–07–236572–2   ISSN 0732-0779   155'.2'05   75–20757

Twentieth Edition

Cover image © 2000 PhotoDisc, Inc.

Printed in the United States of America   1234567890BAHBAH543210   Printed on Recycled Paper

155.2
P43
2000/01

Editors/Advisory Board

Staff

To the Reader

In publishing ANNUAL EDITIONS we recognize the enormous role played by the magazines, newspapers, and journals of the public press in providing current, first-rate educational information in a broad spectrum of interest areas. Many of these articles are appropriate for students, researchers, and professionals seeking accurate, current material to help bridge the gap between principles and theories and the real world. These articles, however, become more useful for study when those of lasting value are carefully collected, organized, indexed, and reproduced in a low-cost format, which provides easy and permanent access when the material is needed. That is the role played by ANNUAL EDITIONS.

New to ANNUAL EDITIONS is the inclusion of related World Wide Web sites. These sites have been selected by our editorial staff to represent some of the best resources found on the World Wide Web today. Through our carefully developed topic guide, we have linked these Web resources to the articles covered in this ANNUAL EDITIONS reader. We think that you will find this volume useful, and we hope that you will take a moment to visit us on the Web at *http://www.dushkin.com* to tell us what you think.

Have you ever watched children on a playground? Some children are reticent; watching the other children play, they sit demurely and shun becoming involved in the fun. Some children readily and happily interact with their playmates. They take turns, share their toys, and follow the rules of the playground. Other children are bullies who brazenly taunt the playing children and aggressively take others' possessions. What makes each child so different? Do childhood behaviors forecast adult behaviors? Can children's (or adults') antisocial behaviors be changed?

These questions are not new. Lay persons and social scientists alike have always been curious about human nature. The answers to our questions, though, are incomplete, because attempts to address these issues are relatively new or just developing. Psychology, the science that can and should answer questions about individual differences, is the primary focus of this book, and has existed for just over 100 years. That may seem old to you, but it is young when other disciplines are considered. Mathematics, medicine, and philosophy are thousands of years old.

By means of psychology and related sciences, this anthology will help you explore the issues of individual differences and their origins, methods of coping, personality changes, and other matters of human adjustment. The purpose of this anthology is to compile the newest, most complete, and readable articles that examine individual behavior and adjustment as well as the dynamics of personal growth and interpersonal relationships. The readings in this book offer interesting insights into both the everyday and scientific worlds, a blend welcomed by most of today's specialists in human adjustment.

The anthology is revised each year to reflect both traditional viewpoints and emerging perspectives about people's behavior. Thanks to the editorial board's valuable advice, the present edition has been completely revised and includes a large number of new articles representing the latest thinking in the field.

Annual Editions: Personal Growth and Behavior 00/01 comprises six units, each of which serves a distinct purpose. The first unit is concerned with issues related to self-identity. For example, one theory, humanism, hypothesizes that self-concept, our feelings about who we are and how worthy we are, is the most valuable component of personality. This unit includes articles that supplement the theoretical articles by providing applications of, or alternate perspectives on, popular theories about individual differences and human adjustment. These include all of the classic and major theories of personality: humanistic, psychoanalytic, and trait theories.

The second unit provides information on how and why a person develops in a particular way—in other words, what factors determine or direct individual growth: physiology, heredity, experience, or some combination. The third unit pertains to problems commonly encountered in the different stages of development: infancy, childhood, adolescence, and adulthood.

The fourth and fifth units are similar in that they address problems of adjustment—problems that occur in interpersonal relationships and problems that are created for individuals by the prevailing social environment or our culture. Unit 4 concerns topics such as competition, love, and friendship, while unit 5 discusses racism, trends in violent crime, and the rapid increase in the use of technology in America. The final unit focuses on adjustment, or on how most people cope with some of these and other issues.

Annual Editions: Personal Growth and Behavior 00/01 will challenge you and interest you in a variety of topics. It will provide you with many answers, but it will also stimulate many questions. Perhaps it will inspire you to continue your study of the burgeoning field of psychology, which is responsible for exploring personal growth and behavior. As has been true in the past, your feedback on this edition would be valuable for future revisions. Please take a moment to fill out and return the postage-paid *article rating form* on the last page. Thank you.

Karen Groves Duffy

Karen G. Duffy
Editor

Contents

UNIT 1

Becoming a Person: Seeking Self-Identity

Six selections discuss the
psychosocial development of an
individual's personality. Attention
is given to values, emotions,
lifestyles, and self-concept.

The concepts in bold italics are developed in the article. For further expansion please refer to the Topic Guide, the Glossary, and the Index.

UNIT 2

Determinants of Behavior: Motivation, Environment, and Physiology

Nine articles examine the effects of culture, genes, and emotions on an individual's behavior.

The concepts in bold italics are developed in the article. For further expansion please refer to the Topic Guide, the Glossary, and the Index.

UNIT 3

Problems Influencing Personal Growth

Eight articles consider aging, development, self-image, depression, and social interaction, and their influences on personal growth.

UNIT 4

Relating
to Others

Eleven articles examine some of the
dynamics involved in relating to
others. Topics discussed include
friendship, love, the importance
of family ties, and self-esteem.

The concepts in bold italics are developed in the article. For further expansion please refer to the Topic Guide, the Glossary, and the Index.

UNIT 5

Dynamics of Personal Adjustment: The Individual and Society

Five selections discuss some of the problems experienced by individuals as they attempt to adjust to society.

The concepts in bold italics are developed in the article. For further expansion please refer to the Topic Guide, the Glossary, and the Index.

UNIT 6

Enhancing Human Adjustment: Learning to Cope Effectively

Nine selections examine some of the ways an individual learns to cope successfully within today's society. Topics discussed include therapy, depression, stress, and interpersonal relations.

The concepts in bold italics are developed in the article. For further expansion please refer to the Topic Guide, the Glossary, and the Index.

The concepts in bold italics are developed in the article. For further expansion please refer to the Topic Guide, the Glossary, and the Index.

Topic Guide

This topic guide suggests how the selections and World Wide Web sites found in the next section of this book relate to topics of traditional concern with the study of personal growth and behavior. It is useful for locating interrelated articles and Web sites for reading and research. The guide is arranged alphabetically according to topic.

The relevant Web sites, which are numbered and annotated on pages 4 and 5, are easily identified by the Web icon (⊙) under the topic articles. By linking the articles and the Web sites by topic, this ANNUAL EDITIONS reader becomes a powerful learning and research tool.

TOPIC AREA	TREATED IN	TOPIC AREA	TREATED IN
Addiction	6. Addicted ⊙ *12, 14, 15, 24, 25*	**Death**	23. Is There Life after Death? 45. Clustering and Contagion of Suicide ⊙ *17*
Adolescents	20. How Well Do You Know Your Kids? ⊙ *1, 9, 13, 14, 16, 17, 18,* *22, 24, 25*	**Depression**	44. Up from Depression ⊙ *26, 27, 28, 29*
Aging	22. Live to 100? No Thanks 27. Friendship and Adaptation across the Life Span ⊙ *15, 26, 27, 28, 29*	**Development**	2. Making Sense of Self-Esteem 3. Raising Kids' Self-Esteem May Backfire 16. Seven Stages of Man 17. Fetal Psychology 18. Clipped Wings 19. Why Children Turn Out the Way They Do 20. How Well Do You Know Your Kids? 21. Invincible kids 22. Live to 100? No Thanks 26. Moral Development of Children 27. Friendships and Adaption across the Life Span ⊙ *1, 7, 9, 12, 13, 14, 15, 16*
Anxiety Disorder	43. Chronic Anxiety: How to Stop Living on the Edge ⊙ *27, 28, 29, 30, 32, 33*		
Apologies	33. Go Ahead, Say You're Sorry		
Autism	10. Autism Is Likely to Be Linked to Several Genes ⊙ *15, 18, 27, 29, 32*		
Behavior/ Behaviorism	4. Private Lives: Discipline and Knowing Where to Draw the Line ⊙ *3, 7, 13*	**Emotional Intelligence**	24. EQ Factor ⊙ *19, 20, 21*
Biochemistry	14. Biology of Joy ⊙ *6, 7, 10, 11*	**Freud, Sigmund**	5. Who Are the Freudians? ⊙ *3, 5*
Brain	12. Revealing the Brain's Secrets 14. Biology of Joy ⊙ *6, 7, 8, 10, 11*	**Gender**	8. Gender Blur ⊙ *8, 10, 12, 21*
Children	2. Making Sense of Self-Esteem 3. Raising Kids' Self-Esteem May Backfire 16. Seven Stages of Man 17. Fetal Psychology 18. Clipped Wings 19. Why Children Turn Out the Way They Do 20. How Well Do You Know Your Kids? 21. Invincible kids ⊙ *1, 12, 14, 15*	**Genes**	7. Is It Nature or Nurture? 8. Gender Blur 9. Optimizing Expression of the Common Genome for Child Development 10. Autism Is Likely To Be Linked To Several Genes 11. Personality Genes ⊙ *11, 31, 32*
		Health	15. Faith & Healing ⊙ *12, 14, 15, 27, 28, 29*
Crime	34. Fistful of Hostility Is Found in Women 37. Psychopathy, Sociopathy, and Crime ⊙ *22, 23, 24*	**Hostility**	34. Fistful of Hostility Is Found in Women ⊙ *23, 24*
Cults	38. Lure of the Cult ⊙ *22*	**Humanistic Psychology**	1. The Last Interview of Abraham Maslow ⊙ *3*
Culture	5. Who Are the Freudians? 25. Face It! ⊙ *5, 20, 21*	**Marriage**	29. Science of a Good Marriage 30. Shattered Vows
		Maslow, Abraham	1. The Last Interview of Abraham Maslow ⊙ *3*
Dating	28. New Flirting Game ⊙ *19, 20, 21*	**Mental Disorder**	43. Chronic Anxiety: How To Stop Living On the Edge

◉ AE: Personal Growth and Behavior

The following World Wide Web sites have been carefully researched and selected to support the articles found in this reader. If you are interested in learning more about specific topics found in this book, these Web sites are a good place to start. The sites are cross-referenced by number and appear in the topic guide on the previous two pages. Also, you can link to these Web sites through our DUSHKIN ONLINE support site at *http://www.dushkin.com/online/*.

The following sites were available at the time of publication. Visit our Web site—we update DUSHKIN ONLINE regularly to reflect any changes.

General Sources

1. National Institute of Child Health and Human Development
   http://www.nichd.nih.gov
 The NICHD conducts and supports research on the reproductive, neurobiologic, developmental, and behavioral processes that determine and maintain the health of children and adults.

2. Psychnet
   http://www.apa.org/psychnet/
 Get information on psychology from this Web site through the site map or by using the search engine. Access *APA Monitor*, the American Psychological Association newspaper; APA Books on a wide range of topics; PsychINFO, an electronic database of abstracts on over 1,350 scholarly journals; and HelpCenter for information on dealing with modern life problems.

Becoming a Person: Seeking Self-Identity

3. Abraham A. Brill Library
   http://plaza.interport.net/nypsan/service.html
 The Abraham A. Brill Library, perhaps the largest psychoanalytic library in the world, contains data on over 40,000 books, periodicals, and reprints in psychoanalysis and related fields. Its holdings span the literature of psychoanalysis from its beginning to the present day.

4. JungWeb
   http://www.onlinepsych.com/jungweb/
 Dedicated to the work of Carl Jung, this site is a comprehensive resource for Jungian psychology. Links to Jungian psychology, reference materials, graduate programs, dreams, multilingual sites, and related Jungian themes are available.

5. Sigmund Freud and the Freud Archives
   http://plaza.interport.net/nypsan/freudarc.html
 Internet resources related to Sigmund Freud can be accessed through this site. A collection of libraries, museums, and biographical materials, as well as the Brill Library archives, can be found here.

Determinants of Behavior: Motivation, Environment, and Physiology

6. American Psychological Society (APS)
   http://www.psychologicalscience.org
 APS membership includes a diverse group of the world's foremost scientists and academics working to expand basic and applied psychological science knowledge. Links to teaching, research, and graduate studies resources are available.

7. Federation of Behavioral, Psychological, and Cognitive Science
   http://www.am.org/federation/
 At this site you can hotlink to the National Institutes of Health's medical database, government links to public information on mental health, a social psychology network, and the Project on the Decade of the Brain.

8. Max Planck Institute for Psychological Research
   http://www.mpipf-muenchen.mpg.de/BCD/bcd_e.htm
 Several behavioral and cognitive development research projects are available on this site.

9. The Opportunity of Adolescence
   http://www.winternet.com/~webpage/ adolescencepaper.html
 This paper calls adolescence the turning point, after which the future is redirected and confirmed, and goes on to discuss the opportunities and problems of this period to the individual and society, using quotations from Erik Erikson, Jean Piaget, and others.

10. Psychology Research on the Net
   http://psych.hanover.edu/APS/exponnet.html
 Psychologically related experiments on the Internet can be found at this site. Biological psychology/neuropsychology, clinical psychology, cognition, developmental psychology, emotions, general issues, health psychology, personality, sensation/perception, and social psychology are addressed.

11. Serendip
   http://serendip.brynmawr.edu/serendip/
 Organized into five subject areas (brain and behavior, complex systems, genes and behavior, science and culture, and science education), Serendip contains interactive exhibits, articles, links to other resources, and a forum area for comments and discussion.

Problems Influencing Personal Growth

12. Ask NOAH About: Mental Health
   http://www.noah.cuny.edu/illness/mentalhealth/mental.html
 This enormous resource contains information about child and adolescent family problems, mental conditions and disorders, suicide prevention, and much more.

13. Biological Changes in Adolescence
   http://www.personal.psu.edu/faculty/n/x/nxd10/ biologic2.htm
 This site offers a discussion of puberty, sexuality, biological changes, cross-cultural differences, and nutrition for adolescents, including obesity and its effects on adolescent development.

14. Facts for Families
   http://www.aacap.org/info_families/index.htm
 The American Academy of Child and Adolescent Psychiatry provides concise, up-to-date information on issues that affect teenagers and their families. Fifty-six fact sheets include many teenager's issues.

15. Mental Health Infosource: Disorders
   http://www.mhsource.com/disorders/
 This no-nonsense page lists hotlinks to psychological disorders pages, including anxiety, panic, phobic disorders, schizophrenia, and violent/self-destructive behaviors.

16. Mental Health Risk Factors for Adolescents
http://education.indiana.edu/cas/adol/mental.html
This collection of Web resources is useful for parents, educators, researchers, health practitioners, and teens. It covers a great deal, including abuse, conduct disorders, and stress.

17. Suicide Awareness: Voices of Education
http://www.save.org
This is the most popular suicide site on the Internet. It is very thorough, with information on dealing with suicide (both before and after), along with material from the organization's many education sessions.

Relating to Others

18. CYFERNET-Youth Development
http://www.cyfernet.mes.umn.edu/youthdev.html
An excellent source of many articles on youth development, this site includes a statement on the concept of normal adolescence and impediments to healthy development.

19. Hypermedia, Literature, and Cognitive Dissonance
http://www.uncg.edu/~rsginghe/metastat.htm
This article, subtitled *The Heuristic Challenges of Connectivity*, discusses EQ (emotional intelligence) in adults and offers an interactive study, the Metatale Paradigm, that is linked to story sources. Click on *http://www.uncg.edu/~rsginghe/metatext.htm for access.*

20. Emotional Intelligence Discovery
http://www.cwrl.utexas.edu/~bump/Hu305/3/3/3/
This site has been set up by students to talk about and expand on Daniel Goleman's book, *Emotional Intelligence*. There are links to many other EI sites.

21. The Personality Project
http://fas.psych.nwu.edu/personality.html
The Personality Project of William Revelle, director of the Graduate Program in Personality at Northwestern University, is meant to guide those interested in personality theory and research to the current personality research literature.

Dynamics of Personal Adjustment: The Individual and Society

22. AFF Cult Group Information
http://www.csj.org/index.html
Information about cults, cult groups, and psychological manipulation is available at this page sponsored by the secular, not-for-profit, tax-exempt research center and educational organization, American Family Foundation.

23. Explanations of Criminal Behavior
http://www.uaa.alaska.edu/just/just110/crime2.html
An excellent outline of the causes of crime, including major theories, which was prepared by Darryl Wood at the University of Alaska Anchorage, can be found at this site.

24. National Clearinghouse for Alcohol and Drug Information
http://www.health.org
This is an excellent general site for information on drug and alcohol facts that might relate to adolescence and the

issues of peer pressure and youth culture. Resources, referrals, research and statistics, databases, and related Internet links are among the options available at this site.

25. Schools Health Education Unit (SHEU)
http://www.ex.ac.uk/~dregis/sheu.html
SHEU is a research unit that offers survey, research, and evaluation services on health and social development for young people.

Enhancing Human Adjustment: Learning to Cope Effectively

26. Clinical Psychology Resources
http://www.psychologie.uni-bonn.de/kap/links_20.htm
This page contains Internet resources for clinical and abnormal psychology, behavioral medicine, and mental health.

27. Health Information Resources
http://nhic-nt.health.org/Scripts/Tollfree.cfm
Here is a long list of toll-free numbers that provide health-related information. None offer diagnosis and treatment, but some do offer recorded information; others provide personalized counseling, referrals, and/or written materials.

28. Knowledge Exchange Network (KEN)
http://www.mentalhealth.org
The CMHS National Mental Health Services Exchange Network (KEN) provides information about mental health via toll-free telephone services, an electronic bulletin board, and publications. It is a one-stop source for information and resources on prevention, treatment, and rehabilitation services for mental illness, with many links to related sources.

29. Mental Health Net
http://www.mentalhealth.net
This comprehensive guide to mental health online features more than 6,300 individual resources. It covers information on mental disorders, professional resources in psychology, psychiatry, and social work, journals, and self-help magazines.

30. Mental Health Net: Eating Disorder Resources
http://www.cmhc.com/guide/eating.htm
This is a very complete list of Web references on eating disorders, including anorexia, bulimia, and obesity.

31. Mind Tools
http://www.psychwww.com/mtsite/
Useful information on stress management can be found at this Web site.

32. NetPsychology
http://netpsych.com/index.htm
This site explores the uses of the Internet to deliver mental health services. This is a basic cybertherapy resource site.

We highly recommend that you review our Web site for expanded information and our other product lines. We are continually updating and adding links to our Web site in order to offer you the most usable and useful information that will support and expand the value of your Annual Editions. You can reach us at: http://www.dushkin.com/annualeditions/.

www.dushkin.com/online/

Unit Selections

1. **The Last Interview of Abraham Maslow,** Edward Hoffman
2. **Making Sense of Self-Esteem,** Mark R. Leary
3. **Raising Kids' Self-Esteem May Backfire, Experts Warn,** Maggie Fox
4. **Private Lives: Discipline and Knowing Where to Draw the Line,** Jan Parker and Jan Stimpson
5. **Who Are the Freudians?** Edith Kurzweil
6. **The Stability of Personality: Observations and Evaluations,** Robert R. McCrae and Paul T. Costa Jr.

Key Points to Consider

❖ What does Abraham Maslow propose about self in his theory? How can his humanistic theory help us produce a more peaceful world and strengthen positive human attributes?

❖ Do you think that the development of self is driven by biology? Why or why not? What else do you think prompts the development of self-concept? Do you believe that self is utilized only to promote our own selfish interests in competition with others? How do you think evaluations from others affect our self-concept, especially self-esteem?

❖ What is behaviorism? What general principles do the theorists subscribe to? Should we utilize punishment to alter or manage children's behaviors? What general principles should we follow when we administer punishment? What principles should we follow when we provide reinforcement? Why is punishment so much more controversial than reinforcement?

❖ Do you believe in the unconscious? Why or why not? If yes, give examples from your own life of its influence. What other concepts are important to Sigmund Freud's concept of humans? Define and give examples of each. How is Freudianism practiced around the world today? How is culture important to the way psychoanalysis is practiced? What do you think Freud would say about how psychoanalysis is used in contemporary society by lay people and by practitioners? How does culture influence the way psychoanalysis is practiced in various parts of the world?

❖ What is a personality trait? Do you think personality traits remain stable over a lifetime? From where do personality traits come? Are they biological or learned? Do traits remain stable across situations; are they carried from church to school, for example? Do traits collectively comprise self-concept or does self comprise more than traits?

❖ Which theory of human personality (humanistic, behavioral, psychoanalytic, or trait) do you think is best and why? How do these theories differ from one another; for example, how does each deal with the "nature" (goodness or badness) of humans? What part of our life experience is most important for each theory?

DUSHKINONLINE **Links**   **www.dushkin.com/online/**

3. **Abraham A. Brill Library**
   http://plaza.interport.net/nypsan/service.html
4. **JungWeb**
   http://www.onlinepsych.com/jungweb/
5. **Sigmund Freud and the Freud Archives**
   http://plaza.interport.net/nypsan/freudarc.html

These sites are annotated on pages 4 and 5.

A baby sits in front of a mirror and looks at himself. A chimpanzee sorts through photographs while its trainer carefully watches its reactions. A college student answers a survey on how she feels about herself. What does each of these events share with the others? All are examples of techniques used to investigate self-concept.

That baby in front of the mirror has a red dot on his nose. Researchers watch to see if the baby reaches for the dot in the mirror or touches his own nose. Recognizing the fact that the image he sees in the mirror is his own, the baby touches his real nose, not the nose in the mirror.

The chimpanzee has been trained to sort photographs into two piles—human pictures or animal pictures. If the chimp has been raised with humans, the researcher wants to know into which pile (animal or human) the chimp will place its own picture. Is the chimp's concept of itself animal or human? Or does the chimp have no concept of self at all?

The college student taking the self-survey answers questions about her body image, whether or not she thinks she is fun to be with, whether or not she spends large amounts of time in fantasy, and what her feelings are about her personality and intelligence.

These research projects are designed to investigate how self-concept develops and steers our behaviors and thoughts. Most psychologists believe that people develop a personal identity or a sense of self, which is a sense of who we are, our likes and dislikes, our characteristic feelings and thoughts, and an understanding of why we behave as we do. Self-concept is our knowledge of our gender, race, and age, as well as our sense of self-worth and more. Strong positive or negative feelings are usually attached to this identity. Psychologists are studying how and when this sense of self develops. Most psychologists do not believe that infants are born with a sense of self but rather that children slowly develop self-concept as a consequence of their experiences.

This unit delineates some of the popular viewpoints regarding how sense of self and personality develop and how, or if, they guide behavior. This knowledge of how self develops provides an important foundation for the rest of the units in this book. This unit explores four major theories or forces in psychology: self or humanistic, behavioral, psychoanalytic, and trait theories.

The first two articles are related to the school of psychology with a strong interest in self-concept, humanistic psychology. In fact, many of the humanistic theorists also are called self-theorists. In "The Last Interview of Abraham Maslow," one of the founders of humanistic psychology discusses the evolution of his theory. In the interview, Maslow talks about his philosophy of human nature and its potential for peaceful living and other positive outcomes for humans. In a companion article, author Mark Leary examines what self-esteem is and where it originates. Leary, in "Making Sense of Self-Esteem," suggests that we need to redefine self-esteem to take into account others' perception of us. In a companion article, author Maggie Fox examines whether trying to raise a child's self-esteem is a sound idea. Several experts cited in the article suggest that such attempts can often backfire, that is, turn children into egotistical, narcissistic individuals.

The fourth article in this unit relates to a different theory—behaviorism. In "Private Lives: Discipline and Knowing Where to Draw the Line," the authors discuss how parents and teachers can better manage a child's behavior by using principles from operant conditioning. Authors Jan Parker and Jan Stimpson provide guidelines on how and when to use reinforcement and punishment, with punishment being the most controversial of the two.

The next essay relates to psychoanalysis, a theory and form of therapy to which humanism and behaviorism were reactions. The main proponent of psychoanalysis was Sigmund Freud, who believed that individuals possess a dark, lurking unconscious that often motivates negative behaviors such as guilt and defensiveness. This essay not only explores Freudian concepts but goes one step further. Edith Kurzweil, in "Who Are the Freudians?" investigates how psychoanalysis is practiced around the world and ultimately declares that Freud, himself, might not recognize the theory today.

The last article in the unit offers a contrasting viewpoint of human nature, known as the trait or dispositional approach. Trait theories in general hold that our personalities are comprised of various traits that are possibly tied together by our self-concept. This review of relevant research claims that most personality traits remain constant over time, a view that is in sharp contrast especially with the growth theory of Abraham Maslow and the psychoanalytic stage theory of Freud.

The Last Interview of

ABRAHAM

MASLOW

When Abraham Maslow first shared his pioneering vision of a "comprehensive human psychology" in this magazine in early 1968, he stood at the pinnacle of his international acclaim and influence.

Edward Hoffman, Ph.D.

About the author: Edward Hoffman received his doctorate from the University of Michigan. A clinical psychologist on New York's Long Island, he is the author of several books, including The Right to be Human: A Biography of Abraham Maslow *(Tarcher).*

HIS ELECTION AS PRESIDENT OF THE AMERIcan Psychological Association some months before capped an illustrious academic career spanning more than 35 productive years, during which Maslow had steadily gained the high regard—even adulation—of countless numbers of colleagues and former students. His best-known books, *Motivation and Personality* and *Toward a Psychology of Being*, were not only being discussed avidly by psychologists, but also by professionals in fields ranging from management and marketing to education and counseling. Perhaps even more significantly, Maslow's iconoclastic concepts like peak experience, self-actualization, and synergy had even begun penetrating popular language.

Nevertheless, it was a very unsettling time for him: Recovering from a major heart attack, the temperamentally restless and ceaselessly active Maslow was finding forced convalescence at home to be almost painfully unbearable. Suddenly, his extensive plans for future research, travel, and lecturing had to be postponed. Although Maslow hoped for a speedy recovery, frequent chest pains induced a keen sense of his own mortality. As perhaps never before, he began to ponder his career's accomplishments and his unrealized goals.

In 1968 PSYCHOLOGY TODAY was a precocious one-year-old upstart, but such was its prestige that it was able to attract perhaps the country's most famous psychologist for an interview.

Maslow likely regarded the PT interview as a major opportunity to outline his "comprehensive human psychology" and the best way to actualize it. At 60, he knew that time permitted him only to plant seeds (in his own metaphor) of research and theory—and hope that later generations would live to see the flowering of human betterment. Perhaps most prescient at a time of global unrest is Maslow's stirring vision of "building a psychology for the peace table." It was his hope that through psychological research, we might learn how to unify peoples of differing racial and ethnic origins, and thereby create a world of peace.

Although the complete audiotapes of the sessions, conducted over three days, disappeared long ago under mysterious circumstances, the written condensation that remains provides a fascinating and still-relevant portrait of a key thinker at the height of his prowess. Intellectually, Maslow was decades ahead of his time; today the wide-ranging ideas he offers here are far from outdated. Indeed, after some twenty-odd years, they're still on the cutting edge of American psychology and social science. Emotionally, this interview is significant for the rare—essentially unprecedented—glimpse it affords into Maslow's personal history and concerns: his ancestry and upbringing; his mentors and ambitions; his courtship, marriage, and fatherhood; and even a few of his peak experiences.

Maslow continued to be puzzled and intrigued by the more positive human phenomenon of self-actualization. He was well aware that his theory about the "best of humanity" suffered from methodological flaws. Yet he had become ever more convinced of its intuitive validity, that self-actualizers provide us with clues to our highest innate traits: love and compassion, creativity and aesthetics, ethics and spirituality. Maslow longed to empirically verify this lifelong hunch.

In the two years of his life that remained, this gifted psychologist never wrote an autobiography, nor did he ever again bare his soul in such a public and wide-ranging way. It may have been that Maslow regarded this unusually personal interview as a true legacy. More than 20 years later, it remains a fresh and important document for the field of psychology.

Mary Harrington Hall, for PSYCHOLOGY TODAY: A couple of William B. Yeats's lines keep running through my head: "And in my heart, the daemons and the gods wage an eternal battle and I feel the pain of wounds, the labor of the spear." How thin is the veneer of civilization, and how can we understand and deal with evil?

Abraham H. Maslow: It's a psychological puzzle I've been trying to solve for years. Why are people cruel and why are they nice? Evil people are rare, but you find evil behavior in the majority of people. The next thing I want to do with my life is to study evil and understand it.

PT: By evil here, I think we both mean destructive action without remorse. Racial prejudice is an evil in our society which we must deal with. And soon. Or we will go down as a racist society.

All the goals of objectivity, repeatability, and preplanned experimentation are things we have to move toward. The more reliable you make knowledge, the better it is.

Maslow: You know, when I became A.P.A. president, the first thing I wanted to do was work for greater recognition for the Negro psychologists. Then I found that there were no Negroes in psychology, at least not many. They don't major in psychology.

PT: Why should they? Why would I think that psychology would solve social problems if I were a Negro living in the ghetto, surrounded by despair?

Maslow: Negroes have really had to take it. We've given them every possible blow.

If I were a Negro, I'd be fighting, as Martin Luther King fought, for human recognition and justice. I'd rather go down with my flag flying. If you're weak or crippled, or you can't speak out or fight back in some way, then people don't hesitate to treat you badly.

PT: Could you look at evil behavior in two ways: evil from below and evil from above? Evil as a sickness and evil as understood compassionately?

Maslow: If you look at evil from above, you can be realistic. Evil exists. You don't give it quarter, and you're a better fighter if you can understand it. You're in the position of a psychotherapist. In the same way, you can look at neurosis. You can see neurosis from below—as a sickness—as most psychiatrists see it. Or you can understand it as a compassionate man might: respecting the neurosis as a fumbling and inefficient effort toward good ends.

PT: You can understand race riots in the same way, can't you?

Maslow: If you can only be detached enough, you can feel that it's better to riot than to be hopeless, degraded, and defeated. Rioting is a childish way of trying to be a man, but it takes time to rise out of the hell of hatred and frustration and accept that to be a man you don't have to riot.

PT: In our society, we see all behavior as a demon we can vanquish and banish, don't we? And yet good people do evil things.

Maslow: Most people are nice people. Evil is caused by ignorance, thoughtlessness, fear, or even the desire for popularity with one's gang. We can cure many such causes of evil. Science is progressing, and I feel hope that psychology can solve many of these problems. I think that a good part of evil behavior bears on the behavior of the normal.

PT: How will you approach the study of evil?

Maslow: If you think only of evil, then you become pessimistic and hopeless like Freud. But if you think there is no evil, then you're just one more deluded Pollyanna. The thing is to try to understand and realize how it's possible for people who are capable of being angels, heroes, or saints to be bastards and killers. Sometimes, poor and miserable people are hopeless. Many revenge themselves upon life for what society has done to them. They enjoy hurting.

PT: Your study of evil will have to be subjective, won't it? How can we measure evil in the laboratory?

Maslow: All the goals of objectivity, repeatability, and preplanned experimentation are things we have to move toward. The more reliable you make knowledge, the better it is. If the salvation of man comes out of the advancement of knowledge—taken in the best sense—then these goals are part of the strategy of knowledge.

PT: What did you tell your own daughters, Ann and Ellen, when they were growing up?

Maslow: Learn to hate meanness. Watch out for anybody who is mean or cruel. Watch out for people who delight in destruction.

PT: How would you describe yourself? Not in personality, because you're one of the warmest and sweetest men I've ever met. But who are you?

Maslow: I'm someone who likes plowing new ground, then walking away from it. I get bored easily. For me, the big thrill comes with the discovering.

PT: Psychologists all love Abe Maslow. How did you escape the crossfire?

Maslow: I just avoid most academic warfare. Besides, I had my first heart attack many years ago, and perhaps I've been unconsciously favoring my body. So I may have avoided real struggle. Besides, I only like fights I know I can win, and I'm not personally mean.

PT: Maybe you're just one of the lucky few who grew up through a happy childhood without malice.

Maslow: With my childhood, it's a wonder I'm not psychotic. I was the little Jewish boy in the non-Jewish neighborhood. It was a little like being the first Negro enrolled in the all-white school. I grew up in libraries and among books, without friends.

Both my mother and father were uneducated. My father wanted me to be a lawyer. He thumbed his way across the whole continent of Europe from Russia and got here at the age of 15. He wanted success for me. I tried law school for two weeks. Then I came home to my poor father one night after a class discussing "spite fences" and told him I couldn't be a lawyer. "Well, son," he said, "what do you want to study?" I answered: "Everything." He was uneducated and couldn't understand my passion for learning, but he was a nice man. He didn't understand either that at 16, I was in love.

PT: All 16-year-olds are in love.

Maslow: Mine was different. We're talking about my wife. I loved Bertha. You know her. Wasn't I right? I was extremely shy, and I tagged around after her. We were too young to get married. I tried to run away with her.

PT: Where did you run?

Maslow: I ran to Cornell for my sophomore year in college, then to Wisconsin. We were married there when I was 20 and Bertha was 19. Life didn't really start for me until I got married.

I went to Wisconsin because I had just discovered John B. Watson's work, and I was sold on behaviorism. It was an explosion of excitement for me. Bertha came to pick me up at New York's 42nd Street library, and I was dancing down Fifth Avenue with exuberance. I embarrassed her, but I was so excited about Watson's behaviorist program. It was beautiful. I was confident that here was a real road to travel: solving one problem after another and changing the world.

PT: A clear lifetime with built-in progress guaranteed.

Maslow: That was it. I was off to Wisconsin to change the world. I went there to study with psychologist Kurt Koffka, biologist Hans Dreisch, and philosopher Alexander Meiklejohn. But when I showed up

> I've devoted myself to developing a theory of human nature that could be tested by experiment and research. I wanted to prove that humans are capable of something grander than war, prejudice, and hatred.

on the campus, they weren't there. They had just been visiting professors, but the lying catalog had included them anyway.

Oh, but I was so lucky, though. I was young Harry Harlow's first doctoral graduate. And they were angels, my professors. I've always had angels around. They helped me when I needed it, even fed me. Bill Sheldon taught me how to buy a suit. I didn't know anything of amenities. Clark Hull was an angel to me, and later, Edward L. Thorndike.

PT: You're an angelic man. I've heard too many stories to let you deny it. What kind of research were you doing at Wisconsin?

Maslow: I was a monkey man. By studying monkeys for my doctoral dissertation, I found that dominance was related to sex, and to maleness. It was a great discovery, but somebody had discovered it two months before me.

PT: Great ideas always go in different places and minds at the same time.

Maslow: Yes, I worked on it until the start of World War II. I thought that working on sex was the easiest way to help mankind. I felt if I could discover a way to improve the sexual life by even one percent, then I could improve the whole species.

One day, it suddenly dawned on me that I knew as much about sex as any man living—in the intellectual sense. I knew everything that had been written; I had made discoveries with which I was pleased; I had done therapeutic work. This was about 10 years before the Kinsey report came out. Then I suddenly burst into laughter. Here was I, the great sexologist, and I had never seen an erect penis except one, and that was from my own bird's-eye view. That humbled me considerably.

PT: I suppose you interviewed people the way Kinsey did?

Maslow: No, something was wrong with Kinsey. I really don't think he liked women, or men. In my research, I interviewed 120 women with a new form of interview. No notes. We just talked until I got some feeling for the individual's personality, then put sex against that background. Sex has to be considered in regard to love, otherwise it's useless. This is because behavior can be a defense—a way of hiding what you feel—particularly regarding sex.

I was fascinated with my research. But I gave up interviewing men. They were useless because they boasted and lied about sex. I also planned a big research project involving prostitutes. I thought we could learn a lot about men from them, but the research never came off.

PT: You gave up all your experimental research in these fields.

Maslow: Yes, around 1941 I felt I must try to save the world, and to prevent the horrible wars and the awful hatred and prejudice. It happened very suddenly. One day just after Pearl Harbor, I was driving home and my car was stopped by a poor, pathetic parade. Boy Scouts and old uniforms and a flag and someone playing a flute off-key.

As I watched, the tears began to run down my face. I felt we didn't understand—not Hitler, nor the Germans, nor Stalin, nor the Communists. We didn't understand any of them. I felt that if we could understand, then we could make progress. I had a vision of a peace table, with people sitting around it, talking about human nature and hatred, war and peace, and brotherhood.

I was too old to go into the army. It was at that moment I realized that the rest of my life must be devoted to discovering a psychology for the peace table. That moment changed my whole life. Since then, I've devoted myself to developing a theory of human nature that could be tested by experiment and research. I wanted to prove that humans are capable of something grander than war, prejudice, and hatred. I wanted to make science consider all the people: the best specimen of mankind I could find. I found that many of them reported having something like mystical experiences.

PT: Your work with "self-actualizing" people is famous. You have described some of these mystical experiences.

Maslow: Peak experiences come from love and sex, from aesthetic moments, from bursts of creativity, from moments of insight and discovery, or from fusion with nature.

I had one such experience in a faculty procession here at Brandeis University. I saw the line stretching off into a dim future. At its head was Socrates. And in the line were the ones I love most. Thomas Jefferson was there. And Spinoza. And Alfred North Whitehead. I was in the same line. Behind me, that infinite line melted into the dimness. And there were all the people not yet born who were going to be in the same line.

I believe these experiences can be studied scientifically, and they will be.

PT: This is all part of your theory of metamotivation, isn't it?

Maslow: But not all people who are metamotivated report peak experiences. The "nonpeakers" are healthy, but they lack poetry and soaring flights of the imagination. Both peakers and nonpeakers can be self-actualized in that they're not motivated by basic needs, but by something higher

PT: Real self-actualization must be rare. What percentage of us achieve it?

Maslow: I'd say only a fraction of one percent.

PT: People whose basic needs have been met, then, will pursue life's ultimate values?

Maslow: Yes, the ultimate happiness for man is the realization of pure beauty and truth, which are the ultimate values. What we need is a system of thought—you might even call it a religion—that can bind humans together. A system that would fit the Republic of Chad as well as the United States: a system that would supply our idealistic young people with something to believe in. They're searching for something they can pour all that emotion into, and the churches are not much help.

PT: This system must come.

Maslow: I'm not alone in trying to make it. There are plenty of others working toward the same end. Perhaps their efforts, aided by the hundreds of youngsters who are devoting their lives to this, will develop a new image of man that rejects the chemical and technological views. We've technologized everything.

PT: The technologist is the person who has fallen in love with a machine. I suppose that has also happened to those in psychology?

Maslow: They become fascinated with the machine. It's almost a neurotic love. They're like the man who spends Sundays polishing his car instead of stroking his wife.

Good psychology should include all the methodological techniques, without having loyalty to one method, one idea, or one person.

PT: In several of your papers, you've said that you stopped being a behaviorist when your first child was born.

Maslow: My whole training at Wisconsin was behaviorist. I didn't question it until I began reading some other sources. Later, I began studying the Rorschach test.

At the same time, I stumbled into embryology and read Ludwig von Bertalanffy's *Modern Theories of Development*. I had already become disillusioned with Bertrand Russell and with English philosophy generally. Then, I fell in love with Alfred North Whitehead and Henri Bergson. Their writings destroyed behaviorism for me without my recognizing it.

When my first baby was born, that was the thunderclap that settled things. I looked at this tiny, mysterious thing and felt so stupid. I felt small, weak, and feeble. I'd say that anyone who's had a baby couldn't be a behaviorist.

PT: As you propose new ideas, and blaze new ground, you're bound to be criticized, aren't you?

Maslow: I have worked out a lot of good tricks for fending off professional attacks. We all have to do that. A good, controlled experiment is possible only when you already know a hell of a lot. If I'm a pioneer by choice and I go into the wilderness, how am I going to make careful experiments? If I tried to, I'd be a fool. I'm not against careful experiments. But rather, I've been working with what I call "growing tip" statistics.

With a tree, all the growth takes place at the growing tips. Humanity is exactly the same. All the growth takes place in the growing tip: among that one percent of the population. It's made up of pioneers, the beginners. That's where the action is.

PT: You were the one who helped publish Ruth Benedict's work on synergy. What's it about?

Maslow: That it's possible to set up social institutions that merge selfishness and unselfishness, so that you can't benefit yourself without benefiting others. And the reverse.

PT: How can psychology become a stronger force in our society?

Maslow: We all should look at the similarities within the various disciplines and think of enlarging psychology. To throw anything away is crazy. Good psychology should include all the methodological techniques, without having loyalty to one method, one idea, or one person.

PT: I see you as a catalyst and as a bridge between many disciplines, theories, and philosophies.

Maslow: My job is to put them all together. We shouldn't have "humanistic psychology." The adjective should be unnecessary. I'm not antibehaviorist. I'm antidoctrinaire.

PT: Abe, when you look back on your own education, what kind would you recommend for others?

Maslow: The great educational experiences of my life were those that taught me most. They taught me what kind of a person I was. These were experiences that drew me out and strengthened me. Psychoanalysis was a big thing for me. And getting married. Marriage is a school itself. Also, having children. Becoming a father changed my whole life. It taught me as if by revelation. And reading particular books. William Graham Sumner's *Folkways* was a Mount Everest in my life: It changed me.

My teachers were the best in the world. I sought them out: Erich Fromm, Karen

Horney, Ruth Benedict, Max Wertheimer, Alfred Adler, David Levy, and Harry Harlow. I was there in New York City during the 1930s when the wave of distinguished émigrés arrived from Europe.

PT: Not everyone can have such an illustrious faculty.

Maslow: It's the teacher who's important. And if this is so, then what we are doing with our whole educational structure—with credits and the idea that one teacher is as good as another? You look at the college catalog and it says English 342. It doesn't even bother to tell you the instructor's name, and that's insane. The purpose of education—and of all social institutions—is the development of full humaneness. If you keep that in mind, all else follows. We've got to concentrate on goals.

PT: It's like the story about the test pilot who radioed back home: "I'm lost, but I'm making record time."

Maslow: If you forget the goal of education, then the whole thing is lost.

PT: If a rare, self-actualizing young psychologist came to you today and said, "What's the most important thing I can do in this time of crisis?" what advice would you give?

Maslow: I'd say: Get to work on aggression and hostility. We need the definitive book on aggression. And we need it now. Only the pieces exist: the animal stuff, the psychoanalytic stuff, the endocrine stuff. Time is running out. A key to understanding the evil which can destroy our society lies in this understanding.

There's another study that could be done. I'd like to test the whole, incoming freshman class at Brandeis University in various ways: psychiatric interviews, personality tests, everything. I want to follow them for four years of college. For a beginning, I want to test my theory that emotionally healthy people perceive better.

PT: You could make the college study only a preliminary, and follow them through their whole life span, the way Lewis Terman did with his gifted kids.

Maslow: Oh yes! I'd like to know: How good a father or mother does this student become? And what happens to his/her children? This kind of long-term study would take more time than I have left. But that ultimately doesn't make any difference. I like to be the first runner in the relay race. I like to pass on the baton to the next person.

Making Sense of Self-Esteem

Mark R. Leary[1]

Department of Psychology, Wake Forest University, Winston-Salem, North Carolina

Abstract

Sociometer theory proposes that the self-esteem system evolved as a monitor of social acceptance, and that the so-called self-esteem motive functions not to maintain self-esteem per se but rather to avoid social devaluation and rejection. Cues indicating that the individual is not adequately valued and accepted by other people lower self-esteem and motivate behaviors that enhance relational evaluation. Empirical evidence regarding the self-esteem motive, the antecedents of self-esteem, the relation between low self-esteem and psychological problems, and the consequences of enhancing self-esteem is consistent with the theory.

Keywords

self-esteem; self; self-regard; rejection

Self-esteem has been regarded as an important construct since the earliest days of psychology. In the first psychology textbook, William James (1890) suggested that the tendency to strive to feel good about oneself is a fundamental aspect of human nature, thereby fueling a fascination—some observers would say obsession—with self-esteem that has spanned more than a century. During that time, developmental psychologists have studied the antecedents of self-esteem and its role in human development, social psychologists have devoted attention to behaviors that appear intended to maintain self-esteem, personality psychologists have examined individual differences in the trait of self-esteem, and theorists of a variety of orientations have discussed the importance of self-regard to psychological adjustment. In the past couple of decades, practicing psychologists and social engineers have suggested that high self-esteem is a remedy for many psychological and social problems.

Yet, despite more than 100 years of attention and thousands of published studies, fundamental issues regarding self-esteem remain poorly understood. Why is self-esteem important? Do people really have a need for self-esteem? Why is self-esteem so strongly determined by how people believe they are evaluated by others? Is low self-esteem associated with psychological difficulties and, if so, why? Do efforts to enhance self-esteem reduce personal and social problems as proponents of the self-esteem movement claim?

PERSPECTIVES ON THE FUNCTION OF SELF-ESTEEM

Many writers have assumed that people seek to maintain their self-esteem because they possess an inherent "need" to feel good about themselves. However, given the apparent importance of self-esteem to psychological functioning, we must ask why self-esteem is so important and what function it might serve. Humanistic psychologists have traced high self-esteem to a congruency between a person's real and ideal selves and suggested that self-esteem signals people as to when they are behaving in self-determined, autonomous ways. Other writers have proposed that people seek high self-esteem because it facilitates goal achievement. For example, Bednar, Wells, and Peterson (1989) proposed that self-esteem is subjective feedback about the adequacy of the self. This feedback—self-esteem—is positive when the individual copes well with circumstances but negative when he or she avoids threats. In turn, self-esteem affects subsequent goal achievement; high self-esteem increases coping, and low self-esteem leads to further avoidance.

The ethological perspective (Barkow, 1980) suggests that self-esteem is an adaptation that evolved in the service of maintaining dominance in social relationships. According to this theory, human beings evolved mechanisms for monitoring dominance because dominance facilitated the acquisition of mates and other reproduction-enhancing resources. Because attention and favorable reactions from others were associated with being dominant, feelings of self-esteem became tied to social approval and deference. From this perspective, the motive to evaluate oneself positively reduces, in evolutionary terms, to the motive to enhance one's relative dominance.

One of the more controversial explanations of self-esteem is provided by terror management theory, which suggests that the function of self-esteem is to buffer people against the existential terror they experience at the prospect of their own death and annihilation (Solomon, Greenberg, & Pyszczynski, 1991). Several experiments have supported aspects of the theory, but not the strong argument that the function of the self-esteem system is to provide an emotional buffer specifically against death-related anxiety.

All of these perspectives offer insights into the nature of self-esteem, but each has conceptual and empirical difficulties (for critiques, see Leary, 1999; Leary & Baumeister, in press). In the past few years, a novel perspective—sociometer theory—has cast self-esteem in a somewhat different light as it attempts to address lingering questions about the nature of self-esteem.

SOCIOMETER THEORY

According to sociometer theory, self-esteem is essentially a psychological meter, or gauge, that monitors the quality of people's relationships with others (Leary, 1999; Leary & Baumeister, in press; Leary & Downs, 1995). The theory is based on the assumption that human beings possess a pervasive drive to maintain significant interpersonal relationships, a drive that evolved because early human beings who belonged to social groups were more likely to survive and reproduce than those who did not (Baumeister & Leary, 1995). Given the disastrous implications of being ostracized in the ancestral environment in which human evolution occurred, early human beings may have developed a mechanism for monitoring the degree to which other people valued and accepted them. This psychological mechanism— the *sociometer*—continuously monitors the social environment for cues regarding the degree to which the individual is being accepted versus rejected by other people.

The sociometer appears to be particularly sensitive to changes in relational evaluation—the degree to which others regard their relationship with the individual as valuable, important, or close. When evidence of low relational evaluation (particularly, a decrement in relational evaluation) is detected, the sociometer attracts the person's conscious attention to the potential threat to social acceptance and motivates him or her to deal with it. The affectively laden self-appraisals that constitute the "output" of the sociometer are what we typically call self-esteem.

Self-esteem researchers distinguish between *state self-esteem*—momentary fluctuations in a person's feelings about him- or herself—and *trait self-esteem*— the person's general appraisal of his or her value; both are aspects of the sociometer. Feelings of state self-esteem fluctuate as a function of the degree to which the person perceives others currently value their relationships with him or her. Cues that connote high relational evaluation raise state self-esteem, whereas cues that connote low relational evaluation lower state self-esteem. Trait self-esteem, in contrast, reflects the person's general sense that he or she is the sort of person who is valued and accepted by other people. Trait self-esteem may be regarded as the resting state of the sociometer in the absence of incoming information relevant to relational evaluation.

SELF-ESTEEM AND ITS RELATIONSHIP TO BEHAVIOR

Sociometer theory provides a parsimonious explanation for much of what we know about self-esteem. Here I examine how sociometer theory answers four fundamental questions about self-esteem raised earlier.

The Self-Esteem Motive

As noted, many psychologists have assumed that people possess a motive or need to maintain self-esteem. According to sociometer theory, the so-called self-esteem motive does not function to maintain self-esteem but rather to minimize the likelihood of rejection (or, more precisely, relational devaluation). When people behave in ways that protect or enhance their self-esteem, they are typically acting in ways that they believe will increase their relational value in others' eyes and, thus, improve their chances of social acceptance.

The sociometer perspective explains why events that are known (or potentially known) by other people have much greater effects on self-esteem than events that are known only by the individual him- or herself. If self-esteem involved only private self-judgments, as many psychologists have assumed, public events should have no greater impact on self-esteem than private ones.

Antecedents of Self-Esteem

Previous writers have puzzled over the fact that self-esteem is so strongly tied to people's beliefs about how they are evaluated by others. If self-esteem is a *self*-evaluation, why do people judge themselves by *other* people's standards? Sociometer theory easily explains why the primary determinants of self-esteem involve the perceived reactions of other people, as well as self-judgments on dimensions that the person thinks are important to significant others. As a monitor of relational evaluation, the self-esteem system is inherently sensitive to real and potential reactions of other people.

Evidence shows that state self-esteem is strongly affected by events that have implications for the degree to which one is valued and accepted by other people (Leary, Haupt, Strausser, & Chokel, 1998; Leary, Tambor, Terdal, & Downs, 1995). The events that affect self-esteem are precisely the kinds of things that, if known by other people, would affect their evaluation and acceptance of the person (Leary, Tambor, et al., 1995). Most often, self-esteem is lowered by failure, criticism, rejection, and other events that have negative implications for relational evaluation; self-esteem rises when a person succeeds, is praised, or experiences another's love—events that are associated with relational appreciation. Even the mere possibility of rejection can lower self-esteem, a finding that

makes sense if the function of the self-esteem system is to warn the person of possible relational devaluation in time to take corrective action.

The attributes on which people's self-esteem is based are precisely the characteristics that determine the degree to which people are valued and accepted by others (Baumeister & Leary, 1995). Specifically, high trait self-esteem is associated with believing that one possesses socially desirable attributes such as competence, personal likability, and physical attractiveness. Furthermore, self-esteem is related most strongly to one's standing on attributes that one believes are valued by significant others, a finding that is also consistent with sociometer theory.

In linking self-esteem to social acceptance, sociometer theory runs counter to the humanistic assumption that self-esteem based on approval from others is false or unhealthy. On the contrary, if the function of self-esteem is to avoid social devaluation and rejection, then the system must be responsive to others' reactions. This system may lead people to do things that are not always beneficial, but it does so to protect their interpersonal relationships rather than their inner integrity.

Low Self-Esteem and Psychological Problems

Research has shown that low self-esteem is related to a variety of psychological difficulties and personal problems, including depression, loneliness, substance abuse, teenage pregnancy, academic failure, and criminal behavior. The evidence in support of the link between low self-esteem and psychological problems has often been overstated; the relationships are weaker and more scattered than typically assumed (Mecca, Smelser, & Vasconcellos, 1989). Moreover, high self-esteem also has notable drawbacks. Even so, low self-esteem tends to be more strongly associated with psychological difficulties than high self-esteem.

From the standpoint of sociometer theory, these problems are caused not by low self-esteem but rather by a history of low relational evaluation, if not outright rejection. As a subjective gauge of relational evaluation, self-esteem may parallel these problems, but it is a coeffect rather than a cause. (In fact, contrary to the popular view that low self-esteem causes these problems, no direct evidence exists to document that self-esteem has any causal role in thought, emotion, or behavior.) Much research shows that interpersonal rejection results in emotional problems, difficulties relating with others, and maladaptive efforts to be accepted (e.g., excessive dependency, membership in deviant groups), precisely the concomitants of low self-esteem (Leary, Schreindorfer, & Haupt, 1995). In addition, many personal problems lower self-esteem because they lead other people to devalue or reject the individual.

Consequences of Enhancing Self-Esteem

The claim that self-esteem does not cause psychological outcomes may appear to fly in the face of evidence showing that interventions that enhance self-esteem do, in fact, lead to positive psychological changes. The explanation for the beneficial effects of programs that enhance self-esteem is that these interventions change people's perceptions of the degree to which they are socially valued individuals. Self-esteem programs always include features that would be expected to increase real or perceived social acceptance; for example, these programs include components aimed at enhancing social skills and interpersonal problem solving, improving physical appearance, and increasing self-control (Leary, 1999).

CONCLUSIONS

Sociometer theory suggests that the emphasis psychologists and the lay public have placed on self-esteem has been somewhat misplaced. Self-esteem is certainly involved in many psychological phenomena, but its role is different than has been supposed. Subjective feelings of self-esteem provide ongoing feedback regarding one's relational value vis-à-vis other people. By focusing on the monitor rather than on what the monitor measures, we have been distracted from the underlying interpersonal processes and the importance of social acceptance to human well-being.

Recommended Reading

Baumeister, R. F. (Ed.). (1993). *Self-esteem: The puzzle of low self-regard.* New York: Plenum Press.

Colvin, C. R., & Block, J. (1994). Do positive illusions foster mental health? An examination of the Taylor and Brown formulation. *Psychological Bulletin, 116,* 3–20.

Leary, M. R. (1999). (See References)

Leary, M. R., & Downs, D. L. (1995). (See References)

Mecca, A. M., Smelser, N. J., & Vasconcellos, J. (Eds.). (1989). (See References)

Note

1. Address correspondence to Mark Leary, Department of Psychology, Wake Forest University, Winston-Salem, NC 27109; e-mail: leary@wfu.edu.

References

Barkow, J. (1980). Prestige and self-esteem: A biosocial interpretation. In D. R. Omark, F. F. Strayer, & D. G. Freedman (Eds.), *Dominance relations: An ethological view of human conflict and social interaction* (pp. 319–332). New York: Garland STPM Press.

Baumeister, R. F., & Leary, M. R. (1995). The need to belong: Desire for interpersonal attachments as a fundamental human motivation. *Psychological Bulletin, 117,* 497–529.

Bednar, R. L., Wells, M. G., & Peterson, S. R. (1989). *Self-esteem: Paradoxes and inno-vations in clinical theory and practice.* Washington, DC: American Psychological Association.

James, W. (1890). *The principles of psychology* (Vol. 1). New York: Henry Holt.

Leary, M. R. (1999). The social and psychological importance of self-esteem. In R. M. Kowalski & M. R. Leary (Eds.), *The social psychology of emotional and behavioral problems: Interfaces of social and clinical psychology* (pp. 197–221). Washington, DC: American Psychological Association.

Leary, M. R., & Baumeister, R. F. (in press). The nature and function of self-esteem: Sociometer theory. *Advances in Experimental Social Psychology.*

Leary, M. R., & Downs, D. L. (1995). Interpersonal functions of the self-esteem motive: The self-esteem system as a sociometer. In M. H. Kernis (Ed.), *Efficacy, agency, and self-esteem* (pp. 123–144). New York: Plenum Press.

Leary, M. R., Haupt, A. L., Strausser, K. S., & Chokel, J. L. (1998). Calibrating the sociometer: The relationship between interpersonal appraisals and state self-esteem. *Journal of Personality and Social Psychology, 74,* 1290–1299.

Leary, M. R., Schreindorfer, L. S., & Haupt, A. L. (1995). The role of self-esteem in emotional and behavioral problems: Why is low self-esteem dysfunctional? *Journal of Social and Clinical Psychology, 14,* 297–314.

Leary, M. R., Tambor, E. S., Terdal, S. J., & Downs, D. L. (1995). Self-esteem as an interpersonal monitor. The sociometer hypothesis. *Journal of Personality and Social Psychology, 68,* 518–530.

Mecca, A. M., Smelser, N. J., & Vasconcellos, J. (Eds.). (1989). *The social importance of self-esteem.* Berkeley: University of California Press.

Solomon, S., Greenberg, J., & Pyszczynski, T. (1991). A terror management theory of social behavior: The psychological functions of self-esteem and cultural worldviews. *Advances in Experimental Social Psychology, 24,* 93–159.

RAISING KIDS' SELF-ESTEEM MAY BACKFIRE, EXPERTS WARN

Maggie Fox

*A seemingly benign attempt by schools and parents to raise the **self**-esteem of children may backfire, creating a violent society, psychologists warn.*

Psychologists Brad Bushman of Iowa State University and Roy Baumeister of Case Western Reserve University in Ohio say that when narcissistic people are criticized, they are likely to react in a violent and unpredictable manner.

Laboratory tests support this theory, they write in the July issue of the American Psychological Association's Journal of Personality and Social Psychology. They conducted two studies of 540 college students and found those who tended to have unrealistically high levels of self-esteem also became aggressive when they were insulted or criticized.

A seemingly benign attempt by schools and parents to raise the self-esteem of children may backfire, creating a violent society, psychologists warn.

Out-of-control self-esteem in the form of a personality disorder known as narcissism could even be responsible for a recent spate of school shootings, they say, although they are quick to add they have no proof of this.

Psychologists Brad Bushman of Iowa State University and Roy Baumeister of Case Western Reserve University in Ohio say that when narcissistic people are criticized, they are likely to react in a violent and unpredictable manner.

Laboratory tests support this theory, they write in the July issue of the American Psychological Association's Journal of Personality and Social Psychology. They conducted two studies of 540 college students and found those who tended to have unrealistically high levels of self-esteem also became aggressive when they were insulted or criticized.

When parents and educators try too hard to raise the self-esteem of children, they may be inadvertently causing narcissism, the psychologists say.

"If kids begin to develop unrealistically optimistic opinions of themselves and those beliefs are constantly rejected by others, their feelings of self-love could make these kids potentially dangerous to those around them," Bushman said in a statement.

Baumeister, author of a book on violent behavior, "Evil—Inside Human Violence and Cruelty," said he had no evidence of any link between recent school shootings and a trend in recent decades in the United States to build the self-esteem of children. But he worries they may have the balance wrong.

"The schools are trying to do it, and if they succeed it could backfire," Baumeister said in a telephone interview.

He said parents are also trying to build the self-esteem of their children and it is not always a good thing, "especially exaggerated or unfounded self-esteem or the desire to think you're better than others, this thing of telling kids that they are doing great no matter how well they do, giving trophies to everybody, having children write stories or lists of all the great things about themselves."

Baumeister's advice to educators: "Forget about self-esteem and concentrate on self-control."

In other words, old-fashioned moral discipline is not always a bad thing, even if it sometimes makes some children feel bad, he said. "Some people should feel bad about themselves when they do something bad," he added.

He said surveys have shown the U.S. population in general already has an inflated view of itself. "The average person thinks that he's above average at present. If we had a population of people who had distorted self-esteem, that would be different. I think inflating it is dangerous."

Other researchers are also warning schools and parents to be careful about just how they go about praising children.

Writing in the same journal, Claudia Mueller and Carol Dweck of Columbia University said praising a child for his or her brains may make the youngster anxious and ill-equipped to deal with failure.

Their study of more than 400 5th-graders found that those who were told they did well on a task because they were smart became timid about failure later and eventually chose to do mainly tasks they knew they would do well at.

Children praised for trying hard, on the other hand, tended to welcome opportunities to learn something new even if they might not perform as well.

Bushman said the study he and Baumeister did conflicts with assertions by some educators and criminal justice experts who say that aggression is caused by low self-esteem.

"We found that low self-esteem definitely does not cause aggression," he said in a telephone interview. He said it is good to give children a feeling of self-worth, but he just does not think people should be praised for no good reason.

"I think people's opinions of themselves should be based on achievement rather than hollow praise. If people are honestly achieving in a valid way they deserve some recognition for that. But praising people regardless of how they behave, if their performance is mediocre, you create this sense of entitlement," he said.

When these people get out into the real world and find that not everyone thinks they are great, they may become angry.

"Reality doesn't cooperate with you if you have a distorted impression of it. If you think you are better than you are then you are more likely to get negative feedback, and if you are emotionally invested in this then you could get violent," Baumeister said.

To prove their theory, Baumeister and Bushman gave 540 undergraduate psychology students personality tests. Then they had each write an essay, which was evaluated by a neutral third party who made comments ranging from strong praise to insults such as "This is one of the worst essays I have read!"

"Narcissists became exceptionally aggressive toward a person who had given them a negative, insulting evaluation," Bushman and Baumeister wrote.

Private Lives: Discipline and knowing where to draw the line

Jan Parker and Jan Stimpson

NO MATTER what you do, how hard you try, there may be times when your child behaves appallingly.

Managing these times so that your child's behaviour improves can be difficult and stressful, but leaving the behaviour unchallenged is worse. Only when you show where you draw the line can a child know which side of it she should be on.

To do this constructively, in ways that bring the results you both need without terrifying or crushing your child in the process, you will sometimes need to be gentle, sometimes tough, often both, and always strong enough to stand your ground.

Thinking ahead and considering your options will make it easier to deal calmly with your child's worst moments. Choosing which discipline strategies, if any, best suit your circumstances is also easier if you know the difference between discipline and punishment.

Discipline is an investment. It teaches children what they have done wrong, the consequences of their behaviour and how they could modify it. It encourages self-discipline and motivates them to do better. It is not a soft option, but can be astonishingly effective.

Punishment involves making children suffer for misbehaviour in an attempt to control it. It aims to shame, frighten or otherwise force children into compliance without them necessarily understanding why. It therefore risks teaching children to modify their behaviour for the wrong reasons, such as the risk of being caught.

The distinction between the two is not always clear-cut and some strategies may involve an element of both, but your *ability* to recognise the type and likely outcome of each approach will help you decide how best to proceed.

Effective discipline strategies

As ever, only consider those approaches that feel right for you and are appropriate to your child's age, understanding and temperament. If any strategy does not work as you hoped, or loses its effectiveness, change it.

Learning to challenge

Challenging is a key skill for turning around a child's behaviour. It takes practice. To those who have never tried it, it may sound too "reasonable" to work in the heat of the moment, but both parents and professionals vouch for its *ability* to stop children in their tracks and praise its effectiveness.

It works on the principle that most children will stop behaving unacceptably if they are told in no uncertain terms how it is affecting others and are given the opportunity to change course without loss of face.

Saying no and meaning it

If you mean it, really mean it, your child is much more likely to get the message. If you don't really mean it your child will pick this up in your expression and body *language* and either ignore you or provoke you until you do.

If you do mean "No", say it in a way that increases its effectiveness. Sometimes you may need to be sharp and stern.

To help your child know you mean business, try getting down to her level so you at least have a chance of eye contact.

Try to stay relaxed and say, calmly but firmly: "No. You are to stop that now—no more." This stops you getting drawn into negotiations and keeps you on very certain ground. Children often echo their parents' emotions; staying in control in an otherwise fiery situation may help them follow suit.

Removing the victim, not the culprit

This is especially useful in educating very young children not to hurt others. It denies the aggressor the attention that may fuel her behaviour and also makes the victim feel safer with you than being left alone.

If your child is hurting another, always explain why you do not like that behaviour and how you would like her to behave instead.

Consequences

Helping children understand the natural consequences of their actions is crucial to their improving their behaviour and learning self-control. This approach can also be used when your child is displaying behaviour you need to stop. For example: Parent (firmly and calmly): "Joe, if you throw your toys someone will get hurt, and you don't want that to happen. Play without throwing, or put it down."

This is often all that is needed to help a child *think* through the consequences of an action—and stop. But what happens when you have told your child the natural consequences of an action and she carries on doing it? Or when you have reminded her of a family rule and she still breaks it? To make it very clear where you draw the line, you may have to impose an (artificial) consequence for crossing it. Eg:

The weapons rule

You may have a family rule that no toys are to be used as weapons to hurt or frighten other children. Whenever nec-essary, you remind her of it and tell her the natural consequence of breaking it (ie "You will hurt"). You may even chal-lenge her behaviour. But two minutes later she hits her brother on the head with a drumstick. What next?

Three strikes and it's out

1. Any toy used as a weapon (ie to hurt or frighten others) is immediately re-moved (for an hour, for the afternoon, for the rest of the day—the older the child the longer the time can be).

2. If it happens again, it is removed again, for longer.

3. If it happens a third time, it is put in the bin.

Standing back

If you react to every misdemeanour you could spend most of your time rein-ing in your child's behaviour, which, by the law of diminishing returns, means she will take less notice and you will be-come increasingly frustrated and angry.

Liberate yourself by choosing times not to react immediately. At the very least, this will allow you time to assess what you want your child to do and how important it is that they do it, or whether you can let it go. If it is behaviour that you feel you must challenge, a consid-ered response is generally much more effective than a knee-jerk one.

———————

'Raising Happy Children' by Jan Parker and Jan Stimpson (Hodder & Stoughton, pounds 9.99)

Who Are the Freudians?

Edith Kurzweil

To answer this question, I began in the late 1970s to undertake a cross-cultural study of psychoanalysis. I had been aware that neither celebrations nor condemnations, neither revisions nor distortions of Freud's and his disciples' insights had attempted to assess the profusion of clinical studies and theories in relation to their local, taken-for-granted cultural assumptions. By then, I already had written a chapter on the French psychoanalyst Jacques Lacan in my book, *The Age of Structuralism: Lévi-Strauss to Foucault* (1980), and had noted that some Parisian psychoanalysts (and not only Lacanians) were elaborating on the early Freudians' discoveries in entirely different directions than were, for instance, the members of the New York Psychoanalytic Society or of the Sigmund Freud-Institut in Frankfurt. At the time, however, I was not yet fully aware that psychoanalysis had so many offshoots, and offshoots of offshoots.

Although I expanded on, and demonstrated, that my previous observations of cultural differences were major elements in the role that psychoanalysis was being accorded within various societies, I still underestimated the personal preferences and affinities among analysts and proponents who are purported to share a specific theory, a culture, and who either belong to the International Psychoanalytic Association or attend its meetings. The very profusion of theories and practices led me, reluctantly, to limit my book to the so-called classical Freudians alone.

As a result of that research, I maintained that "the fragmentation of psychoanalytic theory proves, among other things, that the Freudians primarily are united by their profession rather than by their ideas." And I predicted that even a victory in court by American psychologists, who in 1985 were suing for membership in the American Psychoanalytic Association (APA) and in the International Psychoanalytic Association (IPA), might not bring the equality of prestige and income they expected, and did not bode well for future cooperation among Freudian therapists.

Still, there now are many local attempts to present a united front, but it is not clear that this has put an end to earlier rivalries.

Since *The Freudians. A Comparative Perspective* was published, in 1989, there have been significant changes not only in the make-up of the psychoanalysts' professional organizations, but in specific culturally induced attitudes towards Freud and psychoanalysis, and in the transliteration of practices from one country to another. After the fall of the Berlin Wall and the demise of the Soviet empire, Sandor Ferenczi's "active" clinical method, that is, his advocacy of closer, personal involvement with an analysand than Freud had approved of, began being introduced and pursued in America. This meant that the detached stance advocated by American ego psychologists was being further relaxed—a change in clinical method that appears to be more suitable to analysands accustomed to today's permissive climate. But this shift also has initiated yet other examinations of the disagreements between Ferenczi and Freud, again has questioned Jones's dismissal of Ferenczi as incompetent at the end of his life, and has led Ferenczi's follower, Clara Thompson who criticized psychoanalytic "scientificity" in the 1940s to be taken more seriously. And Ferenczi's assumptions about child abuse, which is of current concern in America (and elsewhere) where more and more instances are being reported, have been useful to researchers investigating psychic and family dynamics. Both medically and psychologically trained therapists, of every school, are engaged in these endeavors.

The political upheavals in such countries as the former Czechoslovakia, the former East Germany, the former Yugoslavia, and in Russia, have allowed, also, for freedom of expression in general, and for psychoanalytic practices as well. New teaching institutes have been set up in these countries, and psychoanalysts from Western Europe have been traveling there, regularly, to conduct seminars and personal analyses.

In Paris, Lacanian therapy has become less pervasive, while its focus on the use of a psychoanalyst's language has become more pronounced, also, among classical Freudians—a phenomenon clearly observable at international gatherings. In Germany, *Sozioanalyse*—which is meant to penetrate to the unconscious elements that allowed the Germans to sit by or participate in the Holocaust—increasingly has been taking a backseat, while psychoanalytic therapy has become more acceptable. A number of studies in the Frankfurt school tradition continue being pursued. In the United States, classical ego psychology has suffered a decline, as have all other long-term therapies, while short-term interventions, and the use of drug induced psychic changes have moved to the fore. And whereas Parisian intellectuals rarely quote

Lacan, some of his ideas, and reverberations of them, have proliferated in many American universities—albeit in non-therapeutic versions of postmodernism.

My predictions, or should I say premonitions, about *psychoanalytic theory*, were based on the dynamic contradictions intrinsic to the following points: 1) clinical approaches grounded in case studies keep evolving and, in turn, reflect personality changes due to cultural pressures; 2) each case study is rooted in the psychic interactions between an analyst and a patient and, therefore, is an objective abstraction from a subjective interpersonal experience; 3) this subjective element is bound to lead every other self-respecting analyst to ponder, or even argue, on how differently he/she might have handled the case; 4) since this holds true for analysts of the same training, the same nationality, the same gender, and the same affiliation as well, the more inclusive of diversity, the more glaring must be the discrepant interpretations; 5) and because psychoanalysts, in the course of their training, must learn to identify fully with their supervisors and analysts, they are bound to have difficulties accepting intrapsychic theories contradicting what, for good reason, have become gut reactions.

My forebodings about the future of *Freud's movement* resulted from my recognition that in the past there were so many dissimilar developments and nationally based interests; 1) all along, to be admitted to membership by the IPA bestowed prestige, but did not add to a psychoanalyst's range or number of patients at home; 2) since "properly" trained psychologists from every country around the world always had been accepted by the IPA, having won the legal right to join was of significance only to Americans, who had restricted admission to medical doctors; 3) although attendance at international meetings, and the possibility of being asked to present a paper, inevitably sparks intellectual activity, American psychologists, who always were free to attend IPA meetings—except for business sessions—would not gain much after becoming members; 4) as in other international organizations, I expected increasing size, diversity of languages, and of cultural assumptions, to lead to more bureaucratization, more internal politicking, and more impersonal contacts, conditions that are anathema to the intimacy on which psychoanalysis thrives.

Still, I had fewer misgivings in relation to *psychoanalytic practice*. For in the course of observing the European scene, I had not noted any major variations in the way clinicians—whatever their formal credentials—were talking about their patients, and about their concerns and practices. Most of them were reiterating the need for rigorous instructional and supervisory standards. This held true for Americans as well: major intellectual disagreements had occurred in-line with specific theoretical stances, with particular details over psychoanalytic formation, and with clinical evaluations of patients. And there had been little contact with therapists of "dubious" training by them all. But, altogether, international ex-changes always had helped broaden individuals' outlook and tolerance, thereby enriching participants' theoretical and clinical knowledge—while introducing them to new perspectives.

The Continuing Conflicts

Unresolvable conflicts continue to ensue when, at international meetings, psychoanalysts assume that the idiom of their own countries, and their own professional societies, ipso facto applies everywhere else; and when, even within the same cultural milieu, they take for granted that clinicians, historians, and postmodernists share similar concerns, or are based on the same premises. In fact, most Freudian scholars in departments of literature, and most historians of psychoanalysis, are much more involved with numerous, and detailed, textual, biographical and historical questions than with clinical issues. However, the foremost focus of practicing analysts is on what goes on in their own and their patients' minds. This activity cannot be successful unless psychoanalysts listen carefully in order to sort out their patients' fantasies from their lives. Since these patients often introduce the relativistic notions of postmodern attitudes, the analysts easily confuse these with the openness to their patients' problems and are influenced in that direction. Nevertheless, the openness of psychoanalysts and the openness of postmodernists are basically opposed to each other. For, ultimately, psychoanalysts try to sort out fantasies from reality, whereas postmodernists have another set of assumptions of what constitutes reality.

Ever since the first psychoanalytic congress in Salzburg, in 1908, Freud's followers have responded to aspects of local conditions and preoccupations, to public demand and professional opportunities, however unconsciously they may have done so. Furthermore, only after traditions have begun to unravel, and after modernization has begun to take its emotional toll, do societies introduce psychoanalytic and related therapeutic means to alleviate the pressures of modern life. At that point, increasing numbers of people start to enter the profession which, in turn, experiences an upsurge of activities. In America, the peak was reached in the 1950s and 1960s, and we now have a surfeit of therapists. Consequently, therapists of many stripes, from the most classical Freudians to the least trained social workers, are competing for patients, sometimes by offering innovative treatment. This trend, though much less pronounced, already is beginning in France, and to some extent in Germany.

The global reach of Freud's hypotheses, his penetration of so many different domains—challenging professionals and amateurs in them all—and his formulations and reformulations of earlier concepts of psychic functioning, has left a grab bag of ideas. In America, for instance, clinicians continue to debate the viability of narrow conceptions of ego psychology versus narcissism, of self-psychology versus interpersonal and relational approaches, whereas social scientists tend to understand narcissism in terms of Christopher Lasch's comments on the behavior of the 1970s generation. That Erik Erikson noted that little girls tend to build enclosed spaces while boys are more likely to construct towers, started the protracted debate with, and among, feminists that still is going on. Such debates, themselves, in recent years, have turned into scholarly subjects. These general polemics, however, are not of particular interest to psychoanalysts. They tend to focus on the clinical advances based on Freud's conceptions, while conceding that here and there he might have been wrong, and going on to explain their differences in more or less psychoanalytic terms. Culturally inclined critics, on the other hand, search for the contradictions within his *oevre* and in the interactions among the disciples. They speculate on the extent to which his cancer of the jaw, or his patriarchal surroundings, might have influenced his thinking. They tend to resort to conspiracy theories, assuming that Ferenczi's concepts were suppressed to uphold Freud's; that Freud rooted seduction by the little girl's father. in fantasy rather than reality, not because he assumed that though it certainly occurred it could not possibly be so frequent, or because treatment failed, but because he deferred to his friend, Wilhelm Fliess; or that he had an affair with his sister-in-law, Minna, because Jung said so in an obscure interview many years after they already had broken up. This is not to say that classical Freudians are on track when they choose to accept Freud's *History of the Psychoanalytic Movement* (1914) as gospel. Moreover, speculations and historical reevaluations have little bearing on what 'clinicians do in their work with patients. All in all, both Freud's followers and his detractors, his imitators and his adversaries, have been able to explore many interesting avenues of research—in line with clinical findings, with professional affinities, and with the general Zeitgeist.

Freud in the Larger Culture

The familiar disputes, as a rule, tend to arise within a national context, and to address specific concerns—a murder trial, a controversial book, a political scandal. But where psychoanalytic thought already permeates the culture, it usually is applied loosely by the media as well. In other words, after a certain time, psychoanalysis becomes everyone's intellectual property. Practicing psychoanalysts, however, take their cues from colleagues within their immediate professional associations, and to a much lesser extent from the leading psychoanalysts within the national and international associations. Thus they frequently overlook that their immediate concerns, for the most part, are rooted in their own societal context. As a result, they tend to judge cultural events and phenomena from a specific vantage point.

The postponement of the Freud exhibit at the Library of Congress, in the fall of 1995, was an example of how professional and personal biases, and interests, intersect in America today, and how a handful of individuals were able to exert political pressure. This is what happened: A few Freud scholars, who are known for their antagonism to psychoanalysts, maintained that "the show was conceived as a means of mobilizing support for the besieged practice of psychoanalysis . . . and [did not account for] the radically different view of Freud from the one promoted by the psychoanalytic establishment." They collected forty-two signatures from people who had intellectual, professional, or personal disagreements with Freudians, mostly from a few historians who wanted immediate access to the Freud archives, and from psychologists who for so long had been kept out of the APA and the IPA. They chose to ignore that this "establishment" is besieged and dwindling. And they apparently were unaware of the fact that this exposition had been initiated, and partially paid for, by the Austrian government—to celebrate the country's millennium as well as the one hundredth birthday of Freud's inception of psychoanalysis. These detractors wanted to have their views represented, to choose the contents of the exhibition, to criticize Freud rather than praise him.

The resulting brouhaha led the Librarian of Congress, James H. Billington, to postpone the exhibit which, by March 1996, induced 180 well-known figures from around the world—psychoanalysts, writers, philosophers, and cinematographers—to protest the cancellation. They could not accept that "as prestigious an institution as the Library of Congress would allow itself to be manipulated by public opinion and to be impressed by the dictatorship by a few intellectuals turned into inquisitors." Essentially, they asked Billington not give in to this "witch hunt," and to reschedule the event "under conditions that would not succumb to a blackmail of fear, and to open the archives to all researchers, from every country and every tendency."

In response, the Librarian of Congress announced that the event had been postponed and would open in the fall of 1998. The critics were placated by having some of their own put on the organizing committee. Ultimately, the exhibit came off, opened with much fanfare and will travel to Los Angeles, New York, London and Vienna. (It is aimed at the general public, whatever that is, and thus features more applications of Freud's ideas in films and comic strips than of his original, significant manuscripts.) But what is astonishing, is the fact that most of the American psychoanalysts to whom I have spoken know very little of what had been going on, although those who do tend to be angry, or to dismiss this affair as "just politics." Unlike their opponents, who, for the most part, were radical graduate students in the late 1960s and now have tenure in universities, they are either unfamiliar with real political tactics or unwilling to waste time on these activities, which take their minds off their analytic work. But French, German, and Chilean psychoanalysts, for instance, and Freud sympathizers from most other countries, are more politically astute, and are differentially integrated into their societies. No matter what their clinical preferences may be, they consider their American colleagues politically naive, their milieu strange and/or provincial, and in this particular instance repressive of freedom of speech as well.

Whether or not this assessment is correct is a moot point. However, disputes within American culture, the psychoanalysts' need for fundamental integrity, and the discounting of milieu generated differences tend, also, to confuse clinical questions with technical ones, and institutional ones with prestige in the public realm. Inevitably, Freudian analysts and Freudian critics talk past each other. Following are some examples of the sources of these disputes:

1. The combination of addressing a public that, generally, is ignorant of history, and preoccupations with personal careers both among practicing psychoanalysts and among Freud scholars cannot help but encourage tunnel vision and superficiality.

2. Clinicians' focus on Freud's past centers on what made him move away from certain theoretical concepts, and to construct others, in the hope to better understand one or another of their patients. Thus they ignore, for the most part, the evolution of these concepts in terms of their historical context; they are not overly concerned with scandals, and, except in rare instances, don't arouse (or titillate) the current Zeitgeist. But reconstructions of this history are meant for academics.

3. Specific disputes and issues in the public realm no longer question the ubiquity of unconscious forces which have changed how we perceive our entire culture. And the very pervasiveness of the therapeutic mindset encourages the public, also, to go for simplistic explanations of intrapsychic dynamics.

4. Freudian therapy has changed medical practices around the world, and psychoanalysis has spread—however differently—over all of Western Europe, Latin America and beyond. This proliferation lulls psychoanalysts into believing that cultural influences—then and now—either don't matter or are the same everywhere.

5. Within the international psychoanalytic realm, multiple theoretical frames are now accepted. Their proponents as a rule present cases that demonstrate one or more clinical successes. In addition to Freudian structural theory, modern ego psychology, Kleinian-Bionian theory, British object relations theory, self-psychology, American object relations theory and Lacanian theories are being debated, always in terms of their viability in working with patients.

6. The current interest in biography, among other things, is unconnected to questions of therapy. Neither is it relevant to the therapy whether psychoanalysis is an art or a science. However, the clinicians' relative ignorance of the ins and outs of the history of their discipline, of the personal animosities among Freud's followers who were responsible for the early theoretical splits, and their defensive stances, are bound to make them lose when debating historians and critics, as well as philosophers of science.

The public, however, expects its psychoanalysts to be on top of all issues—precisely because they are therapists—and does not realize that working with patients all day long keeps them somewhat isolated from the larger cultural trends which, currently, are dominated by postmodern ideas that no one in a university is able to escape.

While talking about The Freudians: A Comparative Perspective in European countries, my listeners reaffirmed the thesis that every country creates the Freud it needs. In fact, the questions I was asked not only reflected the specific cultural context, but allowed me to guess, correctly, whether an interlocutor was a historian, a therapist, or a social critic.

By now, Freud's legacy is claimed by some therapists whose practices he would reject and rejected by some scholars who spend their lives studying his every word. In the meantime, notions of the unconscious are being accepted around the world, Freudian therapies—and their bastard offspring—are introduced in more and more countries, and the city of Vienna, which at first was so unreceptive to psychoanalysis, has proclaimed Freud its most favorite son. As they say, "what goes around comes around," or, to paraphrase Freud, the voice of the intellect moves slowly, but in the end it will win out.

Edith Kurzweil is University Professor of Social Thought at Adeiphi University. She is the editor of Partisan Review. *Her writings have appeared in* Society, Commentary, *and other journals in the United States and Europe. She is the author of several books, including* The Freudians: A Comparative Perspective *and* The Age of Structuralism: From Lévi-Strauss to Foucault, *both published by Transaction.*

The Stability of Personality: Observations and Evaluations

Robert R. McCrae and
Paul T. Costa, Jr.

Robert R. McCrae is Research Psychologist and **Paul T. Costa, Jr.,** is Chief, Laboratory of Personality and Cognition, both at the Gerontology Research Center, National Institute on Aging, National Institutes of Health. Address correspondence to Robert R. McCrae, Personality, Stress and Coping Section, Gerontology Research Center, 4940 Eastern Ave., Baltimore, MD 21224.

"There is an optical illusion about every person we meet," Ralph Waldo Emerson wrote in his essay on "Experience":

> In truth, they are all creatures of given temperament, which will appear in a given character, whose boundaries they will never pass: but we look at them, they seem alive, and we presume there is impulse in them. In the moment it seems impulse; in the year, in the lifetime, it turns out to be a certain uniform tune which the revolving barrel of the music-box must play.[1]

In this brief passage, Emerson anticipated modern findings about the stability of personality and pointed out an illusion to which both laypersons and psychologists are prone. He was also perhaps the first to decry personality stability as the enemy of freedom, creativity, and growth, objecting that "temperament puts all divinity to rout." In this article, we summarize evidence in support of Emerson's observations but offer arguments against his evaluation of them.[2]

EVIDENCE FOR THE STABILITY OF ADULT PERSONALITY

Emerson used the term temperament to refer to the basic tendencies of the individual, dispositions that we call personality traits. It is these traits, measured by such instruments as the Minnesota Multiphasic Personality Inventory and the NEO Personality Inventory, that have been investigated in a score of longitudinal studies over the past 20 years. Despite a wide variety of samples, instruments, and designs, the results of these studies have been remarkably consistent, and they are easily summarized.

1. The mean levels of personality traits change with development, but reach final adult levels at about age 30. Between 20 and 30, both men and women become somewhat less emotional and thrill-seeking and somewhat more cooperative and self-disciplined—changes we might interpret as evidence of increased maturity. After age 30, there are few and subtle changes, of which the most consistent is a small decline in activity level with advancing age. Except among individuals with dementia, stereotypes that depict older people as being withdrawn, depressed, or rigid are unfounded.
2. Individual differences in personality traits, which show at least some continuity from early childhood on, are also essentially fixed by age 30.

Stability coefficients (test-retest correlations over substantial time intervals) are typically in the range of .60 to .80, even over intervals of as long as 30 years, although there is some decline in magnitude with increasing retest interval. Given that most personality scales have short-term retest reliabilities in the range from .70 to .90, it is clear that by far the greatest part of the reliable variance (i.e., variance not due to measurement error) in personality traits is stable.

3. Stability appears to characterize all five of the major domains of personality—neuroticism, extraversion, openness to experience, agreeableness, and conscientiousness. This finding suggests that an adult's personality profile as a whole will change little over time, and studies of the stability of configural measures of personality support that view.
4. Generalizations about stability apply to virtually everyone. Men and women, healthy and sick people, blacks and whites all show the same pattern. When asked, most adults will say that their personality has not changed much in adulthood, but even those who claim to have had major changes show little objective evidence of change on repeated administrations of personality questionnaires. Important exceptions to this generalization include people suffering from dementia and certain

categories of psychiatric patients who respond to therapy, but no moderators of stability among healthy adults have yet been identified.[3]

When researchers first began to publish these conclusions, they were greeted with considerable skepticism—"I distrust the facts and the inferences" Emerson had written—and many studies were designed to test alternative hypotheses. For example, some researchers contended that consistent responses to personality questionnaires were due to memory of past responses, but retrospective studies showed that people could not accurately recall how they had previously responded even when instructed to do so. Other researchers argued that temporal consistency in self-reports merely meant that individuals had a fixed idea of themselves, a crystallized self-concept that failed to keep pace with real changes in personality. But studies using spouse and peer raters showed equally high levels of stability.[4]

The general conclusion that personality traits are stable is now widely accepted. Some researchers continue to look for change in special circumstances and populations; some attempt to account for stability by examining genetic and environmental influences on personality. Finally, others take the view that there is much more to personality than traits, and seek to trace the adult developmental course of personality perceptions or identity formation or life narratives.

These latter studies are worthwhile, because people undoubtedly do change across the life span. Marriages end in divorce, professional careers are started in mid-life, fashions and attitudes change with the times. Yet often the same traits can be seen in new guises: Intellectual curiosity merely shifts from one field to another, avid gardening replaces avid tennis, one abusive relationship is followed by another. Many of these changes are best regarded as variations on the "uniform tune" played by individuals' enduring dispositions.

ILLUSORY ATTRIBUTIONS IN TEMPORAL PERSPECTIVE

Social and personality psychologists have debated for some time the accuracy of attributions of the causes of behavior to persons or situations. The "optical illusion" in person perception that Emerson pointed to was somewhat different. He felt that people attribute behavior to the live and spontaneous person who freely creates responses to the situation, when in fact behavior reveals only the mechanical operation of lifeless and static temperament. We may (and we will!) take exception to this disparaging, if common, view of traits, but we must first concur with the basic observation that personality processes often appear different when viewed in longitudinal perspective: "The years teach much which the days never know."

Consider happiness. If one asks individuals why they are happy or unhappy, they are almost certain to point to environmental circumstances of the moment: a rewarding job, a difficult relationship, a threat to health, a new car. It would seem that levels of happiness ought to mirror quality of life, and that changes in circumstances would result in changes in subjective well-being. It would be easy to demonstrate this pattern in a controlled laboratory experiment: Give subjects $1,000 each and ask how they feel!

But survey researchers who have measured the objective quality of life by such indicators as wealth, education, and health find precious little association with subjective well-being, and longitudinal researchers have found surprising stability in individual differences in happiness, even among people whose life circumstances have changed markedly. The explanation is simple: People adapt to their circumstances rapidly, getting used to the bad and taking for granted the good. In the long run, happiness is largely a matter of enduring personality traits.[5] "Temper prevails over everything of time, place, and condition, and . . . fix[es] the measure of activity and of enjoyment."

A few years ago, William Swann and Craig Hill provided an ingenious demonstration of the errors to which too narrow a temporal perspective can lead. A number of experiments had shown that it was relatively easy to induce changes in the self-concept by providing self-discrepant feedback. Introverts told that they were really extraverts rated themselves higher in extraversion than they had before. Such studies supported the view that the self-concept is highly malleable, a mirror of the evaluation of the immediate environment.

Swann and Hill replicated this finding, but extended it by inviting subjects back a few days later. By that time, the effects of the manipulation had disappeared, and subjects had returned to their initial self-concepts. The implication is that any one-shot experiment may give a seriously misleading view of personality processes.[6]

The relations between coping and adaptation provide a final example. Cross-sectional studies show that individuals who use such coping mechanisms as self-blame, wishful thinking, and hostile reactions toward other people score lower on measures of well-being than people who do not use these mechanisms. It would be easy to infer that these coping mechanisms detract from adaptation, and in fact the very people who use them admit that they are ineffective. But the correlations vanish when the effects of prior neuroticism scores are removed; an alternative interpretation of the data is thus that individuals who score high on this personality factor use poor coping strategies and also have low well-being: The association between coping and well-being may be entirely attributable to this third variable.[7]

Psychologists have long been aware of the problems of inferring causes from correlational data, but they have not recognized the pervasiveness of the bias that Emerson warned about. People tend to understand behavior and experience as the result of the immediate context, whether intrapsychic or environmental. Only by looking over time can one see the persistent effects of personality traits.

THE EVALUATION OF STABILITY

If few findings in psychology are more robust than the stability of personality, even fewer are more unpopular. Gerontologists often see stability as an affront to their commitment to continuing adult development; psychotherapists sometimes view it as an alarming challenge to their ability to help patients;[8] humanistic psychologists and transcendental philosophers think it degrades human nature. A popular account in *The Idaho Statesman* ran under the disheartening headline "Your Personality—You're Stuck With It."

In our view, these evaluations are based on misunderstandings: At worst, stability is a mixed blessing. Those individuals who are anxious, quarrelsome, and lazy might be understandably distressed to think that they are likely to stay that way, but surely those who are imaginative, affectionate, and carefree at age 30 should be glad to hear that they will probably be imaginative, affectionate, and carefree at age 90.

Because personality is stable, life is to some extent predictable. People can make vocational and retirement choices with some confidence that their current interests and enthusiasms will not desert them. They can choose friends and mates with whom they are likely to remain compatible. They can vote on the basis of candidates' records, with some assurance that future policies will resemble past ones. They can learn which coworkers they can depend on, and which they cannot. The personal and social utility of personality stability is enormous.

But it is precisely this predictability that so offends many critics. ("I had fancied that the value of life lay in its inscrutable possibilities," Emerson complained.) These critics view traits as mechanical and static habits and believe that the stability of personality traits dooms human beings to lifeless monotony as puppets controlled by inexorable forces. This is a misunderstanding on several levels.

First, personality traits are not repetitive habits, but inherently dynamic dispositions that interact with the opportunities and challenges of the moment.[9] Antagonistic people do not yell at everyone; some people they flatter, some they scorn, some they threaten. Just as the same intelligence is applied to a lifetime of changing problems, so the same personality traits can be expressed in an infinite variety of ways, each suited to the situation.

Second, there are such things as spontaneity and impulse in human life, but they are stable traits. Individuals who are open to experience actively seek out new places to go, provocative ideas to ponder, and exotic sights, sounds, and tastes to experience. Extraverts show a different kind of spontaneity, making friends, seeking thrills, and jumping at every chance to have a good time. People who are introverted and closed to experience have more measured and monotonous lives, but this is the kind of life they choose.

Finally, personality traits are not inexorable forces that control our fate, nor are they, in psychodynamic language, ego alien. Our traits characterize us; they are our very selves;[10] we act most freely when we express our enduring dispositions. Individuals sometimes fight against their own tendencies, trying perhaps to overcome shyness or curb a bad temper. But most people acknowledge even these failings as their own, and it is well

that they do. A person's recognition of the inevitability of his or her one and only personality is a large part of what Erik Erikson called ego integrity, the culminating wisdom of a lifetime.

Notes

1. All quotations are from "Experience," in *Essays: First and Second Series*, R.W. Emerson (Vintage, New York, 1990) (original work published 1844).

2. For recent and sometimes divergent treatments of this topic, see R.R. McCrae and P.T. Costa, Jr., *Personality in Adulthood* (Guilford, New York, 1990); D. C. Funder, R.D. Parke, C. Tomlinson-Keasey and K. Widaman, Eds., *Studying Lives Through Time: Personality and Development* (American Psychological Association, Washington, DC, 1993); T. Heatherton and J. Weinberger, *Can Personality Change?* (American Psychological Association, Washington, DC, 1994).

3. L.C. Siegler, K.A. Welsh, D.V. Dawson, G.G. Fillenbaum, N.L. Earl, E.B. Kaplan, and C.M. Clark, Ratings of personality change in patients being evaluated for memory disorders, *Alzheimer Disease and Associated Disorders, 5,* 240–250 (1991); R.M.A. Hirschfeld, G.L. Klerman, P. Clayton, M.B. Keller, P. McDonald-Scott, and B. Larkin, Assessing personality: Effects of depressive state on trait measurement, *American Journal of Psychiatry, 140,* 695–699 (1983); R.R. McCrae, Moderated analyses of longitudinal personality stability, *Journal of Personality and Social Psychology, 65,* 577–585 (1993).

4. D. Woodruff, The role of memory in personality continuity: A 25 year follow-up, *Experimental Aging Research, 9,* 31–34 (1983); P.T. Costa, Jr., and R.R. McCrae, Trait psychology comes of age, in *Nebraska Symposium on Motivation: Psychology and Aging,* T.B. Sonderegger, Ed.

(University of Nebraska Press, Lincoln, 1992).

5. P.T. Costa, Jr., and R.R. McCrae, Influence of extraversion and neuroticism on subjective well-being: Happy and unhappy people, *Journal of Personality and Social Psychology, 38,* 668–678 (1980).

6. The study is summarized in W.B. Swann, Jr., and C.A. Hill, When our identities are mistaken: Reaffirming self-conceptions through social interactions, *Journal of Personality and Social Psychology, 43,* 59–66 (1982). Dangers of single-occasion research are also discussed in J.R. Council, Context effects in personality research, *Current Directions in Psychological Science, 2,* 31–34 (1993).

7. R.R. McCrae and P.T. Costa, Jr., Personality, coping, and coping effectiveness in an adult sample, *Journal of Personality, 54,* 385–405 (1986).

8. Observations in nonpatient samples show what happens over time under typical life circumstances; they do not rule out the possibility that psychotherapeutic interventions can change personality. Whether or not such change is possible, in practice much of psychotherapy consists of helping people learn to live with their limitations, and this may be a more realistic goal than "cure" for many patients. See P.T. Costa, Jr., and R.R. McCrae, Personality stability and its implications for clinical psychology, *Clinical Psychology Review, 6,* 407–423 (1986).

9. A. Tellegen, Personality traits: Issues of definition, evidence and assessment, in *Thinking Clearly About Psychology: Essays in Honor of Paul E. Meehl,* Vol. 2, W. Grove and D. Cicchetti, Eds. (University of Minnesota Press, Minneapolis, 1991).

10. R.R. McCrae and P.T. Costa, Jr., Age, personality, and the spontaneous self-concept, *Journals of Gerontology: Social Sciences, 43,* S177–S185 (1988).

Unit 2

Unit Selections

Key Points to Consider

❖ Based on your experience observing children, what would you say most contributes to their personal growth: physiological or environmental factors? Explain why you think different aspects of our behaviors and personalities are accounted for by physiology, experience, or some combination of the two.

❖ Name some bona fide differences between the sexes that are controlled by the brain and that have been discovered by scientists. What sex differences are due to stereotypes and are therefore untrue? Where do these differences originate? Why and how are the boundaries blurring between the sexes?

❖ Why is it important to study heredity? How is genetic research conducted and why is it important to psychologists? If we discover that a certain psychological characteristic, especially a negative one such as criminality, is indeed inherited, why would this be controversial or political?

❖ How do the genes influence specific human features, such as personality traits? Are most mental disorders due to the effects of a single gene or to multiple genes? What is autism and what may cause it?

❖ How can we map the brain? What are the various parts of the brain? Explain whether or not and how you could ascribe certain behaviors to certain parts of the brain. What brain disorders are being studied with modern scientific techniques? How do disorders affect the brain? What role does the brain play in depression and traumatic memory? How is traumatic memory different from other types of memory?

❖ What is the biology of joy? What are endorphins? What other biochemical actions influence our moods, emotions, and behaviors? What anecdotal evidence can you provide that emotions indeed affect us physiologically? Or is it a two-way action; does physiology affect our emotions? That is, do you feel nervous because your hands get clammy and you have a lump in your throat?

❖ What evidence is there that biology is not the only influence on our psychological being? What role do you think the environment plays compared to biology? Do you think the environment's influence grows the further we proceed through life? Defend your arguments with research or anecdotes.

❖ How can our minds affect our physical health? Offer data to support your position.

DUSHKIN ONLINE Links www.dushkin.com/online/

These sites are annotated on pages 4 and 5.

On the front pages of every newspaper, in practically every televised newscast, and on many magazine covers the problems of substance abuse in America haunt us. Innocent children are killed when caught in the crossfire of the guns of drug lords or even of their own classmates. Prostitutes selling their bodies for drug money spread the deadly AIDS virus. The white-collar middle manager loses his job because he embezzled company money to support his cocaine habit.

Why do people turn to drugs? Why doesn't all of the publicity about the ruining of human lives diminish the drug problem? Why can some people consume two cocktails and stop, while others feel helpless against the inebriating seduction of alcohol? Why do some people crave heroin as their drug of choice, while others choose cigarettes or caffeine?

The causes of individual behavior such as drug and alcohol abuse are the focus of this section. If physiology, either biochemistry or genes, is the determinant of our behavior, then solutions to such puzzles as alcoholism lie in the field of psychobiology, the study of behavior in relation to biological processes. However, if experience as a function of our environment and learning creates personality and coping ability and thus causes subsequent behavior, normal or not, then researchers must take a different tack and explore features of the environment responsible for certain behaviors. A third explanation is that ability to adjust to change is produced by some complex interaction or interplay between experience and biology. If this interaction accounts for individual differences in personality and ability to cope, scientists then have a very complicated task ahead of them.

Conducting research designed to unravel the determinants of behavior is difficult. Scientists must call upon their best design skills to develop studies that will yield useful and replicable findings. A researcher hoping to examine the role of experience in personal growth and behavior needs to be able to isolate one or two stimuli or environmental features that seem to control a particular behavior. Imagine trying to delimit the complexity of the world sufficiently so that only one or two events stand out as the cause of an individual's alcoholism. Likewise, researchers interested in psychobiology also need refined, technical knowledge. Suppose a scientist hopes to show that a particular form of mental illness is inherited. She cannot merely examine family genetic histories, because family members can also learn maladaptive behaviors from one another. The researcher's ingenuity will be challenged; she must use intricate techniques such as comparing children to their adoptive as well as to their biological parents. Volunteer subjects may be difficult to find, and, even then, the data may be hard to interpret.

The first two articles in this unit offer general information on the interaction of nature and nurture.

The first article, by Marc Peyser and Anne Underwood, explores the joint contributions of nature and nurture. The article discusses the contributions of genes as well as the relative influence of the environment. The authors clearly but succinctly provide a general overview of the nature/nurture controversy. A companion article discusses the nature/nurture issue in relationship to gender. From where do gender differences and similarities come? Deborah Blum argues in "The Gender Blur" that gender boundaries are becoming less crisp, resulting in more similarities than differences, a situation that makes the study of the origin of gender more complicated.

We next examine the role of nature, in particular of genetics, in determining our behaviors. The article "Optimizing Expression of the Common Human Genome for Child Development" provides an overview of how genes influence the developing person. "The Personality Genes" assesses how much influence DNA exerts on our developing personalities.

Similarly, a related article, "Autism Is Likely to Be Linked to Several Genes," discusses how a disorder is usually influenced by multiple genes. The article is also interesting because it divulges information about a fascinating disorder—autism.

The nervous system is also an important component of the biological determinants of our personalities and behaviors. In her article, Kathleen Allison reveals information about the brain, which is the focal point of the nervous system. She discusses how new techniques in molecular biology are helping us to better understand brain disorders.

The influence of the brain on the expression of specific aspects of human behavior is discussed in the next article. Lynn Nadel and W. Jake Jacobs analyze the results of brain studies and conclude that memory for emotionally laden information may be distorted compared to other memories.

The next article is on another topic related to psychophysiology—biochemistry. Hormones, neurotransmitters, and other biochemicals affect the nervous system and thus affect human behavior. In "The Biology of Joy," Jeremiah Creedon discusses the role of biochemistry with regard to one particular and delightful emotion—joy. Certain neurotransmitters, endorphins, are secreted during pleasurable events. Thus, neurochemistry is important as a determinant of our behaviors and our personalities.

In the final article in this unit, "Faith & Healing," Claudia Wallis suggests that people are turning more and more to forms of healing other than medicine and psychology. Some individuals turn to religion; others look inward and examine their feelings and attitudes. In any event, new research is demonstrating that there is indeed a mind-body connection, and that, for example, those who turn to religion are healthier than those who do not.

The wizards of genetics keep closing in on the biological roots of personality. It's not your imagination that one baby seems born cheerful and another morose. But that's not the complete picture. DNA is not destiny; experience plays a powerful role, too.

Shyness, Sadness, Curiosity, Joy.

Is It Nature or Nurture?

By Marc Peyser and Anne Underwood

IF ANY CHILD SEEMED DESTINED TO GROW UP AFRAID OF her shadow and just about anything else that moved, it was 2-year-old Marjorie. She was so painfully shy that she wouldn't talk to or look at a stranger. She was even afraid of friendly cats and dogs. When Jerome Kagan, a Harvard professor who discovered that shyness has a strong genetic component, sent a clown to play with Marjorie, she ran to her mother. "It was as if a cobra entered that room," Kagan says. His diagnosis: Marjorie showed every sign of inherited shyness, a condition in which the brain somehow sends out messages to avoid new experiences. But as Kagan continued to examine her over the years, Marjorie's temperament changed. When she started school, she gained confidence from ballet classes and her good grades, and she began to make friends. Her parents even coaxed her into taking horseback-riding lessons. Marjorie may have been born shy, but she has grown into a bubbly second grader.

61% of all parents believe that differences in behavior between girls and boys are not inborn but a result

For Marjorie, then, biology—more specifically, her genetic inheritance—was not her destiny. And therein lies our tale. In the last few years scientists have identified genes that appear to predict all sorts of emotional behavior, from happiness to aggressiveness to risk-taking. The age-old question of whether nature or nurture determines temperament seems finally to have been decided in favor of Mother Nature and her ever-deepening gene pool. But the answer may not be so simple after all. Scientists are beginning to discover that genetics and environment work together to determine personality as intricately as Astaire and Rogers danced. "If either Fred or Ginger moves too fast, they both stumble," says Stanley Greenspan, a pediatric psychiatrist at George Washington University and the author of "The Growth of the Mind." "Nature affects nurture affects nature and back and forth. Each step influences the next." Many scientists now believe that some experiences can actually alter the structure of the brain. An aggressive toddler, under the right circumstances, can essentially be rewired to channel his energy more constructively. Marjorie can overcome her shyness—forever. No child need be held captive to her genetic blueprint. The implications for child rearing—and social policy—are profound.

While Gregor Mendel's pea plants did wonders to explain how humans inherit blue eyes or a bald spot, they turn out to be an inferior model for analyzing something as complex as the brain. The human body contains about 100,000 genes, of which 50,000 to 70,000 are involved in brain function. Genes control the brain's neurotransmitters and receptors, which deliver and accept mental messages like so many cars headed for their assigned parking spaces. But there are billions of roads to each parking lot, and those paths are highly susceptible to environmental factors. In his book "The New View of Self," Dr. Larry Siever, a psychiatry professor at Mount Sinai Medical Center, writes about how the trauma of the Holocaust caused such intense genetic scrambling in some survivors that their children inherited the same stress-related abnormalities. "Perhaps the sense of danger and uncertainty associated with living through such a time is passed on in the family milieu and primes the biological systems of the children as well," says Siever. He added that that might explain why pianist David Helfgott, the subject of the movie "Shine," had his mental breakdown.

A gene is only a probability for a given trait, not a guarantee. For that trait to be expressed, a gene often must be "turned on" by an outside force before it does its job. High levels of stress apparently activate a variety of genes, including those suspected of being involved in fear, shyness and some mental illnesses. Children conceived

Scientists estimate that genes determine only about 50 percent of a child's personality

during a three-month famine in the Netherlands during a Nazi blockade in 1945 were later found to have twice the rate of schizophrenia as did Dutch children born to parents who were spared the trauma of famine. "Twenty years ago, you couldn't get your research funded if you were looking for a genetic basis for schizophrenia, because everyone knew it was what your mother did to you in the first few years of life, as Freud said," says Robert Plomin, a geneticist at London's Institute of Psychiatry. "Now you can't get funded *unless* you're looking for a genetic basis. Neither extreme is right, and the data show why. There's only a 50 percent concordance between genetics and the development of schizophrenia."

SCIENTISTS HAVE BEEN DEvoting enormous energy to determining what part of a given character trait is "heritable" and what part is the result of socialization. Frank Sulloway's book "Born to Rebel," which analyzes the influence of birth order on personality, opened a huge window on a universal—and largely overlooked—environmental factor. But that's a broad brushstroke. Most studies focus on remarkably precise slivers of human emotions. One study at Allegheny University in Pennsylvania found that the tendency for a person to throw dishes or slam doors when he's angry is 40 percent heritable, while the likelihood a person will yell in anger is only 28 percent heritable. The most common method for determining these statistics is studying twins. If identical twins are more alike in some way than are fraternal twins, that trait is believed to have a higher likelihood of being inherited. But the nature-nurture knot is far from being untied.

The trick, then, is to isolate a given gene and study the different ways environment interacts with it. For instance, scientists believe that people with the longer variety of a dopamine-4 receptor gene are biologically predisposed to be thrill seekers. Because the gene appears to make them less sensitive to pain and physical sensation, the children are more likely to, say, crash their tricycles into a wall, just to see what it feels like. "These

78% of those polled who are in two-parent families say that they share equality when it comes to setting rules for their young child

are the daredevils," says Greenspan. But they need not be. Given strict boundaries, Greenspan says, thrill-seeking kids can be taught to modulate and channel their overactive curiosity. A risk-taking child who likes to pound his fist into hard objects can be taught games that involve hitting softly as well. "If you give them constructive ways to meet their needs," says Greenspan, "they can become charismatic, action-oriented leaders."

Shyness has been studied perhaps more than any other personality trait. Kagan, who has monitored 500 children for more than 17 years at Harvard, can detect telltale signs of shyness in babies even before they're born. He's found that the hearts of shy children in the womb consistently beat faster than 140 times a minute, which is much faster than the heartbeats of other babies. The shy fetus is already highly reactive, wired to overmonitor his environment. But he can also outgrow this predisposition if his parents gently but firmly desensitize him to the situations that cause anxiety, such as encouraging him to play with other children or, as in Marjorie's fear of animals, taking her to the stables and teaching her to ride a horse. Kagan has found that by the age of 4, no more than 20 percent of the previously shy children remain that way.

Will the reprogramming last into adulthood? Because evidence of the role of genes has been discovered only recently, it's still too early to tell. But studies of animals give some indication. Stephen Suomi at the National Institute of Child Health and Human Development works with rhesus monkeys that possess the same genetic predisposition to shyness that affects humans. He's shown that by giving a shy monkey to a foster mother who is an expert caregiver, the baby will outgrow the shyness. Even more surprising, the once shy monkey will become a leader among her peers and an unusually competent parent, just like the foster mom. Though she will likely pass along her shyness genes to her own child, she will teach it how to overcome her predisposition, just as she was taught. And the cycle continues—generations of genetically shy monkeys become not just normal, but superior, adults

and parents. The lesson, says Suomi: "You can't prejudge anyone at birth. No matter what your genetic background, a negative characteristic you're born with may even turn out to be an advantage."

But parents aren't scientists, and it's not always easy to see how experience can influence a child's character. A baby who smiles a lot and makes eye contact is, in part, determining her own environment, which in turn affects her temperament. As her parents coo and smile and wrinkle their noses in delighted response, they are reinforcing their baby's sunny disposition. But what about children who are born with low muscle tone, who at 4 months can barely hold up their own heads, let alone smile? Greenspan has discovered that mothers of these kids smile at the baby for a while, but when the affection isn't returned, they give up. And so does the baby, who over time fails to develop the ability to socialize normally. "If you move in the wrong patterns, the problem is exacerbated," Greenspan says. He has found that if parents respond to nonsmiling babies by being superanimated—like Bob Barker hosting a game show—they can engage their child's interest in the world.

The ramifications of these findings clearly have the potential to revolutionize child-rearing theory and practice. But to an uncertain end. "Our society has a strong belief that what happens in childhood determines your fate. If you have a happy childhood, everything will be all right. That's silly," says Michael Lewis, director of the Institute for the Study of Child Development in New Jersey and the author of "Altering Fate." Lewis estimates that experience ultimately rewrites 90 percent of a child's personality traits, leaving an adult with only one tenth of his inborn temperament. "The idea that early childhood is such a powerful moment to see individual differences in biology or environment is not valid," he says. "We are too open to and modifiable by experience." Some scientists warn that attempting to reprogram even a narrow sliver of childhood emotions can prove to be a daunting task, despite research's fascinating new insights. "Children are not a 24-hour controlled experiment," says C. Robert Cloninger, a professor of psychiatry and genetics at the Washington University School of Medicine in St. Louis. "If you put a child in a Skinner box, then maybe you could have substantial influence." So, mindful of the blinding insights of geneticists and grateful for the lingering influences of environment, parents must get on with the business of raising their child, an inexact science if ever there was one.

Once there were only two: male and female. Men, mostly, were the big ones, with deep voices and sturdy shoes, sitting with legs splayed. Women, mostly, were the smaller ones, with dainty high heels, legs crossed tightly at the ankle, and painted mouths. It was easy to tell them apart. These days, it's not so easy. Men wear makeup and women smoke cigars; male figure skaters are macho—but Dennis Rodman wears a dress. We can be one gender on the Internet and another in bed. Even science, bastion of the rational, can't prove valid the lines that used to separate and define us. Although researching the biology of gender has answered some old questions, it has also raised important new one. The consensus? Gender is more fluid than we ever thought. Queer theorists call gender a social construct, saying that when we engage in traditional behaviors and sexual practices, we are nothing but actors playing ancient, empty roles. Others suggest that gender is performance, a collection of masks we can take on and off at will. So are we witnessing the birth of thrilling new freedoms, or the disintegration of the values and behaviors that bind us together? Will we encounter new opportunities for self-realization, or hopeless confusion? Whatever the answers, agreeing that our destinies aren't preordained will launch a search that will profoundly affect society, and will eventually engage us all.　　　　　　　　　　—*The Editors*

By Deborah Blum

The Gender Blur

where does biology end and society take over ?

I was raised in one of those university-based, liberal elite families that politicians like to ridicule. In my childhood, every human being—regardless of gender—was exactly alike under the skin, and I mean exactly, barring his or her different opportunities. My parents wasted no opportunity to bring this point home. One Christmas, I received a Barbie doll and a softball glove. Another brought a green enamel stove, which baked tiny cakes by the heat of a lightbulb, and also a set of steel-tipped darts and competition-quality dart-board. Did I mention the year of the chemistry set and the ballerina doll?

It wasn't until I became a parent—I should say, a parent of two boys—that I realized I had been fed a line and swallowed it like a sucker (barring the part about opportunities, which I still believe). This dawned on me during my older son's dinosaur phase, which began when he was about 2 ½. Oh, he loved dinosaurs, all right, but only the blood-swilling carnivores. Plant-eaters were wimps and losers, and he refused to wear a T-shirt marred by a picture of a stegosaur. I looked down at him one day, as he was snarling around my feet and doing his toddler best to gnaw off my right leg, and I thought: This goes a lot deeper then culture.

Raising children tends to bring on this kind of politically-incorrect reaction. Another friend came to the same conclusion watching a son determinedly bite his breakfast toast into the shape of a pistol he hoped would blow away—or at least terrify—his younger brother. Once you get past the guilt part—Did I do this? Should I have bought him that plastic allosaur with the oversized teeth?—such revelations can lead you to consider the far more interesting field of gender biology, where the questions take a different shape: Does love of carnage begin in culture or genetics, and which

drives which? Do the gender roles of our culture reflect an underlying biology, and, in turn, does the way we behave influence that biology?

The point I'm leading up to—through the example of my son's innocent love of predatory dinosaurs—is actually one of the most straightforward in this debate. One of the reasons we're so fascinated by childhood behaviors is that, as the old saying goes, the child becomes the man (or woman, of course.) Most girls don't spend their preschool years snarling around the house and pretending to chew off their companion's legs. And they—mostly—don't grow up to be as aggressive as men. Do the ways that we amplify those early differences in childhood shape the adults we become? Absolutely. But it's worth exploring the starting place—the faint signal that somehow gets amplified.

"There's plenty of room in society to influence sex differences," says Marc

Breedlove, a behavioral endocrinologist at the University of California at Berkeley and a pioneer in defining how hormones can help build sexually different nervous systems. "Yes, we're born with predispositions, but it's society that amplifies them, exaggerates them. I believe that—except for the sex differences in aggression. Those [differences] are too massive to be explained simply by society."

Aggression does allow a straightforward look at the issue. Consider the following statistics: Crime reports in both the United States and Europe record between 10 and 15 robberies committed by men for every one by a woman. At one point, people argued that this was explained by size difference. Women weren't big enough to intimidate, but that would change, they predicted, with the availability of compact weapons. But just as little girls don't routinely make weapons out of toast, women—even criminal ones—

sexual encounters, more offspring, more genetic future. For the female—especially in a species like ours, with time for just one successful pregnancy a year—what's the genetic advantage in brawling?

Thus the issue becomes not whether there is a biologically influenced sex difference in aggression—the answer being a solid, technical "You betcha"—but rather how rigid that difference is. The best science, in my opinion, tends to align with basic common sense. We all know that there are extraordinarily gentle men and murderous women. Sex differences are always generalizations: They refer to a behavior, with some evolutionary rationale behind it. They never define, entirely, an individual. And that fact alone should tell us that there's always—even in the most biologically dominated traits—some flexibility, an instinctive ability to respond, for better and worse, to the world around us.

mal matches. One is that even with this apparently precise system, there's nothing precise—or guaranteed—about the physical construction of male and female. The other point makes that possible. It appears that sex doesn't matter in the early states of embryonic development. We are unisex at the point of conception.

If you examine an embryo at about six weeks, you see that it has the ability to develop in either direction. The fledgling embryo has two sets of ducts—Wolffian for male, Muellerian for female—an either/or structure, held in readiness for further development. If testosterone and other androgens are released by hormone-producing cells, then the Wolffian ducts develop into the channel that connects penis to testes, and the female ducts wither away.

Without testosterone, the embryo takes on a female form; the male ducts vanish and the Muellerian ducts expand into oviducts, uterus, and vagina. In other words, in humans, anyway (the opposite is true in birds), the female is the default sex. Back in the 1950s, the famed biologist Alfred Jost showed that if you castrate a male rabbit fetus, choking off testosterone, you produce a completely feminized rabbit.

We don't do these experiments in humans—for obvious reasons—but there are naturally occurring instances that prove the same point. For instance: In the fetal testes are a group of cells, called Leydig cells, that make testosterone. In rare cases, the fetus doesn't make enough of these cells (a defect known as Leydig cell hypoplasia). In this circumstance we see the limited power of the XY chromosome. These boys have the right chromosomes and the right genes to be boys; they just don't grow a penis. Obstetricians and parents often think they see a baby girl, and these children are routinely raised as daughters. Usually, the "mistake" is caught about the time of puberty, when menstruation doesn't start. A doctor's examination shows the child to be internally male; there are usually small testes, often tucked within the abdomen. As the researchers put it, if the condition had been known from the beginning, "the sisters would have been born as brothers."

Just to emphasize how tricky all this body-building can get, there's a peculiar genetic defect that seems to be clustered by heredity in a small group of villages in the Dominican Republic. The result of the defect is a failure to produce an enzyme that concentrates testosterone, specifically for building

will that wonderful, unpredictable, flexible biology that we have been given allow a shift, so that one day, we will literally be far more alike?

don't seem drawn to weaponry in the same way that men are. Almost twice as many male thieves and robbers use guns as their female counterparts do.

Or you can look at more personal crimes: domestic partner murders. Three-fourths of men use guns in those killings; 50 percent of women do. Here's more from the domestic front: In conflicts in which a woman killed a man, he tended to be the one who had started the fight—in 51.8 percent of the cases, to be exact. When the man was the killer, he again was the likely first aggressor, and by an even more dramatic margin. In fights in which women died, they had started the argument only 12.5 percent of the time.

Enough. You can parade endless similar statistics but the point is this: Males are more aggressive, not just among humans but among almost all species on earth. Male chimpanzees, for instance, declare war on neighboring troops, and one of their strategies is a warning strike: They kill females and infants to terrorize and intimidate. In terms of simple, reproductive genetics, it's an advantage of males to be aggressive: You can muscle your way into dominance, winning more

This is true even with physical characteristics that we've often assumed are nailed down by genetics. Scientists now believe height, for instance, is only about 90 percent heritable. A person's genes might code for a six-foot-tall body, but malnutrition could literally cut that short. And there's also some evidence, in girls anyway, that children with stressful childhoods tend to become shorter adults. So while some factors are predetermined, there's evidence that the prototypical male/female body design can be readily altered.

It's a given that humans, like most other species—bananas, spiders, sharks, ducks, any rabbit you pull out of a hat—rely on two sexes for reproduction. So basic is that requirement that we have chromosomes whose primary purpose is to deliver the genes that order up a male or a female. All other chromosomes are numbered, but we label the sex chromosomes with the letters X and Y. We get one each from our mother and our father, and the basic combinations are these: XX makes female, XY makes male.

There are two important—and little known—points about these chromoso-

the genitals. One obscure little enzyme only, but here's what happens without it: You get a boy with undescended testes and a penis so short and stubby that is resembles an oversized clitoris.

In the mountain villages of this Caribbean nation, people are used to it. The children are usually raised as "conditional" girls. At puberty, the secondary tide of androgens rises and is apparently enough to finish the construction project. The scrotum suddenly descends, the phallus grows, and the child develops a distinctly male body—narrow hips, muscular build, and even slight beard growth. At that point, the family shifts the child over from daughter to son. The dresses are thrown out. He begins to wear male clothes and starts dating girls. People in the Dominican Republic are so familiar with this condition that there's a colloquial name for it: *guevedoces,* meaning "eggs (or testes) at 12."

stances, behave differently than if the individual was a female."

Do the ways that we amplify physical and behavioral differences in childhood shape who we become as adults? Absolutely. But to understand that, you have to understand the differences themselves—their beginning and the very real biochemistry that may lie behind them.

Here is a good place to focus on testosterone—a hormone that is both well-studied and generally underrated. First, however, I want to acknowledge that there are many other hormones and neurotransmitters that appear to influence behavior. Preliminary work shows that fetal boys are a little more active than fetal girls. It's pretty difficult to argue socialization at that point. There's a strong suspicion that testosterone may create the difference.

And there are a couple of relevant animal models to emphasize the point.

consensus seems to be that full-blown "I'm a girl" or "I'm a boy" instincts arrive between the ages of 2 and 3. Research shows that if a family operates in a very traditional, Beaver Cleaver kind of environment, filled with awareness of and association with "proper" gender behaviors, the "boys do trucks, girls do dolls" attitude seems to come very early. If a child grows up in a less traditional family, with an emphasis on partnership and sharing—"We all do the dishes, Joshua"—children maintain a more flexible sense of gender roles until about age 6.

In this period, too, relationships between boys and girls tend to fall into remarkably strict lines. Interviews with children find that 3-year-olds say that about half their friendships are with the opposite sex. By the age of 5, that drops to 20 percent. By 7, almost no boys or girls have, or will admit to having, best friends of the opposite sex. They still hang out on the same playground, play on the same soccer teams. They may be friendly, but the real friendships tend to be boy-to-boy or girl-to-girl.

do the ways that we amplify differences in childhood shape who we become as adults?

It's the comfort level with this slip-slide of sexual identity that's so remarkable and, I imagine, so comforting to the children involved. I'm positive that the sexual transition of these children is less traumatic than the abrupt awareness of the "sisters who would have been brothers." There's a message of tolerance there, well worth repeating, and there are some other key lessons too.

These defects are rare and don't alter the basic male-female division of our species. They do emphasize how fragile those divisions can be. Biology allows flexibility, room to change, to vary and grow. With that comes room for error as well. That it's possible to live with these genetic defects, that they don't merely kill us off, is a reminder that we, male and female alike, exist on a continuum of biological possibilities that can overlap and sustain either sex.

Marc Breedlove points out that the most difficult task may be separating how the brain responds to hormones from how the brain responds to the *results* of hormones. Which brings us back, briefly, below the belt: In this context, the penis is just a result, the product of androgens at work before birth. "And after birth," says Breedlove, "virtually everyone who interacts with that individual will note that he has a penis, and will, in many in-

Back in the 1960s, Robert Goy, a psychologist at the University of Wisconsin at Madison, first documented that young male monkeys play much more roughly than young females. Goy went on to show that if you manipulate testosterone level—raising it in females, damping it down in males—you can reverse those effects, creating sweet little male monkeys and rowdy young females.

Is testosterone the only factor at work here? I don't think so. But clearly we can argue a strong influence, and, interestingly, studies have found that girls with congenital adrenal hypoplasia—who run high in testosterone—tend to be far more fascinated by trucks and toy weaponry than most little girls are. They lean toward rough-and-tumble play, too. As it turns out, the strongest influence on this "abnormal" behavior is not parental disapproval, but the company of other little girls, who tone them down and direct them toward more routine girl games.

And that reinforces an early point: If there is indeed a biology to sex differences, we amplify it. At some point—when it is still up for debate—we gain a sense of our gender, and with it a sense of "gender-appropriate" behavior.

Some scientists argue for some evidence of gender awareness in infancy, perhaps by the age of 12 months. The

There's some interesting science that suggests that the space between boys and girls is a normal part of development; there are periods during which children may thrive and learn from hanging out with peers of the same sex. Do we, as parents, as a culture at large, reinforce such separation? Is the pope Catholic? One of my favorite studies looked at little boys who asked for toys. If they asked for a heavily armed action figure, they got the soldier about 70 percent of the time. If they asked for a "girl" toy, like a baby doll or a Barbie, their parents purchased it maybe 40 percent of the time. Name a child who won't figure out how to work *that* system.

How does all this fit together—toys and testosterone, biology and behavior, the development of the child into the adult, the way that men and women relate to one another?

Let me make a cautious statement about testosterone: It not only has some body-building functions, it influences some behaviors as well. Let's make that a little less cautious: These behaviors include rowdy play, sex drive, competitiveness, and an in-your-face attitude. Males tend to have a higher baseline of testosterone than females—in our species, about seven to ten times as much—and therefore you would predict (correctly, I think) that all of those behaviors would be more generally found in men than in women.

But testosterone is also one of my favorite examples of how responsive biology is, how attuned it is to the way we live our lives. Testosterone, it turns out, rises in response to competition and threat. In the days of our ancestors, this might have been hand-to-hand combat or high-risk hunting endeavors. Today, scientists have measured testosterone rise in athletes preparing for a game, in chess players awaiting a match, in spectators following a soccer competition.

If a person—or even just a person's favored team—wins, testosterone continues to rise. It falls with a loss. (This also makes sense in an evolutionary perspective. If one was being clobbered with a club, it would be extremely unhelpful to have a hormone [under] one to battle on.) Testosterone also rises in the competitive world of dating, settles down with a stable and supportive relationship, climbs again if the relationship starts to falter.

It's been known for years that men in high-stress professions—say, police work or corporate law—have higher testosterone levels than men in the ministry. It turns out that women in the same kind of strong-attitude professions have higher testosterone than women who choose to stay home. What I like about this is the chicken-or-egg aspect. If you argue that testosterone influenced the behavior of those women, which came first? Did they have high testosterone and choose the law? Or did they choose the law, and the competitive environment ratcheted them up on the androgen scale? Or could both be at work?

And, returning to children for a moment, there's an ongoing study by Pennsylvania researchers, tracking that question in adolescent girls, who are being encouraged by their parents to engage in competitive activities that were once for boys only. As they do so, the researchers are monitoring, regularly, two hormones: testosterone and cortisol, a stress hormone. Will these hormones rise in response to this new, more traditionally male environment?

What if more girls choose the competitive path; more boys choose the other? Will female testosterone levels rise, male levels fall? Will that wonderful, unpredictable, flexible biology that we've been given allow a shift, so that one day, we will literally be far more alike?

We may not have answers to all those questions, but we can ask them, and we can expect that the answers will come someday, because science clearly shows us that such possibilities exist. In this most important sense, sex differences offer us a paradox. It is only through exploring and understanding what makes us different that we can begin to understand what binds us together.

Deborah Blum is a Pulitzer Prize-winning science writer, a professor of journalism at the University of Wisconsin-Madison, and author of Sex on the Brain: The Biological Differences Between Men and Women (*Penguin, 1997*).

Optimizing Expression of the Common Human Genome for Child Development

Bernard Brown[1]

Abstract

Molecular biology has moved the gene-environment issue in behavior genetics to how and when expression of the human genome is triggered and maintained. How does environment influence gene expression? How many genes are expressed in producing a given behavior? The genome is a data bank and does not automatically create a working brain. The body and brain grow well when (a) endocrine hormones initiate and promote the expression of genes, (b) nutrition is sufficient to sustain the production of proteins, and (c) stress does not suppress gene expression. The growth of brain synapses also requires appropriate neural stimulation. To study gene expression, it is essential to view the complex biology of the cell from a system context that includes the entire genome plus the biological and psychological environments. Optimizing gene expression for child growth can be achieved by a balance of medicine, nutrition, and appropriate physical, educational, and psychological environments.

Keywords

gene expression; molecular biology; environment; development

The nature-versus-nurture debate is now informed by current research on molecular biology that moves the question from which factor is more important to how and when expression of the human genome is triggered and maintained. The basic behavior genetics issue has become how environment influences gene expression. How do human physiology and biochemistry, which react to the external environment, affect gene expression? Can facilitated gene expression enhance children's development, physical and mental health, and cognitive ability or rehabilitate brain injury and inadequate nurture?

WHAT IS A GENE?

The human cell can be viewed as a protein factor in which genes transmit

From *Current Directions in Psychological Science,* April 1999, pp. 37-41. © 1999 by the American Psychological Society. Reprinted by permission of Blackwell Publishers.

molecular messages to ribosomes to produce protein from amino acids. A gene is a small unit of the DNA molecule that contains information for building a single protein. The genome is the equivalent of a database in a computer ROM memory. Located in the DNA molecule, a long string of genes shaped like a double helix, the genome contains codes that prescribe the structure and function of the cell. A gene is activated when the external environment asks the genome to supply information. The information from the activated gene is then processed by the body's basic operating system, the DNA-ribosome protein factory. The ROM's information is essential for the operation of the protein factory, but it is only information, a blueprint, and not otherwise part of the control system that regulates the factory's production of protein. A vast array of biological structures is built from the information in the human genome's 50,000 to 100,000 genes (Lewin, Siliciano, & Klotz, 1997).

In a critical number of cells affecting human growth, the genetic machinery of the cell does not by itself issue instructions to assemble proteins from the genetic blueprint. Rather, gene expression is triggered by hormones, messenger proteins secreted by endocrine glands. Hormone levels are influenced by biological and psychological environments. Many structural genes that code for proteins remain quiescent until the environment gives rise to hormones and chains of molecules created by hormones, such as steroids, that signal cells to activate genes. An activated gene's structure is copied (transcribed) to produce a new molecule, a messenger RNA molecule, which is then sent to tell a ribosome to produce a protein. To get the messages across the bridge from gene to ribosome, the cell requires biochemical promoters and inhibitors, as well as certain biochemical and physiological conditions within the cell, such as sufficient levels of energy and nutrients (Lewin et al., 1997).

GROWTH AND DIFFERENTIATION

Stress, nutrition, health, endocrine hormones, and the psychological environment all affect the rate and magnitude of brain growth, information processing and storage, and competition among neural networks. The rate at which the brain absorbs, processes, and consolidates information depends on the neural stimulation it receives and on its biochemical resources for processing and absorbing information.

Homeostasis is an organism's tendency to preserve its state. The body is a multiply redundant failsafe system controlled by multiple feedback loops in which genes play a protective role, ensuring function under adverse conditions and survivability across generations. Genes conserve the organism's form, sequence of development, and function, supplying mechanisms for adapting to the environment. Even when severe stress, malnutrition, or lack of stimulation slows the growth of brain structures, the order of gene expression is conserved. Each stage of brain growth follows its predecessor, and the genetic plan still unfolds, albeit more slowly and less perfectly.

After an early period of exponential growth, human children grow in stages of differentiation; simple cells and tissues specialize into more complex forms and functions. The genome specifies the order in which genes are expressed and provides sets of contingency plans for the different conditions the organism may encounter. Hundreds of genes that eventually affect behavior are expressed in each of hundreds of differentiation waves. A child's development reflects a series of genetically programmed steps that start at different ages. As the steps progress, old and newly expressed genes interact with successive environments. In brain growth, neurons (nerve cells) increase in the early stages and connecting tissues (axons and dendrites) increase and organize in later stages. Brain plasticity, the capacity of the brain to change as a result of experience, concerns changes in the number and size of synapses and synaptic networks. When sufficient electrical signals are sent from a neuron through an axon to a synapse (a small attachment point on the dendrite of a second neuron) and the biological environment of the synapse is supportive, the synapse will grow. The brain grows in cycles of synaptic growth and pruning (elimination). If a door opens on a favorable microenvironment, synapses tend to form and neural networks grow. But if the door opens on an unfavorable microenvironment, synapses are more likely to be pruned.

TRIGGERING AND MAINTAINING GENETIC ACTION

Hormones secreted by the endocrine glands are the primary source of genetic action. Stress has a major impact on which hormones are secreted and hence on how children grow. The influence of hormones and neural stimulation on

brain growth also depends on nutrition at the cellular level.

The Endocrine System

As a child grows, the endocrine system —under the influence of its biochemical, biophysical, and psychological environments—generates many hormones, chemicals that signal body cells to change the rates of chemical reactions. Levels of hormones change with nutrition, stress, illness, medication, and mood (Wilson & Foster, 1985). The hormones, in turn, trigger the expression of tens of thousands of genes. Hormonal levels influence the growth and function of the brain at many levels (Kuhn & Shanberg, 1984).

Thyroid hormones trigger gene transcription and accelerate the functional maturation of the brain. Too much thyroid hormone produces adverse effects, such as over-rapid growth. When thyroid hormone levels are insufficient, brain growth slows and cell division persists past the normal time of termination. There are reductions in cell size, synaptic density, and density of brain cell connections, and delayed functional development. Gene expression is slowed, impairing production of proteins and decreasing RNA content and T3 thyroid hormone receptors (Kuhn & Shanberg, 1984).

Steroids, the molecular end products of the thyroid hormone chemical chain, which is activated by stress, profoundly suppress growth in all tissues. Large doses of steroids suppress brain growth. Stress, medication, and some illnesses raise levels of cortisol, the thyroid chain's final end product, delaying development and suppressing DNA synthesis. Steroids affect nervous system plasticity (McEwen, 1992).

Growth hormone directly affects the rate at which genes transcribe their messages to produce proteins. Growth hormone is necessary for normal body and brain development.

Stress

Stress is universal, and children must learn to cope with normal stressful events; however, continuing, uncontrolled stress slows mental growth (Brown & Rosenbaum, 1985). Stress has strong effects on endocrine function (Chrousos & Gold, 1992). High stress-related cortisol levels damage the brain's hippocampus (Sapolsky, 1996) and slow body growth (Wilson & Foster, 1985). Meerson (1984) found that stressed rats increased cellular weight and had higher levels of DNA, RNA, and protein synthesis. The diversion of energy and cellular resources toward the buildup of large stress-resisting cellular structures clearly competes with growth.

Nutrition

The role of nutrition in physical growth and brain growth is well established (Brown, 1972). For example, Bogin (1988) found Guatemalan children raised in the United States gain greater stature than their fathers and children in Guatemala. For optimum gene expression, it is essential to provide nutrients that maintain cellular energy and sufficient cellular concentrations of amino acids (basic protein components; Chan & Hargrove, 1993).

ASPECTS OF GENETIC ACTION

The 19th century saw tremendous scientific progress as physics and biology moved beyond global analysis and examined small subsystems. Developmental biology, influenced by Mendel, adapted a mechanistic model that separated the inside of the body from the outside environment. In Mendelian genetics, the gene was conceptualized as unitary, independent, and the determinant of the final state of the developing organism (Lewontin, 1994). However, molecular biology now shows that gene expression is more complex.

Gene expression has often been measured in terms of the number of gene copies found in a chromosome, a section of the DNA helix. Although relating the number of copies of a gene in a chromosome to the color of peas worked well in Mendel's context, inherited traits are not a simple function of the number of gene copies. Within the various chromosomes of DNA, there are many copies and reverse copies of genes, as well as psuedogenes, all of which may look like true copies but will not be expressed. The alternative to measuring the number of gene copies, and the only sure way to study the likelihood that a given gene has been expressed, is to test for the presence of a specific messenger RNA.

Often, gene expression is measured inadequately in terms of copies of receptor genes. Receptors are molecules, created from receptor genes, that sit on membranes (e.g., the surfaces of cells) and act as entry portals. When a receptor recognizes an incoming molecule and binds to it, a chain of chemical reactions that leads to gene expression

(production of a protein) begins. A receptor gene is not the same as the gene of the molecule that binds to it. Both the receptor and the molecule that binds to it are needed to create a chemical pathway leading to the creation of a protein. Moreover, the number of receptors will change with tissue needs. Hormonal changes can increase the density of receptors at a site by a factor of 10.

The D4DR dopamine receptor gene is an important and well-known gene that has been associated with sensation seeking, risk taking, substance abuse, attention deficit hyperactivity disorder (ADHD), dyslexia, delinquency, and antisocial behavior (Hamer & Copeland, 1998). Practitioners treat these conditions with nutritional regimes, biofeedback, behavior modification, cognitive therapy, and various medications such as ritalin.

The D4DR receptor is part of a larger system that regulates behavior. Many neurons produce the neurotransmitter dopamine. Dopamine is transmitted from a neuron to a synapse on a second neuron and then binds to the second neuron's receptor, delivering the first neuron's message. But the D4DR receptor is only one of many dopamine receptors that sit on the surface of some neurons. Once the dopamine is delivered to the receptor, dopamine transporters return the dopamine across the synapse to the first neuron, to be used again. Mutations in transporter genes can cause the dopamine secreted by the synapse to be returned before it binds to the dopamine receptor and delivers its message. Behavior problems attributed to D4DR may instead result from the level of dopamine; from different kinds of neurons, synapses, receptors, or molecular agents; or from their various combinations. In the brain, synaptic growth and function depend on complex biochemical systems that regulate many different kinds of molecules that act as neurotransmitters, receptors, release agents, and promotors, inhibitors, modulators, and integrators of the chemical reactions that lead to gene transcription and protein production.[2]

Although Mendel viewed both parents as the source of inheritance, molecular pathways are more complex. Lamond and Earnshaw (1998) showed that the cell nucleus (in which DNA resides) has a dynamic structure. Genes are generally kept in inactive nuclear regions, but the most recently activated genes are located at nuclear processing sites in the best position to be processed again if there is an environmental trigger. Human female XX chromosomes, for example, have been observed with one X chromosome (from one parent) in an active re-

gion and the other (from the other parent) in an inactive region, potentially increasing the influence of one parent over the other. The elevated reaction probability of genes in activated nuclear regions may explain many aspects of learning. Mitochondria, the cellular energy sources, are inherited only from the mother. The tiny mitochondrion has a small DNA-like strand with genes for 37 energy-generating molecules. There are about 100 mitochondria per cell. Genetic disorders stemming from mitochondria may be involved in many energy-related behavior problems, especially in the aged (Wallace, 1997). Stressed or malnourished mothers may develop low mitochondrial density and pass the environmental condition on to their children through their ova.

OPTIMIZING GENETIC EXPRESSION

Genes are not destiny. There are many places along the gene-behavior pathway where genetic expression can be regulated. Environmental factors such as temperature; nutrition; light level; the timing, pace, and intensity of stimuli; and effective coping skills can promote or inhibit the expression of specific genes and proteins that lead to specific behaviors. Treatment of a single factor may be too weak to effect change. It is important to use system thinking as treatments for behavior problems are combined and optimized.

Medicine

Physicians use thousands of drugs that alter biochemical pathways to reduce or remove genetically related illness and dysfunction. Some drugs modify physiological pathways through which genes are expressed; many target gene products, proteins. The use of drugs to promote learning in schools has become commonplace. New generations of psychoactive drugs regulate receptor function. Some regulate neurotransmitters in synapses, such as serotonin and dopamine. More than 20 antidepressant drugs, such as Prozac, are regularly prescribed to increase serotonin concentrations in synapses. Benzodiazipines are now used to treat anxiety, insomnia, and seizures. The enormous progress in molecular biology may lead to drugs that improve cognitive ability and cure schizophrenia.

Nutrition

Alternative medicine is developing wellness models, as opposed to deficit models, to meet growth-retarded and ADHD children's nutritional needs. One current approach is a learning-nutrition discipline that adjusts diets to optimize energy and levels of amino acids, vitamins, gene-promoting enzymes, and minerals.

Physical Environment

Physical environment involves factors such as light, temperature, noise, humidity, wind, space, and air pressure. Genes determine the eye's iris color and retinal pigmentation. Children with dark eyes may need more light for optimum visual performance than other children. They would have no problem if school lighting met prescribed standards and teachers did not draw the shades and turn off the lights at 2:00, as children taking ritalin become less tractable because their medicine wears off. This real genetic problem has a simple practical solution. Another example of the relationship between light and behavior concerns the use of high light levels. Intense light is used to treat depression by changing levels of the neurotransmitter serotonin and to regulate daily body rhythms by changing levels of melatonin.

Regulation of home and school temperatures is important. High temperature, which can cause sleepiness in hot classrooms, shunts blood away from the brain into the peripheral vascular system, reducing the energy and nutrient supply needed for gene expression.

Psychological Environment

In child development, gene expression responds to love; security; effective role models; stimulating language and cognitive environments; a positive family environment including support, discipline, values, and positive directions; education; and appropriate management of stress and anxiety. These psychological factors modulate genetic expression through the endocrine system and the brain, and when deficient can be improved through psychotherapy.

Providing stress-coping skills and controlling the intensity, frequency, and duration of stress are essential for optimizing gene expression. Mind-body therapies such as biofeedback and progressive relaxation promote relaxation, improving health and performance.

Adverse psychological environment can slow gene expression, leading to slower mental growth, especially when a child is subject to malnutrition, stress, illness, or suboptimal physical environments. Psychological environment also plays a role in the origins and outcomes of known brain disorders with genetic components, including stress-induced dysfunction of the amygdala and hippocampus, substance abuse, and some disorders of sleep, metabolism, vision, hearing, and speech. In addition to psychotherapy and pharmacology, education has played a vital role in the treatment of these disorders.

Genetic Differences Between the Sexes

Sex, the most obvious genetic difference, has received too little study. When scaled tests are used to measure cognitive differences, the selection of test items to ensure equal responses by males and females obscures male-female differences. Hanlon (1996) found dramatic sex differences in brain growth and in the areas at which brain activity occurs. Young girls are more verbal than young boys, who show better spatial and gross motor ability. Are boys taught to read before genes for reading are expressed? Would the Swedish approach to education, which delays reading instruction, reduce boys' reading disabilities in the United States? Some day genetic testing may help determine when a child is ready for a given educational program.

CONCLUSION

The gene is as a framed canvas, an invariant plane on which the organic environment molds a variegated hormonal surface, upon which the psychological environment paints a person.

The genome gives rise to an enormous, complex array of balanced chemical subsystems highly resistant to change. Regulatory pathways often overlap. Exciting or inhibiting one pathway can affect a series of pathways, sometimes leading to side effects. A single gene by itself may not be sufficiently strong to affect the system. A gene may be present, but there may not be a trigger to express the gene. A gene may lead to dysfunction in one environment yet produce exceptional function in another environment.

To optimize gene expression, it is essential to adopt a multidisciplinary system approach that takes into account the entire genome plus the biological and psychological environments. Even if a gene is the direct source of a behavior problem, there may be ways to alter its expression or to bypass it by promoting alternative genetic pathways. Treatment needs to balance medicine, nutrition, and physical, educational, and psychological environments and must be sensitive to gender differences. A narrow focus on a given gene, a given condition, or a single treatment is not likely to change the system. From the viewpoint of molecular biology, growth involves very complex and continuing interaction of genes and environment. But within the complexity lies a vast number of possibilities for improving children's growth.

Recommended Reading

Bogin, B. (1988). (See References)

Diamond, M.C. (1988). *The impact of the environment on the anatomy of the brain.* New York: Free Press.

Hamer, D.H., & Copeland, P. (1998). (See References)

Notes

1. Address correspondence to Bernard Brown, 182 New Mark Esplanade, Rockville, MD 20850; e-mail: berniebr@ erols.com.

2. Genome database projects now provide excellent information on most gene sequences and protein products. Functional information about what each protein does in the cell and what its metabolic and regulatory pathways are is available on the World Wide Web from the Kyoto University database, www.genome.ad.jp/kegg/. The CMS Molecular Biology Resources database can be visited at www.sdsc. edu/restools/cmshp.html. It is a functional listing of public-domain biological research tools.

References

Bogin, B. (1988). *Patterns of human growth.* Cambridge, England: Cambridge University Press.

Brown, B. (1972). *Growth retardation: A systems study of the educational problems of the disadvantaged child.* Unpublished doctoral dissertation, American University, Washington, DC.

Brown, B., & Rosenbaum, L. (1985). Stress and competence. In J.H. Humphrey (Ed.), *Stress in childhood* (pp. 127–154). New York: AMS Press.

Chan, D.K.-C., & Hargrove, J.L. (1993). Effects of dietary protein on gene expression. In C.D. Berdanier & J.L. Hargrove

(Eds.), *Nutrition and gene expression* (pp. 353–375). Boca Raton, FL: CRC.

Chrousos, G. P., & Gold, P.W. (1992). The concepts of stress and stress system disorders: Overview of physical and behavioral homeostasis. *Journal of the American Medical Association, 267,* 1244–1252.

Hamer, D.H., & Copeland, P. (1998). *Living with our genes.* New York: Doubleday.

Hanlon, H. (1996). Topographically different regional networks impose structural limitations on both sexes in early post-natal development. In K.H. Pribram & J. King (Eds.), *Learning as self-organization* (pp. 311–376). Hillsdale, NJ: Erlbaum.

Kuhn, C., & Shanberg, S. (1984). Hormones and brain development. In C.B. Nemeroff & A.D. Dunn (Eds.), *Peptides, hormones and behavior* (pp. 775–821). New York: SP Medical and Scientific Books.

Lamond, A.I., & Earnshaw, W.C. (1998). Structure and function in the nucleus. *Science, 280,* 547–553.

Lewin, B., Siliciano, P., & Klotz, M. (1997). *Genes VI.* Oxford, England: Oxford University.

Lewontin, R.C. (1994). *Inside and outside: Gene, environment and organism.* Worcester, MA: Clark University.

McEwen, B.S. (1992). Effects of the steroid/thyroid hormone family on neural and behavioral plasticity. In C.B. Nemeroff (Ed.), *Neuroendocrinology* (pp. 333–351). Boca Raton, FL: CRC.

Meerson, F.Z. (1984). *Adaptation, stress and prophylaxis.* New York: Springer-Verlag.

Sapolsky, R.M. (1996). Why stress is bad for your brain. *Science, 273,* 749–750.

Wallace, D.C. (1997). Mitochondrial DNA in aging and disease. *Scientific American, 277,* 40–47.

Wilson, J.D., & Foster, D.W. (1985). *Williams textbook of endocrinology* (7th ed.). Philadelphia: Saunders.

Autism is likely to be linked to several genes

Researchers are close to identifying several genes that influence different aspects of autism.

By Hugh McIntosh

Ever since a study revealed that if one identical twin had autism, the other was likely to have it too, researchers have been searching for genes that cause autism. Now, after 20 years of looking, scientists believe they're closing in on a handful of genes and chromosomal "hot spots" that may be responsible for different aspects of the disorder.

Identification of specific autism-related genes would reveal the proteins the genes produce—knowledge that will boost researchers' ability to diagnose autism and to discover more effective treatments for the disorder, which is characterized by communication problems, social impairment, and unusual or repetitive behaviors.

The discovery of such genes has been hampered by the complex nature of autism. Because the symptoms of people with autism vary dramatically in degree and form, researchers believe the condition might involve two or more of a large number of genes. In fact, a person with autism may have mutations in several of perhaps 20 possible genes. Thus, two people with the disorder might have mutations in two completely different sets of genes.

In the past two years, scientists have identified several candidate genes. Some might alter the effects on the brain of neurotransmitters, others might compromise the immune system enough to allow viral infections that may cause autism, and another may influence embryonic development of the nervous system.

Chromosome 15

Among the most promising findings, say experts, are reports that an autism gene may be on the long arm of chromosome 15, near the centromere—an indented point that holds the two sides of a chromosome together. This region is a well-known spot for genetic abnormalities, including duplications of parts of the chromosome's DNA. Short duplications cause no apparent harm. But longer duplications are associated with about a 50 percent risk for autism.

Last year, the research team of child psychiatrist Edwin Cook, MD, of the University of Chicago, reported that the autism risk associated with longer duplications appears to come through the mother.

Cook suspects that genes in this region of chromosome 15, which encode receptors for the neurotransmitter gamma-amino butyric acid (GABA), might be involved with autism. In fact, three genes for three GABA receptor subunits all are good candidates because they are associated with seizures and anxiety, which are common among autistic children, Cook says.

His team found moderately strong evidence for an association between one GABA subunit and autism—about one of every 70 children studied had a chromosome 15 duplication including this gene. Their study is published in the *American Journal of*

In the past two years, scientists have identified several candidate genes. Some might alter the effects on the brain of neurotransmitters, others might compromise the immune system enough to allow viral infections that may cause autism, and another may influence embryonic development of the nervous system.

Human Genetics (Vol. 62, No. 5, p. 1077–1083).

Duke University researchers say an autism gene might be a little farther away from chromosome 15's centromere, just beyond the GABA receptor genes. A genetic screening of about 50 families with autistic children turned up three positive markers in this area, says molecular geneticist John Gilbert, PhD. An autism susceptibility gene may lie between these markers and the GABA receptor genes. Exactly what that gene might do is still unknown.

To examine the link between chromosome 15 duplications and autism more closely, researchers at the University of California, Los Angeles, hope next year to launch a nationwide study of 100 children with these duplications. Researchers will look for molecular differences that might explain why half the people with this duplication have autism and half do not, says geneticist Carolyn Schanen, MD, PhD. They will also try to determine whether autistic children with this duplication are more likely to have severe language problems.

"In the kids that I know . . . it essentially wipes out language to have this extra piece," Schanen says. In the study, a psychologist will travel around the country to assess the children's phenotype, as well as to collect blood samples for genetic analysis.

A serotonin transporter gene?

Researchers have long found that many autistic persons have elevated blood levels of the neurotransmitter se-rotonin. This finding suggests that people with autism have a defect in the gene that produces serotonin transporter—a substance that sweeps serotonin from the space between two nerve cells, thus ending its effect on the cells.

In the general population, the transporter gene occurs in either a long or a short form. Last year Cook and his colleagues reported finding that children with autism inherited the short form more frequently than expected, based on typical inheritance patterns. This pattern of inheritance, called "preferential transmission," suggests that the gene is a susceptibility gene—one that plays a role in whether a person gets the disorder.

Research groups in France and Germany, however, found preferential transmission of the long form. Though conflicting, these results represent some of the stronger evidence to date for a genetic role in autism.

However, Yale University neurochemist George Anderson, PhD, says that, to him, the findings of the three studies suggest that the serotonin transporter gene may not be a susceptibility gene. Rather, it may be a "quantitative trait locus," which affects the degree of a genetic trait in someone who already has the disorder.

Cook agrees with that possibility but offers another explanation for the findings: The three samples studied may have contained different mixes of autism subtypes. The two other studies, he says, may have enrolled higher proportions of children referred for treatment of severe behavior problems such as aggression. In contrast, his group's sample contained a high proportion of people referred for communication or socialization problems rather than severe behavior problems. To test this possibility, his group has begun collecting data about aggression in people in their sample.

Nervous-system genes

Another autism candidate gene may lie among the genes involved with early development of the nervous system. This idea emerged from a Swedish study of 100 people whose mothers had taken thalidomide during pregnancy.

The study found that five of the 15 people exposed to thalidomide during days 20 to 24 of gestation had autism, says embryologist Patricia Rodier, PhD, of the University of Rochester. This suggests that the damage leading to autism occurred during the development of the hindbrain, long before the cortex and other parts of the forebrain developed. These and other findings have led Rodier and her colleagues to look for mutations in several well-known developmental genes.

"If you have mutations in some of these genes that are critical in the early stages of the development of the nervous system, that in itself may be sufficient to cause the kinds of neuroanatomical changes that we think underlie autism," Rodier says. "But it could also be that that just makes you more sensitive to environmental agents at that time."

For example, the investigators hypothesize that embryonic environmental factors—such as the presence of thalidomide—may act during early embryonic development on the genes being studied.

Immune deficiency?

Gene-environment interaction is the idea behind another candidate autism gene, called C4B, on the short arm of chromosome 6. This gene produces complement C4 protein, which

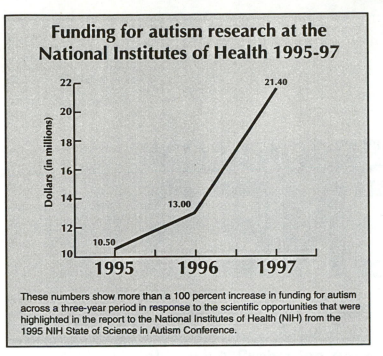

Funding for autism research at the National Institutes of Health 1995-97

These numbers show more than a 100 percent increase in funding for autism across a three-year period in response to the scientific opportunities that were highlighted in the report to the National Institutes of Health (NIH) from the 1995 NIH State of Science in Autism Conference.

Angela e. Terry

works with the antibody immuno-globulin A to fight viruses. Deficiencies in either of these substances reduce the immune system's ability to respond to viral infection.

"Autistic children are chronically ill, which is an indication that they have a deficiency in their immune system," says immunologist Roger Burger, PhD, at Utah State University in Logan.

Immune deficiency might contribute to some cases of autism by allowing a virus to damage the brain or trigger an auto-immune response that causes brain injury, Burger says. Damage might also occur in utero if the mother has an immune deficiency. People with autism have an unusually high frequency of a form of the C4B gene that produces no protein.

Working together

While the University of Utah research team and others follow interesting leads, the National Institutes of Health (NIH) is funding five major collaborative groups to conduct genome screens of families with autism. Earlier this year, one of these consortiums reported in the journal *Human Molecular Genetics* (Vol. 7, No. 3, p. 571–578) that they'd found a hot spot on chromosome 7.

"We think it's a susceptibility gene," says geneticist Anthony Monaco, MD, PhD, of the University of Oxford. "But what gene . . . or what type of gene, we really have no idea." The suspect region includes genes expressed in the brain during development.

Supporting their finding is evidence from another collaborative

group headquartered at Duke University. The researchers screened about 50 families and turned up "a number of interesting regions" on chromosome 7, says Duke geneticist Margaret Pericak-Vance, PhD.

A group at the University of Iowa has evidence for a link between autism and chromosome 13. The group is also exploring the idea that there is a broad autism phenotype that includes people with milder autism-like symptoms, as well as those with classic autistic disorder.

"We're seeing some pretty large pedigrees where there are maybe two autistic kids and an autistic first cousin, and then in between a lot of people who we think have the broad phenotype," says child psychiatrist Joseph Piven, MD. "These pedigrees . . . look more like single-gene disorders" than multigene disorders.

Although a single gene might explain autism in one family, the number of tantalizing prospects turning up from the genome screens suggests several genes are involved in autism, says Marie Bristol-Power, PhD, coordinator of the NIH autism network. She notes that the five collaborative groups together are expected to enroll more than 1,000 families with autistic children, generating plenty of statistical power to root out the genetics of this complex disorder.

Hugh McIntosh is a writer in Chicago.

THE PERSONALITY GENES

Does DNA shape behavior? A leading researcher's behavior is a case in point

By J. MADELEINE NASH

MOLECULAR BIOLOGIST Dean Hamer has blue eyes, light brown hair and the goofy sense of humor of a stand-up comic. He smokes cigarettes, spends long hours in a cluttered laboratory at the National Institutes of Health, and in his free time clambers up cliffs and points his skis down steep, avalanche-prone slopes. He also happens to be openly, matter-of-factly gay.

What is it that makes Hamer who he is? What, for that matter, accounts for the quirks and foibles, talents and traits that make up anyone's personality? Hamer is not content merely to ask such questions; he is trying to answer them as well. A pioneer in the field of molecular psychology, Hamer is exploring the role genes play in governing the very core of our individuality. To a remarkable extent, his work on what might be called the gay, thrill-seeking and quit-smoking genes reflects his own genetic predispositions.

That work, which has appeared mostly in scientific journals, has been gathered into an accessible and quite readable form in Hamer's provocative new book, *Living with Our Genes* (Doubleday; $24.95). "You have about as much choice in some aspects of your personality," Hamer and coauthor Peter Copeland write in the introductory chapter, "as you do in the shape of your nose or the size of your feet."

Until recently, research into behavioral genetics was dominated by psychiatrists and psychologists, who based their most compelling conclusions about the importance of genes on studies of identical twins. For example, psychologist Michael Bailey of Northwestern University famously demonstrated that if one identical twin is gay, there is about a 50% likelihood that the other will be too. Seven years ago, Hamer picked up where the twin studies left off, homing in on specific strips of DNA that appear to influence everything from mood to sexual orientation.

Hamer switched to behavioral genetics from basic research; after receiving his Ph.D. from Harvard, he spent more then a decade studying the biochemistry of metallothionein, a protein that cells use to metabolize heavy metals like copper and zinc. As he was about to turn 40, however, Hammer suddenly realized he had learned as much about metallothionein as he cared to. "Frankly, I was bored," he remembers, "and ready for something new."

Instrumental in Hamer's decision to switch fields was Charles Darwin's *The Descent of Man, and Selection in Relation to Sex*. "I was fascinated to learn that Darwin seemed so convinced that behavior was partially inherited," he remembers, "even though when he was writing, genes had not been discovered, let alone DNA." Homosexual behavior, in particular, seemed ripe for exploration because few scientists had dared tackle such an emotionally and politically charged subject. "I'm gay," Hamer says with

Nature or Nurture?

Many aspects of personality may have a genetic component—such as sexual orientation, anxiety, a tendency to take chances and ...

IMPULSIVENESS   OPENNESS

a shrug, "but that was not a major motivation. It was more of a question of intellectual curiosity—and the fact that no one else was doing this sort of research."

The results of Hamer's first foray into behavioral genetics, published by the journal *Science* in 1993, ignited a furor that has yet to die down. According to Hamer and his colleagues, male homosexuality appeared to be linked to a stretch of DNA at the very tip of the X chromosome, the chromosome men inherit from their mothers. Three years later, in 1996, Hamer and his collaborators at NIH seconded an Israeli group's finding that linked a gene on chromosome 11 to the personality trait psychologists called novelty seeking. That same year Hamer's lab helped pinpoint another gene, this time on chromosome 17, that appears to play a role in regulating anxiety.

Unlike the genes that are responsible for physical traits, Hamer emphasizes, these genes do not cause people to become homosexuals, thrill-seeking rock climbers or anxiety-ridden worrywarts. The biology of personality is much more complicated than that. Rather, what genes appear to do, says Hamer, is subtly bias the psyche so that different individuals react to similar experiences in surprisingly different ways.

Intriguing as these findings are, other experts caution that none has been unequivocally replicated by other research teams. Why? One possibility is that, despite all of Hamer's work, the links between these genes and these particular personality traits do not, in fact, exist. There is, however, another, more tantalizing possibility. Consider the genes that give tomatoes their flavor, suggests Hamer's colleague Dr. Dennis Murphy of the National Institute of Mental Health. Even a simple trait like acidity is controlled not by a single gene but by as many as 30 that operate in concert. In the same way, he

speculates, many genes are involved in setting up temperamental traits and psychological vulnerabilities; each gene contributes just a little bit to the overall effect.

Hunting down the genes that influence personality remains a dauntingly difficult business. Although DNA is constructed out of a mere four chemicals—adenine, guanine, cytosine, thymine—it can take as many as a million combinations to spell out a single human gene. Most of these genes vary from individual to individual by only one chemical letter in a thousand, and it is precisely these minute differences that Hamer and his colleagues are trying to identify. Of particular interest are variations that may affect the operation of such brain chemicals as dopamine and serotonin, which are well-known modulators of mood. The so-called novelty-seeking gene, for example, is thought to affect how efficiently nerve cells absorb dopamine. The so-called anxiety gene is postulated to affect serotonin's action.

How can this be? After all, as Hamer and Copeland observe in their book, " . . . genes are not switches that say 'shy' or 'outgoing' or 'happy' or 'sad.' Genes are simply chemicals that direct the combination of more chemicals." What genes do is order up the production of proteins in organs like the kidney, the skin and also the brain. Thus, Hamer speculates, one version of the novelty-seeking gene may make a protein that is less efficient at absorbing dopamine. Since dopamine is the chemical that creates sensations of pleasure in response to intense experiences, people who inherit this gene might seek to stimulate its production by seeking out thrills.

Still, as critics emphasize and Hamer himself acknowledges, genes alone do not control the chemistry of the brain. Ultimately, it is the environment that determines

how these genes will express themselves. In another setting, for example, it is easy to imagine that Hamer might have become a high school dropout rather than a scientist. For while he grew up in an affluent household in Montclair, N.J., he was hardly a model child. "Today," he chuckles, "I probably would have been diagnosed with attention-deficit disorder and put on Ritalin." In his senior year in high school, though, Hamer discovered organic chemistry and went from being an unruly adolescent to a first-rate student. What people are born with, Hamer says, are temperamental traits. What they can acquire through experience is the ability to control these traits by exercising that intangible part of personality called character.

Over the coming decade, Hamer predicts, scientists will identify thousands of genes that directly and indirectly influence behavior. A peek inside the locked freezer in the hallway outside his own lab reveals a rapidly expanding stash of plastic tubes that contain DNA samples form more than 1,760 volunteers. Among them: gay men and their heterosexual brothers, a random assortment of novelty seekers and novelty avoiders, shy children and now a growing collection of cigarette smokers.

Indeed, while Hamer has maintained a professional distance from his studies, it is impossible to believe he is not also driven by a desire for self-discovery. Soon, in fact, his lab will publish a paper about a gene that makes it harder or easier for people to stop smoking. Judging by the pack of cigarettes poking out of his shirt pocket, Hamer would seem to have drawn the wrong end of that genetic stick. He has tried to stop smoking and failed, he confesses, dozens of times. "If I quit," he says, "it will be an exercise of character." And not, it goes without saying, of his genes.

CONSERVATISM   HOSTILITY   INTELLIGENCE

Revealing the Brain's Secrets

Is space truly the final frontier? Not according to scientists who are probing what they call the most complex and challenging structure ever studied: the human brain. "It is the great unexplored frontier of the medical sciences," said neurobiologist John E. Dowling, professor of natural science at Harvard University. Just as space exploration dominated science in the 1960s and 1970s, the human brain is taking center stage in the 1990s.

It may seem odd to compare an organ that weighs only about three pounds to the immensity of the universe. Yet the human brain is as awe-inspiring as the night sky. Its complex array of interconnecting nerve cells chatter incessantly among themselves in languages both chemical and electrical. None of the organ's magical mysteries has been easy to unravel. Until recently, the brain was regarded as a black box whose secrets were frustratingly secure from reach.

Now, an explosion of discoveries in genetics and molecular biology, combined with dramatic new imaging technologies, have pried open the lid and allowed scientists to peek inside. The result is a growing understanding of what can go wrong in the brain, which raises new possibilities for identifying, treating, and perhaps ultimately preventing devastating conditions such as Alzheimer's disease or stroke.

"The laboratory bench is closer to the hospital bed than it has ever been," said neurobiologist Gerald Fischbach, chairman of neurobiology at Harvard Medical School, where the brain and its molecular makeup are a primary focus of research.

One important challenge is to understand the healthy brain. By studying brain cells and the genetic material inside them, scientists are discovering how groups of specialized cells interact to produce memory, language, sensory perception, emotion, and other complex phenomena. Figuring out how the healthy brain goes about its business is an essential platform that researchers need in order to comprehend what goes wrong when a neurological disease strikes.

There have also been great strides toward elucidating some of the common brain disorders that rob people of memory, mobility, and the ability to enjoy life. The most promising of these fall into several broad categories.

- The discovery of disease-producing genetic mutations has made it possible not only to diagnose inherited disorders, but in cases such as Huntington's disease, to predict who will develop them. These findings have also pointed the way toward new therapies.
- Insights into the programmed death of nerve cells may lead to drugs that can halt the progression of degenerative diseases or contain stroke damage.
- Naturally occurring chemicals that protect nerve cells from environmental assaults may hold clues about preventing disease or reversing neurologic injury.
- Information about brain chemistry's role in mood and mental health has already helped people burdened by depression, for example, and is expected to benefit others as well.

Genetics opens a new door

Discovering a gene associated with a disease is like unlocking a storehouse of knowledge. Once researchers have such a gene, they may be able to insert it into experimental systems such as cell cultures or laboratory animals. This makes it easier to discern the basic mechanisms of the disorder, which in turn helps scientists figure out what diagnostic tests or therapies might be best. When a new treatment is proposed, genetically engineered models of human diseases make testing quicker and more efficient.

In recent years, scientists have found abnormal genes associated with Huntington's disease (HD), Alzheimer's disease (AD), amyotrophic lateral sclerosis (ALS or Lou Gehrig's disease), one form of epilepsy, Tay-Sachs disease, two types of muscular dystrophy, and several lesser-known neurological conditions.

A decade-long search for the HD gene ended in 1993, when Harvard researchers Marcy MacDonald and James Gusella, working with scientists at other institutions, identified a sequence of DNA that produces symptoms

Reprinted with permission from the *Harvard Health Letter*, January 1996. pp. 9–12. © 1996 by the President and Fellows of Harvard College.

of the disease if it is repeated enough times. Huntington's is a progressive and ultimately fatal hereditary disorder that affects about 25,000 people in the United States. It typically strikes at midlife, and the researchers discovered that the more copies of the sequence a person inherited, the earlier symptoms show up.

Scientists quickly developed a highly reliable assay that enables people with a family history of HD to find out if they or their unborn fetus harbors the dangerous mutation. But because no cure for the disease exists, few people have rushed to have themselves tested.

Demand might increase, however, if scientists can use the HD gene to design effective treatments. Genes contain the assembly instructions for proteins, the molecules that carry out the day-to-day operations of the body. Scientists strive to identify the protein made by a disease-producing gene and to figure out what it does, which in turn helps them understand the event that initiates the disease process.

The HD gene codes for a protein that appears to contribute to the premature death of certain neurons. It is the loss of these cells that results in the involuntary movements and mental deterioration typical of Huntington's. When researchers know more about this protein, they may be able to develop drugs or other therapies that could slow the onset of symptoms or even block them entirely.

A downward spiral

The gradual extinction of certain brain cells is also the underlying cause of Alzheimer's disease. In this case, the impact is progressive loss of memory, changes in personality, loss of impulse control, and deterioration in reasoning power. Under the microscope, the brains of people who died with AD are studded with abnormalities called amyloid plaques and neurofibrillary tangles. About 20% of all AD cases are inherited, and these people develop symptoms earlier in life than those with the more common form, which typically appears well after age 65.

In recent years, scientists have discovered several different genetic mutations that can cause the unusual, inherited form of AD. One of these abnormal genes has successfully been introduced into mice by researchers at several pharmaceutical companies, and experts believe that this animal model will help them understand how all forms of the disease progress at the cellular and molecular level.

So far, it looks as though some of the animals' brains develop amyloid plaques like the ones that build up in humans. Long-standing doubt about whether plaques cause symptoms may be resolved by future observations of whether these genetically engineered mice show signs of memory loss. If there is a strong correlation between amyloid accumulation and symptom severity, these mice will be used to test drugs that might keep plaques from forming.

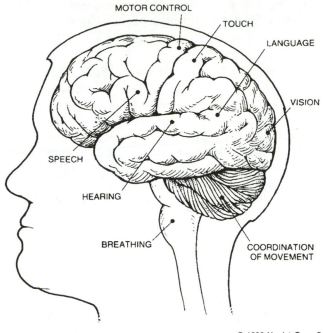

© 1996 Harriet Greenfield

The cell death story

Unlike other types of cells, nerve cells (neurons) are meant to last a lifetime because they can't reproduce themselves. Struck by the realization that abnormal cell death is the key factor in neurologic problems ranging from Alzheimer's to stroke, scientists have embarked on a crusade aimed at understanding why nerve cells die and how this might be prevented.

It's normal to lose some brain cells gradually. Trouble arises when a large population of cells dies all of a sudden, as in a stroke, or when too many of a certain type die over time, such as in Alzheimer's or Parkinson's (PD) disease. While some scientists remain skeptical that inquiries into cell death will ever lead to effective means for preventing or treating neurodegenerative diseases, many others are enthusiastically pursuing this line of research.

Some scientists are racing to develop *neuroprotective* drugs that could guard brain cells against damage and death or even help them regenerate. There are many different ideas about how to do this.

For example, although Harvard scientists have identified the gene for HD and the protein it makes, they don't understand the mechanisms that lead to symptoms. One theory is that a phenomenon called *excitotoxicity* is responsible, and that Huntington's is only one of many diseases in which this process plays a role.

The idea behind excitotoxicity is that too much of a good thing is bad for cells. Glutamate, for example, is an ordinarily benign chemical messenger that stimulates certain routine cellular activities. Under extraordinary circumstances, however, "cells can be so excited by glutamate that they wear themselves out and die," said John

Penney Jr., a neurologist at Massachusetts General Hospital and a Harvard professor of neurology.

Sending a signal

One of the many types of doorways built into the walls of nerve cells is a structure called an NMDA receptor. One of its functions is to allow small amounts of calcium (a substance usually shut out of the cell) to enter it. This happens when the NMDA receptor is stimulated by glutamate. If excess glutamate is present, too much calcium rushes in—an influx that is lethal to the cell.

Someday it may be possible to halt the advance of Huntington's by injecting drugs which block the NMDA receptor so that calcium can't get in. In animal experiments, scientists have demonstrated that such receptor-blocking agents can keep brain cells from dying. Harvard researchers are seeking approval for a clinical trial that will test such neuroprotective drugs in patients with symptomatic disease. If participants obtain any relief from this treatment, the next step will be to determine whether this approach can prevent symptoms in patients who have the gene but do not have symptoms.

Scientists also hope that neuroprotection can be used to limit brain damage due to stroke. When a stroke shuts down the supply of blood to part of the brain, neurons in the immediate area die within minutes. Over the next several hours, more distant cells in the region are killed as excitotoxic signals spread. In an effort to limit the extent of brain damage, researchers are currently treating small numbers of patients with intravenous doses of experimental agents such as NMDA receptor blockers and free radical scavengers. Other neuroprotective agents under development, include protease inhibitors, nitric oxide inhibitors, and nerve growth factors.

"Our dream is a safe and effective neuroprotectant that can be given to the stroke patient in the ambulance or shortly after arrival in the emergency room," said neurologist Seth Finklestein, an associate professor at Harvard Medical School who conducts basic research at Massachusetts General Hospital. "That's the holy grail of neuroprotective treatment."

Applications for Alzheimer's

Neuroprotection is also making waves in Alzheimer's research, as scientists strive to inhibit the type of cell death that typifies this disease. One group of investigators has identified several *peptides* (small protein molecules) that block the formation of amyloid plaque in the test tube, said neurobiologist Huntington Potter, an associate professor at Harvard Medical School. The researchers hope to test these peptides in humans.

Brain cells manufacture several neuroprotective chemicals on their own, which scientists call *neurotrophic* or nerve growth factors. These small proteins may hold the key to keeping cells alive even in the face of stroke, degenerative diseases, or even spinal cord injury.

For example, several different neurotrophic factors are being tested in the laboratory to determine if they could protect the dopamine-producing cells that die prematurely in people with Parkinson's disease. Other uses are being studied as well, and some researchers anticipate that these chemicals will be tested in humans before the decade draws to a close.

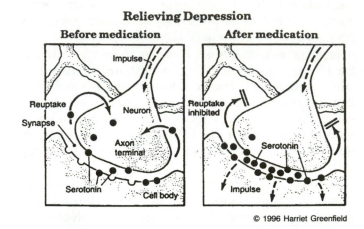

Relieving Depression

© 1996 Harriet Greenfield

People who are depressed have less of the neurotransmitter serotonin than those who aren't. In the picture on the left, the axon terminal of one nerve cell releases serotonin, which travels across the synapse and activates the cell body (receiving cell). Serotonin is then reabsorbed by the sending cell. On the right, a selective serotonin reuptake inhibitor (SSRI), such as the antidepressant Prozac, slows the reabsorption of serotonin, keeping it in the synapse longer and boosting its effect on the receiving cell.

Mood, mind, and brain chemistry

Scientists have discovered that a surprising number of mental disorders, from depression to schizophrenia, are the result of brain chemistry gone awry. And this understanding has led them to design new medications for treating specific mental disorders and behavior problems.

The best known of this new breed of drugs is fluoxetine (Prozac), one of several selective serotonin reuptake inhibitors (SSRIs). It was possible to design these agents, which are widely prescribed to alleviate depression and related disorders, only after scientists came to understand how nerve cells communicate at the molecular level.

Each nerve cell has an *axon,* a long branch that reaches out and touches other nerve cells. A tiny space called a *synapse* separates the axon terminal (which sends a message) and the cell body (that receives it), and this is where the action is. The sending cell releases *neurotransmitters* (chemical messengers) into the synapse which either excite or inhibit a receiving cell that is equipped with the proper receptors. Messages pass from cell to cell in this manner, eventually leading to a physiologic action. In each synapse, the cell that sent the message sops up leftover neurotransmitters and stores them for future use. People who are depressed have less serotonin than those who aren't, and the SSRIs block the reuptake of this chemical, thereby boosting the effect of a small amount on the receiving cell. (*See illustration* "Relieving Depression.")

But Prozac and its relatives are only the tip of the iceberg. As researchers work to understand the roles of different chemical messengers and the highly specific receptors that bind them, a whole new approach to the treatment of mental disorders is evolving. The identification of highly specialized receptors is already paving the way for ever more specific drugs to treat these conditions.

Schizophrenia therapy is a case in point. As devastating as this form of mental illness is, treatments have sometimes appeared worse than the disease. Until very recently, the only drugs that relieved symptoms could also lead to spasmodic, uncontrollable movements known as *tardive dyskinesia*. This is because these agents block all types of receptors for dopamine, a neurotransmitter that is a key player in normal movement as well as in this mental disorder. Now there is a new drug for schizophrenia, clozapine, that blocks only a small subclass of dopamine receptors. It relieves symptoms of the illness in some people without leading to abnormal movements. Still, it can have other serious side effects.

Tailored to fit

The bottom line for the treatment of behavior and emotional disorders may be that drugs will become ever more specialized. Just as computers now help salespeople fit blue jeans to the individual purchasers, it is not inconceivable that psychopharmacologists may someday tailor drugs to the needs of each patient.

What does the future of brain research hold? Dr. Dowling anticipates that medications that can slow the process of degenerative disease, correct the chemical imbalances that cause mental disorders, prevent stroke damage, and repair spinal cord injuries may all be on the horizon. "We have learned so much about the cellular and molecular aspects of the brain," Dr. Dowling said. "We stand at a time of great opportunity, when we can take tremendous advantage of these things and turn them into practical clinical therapies."

—*KATHLEEN CAHILL ALLISON*

Traumatic Memory Is Special

Lynn Nadel and W. Jake Jacobs[1]

Department of Psychology, University of Arizona, Tucson, Arizona

Does the brain represent and store memories for traumatic events differently than memories for everyday autobiographical events (cf. the June 1997 Special Issue of *Current Directions*)? Laboratory evidence is central to answering this question, and hence to understanding clinical trauma. An answer would provide a guide to how "recovered" memories should be interpreted, and would also have implications for treating victims of trauma. In this article, we consider empirical data concerning the neurobiological nature of multiple memory systems, and how stress and trauma affect these systems, and then we briefly discuss the implications of these facts for the clinical issues.

EMPIRICAL DATA

On the basis of several decades of empirical work, most investigators distinguish between at least two types of memory (e.g., explicit and implicit; see Schacter & Tulving, 1994, for a variety of multiple-memory-systems approaches). Going beyond a simple dichotomy, more recent research establishes that each major class of memory encompasses more than one form of memory, and the concomitant involvement of more than one underlying neural substrate. Consider explicit memory, which refers to any and all forms of recollection entering awareness. This sort of memory is most often associated with the medial temporal lobe, an area of the brain that includes the amygdala, rhinal cortex, parahippocampal gyrus, and hippocampal formation. Although there has been a tendency to think of these structures as parts of a larger medial temporal lobe memory system, recent work indicates that each is responsible for different aspects of explicit memory. In the present context, it is particularly important to attend to these distinctions, because stress has differential impact on them.

• *Amygdala.* This structure is thought to be essential in memory for emotionally charged events. Studies in rats, monkeys, and humans have now shown that (a) damage to the amygdala interferes with learning about fearful or unpleasant stimuli (Adolphs, Tranel, Damasio, & Damasio, 1994; Davis, 1992; LeDoux, 1995; McGaugh, Cahill, & Roozendaal, 1996); (b) neurons in the amygdala of experimental animals are activated by stimuli with motivational or emotional import (e.g., Rolls, 1982); and (c) the human amygdala is activated when a person is exposed to emotion-provoking stimuli or events (Morris et al., 1996). By contrast, other regions in the medial temporal lobe are apparently not involved, in any general way, with such stimuli.

• *Rhinal cortex.* This structure is thought to be central to recognition memory, the process by which an organism determines it has, or has not, had prior experience with a particular stimulus or event. A prominent demonstration of this function concerns the laboratory task known as delayed matching (or nonmatching) to sample. In this widely used paradigm, the experimental subject is exposed briefly to a *sample* stimulus, and then after a variable delay, allowed to choose between the sample and another, new, stimulus. In the more commonly used nonmatching case, the subject must choose the new stimulus in order to receive reward. Monkeys, and rats, with damage to the rhinal cortex are severely impaired at this task at a wide range of delay intervals (Mumby, & Pinel, 1994; Murray, Gaffan, & Flint, 1996; Zola-Morgan, Squire, Amaral, & Suzuki, 1989). By contrast, subjects with damage to the hippocampus or amygdala are either not impaired at all or impaired only under a narrow range of as yet poorly understood conditions (e.g., Gaffan, 1994). In addition to the

From *Current Directions in Psychological Science,* October 1998, pp. 154-157. © 1998 by the American Psychological Society. Reprinted by permission of Blackwell Publishers.

evidence from such behavioral studies, electrophysiological analyses of the rhinal area have shown that its neuronal activity reflects recognition memory (e.g., Brown, 1996).

• *Parahippocampal gyrus.* This brain region is now thought to play an important role in some forms of spatial cognition. Thus, this area in humans is activated in circumstances in which individuals are thinking about moving around in space (e.g., Maguire, Frackowiak, & Frith, 1996). In people with damage to the parahippocampal region, learning about the spatial layout of a test environment is severely impaired (e.g., Bohbot et al., 1998).

• *Hippocampal formation.* This region has long been implicated in spatial learning and memory (O'Keefe & Nadel, 1978) and in memory for episodes (Kinsbourne & Wood, 1975; Milner, 1962). How best to characterize its precise role in memory function has been a matter of intense debate in recent years. Many investigators (Metcalfe & Jacobs, 1998; Moscovitch, 1995; Nadel, Willner, & Kurz, 1985; Squire, Cohen, & Nadel, 1984; Teyler & DiScenna, 1985) agree that the hippocampus plays a role "binding" together the elements of an episode, which themselves are represented in dispersed brain systems. That is, the hippocampus provides a mechanism by which disaggregated bits of information making up an episode can be kept in touch with one another (Jacobs & Nadel, in press). There is general agreement that the hippocampus is essential to this function for recent memories; its role in the retrieval of remote memories is a matter of considerable current debate (cf. Moscovitch & Nadel, 1998; Nadel & Moscovitch, 1997).

A key point of this proposal is that various aspects of an episode memory are represented and stored in dispersed brain modules (cf. O'Keefe & Nadel, 1978, p. 100). Also, each module interconnects with the hippocampal complex, so that the collection of representations of the features of an episode can activate within the hippocampal complex an ensemble encoding that episode. This creation of a hippocampal ensemble (or "cognitive map"; O'Keefe & Nadel, 1978) occurs rapidly, through the mechanism of long-term synaptic potentiation (a form of neural plasticity thought by many to underlie learning and memory) within the relevant hippocampal connections. An act of episode retrieval can be accomplished in two ways: first, by activating the relevant hippocampal ensemble, which then activates dispersed extrahippocampal features, or second, by activating some subset of these dispersed features, which then activate the hippo-campal ensemble. In both cases, the hippocampal component is essential to accurate reconstruction of the episodic memory.

STRESS AND MEMORY SYSTEMS

These distinctions among types of explicit memory, and their neural substrates, must be taken into account in any consideration of the ways in which stress affects memory. The data suggest that within physiological limits, stress enhances the function of the amygdala, and consequently strengthens those aspects of explicit memory subserved by this structure (cf. Metcalfe & Jacobs, 1998). The data also firmly establish that high levels of stress or the high levels of the hormone corticosterone (cortisol in humans) typically resulting from stress impair the function of the hippocampus, weakening or totally disrupting those aspects of spatial and explicit memory subserved by this structure. A number of studies, with both humans and animals, have demonstrated this now well-accepted fact (e.g., Bodnoff et al., 1995; de Quervain, Roozendaal, & McGaugh, 1998; Diamond & Rose, 1994; Foy, Stanton, Levine, & Thompson, 1987; Luine, Villegas, Martinez, & McEwen, 1994). For example, Luine et al. (1994) induced stress levels of corticosterone in rats by restraining them in Plexiglas containers in their home cages for 6 hr/day for 21 days. When tested on an eight-arm radial maze, a widely used spatial memory task, these rats were impaired compared with nonstressed control rats (see also Kállai, Kóczán, Szabó, Molnár, & Varga, 1995; Kirschbaum, Wolf, May, Wippich, & Hellhammer, 1996; Lupien et al., 1998, for related studies in humans).

Intriguingly, abnormally low levels of corticosterone, produced by removal of the adrenal glands, can also impair spatial learning (e.g., Conrad & Roy, 1995; Vaher, Luine, Gould, & McEwen, 1994). We, and others, have concluded that the relation between corticosterone and hippocampal function is U-shaped; that is, circulating levels of corticosterone within some optimal range yield normal function. Too little or too much corticosterone impairs function.

Thus, the laboratory data show that the relation between stress and the function of neural structures important for explicit memory is quite complex. Within a certain range, stress could enhance all forms of explicit memory, but high levels of stress could enhance some aspects of explicit memory while impairing others.

And here is the critical point: When stress is high enough to impair the function of the hippocampus, resulting memories will be different from those formed under more ordinary circumstances. These empirical data suggest that memories of trauma may be available as isolated fragments rather than as coherently bound episodes (e.g., van der Kolk & Fisler, 1995). This hypothesis contrasts with the position espoused by Shobe and Kihlstrom (1997), who did not take into account the differential effects of stress on the various memory modules.

CLINICAL IMPLICATIONS

We (Jacobs & Nadel, in press) have argued that these differential effects of stress on the various components of episode memory account for several of the unusual features of memories formed under stress. Traumatic stress can cause amnesia for the autobiographical context of stressful events, but stronger than normal recall for the emotional memories produced by them. That such *emotional hypermnesia* may result from traumatic stress is consistent with early reports (e.g., Charcot, 1887; Janet, 1889). Even in the context of extensive autobiographical amnesia, intrusive emotions or images associated with the trauma (and related events) may appear (Jacobs, Laurance, Thomas, Luzcak, & Nadel, 1996). Intrusions appear in the context of grief, anxiety disorders, mood disorders, and dissociative disorders (syndromes involving disturbances in identity, memory, or consciousness; Brewin, Hunter, Caroll, & Tata, 1996; Gibbs, 1996; Horowitz, 1986; Howe, Courage, & Peterson, 1995), and can also be elicited in the laboratory (van der Kolk, 1994). What distinguishes these intrusive memory states is the absence of the time-and-place contextual information that typically characterizes autobiographical episode memory.

Van der Kolk and Fisler (1995) showed that after an initial phase when traumatic memories are experienced as fragmentary, an autobiographical memory eventually emerges. We have suggested that this emergence reflects a process of "inferential narrative smoothing," whereby disembodied fragments are knit together into a plausible autobiographical episode (Jacobs & Nadel, in press).

The present analysis suggests that at least some memories "recovered" during therapy should be taken seriously. Although such memories may contain emotional experiences accumulated across multiple stressful events, some of this emotional content could be veridical. The narratives associated with these memories are less likely to be veridical in their entirety. These narratives may be composites of real fragments of experience and the emotions elicited by those experiences, filled out by tacit knowledge and logic available to the individual, and shaped by interlocutors such as friends and therapists.

Notes

1. Address correspondence to Lynn Nadel, Department of Psychology, University of Arizona, Tucson, AZ 85721.

Recommended Reading

Jacobs, W.J., & Nadel, L. (1985). Stress induced recovery of fears and phobias. *Psychological Review, 92,* 512–531.

LeDoux, J.E. (1994). Emotion, memory and the brain. *Scientific American, 270,* 50–57.

Lupien, S.J., & McEwen, B.S. (1997). The acute effects of corticosteroids on cognition: Integration of animal and human model studies. *Brain Research Reviews, 24,* 1–27.

Sapolsky, R.M. (1998). *Why zebras don't get ulcers: An updated guide to stress, stress-related diseases, and coping.* New York: W.H. Freeman.

Schacter, D. (1996). *Searching for memory: The brain, the mind, and the past.* New York: Basic Books.

References

Adolphs, R., Tranel, D., Damasio, H. & Damasio, A. (1994). Impaired recognition of emotion in facial expressions following bilateral damage to the human amygdala. *Nature, 372,* 669–672.

Bodnoff, S.R., Humphreys, A.G., Lehman, J.C., Diamond, D.M., Rose, G.M., & Meaney, M.J. (1995). Enduring effects of chronic corticosterone treatment on spatial-learning, synaptic plasticity, and hippocampal neuropathology in young and mid-aged rats. *Journal of Neuroscience, 15,* 61–69.

Bohbot, V., Kalina, M., Stepankova, K., Spackova, N., Petrides, M., & Nadel, L. (1998). Spatial memory deficits in patients with lesions to the right hippocampus and to the right parahippocampal cortex. *Neuropsychologia, 36,* 1217–1238.

Brewin, C.R., Hunter, E., Caroll, F., & Tata, P. (1996). Intrusive memories in depression: An index of schema activation? *Psychological Medicine, 26,* 1271–1276.

Brown, M.W. (1996). Neuronal responses and recognition memory. *Seminars in the Neurosciences, 8,* 23–32.

Charcot, J.M. (1887). *Lecons sur les maladies du système nerveux faites a la Salpêtrière* [Lessons on the illnesses of the nervous system held at Salpetriere] (Vol. 3). Paris: Progres Medical en A. Delahye & Lecorsnie.

Conrad, C.D., & Roy, E.J. (1996). Dentate gyrus destruction and spatial learning impairment after corticosteroid removal in young and middle-aged rats. *Hippocampus, 5,* 1–15.

Davis, M. (1992). The role of the amygdala in fear and anxiety. *Annual Review of Neuroscience, 15,* 353–375.

de Quervain, D.J.-F., Roozendaal, B., & McGaugh, J.L. (1998). Stress and glucocorticoids impair retrieval of long-term spatial memory. *Nature, 394,* 787–790.

Diamond, D.M., & Rose, G.M. (1994). Stress impairs LTP and hippocampal-dependent memory. *Annals of the New York Academy of Sciences, 746,* 411–414.

Foy, M.R., Stanton, M.E., Levine, S., & Thompson, R.F. (1987). Behavioral stress impairs long-term potentiation in rodent hippocampus. *Behavioral and Neural Biology, 48,* 138–149.

Gaffan, D. (1994). Dissociated effects of perirhinal cortex ablation, fornix transection and amygdalectomy: Evidence for multiple memory systems in the primate temporal lobe. *Experimental Brain Research, 99,* 411–422.

Gibbs, N.A. (1996). Nonclinical populations in research on obsessive-compulsive disorder—A critical-review. *Clinical Psychology Review, 16,* 729–773.

Horowitz, M.J. (1986). *Stress response syndromes* (2nd ed.). New York: Jason Aronson.

Howe, M.I., Courage, M.I., & Peterson, C. (1995). Intrusions in preschoolers' recall of traumatic childhood events. *Psychonomic Bulletin & Review, 2,* 130–134.

Jacobs, W.J., Laurance, H.E., Thomas, K.G.F., Luzcak, S.E., & Nadel, L. (1996). On the veracity and variability of recovered traumatic memory. *Traumatology, 2*(1) [Online]. Available: http://rdz.stjohns.edu/trauma/traumaj.html.

Jacobs, W.J., & Nadel, L. (in press). Neurobiology of reconstructed memory. *Psychology of Public Policy and Law.*

Janet, P. (1889). *L'automatisme psychologique.* Paris: Alcan.

Kállai, J., Kóczán, G., Szabó, I., Molnár, P., & Varga, J. (1995). An experimental study to operationally define and measure spatial orientation in panic agoraphobia subjects, generalized anxiety and healthy control groups. *Behavioural and Cognitive Psychology, 23,* 145–152.

Kinsbourne, M., & Wood, F. (1975). Short-term memory processes and the amnesic syndrome. In D. Deutsch & J.A. Deutsch (Eds.), *Short-term memory* (pp. 258–291). New York: Academic Press.

Kirschbaum, C., Wolf, O.T., May, M., Wippich, W., & Hellhammer, D.H. (1996). Stress- and treatment-induced elevations of corti-sol levels associated with impaired declarative memory in healthy adults. *Life Sciences, 58,* 1475–1483.

LeDoux, J.E. (1995). Emotion: Clues from the brain. *Annual Review of Psychology, 46,* 209–235.

Luine, V., Villegas, M., Martinez, C., & McEwen, B.S. (1994). Repeated stress causes reversible impairments of spatial memory performance. *Brain Research, 639,* 167–170.

Lupien, S.J., de Leon, M., de Santi, S., Convit, A., Tarshish, C., Nair, N.P.V., Thakur, M., McEwen, B.S., Hauger, R.L., & Meaney, M.J. (1998). Cortisol levels during human aging predict hippocampal atrophy and memory deficits. *Nature Neuroscience, 1,* 69–73.

Maguire, E.A., Frackowiak, R.S.J., & Frith, C.D. (1996). Learning to find your way: A role for the human hippocampal formation. *Proceedings of the Royal Society of London, 263,* 1745–1750.

McGaugh, J.L., Cahill, L., & Roozendaal, B. (1996). Involvement of the amygdala in memory storage—Interaction with other brain systems. *Proceedings of the National Academy of Sciences, USA, 93,* 13508–13514.

Metcalfe, J., & Jacobs, W.J. (1998). Emotional memory: The effects of stress on 'cool' and 'hot' memory systems. In D.L. Medin (Ed.), *The psychology of learning and motivation: Vol. 38. Advances in research and theory* (pp. 187–222). San Diego: Academic Press.

Milner, B. (1962). Les troubles de la memoire accompagnant des lesions hippocampiques bilaterales. In P. Passouant (Ed.), *Physiologie de l'hippocampe* (pp. 257–272). Paris: Centre National de la Recherche Scientifique.

Morris, J.S., Frith, C.D., Perrett, D.I., Rowland, D., Young, A.W., Calder, A.J., & Dolan, R.J. (1996). A differential neural response in the human amygdala to fearful and happy facial expressions. *Nature, 383,* 812–815.

Moscovitch, M. (1995). Recovered consciousness: A hypothesis concerning modularity and episodic memory. *Journal of Clinical and Experimental Neuropsychology, 17,* 276–290.

Moscovitch, M., & Nadel, L. (1998). Consolidation and the hippocampal complex revisited: In defense of the multiple-trace model. *Current Opinions in Neurobiology, 8,* 297–300.

Mumby, D.G., & Pinel, J.P.J. (1994). Rhinal cortex lesions and object recognition in rats. *Behavioral Neuroscience, 108,* 11–18.

Murray, E.A., Gaffan, E.A., & Flint, R.W., Jr. (1996). Anterior rhinal cortex and amygdala: Dissociation of their contributions to memory and food preference in rhesus monkeys. *Behavioral Neuroscience, 110,* 30–42.

Nadel, L., & Moscovitch, M. (1997). Memory consolidation, retrograde amnesia and the hippocampal formation: A re-evaluation of the evidence and new model. *Current Opinions in Neurobiology, 7,* 217–227.

Nadel, L., Willner, J., & Kurz, E.M. (1985). Cognitive maps and environmental context. In P. Balsam & A. Tomie (Eds.), *Context and learning* (pp. 385–406). Hillsdale, NJ: Erlbaum.

O'Keefe, J., & Nadel, L. (1978). *The hippocampus as a cognitive map.* Oxford, England: Oxford University Press.

Rolls, E.T. (1982). Neuronal mechanisms underlying the formation and disconnection of associations between visual stimuli and reinforcement in primates. In C.C. Woody (Ed.), *Conditioning* (pp. 363–373). New York: Plenum Press.

Schacter, D.L., & Tulving, E. (1994). *Memory systems 1994* (pp. 369–394). Cambridge, MA: MIT Press.

Shobe, K.K., & Kihlstrom, J.F. (1997). Is traumatic memory special? *Current Directions in Psychological Science, 6,* 70–74.

Squire, L.R., Cohen, N.J., & Nadel, L. (1984). The medial temporal region and memory consolidation: A new hypothesis. In H. Weingartner & E.S. Parker (Eds.), *Memory consolidation: Psychobiology of cognition* (pp. 185–210). Hillsdale, NJ: Erlbaum.

Teyler, T.J., & DiScenna, P. (1985). The role of the hippocampus in memory: A hypothesis. *Neuroscience and Biobehavioral Reviews, 9,* 377–389.

Vaher, P., Luine, V., Gould, E., & McEwen, B. (1994). Effects of adrenalectomy on spatial memory performance and dentate gyrus morphology. *Brain Research, 656,* 71–76.

van der Kolk, B. (1994). The body keeps the score: Memory and the evolving psychobiology of posttraumatic stress. *Harvard Review of Psychiatry, 5,* 253–265.

van der Kolk, B., & Fisler, R. (1995). Dissociation and the fragmentary nature of traumatic memories: Overview and exploratory study. *Journal of Traumatic Stress, 8,* 505–525.

Zola-Morgan, S., Squire, L.R., Amaral, D.G., & Suzuki, W.A. (1989). Lesions of perirhinal and parahippocampal cortex that spare the amygdala and the hippocampal formation produce severe memory impairment. *Journal of Neuroscience, 9,* 4355–4370.

THE BIOLOGY OF *Joy*

By Jeremiah Creedon

Scientists are unlocking the secrets of pleasure— and discovering what poets already knew

Pleasure, like fire, is a natural force that from the beginning humans have sought to harness and subdue. We've always sensed that pleasure is somehow crucial to life, perhaps the only tangible payoff for its hardships. And yet many have discovered that unbridled pleasure can also be dangerous, even fatal. Since ancient times, philosophers and spiritual leaders have debated its worth and character, often comparing it unfavorably to its more stable sibling, happiness. No one, however, saint or libertine, has ever doubted which of the pair would be the better first date.

Happiness is a gift for making the most of life. Pleasure is born of the reckless impulse to forget life and give yourself to the moment. Happiness is partly an abstract thing, a moral condition, a social construct: The event most often associated with happiness, some researchers say, is seeing one's children grow up to be happy themselves. How nice. Pleasure, pure pleasure, is a biological reflex, a fleeting "reward" so hot and lovely you might sell your children to get it. Witness the lab rat pressing the pleasure bar until it collapses. Or the sad grin of the crack addict as the molecules of mountain shrub trip a burst of primal gratitude deep in a part of the human brain much like a rat's. Both know all too well that pleasure, uncaged, can eat you alive.

Some scientists claim they're close to knowing what pleasure is, biologically speaking. Their intent is to solve the riddle of pleasure much as an earlier generation unleashed the power of the atom. Splitting pleasure down to its very molecules will have many benefits, they say, including new therapies for treating drug abuse and mental illness. Others note that research on the biology of pleasure is part of a wider trend that's exploding old ideas about the human brain, if not the so-called "Western biomedical paradigm" in general, with its outmoded cleaving of body from mind.

The assumption is that somehow our lives will be better once this mystery has been unraveled. Beneath that is the enduring belief that we can conquer pleasure as we've conquered most everything else, that we can turn it into a docile beast and put it to work. That we've never been able to do so before, and yet keep trying, reveals a lot about who we are, as creatures of a particular age—and species.

Of all the animals that humans have sought to tame, pleasure most resembles the falcon in its tendency to revert to the wild. That's why we're often advised to keep it hooded. The Buddha warned that to seek pleasure is to chase a shadow; it only heightens the unavoidable pain of life, which has to be accepted. Nevertheless, most have chosen to discover that for

 From *Utne Reader*, November/December 1997, pp. 66-71, 106.

themselves. The early Greek hedonists declared pleasure the ultimate good, then immediately began to hedge. Falling in love, for instance, wasn't really a pleasure, given the inevitable pain of falling out of it. The hedonists thought they could be masters of pleasure, not its slaves; yet their culture's literature is a chronicle of impetuous, often unspeakable pleasures to be indulged at any cost.

When the Christians crawled out of the catacombs to make Rome holy, they took revenge on pagan pleasure by sealing it in—then pretended for centuries not to hear its muffled protests. Eclipsed was the Rose Bowl brilliance of the Roman circus, where civic pleasure reached a level of brutal spectacle unmatched until the advent of *Monday Night Football*. Pleasure as a public function seemed to vanish.

The end of the Dark Ages began with the Italian poet Dante, who, for all his obsession with the pains of hell, endures as one of the great, if ambivalent, students of pleasure. His *Inferno* is but a portrait of the enjoyments of his day turned inside out, like a dirty sock. For every kind of illicit bliss possible in the light of the world above, Dante created a diabolically fitting punishment in his theme-park hell below. We can only guess what terrible eternity he has since devised for his countryman, the pleasure-loving Versace, felled in what Dante would have considered the worst of ways—abruptly, without a chance to confess his sins. At the very least he's doomed to wear Armani.

Dante's ability to find a certain glee in the suffering of others—not to mention in the act of writing—goes to the heart of the problem of pleasure. Let's face it: Pleasure has a way of getting twisted. Most people, most of the time, are content with simple pleasures: a walk on the beach, fine wine, roses, cuddling, that sort of thing. But pleasure can also be complicated, jaded, and sick. The darker aspects of pleasure surely lie dormant in many of us, like the Minotaur in the heart of the labyrinth waiting for its yearly meal of pretty flesh. In the words of the Mongol ruler Genghis Khan, "Happiness lies in conquering one's enemies, in driving them in front of oneself, in taking their property, in savoring their despair, in outraging their wives and daughters." He meant pleasure, of course, not happiness—but *you* tell him.

In the Age of Reason, the vain hope that humans could reason with pleasure returned. Thinkers like Jeremy Bentham took up the old Greek idea of devising a "calculus" of pleasure—complex equations for estimating what pleasure really is, in light of the pain often caused by the quest for it. But the would-be moral engineers, rational to a fault, found the masses oddly attached to the older idea of pleasure being a simple sum of parts, usually private parts. As for the foundlings thus multiplied, along with certain wretched venereal ills, well, who would have figured?

The first "scientists of mind" were pretty sure that the secrets of pleasure, and the emotions in general, lay locked beyond their reach, inside our heads. Throughout the 19th century, scientists could only speculate about the human brain and its role as "the organ of consciousness." Even more galling, the era's writers and poets clearly speculated so much better—especially those on drugs.

Two of them, Samuel Taylor Coleridge and Thomas De Quincey, both opium addicts, also may have been early explorers of the brain's inner geography. Images of a giant fountain gushing from a subterranean river in Coleridge's most famous poem—"Kubla Khan; or, A Vision in a Dream" bear an odd resemblance to modern models of brain function, especially brains steeped in mind-altering chemicals. Writing in *The Human Brain* (BasicBooks, 1997), Susan A. Greenfield, professor of pharmacology at Oxford University, describes the "fountainlike" nerve-cell structures that arise in the brain stem and release various chemical messengers into the higher brain areas. As Greenfield notes, and Coleridge perhaps intuited, these geysers of emotion are "often the target of mood-modifying drugs."

De Quincey describes a similar terrain in *Confessions of an English Opium Eater (1821)*. He even suggests that the weird world he envisioned while he was on the drug might have been his own fevered brain projected, a notion he fears will seem "ludicrous to a medical man." Not so. Sherwin B. Nuland, National Book Award winner and clinical professor of surgery at Yale, expresses an updated version of that concept in *The Wisdom of the Body* (Knopf, 1997). In Nuland's view, we may possess an "awareness" distinct from rational thought, a kind of knowledge that rises up from our cells to "imprint itself" on how we interpret the world. "It is by this means that our lives . . . and even our culture come to be influenced by, and are the reflection of, the conflict that exists within cells," he writes.

Maybe De Quincey really could see his own brain. Maybe that's what many artists see. Think of Dante's downward-spiraling hell, or the Minotaur in the labyrinth, even the cave paintings at Altamira and Lascaux. The first known labyrinth was built in Egypt nearly 4,000 years ago, a convoluted tomb for both a pharaoh's remains and those of the sacred crocodiles teeming in a nearby lake. It's an odd image to find rising up over and over from the mind's sunless sea, of subterranean passages leading ever deeper to an encounter with . . . the Beast. In an age when high-tech imaging devices can generate actual images of the brain at work, it's intriguing to think that artists ventured to the primordial core of that process long ago. And left us maps.

Today, Paul D. MacLean, National Institute of Mental Health scientist and author of *The Triune Brain in Evolution* (Plenum, 1990), describes a similar geography. He theorizes that the human brain is "three-brains-in-one," reflecting its "ancestral relationship to reptiles, early mammals, and recent mammals." Peter C. Whybrow, director of the Neuropsychiatric Institute at UCLA, uses this model to explain what he calls "the anatomical roots of emotion." Writing in *A Mood Apart* (BasicBooks, 1997), his study of depression and other "afflictions of the self," Whybrow notes: "The behavior of human beings is more complicated than that of other animals . . . but nonetheless we share in common with many creatures such behaviors as sexual courtship, pleasure-seeking, aggression, and the defense of territory. Hence it is safe to conclude that the evolution of human behavior is, in part, reflected in the evolution and hierarchical development of other species."

Sensuous LIKE ME

How I got back in my body through my nose

Some mornings my head is like a little dog panting, whimpering, and straining at his leash. *Let's go, let's go, let's go!* My head gets me up and leads me around all day. Sometimes it's dinnertime before I remember that I have a body.

And the idea that this body can give me pleasure—well, that's a really hard one. I used to think that because I read hip French books about sexual ecstasy I had somehow escaped my Calvinist heritage—the idea that the body is shameful and only a narcissistic lazybones would pay any attention to it. No such luck. My version of Calvinist body-denial was compulsive reading, and the more I read about French people's ecstasies, which are usually pretty cerebral anyway—the more I hid out from my own body. A body that, let's face it, is plumper, paler, and more easily winded than I would prefer.

Falling in love changed things. Intimacy with a woman who was learning to accept and even love her body gave me new eyes to see (and new nerve endings to feel) my own. I started—just started—to think of my body as a means of communication with the world, not a sausage case for Great Thoughts. I wanted to go further.

It was my wife who found Nancy Conger, professor of the five senses. A slender young woman with apparently bottomless reserves of energy and optimism, she lives in an old farmhouse in western Wisconsin, plays the violin, and teaches people how to get out of debt, simplify their lives, and use their senses for entertainment and joy. She even teaches a one-night class called "Sensuous Living." Laurie and I enrolled.

A class in sensuousness. An idea not without irony, amazing that we actually have to study this stuff. Five perfectly sensible-looking adults perched on plastic chairs in a drab little classroom in Minneapolis, with Nancy presiding in a sleeveless black jumpsuit. On two tables toward the front: nasturtiums in a vase, a strip of fur, a piece of sandpaper, a twig, a violin, a seashell.

"Lick your forearm," said Nancy, "and smell yourself."

Lick my forearm and smell myself?

I looked around me. The matronly woman in the purple blouse and matching shoes was licking her forearm. So was the shy, 40ish guy with the salt-and-pepper beard, and the thin, Italian-looking young woman with the big braid. Finally, feeling uncomfortably canine, I licked myself. I sniffed ("Little, short sniffs, like perfumers use," said Nancy). Hmm. A faintly metallic aroma. Sniff, sniff. Beneath it, something breadlike.

Like a wine, I had a bouquet.

Deciphering the code of art into the language of modern science took most of two centuries. One discipline after another tried to define what feelings like pleasure were, and from where they arose, only to fall short. Darwin could sense that emotions were important in his evolutionary scheme of things, but he was limited to describing how animals and humans expressed them on the outside, using their bodies, especially faces. William James, in a famous theory published in 1884, speculated that the brain only translates various sensations originating below the neck into what we think of as, say, joy and fear. Others saw it the other way around—emotions begin in the brain and the bodily reactions follow. Without knowing what pleasure actually is, Freud could see that the inability to feel it is a kind of disease, or at least a symptom, that he traced to (you guessed it) neurotic conflict.

By then, though, many people were fed up with all the talking. The study of mind had reached that point in the movie where the gung-ho types shove aside the hostage negotiator and shout, *We're going in.*" And with scalpels drawn, they did. In 1872, Camillo Golgi, a young doctor working at a "home for incurables" in an Italian village, discovered the basic component of brain tissue, the neuron. During the 1920s, German scientist Otto Loewi, working with frog hearts, first identified neurotransmitters: chemical messengers that carry information across the gap between the neurons—the synapse—to receptors on the other side. Meanwhile, the Canadian neurosurgeon Wilder Penfield, operating on conscious patients with severe epilepsy, managed to trigger various emotions and dreamlike memories by electrically stimulating their brains. Such work gave rise to the idea that various mental functions might be "localized" in particular brain areas.

In 1954, psychologists James Olds and Peter Milner made a remarkable breakthrough—by accident. While researching the alerting mechanism in rat brains, they inadvertently placed an electrode in what they soon identified as a rat's pleasure-and-reward center: the so-called limbic system deep inside the brain. When the rats were later wired in a way that let them press a lever and jolt themselves, they did so as many as 5,000 times an hour.

This became the basis for current research on the "biology of reward." Scientists like Kenneth Blum have linked what they call reward deficiency syndrome to various human behavioral disorders: alcoholism, drug abuse, smoking, compulsive eating and gambling. Blum traces these disorders to genetically derived flaws in the neurotransmitters and receptors now associated with pleasure, including the pathways tied to the brain chemicals serotonin and dopamine, and the endorphins. Other researchers aren't so sure.

We all know by now that endorphins are the "body's own natural morphine." The discovery of endorphins in the early '70s marked the start of what some have declared the golden age of modern neuroscience. The impact was clear from the beginning to Candace B. Pert, whose work as a young scientist was crucial to the discovery. A few years earlier, she had helped identify the receptors that the endorphins fit into, as a lock fits a key, thus popping the lid of pleasure. According to

Then Nancy got us out of our chairs to wander around and "smell what doesn't seem to have a smell." I put my nose right up next to a big pad of paper on an easel. Faint wheaty aroma like my school tablets in fifth grade. All the sunshiny, chalk-dusty, gentle boredom of elementary school came back, like a tune.

A brick gave off a mysterious musty tang, charged with the past. A quarter smelled sour, a metal door bitter and somehow sad.

"Smell detours right around your thinking brain, back to the limbic system at the bottom of the brain, where memory is," Nancy told us. She also explained that smell can be hugely improved, made more subtle and precise, if you keep sniffing. "Smell dishes. Smell clothes. Smell everything," she exhorted.

I did want to keep on smelling, but we were on to a trust-and-touch experiment. We paired off (I went with the big-braid woman) and took turns blindfolding and leading each other. I put my partner's hand on a brick, a door, a seashell, a twig.

Then I put on the blindfold (it smelled powdery and lusciously feminine), and she led me. Without any visual clues to tell me what things were supposed to feel like, I met each surface with a small thrill of tactile freshness. A metal door, I discovered, was studded with sharp little grains. A twig was as rough as sandpaper, and the sandpaper itself practically made me jump out of my skin. With most of the objects, I enjoyed a few wonderful seconds of pure sensation before the thinking brain clicked in and gave the thing a name. But click in it did; and that's when the magic ended.

The evening concluded with experiments in sound (Nancy played her violin very near each of us so we could feel the vibration in our bodies) and taste (we passed around a loaf of focaccia), but as we drove home I was still hung up on the smell and touch thing.

My nose, which I had mostly used as a passive receiver of pretty large and often alarming signals (skunk crushed on an Iowa road, underarms needing immediate attention, and so on) felt amazingly discriminating, having actually sniffed the difference between a door and a quarter. My fingers still tingled with the thrill of sandpaper and brick and (blessed relief!) fur.

The part of my head that names, makes distinctions, and is vigilant against stupidities pointed out that five middle-class white folks in a certain demographic had just spent three hours rubbing, if not exactly gazing at, their navels.

The honorable side of my Calvinism (as a kid I lived on Calvin Avenue in Grand Rapids, Michigan, just down the street from Calvin College) bridled at the idea of stroking my nerve endings like some French decadent poet, while an entire society—an entire world—splits along economic fault lines.

A third part of me rejoiced: I had discovered the cleverest answer yet to television. It was the exquisite entertainment technology of a body—my body. Anyone's body. It is—or could be—an immediate rebuke and alternative to the technologies of consumerism, which coarsen, obscure, jack up, deny, extend beyond reason, and in general do numbing violence to the subtle, noble equipment for receiving the joys of life that we were all issued at birth.

Anyone can sniff a leaf or reach out to the rough bark of a tree. Anyone can listen for a little while to the world. And anyone can do it now, at the kitchen table, in the schoolroom, at the racetrack, in the hospital bed. And we can keep doing it until we believe again in the wondrous beauty of our own equipment (absolutely no amplification from Sony required).

—Jon Spayde

Pert, "it didn't matter if you were a lab rat, a First Lady, or a dope addict—everyone had the exact same mechanism in the brain for creating bliss and expanded consciousness." As she recounts in *Molecules of Emotion* (Scribner, 1997), her early success led to a career at the National Institute of Mental Health identifying other such messenger molecules, now known as neuropeptides.

Pert's interest in the natural opiates soon took her into uncharted territory—sexual orgasm. Working with Nancy Ostrowski, a scientist "who had left behind her desire to become a nun and gone on instead to become an expert on the brain mechanisms of animal sex," Pert turned her clinical gaze on the sexual cycle of hamsters. "Nancy would inject the animals with a radioactive opiate before copulation, and then, at various points in the cycle, decapitate them and remove the brains," Pert writes. "We found that blood endorphin levels increased by about 200 percent from the beginning to the end of the sex act." She doesn't say what happened to their own endorphin levels while they watched—but Dante has surely kept a log.

Modern students of pleasure and emotion have their differences. Pert, for instance, having worked so much with neuropeptides, doesn't buy the idea that emotions are localized in certain brain areas. "The hypothalamus, the limbic system, and the amygdala have all been proposed as the center of emotional expression," she writes. "Such traditional formulations view only the brain as important in emotional expressivity, and as such are, from the point of view of my own research, too

limited. From my perspective, the emotions are what link body and mind into bodymind."

This apparent reunion of body and mind is, in one sense, Pert's most radical conjecture. And yet, oddly, it's the one idea that many modern researchers do seem to share, implicitly or otherwise, to varying degrees. Most would agree that the process of creating human consciousness is vastly complex. It is also a "wet" system informed and modulated by dozens of neurochemical messengers, perhaps many more, all moving at incredible speeds. Dare we call it a calculus? Not on your life. Any analogy of the brain that summons up a computer is definitely uncool. For now.

There also seems to be a shared sense, not always stated, that some sort of grand synthesis may be, oh, 20 minutes away. In other words, it's only a matter of time before the knowledge of East and West is melded back into oneness, a theory that reunifies body and mind—and, as long as we're at it, everything else. That may be. But given that a similar impulse seems so prevalent throughout the culture, could it be that what we're really seeing is not purely science, but a case of primal yearning, even wishful thinking? A generation of brilliant scientists, their sensibilities formed in the psychedelic '60s, could now be looking back to the vision of mystical union they experienced, or at least heard about over and over again, in their youth. Perhaps they long to reach such a place, abstract though it is, for the same reason a salmon swims to the placid pool where its life began. We, like all creatures, are driven by the hope of an ultimate reward, a pleasure that has no name, a

THE NEW
Pleasure PRINCIPLE

This just in: Pain is not the route to happiness

Don't worry. Be happy.

The philosophy is simple, but living it is not, especially in our achievement-oriented society. According to Los Angeles-based therapist Stella Resnick, that's because we focus on the pain in our lives—getting through it, around it, or over it. Pleasure, the "visceral, body-felt experience of well-being," is a better path to growth and happiness, she contends in her book *The Pleasure Zone* (Conari Press, 1997). If only we knew how to feel it.

Resnick had to learn, too. Her childhood was unpleasant; her father left when she was 5, and, for 10 years, she endured beatings from her stepfather. She hung out on street corners and dated a gang leader. By age 32, she'd had two brief marriages and was involved in another stormy relationship. Although she'd built a successful San Francisco therapy practice, she was lonely and miserable. Nothing helped: not yoga, nor meditation, nor exercise, nor a vegetarian diet. "I was a very unhappy young woman," she recalls. "I'd had the best therapy from the best therapists, but even with all the work I had done on myself, something was missing."

What was missing, she discovered, was the ability to enjoy herself. At 35, after she lost her mother to cancer, she moved to a small house in the Catskill Mountains, where she lived alone for a year and, for the first time, paid attention to what felt good. At first she cried and felt sorry for herself. But by year's end, she was dancing to Vivaldi and the Temptations, and finding creativity in cooking and chopping wood.

She soon realized that most of her patients shared the same pleasure deprivation. "Our whole society diminishes the value of pleasure," she writes. "We think of it as fun and games, an escape from reality—rarely a worthwhile end in itself. Amazingly, we don't make the connection between vitality—the energy that comes from feeling good—and the willingness to take pleasure in moment-by-moment experience."

Therapy too often concentrates on pain and what the mind thinks; Resnick focused on pleasure and what the body feels. But when she first published her ideas in 1978, epithets were hurled: "narcissist," "hedonist," "icon for the Me Decade." It wasn't until research on the positive effects of pleasure and the negative effects of stress began to accumulate in the '80s that people became more receptive. "This is not about creating a society of me-first people," she says of her work. "There's no joy in hoarding all the goodies for our lonesome."

To help people understand pleasure, Resnick divides it into eight "core" categories: primal (the feeling of floating); pain relief (being touched and soothed); elemental (childlike laughter, play, movement, and voice); mental (the fun of learning); emotional (the feeling of love); sensual (the five senses, plus imagination); sexual (arousal, eroticism, orgasm); and spiritual (empathy, morality, and altruism).

Her prescription is body-based and simple. Listen to a fly buzz. Float on your back. Tell a dream. Her number-one tip for falling and staying in love is . . . breathe. Conscious breathing enhances relationships, she claims, because it allows us to let go in sweet surrender, rather than fighting or resisting ourselves or each other.

Experiencing pleasure opens the body, releasing enormous energy, says Resnick. Ironically, this flow is what scares us, causing us to tense up and shut down, because we don't know what to do with it. We can miss the healing power of great sex, for example, by wanting to release the energy as soon as we get turned on. She advises allowing the excitement to build and circulate so that "it's something you feel in your heart. And in your big toes."

Repressing one's desire for pleasure was once considered virtuous, a sign of moral superiority. But Resnick questions whether it's good to continue in that vein. "We have poor race relations, poor man-woman relations, whole segments of society that have problems with parents and institutions," she says. "Could we do better if we enjoyed our relationships more, if people knew how to encourage and inspire themselves instead of being motivated by shame, guilt, and other negative emotions?"

Resnick doesn't advocate always succumbing to immediate gratification—there's pleasure in yearning—or fear and anger, which can inform and protect us. But using negative means to pursue positive ends simply doesn't work. "The secret to success in all things—business, creativity, art, relationships, family, spirituality—is to be relaxed during challenging times," she says. "Don't hold yourself in, or brace yourself for what might go wrong." And if you don't get it at first, don't worry. Even Resnick has to remind herself to breathe.

—*Cathy Madison*

pleasure that in fact may not be ours to feel. Thus, we never conquer pleasure; pleasure conquers us. And for its own reasons, both wondrous and brutal.

None of which makes the alleged new paradigm any less real. As the poets of our day, for better or worse, the modern scientists of mind have already shaped our reality with their words and concepts. Who hasn't heard of the endorphin-driven runner's high, or traced a pang of lover's jealousy to their reptilian brain?

On *Star Trek Voyager,* a medical man of the future waves his magic wand over a crewmate emerging from a trance and declares, "His neuropeptides have returned to normal!"

You didn't have to be a Darwin to see that the news gave Captain Janeway a certain . . . pleasure.

Jeremiah Creedon is a senior editor of Utne Reader.

FAITH & HEALING

**Can prayer, faith and spirituality really improve your physical health?
A growing and surprising body of scientific evidence says they can.**

Claudia Wallis

DRAPED IN EMBROIDERED CLOTH, laden with candles, redolent with roses and incense, the altar at the Santa Fe, New Mexico, home of Eetla Soracco seems an unlikely site for cutting-edge medical research. Yet every day for 10 weeks, ending last October, Soracco spent an hour or more there as part of a controlled study in the treatment of AIDS. Her assignment: to pray for five seriously ill patients in San Francisco.

Soracco, an Estonian-born "healer" who draws on Christian, Buddhist and Native American traditions, did not know the people for whom she was praying. All she had were their photographs, first names and, in some cases, T-cell counts. Picturing a patient in her mind, she would ask for "permission to heal" and then start to explore his body in her mind: "I looked at all the organs as though it is an anatomy book. I could see where things were distressed. These areas are usually dark and murky. I go in there like a white shower and wash it all out." Soracco was instructed to spend one hour a day in prayer, but the sessions often lasted twice as long. "For that time," she says, "It's as if I know the person."

Soracco is one of 20 faith healers recruited for the study by Dr. Elisabeth Targ, clinical director of psychosocial oncology research at California Pacific Medical Center in San Francisco. In the experiment, 20 severely ill AIDS patients were randomly selected; half were prayed for, half were not. None were told to which group they had been assigned. Though Targ has not yet published her results, she describes them as sufficiently "encouraging" to warrant a larger, follow-up study with 100 AIDS patients.

Twenty years ago, no self-respecting M.D. would have dared to propose a double-blind, controlled study of something as intangible as prayer. Western medicine has spent the past 100 years trying to rid itself of remnants of mysticism. Targ's own field, psychiatry, couldn't be more hostile to spirituality: Sigmund Freud dismissed religious mysticism as "infantile helplessness" and "regression to primary narcissism." Today, while Targ's experiment is not exactly mainstream, it does exemplify a shift among doctors toward the view that there may be more to health than blood-cell counts and EKGS and more to healing than pills and scalpels.

"People, a growing number of them, want to examine the connection between healing and spirituality," says Jeffrey Levin, a gerontologist and epidemiologist at Eastern Virginia Medical School in Norfolk. To do such research, he adds, "is no longer professional death." Indeed, more and more medical schools are adding courses on holistic and alternative medicine with titles like Caring for the Soul. "The majority, 10 to 1, present the material uncritically," reports Dr. Wallace Sampson of Stanford University, who recently surveyed the offerings of every U.S. medical school.

This change in doctors' attitudes reflects a broader yearning among their patients for a more personal, more spiritual approach to health and healing. As the 20th century draws to an end, there is growing disenchantment with one of its greatest achievements: modern, high-tech medicine. Western medicine is at its best in a crisis—battling acute infection, repairing the wounds of war, replacing a broken-down kidney or heart. But increasingly, what ails America and other prosperous societies are chronic illnesses, such as high blood pressure, backaches, cardiovascular disease, arthritis, depression and acute illnesses that become chronic, such as cancer and AIDS. In most of these, stress and life-style play a part.

"Anywhere from 60% to 90% of visits to doctors are in the mind-body, stress-related realm," asserts Dr. Herbert Benson, president of the Mind/Body Medical Institute of Boston's Deaconess Hospital and Harvard Medical School. It is a triumph of medicine that so many of us live long enough to develop these chronic woes, but, notes Benson, "traditional modes of therapy—pharmaceutical and surgical—don't work well against them."

Not only do patients with chronic health problems fail to find relief in a doctor's office, but the endless high-tech scans and tests of modern medicine also often leave them feeling alienated and uncared for. Many seek solace in the offices of alternative therapists and faith healers—to the tune of $30 billion a year, by some estimates. Millions more is spent on best-selling books and tapes by New Age doctors such as Deepak Chopra, Andrew Weil and Larry Dossey, who offer an appealing blend of medicine and Eastern-flavored spirituality.

Some scientists are beginning to look seriously at just what benefits patients may derive from spirituality. To their surprise, they are finding plenty of relevant data buried in the medical literature. More than 200 studies that touch directly or indirectly on the role of religion have been ferreted out by Levin of Eastern Virginia and Dr. David Larson, a research psychiatrist formerly at the National Institutes of Health and now at the privately funded National Institute for Healthcare Research. Most of these studies offer evidence that religion is good for one's health. Some highlights:

• A 1995 study at Dartmouth-Hitchcock Medical Center found that one of the best predictors of survival among 232 heart-surgery patients was the degree to which the patients said they drew comfort and strength from religious faith. Those who did not had more than three times the death rate of those who did.

• A survey of 30 years of research on blood pressure showed that churchgoers have lower blood pressure than nonchurchgoers—5 mm lower, according to Larson, even when adjusted to account for smoking and other risk factors.

• Other studies have shown that men and women who attend church regularly have half the risk of dying from coronary-artery disease as those who rarely go to church. Again, smoking and socioeconomic factors were taken into account.

• A 1996 National Institute on Aging study of 4,000 elderly living at home in North Carolina found that those who attend religious services are less depressed and physically healthier than those who don't attend or who worship at home.

• In a study of 30 female patients recovering from hip fractures, those who regarded God as a source of strength and comfort and who attended religious services were able to walk farther upon discharge and had lower rates of depression than those who had little faith.

• Numerous studies have found lower rates of depression and anxiety-related illness among the religiously committed. Nonchurchgoers have been found to have a suicide rate four times higher than church regulars.

There are many possible explanations for such findings. Since churchgoers are more apt than nonattendees to respect religious injunctions against drinking, drug abuse, smoking and other excesses, it's possible that their better health merely reflects these healthier habits.

Some of the studies, however, took pains to correct for this possibility by making statistical adjustments for life-style differences. Larson likes to point out that in his own study the benefits of religion hold up strongly, even for those who indulge in cigarette smoking. Smokers who rated religion as being very important to them were one-seventh as likely to have an abnormal blood-pressure reading as smokers who did not value religion.

Churchgoing also offers social support—which numerous studies have shown to have a salutary effect on well-being. (Even owning a pet has been shown to improve the health of the lonesome.) The Dartmouth heart-surgery study is one of the few that attempts to tease apart the effects of social support and religious conviction. Patients were asked separate sets of questions about their participation in social groups and the comfort they drew from faith. The two factors appeared to have distinct benefits that made for a powerful combination. Those who were *both* religious and socially involved had a 14-fold advantage over those who were isolated or lacked faith.

Could it be that religious faith has some direct influence on physiology and health? Harvard's Herbert Benson is probably the most persuasive proponent of this view. Benson won international fame in 1975 with his best-selling book, *The Relaxation Response.* In it he showed that patients can successfully battle a number of stress-related ills by practicing a simple form of meditation. The act of focusing the mind on a single sound or image brings about a set of physiological changes that are the opposite of the "fight-or-flight response." With meditation, heart rate, respiration and brain waves slow down, muscles relax and the effects of epinephrine and other stress-related hormones diminish. Studies have shown that by routinely eliciting this "relaxation response," 75% of insomniacs begin to sleep normally, 35% of infertile women become pregnant and 34% of chronic-pain sufferers reduce their use of painkilling drugs.

In his latest book, *Timeless Healing* (Scribner; $24), Benson moves beyond the purely pragmatic use of meditation into the realm of spirituality. He ventures to say humans are actually engineered for religious faith. Benson bases this contention on his work with a subgroup of patients who report that they sense a closeness to God while meditating. In a five-year study of patients using meditation to battle chronic illnesses, Benson found that those who claim to feel the intimate presence of a higher power had better health and more rapid recoveries.

"Our genetic blueprint has made believing in an Infinite Absolute part of our nature," writes Benson. Evolution has so equipped us, he believes, in order to offset our uniquely human ability to ponder our own mortality: "To counter this fundamental angst, we are also wired for God."

In Benson's view, prayer operates along the same biochemical pathways as the relaxation response. In other words, praying affects epinephrine and other corticosteroid messengers or "stress hormones," leading to lower blood pressure, more relaxed heart rate and respiration and other benefits.

Recent research demonstrates that these stress hormones also have a direct impact on the body's immunological defenses against disease. "Anything involved with meditation and controlling the state of mind that alters hormone activity has the potential to have an impact on the immune system," says David Felten, chairman of the Department of Neurobiology at the University of Rochester.

It is probably no coincidence that the relaxation response and religious experience share headquarters in the brain. Studies show that the relaxation response is controlled by the amygdala, a small, almond-shaped structure in the brain that together with the hippocampus and hypothalamus makes up the limbic system. The limbic system, which is found in all primates, plays a key role in emotions, sexual pleasure, deep-felt memo-

ries and, it seems, spirituality. When either the amygdala or the hippocampus is electrically stimulated during surgery, some patients have visions of angels and devils. Patients whose limbic systems are chronically stimulated by drug abuse or a tumor often become religious fanatics. "The ability to have religious experiences has a neuroanatomical basis," concludes Rhawn Joseph, a neuroscientist at the Palo Alto VA Medical Center in California.

Many researchers believe these same neuronal and hormonal pathways are the basis for the renowned and powerful "placebo effect." Decades of research show that if a patient truly believes a therapy is useful—even if it is a sugar pill or snake oil—that belief has the power to heal. In one classic 1950 study, for instance, pregnant women suffering from severe morning sickness were given syrup of ipecac, which induces vomiting, and told it was a powerful new cure for nausea. Amazingly, the women ceased vomiting. "Most of the history of medicine is the history of the placebo effect," observes Benson in *Timeless Healing.*

Though Benson devotes much of his book to documenting the power of the placebo effect—which he prefers to call "remembered wellness"—he has come to believe the benefits of religious faith are even greater. "Faith in the medical treatment," he writes, "[is] wonderfully therapeutic, successful in treating 60% to 90% of the most common medical problems. But if you so believe, faith in an invincible and infallible force carries even more healing power ... It is a supremely potent belief."

Do the faithful actually have God on their side? Are their prayers answered? Benson doesn't say. But a true scientist, insists Jeffrey Levin, cannot dismiss this possibility: "I can't directly study that, but as an honest scholar, I can't rule it out."

A handful of scientists have attempted to study the possibility that praying works through some supernatural factor. One of the most cited examples is a 1988 study by cardiologist Randolph Byrd at San Francisco General Hospital. Byrd took 393 patients in the coronary-care unit and randomly assigned half to be prayed for by born-again Christians. To eliminate the placebo effect, the patients were not told of the experiment. Remarkably, Byrd found that the control group was five times as likely to need antibiotics and three times as likely to develop complications as those who were prayed for.

Byrd's experiment has never been replicated and has come under some criticism for design flaws. A more recent study of intercessory prayer with alcoholics found no benefit, while Elisabeth Targ's study of AIDS patients is still too small to produce significant results.

Science may never be able to pin down the benefits of spirituality. Attempts by Benson and others to do so are like "trying to nail Jell-O to the wall," complains William Jarvis, a public-health professor at California's Loma Linda University and the president of the National Council Against Health Fraud. But it may not be necessary to understand how prayer works to put it to use for patients. "We often know something works before we know why," observes Santa Fe internist Larry Dossey, the author of the 1993 best seller *Healing Words*.

A TIME/CNN poll of 1,004 Americans conducted last week by Yankelovich Partners found that 82% believed in the healing power of prayer and 64% thought doctors should pray with those patients who request it. Yet even today few doctors are comfortable with that role. "We physicians are culturally insensitive about the role of religion," says David Larson, noting that fewer than two-thirds of doctors say they believe in God. "It is very important to many of our patients and not important to lots of doctors."

Larson would like physicians to be trained to ask a few simple questions of their seriously or chronically ill patients: Is religion important to you? Is it important in how you cope with your illness? If the answers are yes, doctors might ask whether the patient would like to discuss his or her faith with the hospital chaplain or another member of the clergy. "You can be an atheist and say this," Larson insists. Not doing so, he argues, is a disservice to the patient.

Even skeptics such as Jarvis believe meditation and prayer are part of "good patient management." But he worries, as do many doctors, that patients may become "so convinced of the power of mind over body that they may decide to rely on that, instead of doing the hard things, like chemotherapy."

In the long run, it may be that most secular of forces—economics—that pushes doctors to become more sensitive to the spiritual needs of their patients. Increasingly, American medicine is a business, run by large HMOs and managed-care groups with a keen eye on the bottom line. Medical businessmen are more likely than are scientifically trained doctors to view prayer and spirituality as low-cost treatments that clients say they want. "The combination of these forces—consumer demand and the economic collapse of medicine—are very powerful influences that are making medicine suddenly open to this direction," observes Andrew Weil, a Harvard-trained doctor and author of *Spontaneous Healing*.

Cynics point out that there is an even more practical reason for doctors to embrace spirituality even if they don't believe. The high cost of malpractice insurance gives physicians an incentive to attend to their patients' spiritual needs—and, if necessary, get on their knees and pray with them. Not only might it help restore their image as infallible caregivers, but if something does go wrong, patients who associate their doctors with a higher power might be less likely to sue.

—*Reported by Jeanne McDowell/ Los Angeles, Alice Park/ New York and Lisa H. Towle/Raleigh*

Unit Selections

Key Points to Consider

❖ Individuals face challenges at every phase of development. What are some of the stages of development? What challenges are typical of each stage, as mentioned in this unit? What are other challenges that have not been mentioned? What stage do you believe is most demanding? Most important? Why?

❖ What are the various factors that can influence fetal development? If drugs and other addictive substances have detrimental effects on the fetus, should we hold addicted parents responsible for the care and treatment of their addicted and possibly deformed or developmentally delayed infants? Why or why not? If you answered "yes," what should we do? For example, should we imprison them for neglect? What other factors besides drugs and alcohol influence prenatal life? Are there times when a child can overcome even the most traumatic and debilitating experiences? How so?

❖ According to Judith Harris, are parents necessary to child development? What other individuals do you think can have an impact on a child's development? What role does Harris say genes play in development? What role does the environment play? Do they play an equal role? An interactive role?

❖ Why do you think there has been an epidemic of violence in our high schools? Where is this violence occurring? Does it happen only in poverty-stricken, urban schools? What can parents do to protect their teens from this violence? How can parents develop caring children who will not commit such violence?

❖ What myths do we hold about old age? What truth is there to these myths? Can we live longer? Do people want to live longer? Should we live longer? What must we do to live longer lives?

❖ What is a near-death experience? Do you believe that such experiences exist? Would you like to experience this phenomenon? Why or why not? How can we study such experiences if the person is unconscious?

DUSHKIN ONLINE Links www.dushkin.com/online/

These sites are annotated on pages 4 and 5.

At each stage of development from infancy to old age, humans are faced with new challenges. The infant has the rudimentary sensory apparati for seeing, hearing, and touching but needs to begin coordinating stimuli into meaningful information. For example, early in life the baby begins to recognize familiar and unfamiliar people and usually becomes attached to the primary caregivers. In toddlerhood, the same child must master the difficult skills of walking, talking, and toilet training. This energetic, mobile, and sociable child also needs to learn the boundaries set on his or her behavior by others. As the child matures, not only do physical changes continue to take place, but the family composition may change when siblings are added, parents divorce, or mother and father work outside the home. Playmates become more influential, and others in the community, such as day-care workers and teachers, have an increasing influence on the child. The child eventually may spend more time at school than at home. The demands in this new environment require that the child sit still, pay attention, learn, and cooperate with others for long periods of time—behaviors perhaps never before extensively demanded of him or her.

In adolescence the body changes noticeably. Peers may pressure the individual to indulge in new behaviors such as using illegal drugs or engaging in premarital sex. Some older teenagers are said to be faced with an identity crisis when they must choose among career, education, and marriage. The pressures of work and family life exact a toll on less mature youths, while others are satisfied with the workplace and home.

Adulthood and middle age may bring contentment or turmoil as individuals face career peaks, empty nests, advancing age, and perhaps the death of loved ones, such as parents. Again, some individuals cope more effectively with these events than do others.

At any step in the developmental sequence, unexpected stressors challenge individuals. These stressors include major illnesses, accidents, natural disasters, economic recessions, and family or personal crises. It is important to remember, however, that an event need not be negative to be stressful. Any major life change may cause stress. As welcome as weddings, new babies, and job promotions may be, they, too, can be stressful because of the changes in daily life that they require. Each challenge and each change must be met and adjusted to if the individual is going to move successfully to the next stage of development. Some individuals continue along their paths unscathed; others do not fare so well.

This unit of the book examines major problems in various stages of life from childhood to old age. The first article commences our chronological look at issues of development at various stages of life. In

"The Seven Stages of Man," Costanza Villalba offers an overview of what can go right or wrong for males in various eras of life.

We next look at several stages in more detail. In "Fetal Psychology," Janet Hopson reveals why fetal life is so important and so delicate. Drugs, alcohol, and other substances can adversely affect the fetus. As the article suggests, problems for our development exist even before birth.

Then, in "Clipped Wings," the results of a report on the deleterious effects of drugs, alcohol, and other substances on the fetus are shared with the reader.

We next turn to childhood. Judith Harris recently authored a controversial book on whether children are influenced most by genetics or by the experiences that their parents provide for them. In excerpts from the book, Harris suggests that genes are of utmost importance in child development. In other words, she insists that criminals are born, not made. Harris does suggest, however, that the environment pressures us to express what our genes have given us.

We move next to adolescence. No American who lived through the last few years can have escaped hearing about the violent shootings in America's high schools. Barbara Kantrowitz and Pat Wingert examine this timely issue in "How Well Do You Know Your Kids?" They suggest that caring parents will be involved enough with their teens so that the teens will not become violent.

There are children who, despite early traumas, remain unscathed, unaffected by early ordeals. In "Invincible Kids" these types of children are examined.

Old age is the central issue in "Live to 100? No Thanks." Do people seek the fountain of youth? How long can we really live? What factors induce people to live to older ages? Do people really want to live to 100? The answer is a resounding "no." In a survey of elderly, results demonstrated that people prefer high-quality life to longevity.

The ultimate developmental stage is death. Death is a topic that both fascinates and frightens most of us. In "Is There Life after Death?" Brendan Koerner examines research on the near-death experiences of individuals who have been snatched back from the brink of death. He explores both the psychology and physiology behind these experiences.

The Seven Stages of Man

Men are often portrayed as big boys, differing from their younger selves only in the sums of money they spend on their toys. Indeed, because men can reproduce well into old age, and do not experience cyclical hormonal changes, their health is regarded as fairly static. But medical experts are learning that between the boy and the man stand a variety of genetic, biological and social changes. Understanding these factors may help men prepare for the stages that await them.

CONSTANZA VILLALBA

INFANCY

At the precise moment when a single sperm wiggles its way into an awaiting egg, the sex of the developing baby is defined. If that sperm carries a portly X chromosome, the egg turned embryo will give rise to a baby girl. If that sperm carries a diminutive Y chromosome, the baby will be a boy. With the blueprint for the male architecture, however, come several, often unfortunate genetic predispositions: hemophilia and Duchenne's Muscular Dystrophy afflict boys and men almost exclusively, while boys are more likely than girls to suffer from Fragile-X Syndrome, the nation's leading cause of mental retardation.

But being born a boy also comes with perks. Baby boys are an animated lot who display a marked curiosity about the world. Compared with girls, they are more alert and emotionally interactive with caretakers. They begin suppressing their emotions later in life, suggesting that masculine stoicism is learned, not hard-wired.

BOYHOOD

Once in school, boys tend to excel at mathematics and other tasks controlled by the brain's right side, or hemisphere. These natural aptitudes may be strengthened by the spike of testosterone that infant boys experience before and right after birth. But the biological machinery that gives boys an advantage in math and spatial tasks may predispose them to learning and developmental disorders: that is, in boys the left brain hemisphere, which controls language and facilitates socialization, may be underdeveloped.

On the playground, school-age boys resist playing with girls. They enjoy rough-and-tumble play and have inherent skill at games involving hit-the-target motor and navigational challenges. This time spent among other boys relays lessons—not all of them healthy—about what it means to be male. Chase and target games, for example, may be an evolutionary throwback to when men had to be good hunters.

ADOLESCENCE

Testosterone's effects on boys' development become most obvious during adolescence. As their soprano voices morph into tenors, boys squawk. Muscles begin replacing baby fat. Male hormones are also responsible for teen-age boys' novel interest in sex. Unfortunately, this interest is not always coupled with mature attitudes about safety and promiscuity. Data show that adolescents account for one-quarter of the 12 million cases of sexually transmitted diseases reported each year. The good news is that teen-agers may be getting the message. Gonorrhea among adolescent boys has been decreasing over the last seven years.

Reported cases of gonorrhea, per 100,000, for boys ages 15 to 19.

But boys' interest in girls is not purely sexual. Compared with previous generations, teen-age boys are more likely to have Platonic relationships with girls and to agree with survey statements like "Boys and girls should both be allowed to express feelings."

The hormones that pique boys' interest in sex goad them toward risky and aggressive behavior. At the same time, parental and societal expectations about masculinity may prevent them from expressing confusion or fear about the changes befalling them. These factors make teen-age boys 2.5 times more likely than girls to die of an unintentional injury and 5 times more likely to die from a homicide or suicide.

YOUNG ADULTHOOD

Men are physically in their prime. This period is characterized by a drive for achievement and by the realization that the foolhardiness of youth has unavoidable consequences. Fatherhood gives men the opportunity to redefine masculinity in a healthful way for themselves and their children.

Bad habits, like smoking, become less appealing but more difficult to shake; more than 80 percent of adults who ever smoked began doing so before age 18. Still, men are smoking less than they did and the incidence of lung cancer in men is falling. Although the incidence of smoking—28.8 percent for black men, 27.1 percent for white men—is similar, black men are at much higher risk of lung cancer than white men.

H.I.V. infection, the leading cause of death among men between ages 25 and 44, is often contracted during adolescence, when boys are experimenting with sex and are oblivious to the risks of infection. But with advances in drug therapies, the incidence of H.I.V.-related deaths has declined over the last four years.

MIDDLE AGE

Beginning in their early 40's, men experience a decline in testosterone of 1 percent each year. These reductions coincide with increased depressive symptoms, including anxiety and sexual dissatisfaction. While some doctors consider this stage tantamount to "male menopause," others argue that the hormonal changes are too subtle to account for these symptoms. They note, too, that impotence and other conditions associated with middle age can be caused by ailments that tend to strike men in this age group, like diabetes.

Percentage of men who smoke, by age group

The risk of heart disease, hypertension and diabetes is exacerbated by obesity, and middle age is when men are likely to be overweight. They lose 3 percent to 5 percent of their muscle mass for every decade after age 25. Reduced muscle mass and physical activity conspire to decrease men's resting metabolic rate. As men age, then, they burn less energy while resting and can gain weight even without changing their eating habits. And they do gain—2 to 3 pounds for every year over age 30.

Heart disease continues to be the leading cause of death for men in the United States. But the rate of heart disease-related deaths among men has decreased more than 50 percent since 1950; those who die of heart disease are dying later in life.

EARLY OLD AGE

Because men continue to produce testosterone throughout life, they are protected from—though not immune to—conditions like Alzheimer's Disease and osteoporosis. Their larger bone size also helps protect against this bone-weakening illness. Men can further maintain their mental acuity by engaging in intellectual activities. They can strengthen their bones and stem bone loss by undertaking weight-bearing exercise. The continued production of testosterone, however, can also adversely affect men. Testosterone aggravates hair loss and stimulates growth of the prostate gland. Noncancerous enlargement of the prostate occurs in more than half of men in their 60's and up to 90 percent of men in their 70's and 80's. At the same time, 80 percent of all prostate cancer cases occur in men age 65 and over.

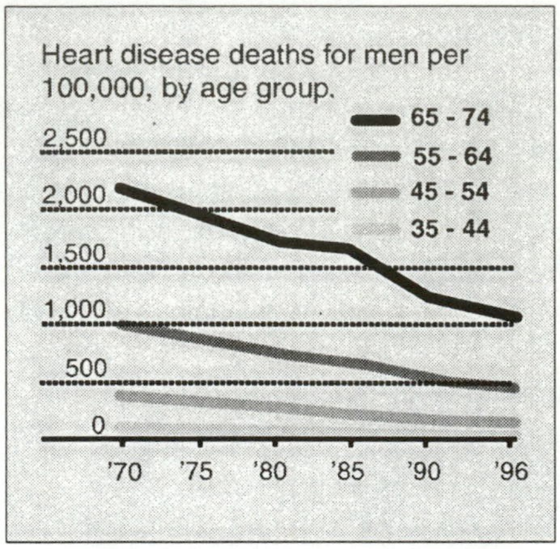

Heart disease deaths for men per 100,000, by age group.

2,500
2,000
1,500
1,000
500
0

'70   '75   '80   '85   '90   '96

65 - 74
55 - 64
45 - 54
35 - 44

LATER OLD AGE

Studies indicate that men are less likely than women to have difficulty maintaining normal routines, like bathing, dressing and using the toilet, as they age.

Still, the trend among the elderly in general is that they become less active, and so need fewer calories. Their appetites diminish, yet their nutritional needs increase because their bodies have lost the ability to synthesize and absorb important vitamins and nutrients. Their skin, for example, no longer easily synthesizes vitamin D when exposed to the sun. The benefits of avoiding potentially harmful foods, such as those high in cholesterol, lessen with age. Maintaining weight and making sure the right nutrients are present in the diet become more important.

FETAL PSYCHOLOGY

Behaviorally speaking, there's little difference between a newborn baby and a 32-week-old fetus. A new wave of research suggests that the fetus can feel, dream, even enjoy *The Cat in the Hat*. The abortion debate may never be the same.

By Janet L. Hopson

The scene never fails to give goose bumps: the baby, just seconds old and still dewy from the womb, is lifted into the arms of its exhausted but blissful parents. They gaze adoringly as their new child stretches and squirms, scrunches its mouth and opens its eyes. To anyone watching this tender vignette, the message is unmistakable. Birth is the beginning of it all, ground zero, the moment from which the clock starts ticking. Not so, declares Janet DiPietro. Birth may be a grand occasion, says the Johns Hopkins University psychologist, but "it is a trivial event in development. Nothing neurologically interesting happens."

Armed with highly sensitive and sophisticated monitoring gear, DiPietro and other researchers today are discovering that the real action starts weeks earlier. At 32 weeks of gestation—two months before a baby is considered fully prepared for the world, or "at term"—a fetus is behaving almost exactly as a newborn. And it continues to do so for the next 12 weeks.

As if overturning the common conception of infancy weren't enough, scientists are creating a startling new picture of intelligent life in the womb. Among the revelations:

• By nine weeks, a developing fetus can hiccup and react to loud noises. By the end of the second trimester it can hear.

• Just as adults do, the fetus experiences the rapid eye movement (REM) sleep of dreams.

• The fetus savors its mother's meals, first picking up the food tastes of a culture in the womb.

A fetus spends hours in the rapid eye movement sleep of dreams.

• Among other mental feats, the fetus can distinguish between the voice of Mom and that of a stranger, and respond to a familiar story read to it.

• Even a premature baby is aware, feels, responds, and adapts to its environment.

• Just because the fetus is responsive to certain stimuli doesn't mean that it should be the target of efforts to enhance development. Sensory stimulation of the fetus can in fact lead to bizarre patterns of adaptation later on.

The roots of human behavior, researchers now know, begin to develop early—just weeks after conception, in fact. Well before a woman typically knows she is pregnant, her embryo's brain has already begun to bulge. By five weeks, the organ that looks like a lumpy inchworm has already embarked on the most spectacular feat of human development: the creation of the deeply creased and convoluted cerebral cortex, the part of the brain that will eventually allow the growing person to move, think, speak, plan, and create in a human way.

At nine weeks, the embryo's ballooning brain allows it to bend its body, hiccup, and react to loud sounds. At week ten, it moves its arms, "breathes" amniotic fluid in and out, opens its jaw, and stretches. Before the first trimester is over, it yawns, sucks, and swallows as well as feels and smells. By the end of the second trimester, it can hear; toward the end of pregnancy, it can see.

FETAL ALERTNESS

Scientists who follow the fetus' daily life find that it spends most of its time not exercising these new abilities but sleeping. At 32 weeks, it drowses 90 to 95% of the day. Some of these hours are spent in deep sleep, some in REM sleep, and some in an indeterminate state, a product of the fetus' immature brain that is different from sleep in a baby, child, or adult. During REM sleep, the fetus' eyes move back and forth just as an adult's eyes do, and many researchers believe that it is dreaming. DiPietro speculates that fetuses dream about what they know—the sensations they feel in the womb.

Closer to birth, the fetus sleeps 85 to 90% of the time, the same as a newborn. Between its frequent naps, the fetus seems to have "something like an awake alert period," according to developmental psychologist William Fifer, Ph.D., who with his Columbia University colleagues is monitoring these sleep and wakefulness cycles in order to identify patterns of normal and abnormal brain development, including potential predictors of sudden infant death syndrome. Says Fifer, "We are, in effect, asking the fetus: 'Are you paying attention? Is your nervous system behaving in the appropriate way?' "

FETAL MOVEMENT

Awake or asleep, the human fetus moves 50 times or more each hour, flexing and extending its body, moving its head, face, and limbs and exploring its warm wet compartment by touch. Heidelise Als, Ph.D., a developmental psychologist at Harvard Medical School, is fascinated by the amount of tactile stimulation a fetus gives itself. "It touches a hand to the face, one hand to the other hand, clasps its feet, touches its foot to its leg, its hand to its umbilical cord," she reports.

Als believes there is a mismatch between the environment given to preemies in hospitals and the environment they would have had in the womb. She has been working for years to change the care given to preemies so that they can curl up, bring their knees together, and touch things with their hands as they would have for weeks in the womb.

Along with such common movements, DiPietro has also noted some odder fetal activities, including "licking the uterine wall and literally walking around the womb by pushing off with its feet." Laterborns may have more room in the womb for such maneuvers than first babies. After the initial pregnancy, a woman's uterus is bigger and the umbilical cord longer, allowing more freedom of movement. "Second and subsequent children may develop more motor experience in utero and so may become more active infants," DiPietro speculates.

Fetuses react sharply to their mother's actions. "When we're watching the fetus on ultrasound and the mother starts to laugh, we can see the fetus, floating upside down in the womb, bounce up and down on its head, bum-bum-bum, like it's bouncing on a trampoline," says DiPietro. "When mothers watch this on the screen, they laugh harder, and the fetus goes up and down even faster. We've wondered whether this is why people grow up liking roller coasters."

FETAL TASTE

Why people grow up liking hot chilies or spicy curries may also have something to do with the fetal environment. By 13 to 15 weeks a fetus' taste buds already look like a mature adult's, and doctors know that the amniotic fluid that surrounds it can smell strongly of curry, cumin,

By 15 weeks, a fetus has an adult's taste buds and may be able to savor its mother's meals.

What's the Impact on Abortion?

Though research in fetal psychology focuses on the last trimester, when most abortions are illegal, the thought of a fetus dreaming, listening and responding to its mother's voice is sure to add new complexity to the debate. The new findings undoubtedly will strengthen the convictions of right-to-lifers—and they may shake the certainty of pro-choice proponents who believe that mental life begins at birth.

Many of the scientists engaged in studying the fetus, however, remain detached from the abortion controversy, insisting that their work is completely irrelevant to the debate.

"I don't think that fetal research informs the issue at all," contends psychologist Janet DiPietro of Johns Hopkins University. "The essence of the abortion debate is: When does life begin? Some people believe it begins at conception, the other extreme believes that it begins after the baby is born, and there's a group in the middle that believes it begins at around 24 or 25 weeks, when a fetus can live outside of the womb, though it needs a lot of help to do so.

"Up to about 25 weeks, whether or not it's sucking its thumb or has personality or all that, the fetus cannot survive outside of its mother. So is that life, or not? That is a moral, ethical, and religious question, not one for science. Things can behave and not be alive. Right-to-lifers may say that this research proves that a fetus is alive, but it does not. It cannot."

"Fetal research only changes the abortion debate for people who think that life starts at some magical point," maintains Heidelise Als, a psychologist at Harvard University. "If you believe that life begins at conception, then you don't need the proof of fetal behavior." For others, however, abortion is a very complex issue and involves far more than whether research shows that a fetus hiccups. "Your circumstances and personal beliefs have much more impact on the decision," she observes.

Like DiPietro, Als realizes that "people may use this research as an emotional way to draw people to the pro-life side, but it should not be used by belligerent activists." Instead, she believes, it should be applied to helping mothers have the healthiest pregnancy possible and preparing them to best parent their child. Columbia University psychologist William Fifer, Ph.D., agrees. "The research is much more relevant for issues regarding viable fetuses—preemies."

Simply put, say the three, their work is intended to help the babies that live—not to decide whether fetuses should.—*Camille Chatterjee*

---

garlic, onion and other essences from a mother's diet. Whether fetuses can taste these flavors isn't yet known, but scientists have found that a 33-week-old preemie will suck harder on a sweetened nipple than on a plain rubber one.

"During the last trimester, the fetus is swallowing up to a liter a day" of amniotic fluid, notes Julie Mennella, Ph.D., a biopsychologist at the Monell Chemical Senses Center in Philadelphia. She thinks the fluid may act as a "flavor bridge" to breast milk, which also carries food flavors from the mother's diet.

FETAL HEARING

Whether or not a fetus can taste, there's little question that it can hear. A very premature baby entering the world at 24 to 25 weeks responds to the sounds around it, observes Als, so its auditory apparatus must already have been functioning in the womb. Many pregnant women report a fetal jerk or sudden kick just after a door slams or a car backfires.

Even without such intrusions, the womb is not a silent place. Researchers who have inserted a hydrophone into the uterus of a pregnant woman have picked up a noise level "akin to the background noise in an apartment," according to DiPietro. Sounds include the whooshing of blood in the mother's vessels, the gurgling and rumbling of her stomach and intestines, as well as the tones of her voice filtered through tissues, bones, and fluid, and the voices of other people coming through the amniotic wall. Fifer has found that fetal heart rate slows when the mother is speaking, suggesting that the fetus not only hears and recognizes the sound, but is calmed by it.

FETAL VISION

Vision is the last sense to develop. A very premature infant can see light and shape; researchers presume that a fetus has the same ability. Just as the womb isn't completely quiet, it isn't utterly dark, either. Says Fifer: "There may be just enough visual stimulation filtered through the mother's tissues that a fetus can respond when the mother is in bright light," such as when she is sunbathing.

Japanese scientists have even reported a distinct fetal reaction to flashes of light shined on the mother's belly. However, other researchers warn that exposing fetuses (or premature infants) to bright light before they are ready can be dangerous. In fact, Harvard's Als believes that retinal damage in premature infants, which has long been ascribed to high concentrations of oxygen, may actually be due to overexposure to light at the wrong time in development.

A six-month fetus, born about 14 weeks too early, has a brain that is neither prepared for nor expecting signals from the eyes to be transmitted into the brain's visual cortex, and from there into the executive-branch frontal lobes, where information is integrated. When the fetus

> A fetus prefers hearing Mom's voice over a stranger's—speaking in her native, not a foreign tongue—and being read aloud familiar tales rather than new stories.

is forced to see too much too soon, says Als, the accelerated stimulation may lead to aberrations of brain development.

FETAL LEARNING

Along with the ability to feel, see, and hear comes the capacity to learn and remember. These activities can be rudimentary, automatic, even biochemical. For example, a fetus, after an initial reaction of alarm, eventually stops responding to a repeated loud noise. The fetus displays the same kind of primitive learning, known as habituation, in response to its mother's voice, Fifer has found.

But the fetus has shown itself capable of far more. In the 1980s, psychology professor Anthony James DeCasper, Ph.D., and colleagues at the University of North Carolina at Greensboro, devised a feeding contraption that allows a baby to suck faster to hear one set of sounds through headphones and to suck slower to hear a different set. With this technique, DeCasper discovered that within hours of birth, a baby already prefers its mother's voice to a stranger's, suggesting it must have learned and remembered the voice, albeit not necessarily consciously, from its last months in the womb. More recently, he's found that a newborn prefers a story read to it repeatedly in the womb—in this case, *The Cat in the Hat*—over a new story introduced soon after birth.

DeCasper and others have uncovered more mental feats. Newborns can not only distinguish their mother from a stranger speaking, but would rather hear Mom's voice, especially the way it sounds filtered through amniotic fluid rather than through air. They're xenophobes, too: they prefer to hear Mom speaking in her native language than to hear her or someone else speaking in a foreign tongue.

By monitoring changes in fetal heart rate, psychologist Jean-Pierre Lecanuet, Ph.D., and his colleagues in Paris have found that fetuses can even tell strangers' voices apart. They also seem to like certain stories more than others. The fetal heartbeat will slow down when a familiar French fairy tale such as *"La Poulette"* ("The Chick") or *"Le Petit Crapaud"* ("The Little Toad"), is read near the mother's belly. When the same reader delivers another unfamiliar story, the fetal heartbeat stays steady.

The fetus is likely responding to the cadence of voices and stories, not their actual words, observes Fifer, but the conclusion is the same: the fetus can listen, learn, and remember at some level, and, as with most babies

and children, it likes the comfort and reassurance of the familiar.

FETAL PERSONALITY

It's no secret that babies are born with distinct differences and patterns of activity that suggest individual temperament. Just when and how the behavioral traits originate in the womb is now the subject of intense scrutiny.

In the first formal study of fetal temperament in 1996, DiPietro and her colleagues recorded the heart rate and movements of 31 fetuses six times before birth and compared them to readings taken twice after birth. (They've since extended their study to include 100 more fetuses.) Their findings: fetuses that are very active in the womb tend to be more irritable infants. Those with irregular sleep/wake patterns in the womb sleep more poorly as young infants. And fetuses with high heart rates become unpredictable, inactive babies.

"Behavior doesn't begin at birth," declares DiPietro. "It begins before and develops in predictable ways." One of the most important influences on development is the fetal environment. As Harvard's Als observes, "The fetus gets an enormous amount of 'hormonal bathing' through the mother, so its chronobiological rhythms are influenced by the mother's sleep/wake cycles, her eating patterns, her movements."

The hormones a mother puts out in response to stress also appear critical. DiPietro finds that highly pressured mothers-to-be tend to have more active fetuses—and more irritable infants. "The most stressed are working pregnant women," says DiPietro. "These days, women tend to work up to the day they deliver, even though the implications for pregnancy aren't entirely clear yet. That's our cultural norm, but I think it's insane."

Als agrees that working can be an enormous stress, but emphasizes that pregnancy hormones help to buffer both mother and fetus. Individual reactions to stress also matter. "The pregnant woman who chooses to work is a different woman already from the one who chooses not to work," she explains.

She's also different from the woman who has no choice but to work. DiPietro's studies show that the fetuses of poor women are distinct neurobehaviorally—less active, with a less variable heart rate—from the fetuses of middle-class women. Yet "poor women rate themselves as less stressed than do working middle-class women," she notes. DiPietro suspects that inadequate nutrition and exposure to pollutants may significantly affect the fetuses of poor women.

Stress, diet, and toxins may combine to have a harmful effect on intelligence. A recent study by biostatistician Bernie Devlin, Ph.D., of the University of Pittsburgh, suggests that genes may have less impact on IQ than previously thought and that the environment of the womb may account for much more. "Our old notion of nature influencing the fetus before birth and nurture after birth needs an update," DiPietro insists. "There is an antenatal environment, too, that is provided by the mother."

Parents-to-be who want to further their unborn child's mental development should start by assuring that the antenatal environment is well-nourished, low-stress, drug-free. Various authors and "experts" also have suggested poking the fetus at regular intervals, speaking to it through a paper tube or "pregaphone," piping in classical music, even flashing lights at the mother's abdomen.

Does such stimulation work? More importantly: Is it safe? Some who use these methods swear their children are smarter, more verbally and musically inclined, more physically coordinated and socially adept than average. Scientists, however, are skeptical.

"There has been no defended research anywhere that shows any enduring effect from these stimulations," asserts Fifer. "Since no one can even say for certain when a fetus is awake, poking them or sticking speakers on the mother's abdomen may be changing their natural sleep patterns. No one would consider poking or prodding a newborn baby in her bassinet or putting a speaker next to her ear, so why would you do such a thing with a fetus?"

Als is more emphatic: "My bet is that poking, shaking, or otherwise deliberately stimulating the fetus might alter its developmental sequence, and anything that affects the development of the brain comes at a cost."

Gently talking to the fetus, however, seems to pose little risk. Fifer suggests that this kind of activity may help parents as much as the fetus. "Thinking about your fetus, talking to it, having your spouse talk to it, will all help prepare you for this new creature that's going to jump into your life and turn it upside down," he says—once it finally makes its anti-climactic entrance.

CLIPPED WINGS

The Fullest Look Yet at How Prenatal Exposure to Drugs, Alcohol, and Nicotine Hobbles Children's Learning

LUCILE F. NEWMAN AND STEPHEN L. BUKA

Lucile F. Newman is a professor of community health and anthropology at Brown University and the director of the Preventable Causes of Learning Impairment Project. Stephen L. Buka is an epidemiologist and instructor at the Harvard Medical School and School of Public Health.

SOME FORTY thousand children a year are born with learning impairments related to their mother's alcohol use. Drug abuse during pregnancy affects 11 percent of newborns each year—more than 425,000 infants in 1988. Some 260,000 children each year are born at below normal weights—often because they were prenatally exposed to nicotine, alcohol, or illegal drugs.

What learning problems are being visited upon these children? The existing evidence has heretofore been scattered in many different fields of research—in pediatric medicine, epidemiology, public health, child development, and drug and alcohol abuse. Neither educators, health professionals, nor policy makers could go to one single place to receive a full picture of how widespread or severe were these preventable causes of learning impairment.

In our report for the Education Commission of the States, excerpts of which follow, we combed these various fields to collect and synthesize the major studies that relate prenatal exposure to nicotine, alcohol, and illegal drugs* with various indexes of students' school performance.

The state of current research in this area is not always as full and satisfying as we would wish. Most of what exists is statistical and epidemiological data, which document the frequency of certain high-risk behaviors and correlate those behaviors to student performance. Such

*The full report for the ECS also addressed the effect on children's learning of fetal malnutrition, pre- and postnatal exposure to lead, and child abuse and neglect.

data are very interesting and useful, as they allow teachers and policy makers to calculate the probability that a student with a certain family history will experience school failure. But such data often cannot control for the effects of other risk factors, many of which tend to cluster in similar populations. In other words, the same mother who drinks during her pregnancy may also use drugs, suffer from malnutrition, be uneducated, a teenager, or poor—all factors that might ultimately affect her child's school performance. An epidemiological study generally can't tell you how much of a child's poor school performance is due exclusively to a single risk factor.

Moreover, the cumulative damage wrought by several different postnatal exposures may be greater than the damage caused by a single one operating in isolation. And many of the learning problems that are caused by prenatal exposure to drugs can be compounded by such social factors as poverty and parental disinterest and, conversely, overcome if the child lives in a high-quality postnatal environment.

All of these facts make it difficult to isolate and interpret the level and character of the damage that is caused by a single factor. Further, until recently, there was little interest among researchers in the effects of prenatal alcohol exposure because there was little awareness that it was affecting a substantial number of children. The large cohort of children affected by crack is just now entering the schools, so research on their school performance hasn't been extensive.

What does clearly emerge from the collected data is that our classrooms now include many students whose ability to pay attention, sit still, or fully develop their visual, auditory, and language skills was impaired even before they walked through our schoolhouse doors. On the brighter side, the evidence that many of these impairments can be overcome by improved environmental conditions suggests that postnatal treatment is possible;

From *American Educator*, Spring 1991, pp. 27–33, 42. Adapted from *Every Child a Learner: Reducing Risks of Learning Impairment during Pregnancy and Infancy*, supported by the Exxon Educational Foundation. Published by the Education Commission of the States. Reprinted by permission.

promising experiments in treatment are, in fact, under way and are outlined at the end of this article.

1. Low Birthweight

The collection of graphs begins with a set on low birthweight, which is strongly associated with lowered I.Q. and poor school performance. While low birth-

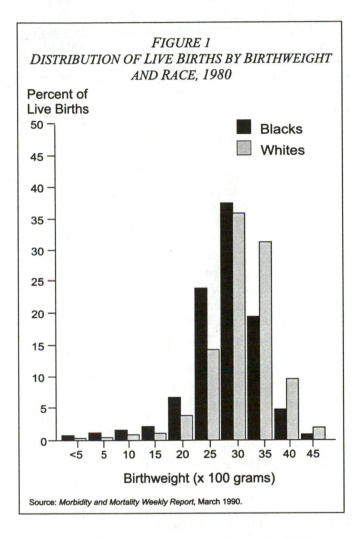

FIGURE 1
DISTRIBUTION OF LIVE BIRTHS BY BIRTHWEIGHT AND RACE, 1980

Source: *Morbidity and Mortality Weekly Report*, March 1990.

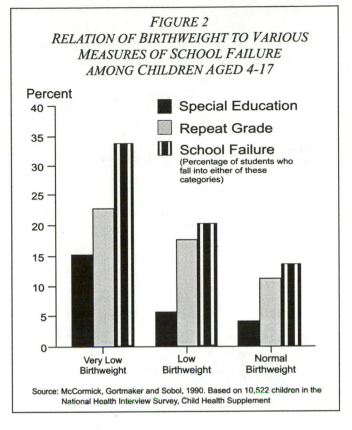

FIGURE 2
RELATION OF BIRTHWEIGHT TO VARIOUS MEASURES OF SCHOOL FAILURE AMONG CHILDREN AGED 4-17

Source: McCormick, Gortmaker and Sobol, 1990. Based on 10,522 children in the National Health Interview Survey, Child Health Supplement

weight can be brought on by other factors, including maternal malnutrition and teenage pregnancy, significant causes are maternal smoking, drinking, and drug use.

Around 6.9 percent of babies born in the United States weigh less than 5.5 pounds (2,500 grams) at birth and are considered "low-birthweight" babies. In 1987, this accounted for some 269,100 infants. Low birthweight may result when babies are born prematurely (born too early) or from intrauterine growth retardation (born too small) as a result of maternal malnutrition or actions that restrict blood flow to the fetus, such as smoking or drug use.

In 1987, about 48,750 babies were born at very low birthweights (under 3.25 lbs. or 1,500 grams). Research estimates that 6 to 8 percent of these babies experience major handicaps such as severe mental retardation or

cerebral palsy (Eilers et al., 1986; Hack and Breslau, 1986). Another 25 to 26 percent have borderline I.Q. scores, problems in understanding and expressing language, or other deficits (Hack and Breslau, 1986; Lefebvre et al., 1988; Nickel et al., 1982; Vohr et al., 1988). Although these children may enter the public school system, many of them show intellectual disabilities and require special educational assistance. Reading, spelling, handwriting, arts, crafts, and mathematics are difficult school subjects for them. Many are late in developing their speech and language. Children born at very low birthweights are more likely than those born at normal weights to be inattentive, hyperactive, depressed, socially withdrawn, or aggressive (Breslau et al., 1988).

New technologies and the spread of neonatal intensive care over the past decade have improved survival rates of babies born at weights ranging from 3.25 pounds to 5.5 pounds. But, as Figures 2 and 3 show, those born at low birthweight still are at increased risk of school failure. The increased risk, however, is very much tied to the child's postnatal environment. When the data on which Figure 2 is based are controlled to account for socioeconomic circumstances, very low-birthweight babies are approximately twice, not three times, as likely to repeat a grade.

Indeed, follow-up studies of low-birthweight infants at school age have concluded that "the influence of the environment far outweighs most effects of nonoptimal prenatal or perinatal factors on outcome" (Aylward et al., 1989). This finding suggests that early assistance can

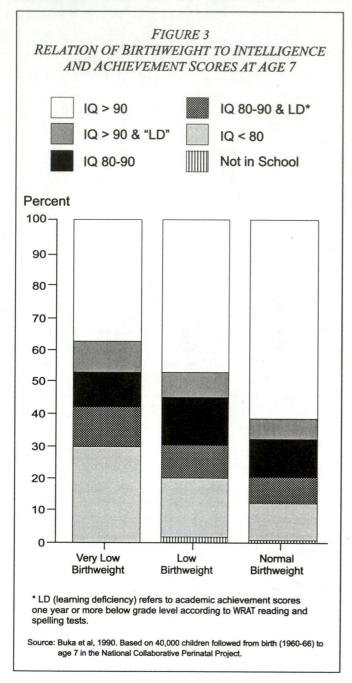

FIGURE 3
RELATION OF BIRTHWEIGHT TO INTELLIGENCE
AND ACHIEVEMENT SCORES AT AGE 7

☐ IQ > 90   ▨ IQ 80-90 & LD*

▨ IQ > 90 & "LD"   ☐ IQ < 80

■ IQ 80-90   ▥ Not in School

* LD (learning deficiency) refers to academic achievement scores
one year or more below grade level according to WRAT reading and
spelling tests.

Source: Buka et al, 1990. Based on 40,000 children followed from birth (1960-66) to
age 7 in the National Collaborative Perinatal Project.

children are particularly subject to hyperactivity and in-attention (Rush and Callahan, 1989).

Data from the National Collaborative Perinatal Project on births from 1960 to 1966 measured, among other things, the amount pregnant women smoked at each pre-natal visit and how their children functioned in school at age seven. Compared to offspring of nonsmokers, children of heavy smokers (more than two packs per day) were nearly twice as likely to experience school failure by age seven (see Figure 4). The impact of heavy smoking is apparently greater the earlier it occurs during pregnancy. Children of women who smoked heavily during the first trimester of pregnancy were more than twice as likely to fail than children whose mothers did not smoke during the first trimester. During the second and third trimesters, these risks decreased. In all of these analyses, it is difficult to differentiate the effects of exposure to smoking before birth and from either parent after birth; to distinguish between learning problems caused by low birthweight and those caused by other damaging effects of smoking; or, to disentangle the effects of smoke from the socioeconomic setting of the smoker. But it is worth noting that Figure 4 is based on children born in the early sixties, an era when smoking mothers were fairly well distributed across socioeconomic groups.

One study that attempted to divorce the effects of smoking from those of poverty examined middle-class children whose mothers smoked during pregnancy (Fried and Watkinson, 1990) and found that the infants showed differences in responsiveness beginning at one week of age. Later tests at 1, 2, 3, and 4 years of age showed that on verbal tests "the children of the heavy smokers had mean test scores that were lower than those born to lighter smokers, who in turn did not perform as well as those born to nonsmokers." The study also indicated that the effects of smoke exposure, whether in the womb or after birth, may not be identifiable until later ages when a child needs to perform complex cognitive functions, such as problem solving or reading and interpretation.

3. Prenatal Alcohol Exposure

Around forty thousand babies per year are born with fetal alcohol effect resulting from alcohol abuse during pregnancy (Fitzgerald, 1988). In 1984, an estimated 7,024 of these infants were diagnosed with fetal alcohol syndrome (FAS), an incidence of 2.2 per 1,000 births (Abel and Sokol, 1987). The three main features of FAS in its extreme form are facial malformation, intrauterine growth retardation, and dysfunctions of the central nervous system, including mental retardation.

There are, in addition, about 33,000 children each year who suffer from less-severe effects of maternal alcohol use. The more prominent among these learning impairments are problems in attention (attention-deficit disorders), speech and language, and hyperactivity. General

improve the intellectual functioning of children at risk for learning delay or impairment (Richmond, 1990).

2. Maternal Smoking

Maternal smoking during pregnancy has long been known to be related to low birthweight (Abel, 1980), an increased risk for cancer in the offspring (Stjernfeldt et al., 1986), and early and persistent asthma, which leads to, among other problems, frequent hospitalization and school absence (Streissguth, 1986). A growing number of new studies has shown that children of smokers are smaller in stature and lag behind other children in cognitive development and educational achievement. These

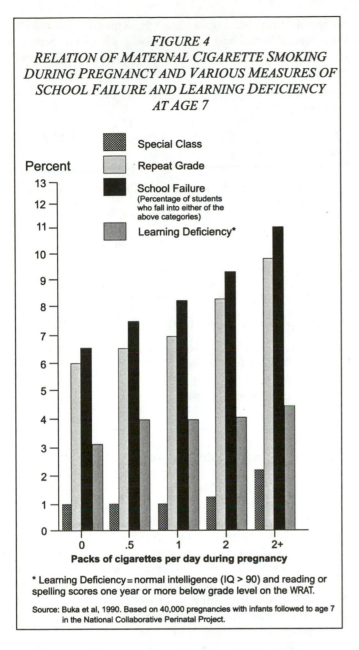

FIGURE 4
RELATION OF MATERNAL CIGARETTE SMOKING
DURING PREGNANCY AND VARIOUS MEASURES OF
SCHOOL FAILURE AND LEARNING DEFICIENCY
AT AGE 7

Special Class
Repeat Grade
School Failure
(Percentage of students who fall into either of the above categories)
Learning Deficiency*

Packs of cigarettes per day during pregnancy

* Learning Deficiency = normal intelligence (IQ > 90) and reading or
spelling scores one year or more below grade level on the WRAT.

Source: Buka et al, 1990. Based on 40,000 pregnancies with infants followed to age 7
in the National Collaborative Perinatal Project.

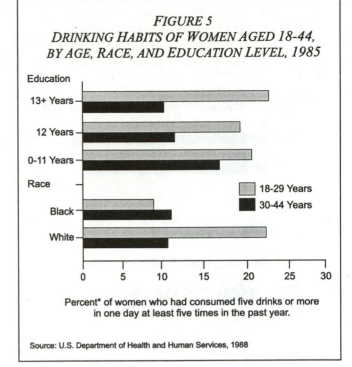

FIGURE 5
DRINKING HABITS OF WOMEN AGED 18-44,
BY AGE, RACE, AND EDUCATION LEVEL, 1985

Percent* of women who had consumed five drinks or more
in one day at least five times in the past year.

Source: U.S. Department of Health and Human Services, 1988

And many of the effects do not appear until ages four to seven, when children enter school.

Nearly one in four (23 percent) white women, eighteen to twenty-nine, reported "binge" drinking (five drinks or more a day at least five times in the past year). This was nearly three times the rate for black women of that age (about 8 percent). Fewer women (around 3 percent for both black and white) reported steady alcohol use (two drinks or more per day in the past two weeks).

4. Fetal Drug Exposure

The abuse of drugs of all kinds—marijuana, cocaine, crack, heroin, or amphetamines—by pregnant women affected about 11 percent of newborns in 1988—about 425,000 babies (Weston et al., 1989).

Cocaine and crack use during pregnancy are consistently associated with lower birthweight, premature birth, and smaller head circumference in comparison with babies whose mothers were free of these drugs (Chasnoff et al., 1989; Cherukuri et al., 1988; Doberczak et al., 1987; Keith et al., 1989; Zuckerman et al., 1989). In a study of 1,226 women attending a prenatal clinic, 27 percent tested positive for marijuana and 18 percent for cocaine. Infants of those who had used marijuana weighed an average of 2.8 ounces (79 grams) less at birth and were half a centimeter shorter in length. Infants of mothers who had used cocaine averaged 3.3 ounces (93 grams) less in weight and .7 of a centimeter less in length and also had a smaller head circumference than babies of nonusers (Zuckerman et al., 1989). The study concluded that "marijuana use and cocaine use during preg-

school failure also is connected to a history of fetal alcohol exposure (Abel and Sokol, 1987; Ernhart et al., 1985). Figure 5 shows the drinking habits of women of childbearing age by race and education.

When consumed in pregnancy, alcohol easily crosses the placenta, but exactly how it affects the fetus is not well known. The effects of alcohol vary according to how far along in the pregnancy the drinking occurs. The first trimester of pregnancy is a period of brain growth and organ and limb formation. The embryo is most susceptible to alcohol from week two to week eight of development, a point at which a woman may not even know she is pregnant (Hoyseth and Jones, 1989). Researchers have yet to determine how much alcohol it takes to cause problems in development and how alcohol affects each critical gestational period. It appears that the more alcohol consumed during pregnancy, the worse the effect.

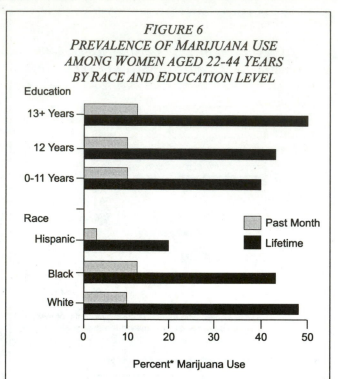

FIGURE 6
PREVALENCE OF MARIJUANA USE
AMONG WOMEN AGED 22-44 YEARS
BY RACE AND EDUCATION LEVEL

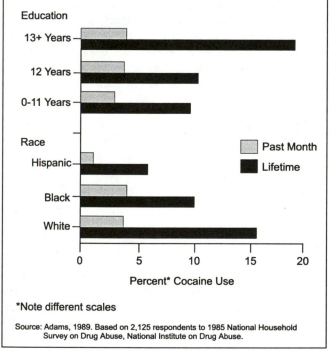

PREVALENCE OF COCAINE USE
AMONG WOMEN AGED 22-44 YEARS
BY RACE AND EDUCATION LEVEL

*Note different scales

Source: Adams, 1989. Based on 2,125 respondents to 1985 National Household Survey on Drug Abuse, National Institute on Drug Abuse.

by the finding that infants born to women who gained little weight, who had smoked one pack of cigarettes a day, and who tested positive for marijuana and cocaine averaged nearly a pound (14.6 ounces or 416 grams)

TABLE 1		
INFANT WEIGHT DIFFERENCES ASSOCIATED WITH SUBSTANCE ABUSE		
Substance Use During Pregnancy at One Prenatal Clinic:		
N = 1,226 Marijuana (n = 330) (27%) Cocaine (n = 221) (18%)		Birthweight difference:
Marijuana users only vs. non-users		− 2.8 oz.
Cocaine users only vs. non-users		− 3.3 oz.
Combination users (marijuana, cocaine, one pack of cigarettes a day, low maternal weight gain) vs. non-users		−14.6 oz.
Source: Zuckerman et al., 1989.		

smaller than those born to women who had normal weight gain and did not use cigarettes, marijuana, and cocaine (see Table 1). The effect of these substances on size is more than the sum of the risk factors combined.

Like alcohol use, drug use has different effects at different points in fetal development. Use in very early pregnancy is more likely to cause birth defects affecting organ formation and the central nervous systems. Later use may result in low birthweight due to either preterm birth or intrauterine growth retardation (Kaye et al., 1989; MacGregor et al., 1987; Petitti and Coleman, 1990). While some symptoms may be immediately visible, others may not be apparent until later childhood (Weston et al., 1989; Gray and Yaffe, 1986; Frank et al., 1988).

In infancy, damaged babies can experience problems in such taken-for-granted functions as sleeping and waking, resulting in exhaustion and poor development. In childhood, problems are found in vision, motor control, and in social interaction (Weston et al., 1989). Such problems may be caused not only by fetal drug exposure but also by insufficient prenatal care for the mother or by an unstimulating or difficult home environment for the infant (Lifschitz et al., 1985).

WHAT CAN be done to ameliorate the condition of children born with such damage? Quite a bit, based on the success of supportive prenatal care and the results of model projects that have provided intensive

nancy are each independently associated with impaired fetal growth" (Zuckerman et al., 1989).

In addition, women who use these substances are likely to smoke and to gain less weight during pregnancy, two factors associated with low birthweight. The cumulative effect of these risk factors is demonstrated

assistance to both baby and mother from the time of birth. These projects have successfully raised the I.Q. of low- and very-low birthweight babies an average of ten points or more—an increase that may lift a child with below-average intelligence into a higher I.Q. category (i.e., from retarded to low average or from low average to average). Generally known as either educational day care or infant day care, these programs provide a developmentally stimulating environment to high-risk babies and/or intensive parent support to prepare the parent to help her child.

In one such program based at the University of California/Los Angeles, weekly meetings were held among staff, parents, and infants over a period of four years. By the project's end, the low-birthweight babies had caught up in mental function to the control group of normal birthweight children (Rauh et al., 1988). The Infant Health and Development Project, which was conducted in eight cities and provided low-birthweight babies with pediatric follow-up and an educational curriculum with family support, on average increased their I.Q. scores by thirteen points and the scores of very-low birthweight children by more than six points. Another project targeted poor single teenage mothers whose infants were at high risk for intellectual impairment (Martin, Ramey and Ramey, 1990). One group of children was enrolled in educational day care from six and one-half weeks of age to four and one-half years for five days a week, fifty weeks a year. By four and one-half years, the children's I.Q. scores were in the normal range and ten points higher than a control group. In addition, by the time their children were four and one-half, mothers in the experimental group were more likely to have graduated from high school and be self-supporting than were mothers in the control group.

These studies indicate that some disadvantages of poverty and low birthweight can be mitigated and intellectual impairment avoided. The key is attention to the cognitive development of young children, in conjunction with social support of their families.

WHY CHILDREN TURN OUT THE WAY THEY DO

Hint: A child's peers matter more than you think.

by Judith Rich Harris

Behavioral genetic studies have proved beyond a shadow of a doubt that heredity is responsible for a sizable portion of the variations in people's personalities. Some people are more hot-tempered or outgoing or meticulous than others, and these variations are a function of the genes they were born with, as well as the experiences they had after they were born. The exact proportion—how much is due to the genes, how much to the experiences—is not important; the point is that heredity cannot be ignored.

But usually it is ignored. Consider the case of Amy, an adopted child. It wasn't a successful adoption; Amy's parents regarded her as a disappointment and favored their older child, a boy. Academic achievement was important to the parents, but Amy had a learning disability. Simplicity and emotional restraint were important to them, but Amy went in for florid role-playing and feigned illnesses. By the time she was ten, she had a serious, though vague, psychological disorder. She was

pathologically immature, socially inept, shallow of character, and extravagant of expression.

Well, naturally. Amy was a rejected child. What makes this case interesting is that Amy had an identical twin, Beth, who was adopted into a different family. Beth was not rejected—on the contrary, she was her mother's favorite. Her parents were not particularly concerned about education, so the learning disability (which she shared with her twin) was no big deal. Beth's mother, unlike Amy's, was empathic, open, and cheerful. Nevertheless, Beth had the same personality problems that Amy did. The psychoanalyst who studied these girls admitted that if he had seen only one of them, it would have been easy to fetch up some explanation in terms of the family environment. But there were two of them. Two, with matching symptoms but very different families.

Matching symptoms and matching genes: unlikely to be a coincidence. Something in the genes that Amy and Beth received from their biological parents—from the woman who gave them up for adoption and the man who got her pregnant—must have predisposed the twins to develop their unusual set of symptoms. If I say that Amy and Beth "inherited" this predisposition from

their biological parents, don't misunderstand me: their biological parents may have had none of these symptoms. Slightly different combinations of genes can produce very different results, and only identical twins have exactly the same combination. Fraternal twins can be surprisingly dissimilar, and the same is true of parents and children: a child can have characteristics seen in neither of her parents. But there is a statistical connection—a greater-than-chance likelihood that a person with psychological problems has a biological parent or a biological child with similar problems.

Heredity is one of the reasons that parents with problems often have children with problems. It is a simple, obvious, undeniable fact; and yet it is the most ignored fact in all of psychology. Judging from the lack of attention paid to heredity by developmental and clinical psychologists, you would think we were still in the days when John Watson was promising to turn a dozen babies into doctors, lawyers, beggar men, and thieves.

Thieves. A good place to begin. Let's see if I can account for criminal behavior in the offspring without blaming it on the environment provided by the parents—on the parents' child-rearing methods or the lack thereof. Don't worry. I am not

Judith Rich Harris is a former writer of college textbooks on child development. Her latest book, *The Nurture Assumption*, brings together insights from psychology, sociology, anthropology, primatology, and evolutionary biology.

From the *Saturday Evening Post*, May/June 1999, pp. 50-53. Reprinted with the permission of The Free Press, a division of Simon & Schuster, from *The Nurture Assumption*. © 1998 by Judith Rich Harris.

going to pin it all on heredity. But I can't do it without heredity, so if that bothers you, go and take a cold shower or something.

How would you go about making a child into a thief? Fagin, of Charles Dickens' *Oliver Twist*, could have told Watson a thing or two. Take four or five hungry boys, make them into an *us*, give them a pep talk and a course in pocket-picking, and sic 'em on *them*, the rich folk. It's intergroup warfare, a tradition of our species, and the potential for it can be found in almost any normal human, particularly those of the male variety. Your schoolboy with his shining morning face is but a warrior in thin disguise.

But Fagin's method, which had worked flawlessly on the London slum children who were his other pupils, didn't work on Oliver. Dickens seemed to think it was because Oliver was born good, but there is another possibility: Oliver didn't identify with the other boys in Fagin's ring. They were Londoners, and he was not. They spoke in a thieves' argot that was almost a foreign language to him. There were too many differences, and Oliver's run-in with the law came too soon to allow him to adapt to his new companions.

Oliver Twist was published in 1838, a time when it was still politically correct to believe that people could be born good or born bad—when it was still politically correct, in fact, to believe that badness could be predicted on the basis of one's racial or ethnic group membership. It was by no means the worst of times, but it was certainly not the best of times.

Today, both the individual explanation—that certain children are born bad—and the group explanation are held to be politically incorrect. Western culture has swung back to the view associated with the philosopher Rousseau: that all children are born good and it is society—their environment—that corrupts them. I'm not sure if this is

optimism or pessimism, but it leaves too much unexplained.

Though we no longer say that some children are born bad, the facts are such, unfortunately, that a euphemism is needed. Now psychologists say that some children are born with "difficult" temperaments—difficult for their parents to rear, difficult to socialize. I can list for you some of the things that make a child difficult to rear and difficult to socialize: a tendency to be active, impulsive, aggressive, and quick to anger; a tendency to get bored with routine activities and to seek excitement; a tendency to be unafraid of getting hurt; an insensitivity to the feelings of others; and, more often than not, a muscular build and an IQ a little lower than average. All of these characteristics have a significant genetic component.

Developmentalists have described how things go wrong when a child who is difficult to manage is born to a parent with poor management skills—something that happens, thanks to the unfairness of nature, more often than it would if genes were dealt out randomly to each new generation. The boy (usually it's a boy) and his mother (often there is no father) get into a vicious spiral in which bad leads to worse. The mother tells the boy to do something or not to do something; he ignores her; she tells him again; he gets mad; she gives up. Eventually, she gets mad, too, and punishes him harshly, but too late and too inconsistently for it to have any educational benefits. Anyway, this is a child who is not very afraid of getting hurt—at least it relieves his boredom.

The dysfunctional family. Oh yes, such families exist—there is no question about it! They are no fun to visit, and you wouldn't want to live there. Even the biological father of this child doesn't want to live there. There's an old joke that goes like this:

Psychologist: You should be kind to Johnny. He comes from a broken home.

Teacher: I'm not surprised. Johnny could break any home.

Difficult for their parents to rear, difficult to socialize. For most psychologists these two phrases are virtually synonymous because socialization is assumed to be the parents' job. For me, they are two different things. It is true that there tends to be a correlation between them, due to the fact that children take their inherited characteristics with them wherever they go. But the correlation is not strong, because the social context within the home, where the rearing goes on, is very different from the social context outside the home, where the socializing goes on. Children who are obnoxious at home are not necessarily obnoxious outside the home. Johnny may be obnoxious everywhere he goes, but fortunately such kids are uncommon.

The word *socialization* is most often used to refer to the training in morality that children are presumed to get at home. Parents are held to be responsible for teaching their children not to steal, not to lie, not to cheat. But here again, there is little correlation between how children behave at home and how they behave elsewhere. Children who were observed to break rules at home when they thought no one was looking were not noticeably more likely than anyone else to cheat on a test at school or in a game on the playground. Morality, like other forms of learned social behavior, is tied to the context in which it is acquired.

Was Dickens right? Are some children born good? Let us do an experiment that John Watson would have approved of. Place in adoptive homes a bunch of infant boys whose biological parents had been convicted (or will later be convicted) of crimes, and a second bunch whose biological parents were, as far as anyone knows, honest. Mix them up: place some of each bunch in homes with honest adoptive parents and let others be reared by crooks. A dastardly experiment, you say?

Well, that's what adoption agencies do. Of course, they don't purposely put babies in the homes of criminals, but sometimes it works out that way, and in places where careful records are kept both of adoptions and of criminal convictions—Denmark, for example—it's possible to study the results. Researchers were able to obtain background data on over 4,000 Danish men who had been placed for adoption in infancy.

As it turned out, criminal convictions were numerous among the biological parents of the adoptees but infrequent among their adoptive parents. Thus, there were not many cases of boys who had honest biological parents being reared in the homes of crooks. Of this small group, 15 percent became criminals. But almost the same percentage (14 percent) was found among the adoptees whose biological parents were honest and whose adoptive parents were also honest. It seems that being reared in a criminal home does not make a criminal out of a boy who wasn't cut out for the job.

The story is a little different for the boys whose biological parents were criminals. Of those who were reared by honest folk, 20 percent became criminals. And of the small group who came up unlucky both times—criminal biological fathers *and* criminal adoptive fathers—almost 25 percent went wrong. So it's not just heredity: it looks like the home environment does count for something after all.

Not so fast. It turns out that the ability of a criminal adoptive family to produce a criminal child—given suitable material to work with—depends on where the family happens to live. The increase in criminality among Danish adoptees reared in criminal homes was found only for a minority of the subjects in this study: those who grew up in or around Copenhagen. In small towns and rural areas, an adoptee reared in a criminal home was no more likely to become a criminal than one reared by honest adoptive parents.

It wasn't the criminal adoptive parents who made the biological son of criminals into a criminal: it was the *neighborhood in which they reared him*. Neighborhoods differ in rates of criminal behavior, and I would guess that neighborhoods with high rates of criminal behavior are exceedingly hard to find in rural areas of Denmark.

People generally live in places where they share a lifestyle and a set of values with their neighbors; this is due both to mutual influence and, especially in cities, to birds of a feather flocking together. Children grow up with other children who are the offspring of their parents' friends and neighbors. These are the children who form their peer group. This is the peer group in which they are socialized. If their own parents are criminals, the friends' parents may also be inclined in that direction. The children bring to the peer group the attitudes and behaviors they learned at home, and if these attitudes and behaviors are similar, in all probability the peer group will retain them.

I have told you about an adoption study of criminality; there are also twin and sibling studies. Behavioral genetic studies of twins or siblings usually show that the environment shared by children who grow up in the same home has little or no effect, but we've come to one of the exceptions. Twins or siblings who grow up in the same home are more likely to match in criminality—to both be criminals or both be honest. This correlation is often attributed to the home environment that the twins or siblings share—in other words, to the influence of the parents. But kids who share a home also share a neighborhood and, in some cases, a peer group. The likelihood that two siblings will match in criminality is higher if they are the same sex and close together in age. It is higher in twins (even if they're not identical) than in ordinary siblings, and higher in twins who spend a lot of time together outside the home than in those who lead separate lives.

The evidence shows that the environment has an effect on criminality but it doesn't show that the relevant environment is the home; in fact, it suggests a different explanation. When both twins or both siblings get into trouble, it is due to their influence on each other and to the influence of the peer group they belong to.

Are some people born bad? A better way of putting it is that some people are born with characteristics that make them poor fits for most of the honest jobs available in most societies, and so far we haven't learned how to deal with them. We are at risk of becoming their victims, but they are victims, too—victims of the evolutionary history of our species. No process is perfect, not even evolution. Evolution gave us big heads, but sometimes a baby has a head so big it can't fit through the birth canal. In earlier times these babies invariably died, as did their mothers. In the same way, evolution selected for other characteristics that sometimes overshoot their mark and become liabilities, rather than assets. Almost all the characteristics of the "born criminal" would be, in slightly watered-down form, useful to a male in a hunter-gatherer society and useful to his group. His lack of fear, desire for excitement, and impulsiveness make him a formidable weapon against rival groups. His aggressiveness, strength, and lack of compassion enable him to dominate his group mates and give him first shot at hunter-gatherer perks.

Unlike the successful hunter-gatherer, however, the career criminal tends to be below average in intelligence. I take this to be a hopeful sign: it suggests that temperament can be overridden by reason. Those individuals born with the other characteristics on the list but who also have above-average intelligence are evidently smart enough to figure out that crime does not pay and to find other ways of gratifying their desire for excitement.

BEYOND LITTLETON

How Well Do You Know Your Kid?

The new teen wave is bigger, richer, better educated and healthier than any other in history. But there's a dark side, and too many parents aren't doing their job.

By Barbara Kantrowitz and Pat Wingert

JOCKS, PREPS, PUNKS, GOTHS, GEEKS. They may sit at separate tables in the cafeteria, but they all belong to the same generation. There are now 31 million kids in the 12-to-19 age group, and demographers predict that there will be 35 million teens by 2010, a population bulge bigger than even the baby boom at its peak. In many ways, these teens are uniquely privileged. They've grown up in a period of sustained prosperity and haven't had to worry about the draft (as their fathers did) or cataclysmic global conflicts (as their grandparents did). Cable and the Internet have given them access to an almost infinite amount of information. Most expect to go to college, and girls, in particular, have unprecedented opportunities; they can dream of careers in everything from professional sports to politics, with plenty of female role models to follow.

But this positive image of American adolescence in 1999 is a little like yearbook photos that depict every kid as happy and blemish-free. After the Littleton, Colo., tragedy, it's clear there's another dimension to this picture, and it's far more troubled. In survey after survey, many kids—even those on the honor roll—say they feel increasingly alone and alienated, unable to connect with their parents, teachers and sometimes even classmates. They're desperate for guidance, and when they don't get what they need at home or in school, they cling to cliques or immerse themselves in a universe out of their parents' reach, a world defined by computer games, TV and movies, where brutality

is so common it has become mundane. The parents of Eric Harris and Dylan Klebold have told friends they never dreamed their sons could kill. It's an extreme case, but it has made a lot of parents wonder: do we really know our kids?

Many teens say they feel overwhelmed by pressure and responsibilities. They are juggling part-time jobs and hours of homework every night; sometimes they're so exhausted that they're nearly asleep in early-morning classes. Half have lived through their parents' divorce. Sixty-three percent are in households where both parents work outside the home, and many look after younger siblings in the afternoon. Still others are home by themselves after school. That unwelcome solitude can extend well into the evening; mealtime for this generation too often begins with a forlorn touch of the microwave.

In fact, of all the issues that trouble adolescents, loneliness ranks at the top of the list. University of Chicago sociologist Barbara Schneider has been studying 7,000 teenagers for five years and has found they spend an average of 3½ hours alone *every day.* Teenagers may claim they want privacy, but they also crave and need attention—and they're not getting it. Author Patricia Hersch profiled eight teens who live in an affluent area of northern Virginia for her 1998 book, "A Tribe Apart." "Every kid I talked to at length eventually came around to saying without my asking that they wished they had more adults in their lives, especially their parents," she says.

Loneliness creates an emotional vacuum that is filled by an intense peer culture, a critical buffer against kids' fear of isolation. Some of this bonding is normal and appropriate; in fact, studies have shown that the human need for acceptance is almost a biological drive, like hunger. It's especially intense in early adolescence, from about 12 to 14, a time of "hyper self-consciousness," says David Elkind, a professor of child development at Tufts University and author of "All Grown Up and No Place to Go." "They become very self-centered and spend a lot of time thinking about what others think of them," Elkind says. "And when they think about what others are thinking, they make the error of thinking that everyone is thinking about *them.*" Dressing alike is a refuge, a way of hiding in the group. When they're 3 and scared, they cling to a security blanket; at 16, they want body piercings or Abercrombie shirts.

If parents and other adults abdicate power, teenagers come up with their own rules. It's "Lord of the Flies" on a vast scale. Bullying has become so extreme and so common that many teens just accept it as part of high-school life in the '90s. Emory University psychologist Marshall Duke, an expert on children's friendships, recently asked 110 students in one of his classes if any of them had ever been threatened in high school. To his surprise, "they all raised their hand." In the past, parents and teachers served as mediating forces in the classroom jungle. William Damon, director of the Stanford University Center for Adolescence, re-

Peril and Promise: Teens by the Numbers

They watch too much television, and their parents may not be around enough, but today's teenagers are committing fewer crimes, having fewer babies and generally staying out of serious trouble. Here's a look at who they are—and what they're up to:

Demographics

THE BREAKDOWN
Teenagers account for roughly 10 percent of the U.S. population.

Teens (13–19)

White	18,199,000	66%
Black	3,992,000	15
Hispanic	3,723,000	14
Asian, Pac. Islander	1,030,000	4
American Indian, Eskimo and Aleut	275,000	1

KIDS HAVING KIDS: A TREND ON THE DECLINE
The birthrate among teens has fallen dramatically, down 16 percent overall.

Birthrates for females 15–19

Percent change, 1991–97 ■ –20% or more ■ –15 to –19.9% ▨ –5 to –14.9%

Lifestyle

SEXUAL ACTIVITY
Almost one out of five teenagers is still a virgin by the age of 20.

Percentage of teens who have had sexual intercourse, 1995

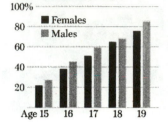

■ Females
▨ Males

Age 15 16 17 18 19

COOLEST BRANDS

Boys	Girls
Nike	Nike
Sony	adidas
Tommy Hilfiger	Tommy Hilfiger
Nintendo	The Gap
adidas	Old Navy

FAVORITE TV SHOWS

Boys	Girls
'The Simpsons'	'Dawson's Creek'
'South Park'	'Friends'
'MTV'	'7th Heaven'
'Home Improve.'	'The Simpsons'
'Friends'	'Buffy the V.S.'

LESS OF THE BAD STUFF: SMOKING, DRINKING AND DOING DRUGS
Today, teens say, they misbehave less than kids in the recent past. The percentage who, in the last 30 days, admit to having used ...

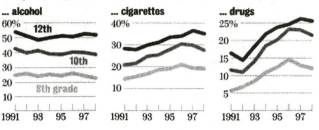

... alcohol   ... cigarettes   ... drugs

12th   10th   8th grade

1991 93 95 97   1991 93 95 97   1991 93 95 97

PARENTS AT WORK
Parents work more, so their teenagers are often left unsupervised.

Families with employed parents

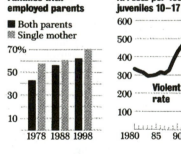

■ Both parents
▨ Single mother

1978 1988 1998

DROP IN CRIME
In 1997, kids were responsible for 17 percent of violent-crime arrests.

Arrests per 100,000 juveniles 10–17

Violent-crime rate

1980 85 90 95

calls writing a satirical essay when he was in high school about how he and his friends tormented a kid they knew. Damon got an "A" for style and grammar, but the teacher took him aside and told him he should be ashamed of his behavior. "That's what is supposed to happen," Damon says. "People are supposed to say, 'Hey, kid, you've gone too far here'." Contrast that with reports from Littleton, where Columbine students described a film class nonchalantly viewing a murderous video created by Eric Harris and Dylan Klebold. In 1999 this apparently was not remarkable behavior.

When they're isolated from parents, teens are also more vulnerable to serious emo-

tional problems. Surveys of high-school students have indicated that one in four considers suicide each year, says Dr. David Fassler, a child and adolescent psychiatrist in Burlington, Vt., and author of "Help Me, I'm Sad: Recognizing, Treating and Preventing Childhood and Adolescent Depression." By the end of high school, many have actually tried to kill themselves. "Often the parents or teachers don't realize it was a suicide attempt," he says. "It can be something ambiguous like an overdose of nonprescription pills from the medicine cabinet or getting drunk and crashing the car with suicidal thoughts."

Even the best, most caring parents can't protect their teenagers from all these problems, but involved parents can make an enormous difference. Kids do listen. Teenage drug use (although still high) is slowly declining, and even teen pregnancy and birthrates are down slightly—largely because of improved education efforts, experts say. More teens are delaying sex, and those who are sexually active are more likely to use contraceptives than their counterparts a few years ago.

In the teenage years, the relationship between parents and children is constantly evolving as the kids edge toward independence. Early adolescence is a period of transition, when middle-school kids move from one teacher and one classroom to a different teacher for each subject. In puberty, they're moody and irritable. "This is a time

when parents and kids bicker a lot," says Laurence Steinberg, a psychology professor at Temple University and author of "You and Your Adolescent: A Parents' Guide to Ages 10 to 20." "Parents are caught by surprise," he says. "They discover that the tricks they've used in raising their kids effectively during childhood stop working." He advises parents to try to understand what their kids are going through; things do get better. "I have a 14-year-old son," Steinberg says, "and when he moved out of the transition phase into middle adolescence, we saw a dramatic change. All of a sudden, he's our best friend again."

IN MIDDLE ADOLESCENCE, ROUGHLY the first three years of high school, teens are increasingly on their own. To a large degree, their lives revolve around school and their friends. "They have a healthy sense of self," says Steinberg. They begin to develop a unique sense of identity, as well as their own values and beliefs. "The danger in this time would be to try to force them to be something you want them to be, rather than help them be who they are." Their relationships may change dramatically as their interests change; in Schneider's study, almost three quarters of the closest friends named by seniors weren't even mentioned during sophomore year.

Late adolescence is another transition, this time to leaving home altogether. "Par-

Online

HOOKED UP
47% of teens are using the computer to go online this year.

WHAT DO THEY DO?
They keep up with each other—and what's out there.

Percentage of teens who go online

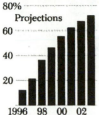

Projections

1996 98 00 02

Top 10 activities

E-mail	83%
Search engine	78
Music sites	59
General research	58
Games	51
TV/movie sites	43
Chat room	42
Own Web page	38
Sports sites	35

EVERY MOVE THEY MAKE
With age comes online freedom. Here's how parents say they monitor their kids while they're on the Net.

	Age 11–15	16–18
Sit with them while online	38%	9%
Kids can log on only with an adult	34	5
Mainly use for online games	28	15
Limit hours for kids' use	47	21
Know which Web sites kids can visit	68	43
Kids are online whenever they want	54	75
Use the Net more than watching TV	19	22

Home life

PASSING THE HOURS
Kids spend more time partying than studying each week. They also like tube time.

Activity	percentage of teens	/hours
Watching TV	98%	11.0
Listening to CDs, tapes, etc.	96	9.9
Doing chores	84	4.1
Studying	59	3.7
Going to parties	58	4.0
Going to religious functions	51	2.5
Working at a regular paid job	32	4.7

WHAT WERE WE TALKING ABOUT?
Parents and kids both say they're discussing important life issues.

Issue discussed	parents	/kids
Alcohol/drugs	98%	90%
How to handle violent situations	83	80
Basic facts of reproduction	76	80
AIDS	78	75

● **85%** of teens said that **Mom** cares 'very much' about them. **58%** said the same about **Dad**.

● **25%** of teens said that their **mom** is 'always' **home** when they return from school. **10%** said their **dad** was.

● Do parents let teenagers make their own decisions about weekend **curfew**? **66%** said no.

● How much are teens '**understood**' by their family members? **35%** said 'quite a bit.'

SPENDING HABITS
Teens average just under $100 in total weekly spending.

Weekly spending
■ Allowance ▦ Own

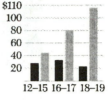

12–15 16–17 18–19

RESEARCH BY BRET BEGUN. SOURCES: CENSUS BUREAU; BLS; NAT'L CENTER FOR JUVENILE JUSTICE; NCHS; TEENAGE RESEARCH UNLIMITED; MONITORING THE FUTURE STUDY, UNIV. OF MICHIGAN; KAISER FAMILY FOUNDATION; NAT'L LONGITUDINAL STUDY OF ADOLESCENT HEALTH; JUPITER COMMUNICATIONS; GREENFIELD ONLINE; THE ALAN GUTTMACHER INST.

ents have to be able to let go," says Steinberg, and "have faith and trust that they've done a good enough job as parents that their child can handle this stuff." Contrary to stereotypes, it isn't mothers who are most likely to mourn in the empty nest. They're often relieved to be free of some chores. But Steinberg says that fathers "suffer from thoughts of missed chances."

That should be the ultimate lesson of tragedies like Littleton. "Parents need to share what they really believe in, what they really think is important," says Stanford's Damon. "These basic moral values are more important than math skills or SATs." Seize any opportunity to talk—in the car, over the breakfast table, watching TV. Parents have to work harder to get their points across. Ellen Galinsky, president of the Families and Work Institute, has studied teenagers' views of parents. "One 16-year-old told us, 'I am proud of the fact that [my mother] deals with me even though I try to push her away. She's still there'." So pay attention now. The kids can't wait.

With ANNE UNDERWOOD

CULTURE & IDEAS

INVINCIBLE KIDS

Why do some children survive
traumatic childhoods unscathed?
The answers can help every child

Child psychologist Emmy Werner went looking for trouble in paradise. In Hawaii nearly 40 years ago, the researchers began studying the offspring of chronically poor, alcoholic, abusive and even psychotic parents to understand how failure was passed from one generation to the next. But to her surprise, one third of the kids she studied looked nothing like children headed for disaster. Werner switched her focus to these "resilient kids," who somehow beat the odds, growing into emotionally healthy, competent adults. They even appeared to defy the laws of nature: When Hurricane Iniki flattened Kauai in 1992, leaving nearly 1 in 6 residents homeless, the storm's 160-mpg gusts seemed to spare the houses of Werner's success stories.

Werner's "resilient kids," in their late 30s when Iniki hit, helped create their own luck. They heeded storm warnings and boarded up their properties. And even if the squall blew away their roofs or tore down their walls, they were more likely to have the financial savings and insurance to avoid foreclosure—the fate of many of Iniki's victims. "There's not a thing you can do personally about being in the middle of a hurricane," says the University of California–Davis's Werner, "but [resilient kids] are planners and problem solvers and picker-uppers."

For many of America's children, these are difficult times. One in five lives in poverty. More than half will spend some of their childhood living apart from one parent—the result of divorce, death or out-of-wedlock birth.

Child abuse, teen drug use and teen crime are surging. Living in an affluent suburb is no protection: Suburban kids are almost as likely as those in violent neighborhoods to report what sociologists call "parental absence"—the lack of a mother and father who are approachable and attentive, and who set rules and enforce consequences.

In the face of these trends, many social scientists now are suggesting a new way of looking at kids and their problems: Focus on survivors, not casualties. Don't abandon kids who fail, but learn from those who succeed.

Such children, researchers find, are not simply born that way. Though genes play a role, the presence of a variety of positive influences in a child's environment is even more crucial; indeed, it can make the difference between a child who founders and one who thrives.

The implications of such research are profound. The findings mean that parents, schools, volunteers, government and others can create a pathway to resiliency, rather than leaving success to fate or to hard-wired character traits. Perhaps most important, the research indicates that the lessons learned from these nearly invincible kids can teach us how to help *all* kids—regardless of their circumstances—handle the inevitable risks and turning points of life. The Search Institute, a Minneapolis-based children's research group, identified 30 resiliency-building factors. The more of these "assets" present in a child's environment, the more likely the child was to avoid school problems, alco-

hol use, early sexual experimentation, depression and violent behavior.

Like the factors that contribute to lifelong physical health, those that create resilience may seem common-sensical, but they have tremendous impact. Locate a resilient kid and you will also find a caring adult—or several—who has guided him. Watchful parents, welcoming schools, good peers and extracurricular activities matter, too, as does teaching kids to care for others and to help out in their communities.

From thug to Scout. The psychologists who pioneered resiliency theory focused on inborn character traits that fostered success. An average or higher IQ was a good predictor. So was innate temperament—a sunny disposition may attract advocates who can lift a child from risk. But the idea that resiliency can be molded is relatively re-

ROBERT DOLE. He came of age during the tough years of the Great Depression. Later, he overcame a nearly fatal war injury.

"Why me, I demanded? ... Maybe it was all part of a plan, a test of endurance and strength and, above all, of faith."

From *U.S. News & World Report*, November 11, 1996, pp. 60-71. © 1996 by U.S. News & World Report. Reprinted by permission.

cent. It means that an attentive adult can turn a mean and sullen teenage thug—a kid who would smash in someone's face on a whim—into an upstanding Boy Scout.

That's the story of Eagle Scout Rudy Gonzalez. Growing up in Houston's East End barrio, Gonzalez seemed on a fast track to prison. By the time he was 13, he'd already had encounters with the city's juvenile justice system—once for banging a classmate's head on the pavement until blood flowed, once for slugging a teacher. He slept through classes and fought more often than he studied. With his drug-using crew, he broke into warehouses and looted a grocery store. His brushes with the law only hardened his bad-boy swagger. "I thought I was macho," says Gonzalez. "With people I didn't like, [it was], 'Don't look at me or I'll beat you up.'"

Many of Gonzalez's friends later joined real gangs. Several met grisly deaths; others landed in prison for drug dealing and murder. More than a few became fathers and dropped out of school. Gonzalez joined urban scouting, a new, small program established by Boy Scouts of America to provide role models for "at risk" youth. At first glance, Gonzalez's path could hardly seem more different than that of his peers. But both gangs and Boy Scouts offer similar attractions: community and a sense of purpose, a hierarchical system of discipline and a chance to prove loyalty to a group. Gonzalez chose merit badges and service over gang colors and drive-by shootings.

Now 20, Gonzalez wears crisply pressed khakis and button-down shirts and, in his sophomore year at Texas A&M, seems well on his way to his goal of working for a major accounting firm. Why did he succeed when his friends stuck to crime? Gonzalez's own answer is that his new life is "a miracle." "Probably, God chose me to do this," he says.

There were identifiable turning points. Scoutmaster John Trevino, a city policeman, filled Gonzalez's need for a caring adult who believed in him and could show him a different way to be a man. Gonzalez's own father was shot and killed in a barroom fight when Rudy was just 6. Fate played a role, too. At 14, using survival skills he'd learned in scouting, Gonzalez saved the life of a younger boy stuck up to his chin in mud in a nearby bayou. The neighborhood hero was lauded in the newspaper and got to meet President Bush at the White

House. Slowly, he began to feel the importance of serving his community—another building block of resiliency. For a Scout project he cleaned up a barrio cemetery.

Something special. Once his life started to turn around, Gonzalez felt comfortable enough to reveal his winning personality and transcendent smile—qualities that contributed further to his success. "When I met him, I wanted to adopt him," says his high school counselor, Betty Porter. "There's something about him." She remembers Gonzalez as a likable and prodigious networker who made daily visits to her office to tell her about college scholarships—some she didn't even know about.

BILL CLINTON. He lost his father in an auto wreck before he was born. Later, he coped with an alcoholic, occasionally violent stepfather.

"My mother taught me about sacrifice. She held steady through tragedy after tragedy and, always, she taught me to fight."

A little bit of help—whether an urban scouting program or some other chance to excel—can go a long way in creating resiliency. And it goes furthest in the most stressed neighborhoods, says the University of Colorado's Richard Jessor, who directs a multimillion-dollar resiliency project for the John D. and Catherine T. MacArthur Foundation. Looking back, Gonzalez agrees. "We were just guys in the barrio without anything better to do," he says. "We didn't have the YMCA or Little League, so we hung out, played sports, broke into warehouses and the school." Adds Harvard University's Katherine Newman: "The good news is that kids are motivated. They want to make it. The bad news is that there are too few opportunities."

Resiliency theory brightens the outlook for kids. Mental health experts traditionally have put the spotlight on children who emerge from bad childhoods damaged and scarred. But statistics show that many—if not most—children born into unpromising

circumstances thrive, or at least hold their own. Most children of teen mothers, for example, avoid becoming teen parents themselves. And though the majority of child abusers were themselves abused as children, most abused children do not become abusers. Similarly, children of schizophrenics and children who grew up in refugee camps also tend to defy the odds. And many Iowa youths whose families lost their farms during the 1980s farm crisis became high achievers in school.

Living well. A person who has faced childhood adversity and bounced back may even fare *better* later in life than someone whose childhood was relatively easy—or so Werner's recently completed follow-up of the Kauai kids at age 40 suggests. Resilient children in her study reported stronger marriages and better health than those who enjoyed less stressful origins. Further, none had been on welfare, and none had been in trouble with the law. Many children of traumatic, abusive or neglectful childhoods suffer severe consequences, including shifts in behavior, thinking and physiology that dog them into adulthood. But though Werner's resilient kids turned adults tended to marry later, there was little sign of emotional turmoil. At midlife, these resilient subjects were more likely to say they were happy and only one third as likely to report mental health problems.

Can any child become resilient? That remains a matter of debate. Some kids, researchers say, simply may face too many risks. And the research can be twisted to suggest that there are easy answers. "Resiliency theory assumes that it's all or nothing, that you have it or you don't," complains Geoffrey Canada, who runs neighborhood centers for New York's poorest youth. "But for some people it takes 10,000 gallons of water, and for some kids it's just a couple of little drops."

In fact, as Canada notes, most resilient kids do not follow a straight line to success. An example is Raymond Marte, whom Canada mentored, teaching the youth karate at one of his Rheedlen Centers for Children and Families. Today, Marte, 21, is a freshman at New York's Bard College. But only a few years ago, he was just another high school dropout and teenage father, hanging out with gang friends and roaming the streets with a handgun in his pocket. "This is choice time," Canada told

DR. RUTH WESTHEIMER. The sex therapist fled the Nazis at 10; her parents died in the Holocaust, and she grew up in a Swiss orphanage.

"The values my family [instilled] left me with the sense I must make something out of my life to justify my survival."

Marte after five of the boy's friends were killed in three months. Marte re-enrolled in school, became an Ameri-Corps volunteer and won a college scholarship. Today, when he walks the streets of his family's gritty Manhattan neighborhood, he is greeted as a hero, accepting high-fives from friends congratulating the guy who made it out.

Good parenting can trump bad neighborhoods. That parents are the first line in creating resilient children is no surprise. But University of Pennsylvania sociologist Frank Furstenberg *was* surprised to find that adolescents in the city's most violence prone, drug-ridden housing projects showed the same resilience as middle-class adolescents. The expectation was that the worst neighborhoods would overwhelm families. Inner-city housing projects do present more risk and fewer opportunities. But good parenting existed in roughly equal proportions in every neighborhood.

Sherenia Gibbs is the type of dynamo parent who almost single-handedly can instill resiliency in her children. The single mother moved her three children from a small town in Illinois to Minneapolis in search of better education and recreation. Still, the new neighborhood was dangerous, so Gibbs volunteered at the park where her youngest son, T. J. Williams, played. Today, six years later, Gibbs runs a city park, where she has started several innovative mentoring programs. At home, Gibbs sets aside time to spend with T. J., now 14, requires him to call her at work when he gets home from school or goes out with friends and follows his schoolwork closely. Indeed, how often teens have dinner with their family and whether they have a curfew are two of the best predictors of teen drug use, according to

the National Center on Addiction and Substance Abuse at Columbia University. How often a family attends church—where kids are exposed to both values and adult mentors—also makes a difference. Says Gibbs: "The streets will grab your kids and eat them up."

Some resiliency programs study the success of moms like Gibbs and try to teach such "authoritative parenting" skills to others. When a kid has an early brush with the law, the Oregon Social Learning Center brings the youth's whole family together to teach parenting skills. Not only is the training effective with the offending youth, but younger brothers and sisters are less likely to get in trouble as well.

Despite the crucial role of parents, few—rich or poor—are as involved in their children's lives as Gibbs. And a shocking number of parents—25 percent—ignore or pay little attention to how their children fare in school, according to Temple University psychology professor Laurence Steinberg. Nearly one third of students across economic classes say their parents have no idea how they are doing in school. Further, half the parents Steinberg surveyed did not know their children's friends, what their kids did after school or where they went at night. Some schools are testing strategies for what educator Margaret Wang, also at Temple, calls "educational resilience."

One solution: teaching teams, which follow a student for a few years so the child always has a teacher who knows him well. In Philadelphia, some inner-city schools have set up "parents' lounges," with free coffee, to encourage moms and dads to be regular school visitors.

Given the importance of good parenting, kids are at heightened risk when parents themselves are troubled. But it is a trait of resilient kids that in such circumstances, they seek out substitute adults. And sometimes they become substitute adults themselves, playing a parental role for younger siblings. That was true of Tyrone Weeks. He spent about half his life without his mother as she went in and out of drug rehabilitation. Sober now for three years, Delores Weeks maintains a close relationship with her son. But Tyrone was often on his own, living with his grandmother and, when she died, with his basketball coach, Tennis Young. Young and Dave Hagan, a neighborhood priest in north

Philadelphia, kept Weeks fed and clothed. But Weeks also became a substitute parent for his younger brother, Robert, while encouraging his mother in her struggle with cocaine. Says Weeks, "There were times when I was lost and didn't want to live anymore."

Like many resilient kids, Weeks possessed another protective factor: a talent. Basketball, he says, gave him a self-confidence that carried him through the lost days. Today, Weeks rebounds and blocks shots for the University of Massachusetts. Obviously, not all kids have Weeks's exceptional ability. But what seems key is not the level of talent but finding an activity from which they derive pride and sense of purpose.

Mon Ye credits an outdoor leadership program with "keeping me out of gang life." Born in a Cambodian refugee camp, Ye has lived with an older brother in a crime-ridden Tacoma, Wash., housing project since his mother's death a few years ago. Outdoor adventure never interested him. But then parks worker LeAnna Waite invited him to join a program at a nearby recreation center (whose heavy doors are dented with bullet marks from gang fights). Last year, Ye led a youth climb up Mount Rainier and now plans to go to college to become a recreation and park supervisor.

It helps to help. Giving kids significant personal responsibility is another way to build resiliency, whether it's Weeks pulling his family together or Ye supervising preteens. Some of the best youth programs value both service to others and the ability to plan and make choices, according to Stanford University's Shirley Brice Heath. The Food Project—in which kids raise 40,000 pounds of vegetables for Boston food kitchens—is directed by the young par-

KWEISI MFUME. The NAACP chief's stepdad was abusive. After his mom died, he ran with gangs and had five sons out of wedlock.

"We're all inbred with a certain amount of resiliency. It's not until it's tested ... that we recognize inner strength."

ticipants, giving them the chance to both learn and then pass on their knowledge. Older teens often find such responsibility through military service.

Any program that multiplies contacts between kids and adults who can offer advice and support is valuable. A recent study of Big Brothers and Big Sisters found that the nationwide youth-mentoring program cuts drug use and school absenteeism by half. Most youth interventions are set up to target a specific problem like violence or teen sex—and often have little impact. Big Brothers and Big Sisters instead succeeds with classic resiliency promotion: It first creates supportive adult attention for kids, then expects risky behavior to drop as a consequence.

The 42,490 residents of St. Louis Park, Minn., know all about such holistic approaches to creating resiliency. They've made it a citywide cause in the ethnically diverse suburb of Minneapolis. Children First is the city's call for residents to think about the ways, big and small, they can help all kids succeed, from those living in the city's Meadowbrook housing project to residents of parkside ranch houses. The suburb's largest employer, HealthSystem Minnesota, runs a free kids' health clinic. (Doctors and staff donate their time.) And one of the smallest businesses, Steve McCulloch's flower shop,

DIANNE FEINSTEIN. The California senator was raised in privilege, but her mother was mentally ill and at times violent.

"I've never believed adversity is a harbinger of failure. On the contrary, [it] can provide a wellspring of strength."

gives away carnations to kids in the nearby housing project on Mother's Day. Kids even help each other. Two high school girls started a Tuesday night baby-sitting service at the Reformation Lutheran Church. Parents can drop off their kids for three hours. The cost: $1.

The goal is to make sure kids know that they are valued and that several adults outside their own family know and care about them. Those adults might include a police officer-volunteering to serve lunch in the school cafeteria line. Or Jill Terry, one of scores of volunteers who stand at school bus stops on frigid mornings. Terry breaks up fights, provides forgotten lunch money or reassures a sad-faced boy about his parents' fighting. The adopt-a-bus-stop program

was started by members of a senior citizens' group concerned about an attempted abduction of a child on her way to school.

Another volunteer, Kyla Dreier, works in a downtown law firm and mentors Angie Larson. The 14-year-old has long, open talks with her mother but sometimes feels more comfortable discussing things with another adult, like Dreier.

Spreading out. St. Louis Park is the biggest success story of over 100 communities nationwide where the Search Institute is trying to develop support for childhood resiliency. In a small suburb, it was relatively easy to rally community leaders. Now Search is trying to take such asset building to larger cities like Minneapolis and Albuquerque, N.M.

In St. Louis Park, resiliency is built on a shoestring budget. About $60,000 a year—all raised from donations—covers the part-time staff director and office expenses. But that's the point, says Children First Coordinator Karen Atkinson. Fostering resiliency is neither complicated nor costly. It's basic common sense—even if practiced too rarely in America. And it pays dividends for all kids.

By Joseph P. Shapiro with Dorian Friedman in New York, Michele Meyer in Houston and Margaret Loftus

Live to 100? No thanks

Most people opt for quality, not quantity, in later years

BY SUSAN L. CROWLEY

Despite stunning medical advances that can extend life, most Americans do not want to live to be 100. They fear the disabilities, impoverishment and isolation commonly thought to accompany old age.

The finding emerged in a wide-ranging AARP survey on attitudes toward longevity. When asked how long they want to live, 63 percent of the 2,032 respondents opted for fewer than 100 years.

"What this says to me," notes Constance Swank, director of research at AARP, "is that people are more interested in the quality of their lives than the length. They don't want to be encumbered by poor health and financial worries in their older years."

Survey respondents reported they would like to live to an average of about 91 years, but expect to live to 80. According to the U.S. Census Bureau, the life expectancy for a child born in 1997 is 76.5 years. A person turning 65 in 1997 could expect to live another 17.6 years.

The telephone survey, conducted from April 9 to 14 for AARP by Market Facts, Inc. of McLean, Va., also found that a huge majority of people are aware that their behavior and habits can affect how well they age.

This was "the real take-home message for me," says Terrie Wetle, deputy director of the National Institute on Aging. "It was very good news that more than 90 percent recognized that they had some control over how they age."

Harvard neuropsychologist Margery Hutter Silver, who is associate director of the New England Centenarian Study, agrees: "Just the fact of thinking you have control is going to have tremendous impact."

Over eight out of 10 respondents reported doing things to stay healthy. Seventy percent said they exercise, 33 percent watch their diets, 10 percent watch their weight and 10 percent maintain a positive attitude.

Most Americans are also optimistic that life will be better for the typical 80-year-old in 2050 and that medical advances will lead to cures for cancer, heart disease, AIDS and Alzheimer's disease.

Yet, even though they are taking steps to age well and are upbeat about the future, most people are still leery of what might befall them if they live to be 100.

That shouldn't come as a surprise, people of all ages told the Bulletin.

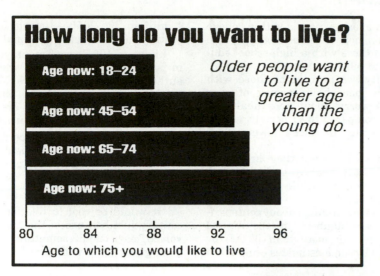

How long do you want to live?

Age now: 18–24

Age now: 45–54

Age now: 65–74

Age now: 75+

Older people want to live to a greater age than the young do.

80   84   88   92   96

Age to which you would like to live

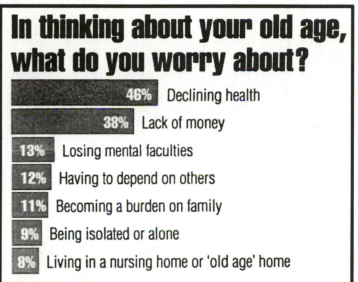

In thinking about your old age, what do you worry about?

46% Declining health

38% Lack of money

13% Losing mental faculties

12% Having to depend on others

11% Becoming a burden on family

9% Being isolated or alone

8% Living in a nursing home or 'old age' home

AARP SURVEY BY MARKET FACTS, INC. MCLEAN, VA.

"Our society bases its economy on young stars and young entrepreneurs," says Lynda Preble, 28, who works for a public relations firm in San Francisco. "I'm sure most people don't understand where they fit in once they are older."

"I was not surprised," says writer and publicist Susan Hartt, 57, of Baltimore. "As the saying goes, 'Old age is not for sissies.'"

Even though disability rates among the old are declining, chronic health problems and poverty are still more likely to appear in advanced age, Wetle says, and "people know that."

"I'm going to hang it up when I'm restricted to bed," say Marion Ballard, 59, a former software company owner in Bethesda, Md.

"A slow mental decline scares me the most," says Lilavati Sinclair, a 32-year-old mother in Bothell, Wash. For Peter Winkert, 47, a sales executive in Cazenovia, N.Y., "running out of income is my biggest concern."

Others express fear of being alone, burdening their families, living in a nursing home or, as one person puts it, "losing my joy and will to keep on living."

How old a person is tends to influence his or her views on age and aging. Among those ages 18 to 24, a person is "old" at 58, according to the survey, while those 65 or older think "old" starts at 75.

"I used to think I would be dead at 30," jokes one woman who just turned 30. "Now that I know I'll be around a while, I want to enjoy life as long as possible."

Not unexpectedly, older people hope and expect to live to greater ages than the young. Survey respondents 75 and older want to live to 96, but for 18- to 24-year-olds, 88 is enough.

Julie Vermillion, 24, who is a public affairs assistant in Washington, D.C., and Erin Laughlin, 23, a dog trainer in Sebastopol, Calif., say that living to 85 is about right.

Yet 85-year-old Lucille Runkel of Cochranton, Pa., is still in good shape and still active. "I wouldn't mind living to be 100 if I'm in good health," she says, "but I don't want to be dependent on my children."

"If I feel well enough," says lawyer Lester Nurick, 84, of Potomac, Md., "I could go on forever....but I would never put a number on it."

"Young people deal with the mythology instead of the reality of aging," says AARP's Swank. "Older people are living it, and many embrace the challenges, the joys. No one wants to be debilitated, but for many, the later years are highly satisfying. So why walk away from it?"

Older people have also witnessed the development of life-saving vaccines, drugs and surgical techniques and are more confident of continuing medical breakthroughs. "What we see here," Swank says, "is the wisdom of age."

Writer Hartt says she wouldn't mind putting up with some infirmities to achieve such wisdom. "So what was adolescence—a day at the beach?"

Lack of information helps fuel the myths of old age. For example, only 28 percent of survey respondents know that the 85-plus age group is the fastest-growing segment of the population.

And many people don't know that most Americans over 65 live independently, with fewer than 5 percent in nursing homes, adds Harvard's Silver.

Other survey highlights:

• On average, people with a college education hope to live longer (to age 92) than those with a high-school education (to 89).

• Fifty-two percent of those with a yearly household income of over $50,000 worry about poor health in old age, compared to 41 percent among those with incomes lower than $50,000.

• Those who say they are doing things to stay healthy and active expect to live to 81, while others expect to live to 76.

Given new findings about centenarians—whose numbers in the United States grew to more than 62,000 by 1998 and by some estimates could reach 1 million by 2050—aiming for the century mark is not unreasonable.

Living to 100 doesn't mean you'll be in poor health, says Silver, who is co-author with Thomas T. Perls, M.D., of "Living to 100" (Basic Books, 1999). To the contrary, centenarians are often healthier than people in their 80s.

But there's a trick, according to their book: "One must stay healthy the vast majority of one's life in order to live to 100."

Some think it's a worthy goal.

"It would be cool to live for over a century, just because of the history involved," says one 30-something. "I can't even guess what will come."

CULTURE & IDEAS

Is there life after death?

Near-death experiences may be physiological. Or they may be peepholes into a world beyond

BY BRENDAN I. KOERNER

On the talk-show circuit and the bestseller list, the tales are legion. After being struck by lightning, a man meets a "Being of Light" who grants forgiveness for a lifetime of violence. In full cardiac arrest on the operating table, a grade-school teacher travels down a long tunnel to "a place filled up with love, and a beautiful bright white light." And Elvis Presley takes her gently by the hand.

As sophisticated medical technology has permitted more and more people to journey back from the brink of death, such seemingly mystical reports have become almost commonplace. Of the nearly 18 percent of Americans who claimed in a recent *U.S. News* poll to have been on the verge of dying, many researchers estimate that a third have had unusual experiences while straddling the line between life and death—perhaps as many as 15 million Americans. A small percentage recall vivid images of an afterlife—including tunnels of light, peaceful meadows, and angelic figures clad in white.

No matter what the nature of the experience, it alters some lives. Alcoholics find themselves unable to imbibe. Hardened criminals opt for a life of helping others. Atheists embrace the existence of a deity, while dogmatic members of a particular religion report "feeling welcome in any church or temple or mosque."

> ## "Most near-death survivors say they don't think there is a God. They Know."
>
> **NANCY EVANS BUSH,** *president emeritus of the International Association for Near-Death Studies*

Such dramatic changes have piqued the imagination of those searching for evidence of the mystical. Bruce Greyson, 50, is a psychiatrist at the University of Virginia Medical School who has spent much of his professional life investigating these events as possible "peepholes" into a world beyond. Greyson says that those who have such experiences "become enamored with the spiritual part of life, and less so with possessions, power, and prestige." Nancy Evans Bush, president emeritus of the International Association for Near-Death Studies, says the experience is revelatory. "Most near-death survivors say they don't *think* there is a God," she says. "They *know*."

Stories about strange events in the borderland between life and death are hardly new. Over two millenniums ago, in the *Republic,* Plato recounted a gravely wounded soldier's journey toward "a straight light like a pillar, most nearly resembling a rainbow, but brighter and purer." Near-death experiences aren't fresh to popular literature, either. Thirteenth-century monks wrote of a farmer who returned from the edge with tales of "corridors of fire" and "icy" paths to the afterlife.

Heavenly cars. And tales from the realm between life and death aren't limited to the West. In Micronesia, "experiencers" have reported that heaven resembles a bustling American city with skyscrapers and plenty of automobiles. In India, the afterlife has frequently been described as a giant bureaucracy, in which survivors are sent back to life because of "clerical error." "There's a lot of cultural overlay," says Greyson, who also edits the *Journal of Near-Death Studies*. It publishes articles on topics ranging from the scholarly ("Near-death Experiences: A Neurophysiological Explanatory Model") to the suspect ("Death and Renewal in *The Velveteen Rabbit*"). "Many people describe it as an ineffable experience, so it's no surprise that they come up with models based on their background," Greyson recounts. Almost all reports from around the world bear similarities to familiar daytime TV fare—the out-of-body feeling, the life review, the presence of deceased relatives on "the other side."

Until recently, however, these anecdotes were usually dismissed as hallucinations or after-the-fact inventions, lumped in with alien abductions. Many who were convinced they had glimpsed an afterlife were afraid to describe their experiences for fear of being labeled crazy. The medical community's perception of these reports began to change in 1975 when Raymond Moody published *Life After Life,* a book that coined the term near-death experience (NDE) to describe this hard-to-define phenomenon. Moody interviewed 150 near-death patients who reported vivid experiences (flashing back to childhood, coming face to face with Christ). He found that those who had undergone NDEs became more altruistic, less materialistic, and more loving.

"NDEs offer a transient reduction in pain and suffering."

DANIEL ALKON, *neuroscientist*

Scores of psychiatrists and neuroscientists have since sought to uncover the roots of these powerful experiences. But serious research into the phenomenon has been difficult. "It's very much like trying to conduct research on humor," says John Sappington, a psychologist at Augusta College. "You can't just get people into the lab and say, 'Now, be funny!'" The task is complicated by the personal nature of the experience; researchers must rely on hearsay that, by definition, cannot be corroborated.

Seeking the greater certainty of controlled observations in the laboratory, a

number of researchers are taking a physiological approach to uncovering the causes behind NDEs. Michael A. Persinger, a neuroscientist at Laurentian University in Sudbury, Ontario, has induced many of the characteristics of an NDE—the sensation of moving through a tunnel, the brilliant white light. He has done so by stimulating the brain's right temporal lobe, the area above the right ear responsible for perception, with mild electromagnetic fields. In England, Karl Jansen has zeroed in on the brain's reaction to shifting levels of ketamine, a powerful neurotransmitter. Often ingested as a recreational drug—its street name is Special K—ketamine frequently causes the out-of-body sensation common to NDEs. The U.S. Navy has managed to replicate many of the sensations of an NDE by subjecting test pilots to massive centrifugal force—a physical stress that can include the presence of a patriarchal figure interpreted by some as God. "There's nothing magical about the NDE," Persinger asserts.

Physiological findings have led many researchers to view NDEs not as glimpses into a world beyond but as insights into the world within the human mind. "I think it is an evolutionary adaptation," says Sherwin Nuland, the National Book Award-winning author of *How We Die.* He ascribes NDEs to the actions of opiate-like compounds known as endorphins, which are released by the brain at times of great physical stress to deaden pain and alleviate fear. He scoffs at those who view NDEs as a temporary bridge to an afterlife. "I think that the mind is just trying to save itself from the horror of unbelievable trauma," he says.

Daniel Alkon, chief of the Neural Systems Laboratory at the National Institutes of Health, says anoxia (oxygen deprivation in the brain) lies at the root of all NDEs. When death appears certain, he argues, the body will often shut down and "play dead" as a last course of action. His skepticism is significant because many years ago, as a result of a hemorrhage, he had a near-death experience himself.

Despite the strides in explaining NDEs through clinical investigation, some researchers believe that the physiological approach is insufficient. "These are just armchair speculations. Finding a chemical change in the brain does not necessarily prove that it causes NDEs," argues Greyson. For Greyson and others

who view NDEs as mystical experiences, the skeptics in the lab are only solving a small part of the puzzle.

"I came away convinced that these are real spiritual experiences."

DIANE KOMP, *pediatric oncologist*

Watching heart patients. A block from the University of Virginia's Charlottesville campus, in an old house labeled Division of Personality Studies, Greyson and Ian Stevenson, 79, are in the middle of a three-year, $250,000 study they hope will answer many of the questions that, in their view, the physiological approach doesn't address. The pair, whose funding comes from a German psychiatric institute rather than the university, have been monitoring cardiac arrest patients. They are searching for insight into notable changes that often accompany the experience, such as heightened zest for life and unconditional love for all humans.

The two are annoyed by those who have made near-death experiences a pop culture fad more likely to be featured in a tabloid alongside a scoop about an 800-pound human baby than in a medical journal. "It makes people take us less seriously," says Greyson. For many scholars, Greyson and Stevenson's work has never threatened to enter the realm of serious inquiry. Nuland debunks near-death research as pseudoscience investigating nothing more than "pleasant illusions." Moody insists "there is no imaginable empirical evidence to prove that there is an afterlife."

Despite the unmuffled snickering of some colleagues, Greyson and Stevenson insist that their research is intellectually rigorous. "Most scientists shy away from the area of the paranormal," says Greyson. "I think the research we're doing here is breaking down some of those prejudices."

Greyson and Stevenson have been instrumental in gathering evidence indicating that religious backgrounds do not affect who is most likely to have an NDE. They have mapped out the conversion-like effects of NDEs that can sometimes lead to hardship. ("They can see the good in all people," Greyson says of people who have experienced the phenomenon: "They act fairly naive, and they often allow themselves to be opened up to con men who abuse their trust.") They have gathered reports of high divorce rates and problems in the workplace following near-death experiences. "The values you get from an NDE are not the ones you need to function in everyday life," says Greyson. Having stared eternity in the face, he observes, those who return often lose their taste for ego-boosting achievement.

Greyson and Stevenson's interest is not limited to the psychological realm, however. They are intrigued by reports of the chronically ill regaining their vigor, and even "miraculous" cures from cancer or HIV infection—claims most of the scientific community put in the same category as snake oil and faith healing. The Virginia researchers are undiscouraged by this scorn. They believe

"Most say that
words cannot describe
the experience."

BRUCE GREYSON, *psychiatrist, with his colleague, Ian Stevenson.*

that they may be pushing the boundaries of human knowledge. "NDEs demonstrate how little we know, and how far we have to go to understand our role in the universe," says Greyson. Stevenson, now in the 35th year of a study of children who claim to recall past lives, concurs. "The evidence for survival after death comes from a wide variety of sources, including NDEs," he says. "Certain communications through mediums deserve attention, too." Operating in terrain disdained by many scientists as a twilight zone, Greyson and Steven-

son hope to peer through a portal into an afterlife.

Not even the diehard skeptics doubt the powerful personal effects of NDEs. "This is a profound emotional experience," explains Nuland. "People are convinced that they've seen heaven." Persinger adds: "The fact that we're studying a neural basis for it doesn't demean its significance." Diane Komp, a pediatric oncologist at Yale, was transformed by witnessing children's NDEs—an 8-year-old with cancer envisioning a school bus driven by Jesus, a 7-year-old leukemia patient hearing a chorus of angels before passing away. "I was an atheist, and it changed my view of spiritual matters," recalls Komp. "Call it a conversion. I came away convinced that these are real spiritual experiences."

For the many Americans who believe they have been privy to a glimpse of life after death, no amount of clinical explanation will shake their faith.

With Joshua Rich

Unit 4

Unit Selections

Key Points to Consider

❖ What is emotional intelligence? How does it develop? How can we tell if we possess it? How do people with EQ differ from people without it? How is EQ related to morality?

❖ Why is the face important in emotional expression? How do researchers study the face and emotionality? Why is it important to understand the emotions of others? Does culture influence emotionality?

❖ What is morality? Why is it such a valuable commodity? What are some theories of the development of conscience? What happens to children who remain self-centered in their conceptions of morality?

❖ What is a friend? What kinds of people attract us to them? How is mental health related to friendship?

❖ How can scientists study marriage? How can we predict whose marriage will end in divorce?

❖ What are some of the signs of an unhappy marriage? Why and how does marital infidelity push a couple toward unhappiness? Can such marriages be saved? Under what circumstances?

❖ What are the causes of shyness? How might others perceive shy individuals?

❖ Why is stress at epidemic proportions in modern American society? How can people better cope with stress? What is the Type A personality? Why are Type A individuals especially prone to stress?

❖ Why is it so hard to apologize? What are the elements of a sincere apology (one that would have the effect of reestablishing trust and friendship)?

❖ Are men and women equally violent and hostile? What causes each to become angry? How can we alter environments to reduce the level of violence and hostility in our society?

 **Links**

www.dushkin.com/online/

These sites are annotated on pages 4 and 5.

People in groups can be seen everywhere: couples in love, parents and their children, teachers and students, gatherings of friends, church groups, theatergoers. People have much influence on one another when they congregate in groups.

Groups spend a great deal of time communicating with members and nonmembers. The communication can be intentional and forceful, such as when protesters demonstrate against a totalitarian regime. Or it can be more subtle, for example, when fraternity brothers reject a prospective brother who refuses to wear the symbols of membership.

Some groups, such as corporations, issue formal rules in writing; discipline for rule breaking is also formalized. Other groups, families or trios of friends, for example, possess fewer, less formal rules and disciplinary codes, but their rules are still quickly learned by and are important to all unit members.

Some groups are large but seek more members, such as nationalized labor unions. Other groups seek to keep their groups small and somewhat exclusive, such as teenage cliques. Groups exist that are almost completely adversarial with other groups. Other groups pride themselves on their ability to remain cooperative, such as neighbors who band together in a community crime watch.

Psychologists are convinced that interpersonal relationships are important to the human experience. There is ample evidence that contact with other people is a necessary part of human existence. Research has shown that most individuals do not like being isolated from other people. In fact, in laboratory experiments they begin to hallucinate the presence of others. In prisons, solitary confinement is often used as a form of punishment. Other research has shown that people who must wait under stressful circumstances prefer to wait with others. This unit examines various types of groups such as friends, dating partners, and married couples. The next unit examines the effects of larger groups, specifically, of society at large on its members.

The first three essays look at what it takes to be socially successful. The first article reviews a hot issue: emotional intelligence, or EQ. Daniel Goleman's pioneering book on this topic suggests that emotional intelligence is more important to our success in life than any other aspect of our being. In her article on this book, Nancy Gibbs discusses the concept and its utility.

The next article also is of a general introductory nature. Individuals who are skilled at EQ are expert at reading others' as well as their emotions. In "Face It!" Deborah Blum describes how we express genuine and faked emotions. The face is the key to our emotional life. Blum describes the research of scientists who study how emotions are both signaled to and read by others.

A concept relevant to successfully interacting with others is morality. Should we take advantage of our friends? Morality is that force or motive that prevents us from doing malicious things to others. In "The Moral Development of Children," William Damon discusses how children learn to move from self-centered morality to higher levels that take into account others' needs. In essence, the moral child is a self-directed child, motivated to behave morally.

We next cover some specific types of interpersonal interactions. The first three social situations involve friendship, dating, and marriage, which are deemed important positive social relationships.

In "Friendships and Adaptation across the Life Span," the authors discuss why friendship is so important and disclose how friendship is construed differently by children and adults. They conclude by explaining our attraction to different types of individuals. It is no surprise that we are most attracted to competent, mentally healthy individuals.

In "The New Flirting Game," Deborah Lott discusses flirting, a form of social interaction that is not new as a means of attracting a date or mate. Lott examines new flirting styles.

In the final of these three articles on positive interactions, we look at marriage. Barbara Kantrowitz and Pat Wingert reveal what science is demonstrating about happy couples and their interactions. Couples in a laboratory are videotaped and other measurements are taken to determine how happy and unhappy couples react to each other, helping us predict who is at risk for divorce.

We then examine some rather negative social interactions. In the next article, we investigate the downside of an unhappy marriage. "Shattered Vows" discusses what happens when romantic relationships turn sour. Marital infidelity is difficult to overcome when it is discovered by the betrayed spouse. This article utilizes both data and anecdote to answer a series of questions about shattered vows.

If we are shy, it is hard for us to make friends in the first place. In "Social Anxiety," the authors discuss research about the millions of Americans who struggle with shyness.

Stress is a modern American plague that affects our physical and psychological being. Benedict Carey suggests, in "Don't Face Stress Alone," that the social support of friends can be highly effective in managing stress. In so doing, Carey also furnishes the reader with helpful information about the Type A or workaholic personality.

Should we find ourselves in a position where we have blemished our friendship, "Go Ahead, Say You're Sorry" explores how and when to apologize.

The final article in this series on negative relations is about hostility in women. Most Americans think that men are the perpetrators of aggression, violence, and hostility. This article discloses statistics about women and crime, showing that women can be quite hostile and violent.

Relating to Others

The EQ Factor

New brain research suggests that emotions, not IQ, may be the true measure of human intelligence

NANCY GIBBS

IT TURNS OUT THAT A SCIENTIST CAN SEE THE future by watching four-year-olds interact with a marshmallow. The researcher invites the children, one by one, into a plain room and begins the gentle torment. You can have this marshmallow right now, he says. But if you wait while I run an errand, you can have two marshmallows when I get back. And then he leaves.

Some children grab for the treat the minute he's out the door. Some last a few minutes before they give in. But others are determined to wait. They cover their eyes; they put their heads down; they sing to themselves; they try to play games or even fall asleep. When the researcher returns he gives the children their hard-earned marshmallows. And then, science waits for them to grow up.

By the time the children reach high school, something remarkable has happened. A survey of the children's parents and teachers found that those who as four-year-olds had the fortitude to hold out for the second marshmallow generally grew up to be better adjusted, more popular, adventurous, confident and dependable teenagers. The children who gave in to temptation early on were more likely to be lonely, easily frustrated and stubborn. They buckled under stress and shied away from challenges. And when some of the students in the two groups took the Scholastic Aptitude Test, the kids who held out longer scored an average of 210 points higher.

When we think of brilliance we see Einstein, deep-eyed, woolly haired, a thinking machine with skin and mismatched socks. High achievers, we imagine, were wired for greatness from birth. But then you have to wonder why, over time, natural talent seems to ignite in some people and dim in others. This is where the marshmallows come in. It seems that the ability to delay gratification is a master skill, a triumph of the reasoning brain over the impulsive one. It is a sign, in short, of emotional intelligence. And it doesn't show up on an IQ test.

For most of this century, scientists have worshiped the hardware of the brain and the software of the mind; the messy powers of the heart were left to the poets. But cognitive theory could simply not explain the questions we wonder about most: why some people just seem to have a gift for living well; why the smartest kid in the class will probably not end up the richest; why we like some people virtually on sight and distrust others; why some people remain buoyant in the face of troubles that would sink a less resilient soul. What qualities of the mind or spirit, in short, determine who succeeds?

The phrase "emotional intelligence" was coined by Yale psychologist Peter Salovey and the University of New Hampshire's John Mayer five years ago to describe qualities like understanding one's own feelings, empathy for the feelings of others and "the regulation of emotion in a way that enhances living." Their notion is about to bound into the national conversation, handily shortened to EQ, thanks to a new book, *Emotional Intelligence* (Bantam; $23.95) by Daniel Goleman. Goleman, a Harvard psychology Ph.D. and a *New York Times* science writer with a gift for making even the chewiest scientific theories digestible to lay readers, has brought together a decade's worth of behavioral research into how the mind processes feelings. His goal, he announces on the cover, is to redefine what it means to be smart. His thesis: when it comes to predict- ing people's success, brainpower as measured by IQ and standardized achievement tests may actually matter less than the qualities of mind once thought of as "character" before the word began to sound quaint.

At first glance, there would seem to be little that's new here to any close reader of fortune cookies. There may be no less original idea than the notion that our hearts hold dominion over our heads. "I was so angry," we say, "I couldn't think straight." Neither is it surprising that "people skills" are useful, which amounts to saying, it's good to be nice. "It's so true it's trivial," says Dr. Paul McHugh, director of psychiatry at Johns Hopkins University School of Medicine. But if it were that simple, the book would not be quite so interesting or its implications so controversial.

This is no abstract investigation. Goleman is looking for antidotes to restore "civility to our streets and caring to our communal life." He sees practical applications everywhere for how companies should decide whom to hire, how couples can increase the odds that their marriages will last, how parents should raise their children and how schools should teach them. When street gangs substitute for families and schoolyard insults end in stabbings, when more than half of marriages end in divorce, when the majority of the children murdered in this country are killed by parents and stepparents, many of whom say they were trying to discipline the child for behavior like blocking the TV or crying too much, it suggests a demand for remedial emotional education. While children are still young, Goleman argues, there is a "neurological window of opportunity" since the brain's prefrontal circuitry, which regulates how we act on what we feel, probably does not mature until mid-adolescence.

And it is here the arguments will break out. Goleman's highly popularized conclusions, says McHugh, "will chill any veteran scholar of psychotherapy and any neuroscientist who worries about how his research may come to be applied." While many researchers in this relatively new field are glad to see emotional issues finally taken seriously, they fear that a notion as handy as EQ invites misuse. Goleman admits the danger of suggesting that you can assign a numerical yardstick to a person's character as well as his intellect; Goleman never even uses the phrase EQ in his book. But he (begrudgingly) approved an "unscientific" EQ test in *USA Today* with choices like "I am aware of even subtle feelings as I have them," and "I can sense the pulse of a group or relationship and state unspoken feelings."

"You don't want to take an average of your emotional skill," argues Harvard psychology professor Jerome Kagan, a pioneer in child-development research. "That's what's wrong with the concept of intelligence for mental skills too. Some people handle anger well but can't handle fear. Some people can't take joy. So each emotion has to be viewed differently."

EQ is not the opposite of IQ. Some people are blessed with a lot of both, some with little of either. What researchers have been trying to understand is how they complement each other; how one's ability to handle stress, for instance, affects the ability to concentrate and put intelligence to use. Among the ingredients for success, researchers now generally agree that IQ counts for about 20%; the rest depends on everything from class to luck to the neural pathways that have developed in the brain over millions of years of human evolution.

It is actually the neuroscientists and evolutionists who do the best job of explaining the reasons behind the most unreasonable behavior. In the past decade or so, scientists have learned enough about the brain to make judgments about where emotion comes from and why we need it. Primitive emotional responses held the keys to survival: fear drives the blood into the large muscles, making it easier to run; surprise triggers the eyebrows to rise, allowing the eyes to widen their view and gather more information about an unexpected event. Disgust wrinkles up the face and closes the nostrils to keep out foul smells.

Emotional life grows out of an area of the brain called the limbic system, specifically the amygdala, whence come delight and disgust and fear and anger. Millions of years ago, the neocortex was added on, enabling humans to plan, learn and remember. Lust grows from the limbic system; love, from the neocortex. Animals like reptiles that have no neocortex cannot experience anything like maternal love; this is why baby

snakes have to hide to avoid being eaten by their parents. Humans, with their capacity for love, will protect their offspring, allowing the brains of the young time to develop. The more connections between limbic system and the neocortex, the more emotional responses are possible.

It was scientists like Joseph LeDoux of New York University who uncovered these cerebral pathways. LeDoux's parents owned a meat market. As a boy in Louisiana, he first learned about his future specialty by cutting up cows' brains for sweetbreads. "I found them the most interesting part of the cow's anatomy," he recalls. "They were visually pleasing—lots of folds, convolutions and patterns. The cerebellum was more interesting to look at than steak." The butchers' son became a neuroscientist, and it was he who discovered the short circuit in the brain that lets emotions drive action before the intellect gets a chance to intervene.

A hiker on a mountain path, for example, sees a long, curved shape in the grass out of the corner of his eye. He leaps out of the way before he realizes it is only a stick that looks like a snake. Then he calms down; his cortex gets the message a few milliseconds after his amygdala and "regulates" its primitive response.

Without these emotional reflexes, rarely conscious but often terribly powerful, we would scarcely be able to function. "Most decisions we make have a vast number of possible outcomes, and any attempt to analyze all of them would never end," says University of Iowa neurologist Antonio Damasio, author of *Descartes' Error: Emotion, Reason and the Human Brain*. "I'd ask you to lunch tomorrow, and when the appointed time arrived, you'd still be thinking about whether you should come." What tips the balance, Damasio contends, is our unconscious assigning of emotional values to some of those choices. Whether we experience a somatic response—a gut feeling of dread or a giddy sense of elation—emotions are helping to limit the field in any choice we have to make. If the prospect of lunch with a neurologist is unnerving or distasteful, Damasio suggests, the invitee will conveniently remember a previous engagement.

When Damasio worked with patients in whom the connection between emotional brain and neocortex had been severed because of damage to the brain, he discovered how central that hidden pathway is to how we live our lives. People who had lost that linkage were just as smart and quick to reason, but their lives often fell apart nonetheless. They could not make decisions because they didn't know how they felt about their choices. They couldn't react to warnings or anger in other people. If they made a mistake, like a bad investment, they felt no regret or shame and so were bound to repeat it.

If there is a cornerstone to emotional intelligence on which most other emotional skills depend, it is a sense of self-awareness, of being smart about what we feel. A person whose day starts badly at home may be grouchy all day at work without quite knowing why. Once an emotional response comes into awareness—or, physiologically, is processed through the neocortex—the chances of handling it appropriately improve. Scientists refer to "metamood," the ability to pull back and recognize that "what I'm feeling is anger," or sorrow, or shame.

Metamood is a difficult skill because emotions so often appear in disguise. A person in mourning may know he is sad, but he may not recognize that he is also angry at the person for dying—because this seems somehow inappropriate. A parent who yells at the child who ran into the street is expressing anger at disobedience, but the degree of anger may owe more to the fear the parent feels at what could have happened.

In Goleman's analysis, self-awareness is perhaps the most crucial ability because it allows us to exercise some self-control. The idea is not to repress feeling (the reaction that has made psychoanalysts rich) but rather to do what Aristotle considered the hard work of the will. "Anyone can become angry—that is easy," he wrote in the *Nicomachean Ethics*. "But to be angry with the right person, to the right degree, at the right time, for the right purpose, and in the right way—that is not easy."

Some impulses seem to be easier to control than others. Anger, not surprisingly, is one of the hardest, perhaps because of its evolutionary value in priming people to action. Researchers believe anger usually arises out of a sense of being trespassed against—the belief that one is being robbed of what is rightfully his. The body's first response is a surge of energy, the release of a cascade of neurotransmitters called catecholamines. If a person is already aroused or under stress, the threshold for release is lower, which helps explain why people's tempers shorten during a hard day.

Scientists are not only discovering where anger comes from; they are also exposing myths about how best to handle it. Popular wisdom argues for "letting it all hang out" and having a good cathartic rant. But Goleman cites studies showing that dwelling on anger actually increases its power; the body needs a chance to process the adrenaline through exercise, relaxation techniques, a well-timed intervention or even the old admonition to count to 10.

Anxiety serves a similar useful purpose, so long as it doesn't spin out of control. Worrying is a rehearsal for danger; the act of fretting focuses the mind on a problem so it can search efficiently for solutions. The danger comes when worrying blocks thinking, becoming an end in itself or a path to resignation instead of perseverance. Over-worrying about failing increases the likelihood of failure; a salesman so concerned about his falling sales that he can't bring himself to pick up the phone guarantees that his sales will fall even further.

But why are some people better able to "snap out of it" and get on with the task at hand? Again, given sufficient self-awareness, people develop coping mechanisms. Sadness and discouragement, for instance, are "low arousal" states, and the dispirited salesman who goes out for a run is triggering a high arousal state that is incompatible with staying blue. Relaxation works better for high energy moods like anger or anxiety. Either way, the idea is to shift to a state of arousal that breaks the destructive cycle of the dominant mood.

The idea of being able to predict which salesmen are most likely to prosper was not an abstraction for Metropolitan Life, which in the mid-'80s was hiring 5,000 salespeople a year and training them at a cost of more than $30,000 each. Half quit the first year, and four out of five within four years. The reason: selling life insurance involves having the door slammed in your face over and over again. Was it possible to identify which people would be better at handling frustration and take each refusal as a challenge rather than a setback?

The head of the company approached psychologist Martin Seligman at the University of Pennsylvania and invited him to test some of his theories about the importance of optimism in people's success. When optimists fail, he has found, they attribute the failure to something they can change, not some innate weakness that they are helpless to overcome. And that confidence in their power to effect change is self-reinforcing. Seligman tracked 15,000 new workers who had taken two tests. One was the company's regular screening exam, the other Seligman's test measuring their levels of optimism. Among the new hires was a group who flunked the screening test but scored as "superoptimists" on Seligman's exam. And sure enough, they did the best of all; they outsold the pessimists in the regular group by 21% in the first year and 57% in the second. For years after that, passing Seligman's test was one way to get hired as a MetLife salesperson.

Perhaps the most visible emotional skills, the ones we recognize most readily, are the "people skills" like empathy, graciousness, the ability to read a social situation. Researchers believe that about 90% of emotional communication is nonverbal. Harvard psychologist Robert Rosenthal developed the PONS test (Profile of Nonverbal Sensitivity) to measure people's ability to read emotional

One Way to Test Your EQ

UNLIKE IQ, WHICH IS GAUGED BY THE FAMOUS STANFORD-Binet tests, EQ does not lend itself to any single numerical measure. Nor should it, say experts. Emotional intelligence is by definition a complex, multifaceted quality representing such intangibles as self-awareness, empathy, persistence and social deftness.

Some aspects of emotional intelligence, however, can be quantified. Optimism, for example, is a handy measure of a person's self-worth. According to Martin Seligman, a University of Pennsylvania psychologist, how people respond to setbacks—optimistically or pessimistically—is a fairly accurate indicator of how well they will succeed in school, in sports and in certain kinds of work. To test his theory, Seligman devised a questionnaire to screen insurance salesmen at MetLife.

In Seligman's test, job applicants were asked to imagine a hypothetical event and then choose the response (A or B) that most closely resembled their own. Some samples from his questionnaire:

You forget your spouse's (boyfriend's/girlfriend's) birthday.
A. I'm not good at remembering birthdays.
B. I was preoccupied with other things.

You owe the library $10 for an overdue book.
A. When I am really involved in what I am reading, I often forget when its due.
B. I was so involved in writing the report, I forgot to return the book.

You lose your temper with a friend.
A. He or she is always nagging me.
B. He or she was in a hostile mood.

You are penalized for returning your income-tax forms late.
A. I always put off doing my taxes.
B. I was lazy about getting my taxes done this year.

You've been feeling run-down.
A. I never get a chance to relax.
B. I was exceptionally busy this week.

A friend says something that hurts your feelings.
A. She always blurts things out without thinking of others.
B. My friend was in a bad mood and took it out on me.

You fall down a great deal while skiing.
A. Skiing is difficult.
B. The trails were icy.

You gain weight over the holidays, and you can't lose it.
A. Diets don't work in the long run.
B. The diet I tried didn't work.

Seligman found that those insurance salesman who answered with more B's than A's were better able to overcome bad sales days, recovered more easily from rejection and were less likely to quit. People with an optimistic view of life tend to treat obstacles and setbacks as temporary (and therefore surmountable). Pessimists take them personally; what others see as fleeting, localized impediments, they view as pervasive and permanent.

The most dramatic proof of his theory, says Seligman, came at the 1988 Olympic Games in Seoul, South Korea, after U.S. swimmer Matt Biondi turned in two disappointing performances in this first two races. Before the Games, Biondi had been favored to win seven golds—as Mark Spitz had done 16 years earlier. After those first two races, most commentators thought Biondi would be unable to recover from his setback. Not Seligman. He had given some members of the U.S. swim team a version of his optimism test before the races; it showed that Biondi possessed an extraordinarily upbeat attitude. Rather than losing heart after turning in a bad time, as others might, Biondi tended to respond by swimming even faster. Sure enough, Biondi bounced right back, winning five gold medals in the next five races. —*By Alice Park*

cues. He shows subjects a film of a young woman expressing feelings—anger, love, jealousy, gratitude, seduction—edited so that one or another nonverbal cue is blanked out. In some instances the face is visible but not the body, or the woman's eyes are hidden, so that viewers have to judge the feeling by subtle cues. Once again, people with higher PONS scores tend to be more successful in their work and relationships; children who score well are more popular and successful in school, even [though] their IQs are quite average.

Like other emotional skills, empathy is an innate quality that can be shaped by experience. Infants as young as three months old exhibit empathy when they get upset at the sound of another baby crying. Even very young children learn by imitation; by watching how others act when they see someone in distress, these children acquire a repertoire of sensitive responses. If, on the other hand, the feelings they begin to express are not recognized and reinforced by the adults around them, they not only cease to express those feelings but they also become less able to recognize them in themselves or others.

Empathy too can be seen as a survival skill. Bert Cohler, a University of Chicago psychologist, and Fran Stott, dean of the Erikson Institute for Advanced Study in Child Development in Chicago, have found that children from psychically damaged families frequently become hypervigilant, developing an intense attunement to their parents' moods. One child they studied, Nicholas, had a horrible habit of approaching other kids in his nursery-school class as if he were going to kiss them, then would bite them instead. The scientists went back to study videos of Nicholas at 20 months interacting with his psychotic mother and found that she had responded to his every expression of anger or independence with compulsive kisses. The researchers dubbed them "kisses of death," and their true significance was obvious to Nicholas, who arched his back in horror at her approaching lips—and passed his own rage on to his classmates years later.

Empathy also acts as a buffer to cruelty, and it is a quality conspicuously lacking in child molesters and psychopaths. Goleman cites some chilling research into brutality by Robert Hare, a psychologist at the University of British Columbia. Hare found that psychopaths, when hooked up to electrodes and told they are going to receive a shock, show none of the visceral responses that fear of pain typically triggers: rapid heartbeat, sweating and so on. How could the threat of punishment deter such people from committing crimes?

It is easy to draw the obvious lesson from these test results. How much happier would we be, how much more successful as individuals and civil as a society, if we were more alert to the importance of emotional

Square Pegs in the Oval Office?

IF A HIGH DEGREE OF EMOTIONAL INTELLIGENCE IS A PREREQUISITE FOR OUTSTANDing achievement, there ought to be no better place to find it than in the White House. It turns out, however, that not every man who reached the pinnacle of American leadership was a gleaming example of self-awareness, empathy, impulse control and all the other qualities that mark an elevated EQ.

Oliver Wendell Holmes, who knew intelligence when he saw it, judged Franklin Roosevelt "a second-class intellect, but a first-class temperament." Born and educated as an aristocrat, F.D.R. had polio and needed a wheelchair for most of his adult life. Yet, far from becoming a self-pitying wretch, he developed an unbridled optimism that served him and the country well during the Depression and World War II—this despite, or because of, what Princeton professor Fred Greenstein calls Roosevelt's "tendency toward deviousness and duplicity."

Even a first-class temperament, however, is not a sure predictor of a successful presidency. According to Duke University political scientist James David Barber, the most perfect blend of intellect and warmth of personality in a Chief Executive was the brilliant Thomas Jefferson, who "knew the importance of communication and empathy. He never lost the common touch." Richard Ellis, a professor of politics at Oregon's Willamette University who is skeptical of the whole EQ theory, cites two 19th century Presidents who did not fit the mold. "Martin Van Buren was well adjusted, balanced, empathetic and persuasive, but he was not very successful," says Ellis. "Andrew Jackson was less well adjusted, less balanced, less empathetic and was terrible at controlling his own impulses, but he transformed the presidency."

Lyndon Johnson as Senate majority leader was a brilliant practitioner of the art of political persuasion, yet failed utterly to transfer that gift to the White House. In fact, says Princeton's Greenstein, L.B.J. and Richard Nixon would be labeled "worst cases" on any EQ scale of Presidents. Each was touched with political genius, yet each met with disaster. "To some extent," says Greenstein, "this is a function of the extreme aspects of their psyches; they are the political versions of Van Gogh, who does unbelievable paintings and then cuts off his ear."

History professor William Leuchtenburg of the University of North Carolina at Chapel Hill suggests that the 20th century Presidents with perhaps the highest IQs—Wilson, Hoover and Carter—also had the most trouble connecting with their constituents. Woodrow Wilson, he says, "was very high strung [and] arrogant; he was not willing to strike any middle ground. Herbert Hoover was so locked into certain ideas that you could never convince him otherwise. Jimmy Carter is probably the most puzzling of the three. He didn't have a deficiency of temperament; in fact, he was too temperate. There was an excessive rationalization about Carter's approach."

That was never a problem for John Kennedy and Ronald Reagan. Nobody ever accused them of intellectual genius, yet both radiated qualities of leadership with an infectious confidence and openheartedness that endeared them to the nation. Whether President Clinton will be so endeared remains a puzzle. That he is a Rhodes scholar makes him certifiably brainy, but his emotional intelligence is shaky. He obviously has the knack for establishing rapport with people, but he often appears so eager to please that he looks weak. "As for controlling his impulses," says Willamette's Ellis, "Clinton is terrible." **—By Jesse Birnbaum. Reported by James Carney/Washington and Lisa H. Towle/Raleigh**

intelligence and more adept at teaching it? From kindergartens to business schools to corporations across the country, people are taking seriously the idea that a little more time spent on the "touchy-feely" skills so often derided may in fact pay rich dividends.

In the corporate world, according to personnel executives, IQ gets you hired, but EQ gets you promoted. Goleman likes to tell of a manager at AT&T's Bell Labs, a think tank for brilliant engineers in New Jersey, who was asked to rank his top performers. They weren't the ones with the highest IQs; they were the ones whose E-mail got answered. Those workers who were good collaborators and networkers and popular with colleagues were more likely to get the cooperation they needed to reach their goals than the socially awkward, lone-wolf geniuses.

When David Campbell and others at the Center for Creative Leadership studied "derailed executives," the rising stars who flamed out, the researchers found that these executives failed most often because of "an interpersonal flaw" rather than a technical inability. Interviews with top executives in the U.S. and Europe turned up nine so-called fatal flaws, many of them classic emotional failings, such as "poor working relations," being "authoritarian" or "too ambitious" and having "conflict with upper management."

At the center's executive-leadership seminars across the country, managers come to get emotionally retooled. "This isn't sensitivity training or Sunday-supplement stuff," says Campbell. "One thing they know when they get through is what other people think of them." And the executives have an incentive to listen. Says Karen Boylston, director of the center's team-leadership group: "Customers are telling businesses, 'I don't care if every member of your staff graduated with honors from Harvard, Stanford and Wharton. I will take my business and go where I am understood and treated with respect.' "

Nowhere is the discussion of emotional intelligence more pressing than in schools, where both the stakes and the opportunities seem greatest. Instead of constant crisis intervention, or declarations of war on drug abuse or teen pregnancy or violence, it is time, Goleman argues, for preventive medicine. "Five years ago, teachers didn't want to think about this," says principal Roberta Kirshbaum of P.S. 75 in New York City. "But when kids are getting killed in high school, we have to deal with it." Five years ago, Kirshbaum's school adopted an emotional literacy program, designed to help children learn to manage anger, frustration, loneliness. Since then, fights at lunchtime have decreased from two or three a day to almost none.

Educators can point to all sorts of data to support this new direction. Students who are depressed or angry literally can-not learn. Children who have trouble being accepted by their classmates are 2 to 8 times as likely to drop out. An inability to distinguish distressing feelings or handle frustration has been linked to eating disorders in girls.

Many school administrators are completely rethinking the weight they have been giving to traditional lessons and standardized tests. Peter Relic, president of the National Association of Independent Schools, would like to junk the SAT completely. "Yes, it may cost a heck of a lot more money to assess someone's EQ rather than using a machine-scored test to measure IQ," he says. "But if we don't, then we're saying that a test score is more important to us than who a child is as a human being. That means an immense loss in terms of human potential because we've defined success too narrowly."

This warm embrace by educators has left some scientists in a bind. On one hand, says Yale psychologist Salovey, "I love the idea that we want to teach people a richer understanding of their emotional life, to help them achieve their goals." But, he adds, "what I would oppose is training conformity to social expectations." The danger is that any campaign to hone emotional skills in children will end up teaching that there is a "right" emotional response for any given situation—laugh at parades, cry at funerals, sit still at church. "You can teach self-control," says Dr. Alvin Poussaint, professor of psychiatry at Harvard Medical School. "You can teach that it's better to talk out your anger and not use violence. But is it good emotional intelligence not to challenge authority?"

SOME PSYCHOLOGISTS GO further and challenge the very idea that emotional skills can or should be taught in any kind of formal, classroom way. Goleman's premise that children can be trained to analyze their feelings strikes Johns Hopkins' McHugh as an effort to reinvent the encoun-ter group: "I consider that an abominable idea, an idea we have seen with adults. That failed, and now he wants to try it with children? Good grief!" He cites the description in Goleman's book of an experimental program at the Nueva Learning Center in San Francisco. In one scene, two fifth-grade boys start to argue over the rules of an exercise, and the teacher breaks in to ask them to talk about what they're feeling. "I appreciate the way you're being assertive in talking with Tucker," she says to one student. "You're not attacking." This strikes McHugh as pure folly. "The author is presuming that someone has the key to the right emotions to be taught to children. We don't even know the right emotions to be taught to adults. Do you really think a child of eight or nine really understands the difference between aggressiveness and assertiveness?"

The problem may be that there is an ingredient missing. Emotional skills, like intellectual ones, are morally neutral. Just as a genius could use his intellect either to cure cancer or engineer a deadly virus, someone with great empathic insight could use it to inspire colleagues or exploit them. Without a moral compass to guide people in how to employ their gifts, emotional intelligence can be used for good or evil. Columbia University psychologist Walter Mischel, who invented the marshmallow test and others like it, observes that the knack for delaying gratification that makes a child one marshmallow richer can help him become a better citizen or—just as easily—an even more brilliant criminal.

Given the passionate arguments that are raging over the state of moral instruction in this country, it is no wonder Goleman chose to focus more on neutral emotional skills than on the values that should govern their use. That's another book—and another debate.

—Reported by Sharon E. Epperson and Lawrence Mondi/New York, James L. Graff/Chicago and Lisa H. Towle/Raleigh

Face It!

How we make and read the fleeting split-second expressions that slip across our countenances thousands of times each day is crucial to our emotional health as individuals and to our survival as a species. BY DEBORAH BLUM

Who hasn't waited for an old friend at an airport and scanned faces impatiently as passengers come hurrying through the gate? You can recognize instantly the travelers with no one to meet them, their gaze unfocused, their expressions carefully neutral; the people expecting to be met, their eyes narrowed, their lips poised on the edge of a smile; the children returning home to their parents, their small laughing faces turned up in greeting. Finally, your own friend appears, face lighting up as you come into view. If a mirror suddenly dropped down before you, there'd be that same goofy smile on your face, the same look of uncomplicated pleasure.

Poets may celebrate its mystery and artists its beauty, but they miss the essential truth of the human countenance. As scientists now are discovering, the power of the face resides in the fleeting split-second expressions that slip across it thousands of times each day. They guide our lives, governing the way we relate to each other as individuals and the way we connect together as a society. Indeed, scientists assert, the ability to make faces—and read them—is vital both to our personal health and to our survival as a species.

Growing out of resurging interest in the emotions, psychologists have been poring over the human visage with the intensity of cryptographers scrutinizing a hidden code. In fact, the pursuits are strikingly similar. The face is the most extraordinary communicator, capable of accurately signaling emotion in a bare blink of a second, capable of concealing emotion equally well. "In a sense, the face is equipped to lie the most and leak the most, and thus can be a very confusing source of information,"

observes Paul Ekman, Ph.D., professor of psychology at the University of California in San Francisco and a pioneer in studying the human countenance.

"The face is both ultimate truth and fata morgana, declares Daniel McNeill, author of the new book *The Face* (Little Brown & Company), a vivid survey of face-related lore from the history of the nose to the merits of plastic surgery. "It is a magnificent surface, and in the last 20 years, we've learned more about it than in the previous 20 millennia."

Today, scientists are starting to comprehend the face's contradiction, to decipher the importance of both the lie and leak, and to puzzle out a basic mystery. Why would an intensely social species like ours, reliant on communication, be apparently designed to give mixed messages? By connecting expression to brain activity with extraordinary precision, researchers are now literally going beyond "skin deep" in understanding how the face connects us, when it pulls us apart. "The face is a probe, a way of helping us see what's behind people's interactions," explains psychology professor Dacher Keltner, Ph.D., of the University of California-Berkeley. Among the new findings:

• With just 44 muscles, nerves, and blood vessels threaded through a scaffolding of bone and cartilage, all layered over by supple skin, the face can twist and pull into 5,000 expressions, all the way from an outright grin to the faintest sneer.

SMILES, the most recognizable signal of HAPPINESS in the world, are so important that we can SEE them far more clearly than any other EXPRESSION—even at 300 feet, the length of a FOOTBALL field.

• There's a distinct anatomical difference between real and feigned expressions—and in the biological effect they produce in the creators of those expressions.

• We send and read signals with lightning-like speed and over great distances. A browflash—the lift of the eyebrow common when greeting a friend—lasts only a sixth of a second. We can tell in a blink of a second if a stranger's face is registering surprise or pleasure—even if he or she is 150 feet away.

• Smiles are such an important part of communication that we see them far more clearly than any other expression. We can pick up a smile at 300 feet—the length of a football field.

• Facial expressions are largely universal, products of biological imperatives. We are programmed to make and read faces. "The abilities to express and recognize emotion are inborn, genetic, evolutionary," declares George Rotter, Ph.D., professor of psychology at Montclair University in New Jersey.

• Culture, parenting, and experience can temper our ability to display and interpret emotions. Abused children may be prone to trouble because they cannot correctly gauge the meaning and intent of others' facial expressions.

Making FACES

Deciphering facial expressions first entails understanding how they are created. Since the 1980s, Ekman and Wallace Friesen, Ph.D., of the University of California in San Francisco, have been painstakingly inventorying the muscle movements that pull our features into frowns, smiles, and glares. Under their Facial Action Coding System (FACS), a wink is Action Unit 46, involving a twitch of a single muscle, the *obicularis oculi*, which wraps around the eye. Wrinkle your nose (Action Unit 09), that's a production of two muscles, the *levator labii superioris* and the *alaeque nasi*.

The smile, the most recognizable signal in the world, is a much more complex endeavor. Ekman and colleagues have so far identified 19 versions, each engaging slightly different combinations of muscles. Consider two: the beam shared by lovers reunited after a long absence and the smile given by a teller passing back the deposit slip to a bank patron.

The old phrase "smiling eyes" is exactly on target. When we are genuinely happy, as in the two lovers' re-

union, we produce what Ekman and Richard Davidson of the University of Wisconsin-Madison call a "felt" smile. The *zygomatic major* muscles, which run from cheekbone to the corner of the mouth, pull the lips upward, while the *obicularis oculi* crinkle the outer corner of the eyes. In contrast, the polite smile offered by the bank teller (or by someone hearing a traveling salesman joke for the hundredth time) pulls up the lips but, literally, doesn't reach the eyes.

It doesn't reach the brain either. Felt smiles, it seems, trigger a sort of pleasurable little hum, a scientifically measurable activity in their creators' left frontal cortex, the region of the brain where happiness is registered. Agreeable smiles simply don't produce that buzz.

Are we taught to smile and behave nicely in social situations? Well, certainly someone instructs us to say, "Have a nice day." But we seem to be born with the ability to offer both felt and social smiles. According to studies by Davidson and Nathan Fox of the University of Maryland, ten-month-old infants will curve their lips in response to the coo of friendly strangers, but they produce happy, felt smiles only at the approach of their mother. The babies' brains light with a smile, it appears, only for those they love.

Evolution's IMPERATIVE

Why are we keyed in so early to making faces? Charles Darwin argued in his 1872 book, *The Expression of the Emotions in Man and Animals*, that the ability to signal feelings, needs, and desires is critical to human survival and thus evolutionarily based. What if infants could not screw up their faces to communicate distress or hunger? Or if foes couldn't bare their teeth in angry snarls as a warning and threat? And what if we couldn't grasp the meaning of those signals in an instant but had to wait minutes for them to be decoded?

Everything known about early hominid life suggests that it was a highly social existence," observes Ekman, who has edited a just-published new edition of Darwin's classic work. "We had to deal with prey and predators; we had a very long period of child rearing. All of that would mean that survival would depend on our being able to respond quickly to each other's emotional states."

We can move PEOPLE from culture to culture and they KNOW how to make and read the same basic expressions: anger, fear, sadness, disgust, surprise, and happiness. The six appear to be HARDWIRED in our brains. EMBARRASSMENT, some suspect, may be a seventh.

Today, the need is just as great. As Ekman points out, "Imagine the trouble we'd be in, if when an aunt came to visit, she had to be taught what a newborn baby's expression meant—let alone if she was going to be a caretaker." Or if, in our world of non-stop far-flung travel, an expression of intense pain was understood in one society but not in another. "And yet," says Ekman, "we can move people from one culture to another and they just know."

Researchers have identified six basic or universal expressions that appear to be hardwired in our brains, both to make and to read: anger, fear, sadness, disgust, surprise, and happiness. Show photos of an infuriated New Yorker to a high-mountain Tibetan or of a miserable New Guinea tribeswoman to a Japanese worker, and there's no translation problem. Everyone makes the same face—and everyone gets the message.

One of the expressions that hasn't made the universal list but probably should is embarrassment. It reflects one of our least favorite emotions: who doesn't loathe that red-faced feeling of looking like a fool? Yet such displays are far less self-centered than has been assumed. Rather than marking a personal humiliation, contends Keltner, embarrassment seems designed to prompt social conciliation.

Think about it. If we accidentally spill a drink on a colleague, stumble into a stranger in the hall, what's the best way to defuse the tension and avoid an escalation into battle? Often, notes Keltner, even before offering a verbal apology, we appease the injured party by showing embarrassment.

When we're embarrassed, our hands tend to come up, partly covering the face. We rub the side of the nose. We cast our eyes downward. We also try to appear smaller, to shrink into ourselves. These behaviors aren't uniquely ours. In awkward social situations, chimpanzees and monkeys do the same thing—and accomplish the same end. The actions defuse hostility, offer a tacit apology, even elicit sympathy in viewers. (When Keltner first tentatively introduced his chosen topic at research meetings, even jaded scientists let out immediate empathetic "oohs" at the slides of people with red faces).

There are physiological changes associated with this," notes Keltner. "If people see an angry face staring at them, they have a heightened autonomic response—rising stress hormones, speeding pulse—all the signs of fear. When they see an embarrassment response, fear is reduced."

A reddened face and downward glance typically start a rapid de-escalation of hostility among children involved in playground quarrels, says Keltner. Parents go easier on youngsters who show visible embarrassment after breaking a household rule, such as playing handball on the living room wall or chasing the dog up and downstairs throughout the house. Adults also go easier on adults. In one of Keltner's studies, jurors in a hypothetical trial meted out much lighter sentences when convicted drug dealers displayed the classic signs of embarrassment.

Cultural RULES

Expressions aren't dictated by biology alone, however; they are deeply influenced by cultural attitudes. De Paul University psychologist Linda Camras, Ph.D., has been exploring why European-American adults seem so much more willing than Asians to express emotion in public. In one experiment, she studied the reactions of European-American and Asian infants, age 11 months, to being restrained by having one arm lightly grasped by a researcher.

European-American and Japanese babies were remarkably similar in their visible dislike of being held still by a stranger's grip. (The scientists let go if the babies cried for seven seconds straight.) Since infants show no apparent inborn difference in the willingness to publicly express dismay, it stands to reason that they must eventually learn the "appropriate" way to express themselves from their families and the society in which they are reared.

Ekman's work clearly shows how culture teaches us to subdue our instinctive emotional reactions. In one set of studies, he asked American and Japanese college students to watch nature films of streams tumbling down mountainsides and trees rustling in the wind, and also graphic tapes of gory surgeries, including limb amputations. Everyone grimaced at the spurting blood at first. But when a note-taking scientist clad in a white coat—the ultimate authority figure—sat in on watching the films, the Japanese students' behavior altered radically. Instead

> When it comes to READING the subtleties of emotion, women are the stronger SEX. While men almost always correctly recognize happiness in a female face, they pick up DISTRESS just 70% of the time. A WOMAN'S face has to be really sad for men to see it.

of showing revulsion, they greeted the bloody films with smiles.

"No wonder that foreigners who visit or live among the Japanese think that their expressions are different from Americans," says Ekman. "They see the results of the cultural display rules, masking and modifying the underlying universal expressions of emotion."

Blank LOOKS

Mental or physical illness, too, can interfere with the ability to make faces—with profound consequences for relationships, researchers are learning. Neurophysiologist Jonathan Cole, of Poole Hospital at the University of Southampton, Great Britain, and author of the new book *About Face* (MIT Press), points out that people with Parkinson's disease are often perceived as boring or dull because their faces are rigid and immobile.

Consider also depression. As everyone knows, it shuts down communication. But that doesn't mean only that depressed people withdraw and talk less. The normal expressiveness of the face shuts down as well.

In one experiment, psychologist Jeffrey Cohn, Ph.D., of the University of Pittsburgh had healthy mothers mimic a depressed face while holding their infants. The women were told not to smile. Their babies responded with almost instant dismay. At first they tried desperately to recruit a response from their mother, smiling more, gurgling, reaching out. "The fact that the babies were trying to elicit their mother's response shows that at an early age, we do have the beginnings of a social skill for resolving interpersonal failures," Cohn notes.

But equally important, the infants simply could not continue to interact without receiving a response. They stopped their efforts. The experiment lasted only three minutes, but by that time, the babies were themselves withdrawn. "When mothers again resumed normal behavior, babies remained distant and distressed for up to a minute," says Cohn. "You can see that maternal depression, were it chronic, could have developmental consequences."

In fact, children of depressed parents tend to become very detached in their relationships with others. They often fail to connect with other people throughout their life and experience difficulties in romantic relationships and marriage, in large part, researchers suspect, because they have trouble producing and picking up on emo-

tional signals. "We think that the lack of facial animation interferes with forming relationships," says Keltner.

Reading FACES

Displays of emotion are only half the equation, of course. How viewers interpret those signals is equally important. "We evolved a system to communicate and a capacity to interpret," observes Keltner. "But much less is known about the interpreting capacity."

What scientists do know for certain is that we are surprisingly bad at discerning the real emotions or intentions behind others' facial expressions. "One of the problems that people don't realize is how complicated face reading is," notes Pollak. "At first glance, it seems very straightforward. But if you break it down—think of all the information in the face, how quickly the brain has to comprehend and analyze it, memories come in, emotions, context, judgments—then you realize that we really can't do it all."

Or can't do it all well. What we seem to have done during our evolution is to learn shortcuts to face reading. In other words, we make snap judgments. "It's not actually a conscious decision," Pollak explains. "But decisions are being made in the brain—What am I going to pay attention to? What am I going to clue into?"

Most of us are pretty good at the strong signals—sobbing, a big grin—but we stumble on the subtleties. Some people are better than others. There's some evidence that women are more adept than men at picking up the weaker signals, especially in women's faces.

In an experiment conducted by University of Pennsylvania neuroscientists Ruben and Raquel Gur, men and women were shown photos of faces. Both genders did well at reading men's expressions. Men also were good at picking up happiness in female faces; they got it right about 90% of the time. But when it came to recognizing distress signals in women's faces, their accuracy fell to 70%.

"A woman's face had to be really sad for men to see it," says Ruben Gur. The explanation may lie in early human history. Charged with protecting their tribes, men had to be able to quickly read threats from other males, suggests Gur. Women, in contrast, en-

Abused children are so POISED to detect anger that they often will READ it into others' faces even when it isn't there. That tendency may serve them well at HOME, where they need all the self defenses they can muster, but it can lead to TROUBLE outside.

trusted with child-rearing, became more finely-tuned to interpreting emotions.

We may be biologically primed to grasp certain expressions, but our individual experiences and abilities also filter the meaning. Mental disorders, apparently, can swamp the biology of facial recognition. People with schizophrenia, for instance, are notoriously bad at face reading; when asked to look at photographs, they struggle to separate a happy face from a neutral one.

Mistaking CUES

Seth Pollak, Ph.D., a psychologist at the University of Wisconsin-Madison, has been exploring how children who have suffered extreme parental abuse—broken bones, burn scarring—read faces. In his studies, he asks these youngsters and those from normal homes to look at three photographs of faces which display classic expressions of fear, anger, and happiness. Mean-while, electrodes attached to their heads measure their brain activity.

Battered children seem to sustain a damaging one-two punch, Pollak is finding. Overall, they have a subdued level of electrical activity in the brain. (So, in fact, do people suffering from schizophrenia or alcoholism. It seems to be a sign of trouble within.) However, when abused youngsters look at the photo of an angry face, they rapidly generate a rising wave of electrical energy, sharper and stronger than anything measured in children who live in less threatening homes.

When Pollak further analyzed the brain activity readings, he found that abused children generate that panicky reaction even when there's no reason to, misreading as angry some of the other pictured faces. They are so primed to see anger, so poised for it, that when making split-second judgments, they tilt toward detection of rage.

This falls in line with findings from DePaul's Camras and other psychologists, which show that abused children struggle significantly more in deciphering ex-

Face SHAPE

Since ancient times, human beings have been making judgments about each other based not just on the expressions that cross the face but on its very structure. The practice of finding meaning in anatomy is enjoying a remarkable renaissance today.

A plethora of pop books ponder the significance of chins, eye slant, and eyebrows. One popular magazine has even started a new face-reading feature. First to be analyzed: President William Jefferson Clinton. His triangular face apparently indicates a dynamic and—big surprise—sexual personality. Among the theories now being trotted out: heavy eyelids denote jealousy, a rosebud mouth promises fidelity, and a hairy brow line ensures restlessness.

Scientists dismiss these readings as no more than facial astrology. "There is as yet no good data to support this practice," observes Lesley Zebrowitz, professor of psychology at Brandeis University.

While many may regard it as a sort of harmless parlor game, face reading does have a more pernicious effect. Charles Darwin noted that he was almost barred from voyaging on the H.M.S. Beagle because the captain thought his nose suggested a lazy nature. In the 1920s, Los Angeles judge Edward Jones insisted that he could, with over 90% accuracy, determine someone was a "born criminal" by his protruding lips and too-close-together eyes.

Though today no one would make such a blatant assessment of character based on anatomy, facial shape at least subconsciously does appear to figure into our judgments. In her book, *Reading Faces*, Zebrowitz meticulously documents her research showing that baby-faced adults, with big eyes and full cheeks and lips, bring out in the rest of us a nurturing protective response, the kind we give to children.

In one remarkable study, she tracked proceedings in Boston small claims court for more than 500 cases and found that, whatever the evidence, chubby-cheeked plaintiffs were more apt to prevail than claimants with more mature-looking faces. Says Zebrowitz: "Although our judicial system talks about 'blind justice,' it's impossible to control the extra-legal factor of stereotyping based on physical appearance."—D.B.

pression. "Overall, there's a relationship between the expressive behavior of the mother and the child's recognition ability," Camras says. "And it's an interesting kind of a difference."

Identifying negative expressions seems to be essential in human interaction; four of the six universal expressions are negative. In most homes, notes Camras, mothers use "mild negative expressions, little frowns, tightening of the mouth." Children from such families are very good at detecting early signs of anger. But youngsters from homes with raging furious moms have trouble recognizing anger. "If the mom gets really angry, it's so frightening, it's so disorganizing for children that it seems they can't learn anything from it."

The Best DEFENSE

So, out of sheer self-protection, if the children from abusive homes are uncertain about what a face says—as they often are—they'll fall back on anger as the meaning and prepare to defend themselves. "They overdetect rage," says Pollak. Does this create problems in their relationships outside the home? It's a logical, if as yet unproven, conclusion.

What Darwin tells us is that emotions are adaptations," Pollak explains. "If a child is physically abused, I'd put my money on an adaptation toward assuming hostile intent. Look at the cost for these kids of missing a threat. So what happens is, they do better in the short run—they're very acute at detecting anger and threat because unfortunately they have to be. But take them out of those maltreating families and put them with other people and their reactions don't fit."

One of Pollak's long-term goals is to find out if such harmful effects can be reversed, if abused children can regain or reconstruct the social skills—that is, reading faces—that are evidently so critical to our design.

Failure to read signals accurately may also figure in juvenile delinquency. "There are studies that have found that juvenile delinquents who are prone to aggression have trouble deciphering certain expressions," says Keltner. "They're not as good as other kids at it. Is that because they're particularly bad at reading appeasement signals like embarrassment? That's something we'd really like to know."

Truth OR LIES?

One area where *everyone* seems to have trouble in reading faces is in detecting deception. We average between 45 and 65% accuracy in picking up lies—pretty dismal when one considers that chance is 50%. Secret Service agents can notch that up a bit to about 64%; sci-

entists suspect that improvement comes only after years of scanning crowds, looking for the faces of potential assassins.

Con artists, too, seem to be especially adept at reading expressions. The latter are also skilled at faking emotions, a trait they share with actors. Not surprising, since success in both careers depends on fooling people.

We seem to be duped particularly easily by a smile. In fact, we tend to implicitly trust a smiling face, just as we do a baby-faced one. In one experiment, Rotter cut out yearbook photos of college students and then asked people to rate the individuals pictured for trustworthiness. In almost every instance, people chose the students with smiling faces as the most honest. Women with the biggest grins scored the best; men needed only a slight curve of the lips to be considered truthful. "Smiles are an enormous controller of how people perceive you," says Rotter. "It's an extremely powerful communicator, much more so than the eyes."

> We do a better job of detecting falsehoods if we listen to a voice or examine body stance than if we read a face.

Incidentally, we aren't suckered only by human faces. We can be equally and easily tricked by our fellow primates. In one classic story, a young lowland gorilla gently approached a keeper, stared affectionately into his face, gave him a hug—and stole his watch. Chimpanzees, too, are famous for their friendly-faced success in luring lab workers to approach, and then triumphantly spraying them with a mouthful of water.

There *are* clues to insincerity. We tend to hold a simulated expression longer than a real one. If we look carefully, a phony smile may have the slightly fixed expression that a child's face gets when setting a smile for a photograph. As we've discussed, we also use different muscles for felt and fake expressions. And we are apt to blink more when we're lying. But not always—and that's the problem. When Canadian researchers Susan Hyde, Kenneth Craig, and Chrisopher Patrick asked people to simulate an expression of pain, they found that the fakers used the same facial muscles—lowering their brows, tightening their lips—as did those in genuine pain. In fact, the only way to detect the fakers was that the expressions were slightly exaggerated and "blinking occurred less often, perhaps because of the cognitive demands to act as if they were in pain," the scientists explain.

We do a better job of finding a falsehood by listening to the tone of a voice or examining the stance of a body than by reading the face, maintains Ekman, who has served as a consultant for police departments, intelligence agencies, and antiterrorist groups. He's even been approached by a national television network—"I can't tell you which one"—eager to train its reporters to better recognize when sources are lying.

Which brings us to perhaps the most provocative mystery of the face: why are we so willing to trust in what the face tells us, to put our faith in a steady gaze, a smiling look? With so much apparently at stake in reading facial cues correctly, why are we so prone to mistakes?

Living SMOOTHLY

Most of us don't pick up lies and, actually, most of us don't care to," declares Ekman. "Part of the way politeness works is that we expect people to mislead us sometime—say, on a bad hair day. What we care about is that the person goes through the proper role."

Modern existence, it seems, is predicated to some extent on ignoring the true meaning of faces: our lives run more smoothly if we don't know whether people really find our jokes funny. It runs more smoothly if we don't know when people are lying to us. And perhaps it runs more smoothly if men can't read women's expressions of distress.

Darwin himself told of sitting across from an elderly woman on a railway carriage and observing that her mouth was pulled down at the corners. A proper British Victorian, he assumed that no one would display grief while traveling on public transportation. He began musing on what else might cause her frown.

While he sat there, analyzing, the woman's eyes suddenly overflowed with tears. Then she blinked them away, and there was nothing but the quiet distance between two passengers. Darwin never knew what she was thinking. Hers was a private grief, not to be shared with a stranger.

There's a lesson in that still, for all of us airport face-watchers today. That we may always see only part of the story, that what the face keeps secret may be as valuable as what it shares.

The Moral Development of Children

It is not enough for kids to tell right from wrong. They must develop a commitment to acting on their ideals. Enlightened parenting can help

by William Damon

With unsettling regularity, news reports tell us of children wreaking havoc on their schools and communities: attacking teachers and classmates, murdering parents, persecuting others out of viciousness, avarice or spite. We hear about feral gangs of children running drugs or numbers, about teenage date rape, about youthful vandalism, about epidemics of cheating even in academically elite schools. Not long ago a middle-class gang of youths terrorized an affluent California suburb through menacing threats and extortion, proudly awarding themselves points for each antisocial act. Such stories make *Lord of the Flies* seem eerily prophetic.

What many people forget in the face of this grim news is that most children most of the time do follow the rules of their society, act fairly, treat friends kindly, tell the truth and respect their elders. Many young-

sters do even more. A large portion of young Americans volunteer in community service—according to one survey, between 22 and 45 percent, depending on the location. Young people have also been leaders in social causes. Harvard University psychiatrist Robert Coles has written about children such as Ruby, an African-American girl who broke the color barrier in her school during the 1960s. Ruby's daily walk into the all-white school demonstrated a brave sense of moral purpose. When taunted by classmates, Ruby prayed for their redemption rather than cursing them. "Ruby," Coles observed, "had a will and used it to make an ethical choice; she demonstrated moral stamina; she possessed honor, courage."

All children are born with a running start on the path to moral development. A number of inborn responses predispose them to act in ethical ways. For example, empa-

thy—the capacity to experience another person's pleasure or pain vicariously—is part of our native endowment as humans. Newborns cry when they hear others cry and show signs of pleasure at happy sounds such as cooing and laughter. By the second year of life, children commonly console peers or parents in distress.

Sometimes, of course, they do not quite know what comfort to provide. Psychologist Martin L. Hoffman of New York University once saw a toddler offering his mother his security blanket when he perceived she was upset. Although the emotional disposition to help is present, the means of helping others effectively must be learned and refined through social experience. Moreover, in many people the capacity for empathy stagnates or even diminishes. People can act cruelly to those they refuse to empathize with. A New York police officer once asked a teenage thug how he could have crippled an 83-year-old woman during a mugging. The boy replied, "What do I care? I'm not her."

A scientific account of moral growth must explain both the good and the bad. Why do most children act in reasonably—sometimes exceptionally—moral ways, even when it flies in the face of their immediate self-interest? Why do some children depart from accepted standards, often to the great harm of themselves and others? How does a child acquire mores and develop a lifelong commitment to moral behavior, or not?

Psychologists do not have definitive answers to these questions, and often their studies seem merely to confirm parents' observations and intuition. But parents, like all people, can be led astray by subjective biases, incomplete information and media sensationalism. They may blame a relatively trivial event—say, a music concert—for a deep-seated problem such as drug dependency. They may incorrectly attribute their own problems to a strict upbringing and then try to compensate by raising their children in an overly permissive way. In such a hotly contested area as children's moral values, a systematic, scientific approach is the only way to avoid wild swings of emotional reaction that end up repeating the same mistakes.

The Genealogy of Morals

The study of moral development has become a lively growth industry within the social sciences. Journals are full of new findings and competing models. Some theories focus on natural biological forces; others stress social influence and experience; still others, the judgment that results from children's intellectual development. Although each theory has a different emphasis, all recognize that no single cause can account for either moral or immoral behavior. Watching violent videos or

The Six Stages of Moral Judgment

Growing up, children and young adults come to rely less on external discipline and more on deeply held beliefs. They go through as many as six stages (grouped into three levels) of moral reasoning, as first argued by psychologist Lawrence Kohlberg in the late 1950s (*below*). The evidence includes a long-term study of 58 young men interviewed periodically over two decades. Their moral maturity was judged by how they analyzed hypothetical dilemmas, such as whether a husband should steal a drug for his dying wife. Either yes or no was a valid answer; what mattered was how the men justified it. As they grew up, they passed through the stages in succession, albeit at different rates (*bar graph*). The sixth stage remained elusive. Despite the general success of this model for describing intellectual growth, it does not explain people's actual behavior. Two people at the same stage may act differently. —*W.D.*

LEVEL 1: SELF-INTEREST
STAGE 1   PUNISHMENT "I won't do it, because I don't want to get punished."
STAGE 2   REWARD "I won't do it, because I want the reward."

LEVEL 2: SOCIAL APPROVAL
STAGE 3   INTERPERSONAL RELATIONS "I won't do it, because I want people to like me."
STAGE 4   SOCIAL ORDER "I won't do it, because it would break the law."

LEVEL 3: ABSTRACT IDEALS
STAGE 5   SOCIAL CONTRACT "I won't do it, because I'm obliged not to."
STAGE 6   UNIVERSAL RIGHTS "I won't do it, because it's not right, no matter what others say."

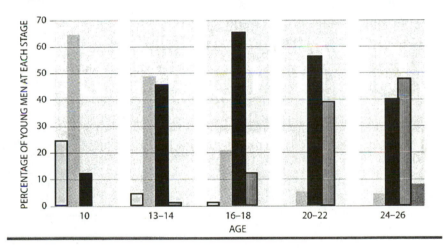

playing shoot-'em-up computer games may push some children over the edge and leave others unaffected. Conventional wisdom dwells on lone silver bullets, but scientific understanding must be built on an appreciation of the complexity and variety of children's lives.

Biologically oriented, or "nativist," theories maintain that human morality springs from emotional dispositions that are hardwired into our species. Hoffman, Colwyn Trevarthen of the University of Edinburgh and Nancy Eisenberg of Arizona State University have established

that babies can feel empathy as soon as they recognize the existence of others—sometimes in the first week after birth. Other moral emotions that make an early appearance include shame, guilt and indignation. As Harvard child psychologist Jerome S. Kagan has described, young children can be outraged by the violation of social expectations, such as a breach in the rules of a favorite game or rearranged buttons on a piece of familiar clothing.

Nearly everybody, in every culture, inherits these dispositions. Mary D. Ainsworth of the University of Virginia reported empathy among Ugandan and American infants; Norma Feshbach of the University of California at Los Angeles conducted a similar comparison of newborns in Europe, Israel and the U.S.; Millard C. Madsen of U.C.L.A. studied sharing by preschool children in nine cultures. As far as psychologists know, children everywhere start life with caring feelings toward those close to them and adverse reactions to inhumane or unjust behavior. Differences in how these reactions are triggered and expressed emerge only later, once children have been exposed to the particular value systems of their cultures.

In contrast, the learning theories concentrate on children's acquisition of behavioral norms and values through observation, imitation and reward. Research in this tradition has concluded that moral behavior is context-bound, varying from situation to situation almost independently of stated beliefs. Landmark studies in the 1920s, still frequently cited, include Hugh Hartshorne and Mark May's survey of how children reacted when given the chance to cheat. The children's behavior depended largely on whether they thought they would be caught. It could be predicted neither from their conduct in previous situations nor from their knowledge of common moral rules, such as the Ten Commandments and the Boy Scout's code.

Later reanalyses of Hartshorne and May's data, performed by Roger Burton of the State University of New York at Buffalo, discovered at least one general trend: younger children were more likely to cheat than adolescents. Perhaps socialization or mental growth can restrain dishonest behavior after all. But the effect was not a large one.

The third basic theory of moral development puts the emphasis on intellectual growth, arguing that virtue and vice are ultimately a matter of conscious choice. The best-known cognitive theories are those of psy-

"Could You Live with Yourself?"

In a distressed neighborhood in Camden, N.J., social psychologist Daniel Hart of Rutgers University interviewed an African-American teenager who was active in community service:

How would you describe yourself?
I am the kind of person who wants to get involved, who believes in getting involved. I just had this complex, I call it, where people think of Camden as being a bad place, which bothered me. Every city has its own bad places, you know. I just want to work with people, work to change that image that people have of Camden. You can't start with adults, because they don't change. But if you can get into the minds of young children, show them what's wrong and let them know that you don't want them to be this way, then it could work, because they're more persuadable.

Is there really one correct solution to moral problems like this one?
Basically, it's like I said before. You're supposed to try to help save a life.

How do you know?
Well, it's just—how could you live with yourself? Say that I could help save this person's life—could I just let that person die? I mean, I couldn't live with myself if that happened. A few years ago my sister was killed, and . . . the night she was killed I was over at her house, earlier that day. Maybe if I had spent the night at her house that day, maybe this wouldn't have happened.

You said that you're not a bad influence on others. Why is that important?
Well, I try not to be a bad role model. All of us have bad qualities, of course; still, you have to be a role model even if you're a person walking down the street. You know, we have a society today where there are criminals and crooks. There are drug users. Kids look to those people. If they see a drug dealer with a lot of money, they want money, too, and then they're going to do drugs. So it's important that you try not to be a bad influence, because that can go a long way. Even if you say, oh, wow, you tell your little sister or brother to be quiet so Mom and Dad won't wake so you won't have to go to school. And they get in the habit of being quiet [laughs], you're not going to school, things like that. So when you're a bad influence, it always travels very far.

Why don't you want that to happen?
Because in today's society there's just really too much crime, too much violence. I mean everywhere. And I've even experienced violence, because my sister was murdered. You know, we need not to have that in future years, so we need to teach our children otherwise.

chologists Jean Piaget and Lawrence Kohlberg. Both described children's early moral beliefs as oriented toward power and authority. For young children, might makes right, literally. Over time they come to understand that social rules are made by people and thus can be renegotiated and that reciprocity in relationships is more fair than unilateral obedience. Kohlberg identified a six-stage sequence in the maturation of moral judgment [see box, "The Six Stages of Moral Judgment]." Several thousand studies have used it as a measure of how advanced a person's moral reasoning is.

Conscience versus Chocolate

Although the main parts of Kohlberg's sequence have been confirmed, notable exceptions stand out. Few if any people reach the sixth and most advanced stage, in which their moral view is based purely on abstract principles. As for the early stages in the sequence, many studies (including ones from my own laboratory) have found that young children have a far richer sense of positive morality than the model indicates. In other words, they do not act simply out of fear of punishment. When a playmate hogs a plate of cookies or refuses to relinquish a swing, the protest "That's not fair!" is common. At the same time, young children realize that they have an obligation to share with others—even when their parents say not to. Preschool children generally believe in an equal distribution of goods and back up their beliefs with reasons such as empathy ("I want my friend to feel nice"), reciprocity ("She shares her toys with me") and egalitarianism ("We should all get the same"). All this they figure out through confrontation with peers at play. Without fairness, they learn, there will be trouble.

In fact, none of the three traditional theories is sufficient to explain children's moral growth and behavior. None captures the most essential dimensions of moral life: character and commitment. Regardless of how children develop their initial system of values, the key question is: What makes them live up to their ideals or not? This issue is the focus of recent scientific thinking.

Like adults, children struggle with temptation. To see how this tug of war plays itself out in the world of small children, my colleagues and I (then at Clark University) devised

How Universal Are Values?

The observed importance of shared values in children's moral development raises some of the most hotly debated questions in philosophy and the social sciences today. Do values vary from place to place, or is there a set of universal values that guides moral development everywhere? Do children growing up in different cultures or at different times acquire fundamentally different mores?

Some light was shed on the cultural issue by Richard A. Shweder of the University of Chicago and his colleagues in a study of Hindu-Brahmin children in India and children from Judeo-Christian backgrounds in the U.S. The study revealed striking contrasts between the two groups. From an early age, the Indian children learned to maintain tradition, to respect defined rules of interpersonal relationships and to help people in need. American children, in comparison, were oriented toward autonomy, liberty and personal rights. The Indian children said that breaches of tradition, such as eating beef or addressing one's father by his first name, were particularly reprehensible. They saw nothing wrong with a man caning his errant son or a husband beating his wife when she went to the movies without his permission. The American children were appalled by all physically punitive behavior but indifferent to infractions such as eating forbidden foods or using improper forms of address.

Moreover, the Indians and Americans moved in opposite directions as they matured. Whereas Indian children restricted value judgments to situations with which they were directly familiar, Indian adults generalized their values to a broad range of social conditions. American children said that moral standards should apply to everyone always; American adults modified values in the face of changing circumstances. In short, the Indians began life as relativists and ended up an universalists, whereas the Americans went precisely the other way.

It would be overstating matters, however, to say that children from different cultures adopt completely different moral codes. In Schweder's study, both groups of children thought that deceitful acts (a father breaking a promise to a child) and uncharitable acts (ignoring a beggar with a sick child) were wrong. They also shared a repugnance toward theft, vandalism and harming innocent victims, although there was some disagreement on what constitutes inno-

Percentage of Kids with Enough Problems to Warrant Psychiatry

1976 ▮▮▮▮ 10%

1989 ▮▮▮▮▮▮▮▮▮ 18.2%

0 2 4 6 8 10 12 14 16 18

KIDS THESE DAYS are likelier to need mental health services, judging from parents' reports of behavioral and emotional problems.

cence. Among these judgments may be found a universal moral sense, based on common human aversions. It reflects core values—benevolence, fairness, honesty—that may be necessary for sustaining human relationships in all but the most dysfunctional societies.

A parallel line of research has studied gender differences, arguing that girls learn to emphasize caring, whereas boys incline toward rules and justice. Unlike the predictions made by culture theory, however, these gender claims have not held up. The original research that claimed to find gender differences lacked proper control groups. Well-designed studies of American children—for example, those by Lawrence Walker of the University of British Columbia—rarely detect differences between boys' and girls' ideals. Even for adults, when educational or occupational levels are controlled, the differences disappear. Female lawyers have almost the same moral orientations as their male counterparts; the same can be said for male and female nurses, homemakers, scientists, high school dropouts and so on. As cultural theorists point out, there is far more similarity between male and female moral orientations within any given culture than between male and female orientations across cultures.

Generational differences are also of interest, especially to people who bemoan what they see as declining morality. Such complaints, of course, are nothing new [see "Teenage Attitudes," by H. H. Remmers and D. H. Radler; SCIENTIFIC AMERICAN, June 1958; and "The Origins of Alienation," by Urie Bronfenbrenner; SCIENTIFIC AMERICAN, August 1974]. Nevertheless, there is some evidence that young people today are more likely to engage in antisocial behavior than those a generation ago were. According to a survey by Thomas M. Achenbach and Catherine T. Howell of the University of Vermont, parents and teachers reported more behavioral problems (lying, cheating) and other threats to healthy development (depression, withdrawal) in 1989 than in 1976 (above). (The researchers are now updating their survey.) But in the long sweep of human history, 13 years is merely an eye blink. The changes could reflect a passing problem, such as overly permissive fashions in child rearing, rather than a permanent trend.

—W.D.

EDWARD BELL; SOURCE; THOMAS M. ACHENBACH AND CATHERINE T. HOWELL

the following experiment. We brought groups, each of four children, into our lab, gave them string and beads, and asked them to make bracelets and necklaces for us. We then thanked them profusely for their splendid work and rewarded them, as a group, with 10 candy bars. Then the real experiment began: we told each group that it would need to decide the best way to divide up the reward. We left the room and watched through a one-way mirror.

Before the experiment, we had interviewed participants about the concept of fairness. We were curious, of course, to find out whether the prospect of gobbling up real chocolate would overwhelm their abstract sense of right and wrong. To test this thoroughly, we gave one unfortunate control group an almost identical conundrum, using cardboard rectangles rather than real chocolate—a not so subtle way of defusing their self-interest. We observed groups of four-, six-, eight- and 10-year-old children to see whether the relationship between situational and hypothetical morality changed with age.

The children's ideals did make a difference but within limits circumscribed by narrow self-interest. Children given cardboard acted almost three times more generously toward one another than did children given chocolate. Yet moral beliefs still held some sway. For example, children who had earlier expressed a belief in merit-based solutions ("The one who did the best job should get more of the candy") were the ones most likely to advocate for merit in the real situation. But they did so most avidly when they themselves could claim to have done more than their peers. Without such a claim, they were easily persuaded to drop meritocracy for an equal division.

Even so, these children seldom abandoned fairness entirely. They may have switched from one idea of justice to another—say, from merit to equality—but they did not resort to egoistic justifications such as "I should get more because I'm big" or "Boys like candy more than girls, and I'm a boy." Such rationales generally came from children who had declared no belief in either equality or meritocracy. Older children were more likely to believe in fairness and to act accordingly, even when such action favored others. This finding was evidence for the reassuring proposition that ideals can have an increasing influence on conduct as a child matures.

Do the Right Thing

But this process is not automatic. A person must adopt those beliefs as a central part of his or her personal identity. When a person moves from saying "People should be honest" to "I want to be honest," he or she becomes more likely to tell the truth in everyday interactions. A person's use of moral principles to define the self is called the person's moral identity. Moral identity determines not merely what the person considers to be the right course of action but also why he or she would decide: "I myself must take this course." This distinction is crucial to understanding the variety of moral behavior. The same basic ideals are widely shared by even the youngest members of society; the difference is the resolve to act on those ideals.

Most children and adults will express the belief that it is wrong to allow others to suffer, but only a subset of them will conclude that they themselves must do something about, say, ethnic cleansing in Kosovo. Those are the ones who are most likely to donate money or fly to the Balkans to help. Their concerns about human suffering are central to the way they think about themselves and their life goals, and so they feel a responsibility to take action, even at great personal cost.

In a study of moral exemplars—people with long, publicly documented histories of charity and civil-rights work—psychologist Anne Colby of the Carnegie Foun-dation and I encountered a high level of integration between self-identity and moral concerns. "People who define themselves in terms of their moral goals are likely to see moral problems in everyday events, and they are also likely to see themselves as necessarily implicated in these problems," we wrote. Yet the exemplars showed no signs of more insightful moral reasoning. Their ideals and Kohlberg levels were much the same as everyone else's.

Conversely, many people are equally aware of moral problems, but to them the issues seem remote from their own lives and their senses of self. Kosovo and Rwanda sound far away and insignificant; they are easily put out of mind. Even issues closer to home—say, a maniacal clique of peers who threaten a classmate—may seem like someone else's problem. For people who feel this way, inaction does not strike at their self-conception. Therefore, despite commonplace assumptions to the contrary, their moral knowledge will not be enough to impel moral action.

The development of a moral identity follows a general pattern. It normally takes shape in late childhood, when children acquire the capacity to analyze people—including themselves—in terms of stable character traits. In childhood, self-identifying traits usually consist of action-related skills and interests ("I'm smart" or "I love music"). With age, children start to use moral terms to define themselves. By the onset of puberty, they typically invoke adjectives such as "fairminded," "generous" and "honest."

Some adolescents go so far as to describe themselves primarily in terms of moral goals. They speak of noble purposes, such as caring for others or improving their communities, as missions that give meaning to their lives. Working in Camden, N.J., Daniel Hart and his colleagues at Rutgers University found that a high proportion of so-called care exemplars—teenagers identified by teachers and peers as highly committed to volunteering—had self-identities that were based on moral belief systems. Yet they scored no higher than their peers on the standard psychological tests of moral judgment. The study is noteworthy because it was conducted in an economically deprived urban setting among an adolescent population often stereotyped as high risk and criminally inclined [see box, "Could You Live with Yourself?"].

At the other end of the moral spectrum, further evidence indicates that moral identity drives behavior. Social psychologists Hazel Markus of Stanford University and Daphne Oyserman of the University of Michigan have observed that delinquent youths have immature senses of self, especially when talking about their future selves (a critical part of adolescent identity). These troubled teenagers do not imagine themselves as doctors, husbands, voting citizens, church members—any social role that embodies a positive value commitment.

How does a young person acquire, or not acquire, a moral identity? It is an incremental process, occurring gradually in thousands of small ways: feedback from others; observations of actions by others that either inspire or appall; reflections on one's own experience; cultural influences such as family, school, religious institutions and the mass media. The relative importance of these factors varies from child to child.

Teach Your Children Well

For most children, parents are the original source of moral guidance. Psychologists such as Diana Baumrind of the University of California at Berkeley have shown that "authoritative" parenting facilitates children's moral growth more surely than either "permissive" or "authoritarian" parenting. The authoritative mode establishes consistent family rules and firm limits but also en-courages open discussion and clear communication to explain and, when justified, revise the rules. In contrast, the permissive mode avoids rules entirely; the authoritarian mode irregularly enforces rules at the parent's whim—the "because I said so" approach.

Although permissive and authoritarian parenting seem like opposites, they actually tend to produce similar patterns of poor self-control and low social responsibility in children. Neither mode presents children with the realistic expectations and structured guidance that challenge them to expand their moral horizons. Both can foster habits—such as feeling that mores come from the outside—that could inhibit the development of a moral identity. In this way, moral or immoral conduct during adulthood often has roots in childhood experience.

As children grow, they are increasingly exposed to influences beyond the family. In most families, however, the parent-child relationship remains primary as long as the child lives at home. A parent's comment on a raunchy music lyric or a blood-drenched video usually will stick with a child long after the media experience has faded. In fact, if salacious or violent media programming opens the door to responsible parental feedback, the benefits can far outweigh the harm.

One of the most influential things parents can do is to encourage the right kinds of peer relations. Interactions with peers can spur moral growth by showing children the conflict between their preconceptions and social reality. During the debates about dividing the chocolate, some of our subjects seemed to pick up new—and more informed—ideas about justice. In a follow-up study, we confirmed that the peer debate had heightened their awareness of the rights of others. Children who participated actively in the debate, both expressing their opinions and listening to the viewpoints of others, were especially likely to benefit.

In adolescence, peer interactions are crucial in forging a self-identity. To be sure, this process often plays out in cliquish social behavior: as a means of defining and shoring up the sense of self, kids will seek out like-minded peers and spurn others who seem foreign. But when kept within reasonable bounds, the in-group clustering generally evolves into a more mature friendship pattern. What can parents do in the meantime to fortify a teenager who is bearing the brunt of isolation or persecution? The most important message they can give is that cruel behavior reveals something about the perpetrator rather than about the victim. If this advice helps the youngster resist taking the treatment personally, the period of persecution will pass without leaving any psychological scars.

Some psychologists, taking a sociological approach, are examining community-level variables, such as whether various moral influences—parents, teachers, mass media and so on—are consistent with one another. In a study of 311 adolescents from 10 American towns and cities, Francis A. J. Ianni of the Columbia University Teachers College noticed high degrees of altruistic behavior and low degrees of antisocial behavior among youngsters from communities where there was consensus in expectations for young people.

Everyone in these places agreed that honesty, for instance, is a fundamental value. Teachers did not tolerate cheating on exams, parents did not let their children lie and get away with it, sports coaches did not encourage teams to bend the rules for the sake of a win, and people of all ages expected openness from their friends. But many communities were divided along such lines. Coaches espoused winning above all else, and parents protested when teachers reprimanded their children for cheating or shoddy schoolwork. Under such circumstances, children learned not to take moral messages seriously.

Ianni named the set of shared standards in harmonious communities a "youth charter." Ethnicity, cultural diversity, socioeconomic status, geographic location and population size had nothing to do with whether a town offered its young people a steady moral compass. The notion of a youth charter is being explored in social interventions that foster communication among children, parents, teachers and other influential adults. Meanwhile other researchers have sought to understand whether the specific values depend on cultural, gender or generational background [see box, "How Universal Are Values?"].

Unfortunately, the concepts embodied in youth charters seem ever rarer in American society. Even when adults spot trouble, they may fail to step in. Parents are busy and often out of touch with the peer life of their children; they give kids more autonomy than ever before, and kids expect it—indeed, demand it. Teachers, for their part, feel that a child's nonacademic life is none of their business and that they could be censured, even sued, if they intervened in a student's personal or moral problem. And neighbors feel the same way: that they have no business interfering with another family's business, even if they see a child headed for trouble.

Everything that psychologists know from the study of children's moral development indicates that moral identity—the key source of moral commitment throughout life—is fostered by multiple social influences that guide a child in the same general direction. Children must hear the message enough for it to stick. The challenge for pluralistic societies will be to find enough common ground to communicate the shared standards that the young need.

The Author

WILLIAM DAMON remembers being in an eighth-grade clique that tormented an unpopular kid. After describing his acts in the school newspaper, he was told by his English teacher, "I give you an A for the writing, but what you're doing is really shameful." That moral feedback has stayed with him. Damon is now director of the Center on Adolescence at Stanford University, an interdisciplinary program that specializes in what he has called "the least understood, the least trusted, the most feared and most neglected period of development." A developmental psychologist, he has studied intellectual and moral growth, educational methods, and peer and cultural influences on children. He is the author of numerous books and the father of three children, the youngest now in high school.

Further Reading

THE MEANING AND MEASUREMENT OF MORAL DEVELOPMENT. Lawrence Kohlberg. Clark University, Heinz Werner Institute, 1981.

THE EMERGENCE OF MORALITY IN YOUNG CHILDREN. Edited by Jerome Kagan and Sharon Lamb. University of Chicago Press, 1987.

THE MORAL CHILD: NURTURING CHILDREN'S NATURAL MORAL GROWTH. William Damon. Free Press, 1990.

ARE AMERICAN CHILDREN'S PROBLEMS GETTING WORSE? A 13-YEAR COMPARISON. Thomas M. Achenbach and Catherine T. Howell in Journal of the American Academy of Child and Adolescent Psychiatry, Vol. 32, No. 6, pages 1145–1154; November 1993.

SOME DO CARE: CONTEMPORARY LIVES OF MORAL COMMITMENT. Anne Colby. Free Press, 1994.

THE YOUTH CHARTER: HOW COMMUNITIES CAN WORK TOGETHER TO RAISE STANDARDS FOR ALL OUR CHILDREN. William Damon. Free Press, 1997.

Friendships and Adaptation Across the Life Span

Willard W. Hartup[1] and Nan Stevens

Institute of Child Development, University of Minnesota, Minneapolis, Minnesota (W.W.H.), and Department of Psychogerontology, University of Nijmegen, Nijmegen, The Netherlands (N.S.)

Abstract

Friends foster self-esteem and a sense of well-being, socialize one another, and support one another in coping with developmental transitions and life stress. Friends engage in different activities with one another across the life span, but friendship is conceived similarly by children and adults. Friends and friendships, however, are not all alike. The developmental significance of having friends depends on the characteristics of the friends, especially whether the friends are antisocial or socially withdrawn. Outcomes also depend on whether friendships are supportive and intimate or fractious and unstable. Among both children and adults, friendships have clear-cut developmental benefits at times but are mixed blessings at other times.

Keywords

friendships; life-span development; relationships

Friendships are important to the well-being of both children and adults. Parents worry if their children do not have friends; adolescents are anxious and upset when they lose their friends; and older adults go to considerable lengths to maintain old friendships and establish new ones. People who have friends generally feel better about themselves and others than do people who do not have friends. Recent studies, however, show that over the life span, the dynamics of friendship are complicated. These relationships sometimes contain a "dark side," and in these instances, developmental benefits are mixed.

In this report, we begin by showing that understanding friendships across the life span requires thinking about these relationships from two perspectives: It is necessary to consider, first, what friendships mean to both children and adults and, second, what distinctive patterns of social interaction characterize friendships. We then suggest that, in order to appreciate the significance of friends over the life span, one must take into account (a) whether a person does or does not have friends, (b) characteristics of the person's friends, and (c) the quality of these relationships.

HOW TO THINK ABOUT FRIENDSHIPS IN LIFE-SPAN PERSPECTIVE

The significance of friendship across the life span can be established only by examining what children and adults believe to be the social meaning (essence) of these relationships, as well as the social exchanges they actually have with their friends. When researchers examine what people believe friendships to be, or what elements constitute a friendship, reciprocity is always involved. Friends may or may not share likes and dislikes, but there is always the sense that one supports and sustains one's friends and receives support in return. Most people do not describe the relation between friends narrowly as a *quid pro quo,* but rather describe the relationship broadly as *mutuality*—that is, friendship involves social giving and taking, and returning in kind or degree. Children, adolescents, newlyweds, middle-aged adults, and soon-to-be retirees differ relatively little from one another in their emphasis on these reciprocities when asked to describe an ideal friend (Weiss & Lowenthal, 1975). Older people describe their friendships more elaborately and with greater subtlety than children do, but then older people generally describe other persons in more complex terms than younger persons do. Consequently, we can assert that the meaning structure specifying friendships changes relatively little from the preschool years through old age; social reciprocities are emphasized throughout the life span (Hartup & Stevens, 1997).

The actual exchanges that occur between friends change greatly with age. Social reciprocities between toddlers are reflected in the time they spend together and the connectedness of their interaction; reciprocities between kindergartners are more elaborated but remain basically concrete ("We play"). Among adolescents, friends engage in common activities (mainly socializing) and social disclosure; among young adults, friendships become "fused" or "blended" with work and parenting. Among older persons, friendships are separated from work once again and centered on support and companionship. The behavioral structures associated with friendship thus change greatly across the life span, generally in accordance with the distinctive tasks or challenges that confront persons at different ages.

HAVING FRIENDS

Occurrence

As early as age 3 or 4, children show preferences for interacting with particular children, and the word "friend" enters their vocabularies. About 75% of preschool-aged children are involved in mutual friendships as identified by mothers or nursery school teachers or measured in terms of the time the children spend together. Mutual friends among school-aged children and older persons are usually identified by asking individuals to name their "best friends," "good friends," or "casual friends," categories differentiated in terms of time spent together and intimacy. Among teenagers, 80% to 90% report having mutual friends, usually including one or two best friends and several good friends. The proportion of people who have friends remains high through adulthood, then declines in old age. More older persons, however, have friends than do not. Small numbers of individuals, about 7%, have no friends in adulthood; after age 65, this friendless group increases to 12% for women and 24% for men.

Friendship networks vary in size according to age and sex. During the nursery school years, boys have an average of two friends, whereas girls have one; during the school years, the number of best friends varies from three to five. Girls' networks are usually smaller and more exclusive than boys' during childhood; this situation reverses, however, in adolescence. Number of friends remains fairly constant through adolescence and early adulthood. Newlyweds have the largest numbers of friends, with fewer friendships being maintained during middle age. Friendship networks increase again before retirement, but a decline occurs following retirement, owing primarily to the loss of casual friends. Close friendships, however, are frequently retained into old, old age (Hartup & Stevens, 1997).

The amount of time spent with friends is greatest during middle childhood and adolescence; in fact, teenagers spend almost a third of their waking time in the company of friends. The percentage of time spent with friends declines until middle age, when adults spend less than 10% of their time with friends. A slight increase occurs at retirement, although it is not as great as one might expect (Larson, Zuzanek, & Mannell, 1985).

Behavior With Friends and Nonfriends

More positive engagement (i.e., more talk, smiling, and laughter) is observed among friends than among nonfriends in childhood and adolescence. Friends also have more effective conflict management and a more mutual orientation when working together (Newcomb & Bagwell, 1995). Differences in behavior between friends and mere acquaintances are similar in adulthood: Self-disclosure occurs more frequently and involves more depth of disclosure among friends than nonfriends; friends are more directive and authoritative with one another than nonfriends.

Companionship and talk continue to distinguish interactions between friends in middle and old age. Sharing, exchange of resources, and emotional support remain salient, especially during crises, such as divorce. Problem solving involves more symmetrical interaction between friends than between nonfriends; conflicts are more effectively managed. Adults' conflicts with friends center on differences in values and beliefs, as well as lifestyles. Conflicts between older friends mainly concern expectations related to age and resource inequities.

Developmental Significance

From early childhood through old age, people with friends have a greater sense of well-being than people without friends. Friendlessness is more common among people who seek clinical assistance for emotional and behavioral problems than among better adjusted persons (Rutter & Garmezy, 1983). But these results mean relatively little: They do not clarify whether friends contribute to well-being or whether people who feel good about themselves have an easier time making friends than those who do not.

Longitudinal studies show that children entering first grade have better school attitudes if they already have friends and are successful both in keeping old ones and making new ones (Ladd, 1990). Similarly, among adolescents, psychological disturbances are fewer when school changes (e.g., from grade to grade or from primary school to middle school) occur in the company of friends than when they do not (Berndt & Keefe, 1992). Once again, the direction of influence is not clear: Does

merely having friends support successful coping with these transitions, or are those people who are better able to cope with these transitions also able to make friends more easily?

Despite these difficulties in interpretation, well-controlled longer term studies extending from childhood into adulthood show similar patterns, thereby strengthening the conclusion that friendships are in some way responsible for the outcome. Self-esteem is greater among young adults who had friends while they were children than among those who did not, when differences in childhood self-esteem are controlled for statistically. Social adjustment in adulthood, however, is more closely related to having been generally liked or disliked by classmates than to having had mutual friends (Bagwell, Newcomb, & Bukowski, 1998).

CHARACTERISTICS OF ONE'S FRIENDS

Although friends may support positive developmental outcomes through companionship and social support, these outcomes depend on who one's friends are. Friendships with socially well-adjusted persons are like money in the bank, "social capital" that can be drawn upon to meet challenges and crises arising every day. In contrast, poorly adjusted friends may be a drain on resources, increasing one's risk of poor developmental outcomes.

Children of divorce illustrate these dynamics: Preadolescents, adolescents, and young adults whose parents have divorced are at roughly three times the risk for psychosocial problems as their peers whose parents are not divorced. Preadolescents who have positive relationships with both custodial and noncustodial parents have a significantly reduced risk if the parents are well-adjusted; friends do not provide the same protection. In contrast, resilience among adolescents whose parents are divorced is influenced by friends as well as family. Specifically, adolescent children of divorce are more resilient (better adapted) if they have both family and friends who have few behavior problems and who are socially mature. Friends continue to promote resilience among the offspring of divorce during early adulthood, but again friends provide this benefit only if they are well-adjusted themselves (Hetherington, in press). Two conclusions can be drawn: First, social capital does not reside merely in having friends, but rather resides in having socially competent friends; and second, whether friends are a protective factor in social development depends on one's age.

Research indicates that the role of friendships as a risk factor also depends on one's age. Friendship risks are especially evident among antisocial children and adolescents. First, antisocial children are more likely to have antisocial friends than other children. Second, antisocial behavior increases as a consequence of associating with antisocial friends. Antisocial children have poor social skills and thus are not good models. Relationships between antisocial children are also problematic: Interactions are more contentious and conflict-ridden, more marked by talk about deviance and talk that is deviant in its social context (e.g., swearing), and more lacking in intimacy than exchanges between nonaggressive children (Dishion, Andrews, & Crosby, 1995). Other studies show that behavior problems increase across the transition from childhood to adolescence when children have stable relationships with friends who have behavior problems themselves (Berndt, Hawkins, & Jiao, in press).

FRIENDSHIP QUALITY

Friendships are not all alike. Some are marked by intimacy and social support, others by conflict and contention. Some friends engage in many different activities, others share narrower interests. Some friendships are relatively stable, others are not. These features of friendships differentiate relationships among both children and adolescents, and define some of the ways that relationships differ from one another among adults.

Friendship quality is related to the psychological well-being of children and adolescents and to the manner in which they manage stressful life events. During the transition from elementary to secondary school, for example, sociability and leadership increase among adolescents who have stable, supportive, and intimate friendships, but decline or do not change among other adolescents. Similarly, social withdrawal increases among students with unstable, poor-quality friendships, but not among students who have supportive and intimate friendships (Berndt et al., in press).

Friendship quality contributes to antisocial behavior and its development. Conflict-ridden and contentious relationships are associated with increases in delinquent behavior during adolescence, especially among young people with histories of troublesome behavior; increases in delinquent behavior are smaller for youngsters who have supportive and intimate friends (Poulin, Dishion, & Haas, in press). Friendship quality is also important to the adaptation of young women from divorced families: Those who have supportive and intimate friendships tend to be resilient, but those who have nonsupportive friendships tend not to be resilient (Hetherington, in press).

Among older adults, support from friends also compensates for missing relationships (e.g., partners). Emotional support and receiving assistance from friends are among the most important protections against loneliness for persons without partners (Dykstra, 1995). There may be two sides to this coin, however: Older widows with "problematic" social ties (e.g., widows with friends who break promises, invade their privacy, and take advantage of them) have lower psychological well-being than widows whose social ties are not problematic (Rook, 1984). In other words, the absence of problematic qualities in these relationships may be as important as the presence of positive qualities.

CONCLUSION

Friendships are developmentally significant across the life span. The meaning assigned to these relationships changes relatively little with age, although the behavioral exchanges between friends reflect the ages of the individuals involved. Whether friendships are developmental assets or liabilities depends on several conditions, especially the characteristics of one's friends and the quality of one's relationships with them.

Recommended Reading

Blieszner, R., & Adams, R. G. (1992). *Adult friendship.* Newbury Park, CA: SAGE.

Bukowski, W. M., Newcomb, A. F., & Hartup, W. W. (Eds.). (1996). *The company they keep: Friendship in childhood and adolescence.* New York: Cambridge University Press.

Hartup, W. W., & Stevens, N. (1997). (See References)

Matthews, S. H. (1986). *Friendships through the life course.* Beverly Hills, CA: SAGE.

Note

1. Address correspondence to Willard W. Hartup, Institute of Child Development, University of Minnesota, 51 E. River Rd., Minneapolis, MN 55455.

References

Bagwell, C. L., Newcomb, A. F., & Bukowski, W. M. (1998). Preadolescent friendship and peer rejection as predictors of adult adjustment. *Child Development, 69,* 140–153.

Berndt, T. J., Hawkins, J. A., & Jiao, Z. (in press). Influences of friends and friendships on adjustment to junior high school. *Merrill-Palmer Quarterly.*

Berndt, T. J., & Keefe, K. (1992). Friends' influence on adolescents' perceptions of themselves in school. In D. H. Schunk & J. L. Meece (Eds.), *Students' perceptions in the classroom* (pp. 51–73). Hillsdale, NJ: Erlbaum.

Dishion, T. J., Andrews, D. W., & Crosby, L. (1995). Anti-social boys and their friends in early adolescence: Relationship characteristics, quality, and interactional process. *Child Development, 66,* 139–151.

Dykstra, P. (1995). Loneliness among the never and formerly married: The importance of supportive friendships and a desire for independence. *Journals of Gerontology: Psychological Sciences and Social Sciences, 50B,* S321–S329.

Hartup, W. W., & Stevens, N. (1997). Friendships and adaptation in the life course. *Psychological Bulletin, 121,* 355–370.

Hetherington, E. M. (in press). Social capital and the development of youth from nondivorced, divorced, and remarried families. In W. A. Collins & B. Laursen (Eds.), *Minnesota Symposia on Child Psychology: Vol. 30. Relationships as developmental contexts.* Hillsdale, NJ: Erlbaum.

Ladd, G. W. (1990). Having friends, keeping friends, making friends, and being liked by peers in the classroom: Predictors of children's early school adjustment? *Child Development, 61,* 1081–1100.

Larson, R., Zuzanek, J., & Mannell, R. (1985). Being alone versus being with people: Disengagement in the daily experience of older adults. *Journal of Gerontology, 40,* 375–381.

Newcomb, A. F., & Bagwell, C. (1995). Children's friendship relations: A meta-analytic review. *Psychological Bulletin, 117,* 306–347.

Poulin, F., Dishion, T. J., & Haas, E. (in press). The peer paradox: Relationship quality and deviancy training within male adolescent friendships. *Merrill-Palmer Quarterly.*

Rook, K. S. (1984). The negative side of social interaction: Impact on psychological well-being. *Journal of Personality and Social Psychology, 46,* 1156–1166.

Rutter, M., & Garmezy, N. (1983). Developmental psychopathology. In P. H. Mussen (Series Ed.) & E. M. Hetherington (Vol. Ed.), *Handbook of child psychology: Vol. 4. Socialization, personality, and social development* (4th ed., pp. 775–911). New York: Wiley.

Weiss, L., & Lowenthal, M. F. (1975). Life-course perspectives on friendship. In M. F. Lowenthal, M. Thurnher, & D. Chiriboga (Eds.), *Four stages of life: A comparative study of women and men facing transitions* (pp. 48–61). San Francisco: Jossey-Bass.

THE NEW
Flirting Game

*IT MAY BE AN AGES-OLD, BIOLOGICALLY-DRIVEN ACTIVITY,
BUT TODAY IT'S ALSO PLAYED WITH ARTFUL SELF-AWARENESS
AND EVEN CONSCIOUS CALCULATION.*

By Deborah A. Lott

To hear the evolutionary determinists tell it, we human beings flirt to propagate our genes and to display our genetic worth. Men are constitutionally predisposed to flirt with the healthiest, most fertile women, recognizable by their biologically correct waist-hip ratios. Women favor the guys with dominant demeanors, throbbing muscles and the most resources to invest in them and their offspring.

Looked at up close, human psychology is more diverse and perverse than the evolutionary determinists would have it. We flirt as thinking individuals in a particular culture at a particular time. Yes, we may express a repertoire of hardwired non-verbal expressions and behaviors–staring eyes, flashing brows, opened palms–that resemble those of other animals, but unlike other animals, we also flirt with conscious calculation. We have been known to practice our techniques in front of the mirror. In other words, flirting among human beings is culturally modulated as well as biologically driven, as much art as instinct.

In our culture today, it's clear that we do not always choose as the object of our desire those people the evolutionists might deem the most biologically desirable. After all, many young women today find the pale, androgynous, scarcely muscled yet emotionally expressive Leonardo DiCaprio more appealing than the burly Tarzans (Arnold Schwartzenegger, Bruce

Willis, etc.) of action movies. Woody Allen may look nerdy but he's had no trouble winning women–and that's not just because he has material resources, but because humor is also a precious cultural commodity. Though she has no breasts or hips to speak of, Ally McBeal still attracts because there's ample evidence of a quick and quirky mind.

In short, we flirt with the intent of assessing potential lifetime partners, we flirt to have easy, no-strings-attached sex, and we flirt when we are not looking for either. We flirt because, most simply, flirtation can be a liberating form of play, a game with suspense and ambiguities that brings joys of its own. As Philadelphia-based social psychologist Tim Perper says, "Some flirters appear to want to prolong the interaction because it's pleasurable and erotic in its own right, regardless of where it might lead."

Here are some of the ways the game is currently being played.

TAKING The Lead

When it comes to flirting today, women aren't waiting around for men to make the advances. They're taking the lead. Psychologist Monica Moore, Ph.D. of Webster University in St. Louis, Missouri, has spent more than 2000 hours observing women's flirting maneuvers in restaurants, singles bars and at par-

Reprinted with permission from *Psychology Today*, January/February 1999, pp. 42-45, 72. © 1999 by Sussex Publishers, Inc.

ties. According to her findings, women give non-verbal cues that get a flirtation rolling fully two-thirds of the time. A man may think he's making the first move because he is the one to literally move from wherever he is to the woman's side, but usually he has been summoned.

Who determined that baring the neck is a sign of female submissivness? It may have a lot more to do with the neck being an erogenous zone.

By the standards set out by evolutionary psychologists, the women who attract the most men would most likely be those with the most symmetrical features or the best hip-to-waist ratios. Not so, says Moore. In her studies, the women who draw the most response are the ones who send the most signals. "Those who performed more than 35 displays per hour elicited greater than four approaches per hour," she notes, "and the more variety the woman used in her techniques, the more likely she was to be successful."

SEXUAL Semaphores

Moore tallied a total of 52 different nonverbal courtship behaviors used by women, including glancing, gazing (short and sustained), primping, preening, smiling, lip licking, pouting, giggling, laughing and nodding, as if to nonverbally indicate, "Yes! yes!" A woman would often begin with a room-encompassing glance, in actuality a casing-the-joint scan to seek out prospects. When she'd zeroed in on a target she'd exhibit the short darting glance—looking at a man, quickly look-

ing away, looking back and then away again. There was something shy and indirect in this initial eye contact.

But women countered their shy moves with other, more aggressive and overt tactics. Those who liked to live dangerously took a round robin approach, alternately flirting with several different men at once until one responded in an unequivocal fashion. A few women hiked their skirts up to bring more leg into a particular man's field of vision. When they inadvertently drew the attention of other admirers, they quickly pulled their skirts down. If a man failed to get the message, a woman might parade, walking across the room towards him, hips swaying, breasts pushed out, head held high.

WHO'S Submissive?

Moore observed some of the same nonverbal behaviors that Eibl-Eibesfeldt and other ethologists had deemed universal among women: the eyebrow flash (an exaggerated raising of the eyebrows of both eyes, followed by a rapid lowering), the coy smile (a tilting of the head downward, with partial averting of the eyes and, at the end, covering of the mouth), and the exposed neck (turning the head so that the side of the neck is bared).

But while many ethologists interpret these signs as conveying female submissiveness, Moore has an altogether different take. "If these behaviors serve to orchestrate courtship, which they do, then how can they be anything but powerful?" she observes. "Who determined that to cover your mouth is a submissive gesture? Baring the neck may have a lot more to do with the neck being an erogenous zone than its being a submissive posture." Though women in Moore's sample used the coy smile, they also maintained direct eye contact for long periods and smiled fully and unabashedly.

Like Moore, Perper believes that ethologists have overemphasized certain behaviors and misinterpreted them as signifying either dominance or submission. For instance, says Perper, among flirting American heterosexual men and women as well as homosexual men, the coy smile is less frequent than direct eye contact and sustained smiling. He suggests that some cultures may use the coy smile more than others, and that it is not always a sign of deference.

In watching a flirtatious couple, Perper finds that a male will perform gestures and movements that an ethologist might consider dominant, such as sticking out his chest and strutting around, but he'll also give signs that could be read as submissive, such as bowing his head lower than the woman's. The woman may also do both. "She may drop her head, turn slightly, bare her neck, but then she'll lift her eyes and lean forward with her breasts held out, and that doesn't look submissive at all," Perper notes.

Men involved in these encounters, says Perper, don't describe themselves as "feeling powerful." In fact, he and Moore agree, neither party wholly dominates in a flirtation. Instead, there is a subtle, rhythmical and playful back and forth that culminates in a kind of physical synchronization between two people. She turns, he turns; she picks up her drink, he picks up his drink.

Still, by escalating and de-escalating the flirtation's progression, the woman controls the pace. To slow down a flirtation, a woman might orient her body away slightly or cross her arms across her chest, or avoid meeting the man's eyes. To stop the dance in its tracks, she can yawn, frown, sneer, shake her head from side to side as if to say "No," pocket her hands, hold her trunk rigidly, avoid the man's gaze, stare over his head, or resume flirting with other men. If a man is really dense, she might hold a strand of hair up to her eyes as if to examine her split ends or even pick her teeth.

PLANNING It Out

Do women make these moves consciously? You bet. "I do these things *incidentally* but not *accidentally*," one adept female flirter told Perper. She wanted her movements and gestures to look fluid and spontaneous but they were at least partly planned. In general, says Perper, women are more aware than are men of exactly what they do, why they do it and the effect it has. A man might simply say that he saw a woman he

Men are able to recite in enormous detail what they do once they are in bed with a woman, but it is women who remember each and every step in the flirtation game that got them there.

was attracted to and struck up a conversation; a woman would remember all the steps in the flirtation dance. "Men can tell you in enormous detail what they do once they are in bed with a woman," declares Perper. But it is the women who know how they got there.

LEARNING The Steps

If flirting today is often a conscious activity, it is also a learned one. Women pick up the moves early. In observations of 100 girls between the ages of 13 and 16 at shopping malls, ice skating rinks and other places adolescents congregate, Moore found the teens exhibiting 31 of the 52 courtship

signals deployed by adult women. (The only signals missing were those at the more overt end of the spectrum, such as actual caressing.) Overall, the teens' gestures looked less natural than ones made by mature females: they laughed more boisterously and preened more obviously, and their moves were broader and rougher.

The girls' clearly modeled their behavior on the leader of the pack. When the alpha female stroked her hair or swayed her hips, her companions copied quickly. "You never see this in adult women," says Moore. "Indeed, women go to great lengths to stand out from their female companions."

Compared with adults, the teens signaled less frequently–7.6 signs per hour per girl, as opposed to 44.6 per woman–but their maneuvers, though clumsy, were equally effective at attracting the objects of their desire, in this case, teen boys.

BEYOND The Straight and Narrow

Flirting's basic purpose may be to lure males and females into procreating, but it's also an activity indulged in by gays as well as straights. How do flirting rituals compare?

Marny Hall, a San Francisco-area psychologist who's been an observer and participant in lesbian courtship, recalls that in the 1950s, gay women adhered to rigid gender-role models. Butches did what men were supposed to do: held their bodies tight, lit cigarettes with a dominating flourish, bought drinks, opened doors and otherwise demonstrated strength and gallantry. "Butches would swagger and wear chinos and stand around with one hip cocked and be bold in their gazes," she observes. "Femmes would sashay and wiggle their hips and use indirect feminine wiles."

Beginning in the late 1960s, such fixed role-playing began to dissolve. Lesbians meeting in consciousness-raising groups rejected gender as-

sumptions. It was considered sexually attractive, says Hall, to "put yourself out without artifice, without deception." In the 90s, however, the butch-femme distinction has returned.

But with a difference. Today's lesbians have a sense of irony and wit about the whole charade that would do Mae West proud. "A butch today might flirt by saying to a femme, 'Can I borrow your lipstick? I'm trying to liberate the woman within,' " she says with a laugh. "The gender roles are more scrambled, with 'dominant femmes' and 'soft butches.' There's more plurality and less polarization."

In San Francisco, gay men are learning the flirting repertoire used by straight women.

Male homosexuals also exhibit a wide range of flirting behaviors. In his studies, Perper has observed two gay men locked in a stalemate of sustained eye contact for 45 minutes before either made the next move. At the other end of the spectrum, he's seen gay dyads go through the entire flirtation cycle–"gaze, approach, talk, turn, touch, synchronize"–and be out the door on the way to one or the other's abode within two minutes.

The advent of AIDS and the greater societal acceptance of long-term gay attachments are changing flirtation rituals in the gay community. A sign of the times may be a courtship and dating course currently offered at Harvey Milk Institute in San Francisco. It instructs gay men in the repertoire of gestures long used by straight women seeking partners—ways of slowing down the flirtation, forestalling physical contact and assessing the other's suitability as a long-term mate. In short, it teaches homosexuals how to employ what the ethologists call a "long-term strategy."

FLIRTING Bi-Ways

When you're a crossdresser, all possibilities are open to you," says a male heterosexual who goes by the name Stephanie Montana when in female garb. In feminine persona, says Montana, "I can be more vulnerable, more animated and use more intermittent eye contact."

On one occasion Montana discovered what women seem to learn early on. A man was flirting with her, and, giddy with the attention, Montana sustained eye contact for a bit too long, gave too many overt sexual signals. In response, the man started acting in a proprietary fashion, frightening Montana with "those voracious male stares." Montana had learned the courtship signals but not the rejection repertoire. She didn't yet know how to put on the brakes.

Bisexuals have access to the entire panoply of male and female gestures. Loree Thomas of Seattle, who refers to herself as a bisexual non-op transsexual (born male, she is taking female hormones and living as a woman, but will not have a sex-change operation), has flirted *four* ways: dressed as a man interacting with men or with women, and dressed as a woman in encounters with women or men.

As a man flirting with a woman, Thomas found it most effective to maintain eye contact, smile, lean close, talk in a low voice and offer sincere compliments about the woman's best features. Man to man, says Thomas, the progression to direct physical contact accelerates. As a woman with a woman, Thomas' flirting has been "more shy, less direct than a man would be." As a woman with a man, she's played the stereotypical female role, "asking the man questions about himself, and listening as if totally fascinated." In all cases, eye contact and smiling are universal flirtation currency.

What the experience of crossdressers reinforces is the degree to which all flirtation is a game, a careful charade that involves some degree of deception and role-playing. Evolutionists talk about this deception in terms of men's tendency to exaggerate their wealth, success and access to resources, and women's strategic use of cosmetics and clothing to enhance their physical allure.

Some of the exhilaration of flirting, of course, lies in what is hidden, the tension between what is felt and what is revealed. Flirting pairs volley back and forth, putting out ambiguous signals, neither willing to disclose more than the other, neither wanting to appear more desirous to the other.

To observers like Moore and Perper, flirtation often seems to most resemble the antics of children on the playground or even perhaps the ritual peek-a-boo that babies play with their caregivers. Flirters jostle, tease and tickle, even sometimes stick out a tongue at their partner or reach around from behind to cover up their eyes. As Daniel Stern, researcher, psychiatrist, and author of *The Interpersonal World of the Infant* (Karnac, 1998), has pointed out, the two groups in our culture that engage in the most sustained eye contact are mothers and infants, and lovers.

And thus in a way, the cycle of flirting takes us full circle. If flirting sets us off on the road to producing babies, it also whisks us back to the pleasures of infancy.

The Science of a Good Marriage

Psychology is unlocking the secrets of happy couples.

BY BARBARA KANTROWITZ AND PAT WINGERT

THE MYTH OF MARRIAGE GOES LIKE this: somewhere out there is the perfect soul mate, the yin that meshes easily and effortlessly with your yang. And then there is the reality of marriage, which, as any spouse knows, is not unlike what Thomas Edison once said about genius: 1 percent inspiration and 99 percent perspiration. That sweaty part, the hard work of keeping a marriage healthy and strong, fascinates John Gottman. He's a psychologist at the University of Washington, and he has spent more than two decades trying to unravel the bewildering complex of emotions that binds two humans together for a year, a decade or even (if you're lucky) a lifetime.

Gottman, 56, comes to this endeavor with the best of qualifications: he's got the spirit of a scientist and the soul of a romantic. A survivor of one divorce, he's now happily married to fellow psychologist Julie Schwartz Gottman (they run couples workshops together). His daunting task is to quantify such intangibles as joy, contempt and tension. Ground zero for this research is the Family Research Laboratory on the Seattle campus (nicknamed the Love Lab). It consists of a series of nondescript offices equipped with video cameras and pulse, sweat and movement monitors to read the hearts and minds of hundreds of couples who have volunteered to be guinea pigs in longitudinal studies of the marital relationship. These volunteers have opened up their lives to the researchers, dissecting everything from the frequency of sex to who takes out

the garbage. The results form the basis of Gottman's new book, "The Seven Principles for Making Marriage Work," which he hopes will give spouses a scientific road map to happiness.

Among his unexpected conclusions: anger is not the most destructive emotion in a marriage, since both happy and miserable couples fight. Many popular therapies aim at defusing anger between spouses, but Gottman found that the real demons (he calls them "the Four Horsemen of the Apocalypse") are criticism, contempt, defensiveness and stonewalling. His research shows that the best way to keep these demons at bay is for couples to develop a "love map" of their spouse's dreams and fears. The happy couples all had such a deep understanding of their partner's psyche that they could navigate roadblocks without creating emotional gridlock.

Gottman's research also contradicts the Mars-Venus school of relationships, which holds that men and women come from two very different emotional worlds. According to his studies, gender differences may contribute to marital problems, but they don't cause them. Equal percentages of both men and women he interviewed said that the quality of the spousal friendship is the most important factor in marital satisfaction.

Gottman says he can predict, with more than 90 percent accuracy, which couples are likely to end up in divorce court. The first seven years are especially precarious; the average time for a divorce in this group is 5.2

years. The next danger point comes around 16 to 20 years into the marriage, with an average of 16.4 years. He describes one couple he first met as newlyweds: even then they began every discussion of their problems with sarcasm or criticism, what Gottman calls a "harsh start-up." Although they professed to be in love and committed to the relationship, Gottman correctly predicted that they were in trouble. Four years later they were headed for divorce, he says.

An unequal balance of power is also deadly to a marriage. Gottman found that a husband who doesn't share power with his wife has a much higher risk of damaging the relationship. Why are men singled out? Gottman says his data show that most wives, even those in unstable marriages, are likely to accept their husband's influence. It's the men who need to shape up, he says. The changes can be simple, like turning off the football game when she needs to talk. Gottman says the gesture proves he values "us" over "me."

Gottman's research is built on the work of many other scientists who have focused on emotion and human interaction. Early studies of marriage relied heavily on questionnaires filled out by couples, but these were often inaccurate. In the 1970s several psychology labs began using direct observation of couples to study marriage. A big boon was a relatively new tool for psychologists: videotape. Having a visual record that could be endlessly replayed made it much easier to study the emotional flow between spouses. In 1978 researchers Paul Ekman and Wallace Freisen devised a coding system for the human face (see box, "Know Your Spouse") that eventually provided another way to measure interchange between spouses.

Although early studies focused on couples in trouble, Gottman thought it was also important to study couples whose marriages work; he thinks they're the real experts. The Love Lab volunteers are interviewed about the history of their marriage. They then talk in front of the cameras about subjects that cause conflict between them. One couple Gottman describes in the book, Tim and Kara, argued constantly about his friend Buddy, who often wound up spending the night on Tim and Kara's couch. The researchers take scenes like this and break down every second of interaction to create a statistical pattern of good and bad moments. How many times did she roll her eyes (a sign of contempt) when he spoke? How often did he fidget (indicating tension or stress)? The frequency of negative and positive expressions, combined with the data collected by the heart, sweat and other monitors, provides a multidimensional view of the relationship. (Tim and Kara ultimately decided Buddy could stay, only not as often.)

Gottman and other researchers see their work as a matter of public health. The average couple who seek help have been having problems for six years—long enough to have done serious damage to their relationship. That delay, Gottman says, is as dangerous as putting off regular mammograms. The United States has one of the highest divorce rates in the industrialized world, and studies have shown a direct correlation between marriage and well-being. Happily married people are healthier; even their immune systems work better than those of people who are unhappily married or divorced. Kids suffer as well; if their parents split, they're more likely to have emotional or school problems.

But going to a marriage counselor won't necessarily help. "Therapy is at an impasse," Gottman says, "because it is not based on solid empirical knowledge of what real couples do to keep their marriages happy and stable." In a 1995 Consumer Reports survey, marriage therapy ranked at the bottom of a poll of patient satisfaction with various psychotherapies. The magazine said part of the problem was that "almost anyone can hang out a shingle as a marriage counselor." Even credentialed therapists may use approaches that have no basis in research. Several recent studies have shown that many current treatments produce few long-term benefits for couples who seek help.

One example: the process called "active listening." It was originally used by therapists to objectively summarize the complaints of a patient and validate the way the patient is feeling. ("So, I'm hearing that you think your father always liked your sister

Know Your Spouse

Test the strength of your marriage in this relationship quiz prepared especially for NEWSWEEK by John Gottman.

TRUE/FALSE

1 I can name by partner's best friends.
2 I can tell you what stresses my partner is currently facing
3 I know the names of some of the people who have been irritating my partner lately
4 I can tell you some of my partner's life dreams
5 I can tell you about my partner's basic philosophy of life
6 I can list the relatives my partner likes the least
7 I feel that my partner knows me pretty well
8 When we are apart, I often think fondly of my partner
9 I often touch or kiss my partner affectionately
10 My partner really respects me
11 There is fire and passion in this relationship
12 Romance is definitely still a part of our relationship
13 My partner appreciates the things I do in this relationship
14 My partner generally likes my personality
15 Our sex life is mostly satisfying
16 At the end of the day my partner is glad to see me
17 My partner is one of my best friends
18 We just love talking to each other
19 There is lots of give and take (both people have influence) in our discussions
20 My partner listens respectfully, even when we disagree
21 My partner is usually a great help as a problem solver
22 We generally mesh well on basic values and goals in life

Scoring: GIVE YOURSELF ONE POINT FOR EACH "TRUE" ANSWER. ABOVE 12: YOU HAVE A LOT OF STRENGTH IN YOUR RELATIONSHIP. CONGRATULATIONS. BELOW 12: YOUR RELATIONSHIP COULD STAND SOME IMPROVEMENT AND COULD PROBABLY BENEFIT FROM SOME WORK ON THE BASICS SUCH AS IMPROVING COMMUNICATION.

better and you're hurt by that.") In recent years this technique has been modified for marital therapy—ineffectively, Gottman says. Even highly trained therapists would have a hard time stepping back in the middle of a fight and saying, "So, I'm hearing that you think I'm a fat, lazy slob."

Happily married couples have a very different way of relating to each other during disputes, Gottman found. The partners make frequent "repair attempts," reaching out to each other in an effort to prevent negativity from getting out of control in the midst of conflict. Humor is often part of a successful repair attempt. In his book, Gottman describes one couple arguing about the kind of

car to buy (she favors a minivan; he wants a snazzier Jeep). In the midst of yelling, the wife suddenly puts her hand on her hip and sticks out her tongue—mimicking their 4-year-old son. They both start laughing, and the tension is defused.

In happy unions, couples build what Gottman calls a "sound marital house" by working together and appreciating the best in each other. They learn to cope with the two kinds of problems that are part of every marriage: solvable conflicts and perpetual problems that may represent underlying conflicts and that can lead to emotional gridlock. Gottman says 69 percent of marital conflicts fall into the latter category. Happy spouses

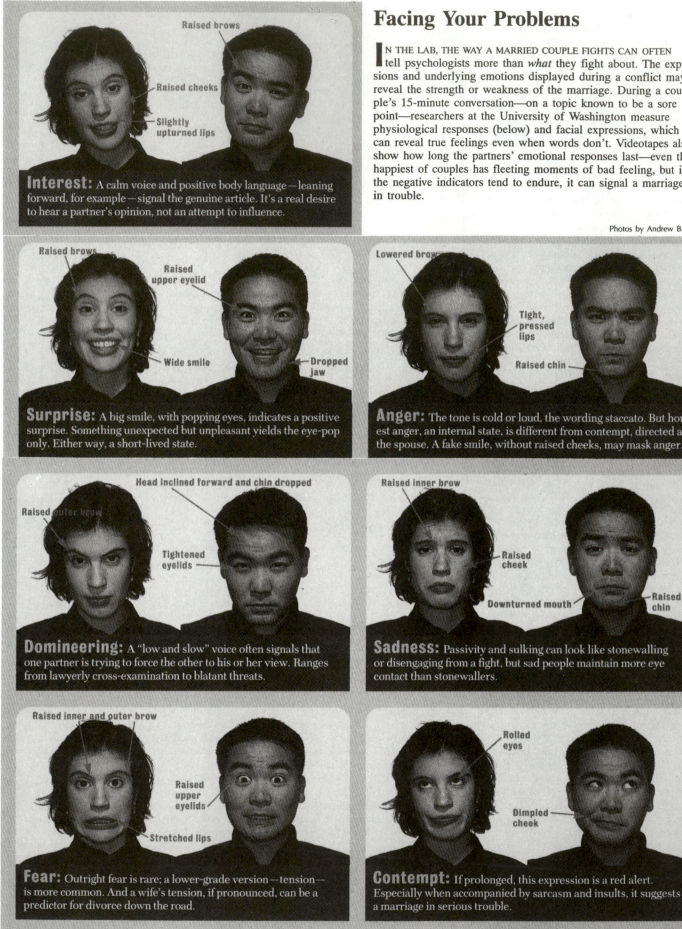

Interest: A calm voice and positive body language—leaning forward, for example—signal the genuine article. It's a real desire to hear a partner's opinion, not an attempt to influence.

Facing Your Problems

IN THE LAB, THE WAY A MARRIED COUPLE FIGHTS CAN OFTEN tell psychologists more than *what* they fight about. The expressions and underlying emotions displayed during a conflict may reveal the strength or weakness of the marriage. During a couple's 15-minute conversation—on a topic known to be a sore point—researchers at the University of Washington measure physiological responses (below) and facial expressions, which can reveal true feelings even when words don't. Videotapes also show how long the partners' emotional responses last—even the happiest of couples has fleeting moments of bad feeling, but if the negative indicators tend to endure, it can signal a marriage in trouble.

Photos by Andrew Brusso.

Surprise: A big smile, with popping eyes, indicates a positive surprise. Something unexpected but unpleasant yields the eye-pop only. Either way, a short-lived state.

Anger: The tone is cold or loud, the wording staccato. But honest anger, an internal state, is different from contempt, directed at the spouse. A fake smile, without raised cheeks, may mask anger.

Domineering: A "low and slow" voice often signals that one partner is trying to force the other to his or her view. Ranges from lawyerly cross-examination to blatant threats.

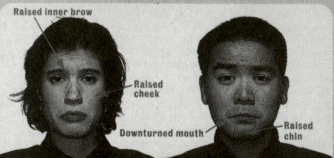

Sadness: Passivity and sulking can look like stonewalling or disengaging from a fight, but sad people maintain more eye contact than stonewallers.

Fear: Outright fear is rare; a lower-grade version—tension—is more common. And a wife's tension, if pronounced, can be a predictor for divorce down the road.

Contempt: If prolonged, this expression is a red alert. Especially when accompanied by sarcasm and insults, it suggests a marriage in serious trouble.

deal with these issues in a way that strengthens the marriage. One couple Gottman studied argued constantly about order in their household (she demanded neatness, and he couldn't care less). Over the years they managed to accommodate their differences, acknowledging that their affection for each other was more important than newspapers piled up in the corner of the living room.

As psychologists learn more about marriage, they have begun devising new approaches to therapy. Philip Cowan and Carolyn Pape-Cowan, a husband-and-wife team (married for 41 years) at the University of California, Berkeley, are looking at one of the most critical periods in a marriage: the birth of a first child. (Two thirds of couples experience a "precipitous drop" in marital satisfaction at this point, researchers say.) "Trying to take two people's dreams of a perfect family and make them one is quite a trick," Pape-Cowan says. The happiest couples were those who looked on their spouses as partners with whom they shared household and child-care duties. The Cowans say one way to help spouses get through the transition to parenting would be ongoing group sessions with other young families to provide the kind of support people used to get from their communities and extended families.

Inside the Love Lab

In the laboratory, video cameras record facial expressions. Motion-sensing jiggle-ometers register fidgeting, and a cluster of sensors reads physiological data.

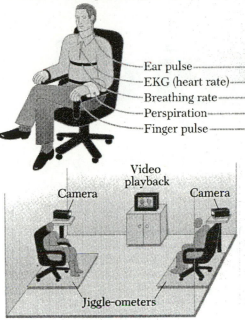

Ear pulse
EKG (heart rate)
Breathing rate
Perspiration
Finger pulse

Video playback
Camera   Camera
Jiggle-ometers

DIAGRAM BY CHRISTOPH BLUMRICH—NEWSWEEK

Two other researchers—Neil Jacobson at the University of Washington and Andrew Christensen at UCLA—have developed what they call "acceptance therapy" after studying the interactions of couples in conflict. The goal of their therapy is to help people learn to live with aspects of their spouse's characters that simply can't be changed. "People can love each other not just for what they have in common but for things that make them complementary," says Jacobson. "When we looked at a clinical sample of what predicted failure in traditional behavior therapy, what we came upon again and again was an inability to accept differences."

Despite all these advances in marital therapy, researchers still say they can't save all marriages—and in fact there are some that *shouldn't* be saved. Patterns of physical abuse, for example, are extremely difficult to alter, Gottman says. And there are cases where the differences between the spouses are so profound and long-standing that even the best therapy is futile. Gottman says one quick way to test whether a couple still has a chance is to ask what initially attracted them to each other. If they can recall those magic first moments (and smile when they talk about them), all is not lost. "We can still fan the embers," says Gottman. For all the rest of us, there's hope.

Shattered Vows

Hold on to your wedding ring. It's difficult, but possible, to repair the damage caused by infidelity. Increasingly, that's what couples want. But let go of assumptions. In an interview with Editor at Large Hara Estroff Marano, a leading expert challenges everything you think you know about the most explosive subject of the year. By Shirley Glass, Ph.D.

Infidelity appears to be the topic of the year. What has struck you most about the reaction to what may or may not be some kind of infidelity in high places?

Whatever horror or dismay people have about it, they're able to separate the way the President is performing in office and the way he appears to be performing in his marriage. That's especially interesting because it seems to reflect the split in his life. We don't know for sure, but he apparently is very much involved in his family life. He's not an absentee father or husband. Whatever it is that they share—and they share a lot, publicly and privately—he has a compartment in which he is attracted to young women, and it is separate from his primary relationships.

Is this compartmentalizing characteristic of people who get into affairs?

It's much more characteristic of men. Most women believe that if you love your partner, you wouldn't even be interested in an affair; therefore, if someone has an affair, it means that they don't love their partner and they do love the person they had the affair with. But my research shows there are many men who do love their partners, who enjoy good sex at home, who nevertheless never turn down an opportunity for extramarital sex. In fact, 56% of the men I sampled who had extramarital intercourse said that their marriages were happy, versus 34% of the women.

That's how I got into this.

Because?

Being a woman, I believed that if a man had an affair, it meant that he had a terrible marriage, and that he probably wasn't getting it at home—the old keep-your-husband-happy-so-he-won't-stray idea. That puts too much of the burden on the woman. I found that she could be everything wonderful, and he might still stray, if that's in his value system, his family background, or his psychodynamic structure.

I was in graduate school when I heard that a man I knew, married for over 40 years, had recently died and his wife was so bereaved because they had had the most wonderful marriage. He had been her lover, her friend, her support system. She missed him immensely. I thought that was a beautiful story. When I told my husband about it, he got a funny look that made me ask, What do you know? He proceeded to tell me that one night when he took the kids out for dinner to an out-of-the-way restaurant, that very man walked in with a young blonde woman. When he saw my husband, he walked out.

How did that influence you?

I wondered what that meant. Did he fool his wife all those years and really not love her? How is it possible to be married for over 40 years and think you have a good marriage? It occurred to me that an affair could mean something different than I believed.

Another belief that was an early casualty was the hydraulic pump theory—that you only have so much energy for something. By this belief, if your partner is getting sex outside, you would know it, because your partner wouldn't be wanting sex at home. However, some people are even more passionate at home when they are having extramarital sex. I was stunned to hear a man tell me that when he left his affair partner and came home he found himself desiring his wife more than he had in a long time, because he was so sexually aroused by his affair. That made me question the pump theory.

Many of our beliefs about the behavior of others come from how we see things for ourselves. A man who associates sneaking around with having sex will, if his wife is sneaking around, find it very hard to believe that she could be emotionally involved without being sexually involved. On the other hand, a woman usually cannot believe that her husband could be sexually involved and not be emotionally involved. We put the same meaning on it for our partner that it would have for us. I call that the error of assumed similarity.

What infidelity research have you done?

My first research study was actually based on a sex questionnaire in *Psychology Today* in the '70s. I analyzed the data, looking at the effect of extramarital sex, length of marriage, and gender difference on marital satisfaction and romanticism. I found enormous gender differences.

Men in long-term marriages who had affairs had very high marital satisfaction—and women in long-term marriages having affairs had the lowest satisfaction of all. Everybody's marital satisfaction went down the longer they were married, except the men who had affairs. But in early marriages, men who had affairs were significantly less happy. An affair is more serious if it happens earlier in the marriage.

Explaining these gender differences was the basis of my dissertation. I theorized that men were having sexual affairs and women emotional affairs.

Are affairs about sex?

Sometimes infidelity is just about sex. That is often more true for men. In my research, 44% of men who said they had extramarital sex said they had slight or no emotional involvement; only 11% of women said that. Oral sex is certainly about sex. Some spouses are more upset if the partner had oral sex than if they had intercourse; it just seems so much more intimate.

What is the infidelity in infidelity?

The infidelity is that you took something that was supposed to be mine, which is sexual or emotional intimacy, and you gave it to somebody else. I thought that we had a special relationship, and now you have contaminated it; it doesn't feel special any more, because you shared something very precious to us with someone else.

There are gender differences. Men feel more betrayed by their wives having sex with someone else; women feel more betrayed by their husbands being emotionally involved with someone else. What really tears men apart is to visualize their partner being sexual with somebody else.

Women certainly don't want their husbands having sex with somebody else, but they may be able to deal with an impersonal one-night fling better than a long-term relationship in which their husband was sharing all kinds of loving ways with somebody else.

Why are affairs so deeply wounding?

Because you have certain assumptions about your marriage. That I chose someone, and the other person chose me; we have the same values; we have both decided to have an exclusive relationship, even though we may have some problems. We love each other—and therefore I am safe.

Voices of *Infidelity*

I was working full-time, as was my wife; I was going to school and we were caring for our son. Little time was left for each other. The night I received my acceptance to medical school, in April, she told me she was unhappy and was attracted to someone else.

We began counseling. A month later, she told me she was in love with him and was very confused. I was feeling insecure in the relationship; it was coming out as anger.

In June, the wife of the guy called and told me that Lori was having an affair with her husband. The heat in my chest began to slowly grow. Lori beeped in on the line; I told her, "I know and I'm on my way" to her office; he worked with her. Now in a full rage, I stalked through the office looking for him, but she had told him I was coming and he'd left the building. I announced that "[He] is screwing my wife!" Then I verbally vented all my anger in front of the building, where Lori was waiting before leaving to get my son from daycare.

When you find out your partner has been unfaithful, then everything you believe is totally shattered. And you have to rebuild the world. The fact that you weren't expecting it, that it wasn't part of your assumption about how a relationship operates, causes traumatic reactions.

And it is deeply traumatic.

It's terrible. The wounding results because—and I've heard this so many times—I finally thought I met somebody I could trust.

It violates that hope or expectation that you can be who you really are with another person?

Yes. Affairs really aren't about sex; they're about betrayal. Imagine you are married to somebody very patriotic and then find out your partner is a Russian spy. Someone having a long-term affair is leading a double life. Then you find out all that was going on in your partner's life that you knew nothing about: gifts that were exchanged, poems and letters that were written, trips that you thought were taken for a specific reason were actually taken to meet the affair partner.

To find out about all the intrigue and deception that occurred while you were operating under a different assumption is totally shattering and disorienting. That's why people then have to get out their calendars and go back over the dates to put all the missing pieces together: "When you went to the drugstore that night and said your car broke down and didn't come home for three hours, what was really happening?"

This is necessary?

In order to heal. Because any time somebody suffers from a trauma, part of the recovery is telling the story. The tornado victim will go over and over the story—"when the storm came I was in my room . . ."—trying to understand what happened, and how it happened. "Didn't we see the black clouds? How come we didn't know?"

And so they repeat the story until it no longer creates unmanageable arousal?

Yes. In fact, sometimes people are more devastated if everything was wonderful before they found out. When a betrayed spouse who suspected something says, "I don't know if I can ever trust my partner again," it is reassuring to tell them that they can trust their own instincts the next time they have those storm warnings. But if somebody thought everything was wonderful, how would they ever know if it happened again? It's frightening.

One question people these days are asking you is, Is oral sex really infidelity?

The question they ask is, Is oral sex really adultery? And that's a different question, because adultery is a legal term. It is also a biblical term. The real issue is, Is

ADVICE TO *Hillary*, ALL DEARLY *betrayed*, AND *nearly* BETRAYED

• Yes, oral sex really is infidelity.

• It's a boundary problem, not a love problem.

• Some woman or other is going to give him a second chance to prove that he can be faithful. Decide if that woman can be you.

• Faithfulness is not a virtue that falls out of the heavens—it's a skill. And it can be learned. . . . [see] (www.smartmarriages.com).

• Disregard what other people say. All that matters is your ability to rebuild trust.

• Recognize your power and use it to renegotiate your relationship from the bottom up.

• Despite the hurt and anger, love can still survive.

• You may want to consider your shared history, shared goals, and shared commitment to important causes.

• Affairs are less a reflection of the partner and the marriage than of broader forces in the culture that undermine monogamy.

• You may look realistically at your partner's other qualities and decide that on balance you prefer your spouse to other potential partners.

—*The Editors, with Peggy Vaughan, author of The Monogamy Myth.*

oral sex infidelity? You don't need to ask a psychologist that—just ask any spouse: "Would you feel that it was an infidelity for your partner to engage in that type of behavior?"

Would women answer that differently from men?

It is not necessarily a function of gender. People might answer it differently for themselves than for their partners. Some people maintain a kind of technical virginity by not having intercourse. However, even kissing in a romantic, passionate way is an infidelity. People know when they cross that line from friendship to affair.

So you don't have to have intercourse to have an affair?

Absolutely. There can be an affair without any kind of touching at all. People have affairs on the Internet.

What is the *sine qua non* of an affair?

Three elements determine whether a relationship is an affair.

One is secrecy. Suppose two people meet every morning at seven o'clock for coffee before work, and they never tell their partners. Even though it might be in a public place, their partner is not going to be happy about it. It is going to feel like a betrayal, a terrible deception.

Emotional intimacy is the second element. When someone starts confiding things to another person that they are reluctant to confide to their partner, and the emotional intimacy is greater in the friendship than in the marriage, that's very threatening. One common pathway to affairs occurs when somebody starts confiding negative things about their marriage. What they're doing is signaling: "I'm vulnerable; I may even be available."

The third element is sexual chemistry. That can occur even if two people don't touch. If one says, "I'm really attracted to you," or "I had a dream about you last night, but, of course, I'm married, so we won't do anything about that," that tremendously increases the sexual tension by creating forbidden fruit in the relationship.

Another question you told me people now ask is, "Are you a liar if you lie about an affair?" How do you answer?

Lying goes with the territory. If you're not lying, you have an open marriage. There may be lies of omission or lies of commission. The lie of omission is, "I had to stop at the gym on my way home." There is the element of truth, but the omission of what was really happening: "I left after 15 minutes and spent the next 45 minutes at someone's apartment."

The lies of commission are the elaborate deceptions people create. The more deception

Lori had asked me not to tell my family we were having problems; thus, I was cut off from my major support system. I wanted to punish her by holding her up to public scrutiny. I gathered everyone from both families and proceeded to tell them the whole story.

After I cooled down, we spent a month "working" on the relationship. Then she filed for divorce. I am left with a huge amount of anger at him and at her even though it is so many months later. I've never had the opportunity to vent my anger at him and still fantasize about tracking him down and beating him senseless. After all the time and emotional investment I'd put into this relationship, they intentionally damaged it until it was unsalvageable.

I am now beginning med school, and we are sharing physical and legal custody of our son. Oh, and her love was fired from his job as a result of this indiscretion.—*BH*

❧

I had an affair with my neighbor. I was friends with his wife. We spent a

and the longer it goes on, the more difficult it is to rebuild trust in the wake of an affair.

The deception makes a tremendous psychological difference to the betrayed spouse. What about to the person who constructed the deception?

Once the affair's been discovered, the involved partner could have a sense of relief, if they hate lying and don't see themselves as having that kind of moral character. They'll say, "I can't understand how I could have done a thing like this, this is not the kind of person I am."

Some people thrive on the game. For them, part of the passion and excitement of an affair is the lying and getting away with something forbidden.

There are some people who have characterological problems, and the affair may be a symptom of that. Such people lie about their accomplishments; they are fraudulent in business. When it's characterological, I don't know any way to rebuild trust; no one can ever be on sure footing with that person.

So there is always moral compromise just by being in an affair?

Which is why some people, no matter how unhappy they are in their marriage, don't have affairs. They can't make the compromise. Or they feel they have such an open relationship with the spouse that they just could not do something like that without telling their partner about it.

Do affairs ever serve a positive function—not to excuse any of the damage they do?

Affairs are often a chance for people to try out new behaviors, to dress in a different costume, to stretch and grow and assume a different role. In a long-term relationship, we often get frozen in our roles. When young couples begin at one level of success and go on to many achievements, the new person sees them as they've become, while the old person sees them as they were.

The unfortunate thing is that the way a person is different in the affair would, if incorporated into the marriage, probably make their spouse ecstatic. But they believe they're stuck; they don't know how to create opportunity for change within the marriage. A woman who was sexually inhibited in marriage—perhaps she married young and had no prior partners—may find her sexuality in an affair, but her husband would probably be thrilled to encounter that new self.

How do you handle this?

After an affair, I do not ask the question you would expect. The spouse always wants to know about "him" or "her": "What did you see in her that you didn't see in me?" Or, "What did you like about him better?" I always ask about "you": "What did you like about yourself in that other relationship?" "How were you different?" and "Of the way that you were in that other relationship, what would you like to bring back so that you can be the person you want to be in your primary relationship?" "How can we foster that part of you in this relationship?"

That's a surprise. How did you come to know that's the question to ask?

There is an attraction in the affair, and I try to understand what it is. Part of it is the romantic projection: I like the way I look when I see myself in the other person's eyes. There is positive mirroring. An affair holds up a vanity mirror, the kind with all the little bulbs around it; it gives a rosy glow to the way you see yourself. By contrast, the marriage offers a makeup mirror; it magnifies every little flaw. When someone loves you despite seeing all your flaws, that is a reality-based love.

In the stories of what happened during the affair, people seem to take on a different persona, and one of the things they liked best about being in that relationship was the person they had become. The man who wasn't sensitive or expressive is now in a relationship where he is expressing his feelings and is supportive.

Can those things be duplicated in the marriage?

That's one of the goals—not to turn the betrayed spouse into the affair partner, but to free the unfaithful spouse to express all the parts of himself he was able to experience in the affair.

I see a lot of men who are married to very competent women and having affairs with very weak women. They feel: "This person needs me." They put on their red cape and do a lot of rescuing. They feel very good about themselves. That makes me sad, because I know that even though their partner may be extremely competent, she wants to be stroked too. She wants a knight in shining armor. Perhaps she hasn't known how to ask.

Do people push partners into affairs?

No. People can create a pattern in the marriage that is not enhancing, and the partner, instead of dealing with the dissatisfaction and trying to work on the relationship, escapes it and goes someplace else.

That is the wrong way to solve the problem?

Yes. Generally when a woman is unhappy, she lets her partner know. She feels better because she's gotten it off her chest. It doesn't interfere with her love. She's trying to improve the relationship: "If I tell him what makes me unhappy, then he will know how to please me; I am giving him a gift by telling him."

Unfortunately, many men don't see it as a gift. They feel criticized and put down. Instead of thinking, "She feels lonely; I will move toward her and make her feel secure," they think, "What is wrong with her? Didn't I just do that?" They pull away. If they come in contact with somebody else who says to them, "Oh, you're wonderful," then they move toward that person. They aren't engaged enough in the marriage to work things out. The partner keeps trying and becomes more unpleasant because he's not responding.

She becomes a pursuer, and he becomes the distancer.

When she withdraws, the marriage is much further down the road to dissolution, because she's given up. Her husband, unfortunately, thinks things are so much better because she's no longer complaining. He doesn't recognize that she has detached and become emotionally available for an affair. The husband first notices it when she becomes disinterested in sex—or after she's left! Then he'll do anything to keep her. That is often too little too late.

By then she is often committed to someone on the outside?

Yes, which is why when women have affairs, it's much more often a result of long-term marital dissatisfaction.

Can you predict which couples will get involved in affairs?

Social context is a predictor. If you're in an occupational or social group where many people have affairs, and there's a sexually per-

lot of time together. (My husband works long hours and all weekend.) I started to work for my neighbor part-time and started to feel excitement build.

The affair lasted five months. We stopped many times but would find ourselves back in each other's arms. The sex was O.K.; I felt that was what I had to give him to get what I wanted—the words about how sexy I was, something I never heard from my husband.

His wife found out and told my husband last year; he left for three months. He would show up nightly after the kids were asleep, call me a whore, and scream at me. I'd be sobbing on the floor. I never wanted to end my marriage.

My husband finally started counseling with me and moved back in. The neighbors moved away three months ago.

My husband told me last week he wants a divorce. After a week of begging him to stay, I found love letters and hotel reservations from a girl in Houston. He said it's his second chance for love. I am devastated. My kids will suffer the rest of their lives for my mistakes.—NC

missive attitude, you're more likely. Also if you come from a family where there's a history of affairs—the most notorious are the Kennedys, where the men have a certain entitlement. Coming from one of the Mediterranean cultures, like the Greek, where the double standard is alive and well, is another predictor.

You're saying that an affair is not always about the marriage. There are often cultural or contextual pulls into affairs. This is important information for women, because women blame themselves.

And society blames women.

So affairs can happen in good marriages. Is the marriage really good?

Sometimes one person thinks the marriage is fine and the other doesn't. That may be because the more dissatisfied person hasn't communicated their dissatisfaction. Or they've communicated it and the partner has discounted it. But after an affair, people often try to justify it by rewriting unhappiness into the marital history. They say, "I never really loved you," or "You never really acted like you loved me." That is just a way to make themselves feel that they didn't do such a terrible thing.

Why do some people in unhappy marriages have affairs and others do not?

Number one is opportunity. Number two is values. Some people do not think an affair is justified for any reason. Others think it's

okay if you're not getting it at home or if you "fall in love" with another person.

Surveys show that for women, the highest justification is for love; emotional intimacy is next. Sex is last on their list of justifications. It's the opposite for men; sex scores the highest.

Is infidelity in a long-standing marriage the same as in one of shorter duration?

It is potentially more threatening to the marriage when it happens earlier, and the chances of the marriage surviving are less, particularly where the woman is having an affair.

Did she choose the wrong mate?

She thinks so, especially if her affair partner is the opposite of her husband.

From your perspective, what's going on?

She's growing and changing, and she chooses somebody she sees as more similar to herself. Usually it's someone at work. Her husband may be working very hard in his profession or going to school and not paying much attention to her. She feels a little lonely, and then she gets involved. Or maybe her husband is very caring, and the relationship is so supportive and stable that it doesn't have a challenge for her.

The opportunities for affairs have changed radically in the past 20 years. Men and women are together all the time in the workplace, and workplaces are sexy places. You dress up, you're trying your best, there's energy in the air.

And you're not cleaning up vomit or the hot water heater that just flooded the basement. And it's not at the end of the day when you're exhausted. Also, you're working together on something that has excitement and meaning.

One of the major shifts is that more married women are having affairs than in the past. There are several reasons. Today's woman has usually had more experience with premarital sex, so she's not as inhibited about getting involved sexually with another man. She has more financial independence, so she's not taking as great a risk. And she is working with men on a more equal level, so the men are very attractive to her.

What do people seek in an affair partner?

Either we choose somebody very different from our partner, or we choose somebody like our partner used to be, but a younger version. A woman married to a really sweet guy who helps with the dishes, who is very nurturing and very secure, may at some point see him as boring and get interested in the high-achieving, high-energy man who may even be a bit chauvinistic. But if she's married to the man with the power and the status, then she's interested in the guy who is sensitive and touchy-feely, who may not be as ambitious.

Is this just the nature of attraction?

It has to do with the fact that people really want it all. Probably the only way to get it all is to be in more than one relationship at the same time. We have different parts of ourselves.

The other flip-flop in choice of affair partner reflects the fact that the marriage often represents a healing of our family wounds. Somebody who lacked a secure attachment figure in their family of origin chooses a mate who provides security and stability. It's healthy to seek that balancing.

But after we've mastered that, we often want to go back and find somebody like that difficult parent and make that person love us. There is a correlation between the nature of the attachment figure and the affair partner; the person is trying to master incomplete business from childhood. As a result, some people will choose an affair partner who is difficult, temperamental, or unpredictable. Under those circumstances, the unfaithful partner is often caught in a triangle.

What do you mean?

The person maintains the marriage, and can't leave it, and maintains the affair, and can't leave that either. Tension arises when either the affair partner or spouse applies pressure on them to get off the fence. The spouse provides security and a sense of family, the affair partner excitement and passion. When the involved spouse says, "I don't know which person to be with," what they really want is to keep both.

The challenge is, how do people satisfy all of their needs within the marriage?

It is a false belief that if I'm incomplete, I have to be completed by another person.

You have to do it through your own life, your own work, for your own pleasure, through individual growth. The more fulfilled you are, in terms of things that you do separately that please you, the more individuated and more whole you are—and the more intimate you can be. Then you're not expecting the other person to make you happy. You're expecting the other person to join you in your happiness.

> When women have affairs, it's much more often a result of long-term marital dissatisfaction.

Are more couples trying to survive affairs these days?

People are more willing to work through them. People are saying, I'm willing to work this through, but we have to solve whatever problems we have; we have to get something out of this; our marriage has to be even better than it was before.

More men are calling to come in for therapy. That's a very positive sign. The downside is, it's often too late. By the time men are alarmed, the woman is too distanced from the marriage.

What other changes do you see in affairs these days?

Cyber affairs are new. For some people the computer is very addictive. They get very caught up in it. It's hiding out, escap-

ing. And an affair is an escape—from the realities of everyday life. These two escapes are now paired.

The other danger on-line is that people can disguise who they are. Think of the roles you can take on if you hide behind a screen. More so than in workplace affairs, you can project anything onto the other person.

You can act out any fantasy you want. You can make this other person become anybody you want them to be. There's a loosening up, because you're not face-to-face with the person.

This attracts only a certain kind of person, doesn't it?

We don't know yet. I always get e-mail questions from people who are concerned because their partner is having an on-line relationship with somebody. Or their partner had an affair with somebody they met on-line. It's very prevalent, and it's very dangerous.

If you're talking to somebody on the computer, and you begin to talk about your sexual fantasies, and you're not talking to your partner about your sexual fantasies, which relationship now has more sexual chemistry? Which has more emotional intimacy? Then your partner walks in the room, and you switch screens. Now you've got a wall of secrecy. It has all the components of an affair. And it's easy.

Technology has impacted affairs in another way, too. Many people have discovered a partner's affair by getting the cellular phone bill, or by getting in the car and pushing redial on the car phone, or by taking their partner's beeper and seeing who's been calling. We're leaving a whole new electronic trail.

Has that changed the dynamics or the psychology of affairs in any way?

In the past, when someone was suspicious they could ask their partner: "What's

'HOW DO I *Know* YOU WON'T *Betray* ME *Again*'

The following are signs of recovery, healing, and hope for a committed future together.

The unfaithful partner:
• recognizes and understands the individual vulnerabilities that contributed to the affair—curiosity, depression, need for excitement, and rescue fantasies are common ones—and views them as danger signals.
• shows empathy for the pain caused by the infidelity.
• assumes responsibility for the betrayal, regardless of any problems that existed in the marriage.

The betrayed partner:
• is able to recognize when his/her partner might be lying again.
• refuses to put his/her head in the sand.
• refuses to give without getting anything back.

Together you develop a united front:
• You can refer to affair-related events with calmness, perhaps humor.
• You can make united decisions concerning fallout from the affair, such as intrusive phone calls or a request for AIDS testing, and jointly manage present and future encounters with the affair partner.
• Your marriage is stronger; there's more reciprocity, more caring and communication, and better conflict management.
• You see eye to eye on the value of exclusivity and monogamy because of the pain the infidelity caused.
• You share responsibility for changing the relationship.
• You make more time for yourselves as a couple, apart from your children's needs, as a way to strengthen the friendship and erotic bond between you.—SG

going on? You seem distant lately." If the partner denied anything was wrong, there wasn't a whole lot a person could do. Now there's tangible evidence people can utilize to find out if their hunches are indeed true.

There is a public conception of affairs as glamorous, but the aftermath is pretty messy. How do we square these views?

They're both true. In those captured moments, there is passion and romance. We're in Stage One of relationship formation—idealizing the partner. This Stage One can go on for years, as long as there's a forbidden aspect.

The admiration and positive mirroring can go on for a long time—until you get to a reality-based relationship. And this is why so many affairs end after the person leaves the marriage.

How many affairs survive as enduring relationships?

Only 10% of people who leave their relationship for affairs end up with the affair partner. Once you can be with the person every day and deal with all the little irritations in a relationship, you're into Stage Two—disillusionment.

How do most affairs get exposed?

Sometimes the betrayed partner will just ask, "Are you involved with somebody else?" Sometimes the affair partner, when it's a woman, does something to inform the wife—she sends a letter or even shows up on the doorstep. She asks, "Do you know where your husband's been?" Her motivation is not to be helpful but to break up the marriage. But often she's the one who then gets left out.

Sometimes people find out in horrible ways. They read about it in the newspaper, or they get a sexually transmitted disease. Or the cell phone bill arrives. Or their partner gets arrested—if there is a sexual addiction, the partner may be caught with prostitutes. Sometimes, somebody is suspicious and checks it out by going to the hotel room to see whether their partner's alone, or by hiring detectives.

Can all relationships be fixed?

No. What I look for is how the unfaithful partner shows empathy for the pain that they have caused when the betrayed spouse starts acting crazy.

In what way do they act crazy?

They're very emotional. They cry easily, their emotions flip-flop. They are hypervigilant. They want to look at the beeper. They have flashbacks. In the car, they hear a country-western song and start crying or accusing. They obsess over the details of the affair. Although these are common post-traumatic reactions to infidelity, their behavior is very erratic and up-

setting to them and their partner. How much compassion the partner has for that is one hallmark.

Another sign of salvageability lies in how much responsibility the unfaithful partner takes for the choice they made, regardless of problems that pre-existed in the marriage. (We definitely need to work on the weaknesses of the marriage, but not to justify the affair.)

If the unfaithful partner says, "You made me do it," that's not as predictive of a good outcome as when the partner says, "We should have gone to counseling to deal with the problems before this happened." Sometimes the unfaithful partner doesn't regret the affair because it was very exciting.

> **People often try to justify an affair by rewriting the marital history. They'll say, 'I never really loved you.'**

One of the big strains between the partners in the primary relationship is the way they perceive the affair partner.

How so?

A lot of the anger and the rage the betrayed spouse feels is directed toward the affair partner rather than the marital partner: "That person doesn't have any morals"; "That person's a home wrecker." To believe that of the marital partner would make it difficult to stay in the relationship.

At the same time, the person who had the affair may still be idealizing the affair partner. The unfaithful spouse perceives the affair partner as an angel, whereas the betrayed person perceives them as an evil person.

It's important at some point in the healing process for the involved person to see some flaws in the affair partner, so that they can partly see what their partner, the betrayed spouse, is telling them. It's also important for the betrayed spouse to see the affair partner not as a cardboard character but as a human being who did some caring things.

Is there anything else that helps you gauge the salvageability of a relationship after an affair?

Empathy, responsibility—and the degree of understanding of the vulnerabilities that made an affair possible.

What vulnerabilities?

There are individual vulnerabilities, such as curiosity. Somebody gets invited for lunch, and they go to the house because they're curious. They must learn that getting curious is a danger sign. Or if some damsel or guy in distress comes with a sad story, they learn to give out the name of a great therapist instead of becoming their confessor and confidante. Knowing what the vulnerabilities are helps you avoid them.

And relationship vulnerabilities?

The biggest one I see today is the child-centered marriage. I tell couples, If you really love your kids, the best gift you can give them is your own happy marriage. You can't have a happy marriage if you never spend time alone. Your children need to see you closing the bedroom door or going out together without them. That gives a sense of security greater than what they get by just by being loved.

Today's parents feel guilty because they don't have enough time with their kids. They think they're making it up to them by spending with them whatever leisure time they do have. They have *family* activities and *family* vacations. To help them rebuild the marriage, I help them become more couple-centered.

There has to be a separate layer of adult relationship?

The affair represents a man and a woman getting together in a dyad and just devoting themselves to each other. Very busy couples sometimes have to actually look at their calendars and find when they can spend time together.

Are there other vulnerabilities?

One is: getting too intimate with co-workers. One way to guard against danger is, if there's somebody you really like at work, then include them as a couple; invite that person and their partner to come over so that there isn't a separate relationship with that person. That's not a guarantee; people do have affairs with their best friend's spouse.

Can you tell whether someone is secretly continuing the affair?

A sign that the affair is continuing is when the unfaithful partner isn't doing anything caring and keeps making excuses—"I don't feel it yet," or "It would be false if I did it now." Sometimes it feels disloyal to the affair partner to be too caring.

Is it hard to get over an affair without a therapist?

It's hard to do *with* a therapist. People can get over it, but I don't know that they resolve the issues. Usually the unfaithful person wants to let it rest at "Hi hon, I'm back. Let's get on with our lives. Why do we have to keep going back over the past?" The betrayed person wants to know the story with all the gory details. They may begin to feel *they're* wrong to keep asking and may suppress their need to know because their partner doesn't want to talk about it. They may stay together, but they really don't learn anything or heal.

Can it ever be the same as it was before?

The affair creates a loss of innocence and some scar tissue. I tell couples things will never be the same. But the relationship may be stronger.

How do you rebuild trust?

Through honesty. First, I have to build safety. It comes about by stopping all contact with the affair partner and sharing your whereabouts, by being willing to answer the questions from your partner, by handing over the beeper, even by creating a fund to hire a detective to check up at random.

It also requires sharing information about encounters with the affair partner before being asked; when you come home, you say, "I saw him today, and he asked me how we're doing; I said, I really don't want to discuss it with you."

That's counterintuitive. People think that talking about it with the spouse will create an upset, and they'll have to go through the whole thing again. But it doesn't. Instead of trying to put the affair in a vault and lock it up, if they're willing to take it out and look at it, then the trust is rebuilt through that intimacy. The betrayed spouse may say, "I remember when such-and-such happened." If the unfaithful spouse can say, "Yeah, I just recalled such-and-such," and they bring up things or ask their partner, "How are you feeling? I see you're looking down today, is that because you're remembering?," trust can be rebuilt.

Eventually, the questioning and revealing assume a more normal level?

Yes, but things will often pop up. Someone or something will prompt them to remember something that was said. "What did you mean when you said that?" Or, "What were you doing when that happened?"

In the beginning, the betrayed partner wants details. Where, what, when. Did you tell them you love them? Did you give them gifts? Did they give you gifts? How often did you see them? How many times did you have sex? Did you have oral sex? Where did you have sex, was it in our house? How much money did you spend? Those kinds of factual questions need to be answered.

> # Unless the unfaithful partner shows empathy for the pain they have caused, the marriage can't be helped.

Eventually the questions develop more complexity. How did it go on so long if you knew that it was wrong? After that first time, did you feel guilty? At that point they're in the final stages of trauma recovery, which is the search for meaning.

And they have come to a joint understanding about what the affair meant?

By combining their stories and their perceptions. A couple builds trust by rewriting their history and including the story of the affair. Some couples do a beautiful job in trying to understand the affair

together, and they co-create the story of what they've been through together. When couples really are healed, they may even tease each other with private little jokes about something that they know about the affair partner or about something that happened during the affair. You can see that they finally have some comfort with it.

One of the signs that they are working in a much more united way is that their perception of the affair partner becomes more integrated—not all evil or all angel, but a human being who perhaps did manipulate but also was caring.

Some people, particularly men, are philanderers; they have repeated affairs. What's going on?

First of all, there are different kinds of philanderers. Sometimes it's easier to deal with this kind of infidelity, because there isn't the emotional involvement; sometimes it's harder, because it's such an established pattern.

One question I explore with somebody who has had lots of sexual relationships is whether it's an addiction or, in the case of men particularly, a sense of entitlement. There are some women now in positions of power who also seem to be treating sex in the same casual way and exploiting power in the same way as male philanderers. Nevertheless, in our culture, there is a sense of male privilege that condones and even encourages affairs.

How does entitlement affect matters?

If a man feels entitled, he experiences little guilt. Also, it is not necessarily a compulsive behavior; he has the ability to choose to stop it—if he changes his attitudes, if he sees what the consequences are, if he comes to believe that marriage means more than being a provider but being a loving father or caring husband. Even if he doesn't see anything wrong with philandering, if he can see the pain it causes someone he loves, he may really make the vow not only to his partner but to himself.

A sexually addicted person usually uses sex the way others use drugs: they get anxious, they say they're not going to do it, but then they're driven toward it. They get a momentary gratification followed by remorse. They decide they're not going to do it again, then they do.

There's a compulsive quality.

There is also often remorse and guilt. If they get into therapy, they may learn what addiction means in their life. Often, there's an emptiness that's linked to a need for excitement. There may be an underlying depression. They then begin to deal with the underlying source of that compulsive behavior.

What is the single most important thing you want people to know about infidelity?

BOUNDARIES. That it is possible to love somebody else, to be attracted to somebody else, even if you have a good marriage. In this collegial world where we work together, you have to conduct yourself by being aware of appropriate boundaries, by not creating opportunities, particularly at a time when you might be vulnerable.

That means that if you travel together, you never invite someone for a drink in the room; if you just had a fight with your spouse, you don't discuss it with a potential partner.

You can have a friendship, but you have to be careful who you share your deepest feelings with. Although women share their deep feelings with lots of people, particularly other women, men are usually most comfortable sharing their feelings in a love relationship. As a result, when a relationship becomes intimate and emotional, men tend to sexualize it.

There may be a history of incest or sexual abuse. Some woman may be turning the tables by using their sexuality to control men rather than be controlled by them, or they may be using sex as a way to get affection, because they don't believe that they can get it any other way. Some people may be acting out like rebellious adolescents against a spouse who is too parental.

What is happening in relationships that are parental or otherwise unequal?

Sometimes there is an over-functioning spouse and an under-functioning spouse. One partner takes on a lot of responsibility—and then resents it. The more a person puts energy into something and tries to work on it, the more committed to the relationship that person is. The other partner, who is only semi-involved in the relationship, is freer to get involved in an affair; they're not as connected to the marriage.

This is interesting because the popular notion is that the person who has the affair wasn't getting enough at home. The reality is that they weren't giving enough at home.

How do you handle that?

In rebuilding that relationship, more equity has to be created. The issue isn't what can the betrayed spouse do to make the partner happy—it's what can the unfaithful spouse do to make their partner happy. In research and in practice, my colleague Tom Wright, Ph.D., and I have observed that when you compare who does more—who is more understanding, who is more romantic, who enjoys sex more—the affair is almost always more equitable than the marriage. Usually, the person was giving more—more time, more attention, more compliments—in the affair than in the marriage. If they can invest in the marriage what they were doing in the affair, they'll feel more.

There is some research showing that people are more satisfied in equitable relationships. When relationships are not equitable, even the over-benefited partners are not as satisfied as those in equitable relationships.

You seem to be constantly reversing the conventional wisdom about affairs.

I've noticed that when younger women get involved in affairs early in the marriage and then leave, often they have not been invested in the marriage. They're working hard, climbing a ladder; the husband is the one making dinner while she's working late. He is the devastated one, because he is really committed and has given a lot. But he is peripheral in her life.

I've seen several couples who had a plan they agreed on, to build a house, or for one partner to go back to school. The person who had the responsibility for carrying out the plan was totally engrossed in it, while the other person felt so neglected that they then had an affair. The betrayed person felt terribly betrayed, because he or she thought he was working for their future. But he didn't necessarily listen to distress signs.

A relationship is like a fire. You can let it go down, but you can't let it go out. Even though you're in another part of the house, you have to go back every once in a while to stoke the coals.

> People think a person having an affair isn't getting enough at home. The truth is, the person isn't giving enough.

Do you ever counsel people directly to leave a relationship?

I would support a betrayed spouse ending the relationship if a period of time has gone by in which they have tried to work on the relationship but the affair continues secretly.

Leaving a bad marriage without trying to repair it first is like buying high and selling low. Better to see how good you can make it, then look at it and ask: Is this good enough?

What percentage of couples make it?

Those who stay in therapy and have stopped the affair have a real good chance. After an affair is first uncovered and the involved person vows to stop it, it usually doesn't stop right away. That would be coitus interruptus; there has to be some kind of closure. There will be secret meetings to say good bye or to make sure that you can really let go. But that should happen in the first few weeks or months.

Are some occupations or settings particularly conducive to affairs?

I don't know any place where the risk is low. When I was doing research for my dissertation, I went to the Baltimore-Washington airport and to an office park and gave out questionnaires. I'd go up to the men, quite imposing in their pinstripe suits and starched collars, and ask if they'd complete an anonymous research questionnaire on marriage.

I was stunned when the forms came back; so many of the men who had looked so conservative had engaged in extramarital sex. It is now known that, while we suspect the liberals, conservative men are actually more likely to be having extramarital affairs—because they split sex and affection. There are the nice girls you marry and the wild girls you have sex with.

The double standard is alive and well.

Men who score high on traits of authoritarianism are more likely to separate sex and affection than men who are low in authoritarianism. Military officers fall into this category.

People in high-drama professions—among doctors, those in the ER, trauma surgeons, cardiologists—engage in a certain amount of living on the edge that is associated with affairs. Certainly, being in the entertainment business is a risk; there's a lot of glamor, and people are away from home a lot. Often you're in a make-believe world with another person.

To hear that a person can be happily married and having an affair is surprising.

I often get asked, "How can women stay with men who have repeated affairs?" Many people believe the Clintons have some kind of an arrangement.

I don't know anything about their marriage, but I do know that it's more comfortable for people to believe they have an arrangement. When something bad happens to others, we distance ourselves from it, try to find an explanation that couldn't possibly apply to us.

You use the metaphor of walls and windows in talking about affairs.

There is almost always a wall of secrecy around the affair; the primary partner does not know what's happening on the other side of that wall. In the affair, there is often a window into the marriage, like a one-way mirror.

To reconstruct the marriage, you have to reverse the walls and windows—put up a wall with the affair partner and put up a window inside the marriage. Answering a spouse's questions about what happened in the affair is a way to reverse the process. It's a matter of who's on the inside and who's on the outside. Sometimes people will open windows but not put up walls. Sometimes they put up walls but don't open the windows. Unless you do both, you cannot rebuild safety and trust in the marriage.

Social Anxiety

For millions of Americans, every day is a struggle with debilitating shyness

BY JOANNIE M. SCHROF AND STACEY SCHULTZ

It is something of a miracle that Grace Dailey is sitting in a restaurant in a coastal New Jersey town having an ordinary lunch, at ease with her world. Her careful, tiny bites of a tuna sandwich may seem unremarkable, but they are in fact a milestone. Back in her grade school cafeteria, she could only sip a bit to drink each day, unable to eat while she imagined her classmates' eyes boring into her. (Her high school teachers mistook her anxiety about eating for anorexia.) Only in her 20s, when panic attacks began to hit, did Dailey learn about the condition called social anxiety disorder, also known as "social phobia." But despite some success with behavioral therapy and anxiety-reducing medication, the 32-year-old still struggles. "I would be a different person in a different place if I didn't have to deal with this on a daily basis," she says, frustration apparent in her furrowed brow.

Shyness is a nearly universal human trait. Most everyone has bouts of it, and half of those surveyed describe themselves as shy. Perhaps because it's so widespread, and because it suggests vulnerability, shyness is often an endearing trait: Princess Diana, for example, won millions of admirers with her "Shy Di" manner. The human species might not even exist if not for an instinctive wariness of other creatures. In fact, the ability to sense a threat and a desire to flee are lodged in the most primitive regions of the brain.

But at some life juncture, roughly 1 out of every 8 people becomes so timid that encounters with others turn into a source of overwhelming dread. The heart races, palms sweat, mouth goes dry, words vanish, thoughts become cluttered, and an urge to escape takes over.

This is the face of social phobia, the third most common mental disorder in the United States, behind depression and alcoholism. Like Woody Allen in the film *Annie Hall*, some social phobics can barely utter a sentence without obsessing over the impression they are making. Others refuse to use public restrooms or talk on the telephone. Sometimes they go mute in front of the boss or a member of the opposite sex. At the extreme, they build a hermitic life, avoiding contact with others (think of young Laura in Tennessee Williams's *Glass Menagerie* or the ghostly Boo in *To Kill a Mockingbird*).

Though social anxiety's symptoms have been noted since the time of Hip-

SUCCESS STORY. In high school, cheerleaders made a sport of saying "hello" to Steve Fox just to watch him blush. Now he is married to one of the girls who used to tease him.

From *U.S. News & World Report*, June 21, 1999, pp. 76-79. © 1999 by U.S. News & World Report. Reprinted by permission.

Coming to you direct

Public service ads—or just a sales pitch?

BY BRENDAN I. KOERNER

Pasted on bus shelters nationwide, the posters ask passersby to imagine being allergic to people. The picture is of a handsome young man, despondently staring at a coffee cup as an apparently happy couple sits at the other end of his table. "Over 10 million Americans suffer from social anxiety disorder," the text reads. "The good news is that this disorder is treatable." A toll-free number and a Web site are listed.

The ads bear the seals of three nonprofit advocacy groups: the American Psychiatric Association, the Anxiety Disorders Association of America, and Freedom From Fear, a trio that together make up the Social Anxiety Disorder Coalition. But funding for their public awareness campaign comes from a far less visible partner: SmithKline Beecham, the pharmaceutical giant whose flagship antidepressant, Paxil, was recently approved by the Food and Drug Administration for the treatment of debilitating shyness, formally known as social anxiety disorder.

Top of the pack. The move made Paxil the first selective serotonin reuptake inhibitor (SSRI) to win that designation. In the crowded SSRI marketplace, which rang up sales of near $7 billion last year, companies are constantly on the lookout for new ways in which their brands can be used—for social phobia, panic disorder, obsessive-compulsive disorder, bulimia. "You really need to keep your brand on the top of the pack," says Sergio Traversa of Mehta Partners, which does investment research on pharmaceutical companies. When you have multiple users, then "it's a relatively cheap alternative to developing new drugs. . . . On one side, it's cheaper, and it also helps keep the brand popular." Not surprisingly, some critics see profit, rather than altruism, as the motive behind SmithKline's financial backing of the "Imagine being allergic to people" campaign, and they question whether the statistics put forward in such advertising are accurate.

Blurring the line between public service and marketing is common practice in the industry. Back in 1996, when Paxil was cleared for the treatment of panic disorder, SmithKline sponsored the "Paxil Report on Panic," in which one third of those surveyed said either they or someone they knew had suffered from a panic attack—a sudden rush of terror or extreme fear. Bristol-Myers Squibb, which sells the antidepressants Serzone and Desyrel, sponsors the popular Depression.com Web site, which includes an "Are You Depressed?" quiz. And Eli Lilly, the maker of Prozac, the top-selling SSRI, launched an "educational television campaign" last month, featuring a 30-minute program chronicling the tales of 10 depression sufferers—all recovered, thanks to its brand.

SmithKline insists that helping the afflicted, not boosting sales, is the goal of the poster blitz. "We find that less than 5 percent of patients are really treated today," says Barry Brand, product director for Paxil. "There's tremendous need out there." The company, he adds, is adamant about deterring frivolous use. "We don't want this to be a pill that you take for shyness," continues Brand. "We don't want you to think, 'Oh, I'll take a Paxil and I'll feel good.'"

Market forces. Hollow words, says Elliot Valenstein, professor of psychology and neuroscience at the University of Michigan and author of *Blaming the Brain.* "[Drug companies] can anticipate criticism very well. But at the same time, their marketing will assume there are many more people out there" whom they will attract. Indeed, the track records of other "lifestyle drugs" show that many are used to achieve modest goals such as shedding a few pounds or becoming more productive at work. "When Prozac came on the market, it was just approved for severe depression," says Sidney Wolfe, director of the Health Research Group of Public Citizen, a consumer advocacy group. "But it was used for all kinds of depression," Just as Prozac became a $3 billion-a-year seller thanks in part to those users, Paxil will bolster its sales by targeting the merely meek, predicts Valenstein. "Shy-ness can't be marketed because most people recognize it as a normal variation on personality," he says. "But 'social phobia' sounds like a disease. I'm sure a lot of thought was given to pushing that particular terminology."

The coalition's brochure is careful to highlight the tag line "It's not just shyness," and the campaign's literature never directly mentions Paxil. But some of the symptoms described are familiar to virtually anyone who has faced pressure: blushing, sweating, dry mouth, pounding heart. And SSRIs are praised as vital to the recovery process. In the campaign's video, a sufferer gives testimony to the healing role of her medication: "I wouldn't have been able to concentrate on therapy and the coping skills" without the drug's ability to "take the edge off." Valenstein says that since Paxil is the only FDA-approved SSRI for the disorder, it will become the prescription of choice for general practitioners, who prescribe the majority of antidepressants.

Alec Pollard, director of the anxiety disorders center at the St. Louis Behavioral Medicine Institute, says the cynicism surrounding Paxil clouds its positive effects, which can be remarkable. "I can't say to you that people won't be given Paxil that don't need it," says Pollard. "But we wouldn't want to judge a treatment based on the fact that sometimes it will be inappropriately applied. That's inevitable. That's why particularly primary-care physicians need to be educated on proper use."

But Wolfe is concerned that the direct-to-consumer marketing approach will drive some patients to demand the medication without proper evaluation. "People are going to ask for it, and they're going to get it," he says. In the realms of managed care, doctors may be only too willing to acquiesce to those demands. "It is possible to give people careful diagnosis," says Erik Parens, an associate at the Hastings Center, a bioethics think tank. "But diagnosis takes time, and it costs money. Therefore, it is cheaper to give people the drug they ask for."

pocrates, the disorder was a nameless affliction until the late 1960s and didn't make its way into psychiatry manuals until 1980. As it became better known, patients previously thought to suffer panic disorder were recognized as being anxious only in social settings. A decade ago, 40 percent of people said they were shy, but in today's "nation of strangers"—in which computers and ATMs make face-to-face relations less and less common—that number is nearing 50 percent. Some psychologists are convinced that the Internet culture, often favored by those who fear human interaction, greases the slope from shyness down to social anxiety. "If people were slightly shy to begin with, they can now interact less and less," says Lynne Henderson, a Stanford University researcher and director of the Shyness Clinic in Menlo Park, Calif. "And that will make the shyness much worse."

Much worse—and, for drug companies, far more lucrative: Recently, Smith Kline Beecham won FDA approval to market the antidepressant Paxil for social phobia, leading to a raft of "public education campaigns"—on top of those already put out by the National Institute of Mental Health and the Anxiety Disorders Association of America. This media blitz has raised concerns that normally shy people will conclude they're social phobics and seek medications for what is a complex, emotional problem, or opt for such drugs merely as "lifestyle" aids to win friends and influence people (story, "Coming to You Direct").

Hard-hitting. Social phobia hit Steve Fox so hard in high school that girls made a sport of saying "hello" just to watch him turn beet red. He refused to speak in class and never dated; even walking in front of other people left him with sweaty palms and gasping for air. By the time Fox was 19, his father was concerned enough to find a doctor, and a combination of medication and therapy has helped him recover. Fox, now

UNABLE TO DRIVE. Roland Bardon had to rely on his mother to chauffeur him when he was overwhelmed by anxiety about what others thought of his driving.

23, recently gave a speech in front of 1,700 people, and he is married to one of the cheerleaders who used to tease him. Normal shyness and serious social phobia are clearly different, but they are related. Emanuel Maidenberg, associate director of UCLA's Social Phobia and Performance Anxiety Clinic, says that shyness is to social phobia what a fair complexion is to skin cancer. "It's a predisposing factor but will only translate into disease under certain circumstances," he says. "For pale people, that might be 10,000 hours in the sun. For shy people, it might be a string of embarrassing events." Even though some people are born with a tendency toward extreme shyness, biology is by no means destiny. Harvard researcher Jerome Kagan has shown that by 8 weeks of age, babies display innate shyness or boldness. Roughly 1 in 5 will consistently be frightened of and avoid anything or anyone new, while the others welcome the unknown, reaching out to touch strangers or to grab new objects. Yet, many shy babies become gregarious 10-year-olds, and some outgoing babies become shy, even socially phobic, adults.

Life experiences can mold the brain to become more or less shy over time. Through a process psychologists call "contextual conditioning," the brain attaches a fear "marker" to the details of a situation that causes trauma (place, time of day, background music). So when a child gets a disparaging tongue-lashing from a teacher, the student will feel at least a bit nervous the next few times he or she steps into that class-

room. But sometimes the brain is too good at making those associations, says Maidenberg, and the anxiety grows like a cancer, attaching itself to the act of entering any classroom or talking to any teacher.

The classic behavior of a child who does not know how to handle these "daggers to the heart," says University of Pennsylvania psychiatrist Moira Rynn, is to avoid any attention at all. In fact, social phobia used to be known as avoidant personality disorder. First, avoidant kids may stop inviting friends over. Some will only speak to certain people, usually their parents, a condition known as "selective mutism" (box, "Suffering in Silence"). Others develop "school refusal." By avoiding the very situations they need to learn the social skills of adulthood, these children end up diminishing their ability to cope. Not only can a parent who is highly critical train a child to cower, but even the gentlest parent can raise a fearful child. "If parents avoid social situations or worry excessively about what the neighbors think of them," says Richard Heimberg, director of the Adult Anxiety Clinic at Temple University in Philadelphia, "the message to a child is that the world is full of danger, humiliation, and embarrassment."

Social phobia affects about half of its victims by age 8, and many others during adolescence, when social fears are more pronounced. Others live with an undetected problem that surfaces when facing a new public arena (college, a new job) that overwhelms them. Grace Dailey, who had managed to suffer qui-

A spectrum of shyness

A touch of timidity is human, but too much shyness can be debilitating

NORMAL SHYNESS

■ You are jittery beginning a public speech, but afterward you are glad you did it.

■ Your mind goes blank on a first date, but eventually you relax and find things to talk about.

■ Your palms sweat in a job interview, but you ask and answer thoughtful questions.

EXTREME SHYNESS

■ You clam up and your heart races when you know people are looking at you.

■ You tremble when speaking up at a meeting, even if it is only to say your name.

etly through high school, was seized with sudden panic attacks in her college classes. The episodes were so distressing that she would race out of lecture halls, and she considered dropping out. She did graduate, with the help of thoughtful professors who let her take tests by herself and who kept classroom doors open so that she didn't feel so trapped.

More women than men are thought to suffer social anxiety, but because shyness and demureness are smiled upon in females and less acceptable in males, more men turn to professionals for help. Roland Bardon, 27, knew he needed to see a psychologist after becoming too anxious to drive a car. "I worry about making other drivers mad," he says. "When people honk, that kind of criticism drives me crazy." He still avoids taking the wheel whenever he can.

Talking to strangers. It's Friday night at the Shyness Clinic in Menlo Park, Calif., time for this week's social phobia information session. But in the tiny room decorated haphazardly with fake flowers, only one man has shown up. The very nature of their disorder often causes social phobics to hide, and revealing themselves to a stranger is the last thing they want to do. Tonight's newcomer put off coming for two months. Clinic patients attend group meetings once a week, but some cannot even bring themselves to show up at all.

When the socially anxious do make it into clinics, they usually start with a few months of cognitive behavioral therapy. The cognitive element fights what psychiatrist Isaac Tylim of the Maimonides Medical Center in Brooklyn calls the intellectual core of social phobia: the belief that others will pass negative judgments on you and that unbearable humiliation will result. "I turn down invitations to go to lunch with people I really admire, even though I desperately want to go," says a Kentucky housewife and mother of two girls who exhibit a similar timidity. "I assume that as soon

as we get together, they'll regret having asked and want to get away from me as soon as possible." These distortions cause an emotional reaction that sends social phobics running away from even the most promising friendships. Through cognitive restructuring—a fancy term for replacing faulty thoughts with realistic ones—many social phobics learn to question the insidious fears that, no matter how irrational, paralyze them in their everyday lives.

Perhaps the most salient feature of social anxiety is what is known as flooding: the sensation of being so overwhelmed that panic sets in. Almost everyone feels mild flooding at the podium during the first minute or so of an important speech, but for most people the discomfort soon subsides. A social phobic can suffer such agony for more than an hour. But even in social phobics, flooding will eventually subside, if only because of sheer exhaustion. That is why behavioral therapists coach social phobics to remain in terrifying situations until the symptoms abate and it becomes clear that nothing bad is going to happen.

The first place that Melinda Stanley, professor of behavioral sciences at the University of Texas-Houston Health Sci-

in front of Stanley and an audience of graduate-student volunteers. Other therapists take social phobics through practice runs of embarrassing situations, like walking through a hotel lobby with toilet paper on their shoes or spilling a drink. It's not unlike physical training, says Henderson. "Just as our gym workouts get easier as time goes by, to stay socially fit we must push ourselves to engage with others until it is second nature."

When a case is so severe that patients cannot even ride an elevator with a therapist, drugs can enable the social phobic to endure behavioral therapy. The perfect medication has yet to be found. Antidepressants known as monoamine oxidase inhibitors (MAOs) have been used for over a decade, but they can cause side effects such as fainting spells, heart palpitations, and blurred vision, and users must follow strict diets excluding everything from coffee to cheese to red wine. Researchers have experimented with Xanax, Valium, and other tranquilizers but have had mixed success, not least because those drugs can cause physical dependence. Some sufferers try beta blockers, which are helpful for surviving a speech or a party but use less as a long-term therapeutic tool.

IN HIDING. Mark Goomishian dropped out of high school and has spent decades in virtual seclusion.

ence Center, takes many patients is the elevator. Riding up and down, the patient practices greeting and making small talk with fellow passengers. "Sometimes it takes 10 or 15 rides, and sometimes it takes all day," says Stanley, "but the phobic's heart will eventually stop racing for fear of what the newcomer might think of him or her." Eventually, the patients progress to giving speeches

Most popular now are the antidepressants known as selective serotonin reuptake inhibitors (SSRIs), which have fewer side effects than the old anxiety drugs. "[Patients treated for depression] were spontaneously reporting that they were losing their social anxiety," explains Murray Stein, director of the anxiety clinic at the University of California-San Diego. Studies of the SSRIs Paxil and

SOCIAL ANXIETY				SEVERE SOCIAL ANXIETY		
■ You avoid starting conversations for fear of saying something awkward.	■ You will do anything, even skip work, to avoid being introduced to new people.	■ You have trouble swallowing in public, making it hard to dine out or go to parties.	■ You feel you never make a good impression and that you are a social failure.	■ You are free of nervousness only when alone and you can barely leave the house.	■ You constantly worry about being embarrassed or humiliated by others.	■ You have panic attacks and often leave the room rather than hold a conversation.

THE SHY CHILD
Suffering in silence

Samantha Williams seems like a typical 11-year-old, enchanted with the prospect of teenage life as she begins to lose interest in childish activities. But at the end-of-the-year cookout she's planning for the girls in her fifth-grade class, Samantha will stand out in one particular way: Most of Samantha's friends have never heard the sound of her voice. Since kindergarten, she has never spoken to any of her teachers or uttered a single word in class, and until very recently, she hasn't made so much as a peep on the playground.

Samantha has a form of childhood social anxiety known as selective mutism. She can comprehend spoken language and she is able to speak, but because she is very shy and anxious around even familiar people, she is unable to talk in public. About 1 percent of kids are like Samantha and have extreme trouble talking to strangers. These children almost always converse easily with their parents—one or both of whom are likely to suffer themselves from some form of social phobia.

Selective mutism has been mistakenly associated in the past with childhood abuse or trauma, charges that researchers say are not supported by scientific evidence. Until recently, it was called "elective mutism," but doctors changed the name because it implied a willful stubbornness of the child that "we've found is really not the case," says Anne Marie Albano, director of the anxiety disorders program at the New York University Child Study Center.

A child's inability to speak in public is not only frustrating for parents, it can also be frightening. When Samantha missed the bus home from school one day, she was unable to tell school officials that she needed to call home for a ride. Instead, she began the 2½-mile trek home, until her mother, in a frantic search of the neighborhood, spotted her. "I worry about her safety," her mother says. "I especially worry that she won't be able to ask for help if she needs it."

Fortunately, behavioral therapy can be effective. Parents, teachers, and friends can play a role, too, says NYU's Albano. "Everyone must maintain the expectation that the child will speak," she says. "We offer rewards and privileges when kids do talk, and we let them experience the consequences when they don't speak," such as earning a poor grade if they miss an oral report in class.

For some children, medication such as Prozac is helpful, but it can take months before the drugs take effect. "One third of the kids we treat get a great deal of benefit from the medication," says Bruce Black, assistant professor of psychiatry at Tufts University School of Medicine. Another third see some benefit, and the rest don't respond at all, he says. Samantha Williams has been taking Paxil, a drug similar to Prozac, for a few months. Her parents hope she will respond as well as 10-year-old Jenna, a selective mute from Maine. After six months of Prozac, Jenna silently decided one day last November that she would talk in school. When she did, her classmates cheered—and her teachers cried. —S.S.

WITHOUT A SOUND. Samantha Williams, 11, has not spoken in school since kindergarten. She is being treated for "selective mutism."

Luvox show great improvement in about half of social phobics, and studies now under way of other new antidepressants, like Effexor and Serzone, are also showing promise. But Henderson urges caution amid the current hoopla over drugs, which she worries are too often used as temporary crutches. "People tend to relapse as soon as they get off the medication," she warns, adding that research indicates that over the long run, therapy might keep a person in better stead. Just as troubling, says Tylim, is the message that only a drug can save them. "These are people whose very problem is a feeling of inadequacy, and the use of drugs can exacerbate that."

Because some social phobics have been out of the habit of talking with others for so long, therapists often have to help patients brush up on the most basic of social skills. For example, it never dawns on many of the most shy that they should introduce themselves to the person standing in front of them. And they often are stuck in the conversation-killing habit of answering questions with one-word answers. "I had to learn that if someone doesn't seem interested in the first sentence out of my mouth, I should not just turn and walk away cold," says Rick Robbins, a 31-year-old who was voted most shy of his Indiana high school class and whose social anxiety led him to drop out of college.

Perhaps the most common thing social phobics have to learn for the first time is to listen. "All kinds of alarm bells and sirens are distracting to social phobics," says Maidenberg. "So it is nearly impossible to hear what a person standing 4 inches away is saying." In fact, it is sometimes difficult for an extremely shy person to even feign interest in a companion's words. "Social phobics don't realize that most people in a room are not taking much notice of them," says Tylim, who says that social phobics in some ways crave the spotlight but fear that humiliation will come from it.

That's why Bernardo Carducci, author of *Shyness* and director of the Shyness Research Institute at Indiana University Southeast, is convinced that shifting the focus away from the self is the most therapeutic thing a shy person can do. "They desperately want to connect with others," he says; otherwise, they would merely be contented introverts or recluses who simply prefer their own company. Carducci sends patients to soup kitchens, hospitals, and nursing homes as a way of escaping the tyranny of self-centeredness. "It works because you get out there and start to see how shy other people can be," says Rick Robbins. "And then you don't feel so all alone, so different from every one else." At first, he tried to pry himself out of his problem with alcohol, what therapists dub "liquid extroversion." Then he forced himself to go to social occasions, where he would sit—miserable, silent, and sick to his stomach. If anything, these kinds of efforts at beating shyness will only aggravate the condition, because they are negative experiences that reinforce the fear.

Learning to cope. And because shyness is at least partially genetic, researchers unanimously agree that it is a mistake to try to become "unshy." Rather, the goal is to take steps to function despite the pounding heart and sweaty palms. Some do advance work for the tough moments. "Before I go out, I come up with four or five topics I would like to talk about," says Robbins. "Usually by the third one I bring up, I find something in common and forget about my nerves." Mark Goomishian, who has trouble even signing a check in public, looks for social arenas where he can be more himself, such as the local coffee shop, where he meets others for regular games of chess. "Because you don't have to talk during the game," he says, "it's a socially anxious person's sport."

In fact, many therapists say that if the socially phobic could rein in their anxiety enough to function, they would help make the world a better place. Many beloved figures in history have suffered shyness, including Eleanor Roosevelt, Robert Frost, and Albert Einstein. Shyness in its milder forms is associated with traits such as greater empathy, more acute perceptiveness, canny intuition, and beneficent sensitivity. All qualities that are nothing to be shy about.

With Brendan I. Koerner and Danielle Svetcov in Menlo Park, Calif.

PANIC ON THE PODIUM
Why everyone gets stage fright

From behind the counter of his Louisville, Ky., smoke shop, Gayle Sallee says he could chat forever with customers who wander through. But when the cigar boom hit in the early 1990s, and requests poured in

TERRORS OF FAME. The cigar craze shoved smoke shop owner Gayle Sallee into the spotlight, where he was forced to overcome his dread of public speaking.

for him to give lectures, seminars, and radio and TV interviews, Sallee says he was petrified: "Even if I was only asked to speak to 10 old slobs who like to smoke, I would get sick just thinking about it."

The fear of public speaking is by far the most prevalent social anxiety, affecting many people who are not the least bit shy in other settings. That makes perfect sense to researchers, who say that stage fright is the same ancient anxiety that hits all creatures when they are in full view of potential predators. But many of us freeze up even before a group of trusted friends. *Shyness* author Bernardo Carducci says this is because of the psychological rule of "salient objects." It is human nature, according to this principle, to scrutinize the most noticeable person in a room (i.e., the professor, the workshop leader, the soloist, the only African-American, the only woman) far more critically than those who blend into the background. And standing in front of a crowd makes us the "salient object," so that we become only too conscious of each gesture and phrase.

Hang in there. Speech coaches say that the self-consciousness fades if nervous speakers don't give up too soon. Many speakers mistakenly assume their cottony mouths and shaking hands means they are failing miserably. "Those sensations are merely signals that you are trying to do something meaningful and important," says Brooklyn psychiatrist Isaac Tylim. That knowledge was small comfort to Sallee as he struggled through months of stammering and stuttering on the cigar circuit. "None of the stuff about picturing people in their underwear worked at all," he recalls. But after six months of weekly presentations, Sallee suddenly realized halfway through a radio interview one Saturday morning that he was relaxed. "Once the fear died down, the fun began," he says. "Now it's to the point where when I'm in an audience, I really wish it was me up there on the stage."

—*J.M.S.*

It's no news that stress can make you sick. But recent research says the solution isn't working less or playing more. It's having someone to confide in.

DON'T FACE STRESS ALONE

By Benedict Carey

THE CURE FOR EXCESSIVE STRESS SHOULD be excessive cash. A fat pile of Microsoft common that provides for limo service and trips to the Seychelles and nannies and someone to vacuum those tumbleweed pet hairs that breed in every corner of the house. Better still, a house that cleans itself. That way we'd have time to read Emerson, learn to play some baroque stringed instrument, and sample Eastern gurus like finger food, accumulating vast reserves of inner peace and healing energy. . . .

We're fooling ourselves. Even stinking rich, most of us would often feel rushed, harassed, afraid that the maid's boyfriend had designs on our Swedish stereo components. We'd lose sleep, lose our tempers, and continue to wonder whether stress was killing us. Not because money doesn't buy

Almost half of Americans say they'd rather be alone when they're stressed. Only 18 percent would call a friend.

tranquility; it buys plenty. But because what we call stress is more than the sum of our chores and responsibilities and financial troubles. It's also a state of mind, a way of interpreting the world, a pattern of behavior.

Think of the people you know. There are those who are so consumed with work that they practically sleep with their cell phones, who go wild when they just have to wait in line at the checkout. And then there are those who breeze through the day as pleased as park rangers—despite having deadlines and kids and a broken-down car and charity work and scowling Aunt Agnes living in the spare bedroom. Back in the 1960s cardiologists Ray Rosenman and Meyer Friedman labeled these polar opposites Type A and Type B. They described Type As as "joyless strivers," people who go through life feeling harried, hostile, and combative. Type Bs, by contrast, are unhurried, even tempered, emotionally secure. In person Type As may be twitchy, prone to interrupt, resentful of conversational diversions. Type Bs are as placid as giraffes, well mannered, affectionately patient. In a landmark 1971 study Rosenman and Friedman found that Type As were about twice as likely to develop coronary artery disease as Type Bs. This was the first evidence of a phenomenon that we now take for granted: People consumed by stress often live short lives.

Often. But not always. Some Type As live long and prosper. Some Type Bs succumb to heart attacks before they turn 50. Rosenman and Friedman's theory represented a giant step in tracing a link between disease and personality. But it only partly explained why stress sometimes damages the heart. So the search has been under way to discover a more specific connection between personality and illness. In the past decade findings in fields as seemingly unrelated as sociology and immunology have begun to converge on a surprising answer. Of course it matters if your life is a high-wire act of clamoring demands and pressing deadlines. And yes, it does make a difference whether you're angry or retiring, effusive or shy, belligerent or thoughtful. But what really matters appears to be something much simpler: whether you have someone in your life who's emotionally on call, who's willing to sit up late and hear your complaints.

HUMAN EMOTIONS ARE a messy affair, fleeting, contradictory, and as hard to define as human beings themselves. So it's no wonder researchers have found themselves groping around the dim and convoluted catacombs of personality, trying to locate the core of the trouble with Type As. Some suspect the real villain may be a specific trait such as hostility, cynicism, or self-centeredness. And indeed, all of these characteristics are prevalent in many people who develop coronary disease. But none has proved terribly useful for predicting who will get sick. The search has been a little like being fitted for glasses: Lens two looks clearer than lens one at first, but then you're not so sure. Still, something's there, all right, and several studies conducted in the late eighties and early nineties have finally brought its ghostly shape into focus.

"If you look across all of these studies for a pattern," says psychologist Margaret Chesney, who has spent the past 20 years doing precisely that, "you see that the hostility questionnaires and the Type A interview and all the other measures—they're all picking up the same thing. It's this person who's often suspicious; who sees people as being in their way; who, when they meet someone new, asks, 'What do you do? Where did you go to school?'—not to make a connection but to assess the competition."

More details emerged in 1989 when psychologists Jerry Suls and Choi Wan of the State University of New York at Albany reviewed the Type A research to look for a common thread. They concentrated on studies whose authors had performed general psychological profiles as well as Type A assessments. As a rule, general psych profiles ask directly about fears, insecurities, childhood traumas, and so on, while the Type A diagnosis focuses on how pressured a person feels and how pleasantly he or she answers aggressive questions.

Suls and Wan had suspected that Type A behavior would be associated with emotional distress. But they found something strange. The Type As did show strains of insecurity and emotional isolation—but none of the anxiety and fear associated with the garden-variety neurotic. These are the sort of people who need counseling but consider therapists overpriced palm-readers. "The picture we're getting is of someone who has deep problems but doesn't admit them," says Suls. "So there are a couple of possibilities here. Either they're in denial. Or they really don't have rich inner lives. They never really think about these things."

They aren't Oprah Winfrey fans, in short. They're happy enough talking about work, fashion, sports—anything but the mushy personal stuff. "If you confront them with that," says Suls, "they get angry. They blow up." As one researcher puts it, "They never let their guard down. If you come close, they wonder, What is this person after?" Spare me the advice, Sigmund, can't you see I'm busy?

This evidence, admittedly raw, is still the subject of much debate, but it has even the most authoritative, skeptical, hard-line figures in the field talking like late-night radio shrinks. Just listen to founding father Rosenman, who has guarded the Type A franchise like a hawk, staring down dozens of psychologists whose work he deemed soft or flawed. "After 40 years of observing and treating thousands of patients, and doing all of the studies, I believe that what's underneath the inappropriate competitiveness of Type As is a deep-seated insecurity. I never would have said that before, but I keep coming back to it. It's different from anxiety in the usual sense, because Type As are not people who retreat. They constantly compete because it helps them suppress the insecurity they're afraid others will sense.

"If I felt this way, how would I cover it up? I'd distract myself, go faster and faster, and win over everybody else. I'd look at everyone as a threat, because they might expose me."

Avoiding exposure inevitably means avoiding close relationships. The person

The people most vulnerable to stress are those who are emotionally isolated. They might have the biggest Rolodex, but they're alone.

Rosenman is describing has friends, sure, but no genuine confidants, no one who's allowed so much as a whiff of frailty. That's why many researchers now believe that the symptom most common among those vulnerable to stress is emotional isolation. As Chesney puts it, "These people might have the biggest Rolodex, but they're alone. They're busy looking for more connections, charming more people. When they feel isolated they get busy. It's a defense mechanism."

According to Jonathan Schedler, a research psychologist affiliated with Harvard

They Touched a Nation

THANKS TO PUBLIC FIGURES who spoke out about their illnesses, we have all grown more comfortable in the past decade confronting health problems that were long shrouded in lonely silence.
—*Rita Rubin*

MUHAMMAD ALI

It was the most arresting moment of the 1996 Olympics in Atlanta: the former boxer, arm trembling, face frozen, raising the torch to light the ceremonial flame. Calls flooded the National Parkinson's Foundation, which adopted a torch as its symbol.

ANNETTE FUNICELLO

In 1992, when the onetime Mickey Mouse Club girl publicly revealed her diagnosis, we all suddenly knew at least one person with MS: Annette. "She is everyone's extended family member," says Arney Rosenblat of the National Multiple Sclerosis Society.

LINDA ELLERBEE

Months after the journalist underwent a double mastectomy, she produced an emotionally charged special on breast cancer. "I can be fair and honest," she says of the disease. "But objective I cannot be."

RONALD REAGAN

Ever-folksy, the former president announced he had Alzheimer's disease in a handwritten letter addressed to "my fellow Americans" in 1994. He called his gesture "an opening of our hearts."

WILLIAM STYRON

The novelist told of his depression in the New York Times and later in *Darkness Visible: A Memoir of Madness.* "The overwhelming reaction made me feel that inadvertently I had helped unlock a closet from which many souls were eager to come out."

CHRISTOPHER REEVE

"You only have two choices," says the actor whose 1995 fall from a horse left him permanently paralyzed and who has raised millions for spinal injury research. "Either you vegetate and look out the window or activate and try to effect change."

GREG LOUGANIS

Mortified that he'd hid his HIV-positive status when his head wound bloodied the Olympic pool in 1988, the diver finally told his story during an interview with Barbara Walters in 1995.

University, the tests researchers use to identify hostile personalities essentially measure something he calls interpersonal warmth. "It has to do with whether you see the people in your life as benevolent or malevolent, whether they offer nourishment or frustration," he says. "The fact is, humans are emotionally frail. We need real support from other people, and those who don't acknowledge it are going to feel besieged."

These notions could easily collapse into sentimentality. Yet scientific evidence for the physical benefits of social support is coming in from all sides. At Ohio State University, for example, immunologist Ron Glaser and psychologist Janice Kiecolt-Glaser have found that the biggest slump in immunity during exam periods occurs in medical students who report being lonely. Analyzing data from the Tecumseh Community Health Study, sociologist James House calculated that social isolation was as big a risk factor for illness and death as smoking was. And these were just the warm-up acts. In 1989 David Spiegel of Stanford Medical School measured the effect of weekly group therapy on women being treated for breast cancer. As expected, those who met in groups experienced less pain than those who didn't. But that wasn't all. The women in counseling survived an average of 37 months—nearly twice as long as those without the group support. Other researchers, including Friedman, have also lengthened some heart patients' lives through group therapy.

The reason remains anyone's guess. Perhaps, as Spiegel has suggested, being in a group makes patients more likely to take their medications, perform prescribed exercise, and so on. Patients may also benefit from advice offered in therapy, which can range from the commonsensical to the corn-ball: from "slow down, spend more time with your family, and don't sweat the little things" to "control your anger, read more poetry, and verbalize affection." Hardly the sort of wisdom that transforms lives.

If these interventions have anything in common, though, it is the presence of other people. This makes sense if you think of stress the way most doctors do, as a hormonal response to pressure. The body perceives a threat, mental or physical, and releases hormones that hike blood pressure and suppress immune response. According to the theory, some of us (the hostile, the troubled, the Type As) have a higher risk of heart disease or cancer because we secrete more of these hormones more frequently than the average joe. This stress response isn't easy to moderate, but one of the few things that seems to help is contact with a supportive person. In several lab experiments, for instance, psychologists have shown that having a friend in the room calms the cardiovascular response to distressing tasks such as public speaking. It's the secret of group therapy: We relax around our own. The simple grace of company can keep us healthy.

Humans are, after all, social by nature. So perhaps it makes sense that the healthiest among us might be the ones who find solace in companionship, who can defuse building pressure by opening up our hearts to someone else. As the late biologist and writer Lewis Thomas observed, human beings have survived by being useful to one another. We are as indispensable to each other as hummingbirds are to hibiscus.

And by finding ways to help each other out, the latest research hints, we forge the emotional connections that could very well sustain us. Thomas understood this. In a *New York Times* interview in 1993, just two weeks before his death, the reporter asked him, "Is there an art to dying?"

"There's an art to living," Thomas replied. "One of the very important things that has to be learned around the time dying becomes a real prospect is to recognize those occasions when we have been useful in the world. With the same sharp insight that we all have for acknowledging our failures, we ought to recognize when we have been useful, and sometimes uniquely useful. All of us have had such times in our lives, but we don't pay much attention to them. Yet the thing we're really good at as a species is usefulness. If we paid more attention to this biological attribute, we'd get a satisfaction that cannot be attained from goods or knowledge."

Benedict Carey has been a staff writer at the magazine since 1988.

Go Ahead, Say You're Sorry

We tend to view apologies as a sign of weak character. But in fact, they require great strength. And we better learn how to get them right, because it's increasingly hard to live in the global village without them

Aaron Lazare, M.D.

Aaron Lazare, M.D., is chancellor/dean of the University of Massachusetts Medical Center in Worcester. He has authored 66 articles and written or edited six books.

A genuine apology offered and accepted is one of the most profound interactions of civilized people. It has the power to restore damaged relationships, be they on a small scale, between two people, such as intimates, or on a grand scale, between groups of people, even nations. If done correctly, an apology can heal humiliation and generate forgiveness.

Yet, even though it's such a powerful social skill, we give precious little thought to teaching our children how to apologize. Most of us never learned very well ourselves.

Despite its importance, apologizing is antithetical to the ever-pervasive values of winning, success, and perfection. The successful apology requires empathy and the security and strength to admit fault, failure, and weakness. But we are so busy winning that we can't concede our own mistakes.

The botched apology—the apology intended but not delivered, or delivered but not accepted—has serious social consequences. Failed apologies can strain relationships beyond repair or, worse, create life-long grudges and bitter vengeance.

As a psychiatrist who has studied shame and humiliation for eight years, I became interested in apology for its healing nature. I am perpetually amazed by how many of my friends and patients—regardless of ethnicity or social class—have long-standing grudges that have cut a destructive swath through their own lives and the lives of family and friends. So many of their grudges could have been avoided altogether or been reconciled with a genuine apology.

In my search to learn more about apologies, I have found surprisingly little in the professional literature. The scant research I've unearthed is mostly in linguistics and sociology, but little or nothing touches on the expectations or need for apologies, their meaning to the offender and offended, and the implications of their failure.

Religious writings, however, in both Christian and Jewish traditions, are a rich source of wisdom on the subject, under such headings as absolution, atonement, forgiveness, penance, and repentance. The *Talmud*, in fact, declares that God created repentance before he created the universe. He wisely knew humans would make a lot of mistakes and have a lot of apologizing to do along the way.

What makes apologies work is an exchange of shame and power between offender and offended.

No doubt the most compelling and common reason to apologize is over a personal offense. Whether we've ignored, belittled, betrayed, or publicly humiliated someone, the common denominator of any personal offense is that we've diminished or injured a person's self-concept. The self-concept is our story about ourselves. It's our thoughts and feelings about who we are, how we would like to be, and how we would like to be perceived by others.

If you think of yourself first and foremost as a competent, highly valued professional and are asked tomorrow by your boss to move into a cramped windowless office, you would likely be personally offended. You might be insulted and feel hurt or humiliated. No matter whether the interpersonal wound is delivered in a profes-sional, family, or social setting, its depth is determined by the meaning the event carries to the offended party, the relationship between offender and offended, and the vulnerability of the offended to take things personally.

No-shows at family funerals, disputes over wills, betrayals of trust—whether in love or friendship—are situations ripe for wounds to the self-concept. Events of that magnitude put our self-worth on the line, more so for the thin-skinned. Other events people experience as personal offenses include being ignored, treated unfairly, embarrassed by someone else's behavior, publicly humiliated, and having one's cherished beliefs denigrated.

So the personal offense has been made, the blow to the self-concept landed, and an apology is demanded or expected. Why bother? I count four basic motives for apologizing:

- **The first is to salvage or restore the relationship.** Whether you've hurt someone you love, enjoy, or just plain need as your ally in an office situation, an apology may well rekindle the troubled relationship.
- **You may have purely empathic reasons for apologizing.** You regret that you have caused someone to suffer and you apologize to diminish or end their pain.

The last two motives are not so lofty:

- **Some people apologize simply to escape punishment,** such as the criminal who apologizes to his victim in exchange for a lesser plea.
- **Others apologize simply to relieve themselves of a guilty conscience.** They feel so ashamed of what they did that, even though it may not have bothered you that much, they apolo-

gize profusely. A long letter explaining why the offender was a half hour late to dinner would be such an occasion. And in so doing, they are trying to maintain some self-respect, because they are nurturing an image of themselves in which the offense, lack of promptness, violates some basic self-concept.

Whatever the motive, what makes an apology work is the exchange of shame and power between the offender and the offended. By apologizing, you take the shame of your offense and redirect it to yourself. You admit to hurting or diminishing someone and, in effect, say that you are really the one who is diminished—I'm the one who was wrong, mistaken, insensitive, or stupid. In acknowledging your shame you give the offended the power to forgive. The exchange is at the heart of the healing process.

ANATOMY OF AN APOLOGY

But in practice, it's not as easy as it sounds. There's a right way and a wrong way to apologize. There are several integral elements of any apology and unless they are accounted for, an apology is likely to fail.

First, you have to acknowledge that a moral norm or an understanding of a relationship was violated, and you have to accept responsibility for it. You must name the offense—no glossing over in generalities like, "I'm sorry for what I have done." To be a success, the apology has to be specific—"I betrayed you by talking behind your back" or "I missed your daughter's wedding."

You also have to show you understand the nature of your wrongdoing and the impact it had on the person—"I know I hurt you and I am so very sorry."

This is one of the most uniting elements of the apology. By acknowledging that a moral norm was violated, both parties affirm a similar set of values. The apology reestablishes a common moral ground.

The second ingredient to a successful apology is an explanation for why you committed the offense in the first place. An effective explanation makes the point that what you did isn't representative of who you are. You may offer that you were tired, sick, drunk, distracted, or in love—and that it will not happen again. Such an explanation protects your self-concept.

A recent incident widely reported in the news provides an excellent, if painful, illustration of the role of an apology in protecting the offender's self-concept. An American sailor apologized at his court-martial for brutally beating to death a homosexual shipmate: "I can't apologize enough for my actions. I am not trying to

make any excuses for what happened that night. It was horrible, but I am not a horrible person."

A successful apology also has to make you suffer. You must express soul-searching regret.

Another vital part of the explanation is to communicate that your behavior wasn't intended as a personal affront. This lets the offended person know that he should feel safe with you now and in the future.

A good apology also has to make you suffer. You have to express genuine, soul-searching regret for your apology to be taken as sincere. Unless you communicate guilt, anxiety, and shame, people are going to question the depth of your remorse. The anxiety and sadness demonstrate that the potential loss of the relationship matters to you. Guilt tells the offended person that you're distressed over hurting him. And shame communicates your disappointment with yourself over the incident.

YOU OWE ME AN APOLOGY

When there's the matter of settling debt. The apology is a reparation of emotional, physical, or financial debt. The admission of guilt, explanation, and regret are meant, in part, to repair the damage you did to the person's self-concept. A well-executed apology may even the score, but sometimes words are just not enough. An open offer of, "Please let me know if there is anything I can do?" might be necessary. Some sort of financial compensation, such as replacing an object you broke, or reimbursing a friend for a show you couldn't make it to, could be vital to restoring the relationship. Or, in long-term close relationships, an unsolicited gift or favor may completely supplant the verbal apology—every other dimension of the apology may be implicit.

Reparations are largely symbolic. They are a way of saying, "I know who you are, what you value, and am thoughtful about your needs. I owe you." But they don't always have to be genuine to be meaningful. Say your boss wrongfully accused you in front of the whole office. A fair reparation would require an apology—in front of the whole office. His questionable sincerity might be of secondary importance.

Ultimately, the success of an apology rests on the dynamics between the two parties, not on a pat recipe. The apology is an interactive negotiation process in which a

deal has to be struck that is emotionally satisfactory to both involved parties.

Nor is the need for an apology confined to intimates. Used strategically, it has great social value within the public domain. The apology is, after all, a social contract of sorts. It secures a common moral ground, whether between two people or within a nation. Present in all societies, the apology is a statement that the harmony of the group is more important than the victory of the individual. Take a look at what will certainly go down in history as one of the world's greatest apologies, F.W. de Klerk's apology to all South Africans for his party's imposition of apartheid.

On April 29, 1993, during a press conference, de Klerk *acknowledged* that apartheid led to forced removals of people from their homes, restrictions on their freedom and jobs, and attacks on their dignity.

He *explained* that the former leaders of the party were *not vicious people* and, at the time, it seemed that the policy of separate nations was better than the colonial policies. "It was not our intention to deprive people of their rights and to cause misery, but eventually apartheid led to just that. Insofar as that occurred, we deeply regret it."

"*Deep regret,*" de Klerk continued, "goes further than just saying you are sorry. Deep regret says that if I could turn the clock back, and if I could do anything about it, I would have liked to have avoided it."

In going on to describe a new National Party logo, he said: "It is a statement that we have broken with that which was wrong in the past and are not afraid to say we are deeply sorry that our past policies were wrong." He promised that the National Party had scrapped apartheid and opened its doors to all South Africans.

De Klerk expressed all the same ingredients and sentiments essential in interpersonal apologies. He enumerated his offenses and explained why they were made. He assured himself and others that the party members are not vicious people. Then he expressed deep regret and offered symbolic reparations in the form of his public apology itself and the new party logo.

In fact, as the world becomes a global village, apologies are growing increasingly important on both national and international levels. Communications, the media, and travel have drawn the world ever closer together. Ultimately we all share the same air, oceans, and world economy. We are all upwind, downstream, over the mountains, or through the woods from one another. We can't help but be concerned with Russia's failing economy, Eastern Bloc toxic waste, Middle Eastern conflicts, and the rain forest, whether it be for reasons of peace, fuel, or just plain oxygen.

In this international community, apologies will be vital to peaceful resolution of conflicts. Within the last several years alone Nelson Mandela apologized for atrocities committed by the African National Congress in fighting against apartheid; Exxon for the *Valdez* spill; Pope John Paul II "for abuses committed by Christian colonizers against Indian peoples"; former Japanese Prime Minister Morihiro Hosokawa for Japanese aggression during World War II; and Russian President Boris Yeltsin apologized for the massacre of 15,000 Polish army officers by Soviet forces during World War II. And that's only the start of it.

But apologies are useful only if done right. There are in the public arena ample examples of what not to do—stunning portraits of failed apologies. They typically take the form of what I call "the pseudo-apology"—the offender fails to admit or take responsibility for what he has done. Recent history furnishes two classics of the genre.

Reel back to August 8, 1974—President Richard Nixon's resignation speech. "I regret deeply any injuries that may have been done in the course of events that have led to this decision. I would say only that if some of my judgments were wrong, and some were wrong, they were made in what I believed at the time to be in the best interest of the nation." Unlike de Klerk, Nixon never acknowledges or specifies his actual offense, nor does he describe its impact. By glossing over his wrongdoing he never takes responsibility for it.

Consider, too, the words of Senator Bob Packwood, who was accused of sexually harassing at least a dozen women during his tenure in Congress. His 1994 apology outfails even Nixon's: "I'm apologizing for the conduct that it was alleged that I did." No acceptance of responsibility or accounting for his alleged offense to be found. An *alleged* apology, not even named.

The most common cause of failure in an apology—or an apology altogether avoided—is the offender's pride. It's a fear of shame. To apologize, you have to acknowledge that you made a mistake. You

have to admit that you failed to live up to values like sensitivity, thoughtfulness, faithfulness, fairness, and honesty. This is an admission that our own self-concept, our story about ourself, is flawed. To honestly admit what you did and show regret may stir a profound experience of shame, a public exposure of weakness. Such an admission is especially difficult to bear when there was some degree of intention behind the wrongdoing.

'The apology is a show of strength. It's an act of generosity, because it restores the self-concept of those we offended.'

Egocentricity also factors into failed or avoided apologies. The egocentric is unable to appreciate the suffering of another person; his regret is that he is no longer liked by the person he offended, not that he inflicted harm. That sort of apology takes the form of "I am sorry that you are upset with me" rather than "I am sorry I hurt you." This offender simply says he is bereft—not guilty, ashamed, or empathic.

Another reason for failure is that the apology may trivialize the damage incurred by the wrongdoing—in which case the apology itself seems offensive. A Japanese-American who was interned during World War II was offended by the U.S. government's reparation of $20,000. He said that the government stole four years of his childhood and now has set the price at $5,000 per year.

Timing can also doom an apology. For a minor offense such as interrupting some-

one during a presentation or accidentally spilling a drink all over a friend's suit, if you don't apologize right away, the offense becomes personal and grows in magnitude. For a serious offense, such as a betrayal of trust or public humiliation, an immediate apology misses the mark. It demeans the event. Hours, days, weeks, or even months may go by before both parties can integrate the meaning of the event and its impact on the relationship. The care and thought that goes into such apologies dignifies the exchange.

For offenses whose impact is calamitous to individuals, groups, or nations, the apology may be delayed by decades and offered by another generation. Case in point: The apologies now being offered and accepted for apartheid and for events that happened in WWII, such as the Japanese Imperial Army's apology for kidnapping Asian women and forcing them into a network of brothels.

Far and away the biggest stumbling block to apologizing is our belief that apologizing is a sign of weakness and an admission of guilt. We have the misguided notion we are better off ignoring or denying our offenses and hope that no one notices.

In fact the apology is a show of strength. It is an act of honesty because we admit we did wrong; an act of generosity, because it restores the self-concept of those we offended. It offers hope for a renewed relationship and, who knows, possibly even a strengthened one. The apology is an act of commitment because it consigns us to working at the relationship and at our self-development. Finally, the apology is an act of courage because it subjects us to the emotional distress of shame and the risk of humiliation, rejection, and retaliation at the hands of the person we offended.

All dimensions of the apology require strength of character, including the conviction that, while we expose vulnerable parts of ourselves, we are still good people.

A Fistful of Hostility Is Found In Women

By ABIGAIL ZUGER

IN the old Punch and Judy shows of the last century, Punch would batter Judy under the stage while the audience roared. But now it seems likely that in their private moments together Judy gave Punch back a bit of his own.

Researchers studying human aggression are discovering that, in contrast to the usual stereotypes, patterns of aggression among girls and women under some circumstances may mirror or even exaggerate those seen in boys and men. And while women's weapons are often words, fists may be used, too.

In a large-scale review of dozens of studies of physical hostility in heterosexual relationships, Dr. John Archer, a psychologist at the University of Central Lancashire in Great Britain, has found that although women sustain more serious and visible injuries than men during domestic disputes, overall they are just as likely as men to resort to physical aggression during an argument with a sexual partner.

Dr. Archer compiled interviews with tens of thousands of men and women in Canada, Great Britain, the United States and New Zealand, and discovered that women who argued with their dates or mates were actually even slightly more likely than men to use some form of physical violence, ranging from slapping, kicking and biting, to choking or using a weapon. The pattern was particularly pronounced among younger women and women who were dating a partner rather than married to or living with him, he said.

"Whatever the base rate of physical aggression in the population, women tended to have a slightly higher rate than men," Dr. Archer said. In contrast, though, most instances of serious violence in his study were caused by men, as were most injuries that required medical care: Women accounted for 65 to 70 percent of those requiring medical help as a result of violence between partners.

Still, "the large minority of men who got injured is fascinating," Dr. Archer said. "It counters a certain entrenched view of partner violence as being exclusively male to female."

Dr. Archer's study was reported at a meeting of the International Society for Research on Aggression held at Ramapo College in Mahwah, N.J., earlier this month. It is an extraordinary study, said Dr. Anne Campbell, a psychologist at the University of Durham in Great Britain, because it lends support to an emerging theory that women may respond to certain environmental stresses with physically aggressive behaviors that are analogous to men's, although often on a different scale of intensity.

For instance, she said, criminologists know that although men are more likely to commit crimes than women, crime rates in the genders are also strongly correlated. In other words, in impoverished, "high crime" areas, rates of both violent and nonviolent crimes increase proportionally among men and women.

"Unlike men, though, women tend to view crime as work rather than adventure," Dr. Campbell said. For example, women spend more of the proceeds of nonviolent crimes on staples rather than on luxuries. And women often commit violent crimes against other women with the very pragmatic purpose of attracting the protection and financial support of a "well-resourced" man.

Patterns of domestic homicide also indicate that women are capable of significant violence, although often only as a last resort. Although the vast majority of all murders are committed by men, "intimate partner" homicides were split about equally between the sexes until about 20 years ago, said Dr. Daniel Nagin, a public policy expert at Carnegie Mellon University in Pittsburgh.

In the last two decades, intimate-partner homicides have declined by about 30 percent. Dr. Nagin noted, however, that the decline has been primarily in rates of women killing men, and correlates strongly with several environmental changes.

"The decline appears to be related to an improved relative economic status of females, and a decline in exposure to violent relationships," Dr. Nagin said.

This drop also correlates with the availability of alternatives to violence for women: In an ongoing study of domestic homicides in 29 cities in the United States, the availability of resources like shelters for battered women and legal advocacy for them has correlated strongly with lower rates of domestic homicide committed by women.

"The resources for women seem to be saving the men's lives," Dr. Nagin said.

The experts in human aggression are now aware that even in childhood similarities between male and female aggression are more substantial than is usually recognized.

Until about five years ago scientists studying aggression tended to include only direct physical or verbal efforts to injure another person. Then they discovered that great damage can be done to another person so subtly that even the victim is unaware. The badmouthing, gossip and smear campaigns that can demolish an opponent as well as direct verbal or physical assaults are now formally known in psychological circles as "indirect aggression," and their patterns are tracked as carefully as punches and kicks.

Research counters the stereotypes of the sexes

With indirect aggression factored in, aggression in childhood is no longer primarily a male affair.

In a large observational study of "trajectories of aggression" in children, Dr. Richard E. Tremblay of the Université de Montreal has found that physical aggression in both sexes seems to peak around age 2, then decline steadily, although it remains consistently more common in boys. Indirect aggression, however, becomes more prevalent as children grow older and is consistently more common in girls.

The effect of external stimuli on these trajectories is still under intensive speculation, but one long-term study suggests that the omnipresent influence of television violence may correlate with overall aggressive behavior in boys and girls in both the short and the long term.

In a 20-year study of more than 300 Chicago-area children, led by Dr. L. Rowell Huesmann at the University of Michigan in Ann Arbor, the more violent television a child watched at ages 6 through 8, the more aggressive behavior that child displayed, no matter what the child's sex.

And in interviews 15 years later with the grown-up study participants, the correlation between the television viewing habits of childhood and adult behavior patterns persisted, Dr. Huesmann said at the Ramapo College meeting. The more television violence the child watched, the more aggressive the man or woman became. The correlation was especially marked among those children who told researchers that they identified with the characters on the television screen, and thought the events depicted were real.

For instance, 16.7 percent of the young women who had been "high violence" television viewers as girls reported having punched, beat or choked another adult, in contrast to 3.6 percent of others. Thirty-seven percent of the "high violence" viewing women had thrown something at a spouse during an argument, in contrast to 16 percent of the others.

"The evidence is pretty compelling that there is a strong longitudinal effect," Dr. Huesmann said.

Unit 5

Key Points to Consider

❖ What is the definition of prejudice? What is it that perpetuates the "isms" (racism, sexism, ageism, and other prejudices)? Do you think some of this is automatic, as suggested by cognitive psychologists? What can we do, if anything, to eliminate or overcome racism, sexism, ageism, and sexual harassment?

❖ What types of media seem to make our society violence-prone? Are the media solely responsible for societal violence; what other factors likely contribute to violence in a society? For what prosocial uses can the media be utilized? Should we censor or restrict certain types of media? Why and for whom? Do you agree that the media should voluntarily make changes? Should such changes be legislated? Why or why not?

❖ What do you think causes the high crime rates in American society? Do you think individuals can inherit a propensity for criminality? What should we do if the answer is "yes"? Are parents responsible for what their children do? If you think that parents are responsible, should we also hold them culpable when their children commit heinous crimes?

❖ What is a cult? Why do people join cults? Would you ever join a cult? What are the advantages to members of cults? What recruiting techniques do cults use? What tragedies seem to follow cults? How could you help a friend who was considering joining a cult?

❖ Do Americans work more today than ever before? Can you provide any anecdotes or statistics to support your answer? If you answered yes, why are Americans working harder? Why are boundaries blurring between free time and work? What can we do to cope better with the demands of work?

 **Links**   # www.dushkin.com/online/

These sites are annotated on pages 4 and 5.

The passing of each decade brings changes to society. Some historians have suggested that changes are occurring more rapidly than in the past. In other words, history appears to take less time to occur. How has American society changed historically? The inventory is long. Technological advances can be found everywhere. Not long ago, few people knew what "user-friendly" and zip drive signified. Today these terms are readily identified with the rapidly expanding computer industry. Twenty years ago, Americans felt fortunate to own a 13-inch television that received three local stations. Now people feel deprived if they cannot select from 200 different worldwide channels on their big, rear-screen sets. Today we can e-mail a message to the other side of the world faster than we can propel a missile to the same place.

In the Middle Ages, Londoners worried about the bubonic plague. Before vaccines were available, people feared polio and other diseases. Today much concern is focused on the transmission and cure of AIDS, the discovery of more carcinogenic substances, and the greenhouse effect. In terms of mental health, psychologists see few hysterics, the type of patient seen by Sigmund Freud in the 1800s. Psychosomatic ulcers and alcohol and drug addiction are more common today. In other words, lifestyle, more than disease, is killing Americans. Similarly, issues concerning the changing American family continue to grab headlines.

Nearly every popular magazine carries a story or two bemoaning the passing of the traditional, nuclear family and the decline in "family values." And as if these spontaneous or unplanned changes are not enough to cope with, some individuals are intentionally trying to change the world. Witness the continuing dramatic changes in Eastern Europe and the Middle East, for example.

This list of societal transformations, while not exhaustive, reflects society's continual demand for adaptation by each of its members. However, it is not just society at large that places stress on us. Smaller units within society, such as our work group, demand constant adaptation by individuals. Work groups expand and contract with every economic fluctuation. Even when group size remains stable, new members come and go as turnover takes place; hence, changes in the dynamics of the group occur in response to the new personalities. Each of these changes, welcome or not, probably places less strain on society as a whole and more stress on the individual, who then needs to adjust or cope with the change.

This unit addresses the interplay between the individual and society in producing the problems each creates for the other.

The first few essays feature ideas about societal problems such as crime and racism. In the unit's first article, "Where Bias Begins: The Truth about Stereotypes," racism is discussed by Annie Paul. Social psychologists disagree with cognitive psychologists about the causes of prejudice and stereotyping. Cognitive psychologists contend that stereotypes are automatic thought processes over which we probably and unfortunately have little control.

The next article is about media violence. Ray Surette blames the media for encouraging our violent behavior. He examines research into media violence. He seems to be telling us that violence is rising in American society and that the causes may be multiple.

Next, David Lykken discusses crime and society. He posits several theories about what causes crime in America and dismisses arguments suggesting that the tendency to commit crime is inherited. Instead he lays the blame squarely on parents.

The article "The Lure of the Cult" offers a sensible and scientific approach to a topic that occasionally appears in the media—cults. Most people find cults abhorrent, but others gladly join. Why they join and the kinds of influences that cults have on their members are investigated in this essay.

Finally, the tendency to be all work and no play places us under immense stress. In "Work, Work, Work, Work!" Mark Hunter discusses how the boundaries between work and home and work and leisure have blurred. We seem to be working all the time, a tendency that Hunter says is unhealthy. Fortunately, Hunter also shares tips for coping with this increased pressure to work endless hours.

WHERE BIAS BEGINS: THE TRUTH ABOUT STEREOTYPES

Psychologists once believed that only bigoted people used stereotypes. Now the study of unconscious bias is revealing the unsettling truth: We all use stereotypes, all the time, without knowing it. We have met the enemy of equality, and the enemy is us.

By Annie Murphy Paul

Mahzarin Banaji doesn't fit anybody's idea of a racist. A psychology professor at Yale University, she studies stereotypes for a living. And as a woman and a member of a minority ethnic group, she has felt firsthand the sting of discrimination. Yet when she took one of her own tests of unconscious bias, "I showed very strong prejudices," she says. "It was truly a disconcerting experience." And an illuminating one. When Banaji was in graduate school in the early 1980s, theories about stereotypes were concerned only with their explicit expression: outright and unabashed racism, sexism, anti-Semitism. But in the years since, a new approach to stereotypes has shattered that simple notion. The bias Banaji and her colleagues are studying is something far more subtle, and more insidious: what's known as automatic or implicit stereotyping, which, they find, we do all the time without knowing it. Though out-and-out bigotry may be on the decline, says Banaji, "if anything, stereotyping is a bigger problem than we ever imagined."

Previously researchers who studied stereotyping had simply asked people to record their feelings about minority groups and had used their answers as an index of their attitudes. Psychologists now understand that these conscious replies are only half the story. How progressive a person seems to be on the surface bears little or no relation to how prejudiced he or she is on an unconscious level—so that a bleeding-heart liberal might harbor just as many biases as a neo-Nazi skinhead.

As surprising as these findings are, they confirmed the hunches of many students of human behavior. "Twenty years ago, we hypothesized that there were people who said they were not prejudiced but who really did have unconscious negative stereotypes and beliefs," says psychologist Jack Dovidio, Ph.D., of Colgate University "It was like theorizing about the existence of a virus, and then one day seeing it under a microscope."

The test that exposed Banaji's hidden biases—and that this writer took as well, with equally dismaying results—is typical of the ones used by automatic stereotype researchers. It presents the subject with a series of positive or negative adjectives, each paired with a characteristically "white" or "black" name. As the name and word appear together on a computer screen, the person taking the test presses a key, indicating whether the word is good or bad. Meanwhile, the computer records the speed of each response.

A glance at subjects' response times reveals a startling phenomenon: Most people who participate in the experiment—even some African-Americans—respond more quickly when a positive word is paired with a white name or a negative word with a black name. Because our minds are more accustomed to making these associations, says Banaji, they process them more rapidly. Though the words and names aren't subliminal, they are presented so quickly that a subject's ability to make deliberate choices is diminished—allowing his or her underlying assumptions to show through. The same technique can be used to measure stereotypes about many different social groups, such as homosexuals, women, and the elderly.

THE UNCONSCIOUS COMES INTO FOCUS

From these tiny differences in reaction speed—a matter of a few hundred milliseconds—the study of automatic stereotyping was born. Its immediate ancestor was the cognitive revolution of the 1970s, an explosion of psychological research into the way people think. After decades dominated by the study of observable behavior, scientists wanted a closer look at the more mysterious operation of the human brain. And the development of computers—which enabled scientists to display information

LIKE THE CULTURE, OUR MINDS ARE SPLIT ON THE SUBJECTS OF RACE, GENDER, SEXUAL ORIENTATION.

very quickly and to measure minute discrepancies in reaction time—permitted a peek into the unconscious.

At the same time, the study of cognition was also illuminating the nature of stereotypes themselves. Research done after World War II—mostly by European émigrés struggling to understand how the Holocaust had happened—concluded that stereotypes were used only by a particular type of person: rigid, repressed, authoritarian. Borrowing from the psychoanalytic perspective then in vogue, these theorists suggested that biased behavior emerged out of internal conflicts caused by inadequate parenting.

The cognitive approach refused to let the rest of us off the hook. It made the simple but profound point that we all use categories—of people, places, things—to make sense of the world around us. "Our ability to categorize and evaluate is an important part of human intelligence," says Banaji. "Without it, we couldn't survive." But stereotypes are too much of a good thing. In the course of stereotyping, a useful category—say women—becomes freighted with additional associations, usually negative. "Stereotypes are categories that have gone too far," says John Bargh, Ph.D., of New York University "When we use stereotypes, we take in the gender, the age, the color of the skin of the person before us, and our minds respond with messages that say hostile, stupid, slow, weak. Those qualities aren't out there in the environment. They don't reflect reality."

Bargh thinks that stereotypes may emerge from what social psychologists call in-group/out-group dynamics. Humans, like other species, need to feel that they are part of a group, and as villages, clans, and other traditional groupings have broken down, our identities have attached themselves to more ambiguous classifications, such as race and class. We want to feel good about the group we belong to—and one way of doing so is to denigrate all those who aren't in it. And while we tend to see members of our own group as individuals, we view those in out-groups as an undifferentiated—stereotyped—mass. The categories we use have changed, but it seems that stereotyping itself is bred in the bone.

Though a small minority of scientists argues that stereotypes are usually accurate and can be relied upon without reservations, most disagree—and vehemently. "Even if there is a kernel of truth in the stereotype, you're still applying a generalization about a group to an individual, which is always incorrect," says Bargh. Accuracy aside, some believe that the use of stereotypes is simply unjust. "In a democratic society people should be judged as individuals and not as members of a group," Banaji argues. "Stereotyping flies in the face of that ideal."

PREDISPOSED TO PREJUDICE

The problem, as Banaji's own research shows, is that people can't seem to help it. A recent experiment provides a good illustration. Banaji and her colleague, Anthony Greenwald, Ph.D., showed people a list of names—some famous, some not. The next day the subjects returned to the lab and were shown a second list, which mixed names from the first list with new ones. Asked to identify which were famous, they picked out the Margaret Meads and the Miles Davises—but they also chose some of the names on the first list, which retained a lingering familiarity that they mistook for fame. (Psychologists call this the "famous overnight-effect.") By a margin of two-to-one, these suddenly "famous" people were male.

Participants weren't aware that they were preferring male names to female names, Banaji stresses. They were simply drawing on an unconscious stereotype of men as more important and influential than women. Something similar happened when she showed subjects a list of people who might be criminals: without knowing they were doing so, participants picked out an overwhelming number of African-American names. Banaji calls this kind of stereotyping *implicit,* because people know they are making a judgment—but just aren't aware of the basis upon which they are making it.

Even further below awareness is something that psychologists call automatic processing, in which stereotypes are triggered by the slightest interaction or encounter. An experiment conducted by Bargh required a group of white participants to perform a tedious computer task. While performing the task, some of the participants were subliminally exposed to pictures of African-Americans with neutral expressions. When the subjects were then asked to do the task over again, the ones who had been exposed to the faces reacted with more hostility to the request—because, Bargh believes, they were responding in kind to the hostility which is part of the African-American stereotype. Bargh calls this the "immediate hostile reaction," which he believes can have a real effect on race relations. When African-Americans accurately perceive the hostile expressions that their white counterparts are unaware of, they may respond with hostility of their own—thereby perpetuating the stereotype.

Of course, we aren't completely under the sway of our unconscious. Scientists think that the automatic activation of a stereotype is immediately followed by a conscious check on unacceptable thoughts—at least in people who think that they are not prejudiced. This internal censor successfully restrains overtly biased responses. But there's still the danger of leakage, which often shows up in nonverbal behavior: our expressions, our stance, how far away we stand, how much eye contact we make.

The gap between what we say and what we do can lead African-Americans and whites to come away with very different impressions of the same encounter, says Jack Dovidio. "If I'm a white person talking to an African-American, I'm probably monitoring my conscious beliefs very carefully and making sure everything I say agrees with all the positive things I want to express," he says. "And I usually believe I'm pretty successful because I hear the right words coming out of my mouth." The listener who is paying attention to non-verbal behavior, however, may be getting quite the opposite message. An African-American student of Dovidio's recently told him that when she was growing up, her mother had taught her to observe how white people moved to gauge their true feelings toward blacks. "Her mother was a very astute ama-

THE CATEGORIES WE USE HAVE CHANGED, BUT STEREOTYPING ITSELF SEEMS TO BE BRED IN THE BONE.

WE HAVE TO CHANGE HOW WE THINK WE CAN INFLUENCE PEOPLE'S BEHAVIORS. IT WOULD BE NAIVE TO THINK THAT EXHORTATION IS ENOUGH.

teur psychologist—and about 20 years ahead of me," he remarks.

WHERE DOES BIAS BEGIN?

So where exactly do these stealth stereotypes come from? Though automatic-stereotype researchers often refer to the unconscious, they don't mean the Freudian notion of a seething mass of thoughts and desires, only some of which are deemed presentable enough to be admitted to the conscious mind. In fact, the cognitive model holds that information flows in exactly the opposite direction: connections made often enough in the conscious mind eventually become unconscious. Says Bargh: "If conscious choice and decision making are not needed, they go away. Ideas recede from consciousness into the unconscious over time."

Much of what enters our consciousness, of course, comes from the culture around us. And like the culture, it seems that our minds are split on the subjects of race, gender, class, sexual orientation. "We not only mirror the ambivalence we see in society, but also mirror it in precisely the same way," says Dovidio. Our society talks out loud about justice, equality, and egalitarianism, and most Americans accept these values as their own. At the same time, such equality exists only as an ideal, and that fact is not lost on our unconscious. Images of women as sex objects, footage of African-American criminals on the six o'clock news,—"this is knowledge we cannot escape," explains Banaji. "We didn't choose to know it, but it still affects our behavior." We learn the subtext of our culture's messages early. By five years of age, says Margo Monteith, Ph.D., many children have definite and entrenched stereotypes about blacks, women, and other social groups. Adds Monteith, professor of psychology at the University of Kentucky: "Children don't have a choice about accepting or rejecting these conceptions, since they're acquired well before they have the cognitive abilities or experiences to form their own beliefs." And no matter how progressive the parents, they must compete with all the forces that would promote and perpetuate these stereotypes: peer pressure, mass media, the actual balance of power in society. In fact, prejudice may be as much a result as a cause of this imbalance. We

create stereotypes—African-Americans are lazy, women are emotional—to explain why things are the way they are. As Dovidio notes, "Stereotypes don't have to be true to serve a purpose."

WHY CAN'T WE ALL GET ALONG?

The idea of unconscious bias does clear up some nettlesome contradictions. "It accounts for a lot of people's ambivalence toward others who are different, a lot of their inconsistencies in behavior," says Dovidio. "It helps explain how good people can do bad things." But it also prompts some uncomfortable realizations. Because our conscious and unconscious beliefs may be very different—and because behavior often follows the lead of the latter—"good intentions aren't enough," as John Bargh puts it. In fact, he believes that they count for very little. "I don't think free will exists," he says, bluntly—because what feels like the exercise of free will may be only the application of unconscious assumptions.

Not only may we be unable to control our biased responses, we may not even be aware that we have them. "We have to rely on our memories and our awareness of what we're doing to have a connection to reality," says Bargh. "But when it comes to automatic processing, those cues can be deceptive." Likewise, we can't always be sure how biased others are. "We all have this belief that the important thing about prejudice is the external expression of it," says Banaji. "That's going to be hard to give up."

One thing is certain: We can't claim that we've eradicated prejudice just because its outright expression has waned. What's more, the strategies that were so effective in reducing that sort of bias won't work on unconscious beliefs. "What this research is saying is that we are going to have to change dramatically the way we think we can influence people's behaviors," says Banaji. "It would be naive to think that exhortation is enough." Exhortation, education, political protest—all of these hammer away at our conscious beliefs while leaving the bedrock below untouched. Banaji notes, however, that one traditional remedy for discrimination—affirmative action—may still be effective since it bypasses our unconsciously compromised judgment.

But some stereotype researchers think that the solution to automatic stereotyping lies in the process itself. Through practice, they say people can weaken the mental links that connect minorities to negative stereotypes and strengthen the ones that connect them to positive conscious beliefs. Margo Monteith explains how it might work. "Suppose you're at a party and someone tells a racist joke—and you laugh," she says. "Then you realize that you shouldn't have laughed at the joke. You feel guilty and become focused on your thought processes. Also, all sorts of cues become associated with laughing at the racist joke: the person who told the joke, the act of telling jokes, being at a party drinking." The next time you encounter these cues, "a warning signal of sorts should go off—'wait, didn't you mess up in this situation before?'—and your responses will be slowed and executed with greater restraint."

That slight pause in the processing of a stereotype gives conscious, unprejudiced beliefs a chance to take over. With time, the tendency to prevent automatic stereotyping may itself become automatic. Monteith's research suggests that, given enough motivation, people may be able to teach themselves to inhibit prejudice so well that even their tests of implicit bias come clean.

The success of this process of "deautomatization" comes with a few caveats, however. First, even its proponents concede that it works only for people disturbed by the discrepancy between their conscious and unconscious beliefs, since unapologetic racists or sexists have no motivation to change. Second, some studies have shown that attempts to suppress stereotypes may actually cause them to return later, stronger than ever. And finally, the results that Monteith and other researchers have achieved in the laboratory may not stick in the real world, where people must struggle to maintain their commitment to equality under less-than-ideal conditions.

Challenging though that task might be, it is not as daunting as the alternative researchers suggest: changing society itself. Bargh, who likens de-automatization to closing the barn door once the horses have escaped, says that "it's clear that the way to get rid of stereotypes is by the roots, by where they come from in the first place." The study of culture may someday tell us where the seeds of prejudice originated; for now the study of the unconscious shows us just how deeply they're planted.

MEDIA, VIOLENCE, YOUTH, AND SOCIETY

Ray Surette

Ray Surette is professor of criminal justice in the School of Public Affairs and Services, Florida International University, North Miami, and author of Media, Crime and Criminal Justice: Images and Realities.

> It is guns, it is poverty, it is over-crowding, and it is the uniquely American problem of a culture that is infatuated with violence. We love it, we glamorize it, we teach it to our children.[1]

The above testimony by Dr. Deborah Prothrow-Stith on gangs and youth violence presented before the U.S. Senate contains two important points concerning the mass media and youth violence. First, it does not mention the media as a factor in violence, lending support to the view that the media are not crucial agents in youth violence. Second, it does cite an American culture that is infatuated with violence, and the glamorization and teaching of violence to our children, as problems. Culture, glamorization, and instruction, however, are areas where the media have been shown to play important social roles. The above statement simultaneously provides support for the position that the media are indeed important players in the production of youth violence and yet paradoxically also supports the position that they are not contributors. The relative validity of these two dichotomous positions, the media as unimportant and the media as central in fostering youth violence, has dominated the public discussion, resulting in much confusion about this issue and

public posturing by various groups and individuals. The actual relationship of the media to youth violence lies somewhere between these two extremes.

Research interest in the relationship of the mass media to social violence has been elevated for most of this century. Over the twentieth century, the issue of the media as a source of violence has moved into and out of

---

If a consensus has emerged from the research and public interest, it is that the media's particular relationship to social violence is extremely complicated.

---

the public consciousness in predictable ten-to-twenty-year cycles. If a consensus has emerged from the research and public interest, it is that the sources of violence are complex and tied to our most basic nature as well as the social world we have created and that the media's particular relationship to social violence is extremely complicated. (See the discussion in this author's *Media, Crime, and Criminal Justice* [1992] and in *Crime and Human Nature* [1985] by J. Wilson and R. Herrnstein.)

Therefore, when discussing the nature of the relationship between the media and violence, it is important not to be myopic. Social violence is embedded in historical, social forces and

phenomena, while the media are components of a larger information system that creates and distributes knowledge about the world. The media and social violence must both be approached as parts of phenomena that have numerous interconnections and paths of influence between them. Too narrow a perspective on youth violence or the media's role in its generation oversimplifies both the problem and the solutions we pursue. Nowhere is this more apparent than in the current concern about media, youth, and violence.

STATISTICS ON YOUTH VIOLENCE

The source of this concern is revealed by a brief review of the statistics of youth violence.[2] Youth violence, and particularly violent crime committed by youth, has recently increased dramatically. Today about 5 out of every 20 robbery arrests and 3 of every 20 murder, rape, and aggravated assault arrests are of juveniles. In raw numbers, this translates into 3,000 murder, 6,000 forcible rape, 41,000 robbery, and 65,000 aggravated assault arrests of youths annually.

The surge in youth criminal violence is concentrated within the past five years. During the first part of the 1980s, there was a general decline in youth arrests for both violent and property crimes. In the latter half of the 1980s, however, youth arrests increased at a pace greater than that of adults for violent crimes. Youth arrests increased substantially between 1981 and 1990 for nonaggravated assault

(72 percent), murder and nonnegligent manslaughter (60 percent), aggravated assault (57 percent), weapons violations (41 percent), and forcible rape (28 percent). Looking over a generational time span from 1965 to 1989, the arrest rate for violent crimes by youths grew between the mid-1960s and the mid-1970s but then leveled off and remained relatively constant until the late 1980s. At that time, the rate again began to increase, reaching its highest recorded level in the most recent years.

Thus, while the proportion of youth in the general population has declined as the baby-boom generation has aged, the rate of violence from our youth has increased significantly. We have fewer youth proportionately, but they are more violent and account for increased proportions of our violent crime. Attempts to comprehend and explain this change have led invariably to the mass media as prime suspects, but decipher-

---

The view of the media as the source of primary effects is often advanced along with draconian policy demands such as extensive government intervention or direct censorship of the media.

---

ing the media's role has not been a simple or straightforward task.

This difficulty in deciphering the media's role is due to the fact that the relationship of media to violence is complex, and the media's influence can be both direct and indirect. Research on their relationship (reported, for example, in George Comstock's 1980 study *Television in America)* has revealed that media effects that appear when large groups are examined are not predictable at the individual subject level. The media are also related to social violence in ways not usually considered in the public debate, such as their effects on public policies and general social attitudes toward violence.

Adding to the complexity of the media's relationship, there are many other sources of violence that either interact with the media or work alone to produce violence. These sources range from individual biology to characteristics of our history and culture. The

importance of nonmedia factors such as neighborhood and family conditions, individual psychological and genetic traits, and our social structure, race relations, and economic conditions for the generation of violence are commonly acknowledged and analyzed, as in Jeffrey Goldstein's 1986 study *Aggression and Crimes of Violence.* The role of the mass media is confounded with these other sources, and its significance is often either lost or exaggerated. One task of this essay is thus to dispel the two popular but polarizing notions that have dominated the public debate. The first is that the media are the primary cause of violence in society. The second is that the media have no, or a very limited, effect on social violence.

The former view of the media as the source of primary effects is often advanced along with draconian policy demands such as extensive government intervention or direct censorship of the media. The counterargument to this position is supported by a number of points. The most basic is that we were a violent nation before we had mass media, and there is no evidence that the removal of violent media would make us nonviolent.[3] Some research into copy-cat crime additionally provides no evidence of a criminalization effect from the media as a cause.[4] The media alone cannot turn a law-abiding individual into a criminal one nor a nonviolent youth into a violent one. In sum, individual and national violence cannot be blamed primarily on the media, and violence-reducing policies directed only at the media will have little effect.

The latter argument, that the media have limited to no effect on levels of social violence, is structured both in posture and approach to the tobacco industry's response to research linking smoking to lung cancer and it rings just as hollow. The argument's basic approach is to expound inherent weaknesses in the various methodologies of the media-violence research and to trumpet the lack of evidence of strong, direct effects, while ignoring the persistent pattern of positive findings. Proponents of the nil effect point out that laboratory experiments are biased toward finding an effect. To isolate the effect of a single factor, in this case the media, and observe a rare social behavior, namely violence, experiments must exaggerate the link between media and aggression and create a setting that will elicit violent behavior. They therefore argue that all laboratory research on the issue is irrelevant. They continue, however, to dismiss the

nonlaboratory research because of a lack of strict variable controls and designs that leave open noncausal interpretations of the results. "No effects" proponents lastly argue that while society reinforces some behaviors shown in the media such as that found in commercials, it does not condone or reinforce violence and, therefore, a violence-enhancing effect should not be expected (a view discussed in "Smoking Out the Critics," a 1984 *Society* article [21:36–40] by A. Wurtzel and G. Lometti).

In reality, the research shows persistent behavioral effects from violent media under diverse situations for differing groups.[5] Regarding the strong behavioral effects apparent in fashion and fad, effects that Madison Avenue touts, the argument of a behavioral effect only on sanctioned behavior but not on unsanctioned violence is specious. The media industry claim of having only positive behavioral effects is as valid as the tobacco industry claiming that their ads do not encourage new smokers but only persuade brand switching among established smokers. First, violence is sometimes socially sanctioned, particularly within the U.S. youth and hypermasculine culture that is the target audience of the most prominently violent media. And although the media cannot criminalize someone not having criminal predispositions, media-generated, copy-cat crime is a significant criminal phenomenon with ample anecdotal and case evidence providing a form for criminality to take.[6] The recurring mimicking of dangerous film stunts belies the argument of the media having only positive behavioral effects. It is apparent that while the media alone cannot make someone a criminal, it can change the criminal behavior of a predisposed offender.

CONFLICTING CAUSAL CLAIMS

The two arguments of primary cause and negligible cause compete for public support. These models not only posit differing causal relations between the media and violence but imply vastly different public policies

---

Figure 1

Primary Cause Model

Violent Media ⟶ Violent Behavior

---

regarding the media as well. The primary-cause model (fig. 1) is that of a significant, direct linear relationship between violent media and violent behavior. In this model, violent media, independent of other factors, directly cause violent behavior. If valid, it indicates that strong intervention is necessary in the content, distribution, and creation of violent media.

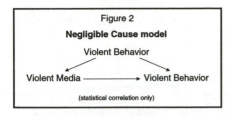

The negligible-cause model (fig. 2) concedes a statistical association between the media and violent behavior but poses the connection as due not to a causal relationship but to persons predisposed to violence simultaneously seeking out violent media and more often behaving violently. As the relationship is associative and not causal in this model, policies targeted at the media will have no effects on violent behavior and the media can be safely ignored.

Both models inaccurately describe the media-violence relationship. The actual relationship between the factors is felt to be bidirectional and cyclical (fig. 3). In addition to violently predisposed people seeking out violent media and violent media causing violent behavior, violent media play a role in the generation of violently predisposed people through their effects on attitudes. And as the made-for-TV movie industry reflects, violent behavior sometimes results in the creation of more violent media. Finally, by providing live models of violence and creating community and home environments that are more inured to and tolerant of violence, violent behavior helps to create more violently predisposed youth in society. Therefore, while the direct effect of media on violence may not be initially large, its influence cycles through the model and accumulates.

An area of research that provides an example of the bidirectional model is the relationship of pornography to sexual violence; a recent (1993) overview of such research can be found in *Pornography,* by D. Linz and N. Malamuth. On one hand, the research establishes that depictions of sexual violence, specifically those that link sex with physical violence toward women, foster antisocial attitudes toward women and lenient perceptions of the crime of rape. Aberrant perceptions, such as increased belief in the "rape myth" (that women unconsciously want to be raped or somehow enjoy being raped), have been reported. Virtually none of the research,

however, reveals strong direct effects from pornography, and even sexually violent media do not appear to negatively affect all male viewers. Many cultural and individual factors appear to mediate the effects and to foster the predisposition to sexually violent media and sexual violence. Researchers in this area have concluded that the media are one of many social forces that affect the development of intervening variables, such as thought patterns, sexual arousal patterns, motivations,

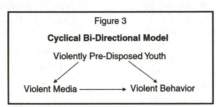

and personality characteristics that are associated with tolerance for sexual violence and perhaps an increase in sexually violent behavior in society.[7] As in other areas of media-violence research, sexually violent media emerge as neither a primary engine nor an innocuous social factor.

THE KEY TO MEDIA EFFECTS

The key to media effects occurring in any particular instance, then, are the intermediate, interactive factors. In terms of the media, there are numerous interactive factors that have been identified as conducive to generating aggressive effects. Among the many delineated in the research, a sample includes: reward or lack of punishment for the perpetrator, portrayal of violence as justified, portrayal of the consequences of violence in a way that does not stir distaste, portrayal of violence without critical commentary, the presence of live peer models of violence, and the presence of sanctioning adults (all discussed in Comstock's *Television in America*). Only unambiguous linking of violent behavior with undesirable consequences or motives by the media appears capable of inhibiting subsequent aggression in groups of viewers.

A list of nonmedia factors deemed significant in the development of crime and the number of violently predisposed individuals can be culled from *Crime and Human Nature* by J. Wilson and R. Herrnstein. The authors list constitutional, developmental, and social-context factors including gender, age, intelligence, personality, psychopathology, broken and abusive families,

schools, community, labor markets, alcohol and heroin, and finally history and culture. As can be seen, most aspects of modern life are implicated, and only tangential factors like diet and climate (which other researchers would have included) are left out. With such a large number of factors coming into play, the levels of interactions and complexity of relationships are obviously enormous.

The research on violence suggests that certain factors are basic to violent crime, as detailed by Wilson and Herrnstein. None of these factors dominates, but none are without significant effects.

Accordingly, the research (contained in this author's 1992 study *Media, Crime and Criminal Justice*) clearly signifies the media as only some of many factors in the generation of youth violence and that media depictions of violence do not affect all persons in the same way. The media contribute to violence in combination with other social and psychological factors. Whether or not a particular media depiction will cause a particular viewer to act more aggressively is not a straightforward issue. The emergence of an effect depends on the interaction between each individual viewer, the content of the portrayal, and the setting in which exposure to the media occurs. This gives the media significant aggregate effects but makes these effects difficult to predict for individuals. There is no doubt, however, that violent children, including those who come to have significant criminal records, spend more time exposed to violent media than do less violent children. The issue is not the existence of a media effect but the magnitude or importance of the effect.

Media violence correlates as strongly with and is as causally related to the magnitude of violent behavior as any other social behavioral variable that has been studied. This reflects both the media's impact and our lack of knowledge about the etiology of violence. Because of the many individual and social factors that come into play in producing any social behavior, one should not expect to find more than a modest direct relationship between the media and violence. Following their review of the research, Thomas Cook and his colleagues conclude:

No effects emerge that are so large as to hit one between the eyes, but early measure of viewing violence adds to the predictability of later aggression over and above the predictability afforded by earlier measures of aggression. These lagged effects

A Brief History of Television and Youth Violence Research

The logic of science requires that in order to establish the causal effect of a variable, one must be able to examine a situation without the variable's effect. In terms of television and violence, this requirement means that a group of subjects (a control group) who have not been exposed to violent television is necessary for comparison with a violent television-exposed group. Television, however, is ubiquitous and an integral part of a modern matrix of influences on social behaviors. Therefore, when the interest is in the effects of television on mainstream citizens in Western industrialized and urbanized nations, finding nontelevision-exposed controls is essentially impossible. In response, artificial laboratory situations are created, or statistical controls and large data sets are employed. Thus, while social sciences abound with research reporting variables that are correlated with one another, research firmly establishing causal relationships is rare. Unlike the content of television, there are few smoking guns in social science. Rather than conclusively proven, cause is more often inferred in a trial-like decision from the predominance of evidence. Such is the case with television and violence.

In a traditional laboratory experiment, two sets of matched, usually randomly assigned, subjects are placed in identical situations except for a single factor of interest. Early research in the television-violence quest were in this vein, with the seminal ones conducted in the 1960s by researchers Bandura, Ross, and Ross.[1] These laboratory studies basically consisted of exposing groups of young children to either a short film containing violence (frequently an adult beating up an inflated Bobo doll) or a similar but nonviolent film. The two groups of children were then placed in playrooms and observed. Children who watched the film where a doll was attacked would significantly more often attack a similar doll if given the opportunity shortly after viewing their film than children who had observed a nonviolent film. These and other studies established the existence of an "observational imitation" effect from visual violence; in short, children will imitate violence they see in the media. It was concluded by many that television violence must therefore be a cause of youth violence.

However, critics of this conclusion argued that because laboratory situations are purposely artificial and contrived to isolate the influence of a single variable, the social processes producing aggression in the laboratory are not equal to those found in the real world. In summary, one

cannot assume that behavior and variable relationships observed in the lab are occurring in the home or street.

In addition to the laboratory studies, at about the same time a number of survey studies were reporting positive correlations between youth aggression and viewing violent television.[2] Efforts to extend the laboratory findings and determine if the correlational studies reflected real-world causal relationships led to two types of research: natural field experiments[3] and longitudinal panel studies.

The better known and most discussed research efforts came from longitudinal panel studies conducted in the 1970s and early '80s. Expensive and time consuming, in panel studies a large number of subjects are selected and followed for a number of years. Three such studies are particularly important due to their renown, similarities in approach, and differences in conclusions.

The first study (called the Rip van Winkle study) by L. Rowell Huesmann, Leonard Eron, and their colleagues used a cross-lag panel design (that is, comparison over time and with different populations) in which television habits at grade three (approximately age eight) were correlated with aggression in grade three and with television viewing and aggression ten years later for a sample of 211 boys.[4] The researchers collected their data in rural New York State from students in the third, eighth, and "thirteenth" grades (one year after graduation). Favorite television programs were rated based on their violent content, and frequency of viewing was

1. See, for example, A. Bandura, D. Ross, and S. A. Ross, "Transmission of Aggression through Imitation of Aggressive Models," *Journal of Abnormal and Social Psychology* 63 (1961), 575–82; and "Imitation of Film-Mediated Aggressive Models," *Journal of Abnormal and Social Psychology* 66 (1963), 3–11.

2. See G. Comstock, et al., *Television and Human Behavior* (New York: Columbia University Press, 1978) for a review.

3. Natural field experiments typically take advantage of a planned introduction of television to a previously unexposed population. This allows both a pretelevision and posttelevision comparison of the new television group and comparisons with similar but still unexposed other groups. Although rare because of the unique circumstances necessary and by definition confined to nonmainstream populations, these studies report significant increases in aggressive behavior for children who watched a lot of television in the new-television populations. See, for example, G. Granzberg, "The Introduction of Television into a Northern Manitoba Cree Community" in G. Granzberg and J. Steinberg, eds. *Television and the Canadian Indian* (Winnipeg, Manitoba; University of Winnipeg Press, 1980); and T. Williams, ed., *The Impact of Television: A Natural Experiment in Three Communities* (New York: Academic Press, 1985).

4. M. Lefkowitz, et al., "Television Violence and Child Aggression: A Follow-up Study" in G. A. Comstock and E. A. Rubinstein, eds. *Television and Social Behavior,* vol. 3, *Television and Adolescent Aggressiveness* (Washington, D.C.: U.S. Government Printing Office, 1971).

obtained from the children's mothers in grade three and from the subjects in grades eight and thirteen. The measure of aggression was a peer-nominated rating obtained from responses to questions such as, "Who starts fights over nothing?" The most significant finding reported was a strong, positive association between violent television viewing at grade three and aggression at grade thirteen. However, this study was criticized for a number of reasons. For example, the measure of aggression used in grade thirteen was poorly worded and phrased in the past tense (i.e., "Who started fights over nothing?") and thus the answers were ambiguous in that the grade thirteen subjects may have been referring to general reputations rather than current behaviors. In addition, cross-lagged correlation analysis has a built-in bias toward finding relationships where none exist. Despite the study's weaknesses, Huesmann and Eron concluded that a causal relationship between television violence and aggression existed. This study had a strong public impact.

A second longitudinal panel study was conducted by Ronald Milavsky and his colleagues in the early 1970s that had an opposite conclusion. This study was based on surveys of about 2,400 elementary students age seven to twelve, and 403 male teenagers age twelve to sixteen in Minneapolis, Minnesota, and Fort Worth, Texas.[5] The subjects were surveyed five to six times over nineteen months. This study also used peer-nominated aggression measures for the younger group and four self-reported measures of aggression for the teenagers.[6] Unlike the "van Winkle" study, which used the children's mothers' selection of favorite programs, this study measured exposure to violent programming based on the subjects' own reports. Their analysis further controlled for earlier levels of aggression and exposure to television violence, in effect searching for evidence of significant incremental increases in youth aggression that could be attributed to past exposure to television violence after taking into account past levels of aggressive behavior.

Huesmann and Eron report meaningful lagged associations between later aggression and a number of prior conditions such as earlier aggression in a child's classroom, father's use of physical punishment, family conflict, and violent environments—but not for prior exposure to violent television. Although some significant positive relationships were found between exposure to television violence and later aggression, the overall pattern and number of findings regarding television were interpreted as inconsistent. These researchers conclude that chance, not cause, is the best explanation for their findings regarding television and aggression.

Partly in response to the Milavsky study and criticisms of their earlier methodology, Huesmann, Eron, and their colleagues conducted a third panel study (the Chicago Circle study) in the late 1970s using first and third graders in Chicago public and parochial schools as subjects.[7] Six hundred seventy-two students were initially sampled and tested for three consecutive years in two groups. One group was followed from first through third grades, the second from third through fifth grades. Aggression was measured once more by a peer-generated scale in which each child designated other children on fifteen descriptive statements, ten of which dealt with aggression. (An example is, "Who pushes and shoves other children?") Exposure to violent television was measured by asking each child to select the show most often watched and frequency of watching from eight different ten-program lists. Each list contained a mix of violent and nonviolent programs.

The study was simultaneously conducted in the United States, Australia, Finland, Israel, the Netherlands, and Poland. Their analysis of the U.S. data showed a significant general effect for television violence on girls but not for boys. However, the interaction of viewing violent television and identification with aggressive television characters was a significant predictor of male aggression. Huesmann and Eron conclude that the relationship between television violence and viewer aggression is causal and significant but bidirectional.

At this time, most reviewers of these studies and the subsequent research that followed conclude that a modest but genuine causal association does exist between media violence and aggression.[8] The fact is that, once introduced, the effect of television on a society or an individual can never be fully extricated from all the other forces that may contribute to violence. Television's influence is so intertwined with these parallel forces that searches for strong direct causal effects are not likely to be fruitful. But similar to smoking/lung cancer research, evidence of a real causal connection of some sort has been established beyond a reasonable doubt for most people.

—R.S.

5. J. Milavsky, et al., *Television and Aggression: A Panel Study* (New York: Academic Press, 1982).

6. Personal aggression toward others, aggression against a teacher (rudeness or unruliness), property aggression (theft and vandalism), and delinquency (serious or criminal behaviors).

7. See Rowell Huesmann and Leonard Eron, "Television Violence and Aggressive Behavior" in D. Pearl, L. Bouthilet, and J. Lazar, eds. *Television and Behavior: Ten Years of Scientific Progress and Implications for the 80's* (Washington, D.C., 1982); and "Factors Influencing the Effect of Television Violence on Children" in Michael Howe, ed., *Learning from Television: Psychological and Educational Research* (New York: Academic Press, 1983).

8. See, for example, L. Heath, L. Bresolin, and R. Rinaldi, "Effects of Media Violence on Children: A Review of the Literature," *Archives of General Psychiatry* 46 (1989), 376–79.

are consistently positive, but not large, and they are rarely statistically significant, although no reliable lagged negative effects have been reported.... But is the association causal? If we were forced to render a judgment, probably yes.... There is strong evidence of causation in the wrong setting (the lab) with the right population (normal children) and in the right setting (outside the lab) with the wrong population (abnormal adults).[8]

MEDIA AMONG MANY FACTORS

In summation, despite the fact that the media are among many factors, they should not be ignored, regardless of the level of their direct impact. Because social violence is a pressing problem, even those factors that only modestly contribute to it are important. Small effects of the media accumulate and appear to have significant long-term social effects.[9] The research strongly indicates that we are a more violent society because of our mass media. Exactly how and to what extent the media cause long-term changes in violent behavior remains unknown, but the fact that it plays an important, but not independent, role is generally conceded.

What public policies are suggested by the knowledge we now possess about media and violence? Not all of the factors discussed above are good candidates for public intervention strategies, but there are three sources of youth violence that government policy can influence. In order of importance, they are: extreme differences in economic conditions and the concentration of wealth in America; the American gun culture; and, exacerbating the problems created by the first two, the media's violence-enhancing messages. Family, neighborhood, and personality factors may be more important for generating violence in absolute magnitude, but they are not easily influenced by public actions.

The magnitude of economic disparity and the concentration of wealth in the United States is greater than in comparable (and, not surprisingly, less violent) societies. Our richest citizens not only earn vastly more than our poorest, but, more important, the wealth in the country is increasingly concentrated in fewer and fewer hands. The trend during this century, which accelerated during the 1980s, is for an ever-shrinking percentage of the richest Americans to control greater proportions of the country's wealth,

The fear and loathing we feel toward criminals—youthful, violent, or not—is tied to our media-generated image of criminality.

while the poorest have access to increasingly smaller proportions. The burden of these economic disenfranchisement, both psychologically and fiscally, falls heavily on the young, and especially on the young who are urban poor minorities, as is shown in Elliott Currie's 1985 study *Confronting Crime.* In a consumerism-saturated society like the United States, hopelessness, bitterness, and disregard for moral values and law are heightened by this growing economic disparity.

And as the economic polarization and violent crime have grown, we also became nationally fixated on heightening and extending our punishment capacities in an attempt to suppress violent behavior, evidenced by Diana Gordon's 1991 study *The Justice Juggernaut.* Since 1975, we have increased the rate of juvenile incarceration steadily. Today we hold in custody approximately one hundred thousand juveniles every year. Despite our strengthened capacity to punish, however, youth violence has not abated.

This result should have been expected because two social mechanisms are needed to reduce violence—punishing violent criminal behavior and rewarding law-abiding, nonviolent behavior. Societies that are more successful in balancing the two mechanisms are less violent, as shown in *Crime and Control in Comparative Perspective,* by H. Heiland and L. Shelley (1992). While punishment of violent behavior is certainly necessary and justified, its emphasis, coupled with the concentration of wealth in America, has resulted in the degrading of the equally important social capacity to reward law-abiding behavior. By emphasizing one, we have lamed and discredited the other. Nonmaterial rewards like social status, an esteemed reputation, and a clear conscience have been losing their legitimacy with the young, while material rewards for law-abiding life-styles such as careers, comfortable incomes and affordable goods are less generally available to our poorest and, not surprisingly, most crime-prone and violent citizens.

We have chosen to emphasize the mechanism, punishment, that is actually the weaker of the two in actually influencing behavior. As operant conditioning theory would predict, punishment, if severe enough, can suppress one type of violent crime. But the suppression of one behavior gives no push toward a desirable replacement activity, and a substitute violent crime will likely emerge. So "smash and grab" robberies give way to "bump and rob" holdups. Shaping behavior requires a credible reward system. In social terms, youth must see law-abiding behavior as credible and potentially rewarding as well as seeing violent behavior as potentially resulting in punishment.

The second area that government policy can immediately address is the gun culture in America. Our culture of violence, referred to in the opening quote, is made immeasurably more deadly by the enfolded gun culture. The availability of guns as cheap killing mechanisms is simply a national insanity. The mass production of these killing "toys" and the easy access to them must he addressed. The most recent statistics show that one out of every ten high school students report that they carry a handgun. Gun buyback programs should be supported, and production and availability must be reduced if a positive net effect is to he expected. Irrespective of the difficulty of controlling the sources of individual violent behavior, the implements of fatal violence should not be ignored.

The third area of policy concern, the mass media, exacerbates the gun culture by portraying guns as glamorous, effective, omnipotent devices. The mass media also heighten the negative effects of economic disparities through their consumer messages in advertising and entertainment. Although both of these effects that add to the problem of youth violence are sometimes discussed, the debate about the media remains tightly focused on measuring and reviewing violent media content. Within this focus, the emphasis has been on counting violent acts rather than on exploring the context of its portrayal. Deciphering the media's moral and value messages about violence has been mostly ignored.

EFFECTS ON CRIMINAL JUSTICE

A closer examination of the context of violence in the media would tell us that we should not try to purge the media of violence, for violent media can be good when programs teach that violence is bad. Our goal should be to reduce graphic, gratuitous, and glorified violence; to portray it not as a problem solver but as a reluctant, distasteful, last resort with tragic, unanticipated consequences. Violence shown consistently as a generator of pain and suffering, not as a personal or social panacea, would be positive media violence. Too

> *Youth violence will not be seriously reduced without violence in other aspects of our culture being addressed.*

often, violence in the media is shown as an effective solution, and, too often, it is simply met by increased counterviolence. But, despite the recurring interest and current debate about media violence, there is little direction for the media industry regarding the context of violence and its effects. A goal should be to provide better information to the industry that details the various contexts and messages of violence and their effects.

Perhaps the most significant social effect of media violence is, however, not the direct generation of social violence but its impact on our criminal justice policy. The fear and loathing we feel toward criminals—youthful, violent, or not—is tied to our media-generated image of criminality. The media portray criminals as typically animalistic, vicious predators. This media image translates into a more violent society by influencing the way we react to all crime in America. We imprison at a much greater rate and make reentry into law-abiding society, even for our nonviolent offenders, more difficult than other advanced (and, not coincidentally, less violent) nations. The predator-criminal image results in policy based on the worst-case criminal and a constant ratcheting up of punishments for all offenders. In its cumulative effect, the media both provide violent models for our youth to emulate and justify a myopic, harshly punitive public reaction to all offenders.

Currently, the debate concerning both the media and youth violence has evolved into "circles of blame" in which one group ascribes blame for the problem to someone else in the circle. Thus,

in the media circle, the public blames the networks and studios, which blame the producers and writers, who blame the advertisers, who blame the public. In the violence circle, the government blames the youth, who blame the community, which blames the schools, which blame the parents, who blame the government. A more sensible, productive process would be a shift to a "ring of responsibility" with the groups addressing their individual contributions to the problem and arriving at cooperative policies. We can't selectively reduce one aspect of violence in a violent society and expect real results. Youth violence will not be seriously reduced without violence in other aspects of our culture being addressed. In the same vein, modifying media violence alone will not have much effect but to ignore it will make efforts on other fronts less successful. Ironically, despite the fact that the media have limited independent effects on youth violence, we need to expand the focus on them. This should incorporate other social institutions, such as the media industry itself, and the social norms and values reflected in the media. We could then derive more general models of media effects and social violence.

Violence is a cultural product. The media are reflections of the culture and engines in the production process. Although they are not the only or even the most powerful causes, they are tied into the other violence-generating engines, and youth pay particular attention to them. The aggregate result of all of these forces in the United States is a national character that is individualistic, materialistic, and violence prone. If we wish to change our national character regarding violence, we cannot take on only some aspects of its genesis. We must address everything we can, such as economic inequities, the gun culture, and the glamorization of violence. And, by a slow, painful, generational process of moral leadership and example, we must work to modify the individual, family, and neighborhood factors that violently predispose youth.

In conclusion, our youth will be violent as long as our culture is violent. The local social conditions in which they are raised and the larger cultural and economic environments that they will enter generate great numbers of violently predisposed individuals. As we have experienced, violently predisposed youth, particularly among our poor, will fully develop their potential and come to prey upon us. Faced with frightful predators, we subsequently

and justly punish them, but the use of punishment alone will not solve the problem. The role that the media play in the above scenario versus their potential role in deglorifying violence and showing our youth that armed aggression is not an American cultural right, will determine the media's ultimate relationship to youthful violence in society.

Notes

1. Dr. Deborah Prothrow-Stith testifying before the Senate Subcommittee on Juvenile Justice, November 26, 1991.
2. Sources of the statistics cited in this essay are drawn from "Arrests of Youth 1990," January 1992, *Office of Juvenile Justice and Delinquency Prevention Update on Statistics;* and *Sourcebook of Criminal Justice Statistics—1992,* Bureau of Justice Statistics, U.S. Department of Justice, 1993.
3. Hugh Davis Graham and Ted Robert Gurr, eds., *Violence in America* (Beverly Hills, CA: Sage, 1979).
4. See S. Milgram and R. Shotland, *Television and Antisocial Behavior: Field Experiments* (New York: Academic Press, 1973) and A. Schmid and J. de Graaf, *Violence as Communication* (Newbury Park, CA: Sage, 1982).
5. T. Cook, D. Kendzierski, and S. Thomas, "The Implicit Assumptions of Television Research," *Public Opinion Quarterly* 47: 161–201.
6. For a listing of examples see S. Pease and C. Love, "The Copy-Cat Crime Phenomenon," in *Justice and the Media* by R. Surette (Springfield, IL: Charles C. Thomas, 1984), 199–211; and A. Schmid and J. de Graaf, *Violence as Communication* (Newbury Park, CA: Sage, 1982).
7. N. Malamuth and J. Briere (1986), "Sexual Violence in the Media: Indirect Effects on Aggression against Women," *Journal of Social Issues* 42, 89.
8. T. Cook, D. Kendzierski, and S. Thomas (1993), "The Implicit Assumptions of Television Research," *Public Opinion Quarterly* 47: 191–92.
9. R. Rosenthal (1986), "Media Violence, Anti-Social Behavior, and the Social Consequences of Small Effects," *Journal of Social Issues* 42: 141–54.

ADDITIONAL READING

George Comstock, *Television in America,* Sage, Newbury Park, Calif., 1980.

Elliott Currie, *Confronting Crime,* Pantheon, New York, 1985.

Jeffrey Goldstein, *Aggression and Crimes of Violence,* Oxford University Press, New York, 1986.

Diana Gordon, *The Justice Juggernaut,* Rutgers University Press, New Brunswick, N.J., 1991.

Joshua Meyrowitz, *No Sense of Place,* Oxford University Press, New York, 1985.

Ray Surette, *Media, Crime, and Criminal Justice,* Brooks/Cole, Pacific Grove, Calif., 1992.

James Q. Wilson and Richard Herrnstein, *Crime and Human Nature,* Simon & Schuster, New York, 1985.

Symposium: Licensing Parents

Psychopathy, Sociopathy, and Crime

David T. Lykken

Since the beginnings of psychiatry in the early nineteenth century, it has been recognized that there are persons whose persisting antisocial behavior cannot be understood in terms of mental disorder or neurotic motivations. Psychiatric befuddlement is evident in the diagnostic labels used to classify these people. The father of French psychiatry, Phillipe Pinel, noted in 1801 that they seemed to behave crazily without actually being crazy, and he coined the term "*manie sans delire.*" Benjamin Rush, the first American psychiatrist, in 1812 described patients with "innate preternatural moral depravity." An English psychiatrist, Pritchard, employed a similar label, "moral insanity," in 1835. The German systematists, like Robert Koch, first used the term "psychopathic" in 1891 for a heterogeneous collection of what we would now call personality disorders, and Emil Kraepelin, in the seventh edition (1915) of his influential textbook, first used "psychopathic personality" specifically to describe the amoral or immoral criminal type. In 1930, an American psychiatrist named Partridge pointed out that these people had in common a disposition to violate social norms of behavior and introduced the term "sociopath." I shall use this term to refer specifically to antisocial personalities whose behavior is a consequence of social or familial dysfunction. I use "psychopath" to refer to those people whose antisocial behavior appears to result from a defect or aberration within themselves rather than in their rearing.

The Psychopath

While not deeply vicious, he carries disaster lightly in each hand.

—Hervey Cleckley, 1982

More than a hundred years after Pinel and Pritchard, an American expert on criminal psychiatry, Benjamin Karpman, concluded: "When all of the cases which I group under symptomatic psychopathy are removed and accounted for, there would still remain a small group which may be designated as primary or idiopathic psychopathy." There seem to be several "species" of psychopath, several different innate peculiarities of temperament or endowment that conduce toward a complete or partial failure of socialization or toward intermittent lapses of socialization and to antisocial behavior. Many of these innate vagaries—choleric temperament or hypersexuality, for example—can be easily identified, but the etiology of what Karpman called "primary psychopathy" is more mysterious and has been the subject of extensive research and debate.

In his classic monograph *The Mask of Sanity*, psychiatrist Hervey Cleckley illustrated the problem of understanding the primary psychopath by means of a collection of vividly drawn case histories from his own practice. Here were people of good families, intelligent

From *Society*, November/December 1996, pp. 29-38. © 1996 by Transaction Publishers. All rights reserved. Reprinted by permission.

and rational, sound of mind and body, who lied without compunction, cheated, stole, casually violated any and all norms of social conduct whenever it suited their whim. Moreover, they seemed surprisingly unaffected by the bad consequences of their actions, whether visited upon themselves or on their families or friends.

Cleckley also cited several examples from literature of the kind of individual he had in mind, including Shakespeare's Iago and Falstaff, Henrik Ibsen's Peer Gynt, and Ferenc Molnár's character Liliom, the prototype of Billy Bigelow in the Rodgers and Hammerstein musical *Carousel.* Unaccountably, however, Cleckley neglected the Shakespearean character who best epitomizes the primary psychopath: Richard III, who, in the first speech of scene 1, declares himself bored, looking for action: "Now is the winter of our discontent / . . . / Why, I, in this weak piping time of peace, / Have no delight to pass away the time."

In the next scene, the Lady Anne enters with bearers carrying the corpse of her husband, Henry VI. It was Richard who had killed Henry, and Anne fears and despises him, yet he commands the bearers to set the coffin down while he proceeds to make love to the grieving widow! Richard talks her around in just three pages—surely one of the greatest tours de force ever essayed by a dramatist or by an actor—and then he gloats: "Was ever woman in this humour woo'd? / Was ever woman in this humour won? / I'll have her; but I will not keep her long. / What, I, that kill'd her husband and his father, / To take her in her heart's extremest hate, / With curses in her mouth, tears in her eyes, / The bleeding witness of my hatred by; / Having God, her conscience, and these bars against me, / And I no friends to back my suit withal / But the plain deveil and dissembling looks. / And yet to win her, all the world to nothing!"

Some female psychopaths in literature include Mildred in Somerset Maugham's *Of Human Bondage;* Sally Bowles, the heroine in *Cabaret;* Ibsen's Hedda Gabler (Hedda is a nice example of a "secondary" psychopath); and Bizet's Carmen. We can see primary psychopathy in the characters played by the actor Jack Nicholson in numerous movies, including *Five Easy Pieces, Chinatown, The Last Detail,* and, especially, *One Flew over the Cuckoo's Nest.* Harry Lyme as portrayed by Orson Welles in the film *The Thin Man* conveys the eerie combination of charm and menace found in some of these individuals. The character played by child actress Patty McCormack in the film *The Bad Seed* and the eponymous hero in Thomas Mann's *The Confessions of Felix Krull, Confidence Man* are contrasting portraits of the psychopath as mendacious manipulator. The brother in Graham Greene's novel *The Shipwrecked* is a good example of the feckless, self- and other-deluding, poseur type of psychopath, as is the protagonist's father in John le Carré's *The Perfect Spy,* a character said to be based on the author's own father. The psychopath in youth can be found as the hero of E. L. Docterow's book *Billy Bath-*

gate, which also provides a more dangerous version in the character of the gangster Dutch Schultz.

As used by the media, "psychopath" conveys an impression of danger and implacable evil. This is mistaken, however, as Cleckley made very clear. Like the unsocialized sociopath, the psychopath is characterized by a lack of the restraining effect of conscience and of empathic concern for other people. Unlike the ordinary sociopath, the primary psychopath has failed to develop conscience and empathic feelings, not because of a lack of socializing experience but, rather, because of some inherent psychological peculiarity that makes him especially difficult to socialize. An additional consequence of this innate peculiarity is that the psychopath behaves in a way that suggests that he is relatively indifferent to the probability of punishment for his actions. This essential peculiarity of the psychopath is not in itself evil or vicious, but combined with perverse appetites or with an unusually hostile and aggressive temperament, the lack of these normal constraints can result in an explosive and dangerous package. Examples of such combinations include the serial killer Ted Bundy, Gary Gilmore, Diane Downs, and the sex-murdering Royal Air Force officer Neville Heath. *Without Conscience: The Disturbing World of the Psychopaths among Us,* a recent and highly readable book by R. D. Hare, the leading researcher in this area, provides numerous sketches of real-life criminal psychopaths.

In marked contrast to these dangerous characters, and illustrative of why psychologists find such fascination in the psychopath, is the case of Oscar Schindler, the savior of hundreds of Krakow Jews, the protagonist of Steven Spielberg's *Schindler's List.* Opportunist, bon vivant, ladies' man, manipulator, unsuccessful in legitimate business by his own admission but wildly successful in the moral chaos of wartime, Schindler's rescue of those Jews can be best understood as a thirty-five-year-old con man's response to a kind of ultimate challenge: Schindler against the Third Reich. Any swine could kill people under the conditions of that time and place; the real challenge—in the words that his biographer may have put in his mouth, the "real power"—lay in rescuing people, especially in rescuing Jews. Some parts of Spielberg's film do not fit with my diagnosis of Schindler as a primary psychopath, in particular, the scene near the end in which Schindler breaks down in tears while addressing his Jewish workers. British filmmaker Jon Blair, whose earlier documentary film *Schindler* was truer to history than Spielberg's feature film, noted this same discrepancy. "It was slightly out of character, and, of course, it never actually happened," Blair said.

Some other biographies of colorful primary psychopaths include N. von Hoffman's *Citizen Cohn,* Neil Sheehan's *A Bright Shining Lie: John Paul Vann and America in Vietnam,* and Daniel Akst's *Wonderboy: Barry Minkow, the Kid Who Swindled Wall Street.* Some historical figures who, I believe, had the talent for psychopathy but who achieved great worldly success include Lyndon Johnson,

Winston Churchill, the explorer Sir Richard Burton, and Chuck Yeager, the first man to break the sound barrier.

The fact that many of these illustrative characters were not adjudicated criminals reminds us that we are talking here about a class of actors rather than a pattern of actions. Psychopaths are at high risk for engaging in criminal behavior, but not all of them succumb to that risk. Even the identical twins of criminal psychopaths, with whom they share all their genes and many of their formative experiences, do not necessarily become criminal themselves. To mention Churchill, Johnson, Burton, and Yeager in this context may seem especially surprising, but all four set out as daring, adventurous, unconventional youngsters who began playing by their own rules early in life. Talent, opportunity, and plain luck enabled them to achieve success and self-esteem through (mainly) licit rather than illicit means. Johnson and Burton were borderline psychopaths, if we can believe their biographers, while Churchill and Yeager seem merely to have shared what I call the "talent for psychopathy." What I believe to be the nature of this talent will be explicated later in this article.

Theories of Psychopathy

Cleckley concluded that the psychopath lacks the normal emotional accompaniments of experience, that the raw feel of his emotional experience is attenuated much as is the color experience of people who are color-blind. Whereas Pritchard and Rush believed that there was an innate lack of moral sensibility, Cleckley took the more modern view that moral feelings and compunctions are not God-given but must be learned and that this learning process is guided and enforced by the power of emotional feelings. When these normal feelings are attenuated, the development of morality—the very mechanism of socialization—is compromised. Thus we can see that Cleckley regarded the primary psychopath as someone for whom the normal socializing experiences are ineffective because of an innate defect, which he thought to be as profound and debilitating as psychosis. As we acknowledged at the outset, some children are harder to socialize than others, and a child whose capacity for emotional experience is innately very weak would presumably be especially difficult.

There is no real evidence, however, that the primary psychopath *is* incapable of genuine emotion. He seems clearly able to feel anger, satisfaction, delight, self-esteem—indeed, if he did not have such feelings, it seems improbable that he would do many of the things, proper and improper, that he does do. As Gilbert and Sullivan pointed out: "When the felon's not engaged in his employment, / Or maturing his felonious little plans, / His capacity for innocent enjoyment, / Is just as great as any honest man's." Other investigators have tried to identify

more focal defects to explain the Cleckley type of psychopath. Several of these conjectured species of this genus are described below.

1. *Lykken's "low fear quotient" theory.* One of the first alternative proposals was my own suggestion in 1957 that the primary psychopath has an attenuated experience not of all emotional states but specifically of anxiety or fear. We are all endowed with the innate tendency to fear certain stimuli—loss of support, snake-like or spider-like objects, strangers, fire—and to associate, or *condition*, fear to stimuli and situations that have been

> A child with a low fear quotient, whose parents nonetheless succeed in instilling the essentials of good citizenship, would grow up to be the kind of person one would like to have on hand when stress and danger threaten.

previously experienced together with pain or punishment. Like all biological variables, fearfulness, or what I have called the innate "fear quotient," varies from person to person. Some individuals have a very high fear quotient and are victimized from childhood on by fearful inhibitions. It is noteworthy that such individuals are especially *unlikely* to become juvenile delinquents or adult sociopaths.

My theory of primary psychopathy is that people at the low end of this same distribution of innate fearfulness are at risk to develop primary psychopathy. The basic idea is that because much of the normal socialization process depends upon punishment of antisocial behavior and because punishment works, when it works, by the fearful inhibition of those impulses toward antisocial behavior the next time that temptation knocks, then someone who is relatively fearless will be relatively harder to socialize in this way. "Harder to socialize" does not mean "impossible to socialize," and it is interesting to note that being less fearful than the average person is not necessarily a disadvantage. A child with a low fear quotient, whose parents nonetheless succeed in instilling the essentials of good citizenship, would grow up to be the kind of person one would like to have on hand when stress and danger threaten. I believe, in short, that the hero and the psychopath may be twigs on the same genetic branch.

An example of a relatively fearless child at risk for developing an antisocial lifestyle is provided in the following excerpt from a letter I received from a single mother in August 1982 after an article of mine on fearlessness appeared in a popular magazine:

> Your article on fearlessness was very informative. I was able to identify with many of the traits. However, being thirty-six and a single parent of three children, I have managed to backpack on the "edge" without breaking my neck. I have a 14-year-old daughter who seems to be almost fearless to anything in her environment. She jumps out second-story windows. When she was in first grade, I came home from work one afternoon and found her hanging by her fingers from our upstairs window. I "calmly" asked her what she was doing. She replied that she was "getting refreshed." Later, she stated that she did things like that when she needed a lift—that she was bored and it made her feel better. Nancy is bright, witty, attractive, charismatic, and meets people easily. She tends to choose friends who are offbeat, antisocial, and into dope, alcohol, etc. During her month's visit here with me, she stole money from my purse, my bank card, etc., etc.

Another letter prompted by my article on fearlessness came from an inmate of a Florida prison, a surfer. He might qualify as a primary psychopath (although better socialized than most, in spite of his being in prison), and it seems clear that his basic attribute is relative fearlessness:

> I am an inmate at Lake Butler Reception and Medical Center, serving a ten year sentence for drug trafficking. Prior to my arrest and conviction, I taught in the public school system, sold real estate, and owned a construction company. In retrospect, I believe that one of the main reasons that I left teaching was the lack of risk. As you know, there is a great deal of risk associated in real estate, running a business, and there certainly is a great deal of risk in drug trafficking and smuggling. I knew a long time ago that the thrill of facing the fear of failure and succeeding were far more important to me that the financial rewards. One group of people that I am familiar with that you might find interesting is surfers. I have surfed for the past 15 years in many parts of the world, meeting surfers from all parts of the globe, and many countries. The one common thread that I find in the group is the total disregard for fear, in fact, it is as if all of us seek it for the adrenaline "rush" you can get, how close to losing your life, and still escape. Witness surfers that ride ten foot waves that break in three feet of water over an urchin-infested coral reef. There certainly is no financial reward, it all must come from the thrill. Needless to say, not all surfers are as fearless as others, but the common thread is there. For years, when smuggling "kingpins" have wanted fearless men to do the actual smuggling, they often have chosen their men from the ranks of the surfing population. It is no accident that many "kingpins" are surfers or ex-surfers themselves.

Another illustrative case is that of Kody Scott, also known as Sanyka Shakur, who was a member of the Eight-Tray Gangster Crips in South Central Los Angeles, where he was known as "Monster"; he is currently serving a seven-year sentence in solitary confinement in a northern California prison. His autobiography required little editing because Monster is intelligent and remarkably articulate, especially considering his negligible education. Kody was initiated into the Eight-Trays when he was twelve and shot his first victim that same night. The name "Monster" resulted from an incident in Kody's early teens, in which a victim Kody was mugging attempted to fight back: Kody stomped him to a bloody pulp.

Kody's mother, Birdie, at twenty-one was a single mother of two, living in Houston, when she met a thirty-three-year-old visitor from Los Angeles; she later moved there to marry him. The marriage was unstable and violent, but Birdie produced four more children before it broke up. One of these four, Kody, was fathered by a professional football player with the L.A. Rams with whom Kody's mother had a brief affair. Kody never knew his biological father, and his mother's husband had gone for good by the time Kody was six.

Kody's mother was a hard worker, mostly at bartending jobs, and the family's circumstances were lower middle class, with the mother, six children, and miscellaneous animals living in a two-bedroom house. There were gangs in the vicinity, and an older brother was briefly involved while in seventh grade; he was caught stealing a leather jacket and spent a night in a juvenile detention center; that one experience stayed with him and he never joined a gang. Kody was different; as M. Horowitz reported in the December 1993 issue of *Atlantic Monthly*:

> Kody was always the daredevil. "He was like a demolition derby," his sister Kendis says, "reckless, wild, and intriguing." "He had no fear," says his older brother Kerwin. Kody built wooden ramps on the street and raced his bike at top speeds, jumping crates like a junior Evil Knieval. "No one else would do it," Kerwin says, "but he would."

A bright, muscular, adventurous boy with no fear and no father, a boy who might have become a professional athlete if his real father had been there to guide and inspire him, or a boxer or policeman or soldier, perhaps even an astronaut—but he became "Monster" instead, a classic example of primary psychopathy in its second-most dangerous form. (The most dangerous form is exemplified by Ted Bundy, the handsome, ingratiating serial killer whose psychopathy was compounded with a perverse sexualized blood lust.) Although they were reared without a father in the same gang-infested neighborhood as was Kody Scott, his siblings were apparently adequately socialized; this is why I would classify him as a psychopath rather than a sociopath, although he exemplifies the frequent overlap between the two groups.

Suppose that Kody Scott's football-player father had started teaching his daredevil son the rudiments of that game when Kody was very small. Suppose his father had enrolled him in a Little League team and shared his triumphs and disappointments with him. What committed Kody to a life of crime early on was his discovery that he was good at it, that he could dominate other boys, beat people up, become feared and respected by his peers. What if he had learned instead that he could dominate and be respected on the football field? I think he might have learned in that context that it is more gratifying to win within the rules than by flouting them. Punishment is an inefficient means of socializing the potential psychopath, whereas pride is an incentive that works as well with him as with anyone.

2. *The Neurobehavioral Theories of Fowles and Gray.* The English psychologist Jeffrey Gray has identified in the brain what he calls the "Behavioral Inhibition System" (BIS), which is activated by cues associated with fear or with "frustrative nonreward" (not getting the expected reward) and which produces the experience of anxiety and the inhibition of ongoing behavior. The BIS organizes passive avoidance by inhibiting previously punished responses, inhibiting the child's impulse to hit someone or take something not his own or to otherwise break the rules.

Another mechanism, the Behavioral Activation System (BAS), a term introduced by the American psychologist Don Fowles, is activated by stimuli associated with reward or with escape from fear or pain. The BAS organizes approach behavior and also active avoidance, that is, behavior to escape from threat. Where freezing in place would be passive avoidance, attacking the threat or running away from it are two examples of active avoidance. Both Gray and Fowles noted that there are individual differences in the strength or reactivity of the BIS and that persons with a relatively weak BIS might show poor passive avoidance, low general anxiety, and the other characteristics of the primary psychopath. This formulation will be seen to be quite similar to my low-fear hypothesis.

Fowles and Gray have also noted that persons with an unusually strong or overreactive BAS might also manifest poor passive avoidance; that is, their normal inhibitions may often be overcome by their abnormally strong desires for the forbidden object or activity. This *secondary psychopath* appears to behave impulsively due to this failure of passive avoidance, and he is likely to get into trouble as a result. Unlike the primary psychopath, however, he is anxious during or after the commission of his crimes (assuming that he has a normal BIS) and is likely to make a poor adjustment to the stresses of prison life.

Also unlike the primary type, the secondary psychopath is likely to show anxiety, irritability, and tension because the lure of temptation leads him to select a stressful and disquieting lifestyle. Whether he would tend to be

as free of guilt and empathic feeling as the primary type will depend on the extent to which his difficult behavior as a child disrupted his parents' attempts to socialize him.

3. *Inhibitory Defect or Underendowment.* As I have already suggested, some psychopathic individuals appear to act impulsively, "without thinking," without giving themselves time to assess the situation, to appreciate the dangers, to foresee the consequences, or even to anticipate how they will feel about their action themselves when they have time to consider it. Although many young children tend to act impulsively, watchful parents

---

> # Even those with strong nervous systems can find themselves temporarily vulnerable when their protective inhibition has been exhausted by an extended period of overuse.

---

will reward more deliberate behavior and, if necessary, interrupt and punish heedless, thoughtless actions because teaching self-control is a part of the socialization process. Once again, however, self-control training is much harder with some children than with others.

Lesions in certain brain areas can cause a decrease in inhibitory control in animals and also in humans; the case of Phineas Gage is one example. Gage was the foreman of a nineteenth-century railway track crew until a construction accident drove a steel rod through his head, destroying much of his frontal lobes. A conscientious worker prior to the accident, Gage subsequently became "fitful, irreverent, indulging at times in the grossest profanity (which had not previously been his custom), manifesting but little deference for his fellows, impatient of restraint or advice when it conflicts with his desires, . . . capricious."

Neurologist A. R. Damasio and colleagues recently described a thirty-five-year-old professional man, "EVR," who was successful and happily married and "who led an impeccable social life, and was a role model to younger siblings." EVR developed a brain tumor that required surgical excision of the frontal orbital (behind the eyes) brain cortex on both sides. After recovery his IQ and memory test scores were uniformly in the superior range, and his performance on several other tests designed to detect frontal lobe damage was entirely normal. EVR's social conduct, however, "was profoundly affected by his brain injury. Over a brief period of time, he entered disastrous business ventures (one of which led to predictable bankruptcy), and was divorced twice (the second marriage, which was to a prostitute, only lasted 6 months). He has been unable to hold any paying job since the time of surgery, and his plans for future activity are defective." Previously a model citizen, EVR now meets criteria for primary psychopathy.

These findings do not, of course, demonstrate that all—or even many—primary psychopaths have lesions or qualitative defects in their frontal cortex areas; they demonstrate merely that frontal lesions can produce a syndrome very similar to primary psychopathy.

4. *The Hysterical Psychopath.* Individuals with a special talent for Freudian repression may be able to avoid fearful apprehension or escape the pangs of guilt simply by repressing awareness of distressing stimuli, including memories or ideas that elicit these unpleasant feelings. Repression involves an inhibition not of overt responding but of the processes of perception, recall, and cognitive processing. All of us have this ability to shut out or attenuate painful or distracting stimuli, whether from internal or external sources, but as is true of all abilities, this one is distributed in varying degrees among different people. Those who are underendowed with this inhibitory capacity, who have what Ivan Pavlov called "weak nervous systems" (or defective "shields," in the idiom of *Star Trek*), are especially vulnerable to the slings and arrows of outrageous fortune and seek sheltered and protective environments.

Even those with strong nervous systems can find themselves temporarily vulnerable (shields down) when their protective inhibition has been exhausted by an extended period of overuse. Most people would agree that they are more irritable, more distractable, more sensitive to pain, and the like, at the end of a tiring day than when they are well rested. One of my colleagues for many years conducted studies of the effect of noise on human hearing and hired healthy undergraduates to sit in a large room filled with loudspeakers that intermittently produced extended blasts of 120-decibel white noise. The subjects could read or try to relax during their six-hour session except while undergoing periodic hearing tests. Subjects willing to tolerate these conditions were presumably self-selected for having strong nervous systems; they were healthy and resilient young people who felt relatively invulnerable to strong stimulation. However, a common report of these subjects was that, after completing a day's stint in this simulated boiler factory, they felt irritable, nervous, unable to relax, and overresponsive to noises; they had difficulty sleeping that first night.

A child unusually well-endowed with such inhibitory capacity might grow up to look very like a fearless, guilt-free psychopath, not because of a lack of these emotional reactions but, rather, because of the ability to shut out or block these feelings—as long as the shields were up.

One such person was Donna, whom I met in 1953 when I was a graduate student in the Psychiatry Depart-

ment of the Minneapolis General Hospital. At that time the hospital boasted one full-time psychologist, a part-time psychiatrist (the Chief, who came around three mornings a week to do rounds and to push the button on the electroconvulsive shock machine), and lots of very crazy patients. In the summer of 1953, the psychologist went off for a three-month tour of Europe while I took her place, trying not to look too foolish to the veteran psychiatric nurses who really ran the place. Donna was a tall, thin nineteen-year-old made by the same firm that created the actress Audrey Hepburn. It was hard to believe that Donna was in the psychiatric ward on referral from the county jail; she had been picked up with a man trying to burglarize a pharmacy for drugs. It was almost impossible to believe that Donna was a heroin addict who had spent the previous three months in Chicago, working as a prostitute to support her pimp and her habit.

You must picture a shy, tremulous, soft-spoken young woman, demure and vulnerable, who could hardly bring herself to speak of these experiences, just as I could hardly imagine her enacting them. The court agreed to put Donna on probation contingent on my taking her as a patient, and the head of psychiatry at the University Hospital agreed to have her transferred there when the summer was over. I saw her daily for the six weeks that she remained an inpatient, then once a week for several months, then intermittently over the next fifteen years.

During those years Donna completed a kind of rake's progress in reverse, from prostitute and heroin addict to becoming the star turn at a local lesbian bar to a serious relationship with a black Army lieutenant and finally to a reasonably stable marriage with a young musician. There was much backsliding along the way, binges of wild self-indulgence, impromptu romances, unplanned trips with new acquaintances. I would not hear from her for months at a time, and then I would hear a faint, frightened voice on the phone: "Dr. Lykken? Can I see you?" I would pry out of her a summary of what she had been up to this time, and always the protagonist of those wild adventures seemed unconnected to the farouche and vulnerable girl who was reluctantly recounting them. It was hard to believe that the person I had come to know was capable of doing the things that other Donna did; my Donna could barely talk about them, much less do them. I saw the other Donna just once, when she dropped in for an unscheduled social visit; it was the only time I saw her laugh or heard her swear. Having burned thus fitfully but at both ends, Donna's candle guttered out; she died of uterine cancer when she was thirty-six.

It is noteworthy that alleged examples of multiple personality, such as the patient described in Cleckley and Thigpen's *The Three Faces of Eve*, often include at least one personality, like Eve Black, one of Eve's three "faces," who appears to be a psychopath. (I doubt that Donna was a true multiple since in her timid state she seemed fully aware of what had happened in her bold state, and vice versa.) It may also be relevant that hysterical personality disorder may have a familial linkage to psychopathy, occurring in higher-than-normal frequency among the relatives of psychopaths. It is also thought that hysterics often are the sex or marriage partners of psychopaths, due to the former's tendency to repress awareness of the dangers of such liaisons, but this assortative-mating hypothesis has not been systematically investigated.

Sociopathy and Crime

Thus, when it comes to the homicidal violence of the contemporary inner city, we are dealing with very bad boys from very bad homes, kids who in most cases have suffered or witnessed violent crimes in the past. These juveniles are not criminally depraved because they are economically deprived; they are totally depraved because they are completely unsocialized.

—J. J. DiIulio, Jr., 1995

Is crime increasing? The U.S. Department of Justice manages two statistical programs for measuring crime, and they paint very different pictures, one reassuring and the other, perhaps, more realistic. The National Crime Victimization Survey (NCVS), begun in 1973, interviews all persons aged twelve or over in a stratified sample of U.S. households, asking who had been victims of various specified crimes. In 1992, for example, most teenagers and adults in 52,000 households nationwide were interviewed, in person or by phone, some 108,000 people altogether. The victimization data suggest that the rate of aggravated assaults (the most common of violent crimes) increased by only 6 percent from 1973 to 1992. Victimization by theft actually decreased by some 35 percent. Although most Americans believe that their homes and streets are more at risk with each passing year, the truth is otherwise—if we can believe the Bureau of Justice Statistics.

The other federal crime-counting program, the FBI's Uniform Crime Report (UCR), provides data on crimes actually reported to the police and then, by local and state police agencies, reported to the FBI. According to the FBI data, the rate of aggravated assaults has increased substantially, more than doubling over the same twenty-year period. Most citizens are inclined to believe, with the FBI, that crime rates have gone up sharply since the 1970s. This is presumably why the U.S. Congress is appropriating still more tens of billions of dollars to combat crime. Citizens, of course, as well as politicians, can be wrong in the impressions gleaned from news reports. I think, however, that they are right in this case, that the FBI statistics tell the truest story in this important instance.

Part of the explanation for the discrepancy between the victimization and FBI trendlines was pointed out in a recent study of violence in the United States by the National Research Council (NRC). The problem with victim surveys is that they undersample those people in the population who are most vulnerable to violent crime. Victims who are currently in jail or in the hospital, and also those who are transients or homeless, do not turn up in household surveys, but if they have been victims of serious crimes, that event is likely to be known to the police. More important, in our inner cities, where crime and violence is most rampant, there are housing projects and, indeed, whole neighborhoods where the survey interviewers are unlikely to venture. Most of the serious crimes tabulated by the FBI occur in urban ghettos, and this is where crime rates have been going up. These same areas are undersampled by NCVS interviewers, and this explains much of the difference between the UCR and NCVS trend lines. The NCVS data tell us about crime in the vast middle-class community where crime rates have been relatively level, while the NRC data—and the nightly television news reports—give us the whole picture, middle-class and also ghetto crime. In 1995, Minneapolis set a new record for number of homicides, but more than two-thirds of those victims (and of their killers) were young, black males, members of the underclass.

The rates of violent crime among the middle class *should have* decreased substantially over the past twenty years for two reasons: (1) The proportion of the population who are elderly has increased, while (2) the proportion of young males, the group that furnishes most criminal predators, has sharply decreased due to the aging of the baby boomers. The people at highest risk to be victims of violent crime are the young; in the United States, those aged fifteen to twenty-four, for example, are ten to fifteen times more likely to be assaulted, robbed, or murdered than are persons aged sixty-five or older. From 1973 to 1992, the proportion of relatively protected seniors in the population increased more than 20 percent, while the proportion of young males aged fifteen to twenty-four—the potential perpetrators—decreased nearly 30 percent.

If we divided the total number of joggers by the total population each year from 1973, it is likely that the jogging-rate trend might also be surprisingly flat because there are proportionately fewer young people now than in 1973 and most of the growing proportion of seniors are at low risk for jogging. But who can doubt that there are relatively more young and middle-aged joggers out there now than twenty-odd years ago? And there are relatively more—many more—violent criminals out there now as well.

The U.S. murder rate is an especially reliable statistic since nearly all murders are reported to the police, who report them in turn to the FBI. The trend since 1973 in murders coincides nicely with the victimization data for other violent crimes; the murder rate has increased only slightly over the past two decades. But in 1973, the murder rate was double what it had been in 1960 (in New

York City, the increase was 400 percent), largely because the proportion of the U.S. population who were males in the most violent age group increased by a third from 1960 to 1973 as the post–World War II baby boomers passed through the ages of highest risk. In 1960, most murders were family affairs, spouse killing spouse and the like. Since then, as the relative numbers of unsocialized young males increased, the number of "stranger murders" has increased apace until now, in our cities, for every victim murdered by a family member there are four persons murdered by strangers.

Beginning about 1980, as the fraction of the population in the high-risk age group started to return to 1960 levels and below, the murder rate should have decreased again—but it did not; the murder rate has actually increased somewhat during the past ten years. Although the proportion of the total population who are young males has decreased substantially in this period, the rate at which those in this murderous age group have been arrested for homicide increased 55 percent from 1973 to 1992. Meanwhile, the proportion of seniors, who are relatively protected from violent crime, has increased by 20 percent. The next male you encounter on the street will be about 30 percent less likely to be aged fifteen to twenty-four than in 1973, but if he is in that age group, he will be 55 percent more likely to be—or to become—a murderer.

The juvenile crime rate, violent crimes committed by offenders under age eighteen, also has increased in recent years. The number of juveniles arrested for aggravated assault in the United States per 100,000 juveniles in the surveyed population increased more than 130 percent from 1973 to 1992 according to FBI age-specific arrest-rate figures. Could this frightening trend be a statistical artifact? Perhaps, but only if we assume that the police for some reason failed to locate and arrest more than half of the juvenile perpetrators in 1973 but not in recent years. More than 200,000 boys between twelve and seventeen years old were arrested in 1992 in the U.S. for murder, forcible rape, aggravated assault, or robbery. By now, most of them are back on the streets with long careers of active predation still ahead of them.

Reared without Fathers

The most urgent domestic challenge facing the United States at the close of the twentieth century is the recreation of fatherhood as a vital social role for men. At stake is nothing less than the success of the American experiment. For unless we reverse the trend of fatherlessness, no other set of accomplishments—not economic growth or prison construction or welfare reform or better schools—will succeed in arresting the decline of child well-being and the spread of male violence. To tolerate the trend of fatherlessness is to accept the inevitability of continued societal recession.

—David Blankenhorn, 1995

The majority of these young criminals are not psychopaths, however. Psychopaths are relatively rare; they can be dangerous, although many are not violent, and I believe that some of them could have been transmuted from a major liability into a useful asset to society by truly skillful parenting. Most recidivistic criminals are *sociopaths*, and sociopaths are just as dangerous and, because of their numbers, an even greater social liability than psychopaths. They are why we lock our doors, stay off the streets at night, carry Mace, and invest in guns and guard dogs and electronic surveillance systems. We are currently producing sociopaths with factory-like efficiency in the United States. Although we do not know how to cure sociopathy, I think we can figure out what needs to be done to prevent it.

Our species was designed by natural selection to live relatively amicably in extended-family groups. Just as we evolved an innate readiness for learning language, so we evolved a proclivity for learning and obeying basic social rules, for nurturing our children and helping our neighbors, and for pulling our own weight in the group effort for survival. But like the ability to acquire language, our innate readiness to become socialized in these ways must be elicited, developed, and practiced during childhood, otherwise we would remain permanently mute and also, perhaps, permanently unsocialized.

In her novel *Breathing Lessons*, Anne Tyler imagines the thoughts of a new mother:

> Wait. Are they going to let me just walk off with him? I don't know beans about babies! I don't have a license to do this.... I mean you're given all these lessons for the unimportant things—piano-playing, typing. You're given years and years of lessons in how to balance equations, which Lord knows you will never have to do in normal life. But what about parenthood? ... Before you can drive a car you need a state-approved course of instruction, but driving a car is nothing, nothing, compared to... raising up a new human being.

In ancestral times, as in traditional societies that still exist today, parents had help from the extended family. With all those uncles and aunts and older children keeping an eye on them, it was hard for the youngsters to get away with much. Moreover, in those societies, this sharing of parental responsibilities provided training in parenting for children as they grew up. In what we call the developed societies of today, although parenting is widely regarded as one of the most difficult as well as the most important of adult responsibilities, it is a task we expect most young people to assume with no training whatever. If we were truly "developed," every high school would include a required course emphasizing the rigors and responsibilities of parenthood and every community college would offer practicum courses for new parents or parents-to-be.

Traditional societies in which children are socialized communally, in the manner to which our species is evolutionarily adapted, have little intramural crime, and any persistent offender is likely to be someone whose innate temperament made him unusually difficult to socialize. These are the people I call psychopaths. Our modern society now entrusts this basic responsibility of socializing children either to the two biological parents collaborating as a team or, with increasing frequency, to single parents, usually single mothers, often single mothers who are immature or unsocialized themselves.

The feral products of indifferent, incompetent, or overburdened parents—the sociopaths—are growing rapidly in number because the proportion of this nation's children who are being reared by (or, rather, domiciled with) such parents is increasing rapidly. Males aged fifteen to twenty-five are responsible for 60 percent of all violent crime in the United States. The proportion of those in this age group who were born out-of-wedlock increased from 4 percent in 1973 to 12 percent in 1992; the proportion whose parents divorced prior to the boy's fifth birthday also tripled over the same period. Most of the first group and many of the second were raised without significant participation of their biological fathers. We know that about 70 percent of the adults and juveniles currently incarcerated were reared without their biological fathers, and we can compute from this that fatherless young males are about *seven times* more likely to become first delinquent and then criminal than are boys reared by both biological parents. The proportion of the high-risk age group whose fathers planted their seed and then moved on has been growing exponentially since the early 1970s.

This is, incidentally, an added reason for believing the crime trends reported by the UCR; if boys reared without fathers are therefore seven times more likely to become criminal, and if the proportion of young males reared without fathers has trebled in the last twenty years, then surely the crime rate has increased, as the UCR indicates, rather than stayed level, as certain ostrich-like commentators would have us believe.

Is There a Solution?

> The idea that every woman has an inherent right to have a child, regardless of other considerations, recurs in every upsurge of feminism. I do not consider this a viable option.
>
> —Margaret Mead, 1979

Causing the existence of a human being is one of the most responsible actions in the range of human life.

> To undertake this responsibility—to bestow a life which may be either a curse or a blessing—unless the being on whom it is to be bestowed will have at least the ordinary chances of a desirable existence, is a crime against that being.
>
> —John Stuart Mill, 1859

Because there is no cure for adult sociopathy, the only useful option is prevention. Gerald Patterson, at the Oregon Social Learning Center, has shown that at least some high-risk parents can be trained to competently socialize their children, but the process is laborious and only a few of those who need such training can be expected to participate. A system of professionalized foster care will be required to salvage most of these children, but no such system currently exists on the scale required. In many states, statutes prevent transracial adoption or foster care and child-protection workers are encouraged to return abused or neglected children to their biological mother or, if the mother is in prison or hopelessly addicted, to the grandparent who failed to socialize that mother in the first place.

Providing healthy and successful rearing environments for the millions of American children now being incompetently reared will be very expensive, but not providing them will be more expensive still. In his important new book, *Licensing Parents,* child psychiatrist Jack Westman estimates that each typical sociopath will cost society about $3 million over the course of his lifetime. That means that each million potential sociopaths now out there on the production line of our American crime factory will end up costing us $3 trillion by the middle of the next century.

The only long-term solution, I believe, is Westman's proposal that we require prospective parents to meet the same minimum requirements that we now expect of couples hoping to adopt a baby: a mature man and woman, sufficiently committed to parenthood to be married to each other, who are self-supporting and neither criminal nor actively psychotic. Such a licensure requirement would offend those who believe that people have an inalienable right to produce as many babies as they wish, no matter how incompetent, immature, abusive, or depraved they may be. Because I am more concerned about the rights of those helpless babies than I am about the alleged procreative rights of their feckless parents—and about the lives of crime, violence, and social dependency that most of these babies are doomed to lead when they grow up—I shall testify in support of a parental licensure bill to be introduced at the next session of the Minnesota State Legislature. The only sanction proposed in this bill for unlicensed parents who produce a child is periodic visits by child-protection caseworkers who will do an annual audit of each child's physical, social, and educational progress. By the time my own grandchildren have grown up, I believe that the incidence of delinquency, school dropout, teenage pregnancy, substance abuse, and other social pathology will be so much greater among these at-risk children than among the children of licensed parents that Minnesotans and their legislative representatives will recognize the need to take one further step. That step, I suggest, should be to take custody of babies born to unlicensed mothers, before bonding occurs, and to place them for adoption or permanent care by professionally trained and supervised foster parents. The result should be a society in which all children are reared by an adult couple, self-supporting and socialized themselves, and thus—unlike millions of American babies today—with a real chance to achieve the American birthright of life, liberty, and the pursuit of happiness.

SUGGESTED FURTHER READING

D. Blankenhorn. *Fatherless America: Confronting Our Most Urgent Social Problem*. New York: Basic Books, 1995.

H. Cleckley. *The Mask of Sanity*. Rev. ed. St. Louis, Mo.: C. V. Mosby, 1982.

R. D. Hare. *Without Conscience: The Disturbing World of the Psychopaths among Us*. New York: Pocket Books, 1993.

D. T. Lykken. *The Antisocial Personalities*. Mahwah, N.J.: Erlbaum, 1995.

G. R. Patterson, J. B. Reid, and T. J. Dishion. *Antisocial Boys*. Eugene, Oreg.: Castalia, 1992.

S. Shakur (AKA Monster Kody Scott). *Monster: The Autobiography of an L.A. Gang Member*. New York: Atlantic Monthly Press, 1993.

J. C. Westman. *Licensing Parents: Can We Prevent Child Abuse and Neglect?* New York: Plenum Press, 1994.

J. Q. Wilson and R. J. Herrnstein. *Crime and Human Nature*. New York: Simon & Schuster, 1985.

Portions of this article were taken, with permission, from my book *The Antisocial Personalities* (Mahwah, N.J.: Erlbaum Associates, 1995).

David T. Lykken is a professor of psychology at the University of Minnesota, where he is director of the Minnesota Twin Registry. He is a past president of the Society for Psychophysiological Research, and in 1990 he received the American Psychological Association's Award for Distinguished Contribution to Psychology in the Public Interest. Dr. Lykken is the author of A Tremor in the Blood: Uses and Abuses of the Lie Detector *(1981) and of* The Antisocial Personalities *(1995).*

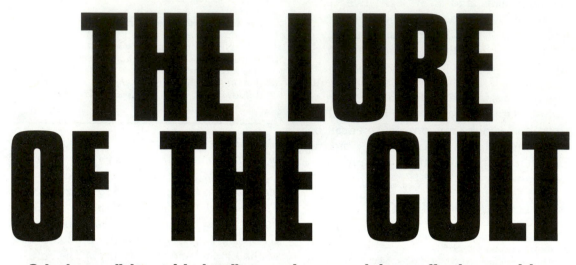

THE LURE OF THE CULT

Out where religion and junk culture meet, some weird new offspring are rising

By RICHARD LACAYO

ON SATURDAY, MARCH 22, AROUND the time that the disciples of Heaven's Gate were just beginning their quiet and meticulous self-extinction, a small cottage in the French Canadian village of St.-Casimir exploded into flames. Inside the burning house were five people, all disciples of the Order of the Solar Temple. Since 1994, 74 members of that group have gone to their death in Canada, Switzerland and France. In St.-Casimir the dead were Didier Quèze, 39, a baker, his wife Chantale Goupillot, 41, her mother and two others of the faithful. At the last minute the Quèze children, teenagers named Tom, Fanie and Julien opted out. After taking sedatives offered by the adults, they closeted themselves in a garden shed to await their parents' death. Police later found them, stunned but alive.

For two days and nights before the blast, the grownups had pursued a remarkable will to die. Over and over they fiddled with three tanks of propane that were hooked to an electric burner and a timing device. As many as four times, they swallowed sedatives, then arranged themselves in a cross around a queen-size bed, only to rise in bleary frustration when the detonator fizzled. Finally, they blew themselves to kingdom come. For them that would be the star Sirius, in the constellation Canis Major, nine light-years from Quebec. According to the doctrines of the Solar Temple, they will reign there forever, weightless and serene.

Quite a mess. But no longer perhaps a complete surprise. Eighteen years after Jonestown, suicide cults have entered the category of horrors that no longer qualify as shocks. Like plane crashes and terrorist attacks, they course roughly for a while along the nervous system, then settle into that part of the brain reserved for bad but familiar news. As the bodies are tagged and the families contacted, we know what the experts will say before they say it. That in times of upheaval and uncertainty, people seek out leaders with power and charisma. That the established churches are too fainthearted to satisfy the wilder kinds of spiritual hunger. That the self-denial and regimentation of cult life will soften up anyone for the kill.

The body count at Rancho Santa Fe is a reminder that this conventional wisdom falls short. These are the waning years of the 20th century, and out on the margins of spiritual life there's a strange phosphorescence. As predicted, the approach of the year 2000 is coaxing all the crazies out of the woodwork. They bring with them a twitchy hybrid of spirituality and pop obsession. Part Christian, part Asian mystic, part Gnostic, part *X-Files*, it mixes immemorial longings with the latest in trivial sentiments. When it all dissolves in overheated computer chat and harmless New Age vaporings, who cares? But sometimes it matters, for both the faithful and the people who care about them. Sometimes it makes death a consummation devoutly, all too devoutly, to be desired.

So the worst legacy of Heaven's Gate may yet be this: that 39 people sacrificed themselves to the new millennial kitsch. That's the cultural by-product in which spiritual yearnings are captured in New Age gibberish, then edged with the glamour of sci-fi and the consolations of a toddler's bedtime. In the Heaven's Gate cosmology, where talk about the end of the world alternates with tips for shrugging off your fleshly container, the cosmic and the lethal, the enraptured and the childish come together. Is it any surprise then that it led to an infantile apocalypse, one part applesauce, one part phenobarbital? Look at the Heaven's Gate Website. Even as it warns about the end of the world, you find a drawing of a space creature imagined through insipid pop dust-jacket conventions: aerodynamic cranium, big doe eyes, beatific smile. We have seen the Beast of the Apocalypse. It's Bambi in a tunic.

By now, psychologists have arrived at a wonderfully elastic profile of the people who attach themselves to these intellectual chain gangs: just about anybody. Applicants require only an unsatisfied spiritual longing, a condition apt to strike anyone at some point in life. Social status is no indicator of susceptibility and no defense against it. For instance, while many of the dead at Jonestown were poor, the Solar Temple favors the carriage trade. Its disciples have included the wife and son of the founder of the Vuarnet sunglass company. The Branch Davidians at Waco came from many walks of life. And at Rancho Santa Fe they were paragons of the entrepreneurial class, so well organized they died in shifts.

The U.S. was founded by religious dissenters. It remains to this day a nation where faith of whatever kind is a force to be reckoned with. But a free proliferation of raptures is upon us, with doctrines that mix the sacred and the tacky. The approach of the year 2000 has swelled the ranks of the fearful and credulous. On the Internet, cults multiply in service to Ashtar and Sananda, deities with names you could find at a perfume counter, or to extraterrestrials—the Zeta Reticuli, the Draconian Reptoids—who sound like softball teams at the *Star Wars* cantina. Carl Raschke, a cult specialist at the University of Denver, predicts "an explosion of bizarre and dangerous" cults. "Millennial fever will be on a lot of minds."

As so often in religious thinking, the sky figures importantly in the New Apocalypse. For centuries the stars have been where the meditations of religion, science and the occult all converged. Now enter Comet Hale-Bopp. In an otherwise orderly and predictable cosmos, where the movement of stars was charted confidently by Egyptians and Druids, the appearance of a comet, an astronomical oddity, has long been an opportunity for panic. When Halley's comet returned in 1910, an Oklahoma religious sect, the Select Followers, had to be stopped by the police from sacrificing a virgin. In the case of Hale-Bopp, for months the theory that it might be a shield for an approaching UFO has roiled the excitable on talk radio and in Internet chat rooms like—what else?—*alt.conspiracy.*

ASTRONOMICAL CHARTS MAY ALSO have helped determine the timing of the Heaven's Gate suicides. They apparently began on the weekend of March 22–23, around the time that Hale-Bopp got ready to make its closest approach to Earth. That weekend also witnessed a full moon and, in parts of the U.S., a lunar eclipse. For good measure it included Palm Sunday, the beginning of the Christian Holy Week. Shrouds placed on the corpses were purple, the color of Passiontide, or, for New Agers, the color of those who have passed to a higher plane.

The Heaven's Gate philosophy added its astronomical trappings to a core of weirdly adulterated Christianity. Then came a whiff of Gnosticism, the old heresy that regarded the body as a burden from which the fretful soul longs to be freed. From the time of St. Paul, some elements of Christianity have indulged an impulse to subjugate the body. But like Judaism and Islam, it ultimately teaches reverence for life and rejects suicide as a shortcut to heaven.

The modern era of cultism dates to the 1970s, when the free inquiry of the previous decade led quite a few exhausted seekers into

---

JONESTOWN, 1978

At the Peoples Temple, more than 900 cult members died because Jim Jones decided it was time

---

intellectual surrender. Out from the rubble of the countercultures came such groups as the Children of God and the Divine Light Mission, est and the Church of Scientology, the robotic political followers of Lyndon LaRouche and the Unification Church of the Rev. Sun Myung Moon. On Nov. 18, 1978, the cultism of the '70s arrived at its dark crescendo in Jonestown, Guyana, where more than 900 members of Jim Jones' Peoples Temple died at his order, most by suicide.

Since then two developments have fostered the spread of cultism. One is the end of communism. Whatever the disasters of Marxism, at least it provided an outlet for utopian longings. Now that universalist impulses have one less way to expend themselves, religious enthusiasms of whatever character take on a fresh appeal. And even Russia, with a rich tradition of fevered spirituality and the new upheavals of capitalism, is dealing with modern cults.

Imported sects like the Unification Church have seen an opening there. Homegrown groups have also sprung up. One surrounds a would-be messiah named Vissarion. With his flowing dark hair, wispy beard and a sing-song voice full of aphorisms, he has managed to attract about 5,000 followers to his City of the Sun. Naturally it's in Siberia, near the isolated town of Minusinsk. According to reports in the Russian press, Vissarion is a former traffic cop who was fired for drinking. In his public appearances, he speaks of "the coming end" and instructs believers that suicide is not a sin. Russian authorities are worried that he may urge his followers on a final binge. In the former Soviet lands, law enforcement has handled cults in the old Russian way, with truncheons and bars. Some have been banned. Last year a court in Kiev gave prison terms to leaders of the White Brotherhood, including its would-be messiah, Marina Tsvigun.

The second recent development in cultism is strictly free market and technological. For the quick recruitment of new congregations, the Internet is a magical opportunity. It's persuasive, far reaching and clandestine. And for better and worse, it frees the imagination from the everyday world. "I think that the online context can remove people from a proper understanding of reality and of the proper tests for truth," says Douglas Groothuis, a theologian and author of *The Soul in Cyberspace.* "How do you verify peoples' identity? How do you connect 'online' with real life?"

"The Internet allows different belief systems to meet and mate," adds Stephen O'Leary, author of *Arguing the Apocalypse,* which examines end-of-the-world religions. "What you get is this millennial stew, a mixture of many different belief systems." Which is the very way that the latest kinds of cultism have flourished. As it happens, that's also the way free thought develops generally. Real ideas sometimes rise from the muck, which is why free societies willingly put up with so much muck.

In Gustave Flaubert's story *A Simple Heart,* an old French woman pines for a beloved nephew, a sailor who has disappeared in Cuba. Later she acquires a parrot. Because it comes from the Americas, it reminds her of him. When the parrot dies, she has it stuffed and set in her room among her items of religious veneration. On her deathbed, she has a vision of heaven. The clouds part to reveal an enormous parrot.

The lessons there for Heaven's Gate? The religious impulse sometimes thrived on false sentiment, emotional need and cultural fluff. In its search for meaning, the mind is apt to go down some wrong paths and to mistake its own reflection for the face of God. Much of the time, those errors are nothing more than episodes of the human comedy. Occasionally they become something worse. This is what happened at Rancho Santa Fe, where foolish notions hardened into fatal certainties. In the arrival of Comet Hale-Bopp, the cult members saw a signal that their lives would end soon. There are many things about which they were badly mistaken. But on that one intuition, they made sure they were tragically correct. **—Reported by Andrew Meier/Moscow, Richard N. Ostling/New York and Andrew Purvis/Toronto**

Work Work Work Work!

It's taking over our lives—invading our homes, haunting our holidays, showing up for dinner. **Should we care?**

by Mark Hunter

YOU'VE HEARD THE JOKE BY NOW, BUT IT RINGS SO true that it bears retelling: A guy reads a headline saying "Clinton creates 8 million jobs," and he cracks wearily, "Yeah, and I got three of 'em."

That gag may be the epitaph of the 1990s. In a very real sense, all of us—not just the 13 percent of us working two or three part-time jobs to survive—have three jobs. There's the work we do for a living, the work we do for ourselves (in many cases, to make sure we still can make a living tomorrow), plus the combination of housework and caregiving. Researchers differ on how much time we put into each of these categories, but most agree on one crucial point: The total keeps growing. As my brother Richard, a vice president of the Gartner Group, a high-tech advisory company, puts it: "It's like trying to fit a size 12 into a size eight shoe."

By far the biggest chunk of our time still goes to the work we do for a living. A survey of some 3,000 employees nationwide by the Families and Work Institute (FWI), a New York nonprofit organization that addresses work and family issues, discovered that over the past two decades, the average time spent at a full-time job has risen from 43.6 to 47.1 hours per week. Over a year, that comes to about four extra weeks—the same figure that Juliet B. Schor arrived at in her controversial 1991 study, *The Overworked American*, one of the first books to document what she called "the decline of leisure."

This fact hit home for me when I returned to the U.S. in 1996 after a decade abroad. I began to notice that not one of the other seven people in my office left their desks at lunchtime, the way folks used to. Throw in that traditional half-hour lunch break, and that's another two-and-a-half hours every week that many people give to work—or about three more weeks per year. Likewise, the Bureau of Labor Statistics reports that since 1985 paid vacation time has declined, and so has the average time that workers take off sick. Not surprisingly, more than one third of the people in the FWI survey said that they "often or very often feel used up at the end of the workday." It's true that some researchers, like John Robinson, a sociology professor at the University of Maryland, argue that it's mainly the well-off among us who are working more, as a matter of choice, and that on average our leisure time has increased. But that's not what I see all around me.

Simultaneously, the old line between work life and private life is vanishing. In trying to understand why employees often refused to take advantage of maternity leave and flex-time, sociologist Arlie Hochschild, author of *The Time Bind*, discovered, to her amazement, that "work has become a form of 'home' and home has become 'work.' "She reports that many people now see their jobs as "a more appreciative, personal sort of social world" compared with their homes, where in the age of divorce and double careers, "the emotional demands have become more baffling and complex." When I interviewed 40 men about their work-life tradeoffs, every one of them said that it was easier to be a success on the job than in his personal relationships. Is it just a coincidence that hit TV shows like *Taxi* or *Murphy Brown* substituted the workplace "family" for the domestic setting of *The Brady Bunch*?

Work has penetrated the home in another potent way, notes market researcher Judith Langer, who has interviewed several hundred people on this subject over the past ten years: "People feel that what they're required to do at work has spilled over into the rest of their lives—reading, keeping up with trends in their fields, keeping up with e-mail and voice mail. We had a guy come into a focus group carrying all the publications that had hit his desk that day and complain, 'Monday weighs 20 pounds.' "

Personal technology has turned what once were hobbies into jobs: When my brother goes home from the office, he fires up his PC and checks the online orders for his self-produced harmonica records. And when the

 From *Modern Maturity*, May/June 1999, pp. 35-49. © 1999 by Mark Hunter. Reprinted by permission.

The distinction between work and leisure no longer exists

one third of Americans with managerial or professional jobs leave home, work follows them on a cell phone, pager, or modem. This past winter I received numerous business-related e-mail messages from an executive who was on a hiking trip deep in the mountains of Utah. (Emergency rescue crews have reported finding stranded hikers in the wilderness who had filled their backpacks with a portable computer, but forgotten to bring enough food and water.) The next time a cell phone rings in a restaurant at dinner-time, notice how many people automatically reach for theirs, because it might be a business call. In the 1960s and 1970s, stress experts called this kind of thing "multiphasic behavior," otherwise known as doing several tasks at once. Nowadays we call it efficiency.

Ironically, the Baby Boomers, who came of age shouting their contempt for the man in the gray flannel suit, have done more than any other generation to erase the line between work and private life. Among the first to spot this paradox was Alvin Toffler in his 1980 futurist manifesto, *The Third Wave*. While most observers took those in the hippie movement for a bunch of unwashed, lazy bums, Toffler realized that they were really the prototype of a new kind of worker, the "prosumer"—people who, like frontier farmers, produce a share of what they consume, from home medicine to clothing (my fiancee creates a wardrobe every two years) to home-baked bread, instead of buying it all in the marketplace. "Once we recognize that much of our so-called leisure time is in fact spent producing goods and services for our own use," he noted, "then the old distinction between work and leisure falls apart."

Just as they turned the home into a workplace, Boomers redefined the ideal workplace as a playground. At the end of the 1970s, pollster Daniel Yankelovich found that this "New Breed" of Americans believed that work should be first and foremost a means to self-fulfillment—unlike their parents, who were taught by the Depression that any job that pays a secure wage was worth keeping. When Catalyst, a New York nonprofit organization that seeks to advance women in business, surveyed more than 800 members of two-career couples about what mattered most to them on the job, at the top of the list were emotional benefits such as supportive management, being able to work on their own, and having control over their product.

Our careers now start earlier and end later, reversing a trend that reached its peak after World War II, when child labor virtually disappeared and retirement became a right. These days, so many teenagers have jobs—and

as a result are cutting back on sleep, meals, and home-work—that the National Research Council has called for strict new limits on the hours they're allowed to work. At the same time, the number of people 55 and older who still are in the labor force has increased by 6 million since 1950, and most of that increase is women. The Department of Labor projects that this number is going to grow by another 6 million by the year 2006.

None of this was supposed to happen. Only a generation ago, the conventional wisdom among economists was that America was turning into an "affluent society," in which ever more efficient technology would produce an abundance of wealth that we could enjoy with less and less labor. Science-fiction novelists like Kurt Vonnegut imagined a society in which a tiny elite ran the show, while everyone else sat around bored. In their vision, work would no longer be a burden, but a privilege for the happy few.

There are a lot of reasons why things didn't turn out quite that way. One is the Vietnam War, which heated the American economy to the boiling point just as the oil shocks of the 1970s arrived—a combination that led to double-digit inflation and sapped the value of wages. Then successive waves of recession, mergers, and downsizing crashed through the American economy during the '80s. With few exceptions, one of the surest ways to raise a company's stock price—and along with it the value of its executives' stock options—was to fire a piece of its workforce. (Fortunately, downsizing appears to be losing steam, as Wall Street begins to suspect it as a desperate attempt to make a company's bottom line look good in the short term.) Gradually, overtime pay replaced wage increases as the main way to stay ahead of the bills.

The Baby Boom played a role here, too. With so many Boomers competing for jobs, they became cheap for employers: "For the first time in recent American history," marvels Landon Y. Jones in *Great Expectations: America and the Baby Boom Generation*, "the relative earnings of college graduates *declined*." In order to maintain or, in many cases to surpass, the lifestyles of their parents—more Baby Boomers now own homes and, on average, bigger homes than Americans did in the 1950s—they have gone deeply into debt. About one fourth of the average family's income now goes to pay various creditors, more than in any previous generation.

Just as the feminist revolution was urging women to do something with their lives besides raise kids and clean house, it became difficult for the average family to make ends meet without two incomes. Today, in nearly four out of five couples—compared with one out of five in 1950—both partners are in the labor force, with women working nearly as many hours for pay as men. One positive result is that since the late 1970s men have taken over a steadily growing (though still smaller) share of the childcare and household chores—nearly two hours' worth per day—that used to be considered women's work.

Yet even visionary feminists like Dorothy Dinnerstein, who predicted this shift in her landmark 1976 book, *The Mermaid and the Minotaur*, did not foresee that it would also have a negative impact on our intimate lives. The Internet site BabyCenter recently polled roughly 2,000 of its new-mother visitors on whether they did or would return to work after their child was born. Two out of three survey participants said that they would go back to work within six months, but only one out of six said that she found the move "satisfying"; twice as many called it "wrenching." Men are also feeling the pinch. "I have absolutely no time for myself or my friends," a married male executive and father complained to a Catalyst researcher. "Not enough time for us as a couple, and even the extended family say they don't see us enough."

Work is focusing us to constantly learn new ways of working

In previous decades, surveys showed that the biggest source of problems for married couples was money; now, when both partners are asked what is the biggest challenge they face, the majority of two-career couples answer "too little time." Not surprisingly, a growing number of leading-edge companies now offer working couples flexible schedules, expanded parental leave, and other benefits that allow their employees to reconcile their jobs with their personal lives.

Paradoxically, the same technology that was supposed to make us all wealthy loafers has contributed to the work-life squeeze. Computers and the changes they wrought have eliminated entire categories of jobs—when was the last time, for example, you talked to a human operator, instead of an automated phone tree, when you called a big company? In his book *The End of Work*, Jeremy Rifkin warned that this trend would end by puffing nearly all of us out of a job—a neat Doomsday inversion of the old "affluent society" prophecy. But many economists argue that new jobs will be created by new technology, just as they always have been. Perhaps, but the pressures to adapt to these rapid technological changes are greater than ever. Computers have even changed the rhythm of our work, giving us more of a say in how the job is done because technology-savvy frontline personnel become responsible for decisions that managers used to make, as they constantly feed information up and down the line. The same applies to managers, whose desktop PCs, equipped with software that does everything from keeping appointments to formatting business letters and writing contracts, have largely replaced personal secretaries. We get more control—which

happens to be one of the key measures of job satisfaction—but in return we end up giving more of ourselves to the job.

Beyond requiring us to put in longer hours for fear of losing our jobs, work is changing us in positive ways. In particular, it is literally forcing us to expand beyond the limits of what we previously thought we could accomplish, to constantly learn new ways of working. A lifelong career now means lifelong retraining. As the Radcliffe Public Policy Institute in Cambridge, Massachusetts, reports, "The qualities that once nearly guaranteed lifelong employment—hard work, reliability, loyalty, mastery of a discrete set of skills—are often no longer enough." That message has come through loud and clear. About one out of 12 Americans moonlights from his or her principal job in order to learn new skills or weave a "safety net" in case that job is lost. And American universities, starved for students only a few years ago as the Baby Boom grew up and out of the classrooms, have found a burgeoning new market in older workers. Census data show that by 1996 an incredible 468,000 college students were age 50 and older—an increase of 43 percent since 1990.

I don't have to look far to see that trend at work. My brother's wife earned her degree as a geriatric nurse in her late 40s, and it's now her part-time career. My mother, who runs her own public-relations agency, is working toward a degree as an English-language teacher, which will become her post-"retirement" career. And I'm riding that same train. This year I began teaching myself to write code for the Internet, just like my friend Randy, a former magazine editor who spent years of evenings learning to make Web pages in order to support his family. Why? Because by the year 2006 there will be fewer jobs for journalists, according to the Department of Labor. Like everyone else, I've got a choice between moving up—or out.

And there's real excitement in acquiring fresh skills—including the joy of proving wrong the adage that old dogs can't learn new tricks. But many older workers are not getting a chance to share in that excitement: They are being shunted aside from the retraining they will need to stay in the labor market at a moment when they are the fastest-growing share of the labor force. And the point at which a worker on the rise becomes a worker who's consigned to history is coming earlier in people's careers, usually around age 44, according to the Bureau of Labor Statistics. This situation persists at a time when a 77-year-old astronaut named John Glenn just went back into space—and while the minimum age for receiving Social Security benefits is rising.

Perhaps more managers should look at the hard science on this question. In a survey of the available research, Paula Rayman, director of the Radcliffe Public Policy Institute notes that there are "at least 20 studies showing that vocabulary, general information, and judgment either rise or never fall before age 60." Despite

six survival tips

THE RULES OF THE GAME MAY HAVE CHANGED, BUT midcareer and older workers still hold a number of aces—among them experience, wisdom, and adaptability. Here's some expert advice on how to play your cards and strengthen your hand for the future, gleaned from John Thompson, head of IMCOR, an interim executive placement firm in Stamford, Connecticut; Peter Cappelli, professor of management at The Wharton School in Philadelphia and author of *The New Deal at Work* (Harvard Business School Press 1999); and management gurus N. Fredric Crandall and Marc J. Wallace, authors of *Work and Rewards in the Virtual Workplace* (AMACOM, 1998)

LEARN WHILE YOU EARN
If your company will pay for you to attend college-level courses to up-grade your skills, great. If not, take them anyway. Anything computer-related is a good bet. Microsoft offers training programs via organizations such as AARP.

FLEX YOUR MUSCLES By offering to work hours that younger workers may shun because of family and other commitments, you set yourself apart, especially in the eyes of employers in service industries who need 24-hour or seven-a-day week staffing. Employers such as the Home Shopping Network now rely on mature workers to fill a variety of positions.

CAST A WIDE NET The World Wide Web has radically changed the employment scene. A growing selection of jobs are being posted there, and so are résumés. Take a look at the Working Options section on AARP's Web site at www.aarp.org/working_options/home.html for career guidance and links to resources, including America's Job Bank.

BECOME AN MVP Do something to make yourself invaluable. For example, consider becoming a mentor to a young, up-and-coming manager who may need just the kind of guidance an experienced hand can offer. Another option: Seek out projects that matter to your boss and allow you to showcase your talents.

TEST THE WATERS Temporary workers are the fastest-growing segment of the labor force, for good reason. Companies faced with budget-cutting pressures are loathe to add full-time, permanent workers who drive up salary and benefit costs. It gives you an opportunity to try out an alternate career to see if it really fits. And temporary work often is the pathway to a permanent gig.

BE A COMEBACK KID
Even if you're planning to retire or cut back from full-time work, don't forget job possibilities with your current employer. GE's information unit in Rockville, Maryland, offers a Golden Opportunity program that lets retirees work up to 1,000 hours a year, and many firms in Southern California use retirees to help with special engineering projects.

Tim Smart

these results, they found that managers "consistently made different hiring, promotion, training, and discipline decisions based *solely* [my emphasis] on the age of the workers."

A recent survey of 405 human-resources professionals found that only 29 percent of them make an active effort to attract and/or retain older workers. Among those employers who have made such efforts, establishing opportunities for advancement, skills training, and part-time work arrangements are the most common. Overall, older employees are rated highly for loyalty and dedication, commitment to doing quality work, reliability in a crisis, solid work performance, and experience. This has given rise to a new phenomenon, in which downsized older workers are coming back to the workplace as consultants, temps. or contingent workers hired to work on specific projects.

Many who possess, skills that are high in demand, like computer experts or financial advisers are finding fresh opportunities: Brokerage firms, for example, have discovered that their clients enjoy having investment counselors whose life experience is written on their faces.

Other countries are grappling with this issue as well. The Danish government, for example now offers salaried one-year training programs to unemployed workers over age 50. The German government has made it more costly for companies to downsize. And the French government is experimenting with ways to reduce the hours people spend on the job, to spread the work around. For Americans, however, the likely solution will depend on the ability of older workers to take control of their careers as never before, to think of themselves as independent contractors—units of one, so to speak—and, to do whatever they can to enhance their value. At a time when work has become, all-encompassing for many of us, it remains an eminently desirable endeavor. And although much is uncertain about the future, one thing is clear: Work will be part of it.

Mark Hunter is the author of five books, including The Passions of Men: Work and Love in the Age of Stress *(Putnam, 1988). He lives in Paris.*

Unit 6

Key Points to Consider

❖ According to "What You Can Change and What You Cannot Change," what does Martin Seligman suggest can be changed by self-determination? With professional assistance? Is the self-approach better than professional help? Discuss what problems seem immune to change. When do you believe professional intervention is necessary? Can most of us effectively change on our own?

❖ According to Emanuel Rosen in "Think Like a Shrink," why has there been a gap between psychiatry and popular culture? What is the author's concept of educational psychotherapy? How might it be applied to the patient and to society in general? What principles will help the laymen to think like a shrink?

❖ Why do some people avoid therapy even when they know it would help? How do people know they need help? Besides resisting therapy, can you think of other self-defeating behaviors that people do? For each, can you think of a way to stop the cycle of self-defeat?

❖ What is anxiety? What is an anxiety disorder? What are the symptoms of anxiety disorder? With what other disorders does anxiety coexist? How can we recognize and treat these disorders?

❖ For anxiety disorder and depression, what seems to cause or exacerbate each problem? What are other types and causes of maladjustment?

❖ Why do people commit suicide? What is a media-inspired suicide? Is it contagious, that is, can the media inspire suicide in viewers? What is a point-cluster suicide? Is this latter type of suicide contagious?

❖ Why do people become addicted to certain substances? What is dopamine? How is it related to addiction? Why is it so hard to become unaddicted?

❖ What is a borderline personality? Do you know anyone with this syndrome? Do you think women are more prone to borderline disorder than men? Why? What can we do to help people with borderline personalities? If you are living with someone with a border personality disorder, what can you do to cope?

❖ What is resiliency? Can you describe how a resilient person would cope with stress? How do others who are not so resilient cope? How can we become more resilient?

These sites are annotated on pages 4 and 5.

On each college and university campus, some students experience overwhelming stress and life-shattering crises. One student learns that her mother has terminal cancer. Another receives the news that his parents are divorcing. A sorority blackballs a student who was determined to become their sister. She commits suicide; the sorority sisters experience guilt.

Fortunately, almost every campus houses a counseling center for students; some universities also offer assistance to employees. At the counseling service, trained professionals offer aid and therapy to troubled members of the campus community.

Many individuals are able to adapt to life's vagaries, even to life's disasters. Others flounder. They simply do not know how to adjust to change. These individuals sometimes seek temporary professional assistance from a therapist or counselor. For these professionals, the difficulty may be how and when to intervene.

There are as many definitions of maladjustment as there are mental health professionals. Some practitioners define mental illness as "whatever society cannot tolerate." Others define it in terms of statistics: "If a majority do not behave that way, then the behavior signals maladjustment." Some professionals suggest that an inadequate self-concept is the cause of maladjustment while others cite a lack of contact with reality. A few psychologists claim that to call one individual ill suggests that the rest are healthy by contrast, when, in fact, there may be few real distinctions among people.

Maladjustment is difficult to define and to treat. For each definition, a theorist develops a treatment strategy. Psychoanalysts press clients to recall their dreams, their childhood, and their intrapsychic conflicts in order to analyze the contents of the unconscious. Humanists encourage clients to explore all of the facets of their lives in order to become less defensive. Behaviorists are usually concerned with observable and therefore treatable symptoms or behaviors. Other therapists, namely psychiatrists who are physicians by training, may utilize these therapies and add drugs and psychosurgery.

This brief list of interventions raises further questions. For instance, is one form of therapy more effective, less expensive, or longer-lasting than another? Is one diagnosis better treated by a particular form of therapy? If two experts disagree on the diagnosis and treatment, how do we decide which one is correct? Should psychologists be allowed to prescribe psychoactive drugs? These questions continue to be debated.

Some psychologists question whether professional intervention is necessary at all. In one well-publicized but highly criticized study, researcher Hans Eysenck was able to show that spontaneous remission rates were as high as therapeutic "cure" rates. Is professional help always necessary? Can people be their own healers? Is support from friends as productive as professional treatment?

The first readings pertain to the process of change as induced by treatments such as psychotherapy. In "What You Can Change and What You Cannot Change," noted psychologist Martin Seligman discusses what can be realistically managed in terms of self-improvement. In "Think Like a Shrink," psychologist Emanuel Rosen discusses some rules of thumb that can be applied to assess our own or others' mental health.

A companion article is "The Doctor's In, The Patient's Not/Even When They Think It Would Help Them, Many People Resist Counseling." In this article Carol Polsky examines why people resist therapy and what factors eventually bring individuals around to the fact that they need assistance.

We next look at a prevalent, underlying cause of mental disorder—anxiety. In the article, "Chronic Anxiety: How to Stop Living on the Edge," anxiety disorders are described. These disorders often coexist with depression. Recognizing and treating anxiety is the focus of this article.

We then look at various, specific adjustment disorders, the first of which is depression. Many Americans have the blues now and then. Clinical depression is so intense that the individual's life is greatly affected. The first article describes the symptoms and treatments of such profound depression. New drug treatments and psychotherapy are offered as treatments for depression.

Three other adjustment problems are discussed next—suicide, substance abuse, and personality disorders. Suicide is a serious problem, often triggered by the severe depression described above. The author of "The Clustering and Contagion of Suicide," asks a cogent question: Is suicide catching? Thomas Joiner's answer is both yes and no, depending on the type of suicide. Suicide, it appears, is contagious when individuals who are suicide-prone have contact with one another in space or time, as in a high school.

Addictions to various substances have plagued humans for centuries. We are just now beginning to understand what causes addiction. J. Madeleine Nash discusses addiction and the question of its origin. She identifies the neurotransmitter dopamine as the likely culprit.

Next, a really baffling disorder, borderline personality, is detailed by Patrick Perry. Individuals with borderline personalities are difficult to manage and often sabotage their best relationships. What the symptomatology is, what these individuals are like, and how to help them are explained here. Profiles of several famous persons who may have had borderline personalities are also shared.

We end on a positive note and examine an interesting concept from psychology, one that is receiving more and more attention—resiliency. Resiliency is the ability to "turn lemons into lemonade." What each of us can do to become better copers is revealed in Deborah Blum's article, "Finding Strength: How to Overcome Anything."

What You Can Change & What You Cannot Change

There are things we can change about ourselves and things we cannot. Concentrate your energy on what is possible—too much time has been wasted.

Martin E. P. Seligman, Ph.D.

This is the age of psychotherapy and the age of self-improvement. Millions are struggling to change: We diet, we jog, we meditate. We adopt new modes of thought to counteract our depressions. We practice relaxation to curtail stress. We exercise to expand our memory and to quadruple our reading speed. We adopt draconian regimens to give up smoking. We raise our little boys and girls to androgyny. We come out of the closet and we try to become heterosexual. We seek to lose our taste for alcohol. We seek more meaning in life. We try to extend our life span.

Sometimes it works. But distressingly often, self-improvement and psychotherapy fail. The cost is enormous. We think we are worthless. We feel guilty and ashamed. We believe we have no willpower and that we are failures. We give up trying to change.

On the other hand, this is not only the age of self-improvement and therapy, but also the age of biological psychiatry. The human genome will be nearly mapped be-

fore the millennium is over. The brain systems underlying sex, hearing, memory, left-handedness, and sadness are now known. Psychoactive drugs quiet our fears, relieve our blues, bring us bliss, dampen our mania, and dissolve our delusions more effectively than we can on our own.

Our very personality—our intelligence and musical talent, even our religiousness, our conscience (or its absence), our politics, and our exuberance—turns out to be more the product of our genes than almost anyone would have believed a decade ago. The underlying message of the age of biological psychiatry is that our biology frequently makes changing, in spite of all our efforts, impossible.

But the view that all is genetic and biochemical and therefore unchangeable is also very often wrong. Many people surpass their IQs, fail to "respond" to drugs, make sweeping changes in their lives, live on when their cancer is "terminal," or defy the hormones and brain circuitry that "dictate" lust, femininity, or memory loss.

The ideologies of biological psychiatry and self-improvement are obviously colliding. Nevertheless, a resolution is apparent. There are some things about ourselves that can be changed, others that cannot, and some that can be changed only with extreme difficulty.

What can we succeed in changing about ourselves? What can we not? When can we overcome our biology? And when is our biology our destiny?

I want to provide an understanding of what you can and what you can't change about yourself so that you can concentrate your limited time and energy on what is possible. So much time has been wasted. So much needless frustration has been endured. So much of therapy, so much of child rearing, so much of self-improving, and even some of the great social movements in our century have come to nothing because they tried to change the unchangeable. Too often we have wrongly thought we were weak-willed failures, when the changes we wanted to make in ourselves

So much child rearing, therapy, and self-improvement have come to nothing.

were just not possible. But all this effort was necessary: Because there have been so many failures, we are now able to see the boundaries of the unchangeable; this in turn allows us to see clearly for the first time the boundaries of what *is* changeable.

With this knowledge, we can use our precious time to make the many rewarding changes that are possible. We can live with less self-reproach and less remorse. We can live with greater confidence. This knowledge is a new understanding of who we are and where we are going.

CATASTROPHIC THINKING: PANIC

S. J. Rachman, one of the world's leading clinical researchers and one of the founders of behavior therapy, was on the phone. He was proposing that I be the "discussant" at a conference about panic disorder sponsored by the National Institute of Mental Health (NIMH).

"Why even bother, Jack?" I responded. "Everyone knows that panic is biological and that the only thing that works is drugs."

"Don't refuse so quickly, Marty. There is a breakthrough you haven't yet heard about."

Breakthrough was a word I had never heard Jack use before.

"What's the breakthrough?" I asked.

"If you come, you can find out."

So I went.

I had known about and seen panic patients for many years, and had read the literature with mounting excitement during the 1980s. I knew that panic disorder is a frightening condition that consists of recurrent attacks, each much worse than anything experienced before. Without prior warning, you feel as if you are going to die. Here is a typical case history:

The first time Celia had a panic attack, she was working at McDonald's. It was two days before her 20th birthday. As she was handing a customer a Big Mac, she had the worst experience of her life. The earth seemed to open up beneath her. Her heart began to pound, she felt she was smothering, and she was sure she was going to have a heart attack and die. After about 20 minutes of terror, the panic subsided. Trembling, she got in her car, raced home and barely left the house for the next three months.

Since then, Celia has had about three attacks a month. She does not know when they are coming. She always thinks she is going to die.

Panic attacks are not subtle, and you need no quiz to find out if you or someone you love has them. As many as five percent of American adults probably do. The defining feature of the disorder is simple: recurrent awful attacks of panic that come out of the blue, last for a few minutes, and then subside. The attacks consist of chest pains, sweating, nausea, dizziness, choking, smothering, or trembling. They are accompanied by feelings of overwhelming dread and thoughts that you are having a heart attack, that you are losing control, or that you are going crazy.

THE BIOLOGY OF PANIC

There are four questions that bear on whether a mental problem is primarily "biological" as opposed to "psychological":

- Can it be induced biologically?
- Is it genetically heritable?
- Are specific brain functions involved?
- Does a drug relieve it?

Inducing panic. Panic attacks can be created by a biological agent. For example, patients who have a history of panic attacks are hooked up to an intravenous line. Sodium lactate, a chemical that normally produces rapid, shallow breathing and heart palpitations, is slowly infused into their bloodstream. Within a few minutes, about 60 to 90 percent of these patients have a panic attack. Normal controls—subjects with no history of panic—rarely have attacks when infused with lactate.

Genetics of panic. There may be some heritability of panic. If one of two identical twins has panic attacks, 31 percent of the cotwins also have them. But if one of two fraternal twins has panic attacks, none of the cotwins are so afflicted.

Panic and the brain. The brains of people with panic disorders look somewhat unusual upon close scrutiny. Their neurochemistry shows abnormalities in the system that turns on, then dampens, fear. In addition, the PET scan (positron-emission tomography), a technique that looks at how much blood and oxygen different parts of the brain use, shows that patients who panic from the infusion of lactate have

What Can We Change?

When we survey all the problems, personality types, patterns of behavior, and the weak influence of childhood on adult life, we see a puzzling array of how much change occurs. From the things that are easiest to those that are the most difficult, this rough array emerges:

Panic	Curable
Specific Phobias	Almost Curable
Sexual Dysfunctions	Marked Relief
Social Phobia	Moderate Relief
Agoraphobia	Moderate Relief
Depression	Moderate Relief
Sex Role Change	Moderate Relief
Obsessive-Compulsive Disorder	Moderate Mild Relief
Sexual Preferences	Moderate Mild Change
Anger	Mild Moderate Relief
Everyday Anxiety	Mild Moderate Relief
Alcoholism	Mild Relief
Overweight	Temporary Change
Posttraumatic Stress Disorder (PTSD)	Marginal Relief
Sexual Orientation	Probably Unchangeable
Sexual Identity	Unchangeable

higher blood flow and oxygen use in relevant parts of their brain than patients who don't panic.

Drugs. Two kinds of drugs relieve panic: tricyclic antidepressants and the antianxiety drug Xanax, and both work better than placebos. Panic attacks are dampened, and sometimes even eliminated. General anxiety and depression also decrease.

Since these four questions had already been answered "yes" when Jack Rachman called, I thought the issue had already been settled. Panic disorder was simply a bio-

We are now able to see the boundaries of the unchangeable.

logical illness, a disease of the body that could be relieved only by drugs.

A few months later I was in Bethesda, Maryland, listening once again to the same four lines of biological evidence. An inconspicuous figure in a brown suit sat hunched over the table. At the first break, Jack introduced me to him—David Clark, a young psychologist from Oxford. Soon after, Clark began his address.

"Consider, if you will, an alternative theory, a cognitive theory." He reminded all of us that almost all panickers believe that they are going to die during an attack. Most commonly, they believe that they are having heart attacks. Perhaps, Clark suggested, this is more than just a mere symptom. Perhaps it is the root cause. Panic may simply be the *catastrophic misinterpretation of bodily sensations.*

For example, when you panic, your heart starts to race. You notice this, and you see it as a possible heart attack. This makes you very anxious, which means that your heart pounds more. You now notice that your heart is *really* pounding. You are now *sure* it's a heart attack. This terrifies you, and you break into a sweat, feel nauseated, short of breath—all symptoms of terror, but for you, they're confirmation of a heart attack. A full-blown panic attack is under way, and at the root of it is your misinterpretation of the symptoms of anxiety as symptoms of impending death.

I was listening closely now as Clark argued that an obvious sign of a disorder, easily dismissed as a symptom, is the disorder itself. If he was right, this was a historic occasion. All Clark had done so far, however, was to show that the four lines of evidence for a biological view of panic could fit equally well with a misinterpretation view. But Clark soon told us about a series of experiments he and his colleague Paul Salkovskis had done at Oxford.

First, they compared panic patients with patients who had other anxiety disorders and with normals. All the subjects read the following sentences aloud, but the last word was presented blurred. For example:

dying
If I had palpitations, I could be
excited

choking
If I were breathless, I could be
unfit

When the sentences were about bodily sensations, the panic patients, but no one else, saw the catastrophic endings fastest. This showed that panic patients possess the habit of thinking Clark had postulated.

Next, Clark and his colleagues asked if activating this habit with words would induce panic. All the subjects read a series of word pairs aloud. When panic patients

Self-Analysis Questionnaire

Is your life dominated by anxiety? Read each statement and then mark the appropriate number to indicate how you generally feel. There are no right or wrong answers.

1. I am a steady person.

Almost never	Sometimes	Often	Almost always
4	3	2	1

2. I am satisfied with myself.

Almost never	Sometimes	Often	Almost always
4	3	2	1

3. I feel nervous and restless.

Almost never	Sometimes	Often	Almost always
1	2	3	4

4. I wish I could be as happy as others seem to be.

Almost never	Sometimes	Often	Almost always
1	2	3	4

5. I feel like a failure.

Almost never	Sometimes	Often	Almost always
1	2	3	4

6. I get in a state of tension and turmoil as I think over my recent concerns and interests.

Almost never	Sometimes	Often	Almost always
1	2	3	4

7. I feel secure.

Almost never	Sometimes	Often	Almost always
4	3	2	1

8. I have self-confidence.

Almost never	Sometimes	Often	Almost always
4	3	2	1

9. I feel inadequate.

Almost never	Sometimes	Often	Almost always
1	2	3	4

10. I worry too much over something that does not matter.

Almost never	Sometimes	Often	Almost always
1	2	3	4

To score, simply add up the numbers under your answers. Notice that some of the rows of numbers go up and others go down. The higher your total, the more the trait of anxiety dominates your life. If your score was:

10–11, you are in the lowest 10 percent of anxiety.

13–14, you are in the lowest quarter.

16–17, your anxiety level is about average.

19–20, your anxiety level is around the 75th percentile.

22–24 (and you are male) your anxiety level is around the 90th percentile.

24–26 (and you are female) your anxiety level is around the 90th percentile.

25 (and you are male) your anxiety level is at the 95th percentile.

27 (and you are female) your anxiety level is at the 95th percentile.

Should you try to change your anxiety level? Here are my rules of thumb:

- If your score is at the 90th percentile or above, you can probably improve the quality of your life by lowering your general anxiety level—regardless of paralysis and irrationality.
- If your score is at the 75th percentile or above, and you feel that anxiety is either paralyzing you or that it is unfounded, you should probably try to lower your general anxiety level.
- If your score is 18 or above, and you feel that anxiety is unfounded and paralyzing, you should probably try to lower your general anxiety level.

got to "breathlessness-suffocation" and "palpitations-dying," 75 percent suffered a full-blown panic attack right there in the laboratory. No normal people had panic attacks, no recovered panic patients (I'll tell you more in a moment about how they got better) had attacks, and only 17 percent of other anxious patients had attacks.

The final thing Clark told us was the "breakthrough" that Rachman had promised.

Issues of the soul can barely be changed by psychotherapy or drugs.

"We have developed and tested a rather novel therapy for panic," Clark continued in his understated, disarming way. He explained that if catastrophic misinterpretations of bodily sensation are the cause of a panic attack, then changing the tendency to misinterpret should cure the disorder. His new therapy was straightforward and brief:

Patients are told that panic results when they mistake normal symptoms of mounting anxiety for symptoms of heart attack, going crazy, or dying. Anxiety itself, they are informed, produces shortness of breath, chest pain, and sweating. Once they misinterpret these normal bodily sensations as an imminent heart attack, their symptoms become even more pronounced because the misinterpretation changes their anxiety into terror. A vicious circle culminates in a full-blown panic attack.

Patients are taught to reinterpret the symptoms realistically as mere anxiety symptoms. Then they are given practice right in the office, breathing rapidly into a paper bag. This causes a buildup of carbon dioxide and shortness of breath, mimicking the sensations that provoke a panic attack. The therapist points out that the symptoms the patient is experiencing—shortness of breath and heart racing—are harmless, simply the result of overbreathing, not a sign of a heart attack. The patient learns to interpret the symptoms correctly.

"This simple therapy appears to be a cure," Clark told us. "Ninety to 100 percent of the patients are panic free at the end of therapy. One year later, only one person had had another panic attack."

This, indeed, was a breakthrough: a simple, brief psychotherapy with no side effects showing a 90-percent cure rate of a disorder that a decade ago was thought to be incurable. In a controlled study of 64 patients comparing cognitive therapy to drugs to relaxation to no treatment, Clark and his colleagues found that cognitive

therapy is markedly better than drugs or relaxation, both of which are better than nothing. Such a high cure rate is unprecedented.

How does cognitive therapy for panic compare with drugs? It is more effective and less dangerous. Both the antidepressants and Xanax produce marked reduction in panic in most patients, but drugs must be taken forever; once the drug is stopped, panic rebounds to where it was before therapy began for perhaps half the patients. The drugs also sometimes have severe side effects, including drowsiness, lethargy, pregnancy complications, and addictions.

After this bombshell, my own "discussion" was an anticlimax. I did make one point that Clark took to heart. "Creating a cognitive therapy that works, even one that works as well as this apparently does, is not enough to show that the *cause* of panic is cognitive." I was niggling. "The biological theory doesn't deny that some other therapy might work well on panic. It merely claims that panic is caused at the bottom by some biochemical problem."

Two years later, Clark carried out a crucial experiment that tested the biological theory against the cognitive theory. He gave the usual lactate infusion to 10 panic patients, and nine of them panicked. He did the same thing with another 10 patients, but added special instructions to allay the misinterpretation of the sensations. He simply told them: "Lactate is a natural bodily substance that produces sensations similar to exercise or alcohol. It is normal to experience intense sensations during infusion, but these do not indicate an adverse reaction." Only three out of the 10 panicked. This confirmed the theory crucially.

Anxiety scans your life for imperfections. When it finds one, it won't let go.

The therapy works very well, as it did for Celia, whose story has a happy ending. She first tried Xanax, which reduced the intensity and the frequency of her panic attacks. But she was too drowsy to work and she was still having about one attack every six weeks. She was then referred to Audrey, a cognitive therapist who explained that Celia was misinterpreting her heart racing and shortness of breath as symptoms of a heart attack, that they were actually just symptoms of mounting anxiety, nothing more harmful. Audrey taught Celia progressive relaxation, and then she demonstrated

the harmlessness of Celia's symptoms of overbreathing. Celia then relaxed in the presence of the symptoms and found that they gradually subsided. After several more practice sessions, therapy terminated. Celia has gone two years without another panic attack.

EVERYDAY ANXIETY

Attend to your tongue—right now. What is it doing? Mine is swishing around near my lower right molars. It has just found a minute fragment of last night's popcorn (debris from *Terminator 2*). Like a dog at a bone, it is worrying the firmly wedged flake.

Attend to your hand—right now. What's it up to? My left hand is boring in on an itch it discovered under my earlobe.

Your tongue and your hands have, for the most part, a life of their own. You can bring them under voluntary control by consciously calling them out of their "default" mode to carry out your commands: "Pick up the phone" or "Stop picking that pimple." But most of the time they are on their own. They are seeking out small imperfections. They scan your entire mouth and skin surface, probing for anything going wrong. They are marvelous, nonstop grooming devices. They, not the more fashionable immune system, are your first line of defense against invaders.

Anxiety is your mental tongue. Its default mode is to search for what may be about to go wrong. It continually, and without your conscious consent, scans your life—yes, even when you are asleep, in dreams and nightmares. It reviews your work, your love, your play—until it finds an imperfection. When it finds one, it worries it. It tries to pull it out from its hiding place, where it is wedged inconspicuously under some rock. It will not let go. If the imperfection is threatening enough, anxiety calls your attention to it by making you uncomfortable. If you do not act, it yells more insistently—disturbing your sleep and your appetite.

You can reduce daily, mild anxiety. You can numb it with alcohol, Valium, or marijuana. You can take the edge off with meditation or progressive relaxation. You can beat it down by becoming more conscious of the automatic thoughts of danger that trigger anxiety and then disputing them effectively.

But do not overlook what your anxiety is trying to do for you. In return for the pain it brings, it prevents larger ordeals by making you aware of their possibility and goading you into planning for and forestalling them. It may even help you avoid them altogether. Think of your anxiety as the "low oil" light flashing on the dashboard of your car. Disconnect it and you will be less distracted and more comfortable for a while. But this may cost you a burned-up engine. Our *dysphoria,* or bad feeling, should, some of the time, be tolerated, attended to, even cherished.

GUIDELINES FOR WHEN TO TRY TO CHANGE ANXIETY

Some of our everyday anxiety, depression, and anger go beyond their useful function. Most adaptive traits fall along a normal spectrum of distribution, and the capacity for internal bad weather for everyone some of the time means that some of us may have terrible weather all of the time. In general, when the hurt is pointless and recurrent—when, for example, anxiety insists we formulate a plan but no plan will work—it is time to take action to relieve the hurt. There are three hallmarks indicating that anxiety has become a burden that wants relieving:

First, is it *irrational?*

We must calibrate our bad weather inside against the real weather outside. Is what you are anxious about out of proportion to the reality of the danger? Here are some examples that may help you answer this question. All of the following are not irrational:

- A fire fighter trying to smother a raging oil well burning in Kuwait repeatedly wakes up at four in the morning because of flaming terror dreams.
- A mother of three smells perfume on her husband's shirts and, consumed by jealousy, broods about his infidelity, reviewing the list of possible women over and over.
- A student who had failed two of his midterm exams finds, as finals approach, that he can't get to sleep for worrying. He has diarrhea most of the time.

The only good thing that can be said about such fears is that they are well-founded.

In contrast, all of the following are irrational, out of proportion to the danger:

- An elderly man, having been in a fender bender, broods about travel and will no longer take cars, trains, or airplanes.
- An eight-year-old child, his parents having been through an ugly divorce, wets his bed at night. He is haunted with visions of his bedroom ceiling collapsing on him.
- A housewife who has an MBA and who accumulated a decade of experience as a financial vice president before her twins were born is sure her job search will be fruitless. She delays preparing her résumés for a month.

The second hallmark of anxiety out of control is *paralysis.* Anxiety intends action: Plan, rehearse, look into shadows for lurking dangers, change your life. When anxiety becomes strong, it is unproductive; no problem-solving occurs. And when anxiety is extreme, it paralyzes you. Has your anxiety crossed this line? Some examples:

- A woman finds herself housebound because she fears that if she goes out, she will be bitten by a cat.
- A salesman broods about the next customer hanging up on him and makes no more cold calls.
- A writer, afraid of the next rejection slip, stops writing.

'Dieting below your natural weight is a necessary condition for bulimia. Returning to your natural weight will cure it.'

The final hallmark is *intensity.* Is your life dominated by anxiety? Dr. Charles Spielberger, one of the world's foremost testers of emotion, has developed well-validated scales for calibrating how severe anxiety is. To find out how anxious *you* are, use the self-analysis questionnaire.

LOWERING YOUR EVERYDAY ANXIETY

Everyday anxiety level is not a category to which psychologists have devoted a great deal of attention. Enough research has been done, however, for me to recommend two techniques that quite reliably lower everyday anxiety levels. Both techniques are cumulative, rather than one-shot fixes. They require 20 to 40 minutes a day of your valuable time.

The first is *progressive relaxation,* done once or, better, twice a day for at least 10 minutes. In this technique, you tighten and then turn off each of the major muscle groups of your body until you are wholly flaccid. It is not easy to be highly anxious when your body feels like Jell-O. More formally, relaxation engages a response system that competes with anxious arousal.

The second technique is regular *meditation.* Transcendental meditation ™ is one useful, widely available version of this. You can ignore the cosmology in which it is packaged if you wish, and treat it simply as the beneficial technique it is. Twice a day for 20 minutes, in a quiet setting, you close your eyes and repeat a *mantra* (a syllable whose "sonic properties are known") to yourself. Meditation works by blocking thoughts that produce anxiety. It complements relaxation, which blocks the motor components of anxiety but leaves the anxious thoughts untouched.

Done regularly, meditation usually induces a peaceful state of mind. Anxiety at other times of the day wanes, and hyperarousal from bad events is dampened. Done religiously, TM probably works better than relaxation alone.

There's also a quick fix. The minor tranquilizers—Valium, Dalmane, Librium, and their cousins—relieve everyday anxiety. So does alcohol. The advantage of all these is that they work within minutes and require no discipline to use. Their disadvantages outweigh their advantages, however. The minor tranquilizers make you fuzzy and somewhat uncoordinated as they work (a not uncommon side effect is an automobile accident). Tranquilizers soon lose their effect when taken regularly, and they are habit-forming—probably addictive. Alcohol, in addition, produces gross cognitive and motor disability in lockstep with its anxiety relief. Taken regularly over long periods, deadly damage to liver and brain ensue.

If you crave quick and temporary relief from acute anxiety, either alcohol or minor tranquilizers, taken in small amounts and only occasionally, will do the job. They are, however, a distant second-best to progressive relaxation and meditation, which are each worth trying before you seek out psychotherapy or in conjunction with therapy. Unlike tranquilizers and alcohol, neither of these techniques is likely to do you any harm.

Weigh your everyday anxiety. If it is not intense, or if it is moderate and not irrational or paralyzing, act now to reduce it. In spite of its deep evolutionary roots, intense everyday anxiety is often changeable. Meditation and progressive relaxation practiced regularly can change it forever.

DIETING: A WAIST IS A TERRIBLE THING TO MIND

I have been watching my weight and restricting my intake—except for an occasional binge like this—since I was 20. I weighed about 175 pounds then, maybe 15 pounds over my official "ideal" weight. I weigh 199 pounds now, 30 years later, about 25 pounds over the ideal. I have tried about a dozen regimes—fasting, the Beverly Hills Diet, no carbohydrates, Metrecal for lunch, 1,200 calories a day, low fat, no lunch, no starches, skipping every other dinner. I lost 10 or 15 pounds on each in about a month. The pounds always came back, though, and I have gained a net of about a pound a year—inexorably.

This is the most consistent failure in my life. It's also a failure I can't just put out of mind. I have spent the last few years reading the scientific literature, not the parade of best-selling diet books or the flood of women's magazine articles on the latest way to slim down. The scientific findings look clear to me, but there is not yet a consensus. I am going to go out on a limb, because I see so many signs all pointing in one direction. What I have concluded will, I believe, soon be the consensus of the scientists. The conclusions surprise me. They will probably surprise you, too, and they may change your life.

Here is what the picture looks like to me:

- Dieting doesn't work.
- Dieting may make overweight worse, not better.
- Dieting may be bad for health.
- Dieting may cause eating disorders—including bulimia and anorexia.

ARE YOU OVERWEIGHT?

Are you above the ideal weight for your sex, height, and age? If so, you are "overweight." What does this really mean? Ideal weight is arrived at simply. Four million people, now dead, who were insured by the major American life-insurance companies, were once weighed and had their height measured. At what weight on average do people of a given height turn out to live longest? That weight is called ideal. Anything wrong with that?

You bet. The real use of a weight table, and the reason your doctor takes it seriously, is that an ideal weight implies that, on average, if you slim down to yours, you will live longer. This is the crucial claim. Lighter people indeed live longer, on average, than heavier people, but how much longer is hotly debated.

But the crucial claim is unsound because weight (at any given height) has a normal distribution, *normal* both in a statistical sense and in the biological sense. In the biological sense, couch potatoes who overeat and never exercise can legitimately be called overweight, but the buxom, "heavy-boned" slow people deemed overweight by the ideal table are at their natural and healthiest weight. If you are a 155-pound woman and 64 inches in height, for example, you are "overweight" by around 15 pounds. This means nothing more than that the average 140-pound, 64-inch-tall woman lives somewhat longer than the average 155-pound woman of your height. It

does not follow that if you slim down to 125 pounds, *you* will stand any better chance of living longer.

In spite of the insouciance with which dieting advice is dispensed, no one has properly investigated the question of whether slimming down to "ideal" weight produces longer life. The proper study would compare the longevity of people who are at their ideal weight without dieting to people who achieve their ideal weight by dieting. Without this study the common medical advice to diet down to your ideal weight is simply unfounded.

This is not a quibble; there is evidence that dieting damages your health and that this damage may shorten your life.

MYTHS OF OVERWEIGHT

The advice to diet down to your ideal weight to live longer is one myth of overweight. Here are some others:

- *Overweight people overeat.* Wrong. Nineteen out of 20 studies show that obese people consume no more calories each day than nonobese people. Telling a fat person that if she would change her eating habits and eat "normally" she would lose weight is a lie. To lose weight and stay there, she will need to eat excruciatingly less than a normal person, probably for the rest of her life.
- *Overweight people have an overweight personality.* Wrong. Extensive research on personality and fatness has proved little. Obese people do not differ in any major personality style from nonobese people.
- *Physical inactivity is a major cause of obesity.* Probably not. Fat people are indeed less active than thin people, but the inactivity is probably caused more by the fatness than the other way around.
- *Overweight shows a lack of willpower.* This is the granddaddy of all the myths. Fatness is seen as shameful because we hold people responsible for their weight. Being overweight equates with being a weak-willed slob. We believe this primarily because we have seen people decide to lose weight and do so in a matter of weeks.

But almost everyone returns to the old weight after shedding pounds. Your body has a natural weight that it defends vigorously against dieting. The more diets tried, the harder the body works to defeat the next diet. Weight is in large part genetic. All this gives the lie to the "weak-willed" interpretations of overweight. More accurately, dieting is the conscious will of the

individual against a more vigilant opponent: the species' biological defense against starvation. The body can't tell the difference between self-imposed starvation and actual famine, so it defends its weight by refusing to release fat, by lowering its metabolism, and by demanding food. The harder the creature tries not to eat, the more vigorous the defenses become.

BULIMIA AND NATURAL WEIGHT

A concept that makes sense of your body's vigorous defense against weight loss is *natural weight.* When your body screams "I'm hungry," makes you lethargic, stores fat, craves sweets and renders them more delicious than ever, and makes you obsessed with food, what it is defending is your natural weight. It is signaling that you have dropped into a range it will not accept. Natural weight prevents you from gaining too much weight or losing too much. When you eat too much for too long, the opposite defenses are activated and make long-term weight gain difficult.

There is also a strong genetic contribution to your natural weight. Identical twins reared apart weigh almost the same throughout their lives. When identical twins are overfed, they gain weight and add fat in lockstep and in the same places. The fatness or thinness of adopted children resembles their biological parents—particularly their mother—very closely but does not at all resemble their adoptive parents. This suggests that you have a genetically given natural weight that your body wants to maintain.

The idea of natural weight may help cure the new disorder that is sweeping young America. Hundreds of thousands of young women have contracted it. It consists of bouts of binge eating and purging alternating with days of undereating. These young women are usually normal in weight or a bit on the thin side, but they are terrified of becoming fat. So they diet. They exercise. They take laxatives by the cup. They gorge. Then they vomit and take more laxatives. This malady is called *bulimia nervosa* (bulimia, for short).

Therapists are puzzled by bulimia, its causes, and treatment. Debate rages about whether it is an equivalent of depression, or an expression of a thwarted desire for control, or a symbolic rejection of the feminine role. Almost every psychotherapy has been tried. Antidepressants and other drugs have been administered with some effect but little success has been reported.

I don't think that bulimia is mysterious, and I think that it will be curable. I believe that bulimia is caused by dieting. The bulimic goes on a diet, and her body attempts to defend its natural weight. With repeated dieting, this defense becomes more vigorous. Her body is in massive revolt—insistently demanding food, storing fat, craving sweets, and lowering metabolism. Periodically, these biological defenses will overcome her extraordinary willpower (and extraordinary it must be to even approach an ideal weight, say, 20 pounds lighter than her natural weight). She will then binge. Horrified by what this will do to her figure, she vomits and takes laxatives to purge calories. Thus, bulimia is a natural consequence of self-starvation to lose weight in the midst of abundant food.

The therapist's task is to get the patient to stop dieting and become comfortable with her natural weight. He should first convince the patient that her binge eating is caused by her body's reaction to her diet. Then he must confront her with a question: Which is more important, staying thin or getting rid of bulimia? By stopping the diet, he will tell her, she can get rid of the uncontrollable binge-purge cycle. Her body will now settle at her natural weight, and she need not worry that she will balloon beyond that point. For some patients, therapy will end there because they would rather be bulimic than "loathsomely fat." For these patients, the central issue—ideal weight versus natural weight—can now at least become the focus of therapy. For others, defying the social and sexual pressure to be thin will be possible, dieting will be abandoned, weight will be gained, and bulimia should end quickly.

These are the central moves of the cognitive-behavioral treatment of bulimia. There are more than a dozen outcome studies of this approach, and the results are good. There is about 60 percent reduction in binging and purging (about the same as with antidepressant drugs). But unlike drugs, there is little relapse after treatment. Attitudes toward weight and shape relax, and dieting withers.

Of course, the dieting theory cannot fully explain bulimia. Many people who diet don't become bulimic; some can avoid it because their natural weight is close to their ideal weight, and therefore the diet they adopt does not starve them. In addition, bulimics are often depressed, since binging-purging leads to self-loathing. Depression may worsen bulimia by making it easier to give in to temptation. Further, dieting may just be another symptom of bulimia, not a cause. Other factors aside, I can speculate that dieting below your natural weight is a necessary condition for bulimia, and that returning to your natural weight and accepting that weight will cure bulimia.

OVERWEIGHT VS. DIETING: THE HEALTH DAMAGE

Being heavy carries some health risk. There is no definite answer to how much,

because there is a swamp of inconsistent findings. But even if you could just wish pounds away, never to return, it is not certain you should. Being somewhat above your "ideal" weight may actually be your healthiest natural condition, best for your particular constitution and your particular metabolism. Of course you can diet, but the odds are overwhelming that most of the weight will return, and that you will have to diet again and again. From a health and mortality perspective, should you? *There is, probably, a serious health risk from losing weight and regaining it.*

In one study, more than five thousand men and women from Framingham, Massachusetts, were observed for 32 years. People whose weight fluctuated over the years had 30 to 100 percent greater risk of death from heart disease than people whose weight was stable. When corrected for smoking, exercise, cholesterol level, and blood pressure, the findings became more convincing, suggesting that weight fluctuation (the primary cause of which is presumably dieting) may itself increase the risk of heart disease.

If this result is replicated, and if dieting is shown to be the primary cause of weight cycling, it will convince me that you should not diet to reduce your risk of heart disease.

DEPRESSION AND DIETING

Depression is yet another cost of dieting, because two root causes of depression are failure and helplessness. Dieting sets you up for failure. Because the goal of slimming down to your ideal weight pits your fallible willpower against untiring biological defenses, you will often fail. At first you will lose weight and feel pretty good about it. Any depression you had about your figure will disappear. Ultimately, however, you will probably not reach your goal; and then you will be dismayed as the pounds return. Every time you look in the mirror or vacillate over a white chocolate mousse, you will be reminded of your failure, which in turn brings depression.

On the other hand, if you are one of the fortunate few who can keep the weight from coming back, you will probably have to stay on an unsatisfying low-calorie diet for the rest of your life. A side effect of prolonged malnutrition is depression. Either way you are more vulnerable to it.

If you scan the list of cultures that have a thin ideal for women, you will be struck by something fascinating. All thin-ideal cultures also have eating disorders. They also have roughly twice as much depression in women as in men. (Women diet twice as much as men. The best estimate is that 13 percent of adult men and 25 percent of adult women are now on a diet.) The cultures without the thin ideal have no eating disor-

ders, and the amount of depression in women and men in these cultures is the same. This suggests that around the world, the thin ideal and dieting not only cause eating disorders, but they may also cause women to be more depressed than men.

THE BOTTOM LINE

I have been dieting off and on for 30 years because I want to be more attractive, healthier, and more in control. How do these goals stack up against the facts?

Attractiveness. If your attractiveness is a high-enough priority to convince you to diet, keep three drawbacks in mind. First, the attractiveness you gain will be temporary. All the weight you lose and maybe more will likely come back in a few years. This will depress you. Then you will have to lose it again and it will be harder the second time. Or you will have to resign yourself to being less attractive. Second, when women choose the silhouette figure they want to achieve, it turns out to be thinner than the silhouette that men label most attractive. Third, you may well become bulimic particularly if your natural weight is substantially more than your ideal weight. On balance, if short-term attractiveness is your overriding goal, diet. But be prepared for the costs.

Health. No one has ever shown that losing weight will increase my longevity. On balance, the health goal does not warrant dieting.

Control. For many people, getting to an ideal weight and staying there is just as biologically impossible as going with much less sleep. This fact tells me not to diet, and defuses my feeling of shame. My bottom line is clear: I am not going to diet anymore.

DEPTH AND CHANGE: THE THEORY

Clearly, we have not yet developed drugs or psychotherapies that can change all the problems, personality types, and patterns of behavior in adult life. But I believe that success and failure stems from something other than inadequate treatment. Rather, it stems from the depth of the problem.

We all have experience of psychological states of different depths. For example, if you ask someone, out of the blue, to answer quickly, "Who are you?" they will usually tell you—roughly in this order—their name, their sex, their profession, whether they have children, and their religion or race. Underlying this is a continuum of depth from surface to soul—with all manner of psychic material in between.

I believe that issues of the soul can barely be changed by psychotherapy or by drugs. Problems and behavior patterns somewhere between soul and surface can be changed somewhat. Surface problems can be changed easily, even cured. What is changeable, by therapy or drugs, I speculate, varies with the depth of the problem.

My theory says that it does not matter *when* problems, habits, and personality are acquired; their depth derives only from their biology, their evidence, and their power. Some childhood traits, for example, are deep and unchangeable but not because they were learned early and therefore have a privileged place.

Rather, those traits that resist change do so either because they are evolutionarily prepared or because they acquire great power by virtue of becoming the framework around which later learning crystallizes. In this way, the theory of depth carries the optimistic message that we are not prisoners of our past.

When you have understood this message, you will never look at your life in the same way again. Right now there are a number of things that you do not like about yourself and that you want to change: your short fuse, your waistline, your shyness, your drinking, your glumness. You have decided to change, but you do not know what you should work on first. Formerly you would have probably selected the one that hurts the most. Now you will also ask yourself which attempt is most likely to repay your efforts and which is most likely to lead to further frustration. Now you know your shyness and your anger are much more likely to change than your drinking, which you now know is more likely to change than your waistline.

Some of what does change is under your control, and some is not. You can best prepare yourself to change by learning as much as you can about what you can change and how to make those changes. Like all true education, learning about change is not easy; harder yet is surrendering some of our hopes. It is certainly not my purpose to destroy your optimism about change. But it is also not my purpose to assure everybody they can change in every way. My purpose is to instill a new, warranted optimism about the parts of your life you can change and so help you focus your limited time, money, and effort on making actual what is truly within your reach.

Life is a long period of change. What you have been able to change and what has resisted your highest resolve might seem chaotic to you: for some of what you are never changes no matter how hard you try, and other aspects change readily. My hope is that this essay has been the beginning of wisdom about the difference.

Yes, you too can see through the defenses people hide behind. To guide you, just consult the handy primer below. Put together by psychiatrist Emanuel H. Rosen, it distills years of Freudian analytical training into a few simple principles that make sense of our psyches.

THINK LIKE A SHRINK

I have always thought it horribly unfortunate that there is such a tremendous gap between psychiatry and popular culture. Psychiatrists are regularly vilified in entertainment, media, and common thought, and our patients are regularly stigmatized. Indeed, I've yet to see a single movie that accurately portrays what we do. From *Silence of the Lambs* to *The Prince of Tides,* we shrinks have a reputation as crazy unbalanced people who can read people's minds. Even the hit comedy *The Santa Clause* made us out to be bimbos.

To some degree, we've gotten just what we deserve. We've allowed ourselves to become, in the public mind at least, mere pill-pushers and to have our uncommon sense dismissed as having zero significance when, in fact, it applies to every moment of every person's life. It is our failure to educate our patients and the general public about the deeper principles of human functioning that have left us so isolated from our communities.

Most patients come to psychiatrists because they recognize that, to some degree, their perceptions contain some distortions. These are usually defensive. For example, a 40-year-old woman may begin her first session with a psychiatrist complaining of a "biological depression" and demanding Prozac. By the end of the hour, however, she may acknowledge that her husband's 10-year refusal to have sex may have as much to do with her unhappy mood.

In my practice, I've engaged in a kind of educational psychotherapy, explaining simply to patients what they are doing and why they are doing it. The result has been not only remarkably effective but catalytic in speeding up the process of psychotherapy The same approach can help the general pub-

> **W**e all play to a hidden audience—Mom and Dad—inside our heads. Especially to Mom, whose nurturing is vital to our self-esteem—though it's not politically correct to say so.

lic delve beneath social images and better understand the deeper struggles of the people around them, and of themselves as well.

Ideas and principles can be introduced directly without the jargon psychiatrists normally hide behind in professional discussions. Doing this in a compassionate and empathic way could lead to a broadening of the vocabulary of the general public and bring about a wider acceptance of certain basic psychological truths.

The core of what we do as psychotherapists is strip away people's protective strategies. If you understand these defensive strategies and the core issues people tend to defend themselves against, you can see through people and, to a lesser extent, yourself.

Here, then, are some general principles to help you think like a shrink. Master them and you will—in some cases dramatically—increase your understanding of the world around you. You *can* see through people. *You* can read their minds.

1.

If you want to know how emotionally healthy someone is, look only at their intimate relationships.

Good-looking, athletic, charismatic, confident, rich, or intelligent people are not always emotionally healthy. For example, chronologically they may be adults, but emotionally, they may be two-year-olds. You will not really be able to make any kind of accurate, in-depth assessment of people until you learn to distinguish their superficial physical qualities from meaningful emotional ones. There are at least three key things you want to know:

• Most importantly how long-lived and committed are their current intimate relationships?

• Secondly, how much negative conflict do they experience in their work environments and how long have they held their current jobs?

• Finally what was their childhood experience like in their family of origin? Or, in plain English, did they get along with their family?

2.

How you feel about yourself (your self-esteem) is significantly determined by how nurturing your mother, father, and siblings were to you when you were growing

up—especially your mother, though it is not politically correct to say so.

It is not that mothers are to blame for all of a patient's problems. It is simply that stable healthy mothering is a strong buffer against a tremendous amount of pathology.

3.

How you relate to intimate people is always based on how you related to your family when you were growing up.

Basically, we all keep our families with us forever. We keep them in our heads. For the rest of our lives, we will have tendencies to either take on the roles of our childhood selves or those of our parents. Examine carefully your relationships with your family. It will tell you a lot about who you are.

4.

We all play to a hidden audience—Mom and Dad—inside our heads.

You often see people do strange things in their interpersonal interactions. "Where did *that* come from," you often ask. It came from a hidden screenplay that was written in that person's head.

Ostensibly he's reacting to you, but in his head, he's reacting to his mother. In fact, the less he remembers of his childhood, the more he is going to act out with you. This leads nicely to. . . .

5.

People who say they "don't remember" their childhood are usually emotionally troubled.

Physically healthy individuals who can't recall their youth have frequently endured some painful experiences that their minds are blocking out. As a result, they really don't know who they are. They have what we psychiatrists call a diminished sense of identity.

6.

Victims like to be aggressors sometimes, and aggressors are often reconstituted victims.

People actually may become more actively aggressive when they feel forced into a passive position.

7.

Yes, Virginia, there is an "unconscious" or "non-conscious" mind, and it basically determines your life, everything from what job you choose to whom you marry.

All the feelings that you had about yourself, your parents, and family are buried in this "unconscious mind." Also buried here are some very deep fears which will be touched on below

The more aware you are of your unconscious mind, the more freedom you will have.

8.

Sex is critical, no matter what anyone says.

Sex has become passé as an important explanatory factor of human behavior. Nowadays, it is more politically correct to emphasize the role of feelings, thoughts, and emotions than the role of sex. Nonetheless, sexual functioning and sexual history *do* tell you a tremendous amount about what people are really like.

9.

Whenever you have two men, or two women, in a room, you have homosexual tension.

It is a core truth that all people have both heterosexual and homosexual drives. What varies is how you deal with those drives. Just because you have a homosexual impulse or idea has absolutely nothing to do with your sexual orientation. You are defined by your sexual *behavior*, not your sexual *impulses*.

The people in our society who are most

against homosexuality are the people who are most uncomfortable with their own homosexual impulses. These impulses are banished from their conscious awareness.

10.

Yes, children do want to be sexual with the opposite sex parent at some point in their young lives, often between the ages of four and six.

Just about everyone is grossed out at the thought of their parents having sex. This is because there is a significant resistance against one's own memory of sexual feelings towards one's parents.

It does not mean, however, that you have to remember your sexual impulses towards a parent to be emotionally healthy. In fact, one of the most common issues an adult has to deal with is the incomplete repression of this core conflict.

11.

There is indeed such a thing as castration anxiety.

In fact, it's the most frightening core fear that people have. It's probably not only evolutionary adaptive, but emotionally important.

12.

Women do not have nearly as much penis envy as men do.

Men are all deep down very preoccupied with their penis. Concerns usually revolve around how big it is, how long, how thick, and how deep it goes.

This is an important issue that will likely never be researched because it makes everyone way too uncomfortable to talk about. There is more mythology on this subject than the Greeks ever wrote.

13.

The Oedipus complex is what keeps psychiatrists in business.

Though lay people tend to think only of the complex's sexual aspects, it really boils down to competition. It's commonly about being bigger, richer, more powerful, a winner or a loser. The feelings surrounding it are universal—and intense.

Getting through the various stages of psychological development—oral, anal, and Oedipal—can be summarized as teach-

> **M**en have much more penis envy than do women. They're all very preoccupied with their penis—how big it is, how long, how thick, and how deep it goes.

ing you three key things:

• To feel stable and secure, to depend on people reasonably

• To feel in control

• To feel able to compete successfully and to feel like a man or a woman.

14.

People are basically the same underneath it all; that is, they all want to satisfy similar deeper needs and quell identical underlying fears.

In general, people all seem to want money, power, and admiration. They want sexual gratification. They want to, as the Bible notes of Judah and Israel, "sit under their vine and fig tree and have none make them afraid." They want to feel secure. They want to feel loved.

Related to this principle: money and intelligence do not protect you. It is only emotional health that keeps you on an even keel; your feelings about yourself and your intimate stable relationships are the only ballast that matters in life.

> **O**ur best defense is a good offense. When people act in an egotistical fashion, their underlying feeling is that they are "dick-less" or impotent.

15.

People often act exactly the opposite of the way they feel, especially when they are unhealthy.

Or: the best defense is a good offense. When people act egotistical, their underlying feeling is that they are "dick-less" or impotent.

16.

More on defenses . . .

Here is human nature in a nutshell. My favorite line from the movie *The Big Chill* is voiced by the character played by Jeff Goldblum. "Where would you be, where would any of us be, without a good rationalization? Try to live without a rationalization; I bet you couldn't do it."

We distort reality both outside and in our minds in order to survive. Distortions of our inner world are common. *Regression*, one of the most intriguing defenses, can be particularly illuminating to acknowledge; it means acting like a kid to avoid the real world.

"Outside" distortions can get us in very serious trouble.

Denial can be fatal whether it involves alcohol abuse or a herd of charging elephants.

Devaluing, or, in simple terms, throwing the baby out with the bath water, comes in handy when we want to insult somebody. But it can be detrimental—for example, causing us to miss a lecturer's important points because we consider the teacher to be a "total jerk."

Idealizing, or putting people on a pedestal, can be hurtful—say when you realize your ex-Navy Seal stockbroker has been churning your brokerage account.

Projecting feelings onto others is a common defensive distortion. Guilt is a painful feeling, so sometimes we may see other people as angry at us rather than feel guilty ourselves. "I know that you are angry that I forgot your birthday" you say. "Don't deny it."

Finally *splitting* our view of the world into good guys and bad guys is a distortion, even if it makes for a great western.

17.

To be successful in the highly competitive American business marketplace requires a personality ethos that will destroy your intimate relationships.

At this point, you are probably experiencing some confusion. After all, I've been saying that it is unhealthy to be striving continuously to compensate for feelings of inferiority or impotency. Yet most people know that it is in fact the strivers who achieve enormous power and success in the world around them.

In order to be emotionally healthy, however, it is necessary for these "winners" to leave their work personalities at the door of their homes and become their natural selves once they cross the threshold. It is absolutely essential that the driven, rushed, acquisitive capitalist ethos not enter into the realm of intimate relationships.

CEOs of corporations and doctors are particularly at risk for this type of contamination of their family life. People who have the best of both worlds—career and rela-

> **S**trangers who blurt out their entire life story at a first meeting, even if it's with a psychiatrist, are likely to be troubled. They have no "boundary"— and they should.

tionships—are those who realize that success in the workplace does not make up for lack of success at home.

18.

How well people deal with death is usually identical to how well they have dealt with life.

19.

How people relate to you in everyday life can tell you a lot about their deeper issues, even in a very short time.

You can tell a tremendous amount about somebody's emotional stability and character by the way they say goodbye to you. People who cling or drag out good-byes often have deep-seated issues with separation. Of course, we all have issues with separation; it's a matter of degree. Those of us from loving stable backgrounds carry around a warm fuzzy teddy bear of sorts that helps us cope with saying good-bye and being alone. Without this security blanket of loving memories, being alone or saying good-bye can be hell.

A stranger who tells you his entire life's story on the first interview even if you are a psychiatrist, is also probably emotionally unhealthy because there is no boundary between that person and you—and there should be. After all, you are a stranger to that person.

20.

Listen with your third ear.

One of my mentors at Duke University Medical Center once defined the "third ear" as follows: "While you're listening to what a patient is saying, with your third ear listen to why they are saying it." Psychiatrists listen in a unique way. A family practitioner examines your ears with an otoscope. A psychiatrist examines your feelings with himself as the tool.

When you are interacting with another person, if you notice yourself feeling a certain way the odds are that your companion is somehow intending you to feel that way. You have to be emotionally stable to accurately use yourself as the examining tool.

When you become adept at identifying what you are feeling, the next step is to determine why. There are usually two reasons. Number one, it may be because you are resonating with what the person is feeling. A second possibility is that you are being subtly provoked to play a complementary emotional role in a scene that has an often hidden script.

The process of using one's own heart as a "scope" is hard work. The fancy term for this process is "counter-transference."

21.

Behind every fear, there is a wish.

Wishes that are often consciously unacceptable can be expressed more easily as "fears." Related to this principle is the maxim: "Beware unsolicited denials." A common example is the seemingly spontaneous statement, "I don't really care at all about money!" Hold on to your wallet.

The Doctor's In, The Patient's Not / Even when they think it would help them, many people resist counseling

By Carol Polsky
STAFF WRITER

Portrait of someone in trouble: The man, a professional in his 30s, was frequently withdrawn. He didn't like socializing at the events his wife dragged him to, he wasn't very involved with his young kids. His wife urged him to get therapy, but he said she exaggerated the problems and there was nothing wrong with him.

The impasse came to a head a few years ago when his wife threatened to leave him unless he went for help. At a psychiatric consultation, his wife gave their history while he sat silently and denied the seriousness of what she described, according to a psychiatrist familiar with the case.

Over the next six months, however, he came for weekly therapy sessions, and eventually improved considerably with a combination of antidepressant medication and psychotherapy. He confessed that he'd considered depression to be a weakness and hadn't wanted to be identified as someone with a problem. And he said he never thought he could have felt so much better.

Such resistance to therapy is not uncommon.

"Some degree of resistance is almost universal," said Dr. John Kane, chief of staff of Hillside Hospital, the psychiatric division of the North Shore-Long Island Jewish Health System. "Most people feel some hesitancy about accepting the need for *treatment*. That's the amazing thing. People are willing to put up with all kinds of limitations in their ability to function or enjoy life rather than seek help."

The reasons can be relatively straightforward. Therapy means a commitment of sometimes scarce time, money and energy. It can mean exposing very personal information to the scrutiny of anonymous insurance company employees in order to get reimbursed. Some people may have had unsatisfactory experiences with therapy in the past. To others, it seems ridiculous to spend so much money just to sit and tell some stranger their problems. And there may be little motivation to rock the boat and seek out a therapist for emotional difficulties as long as life continues along without an immediate crisis.

But resistance often comes from a deeper place. People develop ways to contain the anxiety in their lives, and even though some of these so-called "coping mechanisms" seem self-destructive—obsessive-compulsive behaviors, for example, or denial about an abusive relationship—they keep people going. Giving them up can feel threatening.

"It's like being caught in a raging river hanging onto a tree limb, which is our coping mechanism," said Dr. Naomi Sadowsky of the Center for Psychotherapy in Mineola. "The fear of letting go of that tree limb depends on how well it is working at that moment."

Holding on to that branch, weak though it may be, "feels a whole lot more steady than trusting the words of some stranger who says, 'I'm an expert at getting you across this river, just let go of that tree limb,' " Sadowsky said.

The seemingly dysfunctional behaviors that some people develop may actually give them a feeling of control or deflect attention from deeper problems. "It keeps you on an equilibrium. You're not going forward and resolving a major problem that needs to be dealt with to feel happy and healthy, but you don't fall behind, either," Sadowsky said. There's a "psychic payoff" to seemingly dysfunctional behavior that raises the question of "Does it seem less costly to the psyche than making the changes?"

For many people, the resistance to therapy comes from "an avoidance to facing pain," said Thomas Conway, a therapist and director of the Commack Consultation Center. "You're talking a lot of times about patterns of communication and behavior that have been in place for a long time, and to change them is difficult.

"Everybody has some self-defeating side to their personality," he added. A pattern of coping "might not be comfortable, but it's known."

And once people do get into therapy, they have to dig into the reasons behind their behavior and expectations, he said. "They have to confront the pain behind that. They have to relearn who they are."

And that means giving up control, he said, opening the door to emotional tumult, finding who-knows-what emotional tarantula under what previously unturned stone. And it means making a long-term commitment to expending energy, money and time, and possibly facing disruptive life changes—like admitting a marriage is abusive and must change or end.

One woman, a mother and freelance writer who asked not to be identified, said she quite consciously resisted going into individual therapy even though she felt she might benefit from it in dealing with unresolved childhood and professional issues.

"It's the can of worms," she said. "You don't want to deal with the consequences of opening the can of worms."

"Things may not be ideal, but you have emotional control," she said. "Life and relationships are in a kind of functional standoff . . . There's the fear that if you start messing with that you'll lose that control and then there's a long and arduous process to regain it."

When people are in crisis—when they are becoming overwhelmed by their emotions or aren't able to function comfortably—they are less likely to resist therapy. But fear of being stigmatized by the label of *mental illness* may interfere with getting help even then.

Thomas Raab, a school psychologist in the New Hyde Park school system with a private practice in Dix Hills and Rockville Centre, said that some people avoid *treatment* because they're "fearful of finding something out or having someone tell them there is severe pathology."

Conversely, people might "need to be in counseling to work through a problem—they're depressed, they're down, there are difficulties with kids or family—but they're afraid they shouldn't be in therapy unless they're clinically something or other, that the only people who should be in therapy are those who are very ill, psychotic. Or they are afraid of that, that it will reflect poorly on themselves."

But most people and families in his practice, he said, had no real specific pathology—just life problems they needed help with.

By the time most people get to the therapist's office, they've overcome at least the initial resistance to getting help. Sometimes, they come for a consultation and are not convinced that they will continue. At that point, said Kane of Hillside Hospital, he as the therapist would try to help the patient overcome any fears.

"The first thing is to get the person to acknowlege what kind of problems they are really having and what are the consequences of those problems, and to acknowlege that they would like to do something about it, and accept the possiblity that therapy might help," he said. "What do they have to lose?"

The fear of being stigmatized does keep people from getting proper *treatment*, Kane said, pointing out that at least one in five people in this country will have a diagnosable *mental* disorder at some point in his or her life.

"It was not so long ago that people were embarrassed to admit they had cancer," he said. "Part of the fear of the stigma is, you observe how people are treated if they behave bizarrely or are not behaving normally. If you've seen that, you fear that could happen to you."

But, he said, "the overwhelming majority of people with disorders are not dangerous or going to act in some bizarre clinical way."

The majority of cases involve anxiety and depression, he said. A psychiatric disorder is "beyond what we'd consider to be the normal moods and anxieties people have every day. It's more persistent, more severe."

Research shows, he said, that these are treatable conditions rather than a failure of

willpower, or weakness, or giving in to feelings that should be dealt with on one's own.

Kane said that he and fellow *mental* health professionals were trying to do more public education about the nature of these disorders and the fact that they "are very treatable, that people shouldn't try to deny that anything is wrong."

"It's very sad if someone is not living their life the way they could."

Even with severe *mental illness*, such as schizophrenia, "We can treat them. We can't cure them, but we can bring about tremendous improvement in most cases."

And resistance itself can serve the purpose of feeling better: For Conway, of Commack, resistance is the core of his therapy. If the patient can understand the reasons for resistance and work through it, he said, "you are three-quarters of the way through."

Three Voices Of Experience

WHEN YOU or someone you care about shows signs of persistent unhappiness or sadness, excessive anxiety, anger or irritability, changes in appetite or sleep patterns, preoccupations, inability to concentrate, persistent unresolved conflicts in relationships, irrational or suicidal thoughts, or bizarre behavior, therapy may help.

While it's impossible to force unwilling adults into therapy unless they are actually psychotic, Dr. John Kane, chief of staff at Hillside Hospital, a division of the North Shore-Long Island Jewish Health System, offered some suggestions on how to persuade someone to seek help:

• Suggest that the person go one time for a consultation to determine whether there is a problem.
• offer to accompany him or her.
• Say that there's nothing to lose and no commitment made by going to a consultation.
• Start with the family physician for a recommendation if the person is more comfortable with that.
• In some cases it may be appropriate to tell a loved one, a friend or co-worker that he or she urgently needs to get help because psychological difficulties or behavior are threatening to relationships, job or marriage. "It's very hard because you're afraid to hurt the person or make things worse, but ignoring or denying the severity of a situation can be much

more harmful in the long run," Kane said.
• Call *mental* health clinics, hospitals or your physician for evaluations or referrals, or get a referral from professional societies of social workers, psychotherapists, psychologists or psychiatrists (who are medical doctors and the only *mental* health professionals able to prescribe drugs). Long Island Jewish-Schneider Children's Hospital offers referrals to therapists, local *mental* health clinics and outpatient programs to those calling 888-LIJ-DOCS.
• There are different types of therapies available: long and short-term, behavioral and psychodynamic, individual and group therapy, marriage and family counseling. Ask the *mental* health professional you consult to discuss the available options, what his or her own approach is and what might be most appropriate for you.
• Programs and clinics that treat specific problems, such as eating disorders or phobias, may be appropriate.
• Children and adolescents should be seen by therapists specializing in their age group.
• If financial considerations are an issue, ask about less expensive therapy options.
• If someone is unhappy with a therapist or is not making progress after some weeks or months, discuss the difficulty with the therapist. It may be part of the patient's resistance, and be resolved through further therapy, but patient and therapist may simply be mismatched. If the difficulty persists, get a second opinion with another therapist.

Chronic Anxiety:

How to Stop Living on the Edge

Feeling nervous is a normal response to stressful situations. Sweaty palms, a racing heart, and butterflies in the stomach are felt by everyone from seasoned performers stepping into the spotlight to the person addressing a group for the first time. These sensations are caused by a rush of stress hormones, such as norepinephrine and cortisol, which prepare the body and mind to rise to a challenge.

Chronic anxiety, however, is very different from the healthy feelings of nervousness that make a speaker effective or enable a sprinter to win a race. Indeed, anxiety disorders are, by definition, psychiatric illnesses that are not useful for normal functioning. Instead of calling a person to action, chronic anxiety can damage relationships, reduce productivity, and make someone terrified of everyday experiences.

Anxiety illnesses are among the most common disorders, affecting more than 23 million Americans (about 1 in 9). Fortunately, sufferers often get substantial relief from various forms of talk therapy, medication, or both. But the majority of people with anxiety disorders do not seek help because they may not recognize their symptoms as a psychiatric problem or may fear being stigmatized with a "mental illness."

There is strong evidence that anxiety conditions run in families. And recent findings suggest that a genetic predisposition to anxiety, when triggered by certain

> **Although anxiety disorders are common, many people do not seek help because they don't realize that treatments are available.**

life experiences (such as early losses or trauma), may alter a person's brain chemistry, causing an illness to surface.

The most common of these conditions and, surprisingly, the least understood is *generalized anxiety disorder* (GAD). Believed to affect about 10 million Americans, it is characterized by unrelenting, exaggerated worry and tension; it can keep people from socializing, traveling, getting a better job, or pursuing a sport or avocation. GAD affects people of both sexes and all ages but is diagnosed more often in adult women, possibly because of hormonal differences or because women seek mental health treatment more frequently than men, whose rate of anxiety may be underestimated. Some mental health experts believe that men manifest anxiety (as well as depression) differently from women: they drink more alcohol, smoke more, and are more prone to aggressive behavior.

The psychiatric diagnosis of GAD is chronic, exaggerated worry and tension that has lasted for more than 6 months, although most people with the disorder can trace it back to childhood or adolescence. They may worry excessively about health, money, family, or work, even when there is no sign of difficulty. And they have trouble relaxing and often have insomnia. Many live from day to day with distressing physical symptoms such as trembling, sweating, muscle tension, or headaches, which tend to worsen when they face even mild stress.

GAD frequently coexists with depression, and certain antidepressants seem to work quite well for people with GAD. Many of these medications regulate levels of brain chemicals such as serotonin and norepinephrine, but scientists do not have a complete understanding of the biology of anxiety or depression or why they often go hand in hand.

A March 1998 symposium in Boston, cosponsored by the National Institute of Mental Health and the Anxiety Disorders Association of America, was among the first dedicated to the interplay between fear and anxiety and the workings of the brain. Some scientists are focusing on a brain structure called the *amygdala*, which regulates fear, memory, and emotion. When a person is exposed to a fearful event, the amygdala coordinates the brain's physical responses, such as increased heart rate and blood pressure. And preliminary research suggests that the release of the stress hormones norepinephrine and cortisol may act in a way that greatly increases memory of the fearful or traumatic event, allowing it to remain vivid for years. (For more on stress hormones, see *Harvard Health Letter*, April 1998.)

Because basic research has uncovered chemical and hormonal differences in how males and females respond to fear and anxiety, investigators are studying the role that estrogen and cyclical hormonal changes may play in women with anxiety disorders.

Late-life anxiety

Although studies indicate that the prevalence of major depression and certain anxiety disorders declines in the over-65 population, depression affects about 1 in 7 in this group. But there are no hard data on how many of them are troubled by chronic anxiety. Researchers, however, believe that GAD is the most common form of anxiety in older people. They estimate that up to two thirds of older individuals with depression have GAD, and the same amount with GAD have depression. (For more on late-life depression, see *Harvard Health Letter*, March 1995.)

Doctors may have difficulty diagnosing anxiety disorders in older people because some of the characteristics of anxiety, such as blood pressure elevations or a racing heart, may be attributable to a physical illness. Indeed, anxiety may be overlooked when a potentially serious medical condition captures a doctor's attention.

Getting well

There are two main roads to treating GAD: talk therapy and medication. Some mental health professionals place great value on *cognitive-behavioral therapy* (CBT); instead of focusing on deep-seated childhood feelings, the therapist helps the patient look realistically at the exaggerated or pessimistic beliefs that flood the mind. Eventually, the

Finding Help

The following national organizations can provide referrals for mental health professionals and/or support groups in your area.

American Psychiatric Association
Phone: (202) 682-6220
Internet: http://www.psych.org

American Psychological Association
Phone: (202) 336-5800
Internet: http://www.helping.apa.org

Anxiety Disorders Association of America
Phone: (301) 231-9350
Internet: http://www.adaa.org

National Alliance for the Mentally Ill
Phone: (800) 950-NAMI
Internet: http://www.nami.org

person learns to think rationally about his or her fears, and anxiety is reduced.

However, other mental health experts say that although CBT may have an excellent short-term effect, it is not necessarily a lifetime one. Many psychotherapists believe that the only way to help someone reduce chronic anxiety for good is to work with the patient over time so he or she can talk about and process traumatic or fearful events, which may have occurred years earlier. Indeed, many people experience a substantial reduction in anxious thoughts when they explore childhood fears or secrets with a supportive and knowledgeable psychiatrist, psychologist, or social worker.

Useful medications

Some types of drugs, such as *benzodiazepines* (mild tranquilizers) are taken every day or on an as-needed basis when stress or worry becomes overwhelming; others, such as antidepressants, must be taken daily, sometimes indefinitely. It is best to combine some form of talk therapy with medication, but many people do not feel the need or they lack the financial resources to do both.

Historically, anxiety has been treated with benzodiazepines. These include diazepam (Valium), alprazolam (Xanax), and lorazepam (Ativan). Although many people who consider taking one of these medications or who are currently on one worry that they are addictive, this is usually not the case, particularly if the person has never abused drugs or alcohol in the past. Some individuals may develop a physical dependence on them, which means that they should reduce their dose slowly when going off the medication. Doctors rarely prescribe benzodiazepines for people with addictive tendencies.

Although the medications are generally well tolerated by people who do not abuse them, they can be a problem in older people, because early side effects include drowsiness, impaired reflexes and motor skills, and confusion. Older individuals are more prone to falls and car accidents during the first few weeks of taking a benzodiazepine.

Antidepressants are being used more frequently to treat GAD. They do not generally have the side effects of benzodiazepines and are considered safer and more effective for long-term use. Numerous investigations have shown that the *selective-serotonin reuptake inhibitors* (SSRIs), sold as Prozac, Paxil, and Zoloft, newer antidepressants such as nefazodone (Serzone), and the older tricyclic antidepressants (imipramine, for example) can significantly reduce symptoms of GAD. A drug called buspirone (BuSpar), which is not an antidepressant but is designed specifically for anxiety, is useful for some people.

The first step in getting help is to see your primary care physician, who can refer you to a mental health professional if you want to explore talk therapy. Another way to find a good counselor is to ask friends or family who have worked with one they liked.

Either your primary care doctor or a psychiatrist can prescribe medication. However, primary care physicians generally do not have time to engage in lengthy or ongoing discussions, so you may prefer to see a mental health professional. Whether you've lived with chronic anxiety for 6 months or 60 years, GAD can be treated. You can get the help you need by asking for it.

Up from Depression

Depression is perhaps the most treatable of all mood disorders.

JEFF KELSEY, M.D.

MAJOR DEPRESSION, ALSO KNOWN AS CLINICAL depression, is more than an ordinary case of the blues. The disorder drags on for at least two weeks, draining all the color and meaning out of life. Activities that once brought pleasure become tedious chores. Negative thoughts—guilt, worthlessness, hopelessness—crowd out all others.

• About one in every six of us will suffer an episode of depression. But less than half will be accurately diagnosed—and fewer than 15 percent who are diagnosed will get adequate treatment. Yet depression is perhaps the most treatable of all mood disorders: medication, psychotherapy, or both can relieve suffering and restore wellness in 80 to 90 percent of patients, often in a matter of weeks. • The causes of depression are murky. Just as no single factor is to blame for most heart attacks—family history, chronic illness, and unhealthy behaviors usually share responsibility—no single factor appears to cause depression. • Depression likely results from a convergence of multiple biological, psychological, and social factors, from hormones to hard times. Risk factors for major depression include female gender; lower socio-economic status; separation or divorce; early childhood trauma or parental loss; and other significant negative life events, including major illness or disability. • Heredity may play a role as well. Studies of twins raised apart have demonstrated that depression is genetic. It seems likely that a vulnerability to depression can be inherited. • Some of the most exciting research in depression centers on neurotransmitters, chemical messengers in the brain that carry signals from one neuron to another. Neurotransmitters involved in depression include serotonin, norepinephrine, corticotrophin-releasing factor, dopamine, and substance P. People with depression have alterations in these neurotransmitters.

Treating Depression

MILD TO MODERATE DEPRESSION APPEARS to respond equally well to psychotherapy (talking therapy) or pharmacotherapy (antidepressant medication). Several types of psychotherapy are available for the brief treatment of depression. The effectiveness of two of these types, cognitive-behavioral therapy and interpersonal therapy, has been particularly well-documented. Both focus on the present and take a practical, problem-solving approach to treatment.

Psychotherapy: Cognitive-behavioral therapy helps a depressed patient recognize, challenge, and change negative thought patterns and distorted perspectives, producing positive changes in outlook and mood. A depressed individual cannot simply will himself or herself to feel better. It's a common misconception that depression reflects a weakness of character and that depressed people simply need to "try harder." Before change can occur, negative and distorted thought patterns must be identified.

Interpersonal therapy is based on the theory that interpersonal problems can trigger or aggravate depression. Current interpersonal relationships are explored, and specific problem areas are identified as targets of treatment.

Pharmacotherapy: For more-severe depression, antidepressants should be considered—either alone or in combination with psychotherapy. Many people begin to see an improvement within one to three weeks of starting an antidepressant medication. In contrast, untreated major depression typically lasts from six months to two years.

The more episodes of depression a person has had, the longer treatment should last. Eight to 14 months of antidepressant therapy is appropriate for a first episode. For patients who have suffered three or more episodes of depression—especially if the episodes were severe—longterm treatment is suggested.

Selective serotonin reuptake inhibitors (SSRIs) were introduced more than a decade ago. These agents—including fluoxetine (Prozac); sertraline (Zoloft); paroxetine (Paxil); fluvoxamine (Luvox); and citalopram (Celexa)—are safer and have far fewer side effects than the older antidepressants.

SSRIs are thought to relieve depression by inhibiting the "reuptake" of serotonin by neurons in the brain. Neurotransmitters like serotonin communicate only two messages: "on" and "off." To signal "on," a neurotransmitter binds, or attaches, to a receptor cell. To signal "off," the neurotransmitter detaches from the receptor. Cells that manufacture norepinephrine, serotonin, or dopamine often will sweep up unbound neurotransmitters, repackage them, and release them again. This recycling is referred to as reuptake. SSRIs slow down the reuptake of serotonin, so that neurons in the brain must manufacture more new serotonin molecules each time an "on" signal needs to be sent. As a result, circulating levels of serotonin in the brain increase.

While the SSRIs are much better tolerated than older antidepressant agents, side effects remain. Common side effects include nausea, insomnia, sedation, headaches, sweating, reduced sexual desire, and difficulty reaching orgasm. The side effects may go away after the first few weeks, as the body adjusts to a new medication. Starting at a low dose and gradually increasing to the desired dose may minimize side effects. Taking the medication after meals may reduce nausea. Even when side effects persist, however, many people are happy to trade depression for these relatively minor complaints.

SNRIs: The New Generation of Antidepressants

A NEW GENERATION OF ANTIDEPRESSANTS, serotonin norepinephrine reuptake inhibitors (SNRIs), has revolutionized the treatment of depression. Serotonin and norepinephrine are neurotransmitters that are believed to be involved in the treatment of major depression. SNRIs include antidepressants such as venlafaxine XR (Effexor XR). Studies have shown that venlafaxine XR may be a more effective antidepressant than fluoxetine (Prozac). The studies demonstrate that a significantly greater number of patients receiving venlafaxine XR, compared with fluoxetine, achieve full remission, which means that patients taking venlafaxine XR were able to reduce their symptoms more completely than those taking fluoxetine.

These efficacy data have raised the bar in treating depression. Physicians are now looking for their treatments to provide not only symptomatic improvement, but also the fullest possible recovery for their patients. It is no longer enough for patients to get better; they need to get well.

Other newer antidepressants also are useful for large numbers of patients. Bupropion (Wellbutrin SR) is thought to act through the norepinephrine system and, perhaps, the dopamine system to treat depression. Two other agents, nefazodone (Serzone) and mirtazapine (Remeron), exert their antidepressant effects not by inhibiting reuptake but by preventing neurotransmitters from binding to receptors. Nefazodone blocks the serotonin type-2 receptor, and mirtazapine blocks the serotonin type-2 and type-3 receptors, along with the norepinephrine alpha-2 receptor.

In general, if an antidepressant has not improved symptoms of depression within four to six weeks, it's time to consider another approach to treatment. The American Psychiatric Association (APA) recommends three broad strategies in such cases. One choice is to switch to an antidepressant with a biochemical profile that is different from the first one. If switching is not desirable, the APA suggests adding thyroid hormone or lithium to the original antidepressant. A third choice is to add a second antidepressant to the first.

The monoamine oxidase inhibitors (MAOIs) and tricyclic antidepressants are older-generation antidepressants that represent valuable alternatives for patients who don't respond to any of the newer-generation agents. Developed in the 1950s, the MAOIs and tricyclic antidepressants were the mainstay of depression treatment for three decades before the SSRIs reached the market.

The MAOIs, including phenelzine (Nardil) and tranylcypromine (Parnate), are presumed to work by inhibiting an enzyme, monoamine oxidase, that is responsible for the metabolism of norepinephrine, serotonin, and dopamine. The MAOIs are highly effective at treating depression, but they are generally harder for patients to tolerate than the SSRIs. Not only do the MAOIs cause more troublesome side effects, but patients on MAOIs also must avoid aged or fermented foods and beverages. Another concern is that the

Do You Have Depression?

You may have depression if you have suffered from a depressed mood or loss of interest or pleasure in most activities more days than not for at least two weeks; if at least five of the following symptoms have also been present more days than not, for at least two weeks; and if the symptoms are causing difficulties in your life.

❖ significant weight loss or gain

❖ change in sleeping patterns (either more or less)

❖ being noticeably more agitated or slowed down

❖ fatigue or loss of energy

❖ feelings of worthlessness or excessive guilt

❖ difficulty concentrating or making decisions

❖ recurrent thoughts of death or suicide

It's important to remember that many of these symptoms can be caused by conditions other than depression, such as thyroid deficiency and anemia. In addition, medications prescribed for other illnesses may cause side effects that resemble depression. Anyone who is experiencing symptoms of depression should see a knowledgeable health care provider for an accurate diagnosis.

MAOIs can be fatal when taken with certain other prescription medications.

The tricyclic antidepressants include imipramine (Tofranil and others); nortriptyline (Pamelor); desipramine (Norpramin); and amitriptyline (Elavil). Although tricyclic antidepressants are less expensive than newer-generation agents, their side-effect profile and safety concerns are worrisome. Common side effects include dry mouth, constipation, weight gain, dizziness, and rapid heart rate. In addition, an overdose of a tricyclic antidepressant can cause serious heart damage.

Other Therapy: For an unfortunate minority of patients, no combination of drugs seems to control depression. Two nondrug treatments, electroconvulsive therapy (ECT) and transcranial magnetic therapy, can be life-saving for these individuals. ECT is perhaps the most effective treatment for depression that cannot be controlled with drugs or psychotherapy, and it is very safe as currently performed. ECT is generally reserved for patients who have failed other treatments or have a life-threatening depression, due either to suicidal intentions or failure to eat or drink fluids.

Depression and Anxiety

WHILE DEPRESSION AND ANXIETY ARE considered separate clinical conditions, they often are closely intertwined. Epidemiological studies show that of patients who are treated for anxiety, more than one-third also suffer from depression, and nearly two-thirds are diagnosed with another mood or anxiety disorder. Conversely, up to 90 percent of patients being treated for depression exhibit one or more symptoms of anxiety. A better understanding of the relationship between depression and anxiety may have important clinical implications for the management of patients who suffer from these conditions.

Most people experience anxiety at one time or another due to stressful life situations, such as bereavement or illness. But unlike everyday anxiety, clinical anxiety is a chronic, pathological condition. Clinical anxiety may appear in a wide array of forms, including generalized anxiety disorder (GAD), obsessive-compulsive disorder, panic, phobias (fears), or eating disorders.

A person who experiences both anxiety and depression simultaneously may find that the symptoms of one disorder exacerbate the other. For example, the presence of GAD may predict a worse outcome for people with another psychiatric diagnosis, such as depression. In addition, depressed patients with a high level of anxiety are at an increased risk of committing suicide. While treatments for anxiety do exist, venlafaxine XR has been shown to be the first antidepressant that may treat both depression and anxiety.

Major depression is a source of significant suffering and disability for many people—not only the patients themselves, but also their families, friends, and loved ones. Sadly, depression too often goes untreated, despite the availability of many safe and effective therapies, both biological and psychological.

The goal of treatment is to restore the depressed patient to a state of wellness and vitality, without any depressive symptoms at all. Merely lessening symptoms is not enough. With so many treatment options available, no one needs to accept depression as a way of life.

Dr. Kelsey is Assistant Professor and Director of the Mood and Anxiety Disorders Clinical Trials Program in the Department of Psychiatry and Behavioral Sciences at Emory University School of Medicine

The Clustering and Contagion of Suicide

Thomas E. Joiner, Jr.[1]
Department of Psychology, Florida State University, Tallahassee, Florida

Abstract

Two general types of suicide cluster have been discussed in the literature; roughly, these can be classified as mass clusters and point clusters. Mass clusters are media related, and the evidence for them is equivocal; point clusters are local phenomena, and these do appear to occur. Contagion has not been conceptually well developed nor empirically well supported as an explanation for suicide clusters. An alternative explanation for why suicides sometimes cluster is articulated: People who are vulnerable to suicide may cluster well before the occurrence of any overt suicidal stimulus, and when they experience severe negative events, including but not limited to the suicidal behavior of one member of the cluster, all members of the cluster are at increased risk for suicidality (a risk that may be offset by good social support).

Keywords

suicide clusters; suicide contagion

The phenomena of attempted and completed suicide are troubling and mysterious enough in themselves; the possibility that suicide is socially contagious, even more so. This article considers whether suicide clusters exist, and if so, whether "contagion" processes can account for them.

There is a potentially important distinction between the terms suicide cluster and suicide contagion. A cluster refers to the factual occurrence of two or more completed or attempted suicides that are nonrandomly "bunched" in space or time (e.g., a series of suicide attempts in the same high school or a series of completed suicides in response to the suicide of a celebrity). The term cluster implies nothing about *why* the cluster came to be, only *that* it came to be. By contrast, contagion refers to a possible explanation (as I argue later, a fairly vague explanation) of *why* a cluster developed. Clusters (of a sort) appear to occur, but the status of contagion as the reason for such occurrences is more equivocal.

CLUSTERS—OF A SORT— APPEAR TO OCCUR

Given that attempted and completed suicides are relatively rare, and given that they tend to be more or less evenly distributed in space and time (e.g., suicides occur at roughly the same rate in various regions of the United States and occur at roughly the same rate regardless of the day of the week or the month), it is statistically unlikely that suicides would cluster by chance alone. Yet cluster they do, at least under some circumstances. (Such clustering is often termed the "Werther effect," after a fictional character of Goethe's whose suicide purportedly inspired actual suicides in 18th-century Europe.) Two general types of suicide cluster have been discussed in the literature: mass clusters and point clusters. Mass clusters are media related; point clusters, local.

Point Clusters

Point clusters occur locally, involving victims who are relatively contiguous in both space and time. The prototypical setting is institutional (i.e., a school or a hospital). Probably the best documented example was reported by Brent and his colleagues (Brent, Kerr, Goldstein, & Bozigar, 1989). In a high school of approximately 1,500 students, 2 students committed suicide within 4 days. During an 18-day span that included the 2 completed suicides, 7 other students attempted suicide and an additional 23 reported having suicidal thoughts. It is important to note, though, that Brent and his colleagues found that 75% of the members of the cluster had at least one major psychiatric disorder, which had existed before the students' exposure to the suicides (i.e., they were vulnerable to begin with). Also, victims' close friends appeared to develop suicidal symptoms more readily than students who were less close to victims. In other words, social contiguity was an important factor.

Haw (1994) described a point cluster of 14 suicides within a 1-year period among patients of a London psychiatric unit. Thirteen of the 14 patients suffered from severe, chronic mental illness (e.g., schizophrenia), and most had ongoing therapeutic contact with the psychiatric unit. The author reported that the point cluster's occurrence may have stemmed from patients' valid perceptions that the future of the hospital was uncertain and that their access to medical staff was decreasing and ultimately threatened. Several other point clusters have also been described (see, e.g., Gould, Wallenstein, & Davidson, 1989).

When Point Clusters Do Not Occur

Given that suicidality runs in families, and that the suicide of a family member is an enormously traumatic event, one might imagine that point clusters would be particularly likely within a given family (e.g., the suicide of one family member might be followed closely by the suicide of another family member). However, within-family point clusters appear to be very rare. (Although certainly at least one has occurred, I could find no documented case in the literature. It is possible, however, that they are underreported or underpublicized.) Point clusters also appear not to occur within groupings beyond the institutional (e.g., at the level of a large community; cf. Chiu, 1988)—except, that is, in the (possible) case of mass clusters.

Mass Clusters

Unlike point cluster, mass clusters are media-related phenomena. They are grouped more in time than in space, and are purportedly in response to the publicizing of actual or fictional suicides. Phillips and his colleagues have examined the possible relation of suicide-related media events and the rate of subsequent suicides (see, e.g., Phillips & Carstensen, 1986, 1988). These researchers have argued that the suicide rate in the population increases in the days after descriptions of suicides appear in televised news reports and in newspapers. Indeed, in many of these studies, the suicide rate did appear to rise after a publicized suicide, although the effect did not always occur, and it appeared to be primarily applicable to adolescent suicide. Interestingly, these researchers also found that accidents, such as motor vehicle fatalities, may increase in the days following a publicized suicide, apparently because many such accidents are actually intentional suicides.

However, a study by Kessler, Downey, Milavsky, and Stipp (1988) cast doubt on the conclusion that mass clusters exist. Examining adolescent suicides from 1973 to 1984, the authors found no reliable relation between suicide-related newscasts and the subsequent adolescent suicide rate. Similarly, these researchers obtained no evidence that the number of teenagers viewing the newscasts (as determined by Neilsen ratings) was correlated with the number of adolescent suicides.

In the case of fictional portrayals of suicide (e.g., a television movie in which a character commits suicide), the evidence indicates, at most, a weak effect. Schmidtke and Haefner (1988) studied responses to a serial, broadcast twice in Germany, showing the railway suicide of a young man. After each broadcast, according to these researchers, railway suicides among young men (but not among other groups) increased sharply. However, several other researchers have conducted similar studies and concluded

that there was no relation between fictionalized accounts of suicide and the subsequent suicide rate, for adolescents in particular (Phillips & Paight, 1987; Simkin, Hawton, Whitehead, & Fagg, 1995), as well as for people in general (Berman, 1988).

CLUSTERING DOES NOT CONTAGION MAKE

If suicide clusters exist (and it appears that point clusters do, although mass clusters may not), contagion—the social, or interpersonal, transmission of suicidality from one victim to another—may or may not be involved. With regard to an array of unfortunate events (e.g., disasters, accidents, even illnesses), it is easy to imagine that there would be point clusters of victims without contagion of any sort. For example, the victims of the Chernobyl nuclear disaster were point-clustered, not because of any type of contagion between victims, but because of victims' simultaneous exposure to radiation. Even cases of mass suicide, the victims of which are point-clustered, are best viewed as instances of mass delusion (e.g., Heaven's Gate) or of a combination of delusion and coercion (e.g., Jonestown), rather than of contagion. In cases such as Chernobyl and even Jonestown, the point clustering of victims may be seen as due to the simultaneous effects of some pernicious, external influence, such as radiation, on a preexisting, socially contiguous group of people, such as those working at or living near the Chernobyl plant.

In disease, the agent of contagion (e.g., some microbial pathogen) is specified, and its mechanism of action delineated. By contrast, no persuasive agent or mechanism of suicide contagion has been articulated. Indeed, with one exception, the very definition of suicide contagion has been so vague as to defy analysis. The one exception is behavioral imitation, which, although clearly defined, lacks explanatory power (e.g., in a school, what determines who, among all the students, imitates a suicide?).

A SPECULATION REGARDING POINT-CLUSTERED SUICIDES

I suggest that the concepts of imitation or contagion may not be needed to explain point-clustered suicides. Rather, four sets of findings, taken together, indicate an alternative view. First, severe negative life events are risk factors for suicidality (and the suicidal behavior of a friend or peer qualifies as one of a large array of severe negative life events).

Second, good social support (e.g., healthy family functioning) buffers people against developing suicidal symptoms. Third, there exists an array of person-based risk factors for suicidality (e.g., personality disorder or other psychiatric disorder). Fourth, people form relationships *assortatively*—that is, people who possess similar qualities or problems, including suicide risk factors, may be more likely to form relationships with one another. Therefore, it is possible that people who are vulnerable to suicide may cluster well before the occurrence of any overt suicidal stimulus (i.e., suicide point clusters may be, in a sense, prearranged), and when they experience severe negative events, including but not limited to the suicidal behavior of one member of the cluster, all members of the cluster are at increased risk for suicidality (a risk that may be offset by good social support).

Consider, the example, the point cluster described by Haw (1994), in which victims were assortatively related on the basis of, at least in part, shared suicide risk factors (e.g., the chronic mental illness that brought them all to the same psychiatric unit). Vulnerable people were brought together (through contact with the agency), were exposed to severe stress (potential for dissolution of the agency; lack of access to important caregivers; for some, suicides of peers), and may not have been well buffered by good social support (the chronically mentally ill often have low social support; a main source of support may have been the agency, which was threatened).

Or consider the example of point clusters within high schools. In this case, the assortative relationships—the prearrangement of clusters—may occur in one or both of two ways. First, because they have mutual interests, compatible qualities, or similar problems (including vulnerability to and experience of psychopathology), vulnerable adolescents may gravitate toward one another. A point cluster reported by Robbins and Conroy (1983) demonstrates this possibility. In this cluster, two adolescent suicides were followed by five attempts (all five teenagers were subsequently admitted to the hospital) and one hospital admission for having suicidal thoughts. Of the six hospitalized teens, all had regularly socialized with each other, and all visited each other during their hospitalizations. Second, having social contact (for whatever reason, assortative or not) with an adolescent who completes or attempts suicide appears to lower the threshold at which a teen becomes suicidal (Brent et al., 1989). The mere occurrence, then, of suicidality in one adolescent may automatically arrange a potential cluster.

Although the empirical facts on point clusters are limited, they appear to be consistent with my speculation that severe negative life events, person-based risk, social contiguity (perhaps as a function of assortative relationships), and lack of buffering by social support, taken together, explain the phenomenon. In an effort to provide further empirical support for this view, I conducted an analogue study among college roommates. College roommates provide an interesting "natural laboratory" for studying issues involving assortative relationships, because in many large universities, a sizable proportion of roommates are randomly assigned to each other (by the university housing agency) and the rest assortatively choose to room with each other. I predicted that suicidality levels would be more similar among roommates who chose to room together than among those randomly paired together. Moreover, I predicted that suicidality levels would be particularly consonant among pairs who both chose one another and, by their own reports, had been experiencing negative life events that affected both of them. Results supported the view that prearranged point clusters (in this case, arranged by people choosing to live together) would share suicide-related features (in this case, symptoms), and that clustered suicidality was particularly likely in those prearranged clusters that had been affected by negative life events. It must be emphasized that this study was an analogue study, and that, in general, students' levels of suicidality were quite low, making the generalization to attempted or completed suicide questionable. The results, however, converge with those from reports on actual point clusters to make the explanation offered here, at the least, a candidate for further study.

ADDRESSING POTENTIAL CRITICISMS OF THIS EXPLANATION

Why Don't Point Clusters Happen All the Time?

According to my speculation about why point clusters develop, at least two concepts are key to understanding why they are relatively rare. First, my explanation involves the joint operation of several phenomena that themselves are infrequent in occurrence. Severe negative events, high person-based risk, suicidality itself, and low social support—all jointly operating ingredients of my explanation—are relatively rare; their confluence is even more so. Second, even given the confluence of these factors, attempted or completed suicides represent an extreme and severe psychopathology, the threshold for which is presumably quite high. Thus, even when life events are severely negative, person-based risk is high, and social support is low, the threshold may not be reached.

Why Don't Point Clusters Occur Within Families?

Because suicidality and suicide risk run in families, because the suicide of a family member is arguably the most severe of negative events, and because family members are socially contiguous, families would appear to be likely sources for point-clustered suicides. Apparently, however, they are not. This may be because of the protective action of social support. Social support is, in general, pervasive (indeed, the need to belong has been proposed as a fundamental human motive; Baumeister & Leary, 1995), and it is intensified for families in mourning. Increased social support thus may offset families' risk for additional suicides among family members.

CONCLUSIONS

The evidence for mass clusters is weak or equivocal, whereas point clusters appear to occur. But clustering does not contagion make. By implication at least, suicide clusters often have been explained as analogous to miniepidemics of contagious illness. I have suggested, however, that a more apt analogy is disasters or industrial accidents, in which simultaneous exposure to some external, pernicious agent (e.g., radiation) is the mechanism of action, a mechanism that is particularly harmful to already vulnerable people. Point-clustered suicides may occur similarly: Contiguous people, if exposed to noxious stimuli (e.g., a severe negative life event, such as the suicide of a peer), and if vulnerable but unprotected (by social support), may simultaneously develop suicidal symptoms.

Recommended Reading

Brent, D. A., Kerr, M. M., Goldstein, C., & Bozigar, J. (1989). (See References)
Gould, M. S., Wallenstein, S., & Davidson, L. (1989). (See References)

Kessler, R. C., Downey, G., Milavsky, J. R., & Stipp, H. (1988). (See References)

Note

1. Address correspondence to Thomas Joiner, Department of Psychology, Florida State University, Tallahassee, FL 32306-1270; e-mail: joiner@psy.fsu.edu.

References

Baumeister, R. F., & Leary, M. R. (1995). The need to belong: Desire for interpersonal attachments as a fundamental human motivation. *Psychological Bulletin, 117,* 497–529.

Berman, A. L. (1988). Fictional depiction of suicide in television films and imitation effects. *American Journal of Psychiatry, 145,* 982–986.

Brent, D. A., Kerr, M. M., Goldstein, C., & Bozigar, J. (1989). An outbreak of suicide and suicidal behavior in a high school. *Journal of the American Academy of Child & Adolescent Psychiatry, 28,* 918–924.

Chiu, L. P. (1988). Do weather, day of the week, and address affect the rate of attempted suicide in Hong Kong? *Social Psychiatry & Psychiatric Epidemiology, 23,* 229–235.

Gould, M. S., Wallenstein, S., & Davidson, L. (1989). Suicide clusters: A critical review. *Suicide & Life-Threatening Behavior, 19,* 17–29.

Haw, C. M. (1994). A cluster of suicides at a London psychiatric unit. *Suicide & Life-Threatening Behavior, 24,* 256–266.

Kessler, R. C., Downey, G., Milavsky, J. R., & Stipp, H. (1988). Clustering of teenage suicides after television news stories about suicides: A reconsideration. *American Journal of Psychiatry, 145,* 1379–1383.

Phillips, D. P., & Carstensen, L. L. (1986). Clustering of teenage suicides after television news stories about suicide. *New England Journal of Medicine, 315,* 685–689.

Phillips, D. P., & Carstensen, L. L. (1988). The effect of suicide stories on various demographic groups, 1968–1985. *Suicide & Life-Threatening Behavior, 18,* 100–114.

Phillips, D. P., & Paight, D. J. (1987). The impact of televised movies about suicide: A replicative study. *New England Journal of Medicine, 317,* 809–811.

Robbins, D., & Conroy, R. C. (1983). A cluster of adolescent suicide attempts: Is suicide contagious? *Journal of Adolescent Health Care, 3,* 253–255.

Schmidtke, A., & Haefner, H. (1988). The Werther effect after television films: New evidence for an old hypothesis. *Psychological Medicine, 18,* 665–676.

Simkin, S., Hawton, K., Whitehead, L., & Fagg, J. (1995). Media influence on parasuicide: A study of the effects of a television drama portrayal of paracetamol self-poisoning. *British Journal of Psychiatry, 167,* 754–759.

A D D I C T E D

Why do people get hooked? Mounting evidence points to a powerful brain chemical called dopamine

By J. MADELEINE NASH

IMAGINE YOU ARE TAKING A SLUG OF WHISKEY. A puff of a cigarette. A toke of marijuana. A snort of cocaine. A shot of heroin. Put aside whether these drugs are legal or illegal. Concentrate, for now, on the chemistry. The moment you take that slug, that puff, that toke, that snort, that shot, trillions of potent molecules surge through your bloodstream and into your brain. Once there, they set off a cascade of chemical and electrical events, a kind of neurological chain reaction that ricochets around the skull and rearranges the interior reality of the mind.

Given the complexity of these events—and the inner workings of the mind in general—it's not surprising that scientists have struggled mightily to make sense of the mechanisms of addiction. Why do certain substances have the power to make us feel so good (at least at first)? Why do some people fall so easily into the thrall of alcohol, cocaine, nicotine and other addictive substances, while others can, literally, take them or leave them?

The answer, many scientists are convinced, may be simpler than anyone has dared imagine. What ties all these mood-altering drugs together, they say, is a remarkable ability to elevate levels of a common substance in the brain called dopamine. In fact, so overwhelming has evidence of the link between dopamine and drugs of abuse

become that the distinction (pushed primarily by the tobacco industry and its supporters) between substances that are addictive and those that are merely habit-forming has very nearly been swept away.

The Liggett Group, smallest of the U.S.'s Big Five cigarette makers, broke ranks in March and conceded not only that tobacco is addictive but also that the company has known it all along. While RJR Nabisco and the others continue to battle in the courts—insisting that smokers are not hooked, just exercising free choice—their denials ring increasingly hollow in the face of the growing weight of evidence. Over the past year, several scientific groups have made the case that in dopamine-rich areas of the brain, nicotine behaves remarkably like cocaine. And late last week a federal judge ruled for the first time that the Food and Drug Administration has the right to regulate tobacco as a drug and cigarettes as drug-delivery devices.

Now, a team of researchers led by psychiatrist Dr. Nora Volkow of the Brookhaven National Laboratory in New York has published the

strongest evidence to date that the surge of dopamine in addicts' brains is what triggers a cocaine high. In last week's edition of the journal *Nature* they described how powerful brain-imaging technology can be used to track the rise of dopamine and link it to feelings of euphoria.

Like serotonin (the brain chemical affected by such antidepressants as Prozac), dopamine is a neurotransmitter—a molecule that ferries messages from one neuron within the brain to another. Serotonin is associated with feelings of sadness and well-being, dopamine with pleasure and elation. Dopamine can be elevated by a hug, a kiss, a word of praise or a winning poker hand—as well as by the potent pleasures that come from drugs.

The idea that a single chemical could be associated with everything from snorting cocaine and smoking tobacco to getting good

PRIME SUSPECT

They don't yet know the precise mechanism by which it works, but scientists are increasingly convinced that dopamine plays a key role in a wide range of addictions, including those to heroin, nicotine, alcohol and marijuana

DOPAMINE MAY BE LINKED TO GAMBLING, CHOCOLATE AND EVEN SEX

grades and enjoying sex has electrified scientists and changed the way they look at a wide range of dependencies, chemical and otherwise. Dopamine, they now believe, is not just a chemical that transmits pleasure signals but may, in fact, be the master molecule of addiction.

This is not to say dopamine is the only chemical involved or that the deranged thought processes that mark chronic drug abuse are due to dopamine alone. The brain is subtler than that. Drugs modulate the activity of a variety of brain chemicals, each of which intersects with many others. "Drugs are like sledgehammers," observes Dr. Eric Nestler of the Yale University School of Medicine. "They profoundly alter many pathways."

Nevertheless, the realization that dopamine may be a common end point of all those pathways represents a signal advance. Provocative, controversial, unquestionably incomplete, the dopamine hypothesis provides a basic framework for understanding how a genetically encoded trait—such as a tendency to produce too little dopamine—might intersect with environmental influences to create a serious behavioral disorder. Therapists have long known of patients who, in addition to having psychological problems, abuse drugs as well. Could their drug problems be linked to some inborn quirk? Might an inability to absorb enough dopamine, with its pleasure-giving properties, cause them to seek gratification in drugs?

Such speculation is controversial, for it suggests that broad swaths of the population may be genetically predisposed to drug abuse. What is not controversial is that the social cost of drug abuse, whatever its cause, is enormous. Cigarettes contribute to the death toll from cancer and heart disease. Alcohol is the leading cause of domestic violence and highway deaths. The needles used to inject heroin and cocaine are spreading AIDS. Directly or indirectly, addiction to drugs, cigarettes and alcohol is thought to account for a third of all hospital admissions, a quarter of all deaths and a majority of serious crimes. In the U.S. alone the combined medical and social costs of drug abuse are believed to exceed $240 billion.

F OR NEARLY A QUARTER-CENTURY the U.S. has been waging a war on drugs, with little apparent success. As scientists learn more about how dopamine works (and how drugs work on it), the evidence suggests that we may be fighting the wrong battle. Americans tend to think of drug addiction as a failure of character. But this stereotype is beginning to give way to the recognition that drug dependence has a clear biological basis. "Addiction," declares Brookhaven's Volkow, "is a disorder of the brain

no different from other forms of mental illness."

That new insight may be the dopamine hypothesis' most important contribution in the fight against drugs. It completes the loop between the mechanism of addiction and programs for treatment. And it raises hope for more effective therapies. Abstinence, if maintained, not only halts the physical and

HIGH AND LOWS — Number who used in the past month

Heroin — Triggers release of dopamine; acts on other neurotransmitters	200,000
Amphetamines — Stimulate excess release of dopamine	800,000
Cocaine/Crack — Blocks dopamine absorption	1.5 million
Marijuana — Binds to areas of brain involved in mood and memory; triggers release of dopamine	10 million
Alcohol — Triggers dopamine release; acts on other neurotransmitters	11 million abusers
Nicotine — Triggers release of dopamine	61 million
Caffeine — May trigger release of dopamine	130 million*

Sources: SAMHSA, National Coffee Association   *coffee drinkers

psychological damage wrought by drugs but in large measure also reverses it.

Genes and social forces may conspire to turn people into addicts but do not doom them to remain so. Consider the case of Rafael Rios, who grew up in a housing project in New York City's drug-infested South Bronx. For 18 years, until he turned 31, Rios, whose father died of alcoholism, led a double life. He graduated from Harvard Law School and joined a prestigious Chicago law firm. Yet all the while he was secretly visiting a shooting "gallery" once a day. His favored concoction: heroin spiked with a jolt

WHAT ELSE?

Preliminary evidence suggests that dopamine may be involved even when we form dependencies on things—like coffee or candy—that we don't think of as drugs at all

of cocaine. Ten years ago, Rios succeeded in kicking his habit—for good, he hopes. He is now executive director of A Safe Haven, a Chicago-based chain of residential facilities for recovering addicts.

How central is dopamine's role in this familiar morality play? Scientists are still trying to sort that out. It is no accident, they say, that people are attracted to drugs. The major drugs of abuse, whether depressants like heroin or stimulants like cocaine, mimic the structure of neurotransmitters, the most mind-bending chemicals nature has ever concocted. Neurotransmitters underlie every thought and emotion, memory and learning; they carry the signals between all the nerve cells, or neurons, in the brain. Among some 50 neurotransmitters discovered to date, a good half a dozen, including dopamine, are known to play a role in addiction.

The neurons that produce this molecular messenger are surprisingly rare. Clustered in loose knots buried deep in the brain, they number a few tens of thousands of nerve cells out of an estimated total of 100 billion. But through long, wire-like projections known as axons, these cells influence neurological activity in many regions, including the nucleus accumbens, the primitive structure that is one of the brain's key pleasure centers. At a purely chemical level, every experience humans find enjoyable—whether listening to music, embracing a lover or savoring chocolate—amounts to little more than an explosion of dopamine in the nucleus accumbens, as exhilarating and ephemeral as a firecracker.

Dopamine, like most biologically important molecules, must be kept within strict bounds. Too little dopamine in certain areas of the brain triggers the tremors and paralysis of Parkinson's disease. Too much causes the hallucinations and bizarre thoughts of schizophrenia. A breakthrough in addiction research came in 1975, when psychologists Roy Wise and Robert Yokel at Concordia University in Montreal reported on the remarkable behavior of some drug-addicted rats. One day the animals were placidly dispensing cocaine and amphetamines to themselves by pressing a lever attached to their cages. The next they were angrily banging at the lever like someone trying to summon a stalled elevator. The reason? The scientists had injected the rats with a drug that blocked the action of dopamine.

In the years since, evidence linking dopamine to drugs has mounted. Amphetamines stimulate dopamine-producing cells to pump out more of the chemical. Cocaine keeps dopamine levels high by inhibiting the activity of a transporter molecule that would ordinarily ferry dopamine back into the cells that produce it. Nicotine, heroin and alcohol trigger a complex chemical cascade that raises dopamine levels. And a still unknown chemical in cigarette smoke, a group led by Brookhaven chemist Joanna Fowler reported last year, may extend the activity of dopamine by blocking a mopping-up enzyme, called MAO B, that would otherwise destroy it.

The evidence that Volkow and her colleagues present in the current issue of *Nature* suggests that dopamine is directly responsible for the exhilarating rush that reinforces the desire to take drugs, at least in cocaine addicts. In all, 17 users participated in the study, says Volkow, and they experienced a high whose intensity was directly related to how extensively cocaine tied up available binding sites on the molecules that transport dopamine around the brain. To produce any high at all, she and her colleagues found, cocaine had to occupy at least 47% of these sites; the "best" results occurred when it took over 60% to 80% of the sites, effectively preventing the transporters from latching onto dopamine and spiriting it out of circulation.

SCIENTISTS BELIEVE THE DOPAMINE system arose very early in the course of animal evolution because it reinforces behaviors so essential to survival. "If it were not for the fact that sex is pleasurable," observes Charles Schuster of Wayne State University in Detroit, "we would not engage in it." Unfortunately, some of the activities humans are neurochemically tuned to find agreeable—eating foods rich in fat and sugar, for instance—have backfired in modern society. Just as a surfeit of food and a dearth of exercise have conspired to turn heart disease and diabetes into major health problems, so the easy availability of addictive chemicals has played a devious trick. Addicts do not crave heroin or cocaine or alcohol or nicotine per se but want the rush of dopamine that these drugs produce.

Dopamine, however, is more than just a feel-good molecule. It also exercises extraordinary power over learning and memory. Think of dopamine, suggests P. Read Montague of the Center for Theoretical Neuroscience at Houston's Baylor College of Medicine, as the proverbial carrot, a reward the brain doles out to networks of neurons for making survival-enhancing choices. And while the details of how this system works are not yet understood, Montague and his colleagues at the Salk Institute in San Diego, California, and M.I.T. have proposed a model that seems quite plausible. Each time the outcome of an action is better than expected, they predicted, dopamine-releasing neurons should increase the rate at which they fire. When an outcome is worse, they should

decrease it. And if the outcome is as expected, the firing rate need not change at all.

As a test of his model, Montague created a computer program that simulated the nectar-gathering activity of bees. Programmed with a dopamine-like reward system and set loose on a field of virtual "flowers," some of which were dependably sweet and some of which were either very sweet or not sweet at all, the virtual bees chose the reliably sweet flowers 85% of the time. In laboratory experiments real bees behave just like their virtual counterparts. What does this have to do with drug abuse? Possibly quite a lot, says Montague. The theory is that dopamine-enhancing chemicals fool the brain into thinking drugs are as beneficial as nectar to the bee, thus hijacking a natural reward system that dates back millions of years.

The degree to which learning and memory sustain the addictive process is only now being appreciated. Each time a neurotransmitter like dopamine floods a synapse, scientists believe, circuits that trigger thoughts and motivate actions are etched onto the brain. Indeed, the neurochemistry supporting addiction is so powerful that the people, objects and places associated with drug taking are also imprinted on the brain. Stimulated by food, sex or the smell of tobacco, former smokers can no more control the urge to light up than Pavlov's dogs could stop their urge to salivate. For months Rafael Rios lived in fear of catching a glimpse of bare arms—his own or someone else's. Whenever he did, he remembers, he would be seized by a nearly unbearable urge to find a drug-filled syringe.

Indeed, the brain has many devious tricks for ensuring that the irrational act of taking drugs, deemed "good" because it enhances dopamine, will be repeated. PET-scan images taken by Volkow and her colleagues reveal that the absorption of a cocaine-like chemical by neurons is profoundly reduced in cocaine addicts in contrast to normal subjects. One explanation: the addicts' neurons, assaulted by abnormally high levels of dopamine, have responded defensively and reduced the number of sites (or receptors) to which dopamine can bind. In the absence of drugs, these nerve cells probably experience a dopamine deficit, Volkow speculates, so while addicts begin by taking drugs to feel high, they end up taking them in order not to feel low.

PET-scan images of the brains of recovering cocaine addicts reveal other striking changes, including a dramatically impaired ability to process glucose, the primary energy source for working neurons. Moreover, this impairment—which persists for up to 100 days after withdrawal—is greatest in the

prefrontal cortex, a dopamine-rich area of the brain that controls impulsive and irrational behavior. Addicts, in fact, display many of the symptoms shown by patients who have suffered strokes or injuries to the prefrontal cortex. Damage to this region, University of Iowa neurologist Antonio Damasio and his colleagues have demonstrated, destroys the emotional compass that controls behaviors the patient knows are unacceptable.

Anyone who doubts that genes influence behavior should see the mice in Marc Caron's lab. These tireless rodents race around their cages for hours on end. They lose weight because they rarely stop to eat, and then they drop from exhaustion because they are unable to sleep. Why? The mice, says Caron, a biochemist at Duke University's Howard Hughes Medical Institute

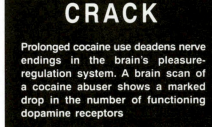

CRACK

Prolonged cocaine use deadens nerve endings in the brain's pleasure-regulation system. A brain scan of a cocaine abuser shows a marked drop in the number of functioning dopamine receptors

laboratory, are high on dopamine. They lack the genetic mechanism that sponges up this powerful stuff and spirits it away. Result: there is so much dopamine banging around in the poor creatures' synapses that the mice, though drug-free, act as if they were strung out on cocaine.

For years scientists have suspected that genes play a critical role in determining who will become addicted to drugs and who will not. But not until now have they had molecular tools powerful enough to go after the prime suspects. Caron's mice are just the most recent example. By knocking out a single gene—the so-called dopamine-transporter gene—Caron and his colleagues may have created a strain of mice so sated with dopamine that they are oblivious to the allure of cocaine, and possibly alcohol and heroin as well. "What's exciting about our mice," says Caron, "is that they should allow us to test the hypothesis that all these drugs funnel through the dopamine system."

Several dopamine genes have already been tentatively, and controversially, linked to alcoholism and drug abuse. Inherited variations in these genes modify the efficiency

COKE'S HIGH IS DIRECTLY TIED TO DOPAMINE LEVELS

A.A.'S PATH TO RECOVERY STILL SEEMS THE BEST

with which nerve cells process dopamine, or so the speculation goes. Thus, some scientists conjecture, a dopamine-transporter gene that is superefficient, clearing dopamine from the synapses too rapidly, could predispose some people to a form of alcoholism characterized by violent and impulsive behavior. In essence, they would be mirror images of Caron's mice. Instead of being drenched in dopamine, their synapses would be dopamine-poor.

The dopamine genes known as D2 and D4 might also play a role in drug abuse, for similar reasons. Both these genes, it turns out, contain the blueprints for assembling what scientists call a receptor, a minuscule bump on the surface of cells to which biologically active molecules are attracted. And just as a finger lights up a room by merely flicking a switch, so dopamine triggers a sequence of chemical reactions each time it binds to one of its five known receptors. Genetic differences that reduce the sensitivity of these receptors or decrease their number could diminish the sensation of pleasure.

The problem is, studies that have purported to find a basis for addiction in variations of the D2 and D4 genes have not held up under scrutiny. Indeed, most scientists think addiction probably involves an intricate dance between environmental influences and multiple genes, some of which may influence dopamine activity only indirectly. This has not stopped some researchers from promoting the provocative theory that many people who become alcoholics and drug addicts suffer from an inherited condition dubbed the reward-deficiency syndrome. Low dopamine levels caused by a particular version of the D2 gene, they say, may link a breathtaking array of aberrant behaviors. Among them: severe alcoholism, pathological gambling, binge eating and attention-deficit hyperactivity disorder.

The more science unmasks the powerful biology that underlies addiction, the brighter the prospects for treatment become. For instance, the discovery by Fowler and her team that a chemical that inhibits the mopping-up enzyme MAO B may play a role in cigarette addiction has already opened new possibilities for therapy. A number of well-tolerated MAO B inhibitor drugs developed to treat Parkinson's disease could find a place in the antismoking arsenal. Equally promising, a Yale University team led by Eric Nestler and David Self has found that another type of compound—one that targets the dopamine receptor known as D1—seems to alleviate, at least in rats, the intense craving that accompanies withdrawal from cocaine. One day, suggests Self, a D1 skin patch might help cocaine abusers kick their habit, just as the nicotine patch attenuates the desire to smoke.

Like methadone, the compound that activates D1 appears to be what is known as a partial agonist. Because such medications stimulate some of the same brain pathways as drugs of abuse, they are often addictive in their own right, though less so. And while treating heroin addicts with methadone may seem like a cop-out to people who have never struggled with a drug habit, clinicians say they desperately need more such agents to tide addicts—particularly cocaine addicts—over the first few months of treatment, when the danger of relapse is highest.

REALISTICALLY, NO ONE BELIEVES better medications alone will solve the drug problem. In fact, one of the most hopeful messages coming out of current research is that the biochemical abnormalities associated with addiction can be reversed through learning. For that reason, all sorts of psychosocial interventions, ranging from psychotherapy to 12-step programs, can and do help. Cognitive therapy, which seeks to supply people with coping skills (exercising after work instead of going to a bar, for instance), appears to hold particular promise. After just 10 weeks of therapy, before-and-after PET scans suggest, some patients suffering from obsessive-compulsive disorder (which has some similarities with addiction) manage to resculpt not only their behavior but also activity patterns in their brain.

In late 20th century America, where drugs of abuse are being used on an unprecedented scale, the mounting evidence that treatment works could not be more welcome. Until now, policymakers have responded to the drug problem as though it were mostly a criminal matter. Only a third of the $15 billion the U.S. earmarks for the war on drugs goes to prevention and treatment. "In my view, we've got things upside down," says Dr. David Lewis, director of the Center for Alcohol and Addiction Studies at Brown University School of Medicine. "By relying so heavily on a criminalized approach, we've only added to the stigma of drug abuse and prevented high-quality medical care."

Ironically, the biggest barrier to making such care available is the perception that efforts to treat addiction are wasted. Yet treatment for drug abuse has a failure rate no different from that for other chronic diseases. Close to half of recovering addicts fail to maintain complete abstinence after a year—about the same proportion of patients with diabetes and hypertension who fail to comply with their diet, exercise and medication regimens. What doctors who treat drug abuse should strive for, says Alan Leshner, director of the National Institute on Drug Abuse, is not necessarily a cure but long-term care that controls the progress of the disease and alleviates its worst symptoms. "The occasional relapse is normal," he says, "and just an indication that more treatment is needed."

Rafael Rios has been luckier than many. He kicked his habit in one lengthy struggle that included four months of in-patient treatment at a residential facility and a year of daily outpatient sessions. During that time, Rios checked into 12-step meetings continually, sometimes attending three a day. As those who deal with alcoholics and drug addicts know, such exertions of will power and courage are more common than most people suspect. They are the best reason yet to start treating addiction as the medical and public health crisis it really is.

—With reporting by Alice Park/New York

PERSONALITY DISORDERS: COPING WITH THE BORDERLINE

*Characterized by stormy relationships, self-mutilation,
and rage, the borderline personality bewilders family, friends,
and the psychiatric community itself.*

by Patrick Perry

After a busy day at work, Bob was looking forward to a quick shower, light supper, and a concert with his new girlfriend, Amanda. But outside his apartment, he froze. On his door the word "CHEATER" had been spray-painted in large black letters. Embarrassed, he scanned the hallway, quietly unlocked the door, and slipped inside.

"Did anyone see who did this?" Bob asked the superintendent.

"Your neighbor said that she recognized the car in the parking lot," he answered. "This is the fourth time somebody's damaged your apartment. Shouldn't we call the police?"

"No," Bob said. "I'll handle it."

He knew who had been there. It was Jennifer.

When he first met Jennifer at a bookstore, he was immediately attracted to the pretty, outgoing 21-year-old. Their first few months together were fantastic. She always wanted to be with him, calling him two or three times a day at the office just to let him know she was thinking about him. Over time, Bob learned more about Jenny—the early sexual assault she had suffered, a broken home, and the barely visible scars on her wrists from a suicide attempt when she was just 17. She had been through a lot in her short life, yet seemed to survive it well.

When the accounting firm where Bob worked picked up a new client, Bob began working late hours. At first, Jenny understood, was even supportive. But as the weeks passed, she became more demanding, wanting to know why he "wanted" to be away from her and if "another woman" was involved. She

telephoned him throughout the day, monitoring his every move. One night after work, he joined old fraternity buddies for a basketball game at the local Y. Jenny unexpectedly showed up. After delivering a barrage of jealous accusations in front of his teammates, she left. Bob thought the flat tire after the game was just a coincidence. On another late night at work, he found her parked alongside him in the garage, and she acted hurt when he questioned her motives.

Jenny's jealousy and demands continued, and soon Bob realized that

> **One moment calm and engaging, the next tempestuous and combative, borderlines bewilder those around them, straining relationships to the breaking point.**

❧

something about the relationship just wasn't right. He decided to break it off. The decision wasn't mutual. Jenny began showing up at his office, at first begging for another chance. When he refused, she flew into a rage in front of his coworkers. When his appointment

book came up missing, he chalked it up to forgetfulness until someone canceled his plane reservations to an important business conference and canceled his doctor's appointments. A late-night phone call from Jenny resulted in a trip to the emergency room and an all-night suicide vigil. Bob now realized that Jenny needed professional help. But when he spoke with her the next day about therapy, she became furious, blaming her hospitalization on him and men like him. He left, feeling ashamed and, for some reason, responsible.

For the next two months, Jenny phoned him at all hours of the night and at the office. She left scathing, often harassing messages on his answering machine. When the office disruptions threatened his job, Bob took out a restraining order against Jenny. Even then, Jenny persisted. On more than one occasion, he saw her peering through restaurant windows or parked outside his apartment building. His mailbox had been tampered with, his tires slashed, an anonymous basket of funeral flowers sent to his office, appointments cancelled, and a defamatory letter sent to his boss. Still, no one would suspect that the pretty, outgoing girl was capable of, much less responsible for, the havoc in his life.

When will it end? Bob thought. *Can I take much more of this?*

* * *

Rage, impulsivity, self-mutilation, guilt, overwhelming fears of abandonment, and volatile relationships—

Jenny's life is a tattered scrapbook of broken relationships, suicide attempts, uncontrollable anger, substance abuse, and violent mood swings. Jenny is a "borderline," short for someone with borderline personality disorder. Five million Americans fit the profile of the borderline personality disorder (BPD), according to the latest estimate. One moment calm and engaging, the next tempestuous and combative, borderlines bewilder those around them, straining relationships to the breaking point. It is this unpredictability and loss of control that baffles both people who love them and the psychiatric community that treats them. BPD is a mysterious malady of the personality that one psychiatrist defines as "a problem with who you are."

The case of Susan Smith, the South Carolina mother who murdered her two children by driving her car into a lake with the children left inside, brought national focus on the subject of personality disorders and the frightening consequences that often result when the disorders are left unchecked.

Unlike depression, a disease frequently episodic in nature and which most people can understand and empathize with, BPD is characterized by enduring and persistent ways of behavior and thought. As such, BPD lies in a unique classification of psychiatric illnesses called personality disorders. According to the current edition of the American Psychiatric Association's *Diagnostic and Statistical Manual of Mental Disorders, 4th Edition, (DSM-IV)*, a personality type is looked upon as a disorder when the traits, or personal habits, that constitute the personality are inflexible and damaging, causing serious distress or impaired function. The *DSM-IV* classifications of personality disorders include: borderline, antisocial, paranoid, narcissistic, avoidant, dependent, obsessive-compulsive, and passive-aggressive.

In her book *Imbroglio,* author Janice M. Cauwels, Ph.D., presents an in-depth look at BPD, exploring the causes and current theories and offering personal histories of patients suffering from the disorder. Dr. Cauwels discovered that many psychiatrists refuse to see these patients because borderlines are seen as provocateurs and expert manipulators. Dr. Cauwels cites a facetious report on BPD patients as "notorious for late-night irrelevant 'emergency' phone calls, no common sense, no redeeming qualities, no income, and no health insur-

ance." The author also noted that one of the supreme ironies in BPD is that borderlines are the neediest people in the world, yet alienate all from whom they crave love.

BPD is the subject of mounting research, innumerable studies, and various theories. While therapists may differ on theory and origin, few would argue with the statement that BPD appears to be one of the most complicated forms of mental illness. The *Post* interviewed leading researchers and clinicians about this crippling mental disorder that affects not only the borderline patients but all who come into contact with them.

What Is Borderline Personality Disorder?

John W. Gunderson, M.D., is regarded as a leading authority on BPD. He is director of psychotherapy and psychosocial research at McLean Hospital in Massachusetts and professor of psychiatry at Harvard Medical School.

Post: How do you describe a borderline personality disorder?

JG: I think of it as a disorder primarily caused by some defect in early attachment that leads to the person searching for some type of protective, nurturing relationship which they feel makes up for what they unfairly did not get in their childhood. It sets in motion a sort of desperate search for some person who will take care of them and stay with them all the time.

Post: When does BPD begin to emerge?

JG: Usually in adolescence, but there's usually enough turmoil in normal adolescence that you're not safe identifying those who will have this disorder until it persists or emerges later in life.

Post: Do borderlines usually focus on one individual at a time?

JG: Yes.

Post: Is this individual a love interest or could it be just a friend?

JG: It could be a friend. It could be a teacher. Most borderline patients feel very secure and can function well, as long as they feel they have someone they believe cares about them and is accessible—someone who will be there. We all need to have caring relationships. What's different here is that the relationship generally evolves around the hope that there will be one person who will

be able to provide all that they need. They get very panicky and have very severe, oftentimes behavioral, reactions when they feel that they're going to be alone. When borderlines feel the threat that somebody needed is going to leave or has lost interest in them, they engage in a lot of angry and manipulative behaviors to prevent the leaving. If they feel that it's futile and that they don't have anyone, they may behave in very desperate ways to become engaged with somebody new—promiscuity, substance abuse, fights. These behaviors—the fights and promiscuity—are often because of the disinhibiting influence of alcohol or other drugs that bring them once again into contact with someone with whom they can recreate the illusion of being loved.

Post: Many people remember the disturbing portrait of borderline disorder in the movie *Fatal Attraction.* What do you think of that movie's portrayal of a borderline patient?

JG: I think, more typically, borderline patients will become self-destructive as a way of evoking some kind of caretaking protective response from others. That's how they prevent people from leaving them.

Post: In the movie, the borderline character's rage grew, eventually leading her to destroy things dear to the man who was the focus of her obsession.

JG: That is a very extreme, dramatic example. Most of the time a borderline patient may start to feel enraged and may have poor control over that rage, and it comes out. It's usually verbal. These people feel that when they have been angry, they are bad, even though they initially felt anger was justified because they had been cruelly mistreated. It's usually hard for them to sustain being angry for long. They soon begin to feel they are evil, then turn the anger toward themselves in very self-destructive ways. Self-destructiveness takes the form of not simply trying to kill themselves, but trying to put themselves in a position where their life is at risk and whether they live or not is in the hands of somebody else. If they are saved, as is usually the case, that's affirmation they are meant to live and deserve to live. If they are not saved, that is an affirmation they are as evil as they thought and deserve to die. They put their lives at risk in a deliberate way where their fate depends upon external intervention.

Post: Could you give a description of how a borderline might react in frustrating situations that all of us encounter—when your car breaks down or you're stuck in a grocery line? Do they react the same way others do?

JG: Most of the time, yes. But consider a patient, for instance, who learns the night before that her boyfriend is going to move out. If then the next day she goes to a grocery store and a child is crying, she might feel inappropriately enraged at the child—so much so that she envisions very primitive things like cutting the kid's tongue out. She is frightened of that thought and says to herself, "This is crazy—I've got to get out of here," because borderlines fear they won't be able to control the anger. She leaves the store. At that point, she hasn't done her grocery shopping, so she feels ashamed of herself for that. She gets into the car and, in an admixture of frustration and guilt, slams into the car in front of her. Feeling that the car in front of her was going too slow and that this is unfair, she'll be enraged at the driver and create a big scene.

Post: What do you consider the two principal diagnostic hallmarks of borderline?

JG: Intolerance of aloneness and self-destructiveness.

Post: Many magazine and professional journal articles mention a relationship between sexual abuse and borderline disorder, particularly among female patients. Were the vast majority of borderline patients sexually abused as children?

JG: Yes, that's well-established, but a "vast majority" overstates it. You can safely say that a large percentage of borderline patients have had abusive experiences in their childhood, but abuse is neither necessary nor specific.

Post: You mean it doesn't matter if the abuse is sexual or if it's, for example, abandonment?

JG: It matters. But the degree of sexual abuse is linked to the high frequency of females with the disorder. With the antisocial personality, you see a familiar frequency of abuse in their childhood, but it's less frequently sexual.

Post: How often are borderlines also antisocial?

JG: About 25 percent.

Post: Is having both traits, borderline and antisocial, a particularly dangerous combination?

Diagnostic Criteria for Borderline Personality Disorder

A pervasive pattern of instability of interpersonal relationships, self-image, and affects, and marked impulsivity beginning by early adulthood and present in a variety of contexts, as indicated by five (or more) of the following:

❶ Frantic efforts to avoid real or imagined abandonment.
❷ A pattern of unstable and intense interpersonal relationships characterized by alternating between extremes of idealization and devaluation.
❸ Identity disturbance: markedly and persistently unstable self-image or sense of self.
❹ Impulsivity in at least two areas that are potentially self-damaging (e.g., spending, sex, substance abuse, reckless driving, binge eating).

❺ Recurrent suicidal behavior, gestures, or threats, or self-mutilating behavior.
❻ Affective instability due to a marked reactivity of mood (e.g., intense episodic dysphoria, irritability, or anxiety usually lasting a few hours and only rarely more than a few days).
❼ Chronic feelings of emptiness.
❽ Inappropriate, intense anger or difficulty controlling anger (e.g., frequent displays of temper, constant anger, recurrent physical fights).
❾ Transient, stress-related paranoid ideation or severe dissociative symptoms.

Source: Diagnostic and Statistical Manual of Mental Disorders, 4th Edition (DSM-IV ™)

JG: "Dangerous" is a strong word because it implies that there's a high risk of violence to other people. I would not say that is the danger, primarily. The problem with the combination of BPD and antisocial disorder is that patients with both these traits are harder to treat and more apt to exploit others without great remorse.

Post: For example?

JG: A babysitter who steals from the employer. They are also, I think, at somewhat higher risk of being irresponsible caretakers. Violence in borderline patients is largely impulsive and under extreme circumstances. It's not something that recurs very often because it's usually followed by intense and suicidal self-accusations. That doesn't mean that such people are not capable of violence. That woman who drowned her children, for example.

Post: Susan Smith, the South Carolina mother who drove her two young children into a lake in a locked car and watched them drown?

JG: Yes. Chances of BPD are quite high in a number of such cases in the news where women have done very violent things to their kids. But that's a little different from antisocial as a recurrent pattern of disregard for social norms and the feelings of others.

Post: When I hear the term borderline, it's often associated with violence, as in the case of Susan Smith. Are cases like this exceptions to the rule when it comes to borderline personalities?

JG: Yes. Violence is usually an act of passion. It's done impulsively under the overriding influence of strong feelings and poor control over impulses. A repeated pattern of systematically being sadistic to others is not typical of borderline patients. It can happen, but that's not typical. Sadism would be much more likely in a purely antisocial person. Someone who really doesn't have any regard for the rights and feelings of others that isn't typical of borderlines.

Post: In what you've read about Susan Smith's history, what led you to label her a borderline personality?

JG: I didn't read very much of the story, so I may be in error. But borderlines have a tremendous dilemma once they become mothers, because an overriding fact of their lives is that they feel that they did not get adequate mothering. That doesn't mean it's true, but that's a very important and central part of their motivations and self-esteem. So they often dream and believe that the highest calling on earth is to become a mother—and a good mother. The problem is, they're psychologically handicapped. Are you a father?

Post: Yes.

JG: You probably know, then, that one's little blighters don't always behave. In fact, they disregard what you tell them to do repeatedly. It takes a lot of sustained limit-setting and frustration tolerance to keep your caretaking role in line, in the face of what could be extremely frustrating circumstances. This overwhelms mothers who are borderline in a variety of ways. One is that the amount of care and attention children legitimately require can tax anybody. But for these women, it's accompanied by a feeling that they themselves are being deprived. It opens up to them how much they aren't getting. In fact, they are giving all the time; it is a depriving stance for everybody. But borderlines feel an enormous sense of deprivation when remaining in this stance for sustained periods of time. In addition, they can't get angry at the little blighters without feeling that they are as bad as, or the embodiment of, the evil mother they hated and renounced. That leads to suicide, because nothing is worse. Susan Smith, as I recall, felt herself to be in a bind where her hoped-for savior—the boyfriend—and his continued availability to her were dependent upon getting rid of the kids. So she sacrificed them—but then couldn't live with herself.

Post: Do borderline patients generally make good mothers?

JG: No, but not for a lack of wanting to. Borderline mothers don't have the psychological resources to manage the feelings normal mothers require in terms of the ability to satisfy personal needs and the ability to get angry in some kind of modulated, controlled, reasonable way—at least without feeling they'll lose control over the anger and do something violent, which they can do. But then they feel terrible about it, often withdrawing from their roles as mothers once it's happened.

Post: How do they withdraw?

JG: They will try to turn the primary care of the child over to someone else. They'll become chronic psychiatric patients. I've known a number of borderline women who found refuge in a psychiatric career because it gave a sort of legitimacy to their inability to mother. They could come back and spend shorter periods of time with the children without being overwhelmed, but they weren't expected to be there all the time. Sometimes they can arrange for someone else to take care of the children. These mothers have some strengths. They may be able to get employment so that they can help with the support in a responsible way, but away from some of the immediate emotional demands.

Post: Is the therapy used to treat borderlines primarily psychodynamic?

JG: I'm primarily psychodynamically oriented, but I have a strong conviction that individual psychodynamic therapy is not usually sufficient for such patients and that you need to integrate psychodynamic therapy with social therapies, like group and family work.

Post: If volatile, unstable relationships are characteristic of borderline people, do they generally end up alone?

JG: Borderline patients usually go from one intense relationship to another. It's the very intensity of their needs that usually makes relationships short-lived. Borderline patients do learn from experience, however. By the time many of them reach their 30s, they will either have modified their interpersonal behaviors enough to sustain relationships, or they will have gone into a more withdrawn situation where they try to avoid getting too involved with people. Instead they try to get their needs met by quite superficial involvements with lots of people. Involvement in self-help groups, churches, or employment situations provide sufficient social contact for them, but they don't get too close to anyone. That's one outcome.

A minority of borderline patients actually improve enough so that they can develop quite reasonably stable, and even relatively healthy, relationships. Those are people who usually have had a corrective relationship somewhere along the line, where they have gotten involved with someone over a long period of time and have become more comfortable with their feelings. Because their self-images have changed, they are less apt to feel that they are bad people. That can happen in the course of a good long-term therapy. Sometimes it may even happen, although I think not quite as completely, through the provision of a good relationship in the outside world.

Post: The *Post* featured an article on bipolar disorder in its March/April 1996 issue. We spoke with Dr. Kay Redfield Jamison, whose books examined a relationship between bipolar disease and creativity. What emerged was a roster of famous people who were highly creative. Are borderline patients also politicians, business leaders, mayors, teachers-of-the-year?

JG: That would be quite unusual, although Marilyn Monroe was probably borderline. Her whole life was tempestuous and maybe more typical of a borderline patient's life. Even when they have done something creative, they are likely to be embedded in a very inconsistent record of productivity, as well as involved in many tumultuous relationships. They would not make for good schoolteachers.

Post: Are borderlines masters at manipulation?

JG: Yes. Some more than others.

Post: Is that why therapists are reluctant to treat borderlines?

JG: Once again, I think it has less to do with their fears about the borderline patient actually hurting them in any physical way, but it may have to do with their apprehensions about being manipulated. Most therapists like to think the best about people, and so they're vulnerable to that kind of thing. But most often the apprehension will have more to do with their borderline patients fears of abandonment and their inability to be alone. The therapist often expects to be disrupted frequently in the middle of the night. Or that patients will want to go with them on vacation, be extremely jealous of the therapist's children, or park out in front of the yard. Those are the most common concerns of therapists.

Diagnosis and Treatment of BPD

BPD researcher, clinician, and author of the book Borderline Personality Disorder: A Multidimensional Approach, *Joel Paris, M.D., is senior psychiatrist, Institute of Community and Family Psychiatry, Sir Mortimer B. Davis-Jewish General Hospital, and professor of psychiatry at McGill University, Montreal.*

Post: How does BPD differ from other personality disorders?

JP: There are ten categories of personality disorder, of which borderline has been the subject of the most research. Borderline personality refers to people who can best be described as emotionally unstable in an extreme way. They tend to have many problems of a particular kind in their relationships. They get involved with other people quickly, but things also sour very quickly. They're impulsive in a number of ways, many of which are related to suicide.

The most characteristic feature of the condition is multiple suicide attempts. These attempts usually occur in the context of a problem in a relationship. These patients come into the emergency room, for example, after a fight with somebody, which leads them to take an overdose or to slash their wrists.

Post: One therapist said that he could diagnose a borderline personality in ten minutes. Are they difficult to diagnose?

JP: I can sometimes do it in ten minutes, but you may miss something. There is a feel about these people. For example, a patient that I saw this morning was dysphoric [depressed], miserable, angry, on edge, and impulsive: she couldn't stand how she felt. She immediately engaged me in a very complicated and unpleasant interaction.

Post: Wouldn't most people be initially hesitant with a stranger?

JP: That's right. Borderlines don't have very good boundaries. When most people see a psychiatrist, they open up slowly. Borderlines will give you deep stuff in minutes—which also makes you think about a borderline diagnosis.

Post: Are borderline personalities resistant to change?

JP: Resistant to change by definition, because all personality disorders are chronic and resistant to change over time. That is how they are defined.

Usually, borderline personalities are very demanding of therapy. The irony is, and this has been shown in research, that if you offer borderlines psychotherapy, about two thirds of them will drop out within a few months—another measure of their impulsivity and emotional instability. In other words, they get frustrated with the therapist. They might say to the therapist, "You're not helping me. You don't care," then storm out.

Post: What brings them to therapy in the first place?

JP: Suicide attempts or suicidal feelings are typical.

Post: Are pharmacological interventions successful?

JP: Borderlines don't respond to drugs very well, even though most of them are on medication. At this point in time, pharmacological treatment doesn't last long and is not very impressive. If I give Prozac to somebody with a classic depression, it's almost like magic. The patient often feels like a new person in a few weeks. But if I give borderline patients Prozac, they might feel a little better, yet in a few weeks we'll be back to square one. Although drugs are given

to many of these patients, we haven't discovered or haven't invented the right one yet.

Post: In your book *Borderline Personality Disorder,* you mentioned abnormally low levels of serotonin—a neurotransmitter affecting mood and behavior in the brain.

JP: Yes, that's a theory. There is indirect evidence supporting it. While it is a subject of intense research, I don't think neurotransmitters fully explain the disorder. If they were just deficient in serotonin, why don't they get better on Prozac?

Post: What about psychotherapy?

JP: This is a very interesting story. The term "borderline" was first used in the 1930s by an analyst who hypothesized that the reason these people don't get better is they are on the borderline of psychosis and neurosis. We are stuck with that term, even though we don't believe in the theory anymore. At the time, this analyst wrote that these people don't respond well to analysis. I think almost everyone since agrees. Nevertheless, a lot of psychotherapists have tried to use modified versions of psychoanalysis, so-

---

Are you coping with someone who has Borderline Personality Disorder?

■ Do you find yourself concealing what you think or feel because you're afraid of the other person's reaction, or because it just doesn't seem worth the horrible fight or hurt feelings that will follow?

■ Do you feel that no matter what you say or do that it will be twisted and used against you? Are you blamed and criticized for everything wrong in the relationship—even when it makes no logical sense?

■ Are you the focus of intense, violent, and irrational rages, alternating with periods when the other person acts perfectly normal and loving? Does no one believe you when you explain that this is going on?

■ Do you feel manipulated, controlled, or even lied to sometimes? Do you feel like you're the victim of emotional blackmail?

■ Do you feel like the person you care about sees you as either all good or all bad, with nothing in between? Is there

sometimes no rational reason for the switch?

■ Are you afraid to ask for things in the relationship because you will be told that you're too demanding or there is something wrong with you? Are you told that your needs are not important?

■ Is the person always denigrating or denying your point of view? Do you feel their expectations of you are constantly changing, so you can never do anything right?

■ Are you accused of doing things you never did and saying things you never said? Do you feel misunderstood a great deal of the time, and when you try to explain the other person doesn't believe you?

■ Are you constantly put down, yet when you try to leave the relationship the other person tries to prevent you from leaving in a variety of ways—anything from declarations of love and promises to change to implicit or explicit threats?

■ Do you have a hard time planning anything (social engagements, etc.) because of the other person's moodiness, impulsiveness, or unpredictability? Do you make excuses for their behavior or try to convince yourself that everything is okay?

From BPD Central, an Internet resource for people who care about someone with borderline personality disorder. BPD Central is a three-star site of Mental Health Net (http://www.cmhc.com/).
Internet Address for BPD Central: http://members.aol.com/BPDCentral.

Editor's Note: *If you would like to share your experiences in living with a person with borderline personality disorder, please write to us. You may use fictitious name(s) to protect the anonymity of the patient. Send your responses to The Saturday Evening Post, P.O. Box 567, Indianapolis, IN 46206.*

called psychoanalytic therapies, with these patients. The problem is that there is no scientific evidence showing whether the therapies do or don't work.

What I wrote in my book was my own clinical experience, using therapy successfully in subgroup classes with high-functioning borderline patients—people, for example, who have good jobs or are attending a university, but whose personal lives are a mess. A lot of studies show that the better functioning you are, the more you get out of psychotherapy. If you are not functioning well anywhere in your life—are on welfare and have few friends—you tend not to do well in psychotherapy. The problem is that a lot of borderline patients are on welfare and also have many problems maintaining friendships.

Post: Structured environments seem to work best for these people?

JP: That is one of the main points in my book. Of course, they've got to have the ability to get into a structured environment. I work part-time in the McGill University health service, so a number of the cases I described were university students. Obviously, these are people who are able to structure themselves. They have higher IQs or other positive personality traits.

I also said in the book that modern society, where it's every man and woman for themselves and where there is such a high level of individualism, might be one factor making BPD more common.

Post: How would a lay person recognize these symptoms?

JP: It's not easy. When you are a psychiatrist, people tell you everything. You discover that you know your patients better than you know your friends. However, many people know someone who is chronically suicidal and has had many treatments for suicidal threats or attempts, usually involving overdoses or wrist cuttings. Attempted suicide is the most characteristic symptom of the disorder.

Post: If people have seven of the nine diagnostic criteria for BPD [see box, "Diagnostic Criteria for Borderline Personality Disorder] but lack the suicidal trait, would they fall outside the diagnosis?

JP: No. If you have seven of the nine, you fit the profile. The way the *DSM-IV* is written, all nine have an equal weight, but they are not independent of each other. But I've never seen anyone who has met the criteria yet

who didn't at least have some suicidal behavior.

Post: Is life with a borderline patient challenging?

> ## "Where other people in the life of borderline patients can go wrong is by trying to do too much. The borderline patient is asking you to be mother, father, lover—everything."

JP: When you're the therapist, you start feeling that you must be a terrible therapist to have somebody hate you or telling you such things as "I'm going to kill myself, and it's your fault, Doctor." I like these patients very much who, with all of their pathology, can be quite engaging, but they are very good at making other people feel sorry for them, guilty about them, and that people close to them haven't done enough to help. Friends and family should distinguish between empathy and sympathy. Empathy doesn't necessarily mean that you agree with the person's actions. There are times when a therapist has to say, "Well, you could kill yourself, but I would rather see you next week for the session."

Where other people in the life of borderline patients can go wrong is by trying to do too much. The borderline patient is asking you to be mother, father, lover—everything. People might think, *Gee, this person really needs me . . . I can understand her better than anyone else.* But after a while, the person gets mad at you, and you're caught.

Post: In your book, you write that the disease is self-limiting.

JP: That is what is called "burnout." Time wears the pathology down. That is true also of antisocial behavior and drug abuse.

The Prevalence of Childhood Sexual Abuse

Paul Soloff M.D., professor of psychiatry at the University of Pittsburgh,

Western Psychiatric Institute and Clinic, is a leading researcher in the psychopharmacology, as well as psychobiology, of BPD.

Post: Is childhood abuse implicated in the incidence of borderline personality disorder?

PS: More recently, the literature has indicated high incidence of abuse—physical abuse or sexual abuse—in the histories of patients with borderline personality disorder. Not all, but many. Some of the percentages are as low as 20 percent, others as high as 70 percent, but always more than in control groups. So the sexual-physical trauma contributes to that interpersonal style of functioning that involves manipulative, dependent relationships. The patients have a chronic low sense of self-esteem, feel bad about themselves, feel like nobody could care for them.

Post: When do borderline patients most often come to the attention of the psychiatric community?

PS: Borderline patients most often come to our attention at times of crisis, usually in the face of a perceived rejection. I use the term "rejection sensitivity." That's one of the buzz words for the mood crashes, the depressive episodes that they have. At a time of perceived rejection, these are the patients who take pills on impulse, cut themselves, or burn themselves. When we see them, they are often in an emergency room with lacerated arms or an overdose of pills. When taking a patient's history, we discover there's a track record and that the patient may have done it many times before.

Post: Self-mutilation could take many forms, is that correct?

PS: Yes, it does, actually. The most common is wrist-cutting or burning with cigarettes. Part of what happens is that these patients usually use the cut or the burn. It has several meanings. One meaning is that the wrist cut or the burn deals with some intense feeling the patient is having. That's its primary purpose—to deal with some intense feeling. In psychiatry, we call that the primary gain. The symptom is doing something for the patient within himself or herself. It's handling this very strong feeling. But in psychiatry we also recognize that symptoms have a personal value to others—an interpersonal meaning. This is called the secondary gain. Now that's fairly easy to understand, because if you cut your wrist and you show it to somebody, what happens? Right away people pay attention. They either put you in the hospital, take care of you, nurture you, or criticize you, but you get a tremendous amount of attention. That's what happens with a borderline patient. Typically, you have a person who, feeling abandoned or alone, does something to himself to deal with that intense feeling. That's the primary gain. The secondary gain is that the patient usually makes sure that somebody else knows about it—the police, the family, or the doctors arrive. The person is the focus of attention. Think of these destructive actions as primitive efforts to obtain help, to force other people to take care of this person—that's a typical kind of borderline dynamic.

Post: Do borderline personalities want therapy?

PS: Patients want therapy. In fact, they're among our most demanding patients because these are people who are seeking care. They manipulate care. They force others to take care of them. That's not the problem. The problem is the forms of treatment that we have so far are not very good. The medications that we have help to palliate the impulsivity and the mood disorder, the mood disregulation. The psychotherapies are in no way curative; they are primarily supportive. You don't cure personality disorders. You help people deal with the symptoms and vulnerabilities that they have. You help them live better.

Post: What's it like to live with a borderline?

PS: I have not had that experience, but my patients certainly have, and I have talked to their spouses. Borderlines are very unstable and argumentative. A family disagreement can result in a trip to the emergency room with her overdosing or his smashing the windows. They're unpredictable in that sense. Borderlines are very rejection-sensitive, so that things you and I would take for granted—criticism, for example—a bor-

derline patient might see as a rejection. Or a partner coming home late for dinner might be taken as rejection. It's the quality of feeling rejected that is important. Abandoned, rejected, that's the critical element here.

Post: Why do you think that three quarters of BPDs are women?

PS: That is part of cultural bias. In this country, three quarters of them are women. In general, that's not true in other countries. There are cultural ways of expressing distress. In this culture, women are taught to express stress by turning their aggression against themselves; men are taught to channel their aggression against others. Men do things that are very dramatic. Male borderlines would, for example, get into fights, stand on bridges, use handguns, create a disturbance—they'll usually end up in jail. Women will end up in mental hospitals: they cut themselves, they burn themselves, they take overdoses. So, the first thing we have to contend with is the cultural bias in symptom expression. What I am saying is that you can have exactly the same problem and, if you're a male, you do something dramatic; you won t cut your wrist. I had one patient who would punch policemen. Another would break picture windows in downtown department stores in broad daylight—smash windows one right after the other. They ended up in jail. They have exactly the same psychodynamic motivation as a woman who might take a handful of pills or cut her wrists when she's feeling rejected. So cultural expression of symptoms is a big part of it.

Comments by
Janice M. Cauwels, Ph.D., writer, consultant, and author of Imbroglio

Post: What was the predominant feature of BPD you encountered in interviews with experts?

JC: The key feature of BPD to experts is that it is the most difficult psychiatric illness to treat. Physicians in other specialties don't like borderlines,

either. While writing my book, for example, I mentioned the topic to a resident in allergy and immunology who had worked for a while in an emergency room. She launched into a tirade against the suicidal borderlines who had appeared or been brought in for treatment while she was on duty, apparently because they had been demanding and troublesome.

Borderlines appear to be very capricious and manipulative. They want to foist all their own responsibility for getting better onto their therapists, with whom they become intensely involved yet they often reject therapists' efforts to help.

Even competent therapists can become so emotionally involved with borderline patients, in turn, that they feel tossed around and make terrible mistakes in treatment. For this reason, knowledgeable therapists insist that ongoing consultation with a colleague about a borderline patient's case is always necessary. But even with such assistance no experienced therapist treats more than one or two borderlines at a time in private practice.

I observed a class on personality disorders in which several psychiatric residents explained that they disliked dealing with borderline instability, dishonesty, distortions, brief psychotic episodes, unbearable anger, demands, and constant threats of suicide. These residents felt scapegoated by the hospital staff for having such troublesome patients.

Writing *Imbroglio* was frustrating because of both the complexity of the subject matter and the objections of therapists to the forthcoming book. Most therapists believed that I had set myself an impossible task; some predicted that I would become a target of borderline rage; many, I think, feared that information about the illness would make their work more difficult by getting borderline patients all stirred up.

FINDING STRENGTH

How to Overcome Anything

Are some of us born more resilient than others? Can strength be taught? Here, a breakthrough report detailing what only decades of research can show—how people overcome terrible trauma, and just what it takes to survive and thrive. Start believing in yourself—now!

By Deborah Blum

For most of us, high-voltage transmission lines are blots on the landscape. They slice up the sky and emit a sinister little hum of energy that translates into "Stay back if you want to see tomorrow. So, for David Miller to like power lines so much—to see in them uplift and promise and future—well, you first have to understand the landscape of a child whose mother decided not to keep him.

He was born in 1960, in Reidsville, North Carolina, in a neighborhood of small, neat ranch houses—in the African-American-only part of town. This was, after all, the deep South of almost forty years ago. He lived with his grandparents. His mother left him

there; she couldn't do it, everyone knew that. She was 24, pregnant by mistake. "It's not that I didn't see my mother," Miller says, "but my grandparents raised me." Yet because his grandparents both worked—his grandfather at a dry cleaners, his grandmother as a laundry attendant—"I was a latchkey kid before the coin was termed."

And when they were home, they had little patience for a small boy's antics. "My grandmother would save up my spankings all week," says Miller. "Friday was judgment day." If the offense was grave enough, he ended up with welts across his back.

You might imagine that he was a child standing on a slippery hillside, his birth merely the first skidding step downward. In his spare time, though, he used to walk under the power lines. "It seemed like hours and miles," he recalls, "but I was pretty small." And he'd follow them with his feet and then his eyes until they disappeared into the clouded edges of the sky. And he'd think about where they went and wonder about the world beyond.

Miller is 37 now and an assistant professor of social work at Case Western Reserve University in Cleveland. He's chosen to study resilience—the ability, let's say, to stand steady on such treacherous hillsides, even to climb them—among other at-risk children, young African-Americans from the poor and drug-overrun neighborhoods of the inner city.

"I'm interested in strengths," he says. "What strengths allow you to deal with the violence, and the guns held to your head, and the fear of being molested? What is it that allows children to grow up in that and not be immobilized?" And when he talks to teenagers there, he remembers his own climb. "I do see myself as resilient. I always believed in my own abilities. I wasn't handcuffed by where I grew up. I'm happy with my life."

And when he travels to New York or Miami or into the power-line neighborhoods of Cleveland, where he lives, he still looks up and watches that unexpected flight of utility hardware to the horizon. And he thinks, "Oh, this is where they were taking me."

WHEN THE RED BALL BOUNCES

Could there be a research field more personal than that of resilience? When we all know that life, even for those who have had the best of childhoods, promises challenge after challenge, year after year? Who doesn't want to know where resilience comes from, how to transcend pain and grief, surmount obstacles and frustrations—to dream along the power lines, if you will? I began thinking about it as a parent. There were days I hated: finding my son standing by a wall in the schoolyard, eyes filling with tears, unwanted by his playmates at that moment. I wanted, oh, I

7 STEPS OF STRENGTH:

- ◆ You have the **ability** right now
- ◆ **Faith**—in the future or in God—counts
- ◆ Recruit **others**
- ◆ Set **goals**
- ◆ **Believe** in yourself
- ◆ Recognize your **strengths**
- ◆ See yourself as a **strategist**

TRIUMPH OVER TORTURE

I HAD NEVER READ A BOOK AS PITI-less, terrifying, and inspiring in my life: a Tibetan woman's account of twenty-seven years of torture in labor camps for resisting China's occupation of her home-land. *Ama Adhe: The Voice That Remembers* (Wisdom Publications) is a memoir that describes—with unutterable calm—acts of unthinkable evil, and the unwavering spirit of the woman who withstood them. But meeting her was the true shock: when I sat with Adhe in my home, she took my hands in hers—strong, vital, calloused, caressing—and it was I, the baby boomer American journalist, who drew strength from her.

She was dressed in typical Tibetan garb—peasant style—and counted her prayer beads from time to time. Now in her sixties, Adhe lives in exile in India under the protection of the Dalai Lama. She has remarried, and speaks reverently of "waking each morning and realizing that I am in freedom, living in the same town that his Holiness the Dalai Lama lives in, and then I am very happy."

The facts: In 1954, when Adhe's son was just a year old, and she was pregnant with her second child, her husband was poisoned and died in front of her. Her husband's mother died soon afterward, of grief. In 1958, nine armed men came to Adhe's home, beat her in front of her children, and arrested her. Several months of physical torture followed, and finally she was brought before a large crowd and forced to watch as her brother-in-law was shot in front of her. "Pieces of his brain and his blood splashed on my dress," Adhe recalls. Her sister, his wife, lost her mind and died soon after.

Adhe, however, was not killed. "They said, 'We want you to suffer for the rest of your life. Now you see who has won.' " Almost three decades of imprisonment, forced labor, near starvation, and beatings followed. Moved from prison to prison, Adhe was not allowed to change or wash her only dress—known in Tibetan as a *chupa*—for years. When she menstruated, she let the blood dry and scraped it off. At one point she fainted while carrying stones; she was believed to be dead and was put in a hut that held the bodies of other dead prisoners. "The bodies looked like skeletons," says Adhe. "The eyes had blackened, the cheekbones were protruding. The sickening smell was overwhelming."

Over time, Adhe became something of a cause célèbre and was finally allowed to visit friends and family in 1979, twenty-one years after she was first imprisoned. She discovered that a friend had raised her daughter, but her son had gone insane after her arrest and one day fell into a river and drowned. "My surviving friends came to see me in the night," she says, "and told me of the fates of most of the women who had worked with me in the resistance. Now they were dead." That may have been Adhe's darkest moment: "There was nothing left. All these years I had been living for nothing, and now I didn't have to try anymore. A terrible restlessness came over me, and I began to wander around muttering to myself, totally unaware of my immediate surroundings."

How does one even use the word "resilience" in this context? It seems too small. There is a quality of indestructible strength and joy in Adhe that seems inborn. However, in her story, one does find the common traits of resilience that researchers have pointed out. For instance, perhaps the cardinal finding about the resilient is that they do not survive alone. Too weak to say her daily prayers (or even to remember them), Adhe sought the advice of an imprisoned monk who crafted her a shortened version of the prayer. Mourning the deaths of fellow women prisoners, Adhe began to make a quilt from their old dresses, and after a few years, it was large enough to sleep on. To this day she keeps the quilt: "My daughter used to beg me to get rid of it, saying, 'I can't stand it. Please throw it in the river.' But somehow I couldn't. It is with me even today."

Later, Adhe was sent food by her brother, and when prison officials wanted to take it away from her, a Chinese doctor at the labor camp who had taken an interest in Adhe's welfare intervened. "He said he would keep the food and give it to me slowly. 'If you overeat at this point, you will die.' " Adhe asked the doctor to use the food to prepare a special soup for all the prisoners. In her memoir, she recalls: "All the prisoners were so happy in getting their share that although it was still very hot, they drank it immediately. You could see their faces glowing red. Some licked the cups, then put in some water, shook the cup, and drank again. Some kissed my hand. They said, 'At least before we die, we are having our native food.' " One Tibetan, a man too weak to walk or stand, gave her his hat, in which a tiny portrait of the Dalai Lama was tied with thread. "After that, I always wore the hat. The most precious gift gave me hope."

When asked how she survived, Adhe says it was through daily prayer. Today, she lives in two rooms with her husband, in Dharmshala, India. She wakes at dawn, makes an offering at her altar, and prays until noon. She then goes to meet and help new Tibetan refugees. She says that though the jailers, labor camps, and suffering of her fellow prisoners comes back to her constantly in dreams, every morning, as soon as she awakens, she is happy again.

The Chinese told her long ago, as they shot her brother-in-law to death in front of her, "Now you see who has won." Yes, now we see who has won.

wanted revenge, although that was pure, lunatic fantasy. I wanted to bundle my son away in some cozy little world without hurt. An even greater fantasy.

Most of all, I wanted to know if I could teach him to bounce back. We all tumble. If we pick ourselves up, and learn from it, and go on with only superficial injury, well—I wanted to know if I could give my son that wonderful ability—that bounce.

I had a powerful visual image of the process. Not Miller's power lines, but the neat, clean, and quick bounce of a ball. The slap, the sting of being down, and then the easy rise, arching into a brighter air. It was a lovely image, really. It made me think of Paul Simon's old lyric about coming back from a failed love affair: "The morning sun is shining like a red rubber ball."

It was such a terrific thought. And this is what I wanted science to tell me: can resilience be deliberately acquired, or must we be born a David Miller, with some marvelous inner ability to see beyond where we stand?

It turns out to be a good time to ask those questions, because so many researchers are also asking them, in a professional capacity. Scientists now study resilience, it seems, in every possible niche: inner cities, tropical islands, families fleeing war or trying to live with it, children coping with the loss of a parent, entire families struggling with the loss of a home. It's part of what American Psychological Association President Martin Seligman, Ph.D., believes is a sea change in psychology, away from focusing on what damages people toward trying to understand what makes them strong.

The first finding, to my chagrin, is that I'm going to have to tuck my red rubber ball image back into the lore of pop-rock. There's no: "Hey, the kid went down, but look, he bounced, he's fine" ending to this story. The ability to rebound is part of the process, sure, but it's not magically pain-free or instantaneous. Psychologists want that message out there. In fact, a professional alarm sounded last year when a national news magazine (okay, *U.S. News and World Report*) published a cover story about resilience research titled "Invincible Children."

"It is a primary example of what I have been calling the myth of the "superkid," who walks between raindrops, confronts any challenge and emerges unscarred and unscathed, never experiences a moment's pain," says Washington, D.C., psychologist Sybil Wolin, Ph.D., who, with husband and clinical psychiatrist Steve Wolin, M.D., co-authored the popular book, *The Resilient Self*.

> One's upbringing does not build a lifelong prison. "The first, biggest surprise to me," says Emmy Werner, Ph.D., "is that so many people recovered" from traumatic childhoods.

"The notion we try to put forth is that resilience embodies a paradox," she says. "We're talking about the capacity to rebound from experience, mixed with all the damage and problems that adversity can cause. It's not an either/or thing. And this 'media resilience' does kids who are struggling no good, does professionals no good in understanding them, has downright dangerous policy implications, and frankly, gives resilience research a bad name."

THE ROCKY CLIMB

Resilience research is often not bright and shiny at all. If you're going to study people climbing upward, you have to start at the very rocky bottom. "I decided to look at adults who'd had traumatic childhoods because I knew some very neat people who had come from that background," said John De-Frain, Ph.D., a professor of family studies at the University of Nebraska. "I thought it would be all warm and fuzzy-feeling. But these were people who were sometimes just barely hanging on. They were surviving as children, but just."

He found that it was in adulthood that people really began to transcend the difficulties of childhood and to rebuild. One man, beaten as a child by his father with belts, razor strops, and tree branches, reached a point in his mid-twenties, when he decided to die. He wrote a suicide note, put the gun to his head, and then suddenly thought, "I'm not going to die because of what someone else did to me." That day for the first time, he called a psychologist and went into counseling.

That dramatically emphasizes one of several key aspects of resilience research:

• **There is no timeline, no set period, for finding strength**, resilient behaviors and coping skills. People do best if they develop strong coping skills as children, and some researchers suggest the first ten years are optimum. But the ability to turn around is always there.

• **About one-third of poor neglected, abused children are capably building better lives** by the time they are teenagers, according to all resilience studies. They are doing well in school, working toward careers, often helping to support their siblings.

• **Faith—be it in the future, the world at the end of the power lines, or in a higher power—is an essential ingredient.** Ability to perceive bad times as temporary times gets great emphasis from Seligman as an essential strength.

• **Most resilient people don't do it alone**—in fact, they don't even try. One of the standout findings of resilience research is that people who cope well with adversity, if they don't have a strong family support system, are able to ask for help or recruit others to help them. This is true for children and adults; resilient adults, for instance, are far more likely to talk to friends and even co-workers about events in their lives.

• **Setting goals and planning for the future is a strong factor in dealing with adversity.** In fact, as University of California-Davis psychologist Emmy Werner, Ph.D., points out, it may minimize the adversity itself. For instance, Werner found that when Hurricane Iniki battered Hawaii in 1993, islanders who were previously identified as resilient reported less property damage than others in the study. Why? They'd prepared more, boarded up windows, invested in good insurance.

• **Believing in oneself and recognizing one's strengths is important.** University of Alabama psychologist Ernestine Brown, Ph.D., discovered that when children of depressed, barely functioning mothers took pride in helping take care of the family, they didn't feel as trapped. "You pick yourself up, give yourself value," Brown says. "If you can't change a bad situation, you can at least nurture yourself. Make yourself a place for intelligence and competence, surround yourself with things that help you stabilize, and remember what you're trying to do."

> An astonishing one-third of children who grow up neglected, poor, or abused, are capable of building better lives by the time they are teenagers.

• **And it's equally important to actually recognize one's own strengths.** Many people don't. Teaching them such self-recognition is a major part of the approach that the Wolins try when helping adults build a newly resilient approach to life. They are among a small group of professionals testing the idea that resilience can be taught, perhaps by training counselors and psychologists to focus on building strengths in their clients.

A WHOLE NEW VIEW OF STRENGTH

Steve Wolin tells a story about one of his clients, a woman whose father—if he felt threatened or challenged in any way—would batter the offender. The woman, who was whipped throughout her childhood, saw herself as helpless. But Wolin encouraged her to see it differently: she was smart; she had learned how to recognize and respond to her father's moods; she was an accomplished strategist. "We encourage people to reframe the way they see themselves," he says. "We call this Survivor's Pride." Insight is only one of the abilities that he tries to persuade his clients to value. Others include humor, independence, initiative, creativity, and morality.

Edith Grotberg, who heads an international resilience project, tries to help people organize their strengths into three simple categories: I have (which includes strong relationships, structure and rules at home, role models); I am (a person who has hope and faith, cares about others, is proud of oneself); and I can (ability to communicate, solve problems, gauge the temperament of others, seek good relationships). She finds, by the way, that men tend to draw most confidence from the "I can" category and women from the "I am."

"But all people have the capacity for resilience," says Grotberg, Ph.D., from the University of Alabama, Birmingham. "We just have to learn to draw it out and to support them."

This is, without hyperbole, a breathtaking change from the approach of psychology just a few decades ago. Seligman describes the old

> I HAVE—strong relationships and role models; I AM—a person who has hope, faith, pride, and cares about others; I CAN—communicate, solve problems, and seek good relationships.

approach—which he says took over after World War II—as victimology, an emphasis on psychological damage driven by the parallel emphasis of the same period on nurture over nature. Psychologists believed that people were shaped by environment—a harmful environment would inevitably result in a bent or skewed or non-functional person.

So powerful was this notion that when Norman Garmezy, Ph.D., of the University of Minnesota, studied children of severely depressed mothers and found that some of them seemed healthy and capable, his first response was that he had misdiagnosed the mothers. Michael Rutter, Ph.D., of the Institute of Psychiatry in London, tracked children of drug-addicted mothers, and reported the same, I-must-have-screwed-up reaction. But their findings—that at least one-fourth of the children seemed both confident and capable—wouldn't go away. Garmezy and Rutter refocused on the coping skills of people in troubled families. Their work laid the foundation for today's entire generation of resilience researchers. This year's annual American Psychological Association meeting is focused on recognizing human strengths.

Garmezy gives credit to Emmy Werner for nurturing the field. "Mother Resilience" is his favorite nickname for her, and it makes her laugh. "Maybe at the age of 68, it needs to be changed to 'Grandmother Resilience,' " she jokes.

Her primary work for the last thirty years, a longitudinal study of native Hawaiians, does provide a terrific case study of resilience research in motion. Werner has followed the same group of islanders from late adolescence into middle age. She titled her last book about them *Overcoming the Odds*.

There are 505 people in Werner's study, born in 1955 on the small and beautiful island of Kauai. About half were born into poverty, mostly the children of sugar plantation workers. It should be noted, from the beginning, that this is almost a guaran-

tee of poverty; the island sugarcane industry has been falling away almost since these children were born. Not surprisingly, many of them grew up in homes dominated by fears of even greater poverty, where alcoholism and anger and abuse were just the way of life.

As Werner says, victim-theory would have predicted that by the time those children reached their twenties, they would have simply sunk into a swamp of crime and unemployment. And most did. Yet there was still that startling number: one-third never seemed to sink at all; they did well in school, began promising careers and—most important—defined themselves as capable and competent adults.

One woman profiled, Leilani, is a working mother of three sons; she is in her thirties, and put it like this: "I am proud of myself as a person now. I have received so much fulfillment in being a wife, mother, and worker. I feel I've finally grown up."

YOUR PAST IS NOT A PRISON

The ground breaking point in Werner's work—which Garmezy calls "the best single study" on resilience in children—is that one's upbringing does not build a lifelong prison. "The first, biggest surprise to me was that so many recovered," Werner said. And when she went back and looked at the islanders in their thirties and forties, she found that even more had determined not to repeat their parents lives. More than half had fallen, as teenagers, into petty crime. Of that group, only 10 percent of the females and one-fourth of males still had criminal records in their thirties. The majority had struggled, but had moved on.

One of the unexpected spinoffs of resilience research, then, is that it has begun breaking down myths of failure—that having a bad beginning makes one a bad person; that abused children grow up to be abusers. In fact, the statistics are very comparable to Werner's resilience study. New studies show that a clear one-third of abused children grow up determined never to lay a hand on their children, and they don't.

And they can choose that even after childhoods that seem to hang on the dark edge of nightmare. John DeFrain and his colleagues—Nikki DeFrain, Linda Ernst,

and Jean Jones—have compiled a horrific portrait of an abusive childhood, based on interviews with forty adults identified as growing up in traumatic family situations.

Consider a typical description from their study: "One time I remember sitting at the dinner table when I was six or seven. My sister was told to say grace and when she finished, my dad slapped her across the face. He told her she said it wrong and to do it over. She started again and he slapped her again. This went on and on, over and over, faster and faster, for what seemed like half an hour. I remember sitting there across from her, paralyzed. I just kept praying, 'Get it right.' The problem was, she was doing it right, just the way we learned it in Sunday School."

Or this one: "I learned to survive by letting myself go. I taught myself how to go numb, to have no feeling. I can feel myself floating out of my body and look down on a little girl screaming. A little dark-eyed girl sits in a big over-stuffed chair. She does not move or whimper, but prays that her mother will forget she is angry at her. 'I'm sorry, I'm sorry' keeps playing in her ears, but she can't remember what for. 'I did my homework,' she reminds herself. 'I made my bed this morning and didn't forget to clean my room.' And then she loses herself in the cracks in the ceiling with the first blows to her head."

No one just bounces back in that type of situation, and DeFrain emphasizes this with great intensity: "I think if society comes to the conclusion that there are some magical little children out there who are somehow inoculated against savagery and violence, we will look the other way as children continue to be traumatized."'

But as his work also emphasizes, if a family situation is insane, most people will build, within it, their own sanctuary and sanity.

They learn the tricks of mental distance, as did the little girl in the big chair. They escape: into music and books. Skills aren't

> Eighty-three percent of adults had transcended troubled childhoods and were proud of it.

only a way to build a better future, they are a safe house. "I took piano and sang in the church choir as well as the school choir," one woman said. "At home, I was quiet and stayed in my room most of the time. Away from home, I was cheerful and upbeat." Many braced themselves with religious faith; in DeFrain's study, people almost unanimously said that they had received little help from people in the church—56 percent said they had no one to talk to—but that they held to the idea of guardian angels or a God who, as one man puts it, "will always love me and forgive me."

DeFrain and his colleagues asked every person in their study if childhood still hurt. "If you're an eight-year-old girl and you're getting pounded every day and all you have is a belief that there's a God out there who loves you, is that a wonderful story?" he asks. Not one person in his study said that they had left their childhood unscarred. Eleven percent said they considered themselves bare survivors, but an astonishing 83 percent said they had moved past, were transcending their childhood, building an adult life they could be proud of.

Ann S. Masten, Ph.D., a professor of psychology at the University of Minnesota, reports a similar balancing of pain and determination in a study of Khmer-American teenagers in Minnesota, children of families who fled Cambodia.

"During the Pol Pot years, from 1975 to 1979," says Masten, "they were very young children, and most lived for many years afterwards under difficult conditions in Thai refugee camps. These children have lived through the unspeakable horrors of war. And most of them have witnessed torture and the death of family and friends from awful violence and starvation, or forced labor and other terribly traumatic events."

There's no arguing that many still suffer the consequences, Masten concedes. "They still have nightmares, periods when they are jumpy and cannot concentrate, or get depressed and anxious. For instance, when the Persian Gulf War was broadcast live on television, many Cambodians experienced an upsurge of the symptoms of trauma from their own wartime experiences."

"Yet these young people are living in Minnesota, getting on with their lives, worrying about what they are going to wear to the prom, or what college they are going to. They are absolute, living testimony to the human capacity for resilience."

RECRUITING HELP: THE MAGIC AND THE MYSTERY

Can one do that on their own, rise above the terrifying parent, the terrible neighborhood, or the trauma of living in a war zone? Resilience researchers find—anecdotally at least—that there are individuals who possess an extraordinary will to transcend, to make their lives work. David Miller, who is studying African-American teenagers living in the drug-plagued neighborhoods of

More than half of resilient people hold to the idea of guardian angels or a God who will always love them.

Cleveland, tells of one boy who made up his mind that he would not do drugs, not join a gang, not fall like his friends around him.

"They wanted him to, but he refused," says Miller. "He was threatened and he was beaten up and he steadfastly remained outside. He took the beatings, and he fought back. He said, 'I'm not doing this.' Eventually they left him alone. He's now a freshman in college."

Can you teach that kind of inner resolve? "No, I don't think so," Miller says. "You can teach people to understand consequences; you can teach them ways to go at life, so that when trauma strikes, they don't become overwhelmed. You can teach them ways to find strength. After all, it doesn't take strength to go the wrong way. It doesn't require any effort."

Miller—and, really, everyone in the field of resilience—emphasizes the importance of someone else's presence. Parents, first and best of all, who believe in you, and, if that fails, neighbors, friends, teachers. The foremost element in transcending trouble is not having to do it alone. Emmy Werner found that many islanders in her study group pulled their lives together when they married. There's an element of obvious common sense here—we all need love and hope and help. At an informational meeting for members of Congress in March 1996, Masten put it like this: "The most important message I have for you today is that there is no magic here."

But Steve Wolin points out that people who emerge successfully from tough times tend to be very good at recruiting people into a support system. He gives the example of a high school boy living in his girlfriend's basement. The boy's parents were drug addicts; his home life was awful, and the girl's mother, who liked him, had offered him a temporary home. He told Wolin that he courted the mother, studying the foods she liked best, bringing gifts like spaghetti sauce and loaves of French bread.

"I want people to see that this is not being manipulative," Wolin said. "This child was not a user. This is a strength." The boy was working after school to provide food for his younger brothers. He was also considering dropping out and taking a second job, to get them better clothes.

Peg Heinzer, who holds joint nursing appointments at LaSalle University in Pennsylvania and Albert Einstein School of Medicine in New York, studied the ways in which children cope with the death of a parent. Heinzer began by trying to help her own five children. Her husband, their father, died a decade ago of lymphoma. Her children ranged from eight to 17 at the time. One of her sons wrote a school paper on role models that began: "The person I most admire is no longer alive."

Determined to provide a strong and loving, single-parent home, she set out to explore whether love really made a difference. To her surprise, the child's attachment to the surviving parent did not directly predict a strong recovery. But children who came from supportive homes had a great ability to build extended networks; they were likable and considerate of others. "They were all delightful," she recalls. "I went into 89 homes and, in every case, the teenagers offered me something to drink or eat and made sure I was comfortable."

The ability to read at grade level by age ten is a startling predictor of resilience in poor and neglected children.

And that quality, she thinks, made them good at asking for help. "We need to be able to talk about the hard times," she says. "And I think we can teach people that it's okay to ask for help."

Miller can still remember the names of everyone on his grandparent's street: there was Mr. Sam and Miss Bertha and the Harrisons and the Watts. Those neighbors hired him to do chores, invited him to drop in for snacks, and urged him on to a better life. He recalls people constantly advising him on good manners, good grades. "It's as if you attract it. People see possibility in you. They would say to me, 'David, you're someone.' It's as if you just attract people who believe in you."

And if one is not a born recruiter, it turns out, organized programs can still make a remarkable difference. For example, a 1996 analysis of the Big Brother/Big Sister program conducted by Public/Private Ventures provided some remarkable statistics of success: The study looked at children from poor, single-parent homes where there was a high incidence of violence. Among children involved in the Big Brother/Big Sister program, first-time drug use was 46 percent lower, school absenteeism was 52 percent lower, and violent behavior was 33 percent lower.

WHY SCHOOL COUNTS

Education remains one of the most important factors in resilience; its greatest side effect is the belief that one is building a roadway out of despair. One girl in Miller's study, the daughter of drug addicts, told him she felt completely isolated, except for school. There she felt competent. She is also now in college, he says. Werner found, in fact, that the ability to read at grade level by age ten was a startling predictor of whether or not poor children would engage in juvenile crime; at least 70 percent of youthful offenders were in need of remedial education by the fourth grade.

This has led some researchers to suggest that intelligence is a key factor in resilient behavior. But Werner argues that we should turn that around: if scholastic competence is important in rising above adversity, then, she says, that suggests we should put more effort into teaching children well in those early years. We don't have to fully understand resilience to concentrate on basics, such as fostering competence in school, learning to find help, learning to plan and set goals.

Peg Heinzer recalls that after her husband died—in a period when she felt that she might simply wash away in grief—she set tiny goals for herself. On her drive to graduate school, there was one particular intersection where she would begin to weep every day. She'd arrive in class with her lap drenched with tears. The first day that she made it through that intersection without weeping, she took as a measure of healing—that she was going to be all right.

"It's more than just surviving," she says now. "I built a new life. I raised five caring

People who've overcome adversity often try to make the world better. It's a kind of antidote to pain.

and close children. I'm proud of myself. I'm happy."

JOY: THE SILVER LINING

Actually, here is one place where we could let the red rubber ball back in. There can be a real joyfulness to the rebound. I've seen it in my son when he goes back to school the next day, plays with his friends again, and that day, partly by pure contrast, is just a wonderful day.

There's a triumph to overcoming the odds, one that doesn't come when you begin on high and stable ground. And many people, once they've made it through, have strong faith in themselves and their strengths, more so than those who have not been tried so hard. "The key person is me," one man told DeFrain. "In some ways I was fortunate to learn to rely on myself. I knew I had to make the change. No one else could do it for me."

DeFrain and his colleagues found that more than 80 percent of the people they talked to, while hating their childhoods, believed they'd become better people because of it: stronger, kinder, and quicker to care for and help others. People who've overcome adversity often try to make the world a better place. One of Steve Wolin's clients came breathlessly to a session after unhesitatingly jumping between an elderly woman and a group of muggers.

"We hear it all the time," Wolin says. "I've been tested and I've prevailed and I'm better for it. We think that kind of reaction

fits right into Survivor's Pride, and that it's an antidote to the pain. And that's part of it too. These are people who have struggled mightily and who have wounds to show for it. No one's story is a clean one; we are all a checkerboard of strengths and scars."

Certainly, Miller sees himself that way. He recognizes how far determination has brought him: "I'll work and work to achieve something. I said that to a friend once, that there are people out there who are smarter than I am, but no one who will work harder." There are still things that come hard for Miller, though. His marriage failed; his wife and 13-year-old daughter live in another state. "Yes," he says, slowly, "there are things I wish I did better, that I work on still."

And his voice falls away from the pure confidence that it holds when he describes his work.

Resilience, as Werner points out, is many different things. It is multifaceted. We all respond differently to different challenges. And no one yet understands how the facets come together; no one can predict when we will be strong or when our strengths will fail us. On that point, there is rare unanimity among researchers: "We aren't there yet," says Peg Heinzer; "We need to evaluate," explains Emmy Werner; "We need more research," replies Ernestine Brown. "We don't want to think we're studying invincibility."

A child may dream along the power lines, if that's the only avenue. And the fact that the child follows the dreams? Does that come from an inner strength we don't understand or one that we do? Miller himself recognizes that his childhood led him, not simply to the town of Cleveland, but far beyond, to begin to map the power of the human soul.

Deborah Blum is a Pulitzer Prize-winning science writer and a professor in the School of Journalism at the University of Wisconsin.

This glossary of psychology terms is included to provide you with a convenient and ready reference as you encounter general terms in your study of psychology and personal growth and behavior that are unfamiliar or require a review. It is not intended to be comprehensive, but taken together with the many definitions included in the articles themselves, it should prove to be quite useful.

abnormal behavior Behavior that contributes to maladaptiveness, is considered deviant by the culture, or that leads to personal psychological distress.

absolute threshold The minimum amount of physical energy required to produce a sensation.

accommodation Process in cognitive development; involves altering or reorganizing the mental picture to make room for a new experience or idea.

acculturation The process of becoming part of a new cultural environment.

acetylcholine A neurotransmitter involved in memory.

achievement drive The need to attain self-esteem, success, or status. Society's expectations strongly influence the achievement motive.

achievement style The way people behave in achievement situations; achievement styles include the direct, instrumental, and relational styles.

acquired immune deficiency syndrome (AIDS) A fatal disease of the immune system.

acquisition In conditioning, forming associations in first learning a task.

actor-observer bias Tendency to attribute the behavior of other people to internal causes and our own behavior to external causes.

acupuncture Oriental practice involving the insertion of needles into the body to control pain.

adaptation The process of responding to changes in the environment by altering responses to keep a person's behavior appropriate to environmental demands.

adjustment How we react to stress; some change that we make in response to the demands placed upon us.

adrenal glands Endocrine glands involved in stress and energy regulation.

adrenaline A hormone produced by the adrenal glands that is involved in physiological arousal; adrenaline is also called epinephrine.

affective flattening Individuals with schizophrenia who do not exhibit any emotional arousal.

aggression Behavior intended to harm a member of the same or another species.

agoraphobia Anxiety disorder in which an individual is excessively afraid of places or situations from which it would be difficult or embarrassing to escape.

alarm reaction The first stage of Hans Selye's general adaptation syndrome. The alarm reaction is the immediate response to stress; adrenaline is released and digestion slows. The alarm reaction prepares the body for an emergency.

all-or-none law The principle that states that a neuron only fires when a stimulus is above a certain minimum strength (threshold), and when it fires, it does so at full strength.

alogia Individuals with schizophrenia that show a reduction in speech.

alpha Brain-wave activity that indicates that a person is relaxed and resting quietly; 8–12 Hz.

altered state of consciousness (ASC) A state of consciousness in which there is a redirection of attention, a change in the aspects of the world that occupy a person's thoughts, and a change in the stimuli to which a person responds.

ambivalent attachment Type of infant-parent attachment in which the infant seeks contact but resists once the contact is made.

amphetamine A strong stimulant; increases arousal of the central nervous system.

amygdala A part of the limbic system involved in fear, aggression, and other social behaviors.

anal stage Psychosexual stage during which, according to Sigmund Freud, the child experiences the first restrictions on his or her impulses.

analytical psychology The personality theory of Carl Jung.

anorexia nervosa Eating disorder in which an individual becomes severely underweight because of self-imposed restrictions on eating.

antisocial personality disorder Personality disorder in which individuals who engage in antisocial behavior experience no guilt or anxiety about their actions; sometimes called sociopathy or psychopathy.

anxiety disorder Fairly long-lasting disruption of a person's ability to deal with stress; often accompanied by feelings of fear and apprehension.

applied psychology The area of psychology that is most immediately concerned with helping to solve practical problems; includes clinical and counseling psychology as well as industrial, environmental, and legal psychology.

approach-approach conflict Occurs when we are attracted to two equally desirable goals that are incompatible.

approach-avoidance conflict When we are faced with a single goal that has positive and negative aspects.

aptitude test Any test designed to predict what a person with the proper training can accomplish in the future.

archetypes In Carl Jung's personality theory, unconscious universal ideas shared by all humans.

arousal theory Theory that focuses on the energy (arousal) aspect of motivation; it states that we are motivated to initiate behaviors that help to regulate overall arousal level.

asocial phase Phase in attachment development in which the neonate does not distinguish people from objects.

assertiveness training Training that helps individuals stand up for their rights while not denying rights of other people.

assimilation Process in cognitive development; occurs when something new is taken into the child's mental picture.

associationism A theory of learning suggesting that once two stimuli are presented together, one of them will remind a person of the other. Ideas are learned by association with sensory experiences and are not innate.

attachment Process in which the individual shows behaviors that promote proximity with a specific object or person.

attention Process of focusing on particular stimuli in the environment.

attention deficit disorder Hyperactivity; inability to concentrate.

attitude Learned disposition that actively guides us toward specific behaviors; attitudes consist of feelings, beliefs, and behavioral tendencies.

attribution The cognitive process of determining the motives of someone's behavior, and whether they are internal or external.

autism A personality disorder in which a child does not respond socially to people.

autokinetic effect Perception of movement of a stationary spot of light in a darkened room.

autonomic nervous system The part of the peripheral nervous system that carries messages from the central nervous system to the endocrine glands, the smooth muscles controlling the heart, and the primarily involuntary muscles controlling internal processes; includes the sympathetic and parasympathetic nervous systems.

aversion therapy A counterconditioning therapy in which unwanted responses are paired with unpleasant consequences.

avoidance conditioning Learning situation in which a subject avoids a stimulus by learning to respond appropriately before the stimulus begins.

avoidant attachment Type of infant-parent attachment in which the infant avoids the parent.

avolition Individuals with schizophrenia who lack motivation to follow through on an activity.

backward conditioning A procedure in classical conditioning in which the US is presented and terminated before the termination of the CS; very ineffective procedure.

basic research Research conducted to obtain information for its own sake.

behavior Anything you do or think, including various bodily reactions. Behavior includes physical and mental responses.

behavior genetics How genes influence behavior.

behavior modification Another term for behavior therapy; the modification of behavior through psychological techniques; often the application of conditioning principles to alter behavior.

behaviorism The school of thought founded by John Watson; it studied only observable behavior.

215

belongingness and love needs Third level of motives in Maslow's hierarchy; includes love and affection, friends, and social contact.

biological motives Motives that have a definite physiological basis and are biologically necessary for survival of the individual or species.

biological response system Systems of the body that are important in behavioral responding; includes the senses, muscles, endocrine system, and the nervous system.

biological therapy Treatment of behavior problems through biological techniques; major biological therapies include drug therapy, psychosurgery, and electroconvulsive therapy.

bipolar disorder Mood disorder characterized by extreme mood swings from sad depression to joyful mania; sometimes called manic-depression.

blinding technique In an experiment, a control for bias in which the assignment of a subject to the experimental or control group is unknown to the subject or experimenter or both (a double-blind experiment).

body dysmorphic disorder Somatoform disorder characterized by a preoccupation with an imaginary defect in the physical appearance of a physically healthy person.

body language Communication through position and movement of the body.

bottom-up processing The psychoanalytic process of understanding communication by listening to words, then interpreting phrases, and finally understanding ideas.

brief psychodynamic therapy A therapy developed for individuals with strong egos to resolve a core conflict.

bulimia nervosa Eating disorder in which an individual eats large amounts of calorie-rich food in a short time and then purges the food by vomiting or using laxatives.

bystander effect Phenomenon in an emergency situation in which a person is more likely to help when alone than when in a group of people.

California Psychological Inventory (CPI) An objective personality test used to study normal populations.

Cannon-Bard theory of emotion Theory of emotion that states that the emotional feeling and the physiological arousal occur at the same time.

cardinal traits In Gordon Allport's personality theory, the traits of an individual that are so dominant that they are expressed in everything the person does; few people possess cardinal traits.

catatonic schizophrenia A type of schizophrenia that is characterized by periods of complete immobility and the apparent absence of will to move or speak.

causal attribution Process of determining whether a person's behavior is due to internal or external motives.

central nervous system The part of the human nervous system that interprets and stores messages from the sense organs, decides what behavior to exhibit, and sends appropriate messages to the muscles and glands; includes the brain and spinal cord.

central tendency In statistics, measures of central tendency give a number that represents the entire group or sample.

central traits In Gordon Allport's personality theory, the traits of an individual that form the core of the personality; they are developed through experience.

cerebellum The part of the hindbrain that is involved in balance and muscle coordination.

cerebral cortex The outermost layer of the cerebrum of the brain where higher mental functions occur. The cerebral cortex is divided into sections, or lobes, which control various activities.

cerebrum (cerebral hemisphere) Largest part of the forebrain involved in cognitive functions; the cerebrum consists of two hemispheres connected by the corpus callosum.

chromosome Bodies in the cell nucleus that contain the genes.

chunking Process of combining stimuli in order to increase memory capacity.

classical conditioning The form of learning in which a stimulus is associated with another stimulus that causes a particular response. Sometimes called Pavlovian conditioning or respondent conditioning.

clinical psychology Subfield in which psychologists assess psychological problems and treat people with behavior problems using psychological techniques (called psychotherapy).

cognition Mental processes, such as perception, attention, memory, language, thinking, and problem solving; cognition involves the acquisition, storage, retrieval, and utilization of knowledge.

cognitive behavior therapy A form of behavior therapy that identifies self-defeating attitudes and thoughts in a subject, and then helps the subject to replace these with positive, supportive thoughts.

cognitive development Changes over time in mental processes such as thinking, memory, language, and problem solving.

cognitive dissonance Leon Festinger's theory of attitude change that states that, when people hold two psychologically inconsistent ideas, they experience tension that forces them to reconcile the conflicting ideas.

cognitive expectancy The condition in which an individual learns that certain behaviors lead to particular goals; cognitive expectancy motivates the individual to exhibit goal-directed behaviors.

cognitive learning Type of learning that theorizes that the learner utilizes cognitive structures in memory to make decisions about behaviors.

cognitive psychology The area of psychology that includes the study of mental activities involved in perception, memory, language, thought, and problem solving.

cognitive restructuring The modification of the client's thoughts and perceptions that are contributing to his or her maladjustments.

cognitive therapy Therapy developed by Aaron Beck in which an individual's negative, self-defeating thoughts are restructured in a positive way.

cognitive-motivational-relational theory of emotion A theory of emotion proposed by Richard Lazarus that includes cognitive appraisal, motivational goals, and relationships between an individual and the environment.

collective unconscious Carl Jung's representation of the thoughts shared by all humans.

collectivistic cultures Cultures in which the greatest emphasis is on the loyalty of each individual to the group.

comparative psychology Subfield in which experimental psychologists study and compare the behavior of different species of animals.

compulsions Rituals performed excessively such as checking doors or washing hands to reduce anxiety.

concept formation (concept learning) The development of the ability to respond to common features of categories of objects or events.

concrete operations period Stage in cognitive development, from 7 to 11 years, in which the child's ability to solve problems with reasoning greatly increases.

conditioned response (CR) The response or behavior that occurs when the conditioned stimulus is presented (after the CS has been associated with the US).

conditioned stimulus (CS) An originally neutral stimulus that is associated with an unconditioned stimulus and takes on the latter's capability of eliciting a particular reaction.

conditioned taste aversion (CTA) An aversion to particular tastes associated with stomach distress; usually considered a unique form of classical conditioning because of the extremely long interstimulus intervals involved.

conditioning A term applied to two types of learning (classical and operant). Conditioning refers to the scientific aspect of the type of learning.

conflict Situation that occurs when we experience incompatible demands or desires; the outcome when one individual or group perceives that another individual or group has caused or will cause harm.

conformity Type of social influence in which an individual changes his or her behavior to fit social norms or expectations.

connectionism Recent approach to problem solving; the development of neural connections allows us to think and solve problems.

conscientiousness The dimension in the five-factor personality theory that includes traits such as practical, cautious, serious, reliable, careful, and ambitious; also called dependability.

conscious Being aware of experiencing sensations, thoughts, and feelings at any given point in time.

conscious mind In Sigmund Freud's psychoanalytic theory of personality, the part of personality that we are aware of in everyday life.

consciousness The processing of information at various levels of awareness; state in which a person is aware of sensations, thoughts, and feelings.

consensus In causal attribution, the extent to which other people react as the subject does in a particular situation.

conservation The ability to recognize that something stays the same even if it takes on a different form; Piaget tested conservation of mass, number, length, and volume.

consistency In causal attribution, the extent to which the subject always behaves in the same way in a situation.

consolidation The biological neural process of making memories permanent; possibly short-term memory is electrically coded and long-term memory is chemically coded.

contingency model A theory that specific types of situations need particular types of leaders.

continuum of preparedness Martin Seligman's proposal that animals are biologically prepared to learn certain responses more readily than they are prepared to learn others.

control group Subjects in an experiment who do not receive the independent variable; the control group determines the effectiveness of the independent variable.

conventional morality Level II in Lawrence Kohlberg's theory, in which moral reasoning is based on conformity and social standards.

convergence Binocular depth cue in which we detect distance by interpreting the kinesthetic sensations produced by the muscles of the eyeballs.

conversion disorder Somatoform disorder in which a person displays obvious disturbance in the nervous system without a physical basis for the problem.

correlation Statistical technique to determine the degree of relationship that exists between two variables.

counterconditioning A behavior therapy in which an unwanted response is replaced by conditioning a new response that is incompatible with it.

creativity A process of coming up with new or unusual responses to familiar circumstances.

critical period hypothesis Period of time during development in which particular learning or experiences normally occur; if learning does not occur, the individual has a difficult time learning it later.

culture-bound The idea that a test's usefulness is limited to the culture in which it was written and utilized.

cumulative response curve Graphed curve that results when responses for a subject are added to one another over time; if subjects respond once every 5 minutes, they will have a cumulative response curve value of 12 after an hour.

curiosity motive Motive that causes the individual to seek out a certain amount of novelty.

cyclothymia disorder A moderately severe problem with numerous periods of hypomanic episodes and depressive symptoms.

death instinct (also called Thanatos) Freud's term for an instinct that is destructive to the individual or species; aggression is a major expression of death instinct.

decay Theory of forgetting in which sensory impressions leave memory traces that fade away with time.

defense mechanisms Psychological techniques to help protect ourselves from stress and anxiety, to resolve conflicts, and to preserve our self-esteem.

delayed conditioning A procedure in classical conditioning in which the presentation of the CS precedes the onset of the US and the termination of the CS is delayed until the US is presented; most effective procedure.

delusion The holding of obviously false beliefs; for example, imagining someone is trying to kill you.

dependent variable In psychology, the behavior or response that is measured; it is dependent on the independent variable.

depersonalization disorder Dissociative disorder in which the individual escapes from his or her own personality by believing that he or she does not exist or that his or her environment is not real.

depolarization Any change in which the internal electrical charge becomes more positive.

depression A temporary emotional state that normal individuals experience or a persistent state that may be considered a psychological disorder. Characterized by sadness and low self-esteem.

descriptive statistics Techniques that help summarize large amounts of data information.

developmental psychology Study of physical and mental growth and behavioral changes in individuals from conception to death.

Diagnostic and Statistic Manual of Mental Disorders (DSM) Published by the American Psychiatric Association in 1952, and revised in 1968, 1980, 1987, and 1994, this manual was provided to develop a set of diagnoses of abnormal behavior patterns.

diffusion of responsibility Finding that groups tend to inhibit helping behavior; responsibility is shared equally by members of the group so that no one individual feels a strong commitment.

disorganized schizophrenia A type of schizophrenia that is characterized by a severe personality disintegration; the individual often displays bizarre behavior.

displacement Defense mechanism by which the individual directs his or her aggression or hostility toward a person or object other than the one it should be directed toward; in Freud's dream theory, the process of reassigning emotional feelings from one object to another one.

dissociative disorder Psychological disorder that involves a disturbance in the memory, consciousness, or identity of an individual; types include multiple personality disorder, depersonalization disorder, psychogenic amnesia, and psychogenic fugue.

dissociative fugue Individuals who have lost their memory, relocated to a new geographical area, and started a new life as someone else.

dissociative identity disorder (multiple personality disorder) Dissociative disorder in which several personalities are present in the same individual.

distinctiveness In causal attribution, the extent to which the subject reacts the same way in other situations.

Down syndrome Form of mental retardation caused by having three number 21 chromosomes (trisomy 21).

dream analysis Psychoanalytic technique in which a patient's dreams are reviewed and analyzed to discover true feelings.

drive Motivational concept used to describe the internal forces that push an organism toward a goal; sometimes identified as psychological arousal arising from a physiological need.

dyssomnia Sleep disorder in which the chief symptom is a disturbance in the amount and quality of sleep; they include insomnia and hypersomnia.

dysthymic disorder Mood disorder in which the person suffers moderate depression much of the time for at least two years.

ego Sigmund Freud's term for an individual's sense of reality.

egocentric Seeing the world only from your perspective.

eidetic imagery Photographic memory; ability to recall great detail accurately after briefly viewing something.

Electra complex The Freudian idea that the young girl feels inferior to boys because she lacks a penis.

electroconvulsive therapy (ECT) A type of biological therapy in which electricity is applied to the brain in order to relieve severe depression.

emotion A response to a stimulus that involves physiological arousal, subjective feeling, cognitive interpretation, and overt behavior.

empiricism The view that behavior is learned through experience.

encoding The process of putting information into the memory system.

encounter group As in a sensitivity training group, a therapy where people become aware of themselves in meeting others.

endorphins Several neuropeptides that function as neurotransmitters. The opiate-like endorphins are involved in pain, reinforcement, and memory.

engineering psychology Area of psychology that is concerned with how work is performed, design of equipment, and work environment; also called human factors psychology.

engram The physical memory trace or neural circuit that holds memory; also called memory trace.

episodic memory Highest memory system; includes information about personal experiences.

Eros Sigmund Freud's term for an instinct that helps the individual or species survive; also called life instinct.

esteem needs Fourth level of motives in Abraham Maslow's hierarchy; includes high evaluation of oneself, self-respect, self-esteem, and respect of others.

eustress Stress that results from pleasant and satisfying experiences; earning a high grade or achieving success produces eustress.

excitement phase First phase in the human sexual response cycle; the beginning of sexual arousal.

experimental group Subjects in an experiment who receive the independent variable.

experimental psychology Subfield in which psychologists research the fundamental causes of behavior. Many experimental psychologists conduct experiments in basic research.

experimenter bias Source of potential error in an experiment from the action or expectancy of the experimenter; might influence the experimental results in ways that mask the true outcome.

external locus of control In Julian Rotter's personality theory, the perception that reinforcement is independent of a person's behavior.

extraversion The dimension in the five-factor personality theory that includes traits such as sociability, talkativeness, boldness, fun-lovingness, adventurousness, and assertiveness; also called surgency. The personality concept of Carl Jung in which the personal energy of the individual is directed externally.

factor analysis A statistical procedure used to determine the relationship among variables.

false memories Memories believed to be real, but the events never occurred.

fast mapping A process by which children can utilize a word after a single exposure.

fetal alcohol syndrome (FAS) Condition in which defects in the newborn child are caused by the mother's excessive alcohol intake.

five-factor model of personality tracts A trait theory of personality that includes the factors of extraversion, agreeableness, conscientiousness, emotional stability, and openness.

fixed action pattern (FAP) Unlearned, inherited, stereotyped behaviors that are shown by all members of a species; term used in ethology.

fixed interval (FI) schedule Schedule of reinforcement where the subject receives reinforcement for a correct response given after a specified time interval.

fixed ratio (FR) schedule Schedule of reinforcement in which the subject is reinforced after a certain number of responses.

flashbulb memory Memory of an event that is so important that significant details are vividly remembered for life.

forgetting In memory, not being able to retrieve the original learning. The part of the original learning that cannot be retrieved is said to be forgotten.

formal operations period Period in cognitive development; at 11 years, the adolescent begins abstract thinking and reasoning. This period continues throughout the rest of life.

free association Psychoanalytic technique in which the patient says everything that comes to mind.

free recall A verbal learning procedure in which the order of presentation of the stimuli is varied and the subject can learn the items in any order.

frequency theory of hearing Theory of hearing that states that the frequency of vibrations at the basilar membrane determines the frequency of firing of neurons carrying impulses to the brain.

frustration A cause of stress that results from the blocking of a person's goal-oriented behavior.

frustration-drive theory of aggression Theory of aggression that states that it is caused by frustration.

functionalism School of thought that studied the functional value of consciousness and behavior.

fundamental attribution error Attribution bias in which people overestimate the role of internal disposition and underestimate the role of external situation.

gate-control theory of pain Theory of pain that proposes that there is a gate that allows pain impulses to travel from the spinal cord to the brain.

gender-identity disorder (GID) Incongruence between assigned sex and gender identity.

gender-identity/role Term that incorporates gender identity (the private perception of one's sex) and gender role (the public expression of one's gender identity).

gene The basic unit of heredity; the gene is composed of deoxyribonucleic acid (DNA).

general adaptation syndrome (GAS) Hans Selye's theory of how the body responds to stress over time. GAS includes alarm reaction, resistance, and exhaustion.

generalized anxiety disorder Anxiety disorder in which the individual lives in a state of constant severe tension, continuous fear, and apprehension.

genetics The study of heredity; genetics is the science of discovering how traits are passed along generations.

genotype The complete set of genes inherited by an individual from his or her parents.

Gestalt psychology A school of thought that studied whole or complete perceptions.

Gestalt therapy Insight therapy designed to help people become more aware of themselves in the here and now and to take responsibility for their own actions.

grandiose delusion Distortion of reality; one's belief that he or she is extremely important or powerful.

group therapy Treatment of several patients at the same time.

groupthink When group members are so committed to, and optimistic about, the group that they feel it is invulnerable; they become so concerned with maintaining consensus that criticism is muted.

growth The normal quantitative changes that occur in the physical and psychological aspects of a healthy child with the passage of time.

GSR (galvanic skin response) A measure of autonomic nervous system activity; a slight electric current is passed over the skin, and the more nervous a subject is, the easier the current will flow.

hallucinations A sensory impression reported when no external stimulus exists to justify the report; often hallucinations are a symptom of mental illness.

hallucinogens Psychedelic drugs that result in hallucinations at high doses, and other effects on behavior and perception in mild doses.

halo effect The finding that once we form a general impression of someone, we tend to interpret additional information about the person in a consistent manner.

haptic Relating to or based on the sense of touch. Also, a predilection for the sense of touch.

Hawthorne effect The finding that behavior can be influenced just by participation in a research study.

health psychology Field of psychology that studies psychological influences on people's health, including how they stay healthy, why they become ill, and how their behavior relates to their state of health.

heuristic Problem-solving strategy; a person tests solutions most likely to be correct.

hierarchy of needs Abraham Maslow's list of motives in humans, arranged from the biological to the uniquely human.

higher order conditioning Learning to make associations with stimuli that have been learned previously.

hippocampus Brain structure in the limbic system that is important in learning and memory.

homeostasis The state of equilibrium that maintains a balance in the internal body environment.

hormones Chemicals produced by the endocrine glands that regulate activity of certain bodily processes.

humanistic psychology Psychological school of thought that believes that people are unique beings who cannot be broken down into parts.

hyperphagia Disorder in which the individual continues to eat until he or she is obese; can be caused by damage to ventromedial hypothalamus.

hypersomnia Sleep disorder in which an individual falls asleep at inappropriate times; narcolepsy is a form of hypersomnia.

hypnosis Altered state of consciousness characterized by heightened suggestibility.

hypochondriasis Somatoform disorder in which the individual is obsessed with fears of having a serious medical disease.

hypothalamus Part of the brain's limbic system; involved in motivational behaviors, including eating, drinking, and sex.

hypothesis In the scientific method, an educated guess or prediction about future observable events.

iconic memory Visual information that is encoded into the sensory memory store.

id Sigmund Freud's representation of the basic instinctual drives; the id always seeks pleasure.

identification The process in which children adopt the attitudes, values, and behaviors of their parents.

identity diffusion In Marcia's adolescent identity theory, the status of individuals who have failed to make a commitment to values and roles.

illusion An incorrect perception that occurs when sensation is distorted.

imitation The copying of another's behavior; learned through the process of observation.

impression formation Developing an evaluation of another person from your perceptions; first, or initial, impressions are often very important.

imprinting A form of early learning in which birds follow a moving stimulus (often the mother); may be similar to attachment in mammals.

independent variable The condition in an experiment that is controlled and manipulated by the experimenter; it is a stimulus that will cause a response.

indiscriminate attachment phase Stage of attachment in which babies prefer humans to nonhumans, but do not discriminate among individual people.

individuation Carl Jung's concept of the process leading to the unification of all parts of the personality.

inferential statistics Techniques that help researchers make generalizations about a finding based on a limited number of subjects.

inferiority complex Adler's personality concept that states that because children are dependent on adults and cannot meet the standards set for themselves they feel inferior.

inhibition Restraint of an impulse, desire, activity, or drive.

insight A sudden grasping of the means necessary to achieve a goal; important in the Gestalt approach to problem solving.

insight therapy Therapy based on the assumption that behavior is abnormal because people do not adequately understand the motivation causing their behavior.

instinct Highly stereotyped behavior common to all members of a species that often appears in virtually complete form in the absence of any obvious opportunities to learn it.

instrumental conditioning Operant conditioning.

intelligence Capacity to learn and behave adaptively.

intelligence quotient (IQ) An index of a person's performance on an intelligence test relative to others in the culture; ratio of a person's mental age to chronological age.

interference Theory of forgetting in which information that was learned before (proactive interference) or after (retroactive interference) causes the learner to be unable to remember the material of interest.

internal locus of control In Rotter's personality theory, the perception that reinforcement is contingent upon behavior.

interstimulus interval Time interval between two stimuli; in classical conditioning, it is the elapsed time between the CS and the US.

intrinsic motivation Motivation inside the individual; we do something because we receive satisfaction from it.

introspection Method in which a subject gives a self-report of his or her immediate experience.

introversion The personality concept of Carl Jung in which the personal energy of the individual is directed inward; characterized by introspection, seriousness, inhibition, and restraint.

James-Lange theory of emotion Theory of emotion that states that the physiological arousal and behavior come before the subjective experience of an emotion.

just noticeable difference (JND) Difference threshold; minimum amount of energy required to produce a difference in sensation.

kinesthesis The sense of bodily movement.

labeling of arousal Experiments suggest that an individual experiencing physical arousal that cannot be explained will interpret those feelings in terms of the situation she or he is in and will use environmental and contextual cues.

language acquisition device (LAD) Hypothesized biological structure that accounts for the relative ease of acquiring language, according to Noam Chomsky.

latent dream content In Sigmund Freud's dream theory, the true thoughts in the unconsciousness; the true meaning of the dream.

latent learning Learning that occurs when an individual acquires knowledge of something but does not show it until motivated to do so.

law of effect Edward Thorndike's law that if a response produces satisfaction it will be repeated; reinforcement.

learned helplessness Condition in which a person learns that his or her behavior has no effect on his or her environment; when an individual gives up and stops trying.

learned social motives Social motives that are learned; include achievement and affiliation.

learning The relatively permanent change in behavior or behavioral ability of an individual that occurs as a result of experience.

learning styles The preferences students have for learning; theories of learning styles include personality differences, styles of information processing, and instructional preferences.

life instinct (also called Eros) Sigmund Freud's term for an instinct that helps the individual or species survive; sex is the major expression of life instinct.

life structure In Daniel Levinson's theory of adult personality development, the underlying pattern of an individual's life at any particular time; seasonal cycles include preadulthood, early adulthood, middle adulthood, and late adulthood.

linguistic relativity hypothesis Proposal that the perception of reality differs according to the language of the observer.

locus of control Julian Rotter's theory in which a person's beliefs about reinforcement are classified as internal or external.

long-term memory The permanent memory where rehearsed information is stored.

love An emotion characterized by knowing, liking, and becoming intimate with someone.

low-ball procedure The compliance technique of presenting an attractive proposal to someone and then switching it to a more unattractive proposal.

magic number 7 The finding that most people can remember about seven items of information for a short time (in short-term memory).

magnetic resonance imaging (MRI) A method of studying brain activity using magnetic field imaging.

major depressive disorder Severe mood disorder in which a person experiences one or more major depressive episodes; sometimes referred to simply as depression.

maladjustment Condition that occurs when a person utilizes inappropriate abilities to respond to demands placed upon him or her.

manic depressive reaction A form of mental illness marked by alternations of extreme phases of elation (manic phase) and depression.

manifest dream content In Sigmund Freud's dream theory, what is remembered about a dream upon waking; a disguised representation of the unconscious wishes.

massed practice Learning as much material as possible in long continuous stretches.

maturation The genetically controlled process of growth that results in orderly changes in behavior.

mean The arithmetic average, in which the sum of scores is divided by the number of scores.

median The middle score in a group of scores that are arranged from lowest to highest.

meditation The practice of some form of relaxed concentration while ignoring other sensory stimuli.

memory The process of storing information so that it can be retrieved and used later.

memory attributes The critical features of an event that are used when the experience is encoded or retrieved.

mental age The age level on which a person is capable of performing; used in determining intelligence.

mental set Condition in which a person's thinking becomes so standardized that he or she approaches new problems in fixed ways.

Minnesota Multiphasic Personality Inventory (MMPI-2) An objective personality test that was originally devised to identify personality disorders.

mnemonic technique Method of improving memory by combining and relating chunks of information.

modeling A process of learning by imitation in a therapeutic situation.

mood disorder Psychological disorder in which a person experiences a severe disruption in mood or emotional balance.

moral development Development of individuals as they adopt their society's standards of right and wrong; development of awareness of ethical behavior.

motivated forgetting (repression) Theory that suggests that people want to forget unpleasant events.

motivation The forces that initiate and direct behavior, and the variables that determine the intensity and persistence of the behavior.

motivator needs In Federick Herzberg's theory, the factors that lead to job satisfaction; they include responsibility, the nature of the work, advancement, and recognition.

motive Anything that arouses the individual and directs his or her behavior toward some goal. Three categories of motives include biological, stimulus, and learned social.

Müller-Lyer illusion A well-known illusion, in which two horizontal lines have end lines either going in or out; the line with the end lines going in appears longer.

multiple approach-avoidance conflict Conflict that occurs when an individual has two or more goals, both of which have positive and negative aspects.

multiple attachment phase Later attachment stage in which the baby begins to form attachments to people other than the primary caretaker.

multiple intelligences Howard Gardner's theory that there exists several different kinds of intelligence.

Myers-Briggs Type Indicator (MBTI) Objective personality test based on Carl Jung's type theory.

narcotic analgesics Drugs that have an effect on the body similar to morphine; these relieve pain and suppress coughing.

naturalistic observation Research method in which behavior of people or animals in their normal environment is accurately recorded.

Necker cube A visual illusion. The Necker cube is a drawing of a cube designed so that it is difficult to determine which side is toward you.

negative reinforcement Removing something unpleasant to increase the probability that the preceding behavior will be repeated.

NEO Personality Inventory (NEO-PI) An objective personality test developed by Paul Costa Jr. and Robert McCrae to measure the five major factors in personality; consists of 181 questions.

neodissociation theory Idea that consciousness can be split into several streams of thought that are partially independent of each other.

neuron A specialized cell that functions to conduct messages throughout the body.

neurosis A Freudian term that was used to describe abnormal behavior caused by anxiety; it has been eliminated from *DSM-IV*.

neutral stimulus A stimulus that does not cause the response of interest; the individual may show some response to the stimulus but not the associated behavior.

norm A sample of scores representative of a population.

normal curve When scores of a large number of random cases are plotted on a graph, they often fall into a bell-shaped curve; as many cases on the curve are above the mean as below it.

observational learning In social learning theory, learning by observing someone else behave; people observe and imitate in learning socialization.

obsessions Fears that involve the inability to control impulses.

obsessive compulsive disorder Anxiety disorder in which the individual has repetitive thoughts (obsessions) that lead to constant urges (compulsions) to engage in meaningless rituals.

object permanence The ability to realize that objects continue to exist even if we can no longer see them.

Oedipus complex The Freudian idea that the young boy has sexual feelings for his mother and is jealous of his father and must identify with his father to resolve the conflict.

olfaction The smell sense.

openness The dimension in the five-factor personality theory that includes traits such as imagination, creativity, perception, knowledge, artistic ability, curiosity, and analytical ability; also called culture or intellect.

operant conditioning Form of learning in which behavior followed by reinforcement (satisfaction) increases in frequency.

opponent-process theory Theory that when one emotion is experienced, the other is suppressed.

optimum level of arousal Motivation theory that states that the individual will seek a level of arousal that is comfortable.

organic mental disorders Psychological disorders that involve physical damage to the nervous system; can be caused by disease or by an accident.

organizational psychology Area of industrial psychology that focuses on worker attitudes and motivation; derived primarily from personality and social psychology.

orgasm The climax of intense sexual excitement; release from building sexual tension, usually accompanied by ejaculation in men.

paired-associate learning A verbal learning procedure in which the subject is presented with a series of pairs of items to be remembered.

panic disorder Anxiety disorder characterized by the occurrence of specific periods of intense fear.

paranoid schizophrenia A type of schizophrenia in which the individual often has delusions of grandeur and persecution, thinking that someone is out to get him or her.

partial reinforcement Any schedule of reinforcement in which reinforcement follows only some of the correct responses.

partial reinforcement effect The finding that partial reinforcement produces a response that takes longer to extinguish than continuous reinforcement.

pattern recognition Memory process in which information attended to is compared with information already permanently stored in memory.

Pavlovian conditioning A bond or association between a neutral stimulus and a response; this type of learning is called classical conditioning.

perception The active process in which the sensory information that is carried through the nervous system to the brain is organized and interpreted; the interpretation of sensation.

persecutory delusion A delusion in which the individual has a distortion of reality; the belief that other people are out to get one.

person perception The process of using the information we gather in forming impressions of people to make evaluations of others.

personal unconscious Carl Jung's representation of the individual's repressed thoughts and memories.

personality disorder Psychological disorder in which there are problems in the basic personality structure of the individual.

phantom-limb pain Phenomenon in which people who have lost an arm or leg feel pain in the missing limb.

phobias Acute excessive fears of specific situations or objects that have no convincing basis in reality.

physiological needs First level of motives in Abraham Maslow's hierarchy; includes the biological needs of hunger, thirst, sex, exercise, and rest.

placebo An inert or inactive substance given to control subjects to test for bias effects.

plateau phase Second phase in the human sexual response cycle, during which the physiological arousal becomes more intense.

pleasure principle In Freudian theory, the idea that the instinctual drives of the id unconsciously and impulsively seek immediate pleasure.

positive reinforcement Presenting a subject something pleasant to increase the probability that the preceding behavior will be repeated.

postconventional morality Level III in Lawrence Kohlberg's theory, in which moral reasoning is based on personal standards and beliefs; highest level of moral thinking.

posttraumatic stress disorder (PTSD) Condition that can occur when a person experiences a severely distressing event; characterized by constant memories of the event, avoidance of anything associated with it, and general arousal.

Prägnanz (law of) Gestalt psychology law that states that people have a tendency to group stimuli according to rules, and that people do this whenever possible.

preconscious mind In Sigmund Freud's psychoanalytic theory of personality, the part of personality that contains information that we have learned but that we are not thinking about at the present time.

preconventional morality Level I of Lawrence Kohlberg's theory, in which moral reasoning is largely due to the expectation of rewards and punishments.

prejudice An unjustified fixed, usually negative, way of thinking about a person or object.

Premack principle Principle that states that, of any two responses, the one that is more likely to occur can be used to reinforce the response that is less likely to occur.

preoperational thought period Period in cognitive development; from two to seven years, the period during which the child learns to represent the environment with objects and symbols.

primacy effect Phenomenon where items are remembered because they come at the beginning of a list.

primary appraisal Activity of determining whether a new stimulus event is positive, neutral, or negative; first step in appraisal of stress.

primary narcissism A Freudian term that refers to the oral phase before the ego has developed; the individual constantly seeks pleasure.

primary reinforcement Reinforcement that is effective without having been associated with other reinforcers; sometimes called unconditioned reinforcement.

probability (p) In inferential statistics, the likelihood that the difference between the experimental and control groups is due to the independent variable.

procedural memory The most basic type of long-term memory; involves the formation of associations between stimuli and responses.

projection Defense mechanism in which a person attributes his or her unacceptable characteristics or motives to others rather than himself or herself.

projective personality test A personality test that presents ambiguous stimuli to which subjects are expected to respond with projections of their own personality.

proximity Closeness in time and space. In perception, it is the Gestalt perceptual principle in which stimuli next to one another are included together.

psyche According to Carl Jung, the thoughts and feelings (conscious and unconscious) of an individual.

psychoactive drug A drug that produces changes in behavior and cognition through modification of conscious awareness.

psychoanalysis The school of thought founded by Sigmund Freud that stressed unconscious motivation. In therapy, a patient's unconscious motivation is intensively explored in order to bring repressed conflicts up to consciousness; psychoanalysis usually takes a long time to accomplish.

psychobiology (also called biological psychology or physiological psychology) The subfield of experimental psychology concerned with the influence of heredity and the biological response systems on behavior.

psychogenic amnesia A dissociative disorder in which an individual loses his or her sense of identity.

psychogenic fugue A dissociative disorder in which an individual loses his or her sense of identity and goes to a new geographic location, forgetting all of the unpleasant emotions connected with the old life.

psychographics A technique used in consumer psychology to identify the attitudes of buyers and their preferences for particular products.

psycholinguistics The psychological study of how people convert the sounds of a language into meaningful symbols that can be used to communicate with others.

psychological dependence Situation in which a person craves a drug even though it is not biologically needed by the body.

psychological disorder A diagnosis of abnormal behavior; syndrome of abnormal adjustment, classified in *DSM*.

psychological types Carl Jung's term for different personality profiles; Jung combined two attitudes and four functions to produce eight psychological types.

psychopharmacology Study of effects of psychoactive drugs on behavior.

psychophysics An area of psychology in which researchers compare the physical energy of a stimulus with the sensation reported.

psychosexual stages Sigmund Freud's theoretical stages in personality development.

psychosomatic disorders A variety of body reactions that are closely related to psychological events.

psychotherapy Treatment of behavioral disorders through psychological techniques; major psychotherapies include insight therapy, behavior therapy, and group therapy.

psychotic disorders The more severe categories of abnormal behavior.

puberty Sexual maturation; the time at which the individual is able to perform sexually and to reproduce.

punishment Any event that decreases the likelihood that the behavior preceding it will be repeated.

quantitative trait loci (QTLs) Genes that collectively contribute to a trait for high intelligence.

rational-emotive therapy A cognitive behavior modification technique in which a person is taught to identify irrational, self-defeating beliefs and then to overcome them.

reaction formation Defense mechanism in which a person masks an unconsciously distressing or unacceptable trait by assuming an opposite attitude or behavior pattern.

reality principle In Freudian theory, the idea that the drives of the ego try to find socially acceptable ways to gratify the id.

reciprocal determinism The concept proposed by Albert Bandura that the behavior, the individual, and the situation interact and influence each other.

reciprocal inhibition Concept of Joseph Wolpe that states that it is possible to break the bond between anxiety-provoking stimuli and responses manifesting anxiety by facing those stimuli in a state antagonistic to anxiety.

reflex An automatic movement that occurs in direct response to a stimulus.

regression Defense mechanism in which a person retreats to an earlier, more immature form of behavior.

reinforcement Any event that increases the probability that the behavior that precedes it will be repeated; also called a reinforcer; similar to a reward.

reinforcement therapy A behavior therapy in which reinforcement is used to modify behavior. Techniques in reinforcement therapy include shaping, extinction, and token economy.

releaser (sign stimulus) Specific environmental cues that stimulate a stereotyped behavior to occur; releasers cause fixed action patterns.

repression Defense mechanism in which painful memories and unacceptable thoughts and motives are conveniently forgotten so that they will not have to be dealt with.

residual schizophrenia Type of schizophrenia in which the individual currently does not have symptoms but has had a schizophrenic episode in the past.

resistance Psychoanalytic term used when a patient avoids a painful area of conflict.

resolution phase The last phase in the human sexual response cycle; the time after orgasm when the body gradually returns to the unaroused state.

Restricted Environmental Stimulation Technique (REST) Research technique in which environmental stimuli available to an individual are reduced drastically; formerly called sensory deprivation.

retroactive interference Interference caused by information learned after the material of interest.

retrograde amnesia Forgetting information recently learned because of a disruptive stimulus such as an electric shock.

reversible figure In perception, a situation in which the figure and ground seem to reverse themselves; an illusion in which objects alternate as the main figure.

risky-shift The tendency for groups to make riskier decisions than individuals.

Rorschach Inkblot Test A projective personality test in which subjects are asked to discuss what they see in cards containing blots of ink.

safety needs Second level of motives in Abraham Maslow's hierarchy; includes security, stability, dependency, protection, freedom from fear and anxiety, and the need for structure and order.

Schachter-Singer theory of emotion Theory of emotion that states that we interpret our arousal according to our environment and label our emotions accordingly.

scheme A unit of knowledge that the person possesses; used in Jean Piaget's cognitive development theory.

schizophrenia Severe psychotic disorder that is characterized by disruptions in thinking, perception, and emotion.

scientific method An attitude and procedure that scientists use to conduct research. The steps include stating the problem, forming the hypothesis, collecting the information, evaluating the information, and drawing conclusions.

secondary appraisal In appraisal of stress, this is the evaluation that an individual's abilities and resources are sufficient to meet the demands of a stressful event.

secondary reinforcement Reinforcement that is effective only after it has been associated with a primary reinforcer; also called conditioned reinforcement.

secondary traits In Gordon Allport's personality theory, the less important situation-specific traits that help round out personality; they include attitudes, skills, and behavior patterns.

secure attachment Type of infant-parent attachment in which the infant actively seeks contact with the parent.

self-actualization A humanistic term describing the state in which all of an individual's capacities are developed fully. Fifth and highest level of motives in Abraham Maslow's hierarchy, this level, the realization of one's potential, is rarely reached.

self-efficacy An individual's sense of self-worth and success in adjusting to the world.

self-evaluation maintenance model (SEM) Tesser's theory of how we maintain a positive self-image despite the success of others close to us.

self-handicapping strategy A strategy that people use to prepare for failure; people behave in ways that produce obstacles to success so that when they do fail they can place the blame on the obstacle.

self-serving bias An attribution bias in which an individual attributes success to his or her own behavior and failure to external environmental causes.

semantic memory Type of long-term memory that can use cognitive activities, such as everyday knowledge.

sensation The passive process in which stimuli are received by sense receptors and transformed into neural impulses that can be carried through the nervous system; first stage in becoming aware of environment.

sensitivity training group (T-group) Therapy group that has the goal of making participants more aware of themselves and their ideas.

sensorimotor period Period in cognitive development; the first two years, during which the infant learns to coordinate sensory experiences with motor activities.

sensory adaptation Tendency of the sense organs to adjust to continuous stimulation by reducing their functioning; a stimulus that once caused sensation and no longer does.

sensory deprivation Situation in which normal environmental sensory stimuli available to an individual are reduced drastically; also called REST (Restricted Environmental Stimulation Technique).

serial learning A verbal learning procedure in which the stimuli are always presented in the same order, and the subject has to learn them in the order in which they are presented.

sex roles The set of behaviors and attitudes that are determined to be appropriate for one sex or the other in a society.

shaping In operant conditioning, the gradual process of reinforcing behaviors that get closer to some final desired behavior. Shaping is also called successive approximation.

signal detection theory Research approach in which the subject's behavior in detecting a threshold is treated as a form of decision making.

similarity Gestalt principle in which similar stimuli are perceived as a unit.

simple phobia Excessive irrational fear that does not fall into other specific categories, such as fear of dogs, insects, snakes, or closed-in places.

simultaneous conditioning A procedure in classical conditioning in which the CS and US are presented at exactly the same time.

Sixteen Personality Factor Questionnaire (16PF) Raymond Cattell's personality test to measure source traits.

Skinner box B. F. Skinner's animal cage with a lever that triggers reinforcement for a subject.

sleep terror disorder (pavor nocturnus) Nonrapid-eye-movement (NREM) sleep disorder in which the person (usually a child) wakes up screaming and terrified, but cannot recall why.

sleepwalking (somnambulism) NREM sleep disorder in which the person walks in his or her sleep.

social cognition The process of understanding other people and ourselves by forming and utilizing information about the social world.

social cognitive theory Albert Bandura's approach to personality that proposes that individuals use observation, imitation, and cognition to develop personality.

social comparison Theory proposed by Leon Festinger that we tend to compare our behavior to others to ensure that we are conforming.

social exchange theory Theory of interpersonal relationships that states that people evaluate the costs and rewards of their relationships and act accordingly.

social facilitation Phenomenon in which the presence of others increases dominant behavior patterns in an individual; Richard Zajonc's theory states that the presence of others enhances the emission of the dominant response of the individual.

social influence Influence designed to change the attitudes or behavior of other people; includes conformity, compliance, and obedience.

social learning theory An approach to social psychology that emphasizes observation and modeling; states that reinforcement is involved in motivation rather than in learning, and proposes that aggression is a form of learned behavior.

social phobia Excessive irrational fear and embarrassment when interacting with other people. Social phobias may include fear of assertive behavior, fear of making mistakes, or fear of public speaking.

social psychology The study of how an individual's behavior, thoughts, and feelings are influenced by other people.

sociobiology Study of the genetic basis of social behavior.

sociocultural Emphasizes the importance of culture, gender, and ethnicity in how we think, feel, and act.

somatic nervous system The part of the peripheral nervous system that carries messages from the sense organs and relays information that directs the voluntary movements of the skeletal muscles.

somatization disorder Somatoform disorder in which a person has medical complaints without physical cause.

somatoform disorders Psychological disorders characterized by physical symptoms for which there are no obvious physical causes.

specific attachment phase Stage at about six months of age, in which the baby becomes attached to a specific person.

split-brain research Popular name for Roger Sperry's research on the syndrome of hemisphere deconnection; research on individuals with the corpus callosum severed. Normal functioning breaks down in split-brain subjects when different information is presented to each hemisphere.

SQ5R A technique to improve learning and memory. Components include survey, question, read, record, recite, review, and reflect.

stage of exhaustion Third stage in Hans Selye's general adaptation syndrome. As the body continues to resist stress, it depletes its energy resources and the person becomes exhausted.

stage of resistance Second stage in Hans Selye's general adaptation syndrome. When stress is prolonged, the body builds some resistance to the effects of stress.

standardization The process of obtaining a representative sample of scores in the population so that a particular score can be interpreted correctly.

Stanford-Binet Intelligence Scale An intelligence test first revised by Lewis Terman at Stanford University in 1916; still a popular test used today.

state-dependent learning Situation in which what is learned in one state can only be remembered when the person is in that state of mind.

statistically significant In inferential statistics, a finding that the independent variable did influence greatly the outcome of the experimental and control group.

stereotype An exaggerated and rigid mental image of a particular class of persons or objects.

stimulus A unit of the environment that causes a response in an individual; a physical or chemical agent acting on an appropriate sense receptor.

stimulus discrimination Responding to relevant stimuli.

stimulus generalization Responding to stimuli similar to the stimulus that had caused the response.

stimulus motives Motivating factors that are internal and unlearned, but do not appear to have a physiological basis; stimulus motives cause an individual to seek out sensory stimulation through interaction with the environment.

stimulus trace The perceptual persistence of a stimulus after it is no longer present.

strange situation procedure A measure of attachment developed by Mary Ainsworth that consists of eight phases during which the infant is increasingly stressed.

stress Anything that produces demands on us to adjust and threatens our well-being.

Strong Interest Inventory An objective personality test that compares people's personalities to groups that achieve success in certain occupations.

structuralism First school of thought in psychology; it studied conscious experience to discover the structure of the mind.

subject bias Source of potential error in an experiment from the action or expectancy of a subject; a subject might influence the experimental results in ways that mask the true outcome.

subjective organization Long-term memory procedures in which the individual provides a personal method of organizing information to be memorized.

sublimation Defense mechanism; a person redirects his or her socially undesirable urges into socially acceptable behavior.

successive approximation Shaping; in operant conditioning, the gradual process of reinforcing behaviors that get closer to some final desired behavior.

sudden infant death syndrome (SIDS) Situation in which a seemingly healthy infant dies suddenly in its sleep; also called crib death.

superego Sigmund Freud's representation of conscience.

surface traits In Raymond Cattell's personality theory, the observable characteristics of a person's behavior and personality.

symbolization In Sigmund Freud's dream theory, the process of converting the latent content of a dream into manifest symbols.

systematic desensitization Application of counterconditioning, in which the individual overcomes anxiety by learning to relax in the presence of stimuli that had once made him or her unbearably nervous.

task-oriented coping Adjustment responses in which the person evaluates a stressful situation objectively and then formulates a plan with which to solve the problem.

test of significance An inferential statistical technique used to determine whether the difference in scores between the experimental and control groups is really due to the effects of the independent variable or to random chance. If the probability of an outcome is extremely low, we say that outcome is significant.

Thanatos Sigmund Freud's term for a destructive instinct such as aggression; also called death instinct.

Thematic Apperception Test (TAT) Projective personality test in which subjects are shown pictures of people in everyday settings; subjects must make up a story about the people portrayed.

theory of social impact Latané's theory of social behavior; it states that each member of a group shares the responsibility equally.

Theory X Douglas McGregor's theory that states that the worker dislikes work and must be forced to do it.

Theory Y Douglas McGregor's theory that states that work is natural and can be a source of satisfaction, and, when it is, the worker can be highly committed and motivated.

therapy In psychology, the treatment of behavior problems; two major types of therapy include psychotherapy and biological therapy.

time and motion studies In engineering psychology, studies that analyze the time it takes to perform an action and the movements that go into the action.

tip-of-the-tongue phenomenon A phenomenon in which the closer a person comes to recalling something, the more accurately he or she can remember details, such as the number of syllables or letters.

token economy A behavior therapy in which desired behaviors are reinforced immediately with tokens that can be exchanged at a later time for desired rewards, such as food or recreational privileges.

trace conditioning A procedure in classical conditioning in which the CS is a discrete event that is presented and terminated before the US is presented.

trait A distinctive and stable attribute in people.

trait anxiety Anxiety that is long-lasting; a relatively stable personality characteristic.

transference Psychoanalytic term used when a patient projects his feelings onto the therapist.

transsexualism A condition in which a person feels trapped in the body of the wrong sex.

trial and error learning Trying various behaviors in a situation until the solution is found.

triangular theory of love Robert Sternberg's theory that states that love consists of intimacy, passion, and decision/commitment.

triarchic theory of intelligence Robert Sternberg's theory of intelligence that states that it consists of three parts: componential, experiential, and contextual subtheories.

Type-A behavior Behavior shown by a particular type of individual; a personality pattern of behavior that can lead to stress and heart disease.

unconditional positive regard Part of Carl Rogers's personality theory; occurs when we accept someone regardless of what he or she does or says.

unconditioned response (UR) An automatic reaction elicited by a stimulus.

unconditioned stimulus (US) Any stimulus that elicits an automatic or reflexive reaction in an individual; it does not have to be learned in the present situation.

unconscious mind In Sigmund Freud's psychoanalytic theory of personality, the part of personality that is unavailable to us; Freud suggests that instincts and unpleasant memories are stored in the unconscious mind.

undifferentiated schizophrenia Type of schizophrenia that does not fit into any particular category, or fits into more than one category.

validity The degree to which you actually measure what you intend to measure.

variability In statistics, variability measures the range of the scores.

variable interval (VI) schedule Schedule of reinforcement in which the subject is reinforced for the first response given after a certain time interval, with the interval being different for each trial.

variable ratio (VR) schedule Schedule of reinforcement in which the subject is given reinforcement after a varying number of responses; the number of responses required for reinforcement is different for every trial.

vestibular sense Sense that helps us keep our balance.

visuo-spatial sketch pad Responsible for visual images involved in geographical orientation and spatial task.

vulnerability-stress model Theory of schizophrenia that states that some people have a biological tendency to develop schizophrenia if they are stressed enough by their environment.

Weber's Law Ernst Weber's law that states that the difference threshold depends on the ratio of the intensity of one stimulus to another rather than on an absolute difference.

Wechsler Adult Intelligence Scale (WAIS) An intelligence test for adults, first published by David Wechsler in 1955; it contains verbal and performance subscales.

Wechsler Intelligence Scale for Children (WISC-III) Similar to the Wechsler Adult Intelligence Scale, except that it is designed for children ages 6 through 16, and helps diagnose certain childhood disorders, such as dyslexia and other learning disabilities.

Wechsler Preschool and Primary Scale of Intelligence (WPPSI-R) Designed for children between the ages of 4 and 7; helps diagnose certain childhood disorders, such as dyslexia and other learning disabilities.

withdrawal Unpleasant physical reactions that a drug-dependent user experiences when he or she stops taking the drug.

within-subject experiment An experimental design in which each subject is given all treatments, including the control condition; subjects serve in both experimental and control groups.

working memory The memory store, with a capacity of about 7 items and enduring for up to 30 seconds, that handles current information.

Yerkes-Dodson Law Popular idea that performance is best when arousal is at a medium level.

Sources for the Glossary:

The majority of terms in this glossary are from Psychology: A ConnecText, 4th Edition, Terry F. Pettijohn. ©1999 Dushkin/ McGraw-Hill, Guilford, CT 06437. The remaining terms were developed by the Annual Editions staff.

AE Article Review Form

We encourage you to photocopy and use this page as a tool to assess how the articles in **Annual Editions** expand on the information in your textbook. By reflecting on the articles you will gain enhanced text information. You can also access this useful form on a product's book support Web site at **http://www.dushkin.com/online/.**

NAME: _____ DATE: _____

TITLE AND NUMBER OF ARTICLE: _____

BRIEFLY STATE THE MAIN IDEA OF THIS ARTICLE: _____

LIST THREE IMPORTANT FACTS THAT THE AUTHOR USES TO SUPPORT THE MAIN IDEA:

WHAT INFORMATION OR IDEAS DISCUSSED IN THIS ARTICLE ARE ALSO DISCUSSED IN YOUR TEXTBOOK OR OTHER READINGS THAT YOU HAVE DONE? LIST THE TEXTBOOK CHAPTERS AND PAGE NUMBERS:

LIST ANY EXAMPLES OF BIAS OR FAULTY REASONING THAT YOU FOUND IN THE ARTICLE:

LIST ANY NEW TERMS/CONCEPTS THAT WERE DISCUSSED IN THE ARTICLE, AND WRITE A SHORT DEFINITION:

ANNUAL EDITIONS revisions depend on two major opinion sources: one is our Advisory Board, listed in the front of this volume, which works with us in scanning the thousands of articles published in the public press each year; the other is you—the person actually using the book. Please help us and the users of the next edition by completing the prepaid article rating form on this page and returning it to us. Thank you for your help!

ANNUAL EDITIONS: Personal Growth and Behavior 00/01

ARTICLE RATING FORM

Here is an opportunity for you to have direct input into the next revision of this volume. We would like you to rate each of the 48 articles listed below, using the following scale:

1. Excellent: should definitely be retained
2. Above average: should probably be retained
3. Below average: should probably be deleted
4. Poor: should definitely be deleted

Your ratings will play a vital part in the next revision. So please mail this prepaid form to us just as soon as you complete it. Thanks for your help!

We Want Your Advice

RATING

ARTICLE

1. The Last Interview of Abraham Maslow
2. Making Sense of Self-Esteem
3. Raising Kids' Self-Esteem May Backfire, Experts Warn
4. Private Lives: Discipline and Knowing Where to Draw the Line
5. Who Are the Freudians?
6. The Stability of Personality: Observations and Evaluations
7. Is It Nature or Nurture?
8. The Gender Blur
9. Optimizing Expression of the Common Human Genome for Child Development
10. Autism Is Likely to Be Linked to Several Genes
11. The Personality Genes
12. Revealing the Brain's Secrets
13. Traumatic Memory Is Special
14. The Biology of Joy
15. Faith & Healing
16. The Seven Stages of Man
17. Fetal Psychology
18. Clipped Wings
19. Why Children Turn Out the Way They Do
20. How Well Do You Know Your Kid?
21. Invincible Kids
22. Live to 100? No Thanks
23. Is There Life after Death?
24. The EQ Factor

RATING

ARTICLE

25. Face It!
26. The Moral Development of Children
27. Friendships and Adaptation across the Life Span
28. The New Flirting Game
29. The Science of a Good Marriage
30. Shattered Vows
31. Social Anxiety
32. Don't Face Stress Alone
33. Go Ahead, Say You're Sorry
34. A Fistful of Hostility Is Found in Women
35. Where Bias Begins: The Truth about Stereotypes
36. Media, Violence, Youth, and Society
37. Psychopathy, Sociopathy, and Crime
38. The Lure of the Cult
39. Work, Work, Work, Work!
40. What You Can Change and What You Cannot Change
41. Think Like a Shrink
42. The Doctor's In, the Patient's Not/Even When They Think It Would Help Them, Many People Resist Counseling
43. Chronic Anxiety: How to Stop Living on the Edge
44. Up from Depression
45. The Clustering and Contagion of Suicide
46. Addicted
47. Personality Disorders: Coping with the Borderline
48. Finding Strength: How to Overcome Anything

(Continued on next page)

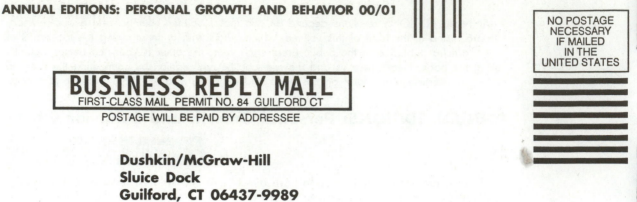

BUSINESS REPLY MAIL

FIRST-CLASS MAIL PERMIT NO. 84 GUILFORD CT

POSTAGE WILL BE PAID BY ADDRESSEE

Dushkin/McGraw-Hill
Sluice Dock
Guilford, CT 06437-9989

IIₗₗₗₗIIₗₗₗIₗIₗIₗₗIIIₗₗₗIIIₗIₗIₗIₗIₗIₗIₗIₗₗIₗIₗI

ABOUT YOU

Name _____ Date _____

Are you a teacher? ☐ A student? ☐
Your school's name _____

Department _____

Address _____ City _____ State ____ Zip ____

School telephone # _____

YOUR COMMENTS ARE IMPORTANT TO US !

Please fill in the following information:
For which course did you use this book?
_____

Did you use a text with this *ANNUAL EDITION*? ☐ yes ☐ no
What was the title of the text?
_____

What are your general reactions to the *Annual Editions* concept?
_____

Have you read any particular articles recently that you think should be included in the next edition?
_____

Are there any articles you feel should be replaced in the next edition? Why?
_____

Are there any World Wide Web sites you feel should be included in the next edition? Please annotate.
_____

May we contact you for editorial input? ☐ yes ☐ no
May we quote your comments? ☐ yes ☐ no